TOURO COLLEGE LIBRARY
Flushing Facility

This volume, "The Empire State" by Dr. Benjamin J. Lossing, is a comprehensive history of the State of New York from the settlement through 1875. It is one of a Series being done by The Reprint Company on the Settlement and Colonial periods of the original Colonies.

The Reprint Company is specializing in Colonial and Revolutionary period history in two distinct divisions: (1) Basic material on the Settlement and Colonial periods and (2) Major Battles and Campaigns of the Revolution.

Basic histories available include: Georgia — Author, Jones; Maryland — Authors, McSherry, McMahon, Bozman; New York, — Authors, O'Callaghan and Lossing; North Carolina — Authors, Hawks, Creecy; New Jersey — Authors, Smith, Barber & Howe; Pennsylvania — Authors, Proud, Gordon; South Carolina — Authors, Stith, Campbell.

Revolutionary period volumes include: Draper's King's Mountain; Stryker's Trenton and Princeton; Tarleton's Campaigns in Southern Provinces (N. C., S. C. & Va.); Schenck's Campaigns and Battles in North Carolina, South Carolina and Virginia; Landrum's Battles in Upper South Carolina; French and Murdock's Concord, Lexington, Bunker Hill and Siege of Boston.

Also completed and available is the 12-volume Heads of Families, First Census of teh United States, 1790, with volumes for the States of South Carolina, North Carolina, Virginia, Pennsylvania, Maryland, New Hampshire, Maine, Rhode Island, Vermont, Connecticut, Massachusetts and New York.

The Reprint Company also has completed and has available a six-volume set on Women of Colonial and Revolutionary Times. The books are: "Martha Washington" and "Dolly Madison" of Virginia; "Eliza Pinckney" of South Carolina; "Catherine Schuyler" of New York; 'Margaret Winthrop" and "Mercy Warren" of Massachusetts.

Volumes on Colonial America and the Revolutionary Battles and Campaigns are constantly being added to our list of reprints.

THE REPRINT COMPANY
154 W. Cleveland Park Drive
Spartanburg, S. C., 29303

First Printing — October, 1968.

An Introduction To
The Author And This Volume

John Benson Lossing was a native New Yorker and one of the most prolific writers of his day. He authored some 40 volumes.

"The Empire State" was undertaken at the urging of friends for a comprehensive history of the state covering the period from the first settlement through the first century of the Republic (1875). These same associates desired a volume which would be extensively illustrated. As a result some 336 sketches are included.

Dr. Lossing was born in the town of Beekman, N. Y., Feb. 12, 1813, of Dutch lineage, his ancestors having been among the first settlers in the valley of the lower Hudson. His parents were Quakers. His father died when he was less than a year old and his mother when he was in his 12th year. He worked on a farm for two years and was then apprenticed to a watchmaker and silversmith in Poughkeepsie.

Mr. Lossing was largely self-educated. While in his teens, he worked for a local newspaper and at 20 entered into a printing partnership. He studied wood engraving in New York so that the paper and a literary magazine he managed could have illustrations. He became a leading and skillful practicioner of the art and pursued it in New York for nearly 30 years.

The first of the some 40 volumes he authored appeared in 1840. Other works, many noted for their illustrations as well as the text, appeared regularly and enjoyed a wide acceptance.

Honorary degrees were awarded Mr. Lossing by Hamilton College and later by Columbia College. In 1873, on recommendation of the Board of Regents, he was awarded a doctorate degree by the University of Michigan. He held an honorary life membership in the Metropolitan Museum of Art in New York City. He was a member of 17 historical, antiquarian and literary societies.

Dr. Lossing made the original drawings of most of his works. He lived quietly for more than 20 years on a farm in Dutchess County in one of the most picturesque sections of his native state. He died June 3, 1891.

This Volume Was Reproduced
From An Original
In The
New York State Library
Albany, New York

Standard Book Numbering:
  No. 8715 2050 8
Library of Congress Catalogue Number: 68-57492

THE NEW STATE HOUSE.

THE
EMPIRE STATE:

A Compendious History

OF THE

COMMONWEALTH OF NEW YORK.

BY BENSON J. LOSSING, LL.D.,

AUTHOR OF

"*Pictorial Field Book of the Revolution*," "*The War of 1812*" and "*The Civil War in America;*"
"*Mount Vernon; or, the Home of Washington;*" "*Illustrated History of the United States;*"
"*Cyclopedia of United States History;*" "*Our Country;*" "*History of the City
of New York;*" "*Story of the United States Navy, for Boys;*"
"*Mary and Martha Washington*," etc., etc.

ILLUSTRATED

By Fac-similes of 333 Pen-and-Ink Drawings

By H. ROSA.

1888.

AMERICAN PUBLISHING COMPANY,

HARTFORD, CONN.

Entered, according to Act of Congress, in the year 1887,

By FUNK & WAGNALLS,

In the Office of the Librarian of Congress at Washington, D. C.

PRESS OF
FUNK & WAGNALLS,
18 and 20 Astor Place,
NEW YORK

PREFACE.

SEVERAL years ago the author of this work received a letter from the late Hon. Horatio Seymour, urging him to supply a conspicuous literary want by writing a compendious history of the State of New York, and illustrating it after the manner of his *Pictorial Field-Book of the Revolution*. No work of the kind was then in existence, nor has there been since.

It has been the chief aim of the author, in the preparation of this work, to embody in one volume, of• moderate size and price, a complete outline narrative of the principal events in the career of the Commonwealth of New York from its inception to the close of the first century of our Republic (1875), so compact, as a whole, that its purchase and perusal will not burden the purses or the leisure of a vast proportion of our people.

As much space has been given to notices of historic events outside of the State of New York as seemed necessary to continually present the Commonwealth to the mind of the reader as a most important part of the great Republic of the West.

The volume contains a brief history of the powerful barbarian republic found by Europeans within the boundaries of the (present) State of New York; a narrative of the explorations, emigrations, and settlements of the Dutch, Swedes, and English in New Netherland; of the Indian wars and desolations; an account of the religious, social, and political organizations under Dutch rule; of the patroon and manorial estates planted along the tide-water region of the Hudson River; of the seizure and occupation of the domain by the English; of the development of democracy at every period of the English rule, with notices of the most interesting events in the political, social, and military history of the Province and State down to the kindling of the old war for independence and to its close; the organization of the State government in 1777; the ever-dominating influence of the State in the national councils; its political, social, and military history as an independent State; its part in the drama of the War of 1812-15; its munificent contributions of men and money during the great struggle for the salvation of the life of the Republic ; the various changes in its constitution ; notices of the vast industrial operations in the State ; its canals and railways ; its agriculture, manufactures, and commerce ; its admirable popular educational system ; its literature, and its marvellous growth in population, wealth, and refinement, with biographical sketches of some of the most prominent actors in public life, from Stuyvesant to Tilden.

Portraiture is made a prominent feature in the graphic illustrations of the work, for we all desire to see the lineaments of the faces of those whose careers interest us. The book contains the portraits of many of the most conspicuous men of New York mentioned in its colonial and State annals, with a brief biography of each. Among them may be found the portraits and biographical sketches of all the governors of the State, from George Clinton, its first chief magistrate in 1777, until 1876. Also pictures of numerous buildings in the State which have been made famous by some historical association. A greater portion of these buildings have been made from drawings by the author from the objects themselves. It also contains a delineation of the seal of every county in the State. The illustrations have been made under the personal guidance of the author, whose special care was to insure accuracy in form, feature, and costume.

BENSON J. LOSSING.

THE RIDGE, DOVER PLAINS, N. Y., October, 1887.

CONTENTS.

CHAPTER I.

What constitutes New York "The Empire State," 1, 2 ; Niagara Falls, 2 ; The Iroquois Confederacy or League, 3–10 ; Henry Hudson and his exploration and discoveries, 10–13 ; Claims for Verazzano, 11 ; Names of the Hudson River, 13.

CHAPTER II.

Fate of Henry Hudson ; Fruits of his discoveries ; Traffic with the Indians opened, 14 ; Planting the seed of empire ; First vessel built on Manhattan Island ; Fort Nassau, on the Upper Hudson ; Adriaen Block, a Dutch navigator, 15 ; A trading company formed, 16, 17 ; Champlain and the Iroquois, 18 ; The Dutch make a treaty with the Indians at Tawasentha, 19 ; Social condition of Holland, 20, 21 ; English Puritans propose to go to New Netherland, 21, 22 ; Dutch West India Company formed, 22, 23 ; An English mariner at Manhattan, 23 ; The Pilgrims at Cape Cod ; The Dutch prepare to plant a colony, 24 ; Walloons emigrate to New Netherland, 25 ; A French vessel at Manhattan, 26 ; Dutch settlements in New Netherland, 26, 27 ; Peter Minuit director-general ; Purchase of Manhattan Island, 27 ; New Netherland created a province, 28.

CHAPTER III.

Fort Amsterdam and a trading-house built ; The beginning of the city of New York ; Robbery and murder of an Indian, 29 ; Trouble with the Mohawks and its effects ; Capture of the Spanish "silver fleet" by the Dutch, 30 ; Charter of Privileges and Exemption, the patroon system, 31 ; Early patroons ; The Van Rensselaer Manor, 32 ; David Pietersen de Vries founds a colony on Delaware Bay, 33 ; Governor Walter van Twiller and his administration, 33, 34 ; First clergyman and schoolmaster in New Netherland ; The first English ship in the Hudson River, 34 ; Van Twiller's absurd conduct, 35, 36 ; The Dutch and English in the valley of the Connecticut, 35, 38 ; Van Twiller recalled, 38 ; William Kieft Governor of New Netherland, 39 ; Condition of public affairs, 40 ; Swedes on the Delaware, 41 ; Trouble with Eastern neighbors and the Indians, 42 ; Impending war with the Indians, 43.

CHAPTER IV.

A new charter for patroons and other landed proprietors ; Colonie of Rensselaerwyck ; Arendt van Curler, commissary, 44 ; Power exercised by Patroon van Rensselaer, 45 ; First clergyman and church at Albany ; A Jesuit missionary and his career among the Mohawks ; First germ of representative government in New Netherland, 46, 47 ; Committee of Twelve, 47 ; Destruction of Indians who sought the hospitality of the Dutch, 48 ; A fierce war kindled, and its consequences, 49, 50 ; The Council of Eight Men, 49, and their memorial to the States-General, 50, 51 ; Condition of the Dutch West

India Company, 51 ; New Sweden, 52 ; Treaty of peace with the Indians ; Dominie Bogardus's boldness, 52 ; Departure of Kieft ; Change in the mode of government ; Peter Stuyvesant appointed governor, 53 ; Arrival of Stuyvesant and his reception, 54 ; Stuyvesant's administration, 55, 56 ; The Committee of Nine, 56 ; Overtures of friendship with the "Pilgrims" in the East, 56, 57 ; Dutch embassy to New Plymouth, 57.

CHAPTER V.

Conference of Dutch and English at Hartford and its results, 58 ; Affairs between the Dutch and the Swedes on the Delaware ; Improvements at the Dutch capital, 59 ; Brandt van Slechtenhorst, commissary of Rensselaerwyck, defies 'Stuyvesant, 60 ; Stuyvesant and the Council of Nine, 61 ; Statement of the Nine to the States-General ; New Amsterdam organized as a city, 62 ; Stuyvesant summoned to Amsterdam, 63 ; The Dutch and New Englanders fraternize ; Republicanism nourished ; A representative assembly and the governor, 64 ; A convention remonstrates against his rule, 65 ; Interview between Stuyvesant and Beeckman and the convention ; Doings of the Swedes on the Delaware, 66 ; Conquest of New Sweden, 67 ; New Amsterdam invaded by Indians, 67, 68 ; Estates ravaged ; Trouble with Indians at Esopus ; Dutch mission to Maryland, 68 ; New Amsterdam and Harlem, 69 ; Social life on Manhattan, 70.

CHAPTER VI.

State tricks ; Stuyvesant and the Quakers, 71 ; Colony of Mennonites, 71, 72 ; New Amstel founded, 72 ; Trouble with Indians at Esopus, 72, 73 ; Secession and revolution on Long Island, 73 ; A General Provincial Assembly ; Seizure of New Netherland by the English contemplated, 74 ; A British force before New Amsterdam, 75 ; Rebellion in the city threatened, 76, 77 ; Surrender of New Amsterdam to the English ; The province and city named New York, 78 ; The Dutch rule in New Netherland, 79 ; Social life at New Amsterdam, 80, 81 ; Character of the Dutch, 81, 82 ; Stuyvesant and the Dutch West India Company, 82.

CHAPTER VII.

Provincial government for New York organized ; Public worship at New York, 84 ; English rule at New York, 85–87 ; Duke's laws, 85 ; Municipal government for the city, 85, 86 ; New Jersey granted to royal favorites, 86 ; The Dutch retake New York, 88, 89 ; Restored to the British crown by treaty, 90 ; The Jesuits among the Iroquois, 90 ; French intrigues with the Iroquois unsuccessful, 91 ; Characters of Governor Andros and the Duke of York, 92 ; Administration of Andros ; King Philip's War, 93 ; An important royal marriage ; Affairs in New Jersey, 94 ; A claim to Staten Island, 95.

CHAPTER VIII.

First popular government for New York, 96, 97 ; Charter of Liberties and Privileges, 97 ; Political divisions of New York, 97, 98 ; Dongan's administration, 99, 100 ; Designs of the French against the Five Nations of the Iroquois, 100 ; Perfidy of King James ; Dongan's patriotism, 101, 102 ; De Nonville's expedition, 102, 103 ; "Dominion of New England ;" Birth of an heir to the British throne, 103 ; Revolution in England, 104 ; Effect of the revolution in New York, 105 ; Leisler's administration of affairs, 106–112 ; Affairs at Albany, 108 ; Conspiracy against the life of Leisler successful, 112 ; Remorse and death of Governor Sloughter, 113.

CHAPTER IX.

Invasion of New York by French and Indians; Destruction of Schenectady, 114; Provincial expeditions against the French in Canada, 115; Failure of these expeditions, 116; Arrival and character of Governor Fletcher; Popular opposition to Fletcher, 117; Invasion by the French led by Frontenac, 118, 119; Fletcher's administration, 119, 120; Appointment and character of Governor Bellomont; Privateering, 121; Captain Kidd and piracy, 122; Bellomont's administration, 122–26; Leislerians and Anti-Leislerians, 123, 124; The French in Canada hostile to the Iroquois; Bellomont defends the latter, 123, 124; Reinterment of Leisler's remains, 124; The Assembly change politically; Fletcher's fraudulent land grants, 125, 126; Death of Bellomont, 126.

CHAPTER X.

Defences against the French strengthened, 128; Leislerians control the government, 128, 129; Contests with Assembly; Lord Cornbury governor, 129; Nicholas Bayard and his fate, 130; Cornbury's character and conduct, 131, 132; Queen Anne's War, 132; Governor Lovelace, 133; Attempt to conquer Canada, 134; Peter Schuyler takes Indians to England, 135; Naval expedition against Quebec, 136; Governor Hunter and his administration, 137, 138; Emigration of Germans to New York; The United Six Nations, 137; First Negro Plot, 138; Governor Burnet and his administration, 139, 140; Inter-colonial traffic prohibited, 140; Governor Montgomery's short administration, 141, 142; Boundary line between New York and Connecticut settled; Governor Cosby and his character, 142; Cosby's contest with Rip Van Dam, 143; Liberty of the press struggled for and vindicated, 143–147; Zenger's trial, 145–147; A popular triumph, 147.

CHAPTER XI.

Social condition of the province of New York, 148, and the city of New York, 149, 150; Aspects of social life at Albany, 151; Lieutenant-Governor Clark, 152; The second Negro Plot, 152, 153; A victim of perjury, 154; Governor Sir George Clinton and his administration, 154–59; King George's War, 155; Surrender of Louisburg and Cape Breton to the English; Saratoga desolated by French and Indians, 156; Preparations to conquer the French dominions in America; William Johnson and the Mohawks, 157; Rancorous party strife prevalent; Political influence of James de Lancey, 158; Governor Sir Danvers Osborne, suicide of, 159; De Lancey acting governor of New York; Governor Sir Charles Hardy; French Jesuits and their influence, 160; Aggressive movements of the French in the West; Colonial convention at Albany, 161; Hostilities between the French and English begun, 162; Conference of governors with General Braddock, 163.

CHAPTER XII.

Expeditions against the French begun, 164; General Lyman and General Johnson, 165–167; King Hendrick, 165, 166; A battle near Lake George; The French defeated at Lake George, 166; Expedition against Forts Niagara and Frontenac unsuccessful; Great Britain declares war against France, and prepares for the conflict, 167; The Seven Years' or French and Indian War, 167–184; Abercrombie's tardy movements; Bradstreet's efficiency; Montcalm's operations, 168; Lord Loudon's inefficiency illustrated, 169, 170; Invasion of New York by French and Indians, 170; Capture of Fort William Henry, 171; A massacre of English troops; Pitt prime-minister, 172; His policy in American affairs; British conquests, 173; Expedition against Ticonderoga,

174 ; English repulsed, 175 ; Fort Frontenac taken ; Expedition against Fort Duquesne successful, 176. 177.

CHAPTER XIII.

A final struggle for the mastery ; Pitt's work, 178 ; Expeditions against Quebec, Fort Niagara, and Montreal, 179 ; Capture of Fort Niagara, 179, 180 ; The French driven from Lake Champlain, 180 ; Capture of Quebec, 181, 183 ; Conquest of Canada, 184 ; France stripped of her possessions in America by treaty at Paris, 185 ; Pontiac's conspiracy ; Civil affairs in New York, 186 ; Important social movements in New York, 187 ; Institutions for intellectual cultivation founded ; A sectarian controversy, 188 ; Dr. Colden acting governor ; An arbitrary royal act, 189 ; Disputes about the New Hampshire Grants, 189–191.

CHAPTER XIV.

Accession of George III., 192 ; His great mistake, 193 ; Governor Monckton, 192, 193 ; Governor Moore and the king's prerogative, 193 ; Writs of Assistance and the Stamp Act, 194 ; Opposition to the Stamp Act, 194–197 ; "Sons of Liberty," 195 ; Stamp Act Congress at New York ; A riot, 196 ; Non-importation league, 197, 198 ; Repeal of the Stamp Act and its effects, 199 ; Troops sent to enslave the New Yorkers, 200 ; Oppressive acts of Parliament, 201 ; Open rebellion imminent ; The Boston massacre, 202 ; Popular committees and patriotic movements, 203 ; Excitement about tea, 204, 205 ; Boston Tea Party, 205, 207 ; A general Congress recommended, 207 ; Great meeting in "The Fields," 208 ; Delegates to a General Congress appointed, 209.

CHAPTER XV.

Committees of Correspondence ; First Continental Congress, 210 ; Its proceedings and effects, 211, 212 ; The American Association, 211 ; Committee to carry it into execution, 212 ; An American episcopate proposed ; The New York Assembly, 213 ; Doings of the Assembly, 214 ; The people aroused, 215 ; New York Provincial Congress, 216, 217 ; Committee of One Hundred, 217 ; Capture of Fort Ticonderoga by the Americans, 218 ; The functions of Congress considered, 219 ; General Wooster with troops near New York ; Reception of Washington and Governor Tryon, 220 ; Political complexion of the Provincial Congress, 221 ; Northern Military Department ; Affairs on Lake Champlain, and the Canadians ; The first Continental Navy created, 222 ; Ethan Allen and his "Green Mountain Boys ;" General Schuyler authorized to invade Canada, 223.

CHAPTER XVI.

The Johnson Family, 224 ; Guy Johnson and Indian councils, 225, 226 ; British coalition with Indians and Tories ; Invasion of Canada begun, 227–229 ; New Yorkers complained of ; A mission to the Canadians, 228 ; St. Johns and Montreal taken, 229 ; Siege of Quebec, 230, 231 ; Schuyler and Sir John Johnson, 231 ; Cannons removed from the Battery at New York, 232 ; Sears's raid on Rivington's printing-house, 233 ; General Lee with troops in New York City ; Siege of Boston, 234 ; Plot to murder Washington, 235, 236 ; Washington's Life Guard, 235 ; Thomas Paine, in *Common Sense*, advocates political independence, 236 ; Congress and colonial legislators advocate independence, 237 ; Change in the New York Provincial Congress ; A capital plan of the British Ministry, 238 ; Commissioners sent to Canada, 239 ; End of the invasion of Canada ; Sir John Johnson and his parole of honor, 240 ; Flees to Canada ; Lady Johnson taken to Albany, 241.

CHAPTER XVII.

A strong British armament appears before New York ; Mission of General and Admiral Howe, 242 ; Washington's successful appeal to the people ; Preparations for battle, 243 ; Battle of Long Island, 244, 245 ; The famous retreat of the Americans from Brooklyn, 245 ; A peace conference ; Condition of the American Army, 246 ; The Americans on Harlem Heights ; Battle on Harlem Plains ; Conflagration in New York City, 247 ; Battle at White Plains, 248 ; The British capture Fort Washington, 248, 249 ; Prisons and prison-ships, 249 ; The British occupy New York City ; Preparations to invade Northern New York, 250 ; Naval operations on Lake Champlain, 251, 252 ; Creation of a navy, 252 ; Flight of the American Army across New Jersey ; Americans victorious at Trenton, 254 ; Battle at Princeton, 255.

CHAPTER XVIII.

Migration of the Provincial Congress ; Convention of representatives of the State of New York, 256, 257 ; Framing a State Constitution and its adoption, 257, 258 ; Jay's desires concerning the Constitution, 258, 259 ; Character of the Constitution, 259, 260 ; A Council of Safety appointed, 260 ; A Vigilance Committee appointed ; An Act of Attainder, and the victim of it, 262 ; State officers chosen, 260–262 ; First meeting of the State Legislature, 262 ; Preparation to invade New York, 263 ; Burgoyne's campaign, 264–282 ; Marauding expeditions ; Baron de Riedesel, 264 ; Indians feasted ; Ticonderoga ; Burgoyne's proclamation, 265 ; Fort Ticonderoga captured, 266 ; Battle of Hubbardton ; The British forces push toward the Hudson River, 267 ; Schuyler's proclamation ; The Jane McCrea tragedy, 268 ; British expedition to Bennington ; Burgoyne's perilous position.

CHAPTER XIX.

St. Leger's invasion ; Fort Schuyler, 270 ; Battle at Oriskany, 271 ; Siege of Fort Schuyler, 272 ; Fort Schuyler relieved, 273 ; Burgoyne perplexed ; Gates supersedes Schuyler in command, 274 ; Burgoyne's army moves forward ; Battle on Bemis's Heights, 275 ; General Arnold in the battle ; Petty jealousy of the opposing commanders, 276 ; Wretched condition of Burgoyne's army ; A council of war, 277 ; Second battle on Bemis's Heights, 278–280 ; Bravery of Arnold, who really won the victory, 279, 280 ; Burgoyne retreats to the Heights of Saratoga, and surrenders, 281 ; The surrendered troops paroled, but detained in America ; Effects of the surrender of Burgoyne, 282.

CHAPTER XX.

The British under Sir Henry Clinton capture Stony Point, 283 ; They capture Forts Montgomery and Clinton, in the Hudson Highlands, 284 ; The boom across the Hudson broken ; Clinton's despatch to Burgoyne and fate of the bearer, 285 ; Marauding British troops burn Kingston ; Battle on the Brandywine Creek ; Americans defeated ; Massacre near the Paoli Tavern, 286 ; Flight of Congress from Philadelphia ; Americans defeated at Germantown, and retire to Whitemarsh, 287 ; Conspiracy against Washington—" Conway's Cabal ;" Loyalty of Lafayette, 288 ; A council with Indians at Johnstown, 289 ; Desolations by Indians and Tories in the interior of New York, 290 ; Massacre at Cherry Valley, 291 ; Invasion of the Wyoming Valley, 292 ; Resistance to the invasion, 293 ; Desolation of Wyoming, 294 ; Alliance with France ; An English peace-commissioner ; The British flee from Philadelphia ; Battle at Monmouth Court-House, 295 ; Hostilities in Rhode Island and off the coast, 297.

CONTENTS.

CHAPTER XXI.

British expedition up the Hudson, 297 ; Capture of Stony Point and Verplanck's Point ; British marauders on the coasts of Connecticut, 298 ; Wayne attacks Stony Point, 299 ; The Americans recapture Stony Point, 300 ; Indian atrocities ; Expedition against the Onondagas ; Tragedy at Minisink, 301 ; Honors to the dead at Goshen, 302 ; Sullivan's campaign, 303, 304 ; Siege of Savannah ; A naval fight ; Sir John Johnson's raid into the Mohawk Valley, 305, 306 ; Schoharie Valley desolated, 306 ; Operations in the Mohawk Valley, 307 ; Battle at "Klock's Field ;" Invasion of a motley army from Canada ; Sir Henry Clinton sails for Charleston ; Surrender of Charleston, 308 ; Operations of Cornwallis in the Carolinas ; Battle of King's Mountain ; Arrival of a land and naval force from France, 309

CHAPTER XXII.

Arnold's treason, 310–315 ; Complot of Arnold and Major André, 311 ; Arrival of Major André, 312 ; Events at Arnold's headquarters, 313, 314 ; Escape of Arnold ; André conveyed to Tappan, 314 ; Trial and execution of André, 314, 315 ; The fate of Arnold and André ; Stirring event on Long Island, 315 ; Civil events in the region of the New Hampshire Grants, or Vermont, 316 ; Leaders in Vermont coquet with British authorities in Canada, 317, 318 ; Settlement of disputes between New York and Vermont ; Continental paper currency and Articles of Confederation, 319 ; Weakness of the general government ; Arnold serving his purchasers in Virginia, 320 ; British troops in Virginia, 321 ; Allied armies and the British in Virginia, 322 ; Surrender of Cornwallis ; War in the South, 323 ; Greene's famous retreat ; Greene turns upon his enemies, 324, 325 ; Battles at Guilford Court-House, near Camden, Fort Ninety-Six, and Eutaw Spring, 324, 325.

CHAPTER XXIII.

Closing events of the Revolution, 326–331 ; Discontents of the soldiers ; A proposal to Washington to become king ; The "Newburg Addresses," 327 ; The results of a meeting of officers, 328 ; Disbanding of the Continental Army begun, 328, 329 ; Latest survivors of the army, 329 ; The Society of the Cincinnati, 329, 330 ; Flight of Tories from New York, and confiscations, 330 ; The British evacuate New York ; Washington parts with his officers, 331 ; Surrenders his commission ; Foundation of a State Government laid, 332, 333 ; Political capital of New York ; Adjustment of boundaries, 333 ; Land cessions by the Six Nations, 334 ; Territorial claims adjusted, 335 ; Formation of a National Constitution, 336 ; Federalists and Anti-Federalists, 337 ; Popular discussions of the Constitution, 338 ; Constituent Convention at Poughkeepsie, 339 ; Adoption of the Constitution ; Members of the National Congress for New York, 341.

CHAPTER XXIV.

Political divisions of New York ; Emigrations and settlements, 342 ; Land purchasers ; A great wagon-road constructed ; Party strife, 343 ; First meeting of Congress under the Constitution, 344 ; Washington inaugurated President of the United States, 345 ; Official appointments ; Spirit of the Constitution of New York ; A political coalition, 346 ; Origin of the canal system in the State, 347, 348 ; The early promoters of the system, 347–349 ; Condition of New York City at the close of the Revolution, 350 ; A Federal celebration, 351 ; A newspaper office mobbed ; Yellow-fever in New York City, 352.

CHAPTER XXV.

Effect of the French Revolution on American politics, 353 ; Jefferson's expectations, disappointments, and suspicions, 353, 354 ; Jefferson the leader of the Republican Party ; Arrival of "Citizen" Genet, 354 ; Reception of Genet in Philadelphia, 355 ; Democratic societies formed ; Conduct of Genet and his friends, 356 ; Reception of Genet in New York ; His recall. 357 ; Social influence of French emigrants in New York ; Jay's treaty, 358, 359 ; The Whiskey insurrection, 358 ; Opposition to Jay's treaty, 359 ; The Tammany Society, or Columbian Order ; Legislative aid for common schools provided, 360, 361 ; State Literature Fund ; Support of popular education, 361 ; Board of Regents, 362 ; Electors ; Abolition of slavery proposed ; Albany made the State capital, 363 ; The alliance with France celebrated ; Political strife, 364 ; Manhattan Water Company and Bank, 365 ; De Witt Clinton ; Jefferson elected President ; Downfall of the Federal Party ; Death of Washington, 366.

CHAPTER XXVI.

Social aspects of New York State and City at the beginning of this century, 367-370 ; The Chamber of Commerce and benevolent societies, 369 ; Churches and country-seats ; First revision of the State Constitution, 370 ; Political influence of two families, 371 ; A bitter personal and political warfare, 372 ; Schism in the Democratic Party ; Hamilton and Burr, 373 ; Hamilton slain by Burr in a duel, 374, 375 ; Burr's political death, and trial for treason ; The West Point Military Academy ; Governor Morgan Lewis, 375 ; Foundation of a permanent school fund laid ; The Free School Society, 376 ; Navigation by steam established, 377 ; Embargo Act, 378 ; Cause of the downfall of the Federal Party ; Coquetting with the "Burrites," 379, 380 ; The State prepares for war ; Governor Tompkins, 380 ; The British Orders in Council unrepealed, 381.

CHAPTER XXVII.

The genesis of the Erie Canal, 382, 385 ; Gouverneur Morris, 382 ; Jesse Hawley, Simeon De Witt, and Joshua Forman, 383 ; Thomas Eddy and a public meeting in New York, 384 ; Beginning of the construction of the Erie Canal, 385 ; Opposition to it, 386 ; Second overthrow of the Federal Party, 386 ; War of 1812-15 ; The *Chesapeake* and *Leopard* affair, 387 ; Peace Party ; Northern frontier of New York, 388 ; Surrender of Detroit ; Militia of New York, 389 ; Beginning of war on the Northern frontier, 390-392 ; Battle of Queenstown, 393-396.

CHAPTER XXVIII.

Doings of the American Navy, 397, 398 ; A bank charter in politics, 399, 400 ; De Witt Clinton a candidate for the Presidency of the United States, 400 ; Hostilities on Lake Ontario and the regions of the St. Lawrence and Niagara rivers, 400, 401 ; War spirit in the West, 403 ; Movements for the recovery of Michigan, 403, 404 ; Belligerent fleets on Lake Erie, 405 ; Battle on Lake Erie, 405, 406 ; The Creek War, 406, 407.

CHAPTER XXIX.

Attack on Ogdensburg, 408 ; The capture of York (Toronto), 409 ; The Niagara River and frontier in possession of the Americans, 410 ; Attack on Sackett's Harbor, 411, 412 ; Affair at the Beaver Dams, 412 ; Operations on the Niagara frontier, 413 ;

Operations on Lake Champlain, 414, 415 ; Expedition against Montreal, 415-417 ; The Niagara frontier desolated, 417 ; Naval operations on the sea, 417, 418 ; Amphibious warfare, 418 ; American naval force in 1813, 419.

CHAPTER XXX.

Wellington's veterans sent to the United States, 420 ; Peace Faction, 420 ; Battle at La Colle Mill ; Struggle for the mastery of Lake Ontario, 421 ; Invasion of Canada, 422, 423 ; Battle of Chippewa, 424 ; Battle of Lundy's Lane, 425 ; Americans victorious at Fort Erie, 426 ; Land and naval contest at Plattsburgh, 427-431 ; Attack on Fort Mackinaw, 432.

CHAPTER XXXI.

Naval and military operations on the coasts of the United States, 433, 434 ; Stirring scenes at New York, 434 ; British invasion of Maryland, 435 ; Battle of Bladensburg ; Incendiarianism at Washington, 436 ; British repulsed at Baltimore, 437 ; Naval operations on the ocean in 1814, 438, 439 ; American privateers, 440 ; New Orleans and Louisiana threatened, 441 ; Battle of New Orleans, 442 ; News of peace at New York, 442, 443 ; The Hartford Convention, 443, 444.

CHAPTER XXXII.

Governors Tompkins and Clinton, 445 ; Common schools and school fund, 446 ; Civil affairs in the State, 447-457 ; Defence against invasion, 448 ; Movements in favor of the construction of the Erie Canal, 449, 450 ; Abolition of slavery proposed, 451 ; Change in the position of political leaders, 452 ; "Bucktails" and "Clintonions," 453 ; Powers of the Councils of Appointment and Revision, 454 ; Revision of the State Constitution, 455 ; Features of the revised Constitution, 456, 457.

CHAPTER XXXIII.

Condition of New York in 1821 ; The Barbary Powers, 458 ; Readjustment of the machinery of the State government, 459 ; The "People's Party ;" De Witt Clinton and the people, 460 ; Lafayette's visit, 461 ; A new era, 462 ; Opening of the Erie Canal, 463 ; Celebration of the opening of the canal, 463-468 ; Grand display in New York Harbor, 465 ; Nuptials of the lakes and the sea, 466 ; Grand procession in New York City, 467 ; Achievements of the Erie Canal, 468-470 ; Buffalo and Rochester in 1813, 469, 470 ; A pagan rite at Rochester, 470 ; The common-school system, 471 ; The Anti-Masonic episode, 471, 472.

CHAPTER XXXIV.

Tariff laws and the "American System ;" Death of Governor Clinton, 473 ; Safety-fund system, 474 ; Anti-Masonic journal and Thurlow Weed, 476 ; A "Workingmen's Party ;" New York fashions, 476 ; Name of the Whig Party—how given, 477 ; Imprisonment for debt abolished, 478 ; Renewal of the United States Bank charter considered, 479 ; Van Buren appointed Minister to England ; Rejected by the Senate, and the result ; Nullification suppressed, 480 ; Actions of the United States Bank ; Equal Rights Party, 481, 482 ; Loco-focos, 481 ; Revolution in journalism, 483 ; Election riots in 1834, 483, 484 ; Native American Party, 484, 485 ; Abolition riots, 485 ; Collapse of the credit system, 485, 486 ; Croton Aqueduct, 487.

CHAPTER XXXV.

Free school libraries established, 487; Normal School at Albany, 488; Lancastrian and Pestalozzian systems of teaching, 488, 489; Revolutionary movements in Canada, 489, 490; "Hero of the Thousand Islands," 490; A disturbing incident on the Niagara frontier, 491; Overthrow of the Democratic Party, 491, 492; Financial achievements of the State, 492; Erie Canal; Mr. Seward's first encounter with the slave power, 493; Seward on general education, 494; John C. Spencer on the same subject, 495; The Roman Catholics and the common-school fund, 496, 497; The Secretary of State and the Legislature at variance, 497; Anti-rentism, 499, 500; The electric telegraph and Professor Morse, 500; Governor Wright on the school fund, 500; The common-school system; The annexation of Texas, 501.

CHAPTER XXXVI.

Third revision of the State Constitution, 503–505; The school system, action upon the, 505–507; John Young governor, 506; Hamilton Fish governor; Whig Party triumphant, 507; Washington Hunt governor; Repeal of the Free School Law, 508; The common-school fund; Horatio Seymour governor, 509; Reorganization of the educational system of the State; Completion of the canals urged, 510; Governor Seymour offends the temperance people by vetoing a prohibitory liquor bill, 510; Myron H. Clark governor, and a stanch prohibitionist, 511; Republican Party organized, 511; Controls the National power, 512; The Lemon slave case, 512, 513; John A. King governor, 513; Edwin D. Morgan governor, 514; Struggle between Freedom and Slavery begun, 515; Conspiracy against the Union, 515, 516.

CHAPTER XXXVII.

Condition of New York State and City in 1861; An approaching tempest watched, 517; A famous and inspiring order, 517, 518; Loyal and patriotic action of the Legislature, 519; Disloyalty of the Mayor of New York, 519; Conservatism of business men; The Crittenden Compromise, 520; A disloyal society, 520, 521; Insolence of a Secession leader; Formation of a league to destroy the republic, 521; Events in Charleston Harbor; The President's call for troops, 522; Response of New York, 522; War meeting at New York, 522, 523; The Union Defence Committee, 523; The Seventh Regiment goes to the field, 524; Patriotic women; The Friends, or Quakers, 524; Action of civil and military authorities, 525; Financial aid given by New York; Women's Relief Associations, 526; United States Sanitary and Christian Commissions, 527–529.

CHAPTER XXXVIII.

Change in political aspects; Financial ability of the State, 530; Soldiers furnished for the war; A new era; Governor Seymour's message, 531; The peace faction and Vallandigham, 532; Seditious movements; The draft, 533; Draft riot in New York City, 534; Union League Club; National currency established, 535; Conspiracies of the Confederates, 536; Men and money furnished for the war; Trophies, 537; Close of the war; Death of President Lincoln, 538; Important legislative action, 539; Revision of the State Constitution; Cornell University, 540; Election in 1868, 541.

CHAPTER XXXIX.

John T. Hoffman governor; Fifteenth Amendment of the National Constitution, 542; A reactionary movement; Amendments of charter, 543; Popular education; Riot in New York City, 544 ; Tweed Ring, 544, 545 ; Plundering of the Treasury of New York City, 545, 546 ; The Exposure of the plunderers, 547, and the result, 548 ; Movements of the colored population ; Liberal Republican Party ; Horace Greeley for President of the United States, 548 ; A social phenomenon (note), 548 ; A Civil Rights Bill ; John A. Dix governor, 549 ; Alterations in the State Constitution ; Compulsory education, 550 ; Laws for the protection of minors, 551 ; Samuel J. Tilden governor, 552.

CHAPTER XL.

Centennial celebration and exhibition ; Savings-banks, 553 ; Investigations ; Frauds discovered, 554 ; Canals in the State, 554 ; Their length and cost, 555 ; Railroads in the State and their operations, 555 ; Public instruction, 556 ; New State House, 556, 557 ; The aggregate public debt ; Movements of population, 557 ; Products of industry, 558, 559 ; Marine architecture, 559 ; State of popular intelligence, 559, 560 ; Books and periodicals ; Money investments ; Benevolent and charitable institutions ; Literary and scientific societies, 560 ; Churches, 560, 561 ; The Hudson River and its associations, 561 ; Manors and manor-houses on the Hudson, 562–565 ; Government House ; Attractions of New York City, 566 ; New York City and its harbor, 566, 567 ; Bartholdi's Statue of Liberty Enlightening the World ; A metropolitan city, 567.

CHAPTER XLI.

Religious and social aspect of New York City ; School of the Collegiate (Dutch Reformed) Church, 568 ; Religious denominations in colonial New York ; An episcopacy opposed, 569 ; Political condition of colonial New York, 569, 570 ; Courts, trade, and population in the colony ; How settlements were discouraged, 571 ; Statesmen, jurists, historians, and other literary men, 572–575 ; Writers on science, 575 ; The fine arts and artists, 575, 576.

APPENDIX.

The organization of the counties of the State ; Governors, colonial and State.

ILLUSTRATIONS.

A.

	PAGE
1. Albany, Seal of the City of.....	102
2. Albany County Seal.............	99
3. Albany, Plan of in 1695.........	128
4. Allegany County Seal...........	578
5. Allerton, Isaac, Signature of....	49
6. Amherst, Jeffrey, Portrait of....	179
7. Armstrong, John, Portrait of....	313
8. Andros, Edmond, Signature of..	91
9. Arnold, Benedict, Portrait of....	310
10. Ato-tar-ho......................	8

B.

11. Battery, Bowling Green, and Fort George..........................	195
12. Baxter, George, Signature of....	58
13. Bayard Arms, The..............	106
14. Bayard, Nicholas, Signature of..	106
15. Beeckman Arms, The...........	111
16. Beeckman, Gerardus, Portrait of.	110
17. Beeckman, Gerardus, Signature of..............................	110
18. Beeckman, William, Signature of..............................	72
19. Bellomont, Earl of, Portrait of..	121
20. Bellomont, Earl of, Signature of..	121
21. Bellows, Henry W., Portrait of..	527
22. Berkeley, John, Signature of....	94
23. Billop House...................	246
24. Binnenhof, The.................	16
25. Bogardus, Everardus, Signature of..............................	34
26. Bolingbroke, Lord, Signature of.	136
27. Bouck, W. C., Portrait of.......	498
28. Bradstreet, John, Signature of...	174
29. Brant, Joseph, Portrait of.......	270
30. Broome County Seal............	578
31. Brown, Jacob..................	396
32. Brown's Monument.............	307
33. Buffalo in 1813................	469
34. Burnet, William, Portrait of....	139
35. Burns's Coffee-House...........	198
36. Burr, Aaron, Portrait of	365

C.

37. Carr, Robert, Signature of......	75
38. Carroll, Charles, Portrait of.....	239
39. Carteret, George, Signature of...	94
40. Carterets, Arms of the..........	86
41. Cartwright, George, Signature of.	75
42. Castle Garden..................	461
43. Cattaraugus County Seal........	578
44. Cayuga County Seal	578
45. Champlain, Samuel, Portrait of.	10
46. Chase, Samuel, Portrait of	239
47. Chautauqua County Seal........	578
48. Chenango County Seal..........	578
49. Cincinnati, Order of the.......	330
50. Clark, Myron H., Portrait of....	511
51. Clarke's Monument.............	152
52. *Clermont, The*.................	377
53. City Hall, The First............	63
54. City Hall in 1700.	126
55. City Hall, Wall Street..........	344
56. Clinton Arms, The	154
57. Clinton County Seal............	578
58. Clinton, DeWitt, Portrait of.....	385
59. Clinton, George, Portrait of.....	399
60. Clinton, James.................	284
61. Clinton's Despatch.............	285
62. Clipper-built Schooner, A......	439
63. Colden, Cadwallader, Seal of....	140
64. Colden, Cadwallader, Signature of...........................	187
65. Colden, Cadwallader, Portrait of.	187
66. Collyer, Vincent, Portrait of....	529
67. Columbia County Seal..........	578
68. Constitution House at Kingston.	258
69. Cook, Lemuel..................	328

ILLUSTRATIONS.

	PAGE
70. Cooper, James Fenimore, Portrait of	574
71. Cornbury, Lord, Signature of	131
72. Cornbury, Lord, Portrait of	131
73. Cortland County Seal	578
74. Costumes of Hollanders, 1630	20
75. Costumes and Furniture, 1740	149
76. Costumes, 1800	368
77. Costumes about 1832	477
78. Cruger, John, Portrait of	369

D.

79. Dearborn, Henry, Portrait of	392
80. Delaware County Seal	579
81. De Laet, John, Signature of	64
82. De Lancey, James, Signature of	158
83. De Lancey, James, Seal of	158
84. De Lancey, Oliver, Signature of	213
85. De Peyster Arms	130
86. De Peyster, Abraham, Portrait of	129
87. De Peyster, Johannes, Seal and Signature of	86
88. De Sille, Signature of	67
89. De Vries, David Pietersen, Portrait of	33
90. Dix, John A., Portrait of	548
91. Dix's Order, Fac-simile of	518
92. Dongan, Governor, Signature of	96
93. Duane, James, Portrait of	350
94. Duchess County Seal	99
95. Duke of York's Seal	84
96. Dunmore, Governor, Signature of	203
97. Dunmore, Governor, Seal of	203
98. Dutch Church at Albany	45

E.

99. Erie County Seal	578
100. Essex County Seal	579
101. Evertsen, Admiral Cornelis, Portrait of	88
102. Executive Privy Seal	504

F.

103. Fac-simile of Journal of the Convention, 1788	340

	PAGE
104. Federal Arms of the Five Nations	7
105. Fenton, Reuben E., Portrait of	537
106. Fish, Hamilton, Portrait of	507
107. Flag of Holland	81
108. Flag of the Dutch West India Company	22
109. Fletcher, Governor, Seal and Signature of	117
110. Fort Plain Block-House	306
111. Franklin, Dr., Portrait of	239
112. Franklin County Seal	579
113. Fulton County Seal	579
114. Fulton, Robert, Portrait of	376
115. *Fulton the First*	378

G.

116. Garden Street Church	125
117. Gardiner Arms, The	42
118. Gates Medal, The	282
119. Genesee County Seal	579
120. Genet, E. C., Portrait of	354
121. George III., Statue of	199
122. Goshen, Monument at	302
123. Gouverneur, Abraham, Signature of	111
124. Government House	566
125. Greene County Seal	579
126. Grinnell, Moses H., Portrait of	523

H.

127. *Half Moon*, The	12
128. Hamilton, Alexander, Portrait of	337
129. Hamilton, Andrew, Portrait of	145
130. Hamilton and the People	146
131. Hamilton County Seal	579
132. Heathcote, Caleb, Portrait of	132
133. Heathcote, Caleb, Signature of	132
134. Hendrick, King, Portrait of	166
135. Herkimer County Seal	579
136. Hoffman, John T., Portrait of	542
137. Hone, Philip, Portrait of	465
138. Howe, Lord George, Portrait of	175
139. Hudson, Henry, Portrait of	11
140. Hughes, Archbishop, Portrait of	496
141. Hunt, Washington, Portrait of	508
142. Hunter, Robert, Signature of	137
143. Hunter, Robert, Seal of	137

ILLUSTRATIONS.

I.

	PAGE
144. Indian Fort, Attack upon	17
145. Ingoldsby, Richard, Signature of	133
146. Iroquois Chieftain	3
147. Irving, Washington	573
148. Izard, George, Portrait of	426

J.

149. James II., Portrait of	101
150. James II., Signature of	101
151. Jay, John, Portrait of	257
152. Jay, William, Portrait of	451
153. Jefferson County Seal	579
154. Jersey Prison Ship	249
155. Jogues, Isaac, Portrait of	47
156. Johnson, Guy, House of	225
157. Johnson, Sir John, Portrait of	231
158. Johnson, Sir William, Portrait of	224
159. Johnson, Sir William, Signature of	225
160. Johnson Hall	226

K.

161. Keg of Erie Water	467
162. Kent, James, Portrait of	448
163. Kieft, William, Signature of	39
164. King, John A	518
165. Kings County Seal	99
166. Knapp, Uzal, Portrait of	235

L.

167. Lamb, John, Portrait of	205
168. Lamb, John, Signature of	205
169. Leisler, Jacob, Seal and Signature of	107
170. Lewis County Seal	579
171. Lewis, Morgan, Portrait of	374
172. Life-Guard, Banner of	236
173. Links of Chain at West Point	253
174. Livingston Arms, The	108
175. Livingston County Seal	579
176. Livingston, John, Portrait of	562
177. Livingston Manor House	563
178. Livingston, Mary, Portrait of	562
179. Livingston, Robert, Portrait of	108
180. Livingston, Philip, Portrait of	221
181. Livingston, Robert R., Portrait of	345
182. Loockermans, Govert, Signature of	56
183. Lovelace, Lord, Signature of	133

M.

184. Macdonough, Thomas, Portrait of	429
185. Macomb, Alexander, Portrait of	430
186. Madison County Seal	579
187. Marcy, William L., Portrait of	479
188. Megopolensis, John, Signature of	77
189. Melyn, Cornelis, Signature of	51
190. Milking-Time at Albany	150
191. Minuit, Peter, Signature of	27
192. Monckton, Robert, Signature of	192
193. Monckton, Robert, Seal of	192
194. Monroe County Seal	579
195. Montgomery County Seal	582
196. Montgomery, Richard, Portrait of	229
197. Mooers, Benjamin, Portrait of	427
198. Moore, Governor, Signature of	193
199. Moore, Governor, Seal of	193
200. Morgan, Edwin D., Portrait of	512
201. Morris Arms, The	143
202. Morris, Gouverneur, Portrait of	382
203. Morris, Lewis, Signature of	143

N.

204. New Amsterdam, 1664	79
205. New Amsterdam, Cottage at	80
206. New Amsterdam, Seal of	67
207. *New Netherland, The*	25
208. New Netherland, Map of	36, 37
209. New Netherland, Seal of	27
210. New State Capital (*Frontispiece*).	
211. New York City, Seal of	95
212. New York County Seal	97
213. New York Province, Seal of	109
214. Niagara County Seal	582
215. Niagara, Fort	402
216. Nicolls, Richard, Signature of	74
217. Nicholson, Francis, Signature of	105
218. Normal School Building	488

O.

219. Oneida County Seal	582
220. Onondaga County Seal	582

ILLUSTRATIONS.

	PAGE
221. Ontario County Seal	582
222. Orange County Seal	99
223. Orleans County Seal	582
224. Oswego County Seal	582
225. Oswego, Fort, in 1750	141
226. Otsego County Seal	582

P.

227. Perry, Oliver H., Portrait of	405
228. Philipse Manor House	565
229. Pike, Zebulon M., Portrait of	409
230. Pleasure Wagon, A Dutch	69
231. Power, Nicholas, Signature of	339
232. Public Instruction, Seal of Department of	510
233. Publishing the Constitution	259
234. Putnam County Seal	582

Q.

235. Queens County Seal	99
236. Queenstown, Incident in the Battle at	394

R.

237. Randolph, Peyton, Portrait of	210
238. Randolph, Peyton, Signature of	211
239. Red Jacket, Portrait of	423
240. Reid, Samuel C., Portrait of	440
241. Rensselaer County Seal	582
242. Richmond County Seal	99
243. Riedesel, Baroness de, Portrait of	265
244. Rivington, James, Portrait of	233
245. Rivington, James, Signature of	234
246. Robinson, Beverly, Portrait of	318
247. Robinson House, The	313
248. Rochambeau, Portrait of	320
249. Rochester in 1813	470
250. Rockland County Seal	582
251. Rogers, Robert, Portrait of	185
252. *Royal Savage, The*	251

S.

253. St. Lawrence County Seal	582
254. Saratoga County Seal	583
255. Schenectady County Seal	583
256. Schoharie County Seal	583

	PAGE
257. Schuyler Arms, The	135
258. Schuyler County Seal	583
259. Schuyler, Peter, Portrait of	134
260. Schuyler, Philip, Portrait of	281
261. Scott, Winfield, Portrait of	422
262. Sears, Isaac, Signature of	208
263. Seal, First Great, of New York	332
264. Seal, Second Great, of New York	333
265. Seneca County Seal	583
266. Seward, William H., Portrait of	492
267. Seymour, Horatio, Portrait of	509
268. Silver Bullet	285
269. Snake Device	212
270. Statue of Liberty, Bartholdi	567
271. Steenwyck, Cornelis, Portrait of	87
272. Steuben, Baron von, Portrait of	322
273. Steuben's Monument	321
274. Steuben County Seal	583
275. Stirling, Lord, Portrait of	245
276. Stone Mill at Plattsburg	428
277. Stone, William L., Portrait of	463
278. Stuyvesant, Peter, Portrait of	53
279. Stuyvesant, Peter, Signature of	78
280. Stuyvesant's Seal	54
281. Suffolk County, Seal of	99
282. Sullivan County Seal	583
283. Sullivan, John, Portrait of	303

T.

284. Tables at Federal Dinner	351
285. Throop, Enos T., Portrait of	478
286. Ticonderoga, Fort, Ruins of	219
287. Tilden, Samuel J., Portrait of	551
288. Tioga County Seal	583
289. Tompkins, Daniel D., Portrait of	380
290. Tompkins County Seal	583
291. Totemic Signatures	6
292. Trinity Church, Old	120
293. Tryon, Governor, Signature of	204
294. Tryon, Governor, Seal of	204

U.

295. Ulster County Seal	99
296. Underhill, John, Signature of	50
297. United States Sanitary Commission Seal	528

ILLUSTRATIONS.

V.

298. Van Buren, Martin, Portrait of.. 446
299. Van Cortlandt Manor House..... 564
300. Van Cortlandt, Oloff S., Seal and Signature of................ 61
301. Van Curler, Arendt, Signature of.......... 44
302. Van Dam, Rip, Portrait of...... 142
303. Van Der Donck, Signature of... 61
304. Van Dincklagen, Lubbertus, Signature of 38
305. Van Rensselaer Arms, The...... 46
306. Van Rensselaer, Killian, Signature of..................... 32
307. Van Rensselaer, Jeremias, Portrait... 74
308. Van Rensselaer Manor House.... 561
309. Van Rensselaer, Stephen, Portrait of 395
310. Van Ruyven, Cornelis, Signature of.......................... 78
311. Van Slechtenhorst, Signature of. 60
312. Van Twiller, Walter, Signature of 34
313. Varick, Richard, Portrait of.... 359

W.

314. Wampum Belt................ 19
315. War Implements, Indian........ 294
316. Warren County Seal............ 583
317. Washington County Seal 583
318. Washington, Colonel George, Portrait of.................. 176
319. Washington's Headquarters, Room in.................... 326
320. Watson, Elkanah, Portrait of... 348
321. Wayne, Anthony, Portrait of.... 299
322. Wayne County Seal............ 583
323. Wayne's Despatch............. 300
324. Webb, James Watson, Portrait of..................... 483
325. West India Company's House... 21
326. Westchester County Sehl.... ... 99
327. Wilkinson, James, Portrait of... 414
328. Willett, Marinus, Portrait of.... 272
329. Windmill, A Dutch 69
330. Wool, John E., Portrait of..... 525
331. Wooster, David, Portrait of..... 230
332. Wright, Silas, Portrait of....... 475
333. Wyoming County Seal......... 583

Y.

334. Yates, Joseph C., Portrait of.... 459
335. Yates County Seal............. 583
336. Young, John, Portrait of....... 506

HISTORY OF
THE STATE OF NEW YORK.

CHAPTER I.

NEW YORK is ranked among the commonwealths of our Republic as "The Empire State." Wherefore? Is it imperial in its various aspects of population, wealth, the products of its industries, its forests and mines, its natural scenery, its commerce, and its institutions of learning and benevolence? Let us see.

The superficial area of New York is 49,000 square miles, including its share of Lakes Erie and Ontario and the St. Lawrence River. Its surface is picturesquely diversified with lofty ranges of the Appalachian chain of mountains, which crown the Atlantic slope of the continent from the Gulf region to the St. Lawrence, and with fertile valleys and uplands, and numerous lakes and rivers.

The loftiest mountain peak in the State is Mount Marcy, the *Ta-ha-was* or "sky-piercer" of the Indians. It is one of the grand Adirondack group in Northern New York, and rises to the altitude of over 5400 feet above tide-water.

The chief river of the State is the Hudson, flowing from the springs of the Adirondack Mountains, receiving numerous swift-running tributaries, and is navigable for large vessels fully 160 miles from the ocean. It traverses a most picturesque and fertile region about 300 miles. Along its whole course its waters and its banks are thickly clustered with exciting and romantic historical and legendary associations.

New York is bisected east and west by the longest and best-equipped canal in the world. It was constructed by the State (1817–25), is 363 miles in length, and cost over $9,000,000. Its subsequent enlargement cost $25,000,000. There are ten other canals owned by the State, the aggregate length of which is over 900 miles. There are 133 railroads in the State, having a total length in operation within the borders of the commonwealth of nearly 7000 miles.

The climate of New York is salubrious and varied, having a range wider than in any other member of the Union. The State lies between the parallels of 40° 29′ and 45° north latitude. Its soil is productive almost everywhere. In the value of its farm lands and general farm products it leads all the other States. In 1880, according to the tenth national census, it had within its borders nearly 242,000 farms, embracing over 23,000,000 acres, of which nearly 18,000,000 acres were improved land. The total value of the farms was more than $1,000,000,000. The State contained, in 1880, nearly 43,000 manufacturing establishments, employing about $515,000,000 of capital, and producing annually goods valued at nearly $1,100,000,000.

The population of the State in 1880 was 5,082,871, or 799,980 more inhabitants than any other State of the Republic, and embracing about one tenth of the entire population of the thirty-eight United States and the Territories. It also carries on its bosom seventeen cities, each having a population of 20,000 and upward. Five of these cities have each a population of over 100,000. Its system of public instruction is unrivalled.

These are a few of the many facts that might be presented in justification of giving to New York the title of "The Empire State."

This mighty fraction of the Great Republic of the West—this populous, wealthy, and powerful State—had its birth two centuries and three quarters ago on the little island of Mannahatta, or Manhattan, lying where the fresh waters of the Hudson River lovingly commingle with the brine of the Atlantic Ocean. Around the cradle in which the infant empire was rocked stood in wonder and awe representatives of an ancient race, dusky and barbarous in aspect, whose early history is involved in the hopeless obscurity of myth and fable.

At the same time there was a barbaric republic in the wilderness, simple, pure, and powerful, its capital seated a hundred leagues from the sea, among the beautiful hills and shadowy forests, glittering lakes and sunny savannas, within the present domain of the State of New York. Its western boundary was the mighty Niagara River, a swift-flowing strait between two great inland seas, broken midway by a cataract which has no equal on the earth in power, grandeur, and sublimity.*

---

* Perhaps the first European who actually saw the Niagara Falls was Father Hennepin, a missionary, who in his *Voyages* gives a description and a rude drawing of the great wonder. He estimated their height much greater than it really was. He also shows in the pictures a portion of the stream spouting from below a rock on the (present) Canada shore, far athwart the great Horse-shoe Fall. There have been many changes within a comparatively few years in the aspect of the Falls, owing to undermining and

The existence of this republic was unknown to the nations beyond the Atlantic, and unsuspected by them until Cartier sailed up the St. Lawrence River; until Champlain penetrated the wilderness of Northern New York, and Hudson voyaged up the beautiful river that bears his name, and touched the eastern border of this marvellous amphictyonic league known in history as "The Iroquois Confederacy." The later history of this league is interwoven with the earlier history of the State of New York, and forms an essential part of it.

The Indian tribes to whom the French gave the name of Iroquois inhabited the State of New York north and west of the Catskill Mountains (the Kaatsbergs) and south of the Adirondack group, a part of Northern Pennsylvania, and a portion of Ohio some distance along the southern shore of Lake Erie. The Hurons or Wyandots, who occupied nearly the whole of Canada south-west of the Ottawa River between Lakes Ontario, Erie, and Huron, seemed by their language to have been a part of the Iroquois family, and these, with the tribes south of the lakes, constituted the Huron-Iroquois nation. They were completely surrounded by the Algonquins, the most extensive and powerful of the aboriginal nations discovered within the present boundaries of the United States by the first European adventurer.

AN IROQUOIS CHIEFTAIN.

The Iroquois Confederacy was originally composed of five related families or nations, called, respectively, *Mohawks, Oneidas, Onondagas, Cayugas*, and *Senecas*. According to their traditions, they had, in a far-back period, been confined under a mountain at the falls of the Oswego River. They were released by *Ta-reng-a-wa-gon*, the Holder of the Heavens, and were led by him to the Mohawk Valley. Wandering eastward, they came to the Hudson River, and descended it to the sea.

---

abrasion by the water. Huge masses of rock have, from time to time, fallen into the gulf below. Table Rock, from the side of which Hennepin's third stream was projected, fell only a few years ago. The writer was upon the rock less than twenty-four hours before it fell.

Returning to the mouth of the Mohawk River, they travelled westward, separated, and seated themselves at various points in the country between the Hudson River and Lake Erie, in the order in which they are above named. At that time there were six families. One of them, the Tuscaroras, soon wandered to the South, and seated themselves on the Neuse River in North Carolina. The five families who remained, though of the same blood, continually waged cruel wars against each other.

The Holder of the Heavens had never ceased his guardianship of these five nations after their release from their subterranean prison. On account of the excellence of his character, his wisdom, and his sagacity, *Ta-reng-a-wa-gon* was called by the people *Hi-a-wat-ha*—" the very wise man." They regarded him with profound veneration, and in all things followed his advice. At length a fierce and powerful tribe of barbarians came from the country north of the lakes, fell upon the Onondagas—the dwellers among the hills—laid waste their country, slaughtered their women and children, and plunged the whole nation into the depths of despair. In their distress they hastened to *Hi-a-wat-ha* for counsel. He advised them to call together all the tribes in a general council to devise means for mutual defence. They agreed to the proposal. He appointed a place for the assembling of the convention on the bank of Onondaga Lake, and promised to meet with them there.

For three days the council fire had blazed before *Hi-a-wat-ha* arrived. He had been devoutly praying in silence to the Great Spirit for guidance. At length he approached in a white canoe, gliding over the waters of the lake, accompanied by his darling daughter, twelve years of age. They were received with joy, and as they landed and walked toward the council fire a sound like a rushing wind was heard, and a dark spot, ever increasing in size, was seen descending from the sky. It was an immense bird swooping down toward the spot where *Hi-a-wat-ha* and his child stood. He was unmoved. The bird fell upon his sweet daughter, crushed her into the earth, and perished itself. For three days *Hi-a-wat-ha* mourned his child. Then he took his seat in the great council, listened to the debates, and said: "Meet me to-morrow, and I will unfold to you my plan." They did so, when the venerated counsellor arose and said:

"Friends and Brothers: You are members of many tribes and nations. You have come here, many of you, a great distance from your homes. We have met for one common purpose—to provide for our common interest—and that is to provide for our mutual safety, and how it shall best be done. To oppose these foes from the north by tribes, singly and alone, would prove our certain destruction. We can make no progress in that way. We must unite ourselves into one common band of brothers. Thus united we may drive the invaders back. This must be done, and we shall be safe.

"You, the *Mohawks*, sitting under the shadow of the 'Great Tree,' whose roots sink deep into the earth, and whose branches spread over a vast country, shall be the first nation, because you are warlike and mighty.

"And you, *Oneidas*, a people who recline your bodies against the 'Everlasting Stone,' that cannot be moved, shall be the second nation, because you give wise counsel.

"And you, *Onondagas*, who have your habitation at the 'Great Mountain,' and are overshadowed by its crags, shall be the third nation, because you are greatly gifted in speech, and are mighty in war.

"And you, *Cayugas*, whose habitation is the 'Dark Forest,' and whose home is everywhere, shall be the fourth nation, because of your superior cunning in hunting.

"And you, *Senecas*, a people who live in the 'Open Country,' and possess much wisdom, shall be the fifth nation, because you understand better the art of raising corn and beans, and making cabins.

"You, five great and powerful nations, must unite and have but one common interest, and no foe shall be able to disturb or subdue you. If we unite, the Great Spirit will smile upon us. Brothers, these are the words of *Hi-a-wat-ha*; let them sink deep into your hearts."

After reflecting upon the subject for a day, the five nations formed a league. Before the council was dispersed *Hi-a-wat-ha* urged the people to preserve the union they had formed. "Preserve this," he said; "admit no foreign element of power by the admission of other nations, and you will always be free, numerous, and happy. If other tribes and nations are admitted to your councils they will sow the seeds of jealousy and discord, and you will become few, feeble, and enslaved. Remember these words; they are the last you will hear from *Hi-a-wat-ha*. The Great Master of Breath calls me to go. I have patiently waited his summons. I am ready to go. Farewell!"

At that moment myriads of singing voices burst upon the ears of the multitude, and the whole air seemed filled with music. *Hi-a-wat-ha*, seated in his white canoe, rose majestically above the throng, and as all eyes gazed in rapture upon the ascending wise man, he disappeared forever in the blue vault of heaven. The music melted into low whispers, like a soft summer breeze. There were pleasant dreams that night in every cabin and wigwam occupied by the members of the Great Council.

and all the Five Nations were made happy by the announcement of the glad tidings among them.

This confederacy was called *Ko-no-shi-oni*—the "cabin-builders"—the "Long House," which extended from the Hudson River to Lake Erie. The Mohawks kept the eastern door and the Senecas the western door. The Great Council Fire, or Federal Capital, was with the Onondagas. This metropolis was a few miles south of (present) Syracuse.

Such is the traditionary history of the formation of the great Iroquois Confederacy. It is, of course, embellished by fancy, but it is undoubtedly correct in every essential particular. At what time this league was formed cannot be accurately determined. It was probably not earlier than the year 1540. Jacques Cartier, who ascended the St. Lawrence to

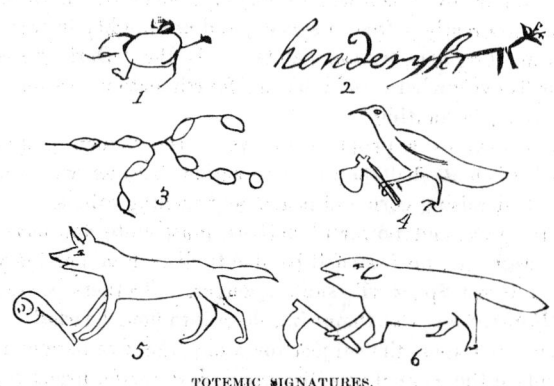

TOTEMIC SIGNATURES.

the site of Montreal in 1535, showed, by a vocabulary of Indian words which he made, that the Iroquois language was spoken there, probably by the Hurons; but he makes no reference to any Indian confederacy.

The polity of the Iroquois League was as purely democratic as possible in spirit, but it took the representative or republican form for convenience. It was a league for mutual defence, not a political union. There was a wide distribution of power and civil organization, which was a safeguard against tyranny. Each canton or nation was a distinct republic, independent of all others in relation to its domestic affairs, but each was bound to the others of the league by ties of honor and general interest. Each canton had eight principal sachems, or civil magistrates, and several inferior sachems. The whole number of civil magistrates in the confederacy amounted to nearly two hundred. There were fifty hereditary sachems.

THE TOTEMIC SYSTEM.

Each canton or nation was subdivided into clans or tribes, each clan having a heraldic insignia called *totem*. For this insignia one tribe would have the figure of a wolf; another, of a bear; another, of a deer; another, of a tortoise, and so on. By this totemic system they maintained a perfect tribal union.* After the Europeans came the sachem of a tribe affixed his *totem*, in the form of a rude representation of the animal that marked his tribe, to documents he was required to sign, like an ancient monarch affixing his seal.†

Office was the reward of merit alone; malfeasance in office brought dismissal and public scorn. All public services were compensated only by public esteem. The league had a president clothed with powers similar to those conferred on the Chief Magistrate of the United States. He had authority to assemble a congress of representatives of the league. He had a cabinet of six advisers, and in the Grand Council he was moderator. There was no coercive power lodged anywhere excepting public opinion.

FEDERAL ARMS OF THE FIVE NATIONS.

---

* The chief totems of the Five Nations—the *bear*, the *wolf*, the *deer*, the *tortoise*, and the *beaver*—were, one of them, the distinguishing mark of the delegate of each nation at the Grand Council or Congress of the Confederation, and appeared on his person. These constituted the Federal arms of the Confederacy when combined.

† There were many totemic symbols besides those named, such as different birds—the eagle, the heron, the turkey, and the plover.

The signatures on page 6 were copied from the originals on documents. Fig. 1 is a *tortoise*; Fig. 2 is the signature of King Hendrick, with his totem, a *deer*; Fig. 3 is a *potato* totem; Fig. 4, an *eagle* totem; Fig. 5, a *wolf* totem, and Fig. 6, a *beaver* totem. Many totemic signatures are rudely drawn, while some are quite artistic and correct.

The *tortoise*, the *wolf*, and the *bear* were the totems of the three families into which each nation was divided. In his stirring metrical romance, *Frontenac*, the late Alfred B. Street, describing the aggressions and the supremacy of the Iroquois, thus alludes to these totemic symbols of a fierce tribe:

> " By the far Mississippi the Illini shrank
> When the trail of the *tortoise* was seen on its bank;
> On the hills of New England the Pequod turned pale
> When the howl of the *wolf* swelled at night on the gale;
> And the Cherokee shook in his green smiling bowers
> When the foot of the *bear* stamp'd his carpet of flowers."

The first chosen president of the league was the venerable *Ato-tar-ho*, a famous Onondaga chief. The Indian traditions invest him with extraordinary attributes. He is represented as living, at the time he was chosen, in grim seclusion in a swamp, where his dishes and drinking-cups, like those of the old Scandinavian warriors, were made of the skulls of his enemies slain in battle. When a delegation of Mohawks went to offer him the symbol of supreme power, they found him sitting in calm repose, smoking his pipe, but was unapproachable because he was clothed with hissing snakes—the old story of Medusa's tresses. They finally invested him with a broad belt of wampum as the highest token of authority.

The military power dominated the civil power in the league. The military leaders were called chiefs. They derived their authority from

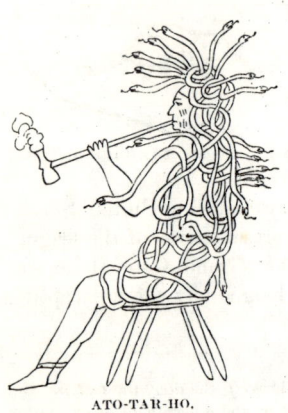

ATO-TAR-HO.

the people, and they sometimes, like the Roman soldiers, deposed sachems or civil rulers. The army was composed wholly of volunteers. Conscription was impossible. Every able-bodied man was bound to do military duty, and he who shirked it incurred everlasting disgrace. The ranks were always full. The war-dances were the recruiting stations. Whatever was done in civil councils was subjected to review by the soldiery, who had the right to call councils when they pleased, and to approve or disapprove public measures. Every important measure was undertaken only after unanimous consent had been given.

The matrons formed a third and most powerful party in the legislature of the league. They had a right to sit in the councils, and held and exercised the veto power on the subject of a declaration of war. They had authority to demand a cessation of hostilities, and they were eminently peace-makers. It was no reflection upon the courage of warriors if, at the call of the matrons, they withdrew from the war-path. These women wielded great influence in the councils of the league, but they modestly delegated the duties of speech-making to some masculine orator. With these barbarians woman was man's coworker in legislation —a thing yet unknown among civilized people. Such was the polity of the Iroquois Confederacy when it was discovered by Europeans.*

* "As I am forced to think," says Dr. Colden (*History of the Five Indian Nations*), "that the present state of the *Indian Nation* exactly shows the *Most Ancient* and *Original Condition* of almost every Nation; so I believe here we may, with more certainty, see

The "inalienable rights of man" were held in such reverence by the Iroquois that they never made slaves of their fellow-men, not even of captives taken in war. By unity they were made powerful; and to prevent degeneracy, members of a tribe were not allowed to intermarry with each other. Like the Romans, they caused the expansion of their commonwealth by conquests and annexation. Had the advent of Europeans in America been postponed a century, the Confederacy might have embraced the whole continent, for the Five Nations had already extended their conquests from the great lakes to the Gulf of Mexico, and were the terror of the other nations East and West.

SAMUEL CHAMPLAIN.

For a long time the French in Canada, who taught the Indians the use of fire-arms, maintained a doubtful struggle against them. Champlain * found the Iroquois at war against the Canada Indians from Lake

---

the *Original Forms of all Governments* than in the *most curious speculations* of the *Learned;* and that the *Patriarchal* and other *Schemes* in *Politicks* are no better than *Hypotheses* in *Philosophy*, and as prejudicial to real knowledge."

The total population of the Confederacy at the advent of the Europeans did not exceed probably 13,000. The Senecas seemed to be the more numerous. They were found to possess many of the better features of civilization. They had framed cabins; cultivated the soil; manufactured stone implements and pottery; made clothing and foot-gear of the skins of animals; fashioned canoes of bark or of logs hollowed by fire and stone axes, and showed some military skill and acumen in the construction of fortifications.

* Samuel Champlain was an eminent French navigator, born at Brouage, France, in 1567; served in the Spanish navy; was pensioned by his king, and was induced by M. de Chastes, Governor of Dieppe, to explore and prepare the way for a colony on the banks of the St. Lawrence River. He was commissioned Lieutenant-General of Canada. He ascended the St. Lawrence in May, 1603, and landed on the site of Quebec. In a subsequent voyage he planted the banner of France at Quebec—the capital of the dominion. In order to gain the friendship of the Indians, he was induced to join them, with a few Frenchmen, in an expedition against their enemies the Iroquois. They went up the Sorel River from the St. Lawrence in twenty-four canoes, into the "Lake of the Iroquois," and on its lower western border (July 29th, 1609) had a sharp engagement with the foe. The arquebuses of the Europeans secured an easy victory. This was the first European invasion of the country of the Iroquois. The fight occurred between Crown Point and Lake George, not far from Schroon (Scarron) Lake. Champlain gave his name to the larger lake.

Huron to the Gulf of St. Lawrence. He fought them on the borders of Lake Champlain in 1609, and from that time until the middle of the century their wars against the Canada Indians and their French allies were fierce and distressing.

The Tuscaroras, in North Carolina, entered into a conspiracy with other Indians in 1711 to exterminate the white people there. They fell like lightning upon the scattered German settlements along the Roanoke River and Pamlico Sound. In one night they slew one hundred and thirty persons. With knife and torch they desolated the settlements along the shores of Albemarle Sound. South Carolinians sped to the rescue of their smitten neighbors in 1712, and in the spring of 1713 the Tuscaroras were driven into their stronghold, where eight hundred of them were made prisoners. The remainder fled to their kindred—the Five Nations—in June, and remaining there, formed the sixth nation of the Iroquois League.

It was after this union that the most important events in the history of the league, as connected with the European inhabitants of the Province and State of New York, occurred. As the wars of the league with other barbarians, which occurred before the advent of the Europeans, have no bearing upon the early history of New York, I will forbear alluding to them.

Upon the walls of the Governor's Room, in the City Hall, New York, hangs a dingy portrait of a man apparently thirty-five or forty years of age. It was painted, probably, about three hundred years ago. His hair is dark and short, and so is his full beard. His forehead is broad, and his eyes are expressive of intelligence and good-nature. His neck is encircled by an ample "ruff," such as men wore late in the reign of Queen Elizabeth. It is claimed that this is an original picture from life of HENRY HUDSON,* a famous English navigator, who, in the service of some London merchants, attempted to make a voyage from Great Britain to China and Japan through the polar waters north of Europe and Asia early in the seventeenth century. He failed, and was afterward employed for the same purpose by the Dutch East India Com-

---

* Henry Hudson was a native of England, born at about the middle of the sixteenth century. Of his early life nothing is known. He appears to have been an expert navigator, and employed, as we have observed in the text, by both English and Dutch merchants in searching for a north-east passage to the East Indies. Failing in this effort, he sailed westward to America, entered a spacious land-locked bay into which poured the waters of a mighty river, and up which he sailed one hundred and sixty miles. His name was given to it, as its discoverer and first explorer. After various tribulations he made a fourth voyage, in 1610, toward the Polar waters, descended the great bay that bears his name, and there perished.

pany. He sailed from the Texel in a yacht of ninety tons named the *Half Moon*, with a select crew, in the spring of 1609. He steered for the coast of Nova Zembla. On the meridian of Spitzbergen he was confronted, as before, by impassable ice and fogs and tempest, and compelled to abandon the enterprise. Then he resolved to sail in search of a north-west passage "below Virginia," spoken of by his friend Captain Smith. He passed the southern capes of Greenland, and in July made soundings on the banks of Newfoundland. Sailing southward, he discovered Delaware Bay. He voyaged as far as the harbor of Charleston, when, disappointed, he turned his prow northward, and early in September sailed into the beautiful New York Bay * and anchored. Sending men ashore in a boat, they saw many almost naked, copper-colored inhabitants, some of whom followed them in their canoes on their return.

HENRY HUDSON.

From his anchorage Hudson saw a broad stream stretching northward. In the purple distance appeared the forms of lofty hills, through and beyond which the dusky inhabitants who swarmed around his ship in canoes told him there was a mighty river which felt the pulsations of the tides of the sea. Believing this stream to be a strait flowing between oceans, he sailed on with joyous hope, not doubting he would be the

---

* A claim has been made that John Verazzano, a Florentine in the maritime service of King Francis I. of France, discovered New York Bay in 1524. It is asserted that he traversed the American coast from Cape Fear to latitude 50° N., when he returned to France. The sole authority upon which this claim rests is a letter alleged to have been written by the navigator to Francis I., in the summer of 1524. This letter was first published at Venice in 1556. No French original is known to exist, nor has there been found in the French archives of that period even an allusion to such a voyage. Verazzano was an adventurer. He was also a corsair, and was captured on the coast of Spain and hanged as a pirate at the village of Pico, in November, 1527. There is good reason for believing that the alleged letter of Verazzano is a forgery. In it is given a most confused account of the "seven hundred leagues of coast" traversed. It is said in it that a bay was discovered, but no data to determine whether it was Delaware, New York, or Narragansett Bay. It is safe to relegate to the realm of pure fiction such a vague and untrustworthy statement, even if the letter was genuine, as a foundation for a belief that Verazzano ever saw New York Bay.

discoverer of the long-sought north-west passage to the Indies. Alas! when he had passed the mountains the water freshened and the stream narrowed. Hope failed him; but he voyaged on through a land of wondrous beauty and fertility—"as beautiful a land as the foot of man can tread upon," he said—a land peopled by vigorous men and beautiful women, who came to his vessel, and abounding with fur-bearing animals. He sailed on until he reached the head of tide-water, and some of his crew in a small boat passed by the foaming cataract of Cohoes at the mouth of the Mohawk River, and went several miles farther. Had Hudson penetrated the wilderness a few leagues farther northward he might have met Champlain, who was then exploring the lower borders of the "Lake of the Iroquois," which afterward bore his own name.

THE HALF MOON.

Hudson returned to his first anchorage in the beautiful harbor into which it has been claimed Verazzano, the Florentine navigator, had sailed more than fourscore years before. He took formal possession of the country in the name of the States-General of Holland, sailed out upon the Atlantic, and hastened to Europe to tell his glad tidings to his employers. He first landed in England, and there told his wonderful story. As he was an English subject, King James claimed the land he had discovered as a rightful possession of the British crown. It was within the bounds of the North Virginia charter which he had granted. Added to these considerations was jealousy of the commercial advantages the Hollanders might derive from Hudson's discovery. The monarch, determined to secure to his crown every political right to the territory and every commercial advantage possible for his subjects, would not allow the navigator and his vessel to leave England for a long time ; but Hudson had sent his log-book, his charts, and a full account of his discoveries to the authorities of the Dutch East India Company at Amsterdam.

These accounts so powerfully excited the cupidity of the Dutch that while King James was devising schemes for British political and commercial advantages, adventurers from Holland had opened a brisk fur trade with the Indians on the island of Manhattan. Acting upon the principle and the practice of the saying, " Possession is nine points of the law," the Dutch, at the mouth of the river discovered by Hudson, kept British authority and dominion at bay more than fifty years.*

---

* The Indians on the upper portion of the great river discovered by Hudson called it *Ca-ho-ha-ta-tea ;* those of the middle portion, *Shat-te-muc,* and the Delawares and the dwellers in its lower portion, *Ma-hi-can-ittuck,* the " place of the Mohicans." The Dutch named it the *Mauritius,* in honor of their great prince, Maurice, Stadtholder of the Netherlands ; and the English named it *Hudson's River* in compliment of its discoverer. Until within a comparatively few years, it was frequently called *North River.* It was so designated at an early period to distinguish it from the Delaware, which was called the *South River.*

CHAPTER II.

In less than three years after his great discovery Hudson and his gallant little yacht perished. Not permitted to leave England, Hudson entered the service of an English company, and in the spring of 1610 he sailed in quest of a north-west passage to India. Passing Iceland, he saw Hecla flaming. Rounding the southern capes of Greenland, he went through Davis's Strait to the ice-floe beyond, and entered the great bay that bears his name. There he endured a dreary winter, and at midsummer, 1611, his mutinous crew thrust him into a frail and open shallop, with his son and seven others, and cast them adrift to perish in the waste of waters. Philip Staffe, the ship's carpenter, obtained leave to share the fate of his commander. The *Half Moon* sailed to the East Indies in the spring of 1611, and in March, the next year, she was wrecked and lost on the island of Mauritius.

Hudson's discovery bore abundant fruit immediately. Wealthy merchants of Amsterdam sent a ship from the Texel laden with cheap merchandise suitable for traffic with the Indians for the furs and peltries of the beaver, the otter, and the bear. As soon as the *Half Moon* returned to New Amsterdam she, too, was sent on a like errand to Manhattan, which became the *entrepot* for the collection and exportation of furs gathered by the Indians from the regions of the Delaware and the Housatonic rivers, and even from the far-off Mohawk Valley, where dwelt the eastern nation of the Iroquois Republic. This was the beginning of peaceful intercourse between the Europeans and the dusky Five Nations.

Many private adventurers were soon engaged in traffic with the Indians, and the Hongers, the Pelgraves, and the Van Tweenhuysens, of Holland, were getting rich on the enormous profits derived from the trade.* Captains De Witt and Christiansen, Block and Mey were becoming famous navigators in connection with this trade before the free cities of Holland had cast a political glance toward the newly-discovered country. But when its importance became manifest, and King

---

* Hans Hongers, Paul Pelgrave, and Lambrecht Tweenhuysen, merchants of Amsterdam, were the earliest Dutch traders for furs with the Indians at Manhattan. In 1612 they equipped two vessels, the *Fortune* and the *Tiger*, for trade along the Hudson River. These vessels were commanded respectively by Captains Christiansen and Block.

James of Great Britain began to growl because the Dutch were monopolizing the fur trade upon his claimed domain, the States-General of Holland * seriously considered the matter.

Within five years after Hudson departed from Manhattan a little seed of empire, less promising than that planted by Dido, Cecrops, or Romulus, but of far higher destiny, was deposited there. In December, 1613, Adrien Block, a bold Dutch navigator, was about to sail from Manhattan for Amsterdam with a cargo of bear-skins when fire reduced his vessel—the *Tiger*—to ashes. The small storehouse of the traffickers could not afford shelter to Block's crew, and the wigwams of the Indians, freely offered, could not shield them from the biting frosts; so they built log-cabins, and from the stately oaks which towered around them they constructed another vessel, which they called the *Onrust*—the "Restless"—forty-four feet long and eleven feet wide, and of sixteen tons burden. With another cargo of furs the *Onrust* sailed for Holland in the spring of 1614.† That little collection of huts on the site of the stately warehouses of Beaver Street, and that little vessel, which was launched at the foot of Broadway, composed the fertile little seed of empire planted on Manhattan—the tiny beginning of the great commercial metropolis of the Western Hemisphere.

Doubtful as to the real disposition of the Indians around them, the Dutch seem to have palisaded their storehouses at the southern end of Manhattan Island for a defence if necessary. In 1614 Captain Christiansen, who had made ten voyages to Manhattan Island, sailed up the Mauritius (now the Hudson River), and on an island a little below the site of Albany he erected a fortified trading-house, and called it Fort Nassau. This was on the borders of the Iroquois Republic. The islet was afterward called Castle Island.

Meanwhile the several United Provinces of the Netherlands had petitioned the States-General or Congress of Holland to pass an ordinance securing a monopoly of the trade with the Indians on the Mauritius for a limited time to Dutch adventurers who might undertake the business. This was done in the spring of 1614.

Merchants of Amsterdam and Hoorn formed a company, and at the

---

* The name given to the Parliament or Congress of the United Provinces of Holland.

† Block, the first shipbuilder on Manhattan Island, sailed up the East River into Long Island Sound; discovered the Connecticut River; explored the New England coasts eastward; entered and explored Narragansett Bay; sailed to Martha's Vineyard and Cape Cod, and at the latter place left the *Onrust*, and proceeded to Holland in a vessel commanded by Captain Christiansen. He was afterward sent in command of some vessels employed in the whale-fishery near Spitzbergen, in 1615.

middle of August, 1614, they sent a deputation to the Dutch court at the Hague to obtain a charter of special privileges promised by the ordinance. Before an oval table in the Binnenhof, a room in the ancient palace of the Counts of Holland, the chief representative of the merchants, Captain Hendricksen, stood and spread before their High Mightinesses, the members of the States-General, twelve in number, a " figurative map" of their discoveries in the Western Hemisphere. He gave details of the adventures of the navigators and traders, their expenses and losses.

THE BINNENHOF

(The Palace of the Counts of Holland at the Hague*).

The leading representative of the State, before whom Hendricksen pleaded, was the famous John Van Olden Barneveldt,† the Advocate of Holland.

---

* For four hundred years the Counts of Holland made their residence at the Hague. There yet stands a straggling pile of buildings surrounding a vast quadrangle on one side of which is the Binnenhof, the palace of the Counts of Holland for many generations. There, in a spacious hall, the States-General constantly held their ordinary meetings.

† Barneveldt was a most liberal and enlightened statesman of Holland, and one of the most loyal of citizens. He was persecuted by political and religious fanaticism, and the spite of Prince Maurice, the Stadtholder, and was finally beheaded in front of the Binnenhof on May 19th, 1619, condemned on a false charge of treason.

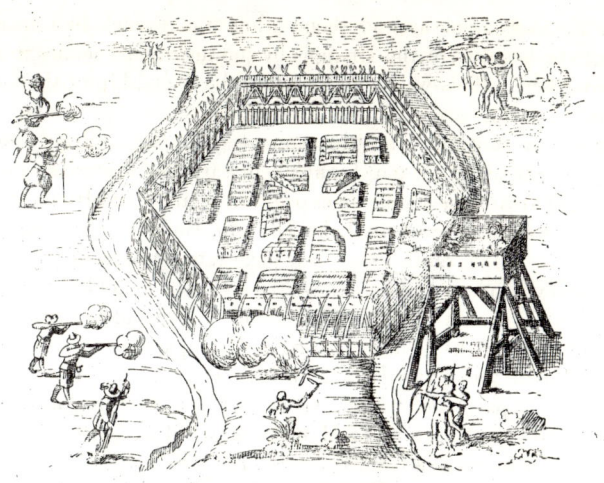

CHAMPLAIN'S ATTACK ON THE INDIAN FORT.*
(From a print in a narrative of his voyages.)

A charter was granted to the merchants on October 14th, 1614, which defined the region wherein they were permitted to operate as "between the fortieth and forty-fifth degree" of north latitude—between the parallels of Cape May and Nova Scotia. In that document the name of NEW NETHERLAND was given to the domain lying "between Virginia and New France." Notwithstanding this domain was included in the royal grant to the Plymouth Company of England, no settlement had been made by the English above Richmond, in Virginia, and no formal territorial jurisdiction had been claimed by them; and the Dutch were not disturbed in their traffic or political jurisdiction for a long time.

The Dutch on Manhattan Island and at Fort Nassau were continually exploring the neighboring regions and assiduously cultivating the friend-

---

* The fort was really the fortified "walls" that enclosed an Iroquois village. It was composed of quadruple palisades of large timber, thirty feet high, "interlocked the one with the other," wrote Champlain, "with an interval of not more than half a foot between them, with galleries in the form of parapets, defended by double pieces of timber, proof against our arquebuses, and on one side they had a pond with a never-failing supply of water, from which proceeded a number of gutters which they had laid along the intermediate space, throwing the water without, and rendering it effectual inside, for the purpose of extinguishing fire." The galleries were well supplied with stones which the garrison hurled upon their enemies. An attempt was made to set fire to the fort, but failed. The assailants constructed movable towers of timber to overlook the parapets, in which to place four or five arquebusiers. See next page.

ship of the barbarians around them, while the French in Canada were arousing the hostility of the Iroquois by joining their enemies in making war upon them. This was done to secure the friendship of the Canadian Indians.

In the early autumn of 1615 Samuel Champlain (already noticed), then at Montreal, with ten Frenchmen carrying fire-arms, joined the Hurons and Adirondacks in an expedition against the Iroquois. They went up the St. Lawrence to Lake Ontario, landed on its south-eastern shore, and moving south-westward, penetrated the country to Lakes Oneida and Onondaga. There they attacked a stronghold of the Iroquois, and after a severe struggle for four hours, the invaders were repulsed, and finally retreated. During the fight Champlain was twice wounded, and, unable to walk, was carried on a frame of wicker-work. He was compelled to pass the winter in the Huron country north of Lake Ontario, and did not return to Montreal until May, 1616, where he was received with joy as one risen from the dead.

The Indians who immediately surrounded the Dutch on Manhattan were the Metowacks on Long Island, the Monatons on Staten Island, the Raritans and Hackensacks on the New Jersey shore, and the Weckquaesgeeks beyond the Harlem River. The Manhattans occupied the island that bears their name.

In 1616 Captain Hendricksen sailed from Manhattan in the little *Restless* built by Block, on an exploring voyage. He entered Delaware Bay, which Hudson had discovered seven years before, and explored the adjoining coasts and the river above as far as the rapids at Trenton. He was charmed with the beauty and evident fertility of the country around these waters. On the site of Philadelphia (which was founded sixty-six years afterward) he ransomed three captive Dutchmen. On his return to Manhattan this first European explorer of Delaware Bay and River proceeded to Holland to assist his employers in obtaining a separate charter which would give them the monopoly of trade with the inhabitants of the newly-discovered territory.

Again the energetic Captain Hendricksen appeared before their High Mightinesses in the Binnenhof, displayed his maps and arguments, and gave a glowing account of his discoveries. Doubtful of their right to any territorial jurisdiction below the fortieth degree, the States-General, after due deliberation, decided to postpone the matter "indefinitely."

The floods of the Mohawk River sweeping in fury down the **Mauritius** with their heavy burden of floating ice compelled the Dutch to abandon Fort Nassau, on Castle Island, in the spring of 1617. The island was submerged, and the fort was almost demolished. A new one was built on the main at the mouth of the Tawasentha Creek (now Norman's Kill), and there soon afterward the first formal treaty of alliance between the Dutch and the Iroquois Confederacy was consummated. It was renewed in 1645, and in 1664 a new league of friendship with the barbarians was formed by the English. This remained inviolate until the kindling of the old war for American independence in 1775.

At the great council at Tawasentha other powerful tribes were represented, but the supremacy of the Five Nations was affirmed and acknowledged by the others, even with tokens of great humiliation. When the long belt of peace and alliance was held by the Dutch at one end and by the Iroquois at the other end, the middle portion rested upon the shoulders of the Mohicans (Mohegans) and the Minsees, and also upon the shoulders of the Lenni-Lenapes as a "nation of women." So the Hollanders wisely and righteously acquired the friendship of these "Romans of the West."

Success had attended the Dutch in New Netherland from the beginning, and wise men in Holland were beginning to prophesy that a flourishing Belgic Empire would arise beyond the Atlantic.

A WAMPUM BELT.*

Speculations concerning the bright future of Holland were everywhere indulged in. The sovereignty of the United Provinces had lately been recognized, and the Netherlands now ranked among the leading nations of the earth. For fully twoscore years political and religious toleration had prevailed in the Low Countries, as Holland was called. There was no official restraint upon conscience. Holland had become an asylum for the persecuted in all lands—of the active thinkers and workers who had been compelled to seek a refuge somewhere for conscience' sake. The world

---

* Wampum was the currency of the Indians, especially of those who lived in the region of the sea. It was made of portions of the common clam shell in the form of cylindrical beads, white and bluish black. Each color had a distinct and fixed value. They were strung in little chains, or fastened upon deer-skin belts, often in alternate layers of white and black. As currency their value was estimated at about two cents of our coins for three black beads, or six of white beads. A fathom in length and three inches in width of white wampum was valued at about $2.50, and a fathom of blue black, at about $5.

of bigots outside sneered. Amsterdam was pointed at as a "common harbor of all opinions and all heresies." Holland was stigmatized as a "cage of unclean birds," where "all strange religions flock together," and an English poet wrote of Amsterdam,

"The Universal Church is only there."

Occasionally, however, the old spirit of intolerance would crop out and acts of violence would be performed when political ambition, dis-

COSTUMES OF THE HOLLANDERS, 1630.

guised under the form of religious controversy, actuated the authorities of State, as in 1619, when Grotius, the eminent scholar, was condemned to imprisonment for life, and the venerable patriot, John Van Olden Barneveldt, was doomed to decapitation. It was at this juncture that schemes for the establishment of a colony of families in New Netherland began to be contemplated. Excellent materials for such a colony were then abundant in Holland, and the political and social condition of the

Low Countries favored such an enterprise. The feudal system there had begun to decay. Industry was made honorable. In the new era which had gradually dawned on the Netherlands the owner of the soil was no longer the head of a band of armed depredators who were his dependents, but the careful proprietor of broad acres, and devoted to industry and thrift. The nobles, who composed the landlord class, gradually came down from the stilts of exclusiveness, and in habits, and even in costume, imitated the working people in a degree. The latter became elevated in the social scale ; their rights were respected, and their relative value in the State was duly estimated. Ceaseless toil in Holland was necessary to preserve the hollow land from the invasion of

DUTCH WEST INDIA COMPANY'S HOUSE.

the sea, and the common needs assimilated all classes in a country where all must work or drown.

Stimulated by the glowing accounts of the country and climate in the region of America watered by the Mauritius, and satisfied with the scant liberty accorded them by the Dutch Government, the English Puritan congregation of the Rev. John Robinson, then at Leyden, earnestly desired to emigrate to New Netherland. They proposed this enterprise to the Associated Merchants in 1618, whose charter of privileges had just expired. Mr. Robinson proposed to form a colony at Manhattan under "the Prince of Orange and their High and Mighty Lords, the States-General."

The Association of Merchants eagerly listened to Robinson's proposal. They offered to transport his whole congregation to Manhattan free of cost, and to furnish each family with cattle. They petitioned the Prince of Orange to sanction the scheme. Maurice referred the matter to the States-General. That body had a more ambitious scheme in contemplation. Nearly thirty years before, the wise Usselincx had suggested the formation of a Dutch West India Company. The project was now revived, and the States-General authorized the organization of such a company—a grand commercial monopoly. A charter was granted on June 3d, 1621. Colonization was neither the motive nor the main object of the establishment of the Dutch West India Company. The grand idea was the promotion of trade. That was an age of great monopolies, and the Dutch West India Company was one of the greatest monopolies of the time. It was incorporated for twenty-four years, with a pledge of a renewal of its charter; and it became the sovereign of the central portion of the original United States of America. It was vested with the exclusive privilege to traffic and plant colonies on the coast of Africa from the Tropic of Cancer to the Cape of Good Hope, and on the coasts of America from the Strait of Magellan to the remotest north. It provided that none of the inhabitants of the United Provinces of the Netherlands should be permitted to sail thence to the coasts of Africa between the points specified, nor to the coasts of America or the West Indies between Newfoundland and Cape Horn, upon pain of a forfeiture of ships and cargoes.

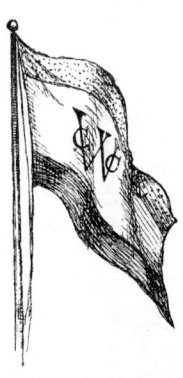

DUTCH WEST INDIA COMPANY'S FLAG.

This great monopoly was vested with enormous powers and immense franchises that it might act with independence. It might conquer provinces at its own risk, hoist its flag of red, white, and blue over fortresses, and make contracts and alliances with princes and other rulers within the limits of its charter. It might build forts; appoint and discharge governors and other officers and soldiers; administer justice and regulate commerce.

The States-General gave to the company a million guilders ($380,000), and became stockholders to the same amount. They agreed to defend the company against every person, in free navigation and

THE DUTCH WEST INDIA COMPANY.

traffic, but not any specified territory. They also agreed, in case of war, to assist the company by furnishing sixteen war-ships of three hundred tons burden and four yachts of eighty tons, all fully equipped. The vessels were to be manned and supported by the company. The whole fleet was to be under an admiral appointed by the States-General. In war the latter was to be known only as allies and patrons.

The company had five separate chambers of management, one in each of five principal cities in the Netherlands. The general executive powers were vested in nineteen delegates, entitled *The College of Nineteen*. In this college the States-General had one representative. The special charge of New Netherland was entrusted to the branch at Amsterdam.* Thus the Government gave to a new mercantile corporation almost unlimited powers to subdue, colonize, and govern the unoccupied regions of Africa and America. The company was not finally organized until June, 1623. On the 21st of that month its books of subscription were closed, and the company began to prosecute their purposes with energy.

Although the Dutch West India Company was primarily a commercial corporation, its first grand effort was the planting of a colony in New Netherland. Good policy dictated this step. In the summer of 1619 an English vessel sent by the Plymouth Company on a voyage of discovery, attempting to pass the dangerous eddies at Hell Gate,† lost its anchor, and was carried by the strong currents of the East River far into the broad bay at Manhattan. Her commander (Captain Dermer) did not stop to parley with the Dutch traffickers, who saluted him, but sailed on to Virginia. On his return he stopped at Manhattan and warned the Dutch traders to leave "His Majesty's domain" as quickly as possible.

"We found no English here, and hope we have not offended," said the good-natured Dutchmen, and went on smoking their pipes, planting their gardens, catching beavers and otters, and buying furs and peltries of the Indians as complacently as if they had never heard of his English Majesty.

Dermer's report of what he saw at Manhattan aroused the slumbering energies of the English, and especially of the Plymouth Company, char-

---

* The most active members of the Amsterdam Chamber were Jonas Witsen, Hendrick Hamel, Samuel Godyn, Samuel Blommaert, John de Laet (the historian), Killian van Rensselaer, Michael Pauw, and Peter Evertsen Hult.

† Formerly a dangerous passage at the entrance to the East River from Long Island Sound, made so by a whirlpool caused by a sunken reef of rocks at certain times of the tide. The danger has been removed by the action of exploded nitro-glycerine applied by a Government engineer. The early Dutch navigators gave it the name of "Helle Gat."

tered by King James in 1606. They had made feeble attempts to plant colonies on the shores of the vast wilderness now known as New England. In 1614 the famous John Smith, the real founder of Virginia, explored its coasts and principal rivers, and gave it the name which it bears. He attempted to plant a colony there under the auspices of the company, but failed. At length (1620) the company obtained a new charter (under the name of *Council of Plymouth*), which extended the limits of their domain to the forty-eighth degree of latitude. The company immediately put forth energetic efforts to establish a colony there.

Pastor Robinson's congregation in Holland were still eager to emigrate to America. They obtained a patent from the Virginia Company to settle in the unoccupied region in the "northern part of Virginia," which extended to the fortieth degree of latitude. They formed a partnership with London capitalists, and late in 1620 one hundred and one men, women, and children of the congregation—pioneers—crossed the stormy Atlantic in the little *Mayflower*, intending to land on the coasts of Delaware or Maryland. By accident or by the providence of God they reached the continent on the shores of Cape Cod Bay. Finding themselves far north of the region designated in their charter, the principal emigrants drew up and signed a democratic constitution, in the cabin of the *Mayflower*, for their government, and chose a governor, their spiritual head being Elder William Brewster. These "Pilgrims," as they called themselves, landed in the deep snow on the bleak coast of Massachusetts late in December, and at a spot which they named New Plymouth they built a little village of log-huts and laid the foundations of a State.

This significant movement admonished the Dutch that the English were preparing to dispute the right of the Hollanders to a foothold within the domain embraced in the charter of the Plymouth Company. Indeed, at this juncture the British Privy Council had instructed Sir Dudley Carleton, the British ambassador at the Hague, to peremptorily demand of the States-General an immediate prohibition of any further prosecution of commercial enterprises or settlements by the Dutch within the region claimed by the English. It was done. The States-General having put the whole matter under the control of the then just chartered Dutch West India Company, paid very little attention to the demand, or to the bluster of the British monarch and his ambassador. But the company, for obvious reasons, took immediate measures for planting a colony and laying the foundations of a State at Manhattan.

Like the Plymouth Company, the Dutch West India Company found in Holland excellent and ample materials for a colony. Thousands of

Protestant refugees of French extraction, known as Walloons, had fled from fiery persecution in the southern Belgic provinces bordering on France, and had taken refuge in Holland. They were mostly skilled artisans and industrious agriculturists. Like the English Puritans in Holland, they were animated by a strong desire to go to America. They asked the Plymouth Company for permission to settle in Virginia. It was denied. They asked the Dutch West India Company for a similar privilege. The Amsterdam Chamber of the company gladly complied, and in the spring of 1623 they equipped the *New Netherland*, of two hundred and sixty tons burden, commanded by Captain Adriaen Joris, and sent her to Manhattan, bearing thirty Walloon families numbering one hundred and ten men, women, and children.* She arrived at Manhattan at the beginning of May. The superintendence of the expedition was intrusted to Captain Cornelis Jacobsen May,† of Hoorn, who was to remain in New Netherland as the first director of the colony. Captain Joris went out as his lieutenant in the management of the colony.

NEW NETHERLAND:

---

* The Walloons (Flemish, *Waelen*) were of a mixed Gallic and Teutonic blood, and most of them spoke the old Teutonic tongue. They inhabited the southern Belgic provinces and adjoining parts of France. When the northern provinces of the Netherlands formed their political union, at Utrecht, in 1579, the southern provinces, whose inhabitants were chiefly Roman Catholics, declined to join the Confederation. Many of the people were Protestants, and against these the Spanish Government at once began the most cruel persecutions. Thousands of them fled to Holland, and were welcomed and protected. At the time of their dispersion (1580), the Walloons numbered over 2,000,000.

† May was an active navigator and explorer. He went up the James River as far as Jamestown, and penetrated other streams on the coast south of Manhattan. The southern coast of New Jersey was named in his honor, and still retains the title of Cape May. He was the first director or governor of New Netherland.

A French vessel had just entered Manhattan harbor, and her captain insisted upon setting up the French arms and taking possession of the country in the name of his sovereign because it was claimed that Verazzano, in the employment of a French monarch, had entered the harbor a century before. Now was presented the spectacle of three European nations claiming the ownership of an undefined territory in a wilderness more than three thousand miles from their respective capitals, on the plea of "first discovery"—the robber's right conferred by the mailed hands of power. The Dutch, having possession—the "nine points of the law"—held on. The Frenchman was driven out to sea by two cannons on the little yacht *Mackerel*, and the English were defied.

The colonists were soon dispersed and settled in permanent homes. Captain Joris, with eighteen families, sailed up the Mauritius as far as the site of Albany, where a fort was constructed and named Orange in honor of their prince. He left a few settlers at Esopus, now Kingston. The colonists built huts, "put in the spade," and began farming vigorously near Fort Orange. Representatives of Indian tribes came and made "covenants of friendship" with Joris. Four couples of the emigrants, with eight seamen, went to the Delaware River and settled on the left bank four miles below the site of Philadelphia, where Fort Nassau was built. Two families and six men were sent to the Connecticut River to build a fort (which was named Good Hope) near the site of Hartford, and to take formal possession of the country by virtue of Block's discovery of that stream in 1614. The remainder of these pioneer colonists settled on the site of Brooklyn.* Other emigrants from Holland soon joined them, and near the site of the Navy Yard at Brooklyn, Sarah Rapelye, the first child of European blood born in the province of New Netherland, inhaled her first breath.

In 1624 a shadow of civil government for the Dutch colony was provided by the installation of Captain Cornelis Jacobsen May as first director of New Netherland. He ruled as an autocrat wisely for about a year, when he was succeeded by William Verhulst as second director of New Netherland. Verhulst also ruled wisely one year.

Meanwhile events in Europe were strengthening the position of Holland and promising increased prosperity to the Dutch West India Company. The foreign relations of Great Britain had become so critical that King James found it expedient to form an alliance with the Netherlands in 1624, and he and his Privy Council wisely concluded that it would be

---

* Brooklyn is a corruption of its original Dutch appellation, Breuckelen—English Brookland or "marshy land"—a pretty village about eighteen miles from Amsterdam, on the road to Utrecht.

impolitic to offend the powerful commercial company by acting as champions of the Council of Plymouth when they complained of aggressions upon their chartered rights. Encouraged by these circumstances, the company proceeded to strengthen the political, social, and commercial powers of the new colony by sending more families and also needed supplies of stock and implements of labor. They commissioned Peter Minuit, of Weser, one of their number, director-general, or governor of New Netherland, and gave him as assistants in his civil administration a council of five persons, a "koop man" or commissary-general, who was also secretary of the province, and a "schout" or public procurator and sheriff.*

SIGNATURE OF PETER MINUIT.

Minuit arrived in May, 1626, in the ship *Sea Mew*, commanded by Captain Joris, and began his administration with vigor. He and his council were invested with legislative, judicial, and executive power, subject to the supervision and appellate jurisdiction of the Chamber at Amsterdam. They had power to fine and imprison criminals, but in cases where capital punishment was the penalty of a crime the culprit was to be sent to Amsterdam.

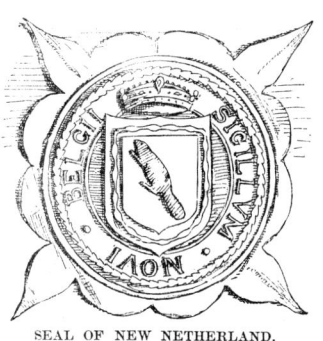

Hitherto the Dutch had possession of Manhattan Island only by the dubious right of first discovery and occupation. Minuit proceeded to place the right upon the sure foundation of justice. He called together the representatives of the barbarians of the island, and made a treaty for the purchase of the domain from them which was mutually satisfactory. It was a treaty as honorable, as important, and as noteworthy as was the famous alleged treaty between William Penn and the Indians beyond the Delaware under the broad Shackamaxon Elm which has been immortalized by history, painting, and poetry. The price paid by the Hollanders for the territory, estimated at twenty-two

SEAL OF NEW NETHERLAND.

---

* The members of the first council were Peter Byveldt, Jacob Elvertsen Wissinck, Jan Janssen Brouwer, Simon Dircksen Pos, and Reynert Harmenssen. Isaac de Rassieres was the commissary and secretary, and Jan Lampo was the schout or sheriff.

thousand acres in extent, was not extravagant—about twenty-four dollars. Nearly all of the island is now covered by buildings, parks, or streets.

The territory called New Netherland was created a province or county of Holland, and the armorial distinction of an earl or count was granted. The seal of New Netherland bore an escutcheon on which was the figure of a beaver, emblematic of the chief wild animal product of the region, and the crest was the coronet of an earl. The organization of a provisional civil government, the purchase of territory, and the erection of New Netherland into a province of Holland, in 1626, is justly regarded as the period of the germination of the fruitful seed which has expanded into the mighty Empire State of New York.

CHAPTER III.

So soon as the purchase of Manhattan was effected, Director Minuit caused a redoubt to be built at the southern extremity of the island near the site of the modern Battery and the Bowling Green. It was quadrangular in form, was constructed of earth faced with stone, and was surrounded with strong palisades of cedar. This redoubt was upon an elevation, and commanded the waters of the bay in front and of the Hudson (Mauritius) and East rivers on its flanks. The work was completed in 1627, and was named Fort Amsterdam. The village that grew up near it was called Manhattan until Stuyvesant came, in 1647, when it was named New Amsterdam.

Each settler on Manhattan owned the rude house in which he lived. It was his inviolable castle. He kept cows, tilled the soil, traded with the Indians, and deposited his furs in the trading-house, which was built of stone and thatched with reeds. This was the embryo of the vast warehouses of the city of New York. There were no idlers. All were producers as well as consumers. In the year in which the fort was completed furs of the value of nearly $20,000 were sent from Manhattan to Amsterdam. The settlers were at peace with all their dusky neighbors, and the future of the colony seemed dazzling to the seers.

But a bright morning is not always a sure harbinger of a pleasant day. While the fort was a-building an event occurred which became the progenitor of many fearful scenes, and of injuries to the colony. One morning a chief from beyond the Harlem River, accompanied by his little nephew and a young warrior, was sauntering with a bundle of beaver skins along the shores of the little lake whose waters once sparkled in the hollow where the Halls of Justice (the Tombs), in the city of New York, now stand. Three of the director's farm servants robbed them and murdered the chief. His nephew fled to the thick woods that bordered the East River and escaped. The lad left behind him a curse upon the white man, and solemnly vowed vengeance when mature manhood should give him strength. We shall observe hereafter how that vow was fulfilled. The surrounding barbarians were made jealous, suspicious, and vengeful.

Trouble now appeared beyond the mountains in the north. Daniel van Krieckenbeeck had been made deputy-commissary and commander at Fort Orange (now Albany), and managed prudently and successfully until he was induced to take a foolish step. The Mohicans had a stockaded village on the opposite side of the river (now East Albany). Enmity had suddenly appeared between them and the Mohawks. The Mohicans crossed the river and asked the Dutch commander to join them in a foray upon the Mohawks. He unwisely assented, and with six of his men marched with his dusky allies into the pine woods, where they were terribly smitten and dispersed by a band of Mohawks. Krieckenbeeck and three of his men were slain. Distrust of the Dutch by the Indians in all that region ensued. The Dutch families fled for safety to Manhattan from Fort Orange. Only a small garrison, without women, remained. At the same time indications of an unfriendly feeling toward the Hollanders among the Raritans in New Jersey caused the Dutch families seated on the left bank of the Delaware River also to flee to Manhattan for safety. These unfortunate events severed the links of trustful friendship which had bound the Dutch and Indians, and many distressing scenes followed the rupture. Emigration to New Netherland was checked for a while, and the tide of its prosperity seemed to be ebbing.

Meanwhile the Dutch West India Company had been gaining great accessions of wealth and power by the success of their war-ships against Spanish merchantmen. Spain was then at war with Holland. The fleets of the two India companies which indirectly governed the State, formed the strong right arm of the Dutch naval power at that time. In 1627 low-born Peter Pietersen Heyn won the title and official position of admiral by his achievements on the coast of Cuba. There he met the Spanish "silver fleet" on its way from Yucatan with the spoils of plundered princes of Mexico and Peru. He captured the whole flotilla, and put almost $5,000,000 in the coffers of his employers. Heyn perished soon after this victory, and was buried with regal pomp by the side of the Prince of Orange (who died in 1625) in the old church at Delft. When the States-General sent a letter of condolence to Heyn's peasant mother, she exclaimed:

"Ay, I thought that would be the end of him. He was always a vagabond. He has got no more than he deserved."

Holland gained the glory of the conquests by the Dutch West India Company, while the company itself gained the solid profits. In the space of two years their ships captured more than one hundred prizes. In 1629 the company divided fifty per cent profits. They soon added Brazil to their possessions, and gave maritime supremacy to the Netherlands.

Wealth and power made the Dutch West India Company more grasping and ambitious. The moderate profits derived from New Netherland appeared insignificant, and they devised new schemes for increasing their gains.

The great want of New Netherland was tillers of the soil. A manorial plan similar to that already in operation in Holland was devised, and this feature of the old feudal system of Europe was soon transplanted into America. It was approved by the States-General. In 1629 the College of Nineteen issued a "Charter of Privileges and Exemptions," which granted to every member of the company extensive domains in New Netherland outside of Manhattan Island, with specified benefits, provided he should, within the space of four years, place upon his lands so granted at least fifty adults as actual settlers, who should become his tenants. Such proprietor was constituted the feudal chief of his domain, with the title of *patroon*—a patron or defender.

It was provided that the lands of each patroon should be limited to sixteen miles in linear extent along one shore of a navigable stream, or to eight miles if he occupied both shores; but he might extend it indefinitely into the interior. It was also provided that if any proportionally greater number of emigrants should be settled by a proprietor, the area of his domain should be extended in the same ratio. He was to be absolutely lord of the manor, political and otherwise. He might hold inferior courts for the adjudication of petty civil cases; and if cities should grow up on his domain he was to have power to appoint the magistrates and other officers of such municipalities, and have a deputy to confer with the governor or first director of New Netherland.

The settlers under the patroons were to be exempted from all taxation and tribute for the support of the provincial government for ten years; and for the same period every man, woman, and child was bound not to leave the service of the patroon without his written consent. The colonists were forbidden to manufacture cloth of any kind on pain of banishment; and the company agreed to furnish them with as many African slaves as they "conveniently could," and also to protect them against foes. Each colony was bound to support a minister and a school-master, and so provide a comforter for the sick and a teacher for the illiterate. It was also provided that every proprietor, whether a patroon or an independent settler, should make a satisfactory arrangement with the Indians for the lands they should occupy. It recognized the right of the aborigines to the soil; invited independent farmers, to whom a homestead should be secured; promised protection to all in case of war, and encouraged religion and learning.

There was neither a settled clergyman nor a school-master in the province during Minuit's administration of six years, but provision was made for two "consolers of the sick," whose duty required them to read the Scriptures and creeds to the people gathered in a horse-mill on Sundays. A bell-tower was erected on the mill, and in it were hung some Spanish bells which the company's fleet had captured at Porto Rico.

There was some sharp practice performed by some of the members of the Amsterdam Chamber in securing valuable manors. Samuel Godyn and Samuel Blommaert, leading members, bought of the barbarians a tract of land stretching along Delaware Bay from Cape Hinlopen north over thirty miles and two miles in the interior, while the charter was under consideration. Soon afterward Killian van Rensselaer, another shrewd director, a wealthy pearl merchant of Amsterdam,

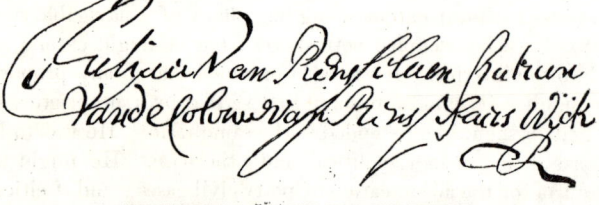

SIGNATURE OF KILLIAN VAN RENSSELAER.

informed by his friend Krol, the deputy secretary and commissary at Fort Orange, of the excellence and good situation of the country in that vicinity, instructed that friend to purchase a large tract of land of the Indians. It was done, and lands were secured on both sides of the river. Michael Pauw, another wide-awake director, secured by purchase of the barbarians, in a similar manner, a large tract of land in New Jersey, opposite Manhattan; also the whole of Staten Island.

This adroit forestalling in the purchase of some of the best lands in the province as to eligibility of situation—this "helping themselves by the cunning trick of merchants"—created much ill feeling among the members for a while; but it was allayed by admitting other directors into partnership. This concession was necessary in order to secure the confirmation of the charter of privileges by the College of Nineteen. This done, steps were immediately taken to colonize the manors. That of Van Rensselaer was the most extensive. It included a territory on both sides of the Mauritius or Hudson River, comprehending a large part of (present) Albany, Rensselaer, and Columbia counties. It was called the "Colonie of Rensselaerwyck."

These patroons—grasping, energetic men—soon gave the company great uneasiness. Their large estates once secured, they entered into competition with the company in the trade with the Indians. They were encouraged by Governor Minuit, who had assisted them in securing their estates, and found it profitable to be their friend. The company, perceiving this, recalled Minuit in 1631, and the colony remained without a governor more than two years.

One of the best, the clearest-headed and most liberal-minded of the directors who became a patroon was David Pietersen de Vries, an eminent navigator in the service of the Dutch East India Company, who came to Manhattan at about the time when Minuit was recalled, and for ten years occupied a conspicuous position in the public and private affairs of New Netherland. He was a friend of Patroon Godyn, and was very active in founding a colony near the site of Lewiston, on Delaware Bay, which was named Swaanendael. The Dutch took possession of the country in the name of the States-General. There thirty emigrants, with cattle and implements, were seated, but they

DAVID PIETERSEN DE VRIES.

were murdered by the Indians the next year, and their dwellings were laid in ruins.

In the spring of 1633 Walter van Twiller, a narrow-minded clerk in the company's warehouse at Amsterdam, who had married a niece of Van Rensselaer and had served that director well in shipping cattle to his manor on the Hudson River, succeeded Minuit as governor. According to all accounts, he was a most absurd man in person, character, and conduct. Washington Irving, in a pleasant pen caricature of him, described his person as "exactly five feet six inches in height and six feet five inches in circumference;" his head "a perfect sphere;" "his face a vast expanse, unfurrowed by any of those lines and angles which disfigure the human countenance with what is termed expression," and his cheeks "were curiously mottled and streaked with dusky red, like a Spitzenberg apple." He "daily took four stated meals, appropriating exactly one hour to each; smoked and doubted eight hours, and slept the remaining twelve of the four-and-twenty."

Van Twiller was totally unfitted by nature and education for the position he was placed in. He was self-indulgent to the last degree, and was profoundly ignorant of public affairs; yet during his administration the colony flourished in spite of him. He came attended by about one hundred and forty soldiers, the first that appeared in the colony.

With Governor Van Twiller came the Rev. Everardus Bogardus, the first clergyman seen in New Netherland;

SIGNATURE OF WALTER VAN TWILLER.

also Adam Roelandsen, the first school-master in the colony. Bogardus was a man of energy. He was bold and faithful, and did not hesitate to reprove the governor for his shortcomings in duty, official, moral, and religious. On one occasion he called him a "child of the devil" to his face and before high officials, and told him that if he did not behave himself he would "give him such a shake from the pulpit" the next Sunday as would make him tremble like a bowl of jelly.

Trouble with the English began with the advent of Van Twiller. A former commissary at Fort Orange (now Albany) named Eelkens, who had been dismissed from the company's service, went to England and, in the employ of London merchants, sailed for the Hudson River in the ship *William*, determined to trade with the Indians in its upper waters, with whom he was acquainted. Van Twiller forbade his ascending the river. Eelkens, knowing the weakness of the governor, treated him with scorn. Van Twiller, mildly offended, caused the Orange flag to be unfurled over Fort Amsterdam and a salute of three guns to be fired in

SIGNATURE OF EVERARDUS BOGARDUS.

honor of the Prince of Orange to fill the intruder with terror. Eelkens, not at all dismayed, ran up the British flag, fired three guns in honor of Charles of England, and sailed up the river.

For once Van Twiller seemed to be really angry. He gathered the garrison at the door of the fort, tapped a cask of wine, filled capacious glasses, swore terribly in Low Dutch, and called upon the people, who stood laughing in his face, to assist him in wiping out this stain upon the honor of himself and Holland. De Vries, who dined with the governor that day, told him he had acted like a fool. Van Twiller did not deny that he was a fool, and meekly assented to the demand of the fiery captain that an expedition should be sent to bring Eelkens back, and thus vindicate the honor and courage of the State. Van Twiller hesitated long, but finally sent a small flotilla fairly armed, and at the end of a month from the day when the offence was committed the *William* was brought back and driven out to sea. Eelkens was foiled. This was the first hostile encounter between the Dutch and English in New Netherland. The *William* was the first English ship whose keel ploughed the waters of the Hudson River.

Already a little cloud had brooded in the east. When the Puritans of Massachusetts were assured of the beauty and fertility of the soil of the valley of the Connecticut River, they yearned for its possession. The Dutch had already assumed that right, in accordance with the British doctrine of first discovery; for, as we have seen, Adriaen Block discovered the Connecticut River nearly six years before the Puritans came to Cape Cod Bay. The Dutch had obtained a more righteous title by a purchase of the whole Connecticut Valley from the barbarians. They had set up the arms of Holland on a tree at the mouth of the river, and had nearly completed the fort a little below the site of Hartford, and named it "Good Hope."

Unmindful of the claims of the Dutch, the Plymouth Company granted a charter to certain parties to settle in the lovely Connecticut Valley. During the bland Indian summer in 1633 a small company of Puritans under Captain Holmes sailed up the Connecticut in a sloop, with the frame of a house all prepared for erection, to plant a settlement on the shore of that stream. The energetic commissary, Jacob van Curler (or Corlear), was then at the fort, on which were mounted two cannons. He demanded a sight of Holmes's commission, and on his refusal to show it Van Curler forbade his going further up the river, and threatened him with destruction if he should attempt to pass the fort. The Yankee filibuster was as careless as a Turk of the shotted cannon. He sailed quietly by, while the Dutch "let the shooting

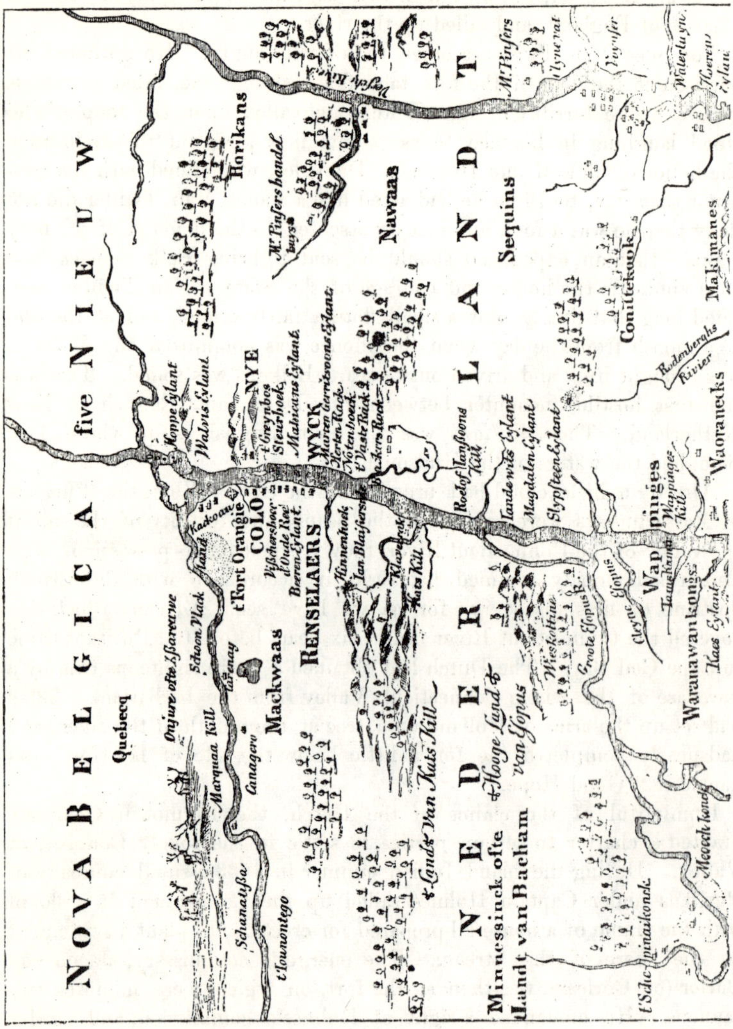
NOVA BELGICA five NIEUW NEDERLANDT
Quebecq
Horikans
Nawaas
Sequins
Mackwaas
RENSELAERS WYCK
COLO NYE
t'Fort Orangie
Walvis Eylant
Mahicans Eylant
M. Tinsers handel huys
M. Tinsers
Marquaa Kill
Canagero
Schanatissa
t'Iounontego
Minnessinck ofte Landt van Bacham
t'Hooge Land van Esopus
t'Lands van Kats Kill
Kats Kill
Roelof Jansoons Kill
Magdalen Eylant
Slyppsteen Eylant
Groote Esopus
Cleyne Esopus
Wappinges
Wappinges Kill
Waranawankongs
Kaes Eylant
Waoranecks
Rodenberghs Rivier
Conittekook
Makimanes

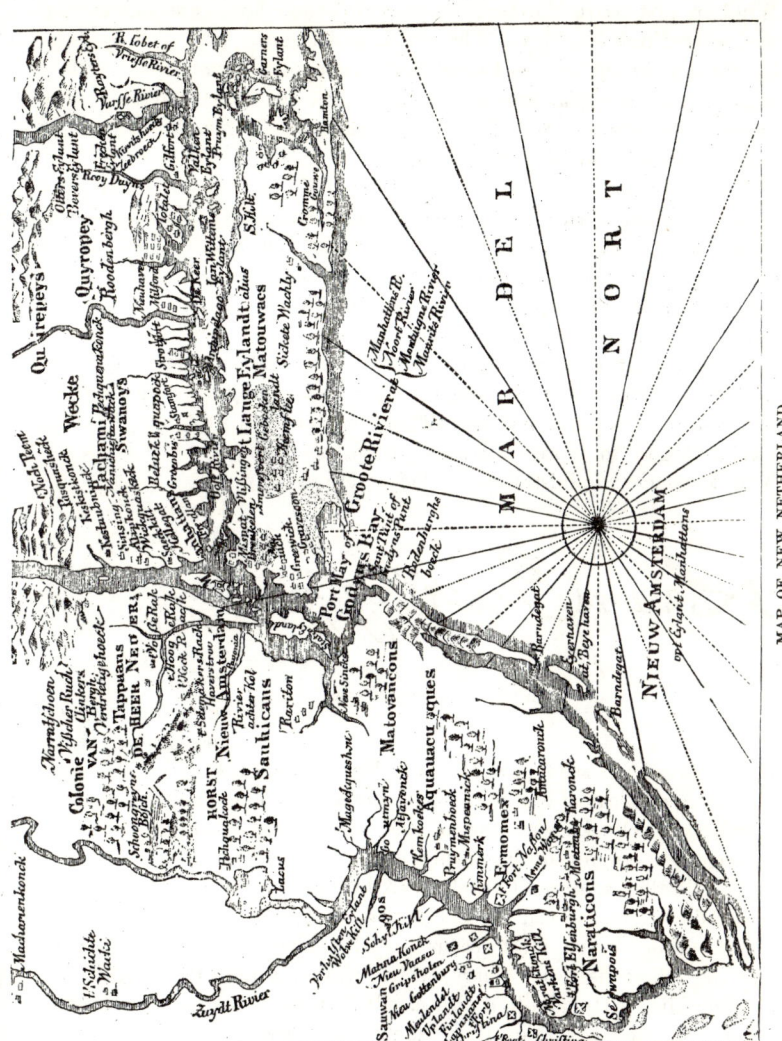

MAP OF NEW NETHERLAND.

stand." Holmes and his little party soon landed, and on the site of Windsor, just above Hartford, they erected their house and planted the seed of an English colony. The Dutch and English quarrelled concerning the ownership of the Connecticut Valley for about twenty years, when the question was amicably settled. The Dutch withdrew, and the present line between New York and Connecticut was established as the eastern boundary of New Netherland.

The new State yet lacked a prime element of perpetuity. There were no independent farmers in New Netherland cultivating their own lands, for the soil belonged to the Dutch West India Company, excepting that of the patroon estates. These wealthy monopolists carried on all agricultural operations off the public domain. The tiller might own his house, but he held no fee-title to the soil. Thousands of fertile acres in the province remained uncultivated, for commercial advantages alone occupied the attention of the company. The feudal system, internal discord between the patroons and the officers of the company, and external dangers began to repress the energies of the people before the end of Van Twiller's administration. Many were sighing for "fatherland." The machinery of the local government generally moved sluggishly and often viciously. The governor lost all personal influence, and became a target for coarse jests. We have seen how Dominie Bogardus treated him. His own subordinates treated him with equal contempt. The schout-fiscal, Lubbertus van Dincklagen, one of the most learned and honest men among them, reproved him openly.

SIGNATURE OF LUBBERTUS VAN DINCKLAGEN.

Van Twiller ventured to strike back in this case, but the blow he gave Van Dincklagen proved to be like that of a boomerang. It wounded the governor himself most seriously. His blow consisted in refusing to pay the schout-fiscal his salary, which was in arrears three years, and sending him to Holland in disgrace. It was a sad day for the governor when Van Dincklagen departed, for the schout-fiscal was a man of pluck, and held a ready pen. He sent such damaging memorials to the States-General, the truths of which were verified by the testimony of De Vries before the Amsterdam Chamber, that Van Twiller was recalled at the moment when he had purchased Nutten and other islands around Manhattan, in expectation of vegetating and dying in official dignity in New Netherland.

We have no memorial of Van Twiller left in the name of any State, village, institution, water-craft, or domain excepting the isle of Nuts, which lies in the bay of New York, within earshot of the place of his final departure for the Zuyder Zee. It is called "The Governor's Island" to this day. At his departure he was one of the most extensive land-owners in the province, and the herds of cattle which stocked his farms gave occasion for the suspicion that the governor had enriched himself at the expense of the company's interests.*

Van Twiller was succeeded by William Kieft, a man of great energy, but lacking in moral qualities. Little is known of him before his appearance at New Amsterdam. He had lived in Rochelle, in France, where, for some misdemeanor, the people hung him in effigy. De Vries, who knew him well, ranked him among the "great rascals of the age."

He was energetic, spiteful, and rapacious; fond of quarrels, and never happy except when in trouble—the reverse of Van Twiller, who loved ease and quiet. His first council was composed of men of similar humor.

Kieft began his administration by concentrating all executive power in his own hands.

SIGNATURE OF WILLIAM KIEFT.

He and his council assumed so much dignity that it became a "high crime to appeal from the judgments" of the governor and his subordinate officials. Yet he was really a better man for the company and the people than his predecessor. He was as busy as a brooding hen, and attempted reforms in government, society, and religion on a scale altogether beyond the capacities of himself and his "subjects," as he sometimes styled the people. He had an exalted opinion

---

* Van Twiller was a native of Nieuwkerk. He married a niece of Patroon Van Rensselaer, through whose influence the incompetent clerk was appointed governor. Recalled in 1637, he publicly abused the Dutch West India Company after his return to Holland with considerable wealth. He vilified the administration of Stuyvesant. The company were indignant, and spoke of Van Twiller as an ungrateful man, who had "sucked his wealth from the breast of the company which he now abuses." Van Rensselaer seems to have had confidence in him, for he made Van Twiller executor of his last Will and Testament.

of Minuit as a governor, and he resolved to imitate his example ; but Minuit became the bane of his peace almost from the beginning.

Kieft found public affairs in New Netherland in a wretched condition, and he put forth strength to bring order out of confusion. Abuses abounded, but measures of reform which he adopted almost stripped the citizens of their privileges. Fort Amsterdam was repaired, and new warehouses for the company were erected. He caused orchards to be planted and gardens cultivated on Manhattan. He had police ordinances framed and enforced. He caused religion and morality to be fostered, regular religious services to be publicly conducted, and a spacious stone church to be built within the fort, in the wooden tower of which were hung the Spanish bells already mentioned as giving out their chimes from the bell-tower of the horse-mill. It was a gala day in New Amsterdam (1642) when the Connecticut architects, John and Richard Ogden, hung those bells, and the governor gave a supper to the builders and the magnates of the village at his *harberg* for strangers, a stone building at the head of Coenties Slip, which was called the " City Tavern" in Stuyvesant's time.*

A more liberal policy in respect to private ownership of land (to be mentioned presently) caused immigration to increase. The freedom of conscience which prevailed in the Fatherland prevailed also in New Netherland. All that Kieft required of new settlers was an oath of allegiance to the States-General of Holland. When they could answer the question affirmatively, " Do you want to buy land and become a citizen ?" it was the extent of the catechism.

Kieft had eaten but few dinners at New Amsterdam when he was informed of the impertinence of the Swedes in buying enough land between two trees to build a house upon, and then claiming the whole territory west of the Delaware from Cape Hinlopen to the falls at Trenton ; lands the most of which were already in possession of patroons. Upon what foundation was this claim laid ? Let us see.

Usselincx, the original projector of the Dutch West India Company, had left Amsterdam in a passion, and laid before Gustavus Adolphus,

---

* The shrewd governor took advantage of the occasion of a wedding feast to secure ample subscriptions for the building of the church. It was the wedding of a daughter of Dominie Bogardus. At the wedding feast, at which the principal people of Manhattan were gathered, after " the fourth or fifth round of drinking," Kieft proposed a subscription for the church, and gave liberally himself. All the company, with light heads made dizzy with drink, vied with each other in " subscribing richly." Some of them, when they became sober, " well repented of their reckless extravagance," but " nothing availed to excuse it."

King of Sweden, the great champion of Protestantism, a well-arranged plan for establishing a Scandinavian colony on the South or Delaware River. Gustavus was delighted, for it promised an asylum in America for all persecuted Protestants. But while the scheme was ripening the Swedish monarch was called to the field, where he fell in battle, near Lutzen. He did not forget the great prospective enterprise. Only a few days before his death he recommended it as "the jewel of his kingdom." The Count of Oxenstierna, who ruled Sweden in behalf of Christina, the daughter of Gustavus—"the sweet little jessamine bud of the royal conservatory" (alas! for its full development)—ardently supported the enterprise. Four years before the wasp of Rochelle succeeded Van Twiller, Oxenstierna gave a charter to the *Swedish West India Company*, and Peter Minuit, the dismissed Governor of New Netherland, was appointed the first governor of the Swedish colony to be founded on the Delaware River. Toward the close of 1637, Minuit sailed for the Delaware in the good ship *Key of Calmar* with a company of emigrants. It was this apparition that startled Kieft soon after his arrival at Manhattan.

At first Kieft was astonished, then affronted, and at last he rubbed his hands with delight, for he saw a clear opportunity for a quarrel and a display of his diplomatic powers. The whole breadth of the present State of New Jersey lay between him and the intruders, and that was a comfort. He fearlessly issued a proclamation with an imperial flourish, protesting against the intrusion and declaring that he would not be "answerable for any mishap, bloodshed, trouble, or disaster" which the Swedes might suffer from his anger and valor.

Minuit laughed at Kieft and went on to build a stronghold on the site of Wilmington, which he named Fort Christina, in honor of his young queen, and pushed a profitable trade with the Indians. The fiery Kieft hurled protest after protest against the Swedes, but they were as little heeded as were the paper bulls sent by Clement to bellow excommunication through the realm of Henry the Eighth of England. Swedish vessels filled with Swedish men, women, and children, intent on empire and happiness in America, came thicker than Belgic proclamations; and in spite of Kieft's majesty, the Scandinavian colonists laid the foundations of the capital of "New Sweden" on an island not far from the site of Philadelphia. More than forty years before Penn,

> "the Quaker, came,
> To leave his hat, his drab, and his name,
> That will sweetly sound from the trump of fame
> Till its final blast shall die,"

they spread the tents of empire on the soil where now flourish in regal pride the commonwealths of Pennsylvania and Delaware.

The English on the east became as troublesome as the Swedes on the south. Like busy ants they were spreading over the fertile lands west of the Housatonic River, and under the provisions of a charter given to Lord Stirling by the Council of Plymouth, they actually claimed the whole of Long Island. They disregarded Dutch proclamations and Indian title-deeds. Filibusters from Massachusetts cast down the arms of Holland which had been set up at Cow Bay on the island, and mocked the officials at Manhattan.

Kieft with great energy soon put an end to these encroachments. He bought for the company from the Indians all the territory comprised within present Kings and Queens counties, and immediately planted settlements within that domain. Colonies were established on Staten Island and on the west side of the Hudson River; while settlements were made by the English on the eastern portions of Long Island without interference by the Dutch.

Lyon Gardiner, the English military commander at the mouth of the Connecticut River, bought of the barbarians the island that bears his name. He removed from Saybrook to his island, where his wife gave birth to a daughter, and so the first permanent English settlement was made within the present limits of the State of New York. Peace might long have reigned in New Netherland had not acquisitiveness arisen in rebellion against justice, and engendered a terrible storm of vengeance among the dwellers of the forest.

THE GARDINER ARMS.

The partiality of the Dutch for the Mohawks made the River Indians (as the dwellers along the Hudson south of Fort Orange were called) jealous, and their friendship for the white people was greatly weakened by the dishonesty of traders, who stupefied them with rum and then cheated them in traffic. Kieft not only winked at these things, but, under the false plea of "express orders" from his principals, he demanded tribute of furs, corn, and wampum from the tribes around Manhattan. They sullenly complied, but with an inward protest against this rank injustice. When they cast the costly tribute at the feet of the Hollanders they turned away with a curse bitter and uncompromising.

When the governor clearly perceived this black cloud on the brows of the barbarians, surcharged with the lightnings of vengeance, his fears and his cruelty were awakened. With the usual instinct of a bad nature, he sought an opportunity to injure those he had deeply wronged. The opportunity was not long delayed. Some swine had been stolen from a plantation on Staten Island. Kieft charged the innocent Raritans with the theft, and sent armed men to chastise them. Several Indians were killed. This outrage kindled the anger of all the surrounding tribes, even beyond the Hudson Highlands.

At this juncture the little nephew of the Westchester chief who had been murdered by Minuit's men fifteen years before had grown to lusty manhood, and proceeded to execute his vow of revenge made when he saw his uncle slain near the spot where the Halls of Justice now stand. He came to Manhattan, crept stealthily to the solitary cabin of Claas Schmidt, a harmless wagon-maker at Turtle Bay, on the East River, slew him with an axe, and plundered his dwelling. Kieft demanded the murderer from his tribe. His chief refused to give him up. Here was a cause for war. Kieft chuckled with delight; but cooler heads and better hearts averted a dire calamity. The people absolutely refused to shoulder their fire-arms at the governor's bidding, and said to him plainly:

"You wish to have war that you may make a wrong reckoning with the company."

Kieft had stormed and threatened, but this unexpected revelation of the people's insight into his real character suddenly transformed the bullying autocrat into a seeming republican. He called together all the masters and heads of families ostensibly to consult upon public affairs. It was only to make them unconscious cat's-paws in the prosecution of his designs, and have them bear a part of the responsibility.

CHAPTER IV.

In 1640 a new charter for patroons was granted which greatly modified the obnoxious features of that of 1629. It allowed "all good inhabitants of the Netherlands to select lands and form colonies in New Netherland." The proposed land grants were comparatively small in extent, comprehending only two miles along the shores of any bay or river, and extending four miles into the country. These inferior patroons were endowed with many of the privileges of the superior patroons.

Provision was also made for another class of proprietors. Whoever should convey to New Netherland five grown persons besides himself was to be recognized as a "master or colonist," and could occupy two hundred acres of land, with the privilege of hunting and fishing. Commercial privileges, which the first charter had restricted to the patroons, were now extended to all "free colonists." These wiser provisions, notwithstanding onerous imposts for the benefit of the company were exacted from the colonists, stimulated emigration and promised perpetuity and prosperity to the province.

SIGNATURE OF ARENDT VAN CURLER.

Meanwhile the Colonie of Rensselaerwyck had greatly prospered under the energetic management of the patroon's commissary, Arendt van Curler.* Around Fort Orange within that domain had grown a

---

* Arendt van Curler is represented as a man "of large benevolence and unsullied honor," bold and energetic, to whom the patroon delegated his entire power at Rensselaerwyck. His jurisdiction included all the territory on both sides of the Hudson River, between Beaver Island and the mouth of the Mohawk River, excepting the precinct of Fort Orange. This post, which was the property of the Dutch West India Company when the first purchases in the neighborhood were made by Van Rensselaer, was always occupied by a small garrison commanded by officers under the immediate direction of the provincial authorities at Manhattan.

Van Curler or Corlear was one of the best and most sagacious of the earlier founders of New York State. He was a first cousin of the first Patroon Van Rensselaer, and

little village called Beverswyck. This was the beginning of the city of Albany, now the political capital of the State of New York.

Patroon Van Rensselaer through Commissary Van Curler was beginning to exercise power almost co-ordinate with that of the director-general or governor at Manhattan. He had his koop-man, his schout-fiscal, and his council under his commissary, and he was invested with power to administer justice, pronounce and execute sentences for all degrees of crime, even the penalty of death; and he was the executor within his domain of all the laws and ordinances of the civil code that

DUTCH REFORMED CHURCH AT ALBANY.*

governed New Netherland. In addition to this, the colonists upon his great manor were subjected to such laws and regulations as the patroon or his deputy might establish. They had the legal right to appeal to the governor and Council at Manhattan; but this right was virtually annulled by the obligation under which the colonists upon the manor were compelled to come—namely, not to appeal from the manorial tribunals.

---

came to America in 1630. His wise and humane treatment of the Indians caused him to be beloved by them all, and his policy toward them did more to secure a peaceful settlement of the Mohawk Valley by the white people than the efforts of any other man. The first act of the English governor after the conquest of the domain from the Dutch in 1664 was to send for Curler, to profit by his advice concerning an Indian policy. He was an efficient promoter of sobriety, morality, and religion. Returning from a visit to Canada on the invitation of the governor, in 1667, his boat was capsized in a squall on Lake Champlain, and he was drowned. For a long period the lake was known to the English as Curler's or Corlear's Lake.

* The first church edifice built at Albany was a wooden structure thirty-four feet long by nineteen wide. It stood among other buildings clustered around Fort Orange. It had pews for the magistrates and deacons, and nine benches for the congregation. The expense of all was thirty-two dollars. In 1656 a larger church was built of stone at the junction of (present) State Street and Broadway. Its pulpit and bell were sent over by the Dutch West India Company. It served the congregation a century and a half, or until 1806. One of its windows bore the arms of the Van Rensselaer family.

In government, as in other matters, the Van Rensselaer Manor or Colonie of Rensselaerwyck exhibited some of the most conspicuous features of feudalism. It was almost an autocracy within a State, and as such it sometimes gave much trouble to the superior authorities at Manhattan. Only Fort Orange and its immediate surroundings were exempt from the patroon's control.

Impressed with the necessity of sound religious instruction in his colony, Patroon Van Rensselaer, in 1642, sent to Rensselaerwyck John Megopolensis, D.D., a learned clergyman belonging to the classis of Alckmaer. A substantial church edifice was constructed, and very soon a flourishing church was established upon the theological foundation formulated by the Synod of Dordrecht. The influence of Dr. Megopolensis on the Hollanders and the Indians was most salutary.

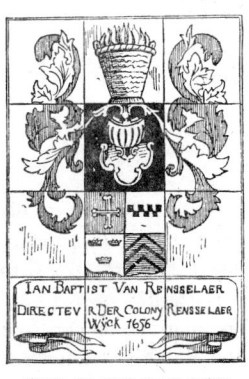

Soon after the arrival of this minister an occasion tested the humanity, the toleration, and the broad Christianity of the Dutch. A Jesuit missionary (Father Jogues) and two other Frenchmen were taken prisoners by the Iroquois and conducted to the Mohawk country, where they frequently suffered tortures. Informed of this, Van Curler attempted to rescue them. With two others he rode on horseback into the Mohawk country, where they were joyfully received, for the commissary was beloved by the Mohawks. He offered munificent ransoms for the Frenchmen, but the Indians refused to give them up. The barbarians saved the life of Father Jogues, but murdered his companions. He finally escaped to Fort Orange, went to Europe, returned to Canada in 1646, ventured among the Mohawks as a missionary, and was slain by them at Caughnawaga soon afterward.

ARMS OF THE VAN RENSSELAER FAMILY.

The "free colonists," as we have observed, were the "masters" who, with the "heads of families," were called in consultation with the governor concerning an attack upon neighboring Indians. By this act the ambitious Kieft, who strove to exercise the powers of an autocrat in the government of New Netherland, unwittingly planted the first seeds of democracy—the first germ of representative government among Europeans within the domain of the State of New York. The "masters and heads of families" who came together at the bidding of the governor in the summer of 1641, chose twelve discreet men as a committee to act for them.

The names of the members of this first representative assembly ever convened for political purposes in New Netherland should never be forgotten. They were: Jacques Bentyn, Maryn Adriaensen, Jan Jansen Dam, Hendrick Jansen, David Pietersen de Vries, Jacob Stoffelsen, Abraham Molenaar, Frederick Lubbertsen, Jochem Pietersen Kuyter, Gerrit Dircksen, George Rapelye, and Abram Planck. They were all emigrants from Holland, and had enjoyed the blessings of popular freedom in that garden of Western Europe. They were the first representatives and asserters within the boundaries of New York of the germinal doctrines of the Declaration of Independence promulgated at Philadelphia more than sixscore years afterward.

The Committee of Twelve chose the energetic De Vries for their president. He had suffered deeply from the barbarians in the destruction of Swaanendael, on the Delaware, and had lost much property by their depredations on Staten Island, yet both humanity and expediency counselled him to preserve peace with the Indians. This condition he strenuously advocated. His colleagues agreed with him, and the sanguinary governor was astonished and puzzled. The senators were firm, and hostilities were deferred.

Meanwhile the Committee of Twelve were busy in maturing a plan for establishing at Manhattan the popular form of government that prevailed in Holland. Kieft was alarmed, for he perceived that a scheme was on foot to abridge the absolute power with which he was clothed. He suggested a compromise, and the confiding representatives of the people, who met early in 1642, put their trust in his promises. He offered concessions of popular freedom on the condition of being allowed to chastise the Westchester Indians for the murder of Schmidt. A reluctant consent was finally given. When the perfidious governor had procured this consent he dissolved the Committee of Twelve, in February, 1642, by an arbitrary order, telling them that the business for which they had been convened was completed. This done, he forbade any popular assemblages thereafter. Thus ended the first attempt to establish popular sovereignty in New Netherland.

Kieft now sent an armed force into Westchester to chastise the Weckquaesgeeks, the tribe of the murderer. The expedition was fruitless, and was followed by concessions and a treaty which prevented bloodshed. The governor was disappointed, but his bloodthirstiness was partially slaked not long afterward. The River Indians were tributary to the Mohawks, and at midwinter in 1643 a large war-party of the latter came down from near Fort Orange to collect tribute of the Weckquaesgeeks in lower Westchester and the Tappans on the west side of the Hudson River.

The terrified Algonquins—men, women, and children, fully five hundred strong—fled before the dreaded Iroquois, and sought refuge with the Dutch. The latter now had a rare opportunity to win the sincere and lasting friendship of their barbarian brethren around them by exercising the virtues of hospitality, common humanity, and a Christian spirit. Such a course De Vries and Bogardus strongly advised; but there were other leading spirits bent on war and revenge who advised the very willing governor to improve the occasion for avenging the murder of Schmidt. Three of the ex-senators, speaking falsely in the name of the Twelve, urged the governor to "fall upon them." The governor was delighted, and at once ordered Sergeant Rudolf to lead eighty well-armed men across the river and attack the fugitive Tappans, who had taken refuge with the Hackensacks at Pavonia or Hoboken, near the Dutch settlement of Vriesdael.

De Vries, representing the majority of the citizens, vainly tried to dissuade the governor from his bloodthirsty purpose. He warned him that he would bring dire calamity upon the province. The fiery magistrate spurned the captain's advice and admonitions, saying: "The order has gone forth; it cannot be recalled." In that order he impiously said the work had been undertaken "in the full confidence that God will crown our resolutions with success."

At the middle of a cold night late in February, 1643, Sergeant Rudolf and his men fell upon the defenceless Tappans at Hoboken, who were sleeping in fancied security. At the same time Sergeant Adriaensen smote the Weckquaesgeeks, who had taken refuge with the Dutch on Manhattan at Corlear's Hook, now the foot of Grand Street He killed forty of them. Rudolf made the deep snows at Hoboken red with the blood of about a hundred unoffending pagans, sparing neither age nor sex in the execution of his cowardly master's will. "Warrior and squaw, sachem and child, mother and babe," says Brodhead, "were alike massacred." The next morning, when the armed Hollanders returned to Fort Amsterdam—a ghastly train—with thirty prisoners and the heads of several Indians on pikes, Kieft shook their bloody hands with delight, and gave them presents.

This massacre and other outrages committed by order of Kieft aroused the fiery hatred of all the surrounding tribes. A fierce war was kindled. Villages and farms were desolated. The white people were butchered wherever found by the enraged barbarians.* The Long Island Indians, hitherto friendly, joined their dusky kindred, and the very existence of the colony was imperilled.

The fierce blaze kindled by the folly and wickedness of Kieft appalled him. He again called upon the "Commonalty" to appoint a committee to consider propositions which he would lay before them. They choose eight men, one of whom was Isaac Allerton, a passenger in the *Mayflower*, who was then a prosperous merchant at Manhattan. The Council of Eight counselled peace with the Long Island tribes and war upon the Westchester Indians, who had desolated settlements and plantations there. It was done.

SIGNATURE OF ISAAC ALLERTON.

---

* Among the victims was Mrs. Anne Hutchinson, who was an advocate of the right of private judgment in religious matters, and had been banished from Boston because it was said she was "weakening the hands and hearts of the people toward the ministers," and was "like Roger Williams, or worse." She went to Rhode Island, but found her abode there undesirable, so she sought the protection of the more tolerant Dutch for the exercise of soul liberty. In the summer of 1642 she removed, with all her family, to Pelham Neck, in Westchester County, within the Dutch domain. It was near New Rochelle, and the spot was called "Annie's Hoeck." The Dutch named Westchester "The Land of Peace." In the fierce war of 1643 the widowed Anne Hutchinson and all her family, excepting a little granddaughter, eight years old, were murdered by the Indians. The child was made a captive, and was ransomed by the authorities at Manhattan.

Lady Deborah Moody, an Englishwoman, who, like Mrs. Hutchinson, had fled from persecution at Salem, established herself at Gravesend, on the western end of Long Island. She had scarcely become settled before the Indians attacked her plantation. Forty resolute colonists bravely defended it, and drove the assailants away. Gravesend escaped the fate that befell all the neighboring settlements on Long Island. Two years afterward Kieft granted Lady Moody, her son, Sir J. Henry Moody, and others a patent for land adjoining Coney Island, now known as Gravesend. She and other inhabitants were allowed to nominate their magistrates. Her home was again attacked by the barbarians during the excitement while Stuyvesant was on his expedition against the Swedes, in 1655.

War raged fearfully again, and the colony, after a dreadful struggle, was on the verge of ruin. At length a company of Englishmen under Captain John Underhill, a brave and restless soldier of New England then living at Stamford, Conn., was called to the assistance of the Dutch. The Indians were subdued, and peace was partially restored. Yet the dreadful war-cloud hung ominously over the Hollanders, charged with the lightnings of suppressed wrath. Kieft trembled at the aspect, and again convoked the Council of Eight. The people had lost all confidence in the governor—nay, they despised and hated him. Their hopes in this hour of their distress rested solely upon their representatives, the Council of Eight. But that council possessed no legal executive power, and the stubborn governor seldom followed their advice. Retrievement seemed almost hopeless. Distant settlements remained desolated. Disorder everywhere prevailed. The Swedes were building up a strong empire on the southern borders of New Netherland, and the Puritans

SIGNATURE OF JOHN UNDERHILL.

were not only claiming absolute title to undoubted Dutch territory, but many of them were becoming citizens under the liberal charter of the company, and were wielding much influence in social life at Manhattan.

At this juncture, and in order to invoke wholesome interference with Kieft's destructive policy, the Council of Eight addressed a memorial to the States-General, giving a full account of public affairs in the province, and asking the recall of the obnoxious governor. At this juncture also De Vries, one of the best and most useful citizens, who had been ruined financially by the war, left the province forever and returned to Holland.* On taking leave of Kieft his last words addressed to the governor

---

* De Vries had accepted an invitation from a Rotterdam skipper to pilot his vessel, laden with Madeira wine, from Manhattan to Virginia. They stopped on the way at the capital of New Sweden, where De Vries was hospitably entertained by the governor (Printz) for five days, while the skipper traded wine and confectionery for beaver-skins. De Vries spent the winter in Virginia, and reached Amsterdam in June, 1644. He seems never to have revisited America. His story of his *Voyages* was published at Alckmaer, in 1655, with a portrait of him. It was translated into English by the late Henry C. Murphy, of Brooklyn, and has been of essential service in the preparation of this volume.

uttered the awful prophecy : " The murders in which you have shed so much innocent blood will yet be avenged upon your own head."

The people endured the rule of Kieft until it could not be longer borne with safety to the colony, and the Council of Eight, representing the commonalty, addressed a second memorial to the States-General and the College of Nineteen, in which they set forth in detail the causes which threatened the absolute ruin of New Netherland.* They said in conclusion :

" This is what we have, in the sorrow of our hearts, to complain of : That one man, who has been sent out, sworn and instructed by his lords and masters, to whom he is responsible, should dispose here of our lives and property according to his will and pleasure, in a manner so arbitrary that a king would not be suffered legally to do." They asked for a better governor for the colonists or permission to return with their " wives and children to their dear Fatherland."

The Dutch West India Company was then nearly bankrupt. Immediate action was necessary to avert the absolute ruin of New Netherland and to prevent the colonists " returning with their wives and children to their dear Fatherland." The company resolved to recall Kieft, and Van Dincklagen, Van

SIGNATURE OF CORNELIS MELYN.

Twiller's disgraced schout-fiscal, was made provisional governor. The people at Manhattan were greatly delighted when they heard of the intended change. Some pugnacious burghers threatened Kieft with personal chastisement when he should " take off the coat with which he was bedecked by the lords his masters."

During Kieft's administration the Swedes had obtained a firm foothold on the Delaware. They claimed territorial jurisdiction on the right side of the Delaware Bay and River from Cape Hinlopen to the falls at Trenton.

---

* It was written by Cornelis Melyn, one of the Eight Men, who came to Manhattan in 1640 to see the country, and was so much pleased with it that he hastened to Antwerp to bring his family to America. He afterward rose to prominence in New Netherland. He was President of the Council of Eight. He had become a *patroon* of Staten Island, and began a colony there. He suffered much in body and estate under Kieft, and brought his grievances before the States-General. He was a stubborn subject under Stuyvesant, and resisted the director's arbitrary power. He finally (1661) surrendered his manor into the hands of the Dutch West India Company for a consideration, and returned to Amsterdam.

Governor Minuit died at Fort Christina in 1642. His lieutenant, Peter Hollandare, at the end of a year and a half afterward returned to Sweden, when the queen commissioned John Printz, a lieutenant of cavalry, governor of New Sweden, and furnished him with officers and soldiers to support his authority.

Printz arrived at Fort Christina early in 1642. He was instructed to maintain and cultivate friendship with the Dutch at Fort Nassau and Manhattan and the English in Virginia, and not to disturb the Dutch settlers within his domain in their forms of divine worship. He made Tinicum Island, near Chester, about twelve miles below Philadelphia, the capital of New Sweden, built a fort upon it of hemlock logs, which he named " New Gottenburg," and erected a dwelling, which was called " Printz Hall." He was instructed not to allow any trade in peltries excepting by the agents of the Swedish Company, and to secure all the Indian trade against the competition of the Dutch.

The attitude of the Swedes very much disturbed the authorities at Manhattan. They were then powerless in regard to the intruders. Added to this cause of irritation was the absurd claim of a British baronet (Sir Edmund Plowden) to nearly all the territory of New Jersey by virtue of a charter granted to him by the Viceroy of Ireland ! The New Englanders, too, annoyed the Dutch by persistent efforts to participate in the profitable fur trade which the Hollanders were determined to monopolize.

Impelled by the force of public opinion and a stern voice of warning from the Amsterdam Chamber, Kieft had consented to treat for peace with the Indians. Representatives of the surrounding tribes of barbarians had come to Manhattan, and in front of the fort on the spot now known as the " Bowling Green" they had sat and smoked the calumet, or pipe of peace, and agreed to a treaty of amity between the Dutch and themselves. That treaty was signed on the last day of summer, 1645. Then a proclamation went forth from Manhattan for the observance of September 6th as a day of thanksgiving throughout New Netherland. This great Indian treaty was ratified at Amsterdam.

Kieft exercised his waning power and indulged his petty spite and tyranny a little longer. When it was known that he was to be recalled, the people became more outspoken in their utterances of contempt for him. Dominie Bogardus was foremost in boldness and plainness of speech. " What are the great men of the country," he exclaimed from the pulpit one Sunday, " but vessels of wrath and fountains of woe and trouble ! They think of nothing but to plunder the property of others, to dismiss, to banish, to transport to Holland." The enraged governor, who was present, never entered the church again. He retaliated by encouraging the officers and soldiers to practise all sorts of noisy games about the church, and even to beat drums and fire cannons during preaching.

After a little more strife with the Swedes and New Englanders, and falsely accusing the people of Manhattan of instigating the late disastrous war with the Indians, Kieft ended his inglorious sojourn in America forever by leaving the shores of New Netherland in August, 1643, in the ship *Princess* bound for Holland, and carrying with him more than $100,000 of ill-gotten wealth. Dominie Bogardus sailed in the same ship, and with about fourscore others perished with Kieft when the vessel was wrecked. The prophecy of De Vries was fulfilled.

The College of Nineteen had changed the mode of government in New Netherland to conform more nearly to that of Holland.

PETER STUYVESANT.

All power for the management of the concerns of the colony was vested in a Supreme Council composed of a director-general or governor, a vice-director, and fiscal or treasurer. At that time Peter Stuyvesant,* a Frieslander, a scholar, and a brave soldier in the service of the Dutch West India Company, and who had lost a leg in an attack upon the Portuguese island of St. Martin, was at Amsterdam receiving surgical treatment. He had been governor of the company's colony of Curaçoa, in which capacity he had shown great vigor and wisdom. He was then forty-four years of age ; strong in physical constitution ; fond of official

---

* Peter Stuyvesant was born in Triestan, in 1602. He became a brave soldier in the Dutch military service, in the West Indies, and was appointed Governor of Curaçoa. He was a strong-headed and sometimes a wrong-headed official, but ruled with equity and fidelity to his country. Made governor of New Netherland in 1645, as "redressor general" of all abuses, he became conspicuous for his energy and patriotism. Compelled to surrender the province to the English in 1664, he retired to private life. The next year he went to Holland to report to his superiors. Returning, he spent the remainder of his days at his seat on Manhattan Island, near the East River, where he died in August, 1682. His remains rest in St. Mark's Churchyard, New York City.

show; admiring the arbitrary nature of military rule, under which he had been educated; aristocratic in all his notions; haughty in his deportment toward subordinates; a thorough disciplinarian; a stern, inflexible patriot, and a just and honest man. He was appointed governor of New Netherland. He was not fitted to govern a simple people with republican tendencies, yet his administration of the affairs of New Netherland for about seventeen years contrasted most favorably with those of his predecessors in office, and he became the most renowned of the officials of the Dutch West India Company.

Owing to a disagreement concerning some of the details of policy in the management of New Netherland, Stuyvesant did not arrive at Manhattan until late in May, 1647. He bore the commission of director-general over New Netherland and "adjoining places" (New Sweden and the Connecticut Valley), and also of the islands of Curaçoa, Buenaire, Aruba, and their dependencies. He was accompanied by Lubbertus van Dincklagen, Van Twiller's dismissed schout-fiscal (who had been instrumental in causing the recall of that governor and also of Kieft), as vice-director or lieutenant-governor. With him also came the fiscal, Hendrick van Dyck, and Commissary Adriaensen. They came with a little squadron of four ships, bearing "free colonists" and private traders.

STUYVESANT'S SEAL.*

The new director-general was received at Manhattan with great joy. The arrival was on a clear and warm May morning. The whole community turned out under arms, and almost exhausted the breath and gunpowder of the town in shouting and firing. Stuyvesant marched to the fort in great pomp, displaying a silver-mounted wooden leg of fine workmanship. After keeping several of the principal inhabitants who went to welcome him waiting some hours bareheaded in the sun, while he remained covered, "as if he were the Czar of Muscovy," he addressed the people. He told them that he should govern them "as a father his children, for the advantage of the chartered Dutch West India Company and these burghers and their land," and he declared that every one should have justice done him. The people went to their homes with hopeful anticipations. Yet a few of the more thoughtful

---

* Stuyvesant's official seal was made of silver. The engraving is of the exact size of the original. As it was his private property, having had it struck at his own expense, he carried it with him to New Netherland.

ones shook their heads in doubt, for they somewhat feared that his haughty carriage denoted a despot's will rather than a father's tender and affectionate indulgence.

Stuyvesant was too frank and honest to conceal his opinions and intentions. At the very outset he asserted the prerogatives of the directorship, and frowned upon every expression of republican sentiment. He regarded the people as his subjects, to be obedient to his will. In this he was not a whit behind his predecessors. On one occasion he declared it to be "treason to petition against one's magistrates, whether there be cause or not." He defended Kieft's conduct in rejecting the interference of "The Twelve" in public affairs, and plainly told the people: "If any one during my administration shall appeal I will make him a foot shorter and send the pieces to Holland, and let him appeal in that way." With such despotic sentiments he began his iron rule.

Stuyvesant was despotic, and yet honesty and wisdom marked all his acts. He truly described New Netherland as in "a low condition" on his arrival. Excepting the Long Island settlements, scarcely fifty bouweries or cultivated farms could be counted; and the whole province could not furnish more than three hundred men capable of bearing arms. He set about reforms with promptness and vigor. The morals of the people, the sale of liquor to the Indians, the support of religion, and the regulation of trade commanded his immediate attention and became subjects for numerous proclamations and ordinances. It was not long before he infused his own energy into the community, and very soon the life-blood of enterprise began to circulate freely through every vein and artery of society.

With the same energy Stuyvesant applied himself to the adjustment of his "foreign relations." He despatched a courier to Governor Printz, of New Sweden, with a decided protest against his occupation of a portion of the domain of New Netherland without the consent of the Dutch West India Company, and he made arrangements to meet commissioners of New England in council to determine the mutual rights of the Dutch and English. He treated the surrounding Indians with the utmost kindness. Because the new director won the warm friendship of those who were lately brooding in sullen hate over the murder of sixteen hundred of their people, the foolish story got abroad in the east that Stuyvesant was forming a coalition with the Indians to exterminate the English!

Financial embarrassments in New Netherland at this time were favorable to the implantation and growth of representative government in the colony. Since 1477 Holland had maintained the just principle that

"Taxation and representation are inseparable." The denial of this principle as applied to the English-American colonies at near the middle of the last century led to a war which dismembered the British Empire and gave political independence to the United States. They formulated the Holland principle in the grand political postulate: "Taxation without representation is tyranny," and fought successfully in its defence.

Stuyvesant dared not tax the colonists without their consent for fear of incurring the censure of the States-General. It could be done in only one way, and that way he adopted. He called a convention of the people and directed them to choose eighteen proper men, nine of whom he might appoint as the representatives of the "commonalty" to form a co-ordinate branch of the local government. Although their prerogatives were hedged round by provisos and limitations, and the first Nine chosen by the governor were to nominate their successors without the voice of the commonalty thereafter, this was an important advance toward the popular government of later times.

THE NINE formed a salutary check upon the director, and kept his power within due bounds. They were heard with respect in the Fatherland, and they were ever the habitual guardians of the rights of the people. They had far more power than THE TWELVE or the EIGHT under Kieft. They nourished the prolific germs of democracy which burst into vigorous life in the time of Leisler, nearly fifty years later. These senators were Augustine Heermans, Arnoldus van Hardenburg, and Govert Loockermans from among the merchants; Jan Jansen Dam, Jacob Wolfertsen van Couwenhoven, and Hendrick Hendricksen Kip from the citizens, and Michael Jansen, Jans Evertsen Bout, and Thomas Hall from the farmers.

SIGNATURE OF GOVERT LOOCKERMANS.

Soon after his inauguration Stuyvesant sent letters to the governors of neighboring colonies expressing his desire to cultivate friendly relations with them, at the same time stating the nature of the territorial claims of the Dutch, the prolific cause of irritation since the administration of Governor Minuit, when the Dutch West India Company claimed jurisdiction over the whole valley of the Connecticut, and Dutch trappers and traders were seen on the waters of Narraganset and Cape Cod bays.

When Minuit made overtures to the "Pilgrims" at Plymouth for the establishment of friendly intercourse, Governor Bradford expressed his willingness to do so, but warned the Dutch not to occupy or carry on trade in the country north of the fortieth degree of latitude, as it belonged to the Council of Plymouth. This excluded the whole of New England and more. Minuit, in reply, claimed the right of the Dutch to trade with the Narraganset Indians as they had done for years. Bradford made no response. Finally Minuit sent a deputation (1627) to New Plymouth to confer with the authorities there. At their head was Rassieres, the Secretary of New Netherland, an accomplished gentleman of French blood. They entered New Plymouth with the sound of a trumpet which heralded their approach from the little vessel which had brought them to that shore. They were kindly received and entertained for several days. The special object of the mission was not attained, but the deputies made a profitable study of the political and social policy of the Puritans. They carried back to Manhattan ideas which, diffused among the people there, led in time to an enlargement of their liberties. The embassy were accompanied to their vessel by an escort of Puritans.

At that conference soft words were used by both parties, kindly feelings were engendered, and while both the Dutch and the English were equally resolved to maintain their respective rights, there were no words of defiant anger uttered. Their farewell and parting were most friendly. Diplomacy and contention between the Dutch and their neighbors continued fully twenty years, when the whole matter was settled, as far as possible, in 1650.

CHAPTER V.

Governor Stuyvesant, peacefully inclined, determined to attempt a settlement of the disputes between New Netherland and New England by diplomacy. He made arrangements for a conference at Hartford between himself and commissioners appointed by the united New England colonies.* Late in September, 1650, accompanied by George Baxter, his English secretary, and a large suite, he sailed from Manhattan, touching at several settlements on the shores of Long Island Sound. He arrived at Hartford on the fourth day of the voyage.

SIGNATURE OF GEORGE BAXTER.

Negotiations began on September 23d. After a discussion for five days it was agreed that "all differences should be referred to two delegates on each side." The commissioners appointed Simon Bradstreet and Thomas Prence, and Stuyvesant chose Captain Thomas Willett and Ensign George Baxter, both Englishmen. The referees recommended that a line drawn from the westerly side of Oyster Bay directly across Long Island to the sea should be made the boundary between the Dutch on the west side of the line and the English on the east side of the line. Also that a line from the west side of Greenwich Bay, in Long Island Sound, extending north twenty miles, and after that not less than ten miles from the Hudson River should be the boundary line between New Netherland and New England on the mainland. Judgment as to what had already happened between the Dutch and New Haven Colony, in Kieft's time, was postponed until advice should be received from Holland. The former, regardless of the warnings of Governor Kieft, had bought

SIGNATURE OF THOMAS WILLETT.

---

* In 1643 delegates from Connecticut, New Haven, Plymouth, and the General Court of Massachusetts assembled at Boston to consider measures against common danger from the Dutch on Manhattan and the Indians. Rhode Island, considered schismatic, was not invited to the conference. A Confederacy was formed of the colonies named, under the title of "United Colonies of New England." It continued for more than forty years, **1643-86**.

lands of the Indians on both sides of the Delaware within the Dutch domain, and proceeded to make settlements there. These settlements were speedily broken up by military force.

The recommendations of the referees were adopted. The two chosen by Stuyvesant, being Englishmen, his countrymen felt slighted, nay, insulted, and accused the governor of partiality for the interests of the English and neglect of theirs. They opposed the treaty, and made new demands for more popular liberty.

Having so far settled all differences with the New Englanders, Stuyvesant turned his attention to the Swedes on the Delaware, whom he regarded as intruders upon Dutch territory. The accession of a new monarch to the throne of Sweden made an adjustment of the long-pending dispute desirable.

Stuyvesant had been directed to act firmly, but discreetly, in the matter. Accompanied by his suite of officers, he went to Fort Nassau, and thence sent to Governor Printz an abstract of the title of the Dutch to the domain, and called a council of the Delaware Indians. Sachems and chiefs in the council declared the Swedes to be usurpers, and by a solemn treaty gave all the land to the Dutch. Then Stuyvesant crossed the river, and near the site of New Castle, Del., built a fort, and named it Casimer. Returning he demolished Fort Nassau. Printz protested in vain. He and Stuyvesant held friendly conferences, and agreed to "keep neighborly friendship and correspondence together." That was in the year 1651.

Meanwhile the director-general had done much to improve his capital, which now had a population of nearly seven hundred persons. He found it an irregularly built and straggling village, without sanitary appliances and very little government. Each burgher was a law unto himself. Various ordinances were now promulgated by the governor and enforced by him for the regulation of the construction of buildings in reference to street lines; for the maintenance of order, cleanliness, and sobriety; for the prevention of conflagrations, the support of religion, the promotion of morality, and the regulation of emigration and trade. Scores of other matters for the general good of society were attended to by the director-general, until Manhattan was made a very pleasant dwelling-place. Though Stuyvesant was a strict member of the Dutch Reformed Church, beliefs and divine worship in any form were tolerated. With a patriotic feeling the director-general dropped the pretty Indian name of the village of Manhattan, and called it New Amsterdam.

Stuyvesant had some unpleasant experience in the spring and summer of 1648 with Brandt van Slechtenhorst,* the patroon's commissary at Rensselaerwyck, who assumed an independent position for "the Colonie." The director-general issued a proclamation for the observance of a fast day throughout New Netherland. The patroon's commissary protested against it as an invasion of "the rights of the lord patroon." This controversy and the fact that illicit trade was carried on with the Colonie induced Stuyvesant to visit Fort Orange at midsummer. He was loyally received at the fort. He summoned Van Slechtenhorst to answer for his contempt of the company's authority. The commissary answered by complaining of Stuyvesant's infringement of the privileges of the patroon. The director-general, incensed by the commissary's words and manner, had no further oral communication with him, but by writing he forbade him to put up any building within the range of the guns of Fort Orange; to make any new ordinances affecting trade with the Colonie without the assent of the officers of the company, and declared the pledge which the patroons exacted from the colonists not to appeal from the decisions of the manorial courts a "crime." He also demanded from the commissary an annual return to him of all the affairs of the Colonie. Then he returned to Manhattan.

"You act as if you were the lord of the patroon's Colonie," was the answer which the stubborn commissary sent after the irate director-general, and persisted in defying that officer's orders.

SIGNATURE OF VAN SLECHTENHORST.

He forbade the commissary of the company to quarry stone or cut timber within the Colonie, and erected houses close by Fort Orange. Stuyvesant sent troops to restrain Van Slechtenhorst and to bring him to Manhattan if he would not desist. They failed to do so. Then the commissary was ordered by a peremptory summons to appear at Fort Amsterdam the next spring.

In the mean time popular discontents were everywhere manifest. THE NINE were compelled to act in behalf of the commonalty, but were

---

* Van Slechtenhorst was a native of Guelderland, bold, fiery in disposition, self-willed, and honest. He had been appointed commissary for the young patroon, whose father, Killian van Rensselaer, had lately died. His persistent practical assertion of the independence of Rensselaerwyck made him a rankling thorn in the side of Stuyvesant. Among other offences, he acquired a cession of lands at Kaatskill, which had already been granted, and refused to recede. He also purchased lands at Claverack, opposite, for the patroon. He soon got into trouble, and was arrested and confined at New Amsterdam. He escaped, and sent his son to explore the Kaatsbergs in search of silver. He bought the land on which the city of Troy now stands, and finally returned to Holland.

thwarted at every step by the sturdy director. At the next election (1649) the energetic Adriaen van der Donck, who had been the schout-fiscal of Rensselaerwyck, and Oloff Stevensen van Cortlandt became members of the COUNCIL OF NINE. Stuyvesant stoutly persisted in maintaining his dictatorial power. At the same time he carried on controversial correspondence with the New Englanders, which was terminated by the conference at Hartford already mentioned.

The contest between THE NINE and the director continued. The

SIGNATURE OF VAN DER DONCK.

latter proceeded with a high hand. He seized the papers of THE NINE and imprisoned Van der Donck for "calumniating the provincial officers." But the popular desire for reform and freedom could not be repressed. Finally THE NINE, in the name of the commonalty, prepared a "Memorial" and a "Remonstrance" to the States-General boldly setting forth the grievances of the people and asking for the establishment of a burgher government in the colony such as their "High

SIGNATURE AND SEAL OF VAN CORTLANDT.

Mightinesses should consider adapted to the province and resembling somewhat the laudable government of our Fatherland." These papers were drawn up by Van der Donck, and he and two others of THE NINE took them to Holland to present them in person.

Again, when Stuyvesant had concluded his treaty at Hartford and threatened to abolish THE NINE and rule as an autocrat, the popular representatives presented a statement of affairs in New Netherland to the States-General, and Van der Donck in Holland strongly pleaded the cause of the commonalty, who yearned for the freer system of government which prevailed in New England. In this memorial and plea Van Dincklagen, the vice-director, and Van Dyke, the fiscal, joined, and Melyn, who had been cruelly persecuted by Kieft and Stuyvesant, added his powerful support.

At length, after Stuyvesant had administered the government of New Netherland more than four years, continually making arbitrary efforts to repress the spirit of popular freedom, the voice of the commonalty of New Amsterdam and its vicinity was heeded by the College of Nineteen, and they informed the headstrong director-general, in the spring of 1652, that they had given their assent to the establishment of a "burgher government" on Manhattan—a government like that of the

SIGNATURE OF VAN TIENHOVEN.

free cities of Holland, the officers, however, to be appointed by the governor. The soul of Stuyvesant was troubled by this "imprudent intrusting of power with the people," as he said.

In February, 1653, New Amsterdam was formally organized as a city by the installation of Cornelis van Tienhoven,[*] *schout;* Arendt van Hattem and Martin Kregier, *burgomasters*, and Paul L. Van der Grist, Maximilian van Gheel, Allard Anthony, William Beeckman, and Peter

---

[*] Van Tienhoven was a conspicuous character in the early history of New Netherland. He came with Van Twiller, became the company's book-keeper, and afterward provincial secretary and schout-fiscal. He purchased lands in Westchester, led an expedition against the Raritans, made a treaty at Bronx River, and urged Kieft to attack the Indians. Retained as provincial secretary by Stuyvesant, the latter sent him to Holland as his representative. He was sent to negotiate with Virginia, also to New Haven for the same purpose. He superintended the South River Expedition against the Swedes in 1655. In 1656 he, a schout-fiscal, was charged with malfeasance in office; so also was his brother, and both were dismissed from the public service, when Cornelis returned to Amsterdam.

Wolfertsen van Couwenhoven, *schepens*.* Jacob Kip was appointed secretary to the municipal government. A building known as the City Tavern, standing at the head of Coenties Slip, which had been taken for the public use, was now named the State House or City Hall.† The city then contained about seven hundred and fifty inhabitants, and embraced the whole island of Manhattan.

Stuyvesant had scarcely recovered from his chagrin at this turn in public affairs when, through the influence of the democratic Van der Donck, he was summoned to appear before the States-General to answer concerning his government in New Netherland. This summons amazed the Amsterdam Chamber of the company. They wrote to Stuyvesant to delay his departure from America. Political considerations soon afterward caused the revocation of the order, and Stuyvesant never left Manhattan until after the sceptre had departed from the Dutch.

THE FIRST CITY HALL.

Another trouble vexed the soul of Peter Stuyvesant. A new element of social progress had begun to work vigorously in New Netherland, and in harmony with the free spirit of Dutch policy in social and political life. "Numbers, nay, whole towns," wrote De Laet, the historian,‡

---

* The *schout* was a prosecuting attorney, a judge, and a sheriff; a *burgomaster* was a governing magistrate, and a *schepen* was an alderman.

† This was a large stone building erected by Governor Kieft for the entertainment of strangers. He called it his *harberg*, or house of entertainment. It was known as the City Tavern after Stuyvesant came, and until he appropriated it to the public use.

‡ John de Laet was one of the most influential directors of the Dutch West India Company. In 1625 he published at Leyden, in a folio, black-letter volume, a *History of the New World; or Description of the West Indies*, which he dedicated to the States-Gen-

"to escape from the persecutions of the New England Puritans, who made their narrow human creed the higher law," had come to New Netherland to enjoy the theoretic liberty of conscience in Church and State under Belgic rule. They had lands assigned them all around Manhattan. New Englanders intermarried with the Dutch. Being free to act as citizens, they exercised much influence in public affairs.

More than ten years before New Amsterdam became a city an English secretary (George Baxter, already mentioned) had been employed by the director-general. The "strangers" readily adopted the republican ideas of the Dutch commonalty, and bore a conspicuous part in the democratic movements which gave Stuyvesant so much trouble during the latter years of his administration. The Dutch sighed for the freedom enjoyed in Fatherland, and the English settlers were determined to exercise the liberty which British subjects then enjoyed under the rule of Cromwell. Stuyvesant saw the tidal wave of popular feeling rising, but, firm in his integrity and convictions of the righteousness of his course, he maintained his position until he was compelled to yield or perish.

SIGNATURE OF JOHN DE LAET.

Republicanism, like any other truth, has remarkable vitality. It is nourished by persecution. The more Stuyvesant attempted to stifle it, the more widely it spread and blossomed. The popular will, fully bent on reforms, became bold enough, in the autumn of 1653, to call a convention of nineteen delegates, who represented eight villages or communities, to assemble in the City Hall at New Amsterdam, ostensibly to take measures to secure themselves against the depredations of barbarians and pirates. They met on November 26th. Stuyvesant tried to control their action, but they paid very little attention to his wishes and none to his commands; yet they treated him with great courtesy. When they adjourned they gave a parting collation, to which the director-general was invited. Of course he would not sanction their proceedings by his presence. The delegates told him plainly that there would be another

---

eral. He quoted largely from Hudson's private journal. In 1630 he became a shareholder in the estate of Rensselaerwyck, which the proprietor had divided into five shares. He also became interested in Swaanendael, on the shore of Delaware Bay.

convention soon, and that he might act as he pleased, and prevent it if he could.

This revolutionary movement in his capital aroused the ire of the director-general. He stormed and threatened, but prudently yielded to the demands of the people that he should issue a call for another convention, and so give legal sanction for the election of delegates thereto. They were chosen, and assembled at the City Hall on December 10th.* The object of the convention was to prepare and adopt a true statement of public affairs in New Netherland, and a remonstrance against the tyrannous rule of the director-general.

This paper was drawn up by Baxter, Stuyvesant's former secretary,† and signed by every delegate. After expressions of loyalty to the States-General, it proceeded with a narrative, arranged under six heads, of the grievances which the colonists had endured. That narrative was a severe indictment of Stuyvesant for maladministration or mismanagement of public affairs. The paper was sent to the governor with a demand for a "categorical answer" to each of its heads.

Stuyvesant met this document with his usual pluck. He denied the right of some of the delegates to seats in the convention. He denounced the whole thing as the wicked work of the English, and expressed a doubt whether "George Baxter, the author, knew what he was about." He wanted to know if there was no one among the Dutch in New Netherland "sagacious and expert enough to draw up a remonstrance to the director and council;" and he severely reprimanded the city government of New Amsterdam for "seizing this dangerous opportunity for conspiring with the English [with whom Holland was then at war], who

---

* As this was the first real representative assembly in the great State of New York, I give here the names in full of the delegates and the districts which they represented. The metropolis (New Amsterdam) was represented by Arendt van Hattem, Martin Kregier, and P. L. Van der Grist; Breuckelen (Brooklyn), by Frederick Lubbertsen, Paul Van der Beech, and William Beeckeman; Flushing, by John Hicks and Tobias Flake; Newtown, by Robert Coe and Thomas Hazard; Heemstede (Hempstead), by William Washburn and John Somers; Amersfoort (Flatlands), by P. Wolfertsen van Couwenhoven, Jan Strycker, and Thomas Swartwout; Midwout (Flatbush), by Elbert Elbertsen and Thomas Spicer; Gravesend, by George Baxter and J. Hubbard.

† George Baxter was an exile from New England, and was appointed English secretary and interpreter by Kieft in 1642. Stuyvesant retained him as such, and he gave the director efficient service for several years. He became a leader in seditious proceedings at Gravesend, where he hoisted an English flag. He was arrested and imprisoned at New Amsterdam, but escaped, went to New England, and thence to London in 1663, where he stimulated the animosity of the English against the Dutch. With Samuel Maverick (who had lived in Massachusetts from his boyhood) and Scott he advised the Council of Foreign Plantations as to the best means for subduing New Netherland.

were ever "hatching mischief, but never performing their promises, and who might to-morrow ally themselves with the North," meaning Sweden and Denmark.

This bluster did not turn the convention from its purpose. Beeckman, of Breuckelen, was sent to tell the governor that if he refused to consider the several points of the remonstrance they would appeal to the States-General. This threat enraged Stuyvesant, and seizing his heavy cane, he ordered Beeckman to leave his presence. The plucky ambassador of the convention folded his arms and silently defied the governor. When Stuyvesant's wrath had subsided he politely begged his visitor to excuse his sudden ebullition of passion, assuring him that he had great personal regard for him. But he was less courteous toward the convention as a body. He ordered the members to disperse on pain of incurring his "high displeasure." "We derive our authority," he said, "from God and the company, not from a few ignorant subjects; and we alone can call the inhabitants together." The convention executed its threat, and appealed to the States-General.

While thus perplexed by domestic annoyances, the tranquillity of the director-general's "foreign relations" was seriously disturbed. The pacific and "neighborly" Governor Printz had left New Sweden, and was succeeded in office by John Risingh, a more warlike magistrate, who came to the Delaware bringing with him some soldiers commanded by the bold Swen Shute. These speedily appeared before Fort Casimer, which Stuyvesant had built, on Trinity Sunday, 1654. "What can I do? I have no powder," said the commander of the little stronghold to the Dutch settlers who flocked to it for protection. He could do nothing; so he walked out of the fort, leaving the gate wide open, and shaking hands with Shute and his men, welcomed them as friends. The Swedes fired two shots over the fort in token of its capture, and then blotting out its Dutch garrison and its name, occupied it and called it Fort Trinity.

When news of this event reached Stuyvesant he was made very angry and perplexed, for he was hourly expecting an attack from a British force, and he was at his wit's end. But the cloud soon passed. The English did not come, for the war was suddenly closed by treaty. Then Stuyvesant made a voyage to the West Indies for the purpose of establishing a trade between New Netherland and those islands. Before he left he delivered to the authorities of the city of New Amsterdam the painted coat-of-arms of the municipality, the seal, and the silver signet which the College of Nineteen had just sent over. They soon afterward sent an order to the director-general to retake Fort Casimer and to wipe out the stain which the "infamous surrender" of that post had imparted to Belgic heroism. He was also ordered to annihilate Swedish dominion on both sides of the Delaware.

This important task the director-general undertook in the summer of 1655, and accomplished it speedily and without bloodshed. After a day of fasting and prayer (August 25th), and "after sermon" on Sunday, September 5th, a squadron of seven vessels, bearing more than six hundred soldiers (mostly volunteers), sailed from New Amsterdam for the Delaware. The flag-ship was the *Balance*, commanded by the valiant Frederick de Konick. In her cabin might have been seen the director-general, Vice-director Nicasius de Sille, and Dominie Megopolensis. The squadron

SEAL OF NEW AMSTERDAM.

ascended the Delaware. The troops landed not far from Fort Christina, and an ensign and a drummer were sent to demand the surrender of Fort Casimer. This demand was speedily complied with. Then the commander drank the health of Stuyvesant in a glass of Rhenish wine; and so ended the expedition, without firing a gun or shedding a drop of blood. So also ended Swedish dominion on the Delaware, and "New Sweden" perished in a day. Like Alfred of England, the director-general wisely made citizens of many of the conquered Swedes, who generally became the most loyal friends of the Dutch. They prospered exceedingly, and when, nearly thirty years afterward, they welcomed William Penn as their governor, they declared that it was the happiest day of their lives.

SIGNATURE OF DE SILLE.

During the absence of the expedition New Amsterdam was menaced with destruction. Van Dyck, a former civil officer, detected an Indian woman stealing peaches and slew her. The fury of her tribe was kindled. The long peace with the barbarians was suddenly broken. Before daybreak one morning almost two thousand River Indians in sixty canoes appeared before New Amsterdam. They landed, and with the pretence of looking for hostile Indians they distributed themselves through the town and broke into several houses in search of the murderer. The alarmed citizens held a council at the fort and summoned the Indian leaders before them. The latter agreed to leave the city and pass over to Nutten (Governor's) Island before sunset. They broke their promises, shot Van Dyck, menaced others, and filled the inhabitants with alarm. The citizens flew to arms and drove the Indians to their canoes, when they crossed over the Hudson River and ravaged a large region in New Jersey and on Staten Island. Within three days one hundred white people were slain, one hundred and fifty were made captive, and more than three hundred estates were utterly ruined.

Stuyvesant returned from the Delaware when the excitement in New Amsterdam was at its height. He soon brought order out of confusion. Yet distant settlements were broken up, the inhabitants flying in fear to Manhattan for protection. To prevent a like calamity in the future, Stuyvesant issued a proclamation ordering all who lived in secluded places in the country to gather themselves into villages "after the fashion of our New England neighbors." The Dutch had very little trouble with the Indians afterward while the former remained masters of New Netherland.

Excepting troubles occasioned by the arbitrary rule of the director-general, the religious intolerance practised and fostered by him, and occasional outside pressure from the Puritans and others, New Netherland enjoyed peace and prosperity for almost ten years after the conquest of New Sweden and the suppression of Indian hostilities.

There was some serious trouble at one time in 1659 with the barbarians at Esopus, in (present) Ulster County, among whom the Dutch had made a settlement. The latter brought a dreadful calamity that befell them upon themselves. Some Indians, sleeping off the effects of a drunken carouse, were wantonly fired upon by the soldiers of a Dutch garrison on the site of Rondout, and several were killed. The Indians flew to arms. Farms were desolated, buildings were burned, cattle and horses were killed, and many human beings perished. Stuyvesant, when he heard of the trouble, hastened to Esopus and soon quelled the great disturbance.

The Dutch were also much disturbed in 1659 by claims made for the proprietor of Maryland to the whole region embraced in New Sweden. An embassy composed of two sturdy burghers—Heermans and Waldron—was sent to Maryland to confer with the authorities there. Dining with Secretary Calvert, they were surprised by his claiming that Maryland extended to the limits of New England.

"Where, then, would remain New Netherland?" asked the envoys.

"I do not know," replied the secretary, with provoking calmness.

The envoys were provoked. They utterly "denied, disowned, and rejected" the claim for Lord Baltimore, and with great spirit maintained that of the Dutch. The conference was ended without any immediate results, and the envoys returned to New Amsterdam.

The New Englanders were again pressing territorial claims, and within and without New Netherland the Anglo-Saxon progressive element was menacing the integrity of the Dutch realm in America. New Amsterdam increased in wealth and population. A wooden palisade or "wall," extending from river to river along the line of (present) Wall Street, from which it derives its name, was constructed. A village was founded on a fertile plain in the upper part of Manhattan Island, and it was called "Harlem." It was planted there "for the promotion of agricultural gardening—and the amuse-

A DUTCH WIND-MILL.

A DUTCH PLEASURE WAGON.

ment for the people of New Amsterdam." They erected a wind-mill there like those in Holland. Between the city and the village might frequently be seen farm wagons on the only road, laden with garden products, and occasionally a Dutch pleasure wagon so familiar to travellers in Holland, at that time, conveying a part of the family to a social gathering. The little city contained many happy homes, where people of cheerful but often uncultivated minds and affectionate hearts domiciled, and life was enjoyed in a dreamy, quiet blissfulness which is quite unknown in these days of bustle and noise. Very little attention was given to political matters by the commonalty or the mass of the people, but there were many thoughtful men and women who were restive under the rule of the director-general. Some of them declared they would be willing to endure English rule for the sake of English liberty. They were soon given an opportunity to try the experiment.

CHAPTER VI.

A crisis in the affairs of New Netherland now approached. Monarchy was restored in England in 1660, and a son of the decapitated Charles I. was set upon the throne of his father as Charles II. This had not been done by the voice of even a majority of the people, and the new monarch, wishing to conciliate all parties, proclaimed "liberty to tender consciences" in all his dominions. But this was only a State trick, as the sad experience of the Dissenters soon taught them.

The Dutch West India Company determined to follow the example of King Charles by expressing "tenderness" for consciences, for their own benefit. They claimed the domains of New Jersey as a part of the realm of New Netherland. It was almost wholly unoccupied by settlers. Desiring to allure the disappointed and persecuted Dissenters in England to their domain, they prepared a charter, which was approved by the States-General, to meet the aspirations of tender consciences. The States-General passed an act in February, 1661, granting to "all Christian people of tender consciences, in England or elsewhere oppressed, full liberty to erect a colony in the West Indies, between New England and Virginia, in America, now within the jurisdiction of Peter Stuyvesant, the States-General's governor for the Dutch West India Company." All concerned were forbidden to hinder Dutch colonists, and were enjoined to afford them "all favorable help and assistance where it shall be needful."

This widening of the tents of toleration and the freedom of the citizens again troubled the soul of the aristocratic Stuyvesant, who was bigotedly loyal to the doctrines and discipline of the Dutch Reformed Church, and he now began those petty persecutions already alluded to which made the Manhattan people more than ever displeased with his administration. He seemed to have a special dislike of the Quakers, and disciplined them with imprisonments and banishments. To a fiery temper like that of Stuyvesant their imperturbability was an offence and annoyance. Their serenity of deportment made him angry. But his persecutions had very little effect in suppressing the aspirations of the people.

Emigrants from Old and New England settled here and there between the Hudson and Delaware rivers, and in 1662 a colony of Mennonites from Holland—followers of Simon Menno, who were Anabaptists—settled on the Hore Kill, in the region of ruined Swaanendael (see p. 33), and there formed an association and adopted seventeen articles of agreement for their government. The Association was composed of married men, at least twenty-four years of age, and out of debt. No clergyman was admitted to the Association. Their religious rites were few and simple. Desirous of maintaining harmony, they excluded "all intractable people—such as those in communion with the Roman See; usurious Jews; English stiff-necked Quakers; Puritans; foolhardy believers in the Millennium, and obstinate modern pretenders to revelation." With Peter Plockhoy as their leader, they flourished until the colony was plundered and ruined by the English, in 1664, "not sparing even a raile."

Another Dutch colony was founded on the Delaware in 1656 by the city of Amsterdam and named New Amstel. The land was bought by the city from the Dutch West India Company. It suffered many misfortunes, and finally perished with New Netherland. This colony was

SIGNATURE OF WILLIAM BEECKMAN.

planted under Stuyvesant's jurisdiction, who, in order to have more direct and sure control of its affairs, appointed William Beeckman Vice-Director and Commissary of New Amstel.*

In the summer of 1663 the peace which had reigned at Esopus for three years was suddenly broken. A new village called Wiltwyck (now Kingston) had been built up, and in comfortable log cottages the inhabitants had been living in fancied security for some time. The village

---

* William Beeckman was born in Overyssel in 1623, and came to New Netherland in the same ship with Stuyvesant. His wife was Catharine de Bergh, by whom he had six children, one of whom married a son of the governor, Nicholas William Stuyvesant. Beeckman was a schepen or alderman of New Amsterdam, secretary and vice-director of New Amstel, where he managed judiciously in diplomacy with the English representatives of Maryland. He was at one time commissary at Esopus. He was alderman in 1679 under English rule, having been burgomaster when the Dutch last possessed the city. He retired from public life in 1696, and died in 1707, in the eighty-fifth year of his age. "William" and "Beekman" streets, in New York, derived their names from him, and still retain them.

was palisaded, and at the mouth of Rondout Creek the Dutch built a *ronduit*—a redoubt—which made the Indians suspicious of their intentions. One day in early June, while the men were working in the fields and the village gates were wide open, bands of barbarians entered, and with friendly pretence offered beans and corn for sale at the doors of the cottages. Suddenly they began to plunder, burn, and murder. As the men rushed from the fields toward their blazing dwellings they were shot down. The living men were finally rallied by the schout, Swartwout, and drove the Indians away. Twenty-one lives had been sacrificed, nine persons were wounded, and forty-five, mostly women and children, were carried away captives.

Great alarm was spread throughout the province, and expeditions were sent against the Esopus Indians from Fort Amsterdam and Fort Orange. These chased the offenders far into the wilderness. Thirty miles from Wiltwyck they destroyed an Indian fort and rescued many of the captives.

The power of the barbarians was now broken, and it was soon crushed. Meanwhile the hostilities of the Indians among themselves on the borders of the white settlements made the Europeans constantly fearful and vigilant. At the same time the Connecticut people were continually encroaching. There was a revolt on Long Island, and the very existence of New Netherland was threatened. There were ever premonitions of such an event, which actually occurred the next year.

Informed late in 1663 that King Charles had granted to his brother James, Duke of York, the whole of Long Island, several of the principal English settlements combined in forming a sort of provisional government in that region. There was then among them Captain John Scott, who had been a disturber of the peace for several years. He had lately come back from England with pretended powers. He had claimed that the Indians had sold to him a large portion of Long Island, and he issued fraudulent deeds. This man the combined English settlements made their provisional president until "His Majesty's mind should be known." With an armed party he sought to force Dutch settlements to join the league, but failed. At the beginning of 1664 Scott departed for England after a conference at Hempstead with representatives of Stuyvesant, when he informed them that the Duke of York was resolved to possess himself not only of Long Island, but of the whole of New Netherland. Stuyvesant was startled and perplexed by this announcement of the "usurper," as he called Scott, and he asked the advice of his Council and the municipal authorities of New Amsterdam. They recommended the complete fortifying of the city. The director-general then ordered an election of delegates for a General Provincial Assembly, to meet in New Amsterdam in April. They assembled in the City Hall. There were delegates from Fort Orange, Rensselaerwyck, Esopus, and all the Dutch settlements; but they were powerless to avert the impending blow, which was to annihilate Dutch dominion in North America.*

The profligate British monarch resolved to rob the Dutch of all New Netherland. With no more right to the domain than had the arch-tempter to "all the kingdoms of the earth," but governed by the ethics of the mailed hand—"might makes right"—and that cannons are the "last arguments of kings," he gave to his royal brother, the Duke of York, a patent for the Dutch territory—"all the lands and rivers from the west side of Connecticut River to the east side of Delaware Bay." The patent included Long Island, Staten Island, and all the adjacent islands.

JEREMIAS VAN RENSSELAER.

As Lord High Admiral of the Royal Navy, the duke at once detached four ships-of-war for service in asserting his claim by force of arms, if necessary. The king provided four hundred and fifty regular soldiers for the same purpose, and intrusted the command of the expedition to Colonel Richard Nicolls, a stanch Royalist and court favorite, who had served under the great

SIGNATURE OF RICHARD NICOLLS.

---

* This General Provisional Assembly was presided over by Jeremias van Rensselaer, the second patroon and director of Rensselaerwyck. New Amsterdam was represented by Cornelis Steenwyck, burgomaster, and Jacob Bachker; Rensselaerwyck, by Jeremias van Rensselaer and Dirck van Schelluyne, its secretary; Fort Orange (Albany), by Jan Verbeek and Gerritt van Slechtenhorst; Breuckelen, by William Bredenbent and Albert Cornelis Wantenaar; Midwout, by Jan Strycker and William Guillians; Amersfoort, by Elbert Elbertsen and Coert Stevensen; New Utrecht, by David Jochemsen and Cornelis Beeckman; Boswyck (Bushwick), by Jan van Cleef and Gyshert Teunissen; Wiltwyck, by Thomas Chambers and Gyshert van Imbroeck; Bergen, by Engelbert Steenhuysen and Hermann Smeeman; and Staten Island, by David de Marest and Pierre Billou. This was the third and last popular assembly convened at New Amsterdam.

Marshal Turenne, and bore the commission of governor of the province after it should be secured to the duke. Associated with Nicolls were Sir Robert Carr, Colonel George Cartwright, and Samuel Maverick, as royal commissioners, instructed to visit the several colonies in New England and demand their assistance in reducing the Dutch to submission.

Stuyvesant had been assured by the misled Amsterdam Chamber that no danger need be apprehended from the British expedition, for it had been sent out to visit the English-American colonies to settle affairs among them and to introduce episcopacy. Soothed by this assurance, the work of fortifying New Amsterdam was suspended, vigilance was relaxed, and the director-general went up to Fort Orange at near the close of July to look after affairs there.

SIGNATURES OF CARR AND CARTWRIGHT.

This dreamed-of security was suddenly dispelled. Early in August intelligence came from Boston that the expedition was actually on the New England coast on its way to New Amsterdam. Stuyvesant, apprised of the fact, hastened back to his capital, and the municipal authorities ordered one third of the inhabitants, without exceptions, to labor every third day in fortifying the city. A permanent guard was organized, and a call was made on the provincial government for artillery and ammunition. Twenty great guns and a thousand pounds of powder were immediately furnished. But the inhabitants did not work with much enthusiasm in preparations for defence, for English influence and the director-general's temper and deportment had alienated the people, and they were indifferent. Some of them regarded the expected invaders as welcome friends. Stuyvesant had shorn himself of strength, and when now, in his extremity, he began to make concessions to the people, it was too late. The sceptre had departed from him. Loyal to his masters in Holland, he resolved to defend the city until the last, and entreated the people to sustain him.

At the close of August the British armament anchored outside the Narrows—the entrance to the harbor of New Amsterdam—and on Saturday, the 30th, Nicolls sent to Stuyvesant a summons to surrender the fort and city. He also sent a proclamation to the inhabitants promising perfect security of person and property to all who should submit to "His Majesty's Government." Stuyvesant immediately called his council and the burgomasters to a conference at the fort. He would not allow the terms offered by Nicolls to the people to be communicated to them. "It would not be approved in Fatherland," he said, for he believed " calamitous consequences" would follow by making them insist upon capitulating. There was also a meeting of other city officers and the burghers, at the City Hall, who determined to prevent the enemy from surprising the town, if possible, and yet they leaned toward submission, seeing resistance would be in vain.

The Sabbath passed by and no answer was returned to the summons of Nicolls. The people, uncertain as to what was going on, became much excited. On Monday the citizens assembled, when the burgomasters explained to them the terms offered by Nicolls. This was not sufficient. They demanded a sight of the proclamation. Stuyvesant went in person to the meeting, and told the people that such a course would " be disapproved in Fatherland." They were not satisfied, and clamored for a sight of the proclamation.

Meanwhile, Governor Winthrop, of Connecticut, who was on friendly terms with Stuyvesant and had joined the squadron, received from Nicolls a letter repeating his terms offered in the proclamation, and authorizing Winthrop to assure the Dutch governor that Hollanders, citizens or merchants, should have equal privileges with the English if he would quietly surrender.

Winthrop, under a flag of truce, delivered this letter to Stuyvesant outside the fort and urged him to surrender. The proud director-general promptly refused, and withdrawing to the Council-room within he opened and read the letter before the assembled Council and burgomasters. They urged him to communicate the letter to the people, as " all which regarded the public welfare ought to be made public."

The governor stoutly refused to yield. The Council and burgomasters as stoutly insisted upon the just measure, when the director-general, who had fairly earned the title of " Peter the Headstrong," unable to control his passions, tore the letter in pieces and threw it upon the floor. When the people who were at work on the palisades heard of this scene they dropped their implements and hastened to the City Hall. Thence they sent a deputation to Stuyvesant to demand the letter. In vain he attempted, in person, to satisfy the burghers and urge them to go on with the fortification. They would not listen to him, but uttered curses against his administration.

" The letter! the letter!" they shouted.

The governor stormed. The people shouted more vociferously:

" The letter! the letter!"

The burghers were on the verge of open insurrection. To avert such a calamity, the sturdy old governor yielded. He allowed the fragments of the torn letter to be picked up from the floor of the Council chamber and a fair copy to be made and given to the people; and he sent off in silence that night, through the dangerous strait of Hell Gate, in a small Dutch vessel, a despatch to the Amsterdam Chamber, saying: "Long Island is gone and lost; the capital cannot hold out long." This was Stuyvesant's last official despatch as Governor of New Netherland.

Receiving no reply from Stuyvesant, Nicolls landed some troops and anchored two ships-of-war in the channel between Fort Amsterdam and the Governor's Island. Stuyvesant saw all this from the ramparts of his fort, but would not yield. He knew the extreme weakness of the fort and city, yet his proud will would not readily bend. Yielding at length to the persuasions of Dominie Megopolensis * (who had led him from the ramparts), he sent a deputation to Nicolls with a letter, in which he said that, though he felt bound to "stand the storm," he desired, if possible, to arrange an accommodation. Nicolls curtly replied:

"To-morrow I will speak with you at Manhattan." Stuyvesant as curtly replied:

"Friends will be welcome if they come in a friendly manner."

SIGNATURE OF JOHN MEGOPOLENSIS.

"I shall come with ships and soldiers," answered Nicolls. "Raise the white flag of peace at the fort, and then something may be considered."

When this imperious message became known men, women, and children flocked to the director-general beseeching him to submit. The brave old soldier said: "I would much rather be carried out dead;"

---

* Dr. John Megopolensis, a learned clergyman, was brought to Rensselaerwyck with his family from Holland at the expense of the patroon, and employed there as a clergyman for six years, when he went home. He soon came back, became a patentee of Flatbush, on Long Island, and organized a church there. His jealousy of and intolerant conduct toward the Lutherans called an admonition from Holland. He was a man greatly beloved by Stuyvesant, and became the governor's most trusted adviser in public affairs. He accompanied Stuyvesant on his expedition against the Swedes in 1655. His earnest missionary spirit caused him to form a warm friendship for Father Le Moyne, the French Roman Catholic missionary among the Indians. He bore communications to Nicolls from Stuyvesant, and advised the surrender of the province to the English. After the surrender he and the English chaplain preached alternately in the church at the fort. He preached on Long Island also. Dominie Megopolensis died in New York, when his widow returned to Holland.

but when the city authorities, the clergy, and the principal inhabitants of the city, and even his own son, Balthazar, urged him to yield, "Peter the Headstrong," who had a heart "as big as an ox and a head that would have set adamant to scorn," consented to capitulate.

On the morning of September 8th, 1664, the last of the Dutch governors of New York led his soldiers from the fort down Beaver Lane to the place of embarkation for Holland. An hour later an English corporal's guard took possession of the fort and raised over it the red cross of St. George, when its name was changed to Fort James, in honor of the duke. Nicolls and Carr, with nearly two hundred soldiers, then entered the city, when the burgomasters duly proclaimed the former the deputy-governor of the province, which, with the city of New Amsterdam, he named "New York" in honor of the duke's first or English

SIGNATURES OF STUYVESANT AND HIS SECRETARY, VAN RUYVEN.*

title. The surrender of the garrison at Fort Orange soon followed, and the name of that post was changed to "Albany" in honor of the duke's second or Scotch title. Long Island was named "Yorkshire," and the region now known as New Jersey was named "Albania." Very soon

---

* Cornelis van Ruyven was appointed provincial secretary in 1653, and performed excellent service for Governor Stuyvesant for about eleven years. He was employed in diplomacy at various points in the province, on the South River and at Hartford. He was one of a committee who carried the letter from Governor Stuyvesant to Colonel Nicolls consenting to a surrender of the province to the English. Above is the signature of Van Ruyven signed officially below that of Stuyvesant to a Dutch document in my possession, dated May, 1664. The document bears the seal of New Netherland, seen on page 27 of this volume. Stuyvesant also had an English secretary—George Baxter—for a few years.

every part of New Netherland quietly submitted to the English, and so passed away forever Dutch dominion in North America.

The government of New Netherland under Dutch rule was little better than a caricature of the political system under which the Dutch colonists had lived happily in their native land. The province during its whole career of forty years had been controlled by a close commercial corporation, whose chief aim was the selfish one of pecuniary profit. The magistrates sent to preside over its public affairs were selected as supposed fit representatives of the great monopoly's aims and interests, and are not to be judged by the standard of those in power, whose chief aim is the happiness of the people and the building up of a State on the permanent foundations of wisdom and justice. The Dutch then (as now) were distinguished for their honesty, integrity, industry, thrift, and frugality.

NEW AMSTERDAM, 1664.

The purity of their morals and the decorousness of their manners were always conspicuous. This may, perhaps, be justly ascribed to the influence of their women, who were devoted wives and mothers and modest maidens. The women were remarkable for their executive ability in managing affairs, and their housekeeping was perfect in cleanliness and order.

As population and wealth increased at New Amsterdam much taste was frequently displayed in their dwellings. At the time of the surrender the city, within the palisades, or below Wall Street, contained about three hundred houses and fully fifteen hundred inhabitants.

Colonel Nicolls described it as "the best of His Majesty's towns in America." At first the houses were built of logs; the roofs were thatched with reeds and straw; the chimneys were made of wood, and the light of their windows entered through oiled paper. Finally the thatched roofs and wooden chimneys gave place to tiles and shingles and brick. The better houses were built of brick imported from Holland, until some enterprising citizens established a brickyard on the island during the administration of Stuyvesant.

A COTTAGE AT NEW AMSTERDAM.

Every house was surrounded by a garden, in which the chief vegetable cultivated was cabbage, and the principal flowers were tulips. The houses were plainly but sometimes richly furnished. It is said that the first carpet—a Turkey rug—seen in the city belonged to Sarah Oort, wife of the famous Captain Kidd. The clean floors were strewn daily with white beach sand wrought into artistic forms by the skilful use of the broom. Huge oaken chests filled with household linen of domestic manufacture were seen in a corner in every room, and in another corner a triangular cupboard with a glass door, sometimes, in which were displayed shining pewter and other plates. The wealthier citizens sometimes had china tea-sets and solid silver tankards, punch bowls, porringers, ladles, and spoons. Tea had only lately found its way to New York. Good horses were rare until they began to import them from New England, but their swine and cows were generally of excellent quality. There were no carriages until after the revolution of 1688. The first hackney coach seen in the city of New York was imported in 1696.

Clocks and watches were almost unknown. Time was measured by sun-dials and hour-glasses. The habits of the people were so regular that they did not need clocks and watches. They arose at cock-crowing, breakfasted at sunrise, and dined at eleven o'clock. At nine o'clock in the evening they all said their prayers and went to bed. Dinner-parties were unknown, but tea-parties were frequent. These parties began at three o'clock in the afternoon in winter, and ended at six o'clock, when the participants went home in time to attend to the milking of the cows.

In every house were spinning-wheels, large and small, for making threads of wool and flax ; and it was the pride of every family to have an ample supply of home-made linen and woollen cloth. The women knit, spun, and wove, and were steadily employed. Nobody was idle. Nobody was anxious to gain wealth. A man worth $1000 was regarded as rich. All practised thrift and frugality. Books were rare luxuries, and in most houses the Bible and prayer-book constituted the stock of literature. The weekly discourses of the clergymen satisfied their intellectual wants, while their own hands, industriously employed, satisfied all their physical necessities. Utility was as plainly stamped upon all their labors as is the maker's name upon silver spoons. Yet they were a cheerful people, and enjoyed rollicking fun during hours of leisure and social intercourse. These were the "good old days" in the city of New York— days of simplicity, comparative innocence and positive ignorance, when the commonalty no more suspected the earth of the caper of turning over like a ball of yarn every day than Stuyvesant did the Puritans of candor and honesty.

"The pioneers of New York," says Brodhead, "left their impress deeply upon the State. Far-reaching commerce, which had made old Amsterdam the Tyre of the seventeenth century,

THE FLAG OF HOLLAND.

early provoked the envy of the colonial neighbors of New Amsterdam, and in the end made her the emporium of the Western world. . . . Cherished birthdays yet recall the memories of the genial anniversaries of the Fatherland ; and year by year the people are invited to render thanks to their God, as their fathers were invited, long before Manhattan was known, and while New England was yet a desert. These forefathers humbly worshipped the King of kings, while they fearlessly rejected the kings of men.

"The emigrants who first explored the coasts and reclaimed the soil of New Netherland, and bore the flag of Holland to the wigwam of the Iroquois, were generally bluff, plain-spoken, earnest, yet unpresumptuous men, who spontaneously left their native land to better their condition and bind another province to the United Netherlands. They brought over with them the liberal ideas and honest maxims and homely virtues of their country. They introduced their church and their schools, their dominies and their school-masters. They carried along with them their huge clasped Bibles, and left them heirlooms in their families. . . The Dutch province always had both popular freedom and public spirit enough to attract within its borders voluntary immigrants from the neighboring British colonies. If the Fatherland gave an asylum to self-exiled Puritans of England, New Netherland as liberally sheltered refugees from the intolerant governments on her eastern frontier. . . . Without underrating others, it may confidently be claimed that to no nation in the world is the Republic of the West more indebted than to the United Provinces for the idea of a confederation of States ; for noble principles of constitutional freedom ; for magnanimous sentiments of religious toleration ; for characteristic sympathy with the subjects of oppression ; for liberal doctrines in trade and commerce ; for illustrious patterns of private integrity and public virtue, and for generous and timely aid in the establishment of independence. Nowhere among the people of the United States can any be found excelling in honesty, industry, courtesy, or accomplishments the posterity of the early Dutch settlers in New Netherland." *

Upon such a foundation—a people who made the hearth-stone the test of citizenship, and demanded residence and loyalty as the only guarantee of faithfulness as citizens—and a happy mixture, in time, of various nationalities and theological ideas, has been reared the grand superstructure of the Empire State of New York.

The Dutch West India Company tried to shift the responsibility of the loss of New Netherland from their own shoulders to those of Stuyvesant. They declared that he had not done his duty well, and asked the States-General to disapprove the " scandalous surrender" of New Amsterdam. The sturdy old Frieslander made serious counter-charges of remissness in duty against the company, and sustained them by sworn testimony taken at New York. He went to Holland in 1665 and urged the States-General to make a speedy decision of his case. There was delay. The dispute was finally ended in 1667 by the peace between Holland and England, concluded at Breda. Then Stuyvesant returned to America, where he was cordially welcomed by his old friends, and kindly received by his political enemies, who had already learned from experience that he was not a worse governor than the duke had sent

---

* Brodhead's *History of the State of New York*, i. 747.

them. He retired to his *bouwerie* or farm on the East River, where he enjoyed the respect of his fellow-citizens. There he died in 1682, at the age of eighty years. Under the venerable church of St. Mark his mortal remains repose. In the northern wall of that venerable fane may be seen a free-stone slab on which is engraved a memorial inscription.

With all his faults, Peter Stuyvesant was a grand man of the time in which he lived. Obedient to every behest of duty and conscience; zealous in his patriotic devotion to the interests of his people and country; lion-hearted in the maintenance of what he deemed to be right and just; with unswerving loyalty to religious and political creeds, in his day, and viewing with supreme contempt the treachery of one of the most despicable of the British monarchs toward his unsuspecting ally, he felt it to be a degradation to yield an iota to the demands of the royal robber, who was incapable of exercising any truly noble aspiration or truly generous impulse.

CHAPTER VII.

The surrender of New Netherland to the English being accomplished, a new provincial government for New York was organized under Colonel Nicolls as chief magistrate. Matthias Nicolls was made secretary of the province. The governor chose for his Council, Robert Needham, Thomas Delavall, Secretary Nicolls, Thomas Topping, and William Wells. Mr. Delavall was made collector and receiver-general of New York. The Dutch municipal officers of New Amsterdam were retained.

A few days after the surrender the burgomasters wrote to the Dutch West India Company giving an account of the event, and adding: "Since we are no longer to depend upon your honors' promises or protection, we, with all the poor, sorrowing, and abandoned commonalty, must fly for refuge to the Almighty God, not doubting but He will stand by us in this sorely afflicting conjunction."

A harmonious arrangement was made for divine worship in New York. The Dutch church in the fort was the only fane in the city dedicated to Jehovah, and it was cordially agreed that after the Dutch morning service on the Sabbath the English chaplain should read the English Episcopal service to the governor and the garrison. Upon this footing the English Episcopal Church and the Dutch Church in New York remained for more than thirty years.

SEAL OF THE DUKE OF YORK.*

The dreams of freedom under British rule in New York were never realized by the Dutch. They soon found that a change of masters did not increase their prosperity or happiness. "Fresh names and laws did

---

* Burke says the Duke of York was directed, by a royal warrant issued in 1652, to use a seal, delineated above, which bore the royal arms of the Stuarts quartered with those of France and England. It was used as the first seal of the province of New York under the English. It was both pendant and incumbent. The engraving represents a pendant seal attached to the first charter of the city of Albany, 1686.

not secure fresh liberties. Amsterdam was changed to York, and Orange to Albany; but these changes only commemorated the titles of a conqueror. It was nearly twenty years before that conqueror allowed for a brief period to the people of New York even that faint degree of representative government which they had enjoyed when the tri-colored ensign of Holland was hauled down from the flag-staff of Fort Amsterdam. New Netherland exchanged Stuyvesant and the Dutch West India Company and a republican sovereignty for Nicolls and a royal proprietor and a hereditary king. The province was not represented in Parliament; nor could the voice of the people reach the chapel of St. Stephen at Westminster as readily as it had reached the chambers of the Binnenhof at the Hague." *

Governor Nicolls required the Dutch inhabitants, who numbered about two thirds of the population of New Netherland, to take an oath of allegiance to the British monarch. The king having authorized the duke to make laws for the colony; the latter empowered Governor Nicolls and his Council to do so without the concurrence of representatives of the people. The code so prepared, and known as "The Duke's Laws," was promulgated in the spring of 1665.†

In order to gain the good-will of the Dutch, Nicolls allowed the municipal government of the city to continue in the form in which he found it. When, in February, 1665, the terms of the municipal officers expired, they were allowed, as usual, to nominate their successors. They chose Oloff Stevens van Cortlandt, burgomaster; Timothy Gabry, Johannes van Brugh, Johannes de Peyster,‡ Jacob Kip, and Jacques Coosseau, aldermen; and Allard Anthony, sheriff.

A little later the government of the city of New York was changed so as to make it more "conformable to the English." The governor selected Thomas Willett, Stuyvesant's wise counsellor in diplomacy, and then a resident of New Plymouth, to be the first Mayor of New York.

---

* Brodhead's *History of the State of New York*, ii. 44.

† There was only a pretence of consultation with representatives of the people in the construction of these laws. A meeting of thirty-four delegates was held at Hempstead, on the call of Governor Nicolls, who laid before them the laws he had caused to be compiled from those of New England; but when the delegates proposed any amendments they found that they had been assembled merely to accept laws which had been prepared for them. They had merely exchanged the despotism of Stuyvesant for English despotism.

‡ Johannes de Peyster was the first of his name who came to New Netherland. He was a man of wealth, and became active in public affairs. He was chosen burgomaster in 1673, while the Dutch had temporary possession of the province, and afterward suffered much from the petty tyranny of Governor Andros. He was the ancestor of the De Peyster family in America, some of whom have been distinguished in the history of our country.

One hundred and forty-two years afterward (1807) Marinus Willett, his great-great-grandson, was mayor of that city, then freed from British rule. It was in May, 1665, that the first Mayor and Board of Aldermen

SIGNATURE AND ARMS OF JOHANNES DE PEYSTER.

for the city of New York were appointed. Three of them were Englishmen—Willett, Delavall, and Lawrence—and four of them were Hollanders—Van Cortlandt, Van Brugh, Van Ruyven (former secretary of Stuyvesant), and Anthony.

War between Holland and Great Britain broke out again early in 1665. The Dutch had resolved no longer to submit to the domination of the English. The States-General authorized the Dutch West India Company to "attack, conquer, and ruin the English, both in and out of Europe, on land and water." The conflict raged chiefly on the ocean, and was terminated by a treaty at Breda at the close of June, 1667, when New Netherland was formally given up to Great Britain.

Meanwhile two royalist favorites—Lord Berkeley and Sir George Carteret—had persuaded the duke to convey to them a part of the magnificent domain in America, which was not yet in his possession, for the expedition sent to seize it was still (June, 1664) out upon the ocean. These favorites had been prompted to ask this grant by the "usurper" Scott—"born to work mischief"—for the purpose of injuring the duke, who had refused to let him have Long Island. The duke conveyed the whole of the beautiful territory between the Hudson River and the Delaware to Berkeley and Carteret, and in memory of the gallant defence of the island of Jersey by the latter, he named the domain in the charter Nova Cæsarea, or New Jersey.

ARMS OF THE CARTERETS.

Richard Nicolls * governed New York judiciously and wisely for about four years, when he resigned the government into the hands of his appointed successor, Francis Lovelace. The latter had visited Long Island in 1652 under a pass from Cromwell's Council of State, and passed thence into Virginia. He was a phlegmatic, indolent, and good-natured man, and of a mild and generous disposition, his weakness causing him occasionally to exercise petty tyranny. He was unfitted to encounter great storms, yet he showed considerable energy in dealing with the French and Indians on the northern frontier of New York during his administration.

One of Lovelace's wisest counsellors and the most influential man in the province at that time was Cornelis Steenwyck,† a wealthy citizen, and who held the office of mayor for three years during the administration of Lovelace. It was at his large storehouse that the corporation gave a banquet to Governor Nicolls on his retirement from office.

CORNELIS STEENWYCK.

---

* Nicolls was born in Bedfordshire in 1624, the son of a London barrister. He was a descendant of the Earl of Elgin. At the breaking out of the civil war he joined the royal forces, leaving college for the purpose, and soon obtained command of a troop of horse. As an *attaché* of the Duke of York, after the death of Charles, he served in France, first under Marshal Turenne, and then under the Prince of Condé. After the Restoration he returned to England, found employment at court, became a favorite, and was made the duke's deputy governor of New York. He returned to England in 1668.

† Cornelis Steenwyck emigrated to New Netherland from Haarlem, Holland. He was a merchant, who arrived at New Amsterdam about 1652, and engaged in trade, principally in tobacco for the European market. He was rated among the most wealthy citizens in 1655. In 1658 he married Margaretta de Riemer, daughter of a widow who conducted a small mercantile establishment in New Amsterdam. The widow was married the next year to Dominie Drissius, the Dutch clergyman of New Amsterdam. Steenwyck had a fine residence on the south-west corner of (present) Whitehall and Bridge streets. He was a very active man in public affairs as burgomaster, delegate to the General Assembly, and colleague of De Ruyven in carrying Stuyvesant's letters to ·Nicolls, and in the business of surrender.

Lovelace held friendly intercourse with the people of New England, and when, in 1673, there was war again between Holland and Great Britain, and a Dutch squadron appeared before his capital in August, he was on a friendly visit to Governor Winthrop, of Connecticut. With disaffection to his government he was always impatient; and when the inhabitants in the territory of "New Sweden," on the Delaware, and also on Long Island, showed a rebellious spirit, he, at the suggestion of a Swede, levied heavy taxes upon them, and told them that they should have no liberty for any other thought than how they should pay their assessments.

At the close of July, 1673, a Dutch squadron, commanded by Admirals Evertsen and Binckes, twenty-three vessels in all, including numerous prizes, and bearing six hundred land troops, arrived off Sandy Hook, and soon anchored above the Narrows in sight of New York. The admirals sent a summons to the commander of the fort there to surrender. The English were taken by surprise. Captain John Manning, who was in command of the fort, sent a messenger to Governor Lovelace in Connecticut, ordered the drums to beat for volunteers, and sent to the nearest towns on Long Island for re-enforcements. None came. The Dutch in the city showed signs of serious disaffection. The call for volunteers was little heeded. Few appeared, and those who did respond came as enemies instead of friends, and spiked the cannon parked in front of the City Hall. In this extremity Manning sent a deputation to the Dutch commander to inquire why he had come "in such a hostile manner to disturb His Majesty's subjects."

"We have come," he replied, "to take what is our own, and our own we will have."

ADMIRAL CORNELIS EVERTSEN.

Manning tried to gain time by procrastination. The war-ships floated up with the tide within musket-shot of the fort without firing a gun. At the end of half an hour the ships fired broadsides and killed and wounded some of the garrison. The fort returned the fire, and shot the flag-ship "through and through." Then six hundred men were landed, when about four hundred armed burghers encouraged their countrymen to storm the fort.

Perceiving resistance under the circumstances to be useless, a white flag was displayed over the fort, and a deputation was sent out to meet the advancing storming party at near sunset. A capitulation was soon effected, when the fort and garrison were surrendered with the honors of war. The Dutch soldiers marched into the fort and the English soldiers marched out of it with colors flying and drums beating, and grounded their arms. Then the English garrison was ordered back, and were made prisoners of war in the church within the fort. The tricolored banner of the Dutch Republic took its old place on the flag-staff of the fort, and the heart of Stuyvesant, who was a witness of the event, was filled with joy. New Amsterdam had been snatched from the Dutch by an English robber, who came stealthily while Holland and Great Britain were at peace. New York had been honorably taken by a Dutch squadron—an open enemy—engaged in war with Great Britain. The name of New Netherland was now restored to the reconquered territory. It then had three chief towns, thirty villages, and between six and seven thousand Dutch inhabitants. Fort James was renamed Fort William Henry in honor of the Prince of Orange. Captain Anthony Colve* was chosen to be governor-general of the province, his commission defining it as extending from "fifteen miles south of Cape Hinlopen to the east end of Long Island and Shelter Island;" on the main north from Greenwich as defined in 1650, and including "Delaware Bay and all intermediate territory possessed by the Duke of York."

The name of the city of New York was changed to New Orange, and Albany to Willemstadt. The municipal government was re-established after the Dutch pattern. Anthony de Milt was appointed *schout*, Johannes van Brugh, Johannes de Peyster, and Ægidius Luyck were chosen *burgomasters*, and William Beeckman, Jeronimus Ebbing, Jacob Kip, Laurens van der Spiegel, and Gelyn Ver Planck were made *schepens*.† Evertsen and Binckes issued a proclamation ordering

---

* Colve was "a man of resolute spirit, and passionate," whose arbitrary nature had not been improved by military training. When made governor, he sought to magnify the office by setting up a coach drawn by three horses. He ruled with energy and sometimes with severity. When an English force demanded the surrender of the province to English rule, provided by treaty, and Edmond Andros claimed the right to take the seat of Colve, the latter yielded to the inevitable with grace. He even went so far as to present to Andros his coach and three horses. After the formal surrender Colve returned to Holland.

† After the recovery of New York by the English Captain Manning was tried by a court-martial on a charge of cowardice and treachery, found guilty, and sentenced to have his sword broken over his head by the executioner in front of the City Hall, and forever incapacitated to hold any office, civil or military, in the gift of the crown. Governor Lovelace was severely reprimanded, and his estates were confiscated and given to

the seizure of all property and debts belonging to the kings of France and England, or their subjects, and urging every person to report such property to the Secretary of the Province, Nicholas Bayard. De Ruyven, who had been made the receiver of the duke's revenue, although an old Dutchman, was required to give a strict account.

The swift reconquest of New York startled the other English colonies in America, and some of them prepared for war. Connecticut foolishly talked of an offensive war. Colve was wide awake, and watched current events around him with great vigilance. He kept his eye on the movements of the Frenchmen and barbarians on the north; watched every hostile indication on the east, and compelled hesitating boroughs on Long Island and in Westchester to take the oath of allegiance to the Prince of Orange. He made strong the fortifications of New York, planting no less than one hundred and ninety cannons around the city and on the fort.

The triumph of the Dutch was of short duration. The reconquest was an accident, not the result of a preconceived plan. The happy dreams of a Belgic empire in America were, in a few months, suddenly dispelled, for a treaty negotiated at Westminster (London) early in 1674 ended the war, and upon the principle of reciprocal restitution, New Netherland was restored to the British crown, and remained thereafter a British province until the war for independence in 1775–83. Doubts having arisen respecting the effects of these political changes upon the duke's title to his American possessions, the king confirmed it by issuing a new charter in June, 1674.

Meanwhile France had been endeavoring to establish and extend her dominion on the borders of the great lakes, especially Ontario. The strong right arm of her power in this work was composed of Jesuit missionaries, who carried the lilies of France wherever they displayed the emblems of Christianity. French soldiers followed in the path of these missionaries. Wars between the French and barbarians within the domain of the State of New York, as well as alliances, had taken place. In the hearing of the barbaric tribes the imposing ritual service of the Church of Rome had been read and chanted for more than a score of years.

At the period of the political changes in New York here mentioned, the Jesuits were active among the Iroquois. They had established a sort

---

the Duke of York. Admiral Evertsen, the commander of the Dutch forces that retook New Netherland, assisted in conveying the forces of William, Prince of Orange, to England in 1688.

of metropolitan station among the Mohawks at Caughnawaga, on the north side of the Mohawk River, in (present) Fulton County, and were successful in making converts among the Mohawks and Oneidas.

Working in concert with the missionaries, for State purposes, was the able Governor-General of Canada, Count Louis Frontenac. Learning from the Jesuits early in 1673 that the Iroquois were not well disposed toward the French, he made a pompous visit to the eastern end of Lake Ontario and there held a conference with delegates from the Five Nations, whom he had invited to meet him. The object of the conference was to impress the barbarians with a sense of the power of Canada. With two bateaux gaudily painted, each carrying sixteen men and a small cannon mounted, accompanied by one hundred and twenty canoes and four hundred men, he ascended the St. Lawrence. The conference was held on the site of Kingston. It was exceedingly friendly. The count tried to persuade the Iroquois sachems and chiefs to consent to allow their youths to learn the French language. He called the Five Nations his "children," and in every way tried to win their supreme affection for the French. But he was unsuccessful; he only won their friendly feelings, and a safeguard for the missionaries among them. He did not weaken in the least degree their attachment to the Dutch.

Frontenac had begun a fort—the afterward famous Fort Frontenac of history —where the conference was held, when, leaving a small garrison in the fort, he returned to Montreal. The great minister of Louis XIV., Colbert, sent word to Frontenac that he had better imitate the Dutch at Manhattan and Orange, and instead of "prosecuting distant discoveries, to build up towns and villages in Canada."

SIGNATURE OF EDMOND ANDROS.

On the reconquest of New York by the English the important question arose: "Who shall be sent to govern the province?" Nicolls was dead, and Lovelace was incompetent. The king commissioned Sir Edmond Andros,* major of dragoons, who was then thirty-seven years of age, to

---

* Sir Edmond Andros was born in London in 1637. His family were distinguished on the island of Guernsey. After serving as Governor of New York from 1674 to 1684 he returned to England, and entered the service of his king at the palace. Appointed Governor of New England, New York, and New Jersey in 1688, he exercised arbitrary power until the Revolution dethroned his master, King James II., that year, when he was deposed and sent to England. In 1692 Andros was made Governor of Virginia, and so remained until 1698. In 1704 he was created Governor of Guernsey, and died at Westminster in 1713.

fill that station. He had been brought up in the royal household; was a favorite of the king and the duke; a good French and Dutch scholar; a thorough royalist; an obedient servant of his superiors, and was well fitted to perform the part which his masters appointed him to play. His private character was without blemish, and the evil things spoken of him relate to his public career. This man played a conspicuous part in American history for a few years.

Andros received the government of New York from Colve in October, 1674. With all their political disabilities under him, the people of that province prospered and were comparatively happy. Luxury had not corrupted their tastes, and their wants were few. A man worth three thousand dollars was considered rich; the possessor of five thousand dollars was considered opulent. There was almost a dead level of equality in society. Beggars were unknown. "Ministers were few, but religions many," and out of matters of faith grew many controversies. There seemed little reason for the twenty thousand inhabitants of the domain to be unhappy; but the divine instinct of freedom, which demanded a free exercise of the rights of self-government, made many of them discontented and in some places mutinous. The career of Andros in America outside of New York was more striking—more dramatic than within that domain.

Andros in his zeal exceeded his master's instructions, and very soon he acquired the just title of "tyrant." The duke, his master, was a strange compound of wickedness and goodness, slow to perceive right from wrong, and seldom seeing truth in its purity. Bancroft says of him: "A libertine without love, a devotee without spirituality, an advocate of toleration without a sense of the natural right to freedom of conscience—to him the muscular force prevailed over the intellectual. He was not bloodthirsty; but to a narrow mind fear seems the most powerful instrument of government, and he propped his throne [when he became king] with the block and gallows. He floated between the sensuality of indulgence and the sensuality of superstition, hazarding heaven for an ugly mistress, and, to the great delight of abbots and nuns, winning it back again by pricking his flesh with sharp points of iron and eating no meat on Saturdays." The Duke of Buckingham said well that "Charles would not and James could not see."

One of the first of the acts of petty tyranny of Andros was the imprisonment of leading citizens of New York—Steenwyck, Van Brugh, De Peyster, Bayard, Luyck, Beeckman, Kip, and De Milt—on a charge of "disturbing the government and endeavoring a rebellion." Their offence consisted in an expressed desire not to take an unconditional oath of allegiance to Charles Stuart, and petitioning the governor for leave to sell their estates and to remove elsewhere.

Andros proceeded to enforce jurisdiction over every foot of territory included in the duke's charter of 1664—Pemaquid, in Maine, the islands of Martha's (Martin's) Vineyard and Nantucket, and disputed domains on the Delaware. He also claimed jurisdiction over all the territory west of the Connecticut River. The authorities of Connecticut disputed the claim, and Andros denounced their action as "rebellion against the duke."

Finding the French were tampering with the Iroquois, Andros went to Albany, regulated some affairs at Schenectady, and penetrated the Mohawk Valley a hundred miles beyond. On his return to Albany he received solemn assurances of the friendship of the Five Nations, and then he organized the first "Board of Commissioners for Indian Affairs." This was a most important measure, and its operations were salutary for a hundred years. He appointed as its secretary Robert Livingston, then town clerk of Albany, a shrewd Scotchman who had lately come over from Rotterdam, and who afterward became prominent in colonial affairs. The Five Nations gave Andros the name of "Corlear," in memory of their good friend, Arendt van Curler or Corlear, who, as we have observed, was commissary of Rensselaerwyck, and who was drowned in Lake Champlain.

It was at this juncture that King Philip's War * broke out and spread great alarm throughout New England. Andros sympathized with his countrymen in their distress, but could not spare a military force to aid them; but he sent six barrels of gunpowder to the Rhode Islanders (who were excluded from the New England Confederacy), and invited any of them who should be driven out by the Indians to come to New York and be welcomed as guests. There was no good feeling between the "United Colonies of New England" (see p. 58) and Andros.

---

* Massasoit, the warm friend of the "Pilgrim Fathers" at New Plymouth, had two sons, called respectively by the English, Philip and Alexander. The former was the elder, and succeeded his father as sachem. Perceiving that the English were undoubtedly determined to deprive him of his domain, he listened favorably to the counsels of his hot young braves, and began a war for the extermination of the white intruders. At his seat at Mount Hope, in Rhode Island, he planned a federation of all the New England tribes for that purpose. Exasperated by an untoward occurrence, he suddenly struck the first blow thirty miles from New Plymouth, and for about a year he spread terror and desolation far and wide. Finally he was killed in a hiding-place by another Indian. His wife and little son had been made prisoners. The Christians of Massachusetts deliberated whether to kill or sell into slavery to fellow-Christians in Barbadoes this innocent pagan boy. The latter measure was the most *profitable*, and it was adopted.

Late in 1677 Andros went to England to look after his private affairs, leaving Anthony Brockholls * in charge of the government of New York. Brockholls administered public affairs wisely for a few months. Meanwhile the governor had been knighted by King Charles, and he returned to New York Sir Edmond Andros. During his absence a royal marriage had taken place which had an important bearing upon the destinies of New York—nay, of the world. It was the marriage of William, Prince of Orange, the acknowledged leader of the Protestants of Europe, to his cousin Mary, daughter of the Duke of York. The duke was a Roman Catholic by conviction, and the marriage was distasteful to him.

The duke, regardless of the rights of Berkeley and Carteret, had given Andros sufficient authority to allow him to annoy these proprietors and the settlers in their domain. Berkeley sold his interest to English "Friends" or Quakers, and Carteret consented to a division of the territory into East and West Jersey. He held East Jersey. The proprietors of West Jersey, making liberal concessions to settlers, soon attracted a numerous population to that region. But Andros was a chronic disturber. He caused the duke to claim the right to rule all New Jersey, and Andros attempted to exercise it. A judicial decision soon freed it absolutely from the duke's control, and late in 1681 the first Representative Assembly met at Salem, in West Jersey, and adopted a code of laws. East Jersey was also sold to Quakers, and numerous settlers came there also.

SIGNATURE OF SIR JOHN BERKELEY AND SIR GEORGE CARTERET.

Meanwhile William Penn, an English Quaker, son of Admiral Penn (who was a friend of the king and the duke), had become a proprietor of West Jersey, having obtained from Charles a grant of a domain (March, 1681) including "three degrees of latitude and five degrees of longitude," west of the Delaware River, in payment of a loan made by the king from

---

* Anthony Brockholls was of a Roman Catholic family in Lancashire, England, and was a "professed Papist" himself. He came to New York at about the time of its surrender to the Dutch in 1674, and was named as the successor of Governor Andros in the event of the death of the latter. In 1681 he was appointed receiver-general of the province, and in 1683 he became one of the council of Governor Dongan. For fully thirty years Brockholls was a very active man in public affairs in the province of New York.

Penn's father. The domain was named in the charter "Pennsylvania." Penn obtained, by grant and purchase of the duke, the territory comprised in the present State of Delaware, and on coming to America the next year, the agent of the duke surrendered it to Penn.

Andros had been suddenly recalled from New York in the autumn of

SEAL OF NEW YORK CITY, 1686.

1682, and Brockholls again became acting governor. Nothing of special interest in public affairs occurred during his administration of nearly three years, excepting a claim to Staten Island as a part of East Jersey, made by Lady Carteret, widow of the deceased proprietor. The matter was soon settled by the sale of East Jersey.

CHAPTER VIII.

SIR EDMOND ANDROS had ruled New York about nine years with vigor. He had kept peace with the Iroquois Confederacy; crushed religious enthusiasts; frowned upon every sign of republicanism, and asserted with great tenacity the power of the duke, his master, within the chartered limits of his territory. Meanwhile the duke had listened to the appeals of the inhabitants of New York and heeded the judicious advice of his friend, William Penn, to give the people more liberty; and he sought an able and enlightened governor to take the place of Andros. He found such a man in Thomas Dongan,* a younger son of an Irish baronet, and then about fifty years of age. He was a Roman Catholic, enterprising and active, a "man of integrity, moderation, and genteel manners."

Under instructions from the duke, Dongan ordered an election of a General Assembly of Representatives of the people, their number not to exceed eighteen. Their functions were to assist the governor and Council in framing laws for the "good of the colony," the duke reserving to himself the right to examine and approve or reject such laws. The representatives were to be allowed free debate among themselves in considering proposed laws. Thus the people of New York were first allowed to share the colonial political authority.

SIGNATURE OF GOVERNOR DONGAN.

It was a notable event in the history of the State of New York when, on October 17th, 1683, the first General Assembly of the Province of New York, composed of ten councillors and seventeen representatives of the people, met at the City Hall and were addressed by Governor

---

* Governor Dongan had served in the French army; was a colonel in the royal army, and had been Lieutenant-Governor of Tangier. When he resigned his office of Governor of New York to Andros, in 1688, he retired to his farm on Long Island. With the assumption of power by Leisler, a strong anti-Roman Catholic spirit was fostered, and Dongan being a Papist, was wrongfully regarded with suspicion. Because he had a brigantine constructed to carry him on a visit to England, he was charged with a treasonable design against William and Mary, in favor of dethroned King James. He went to Boston, sailed thence to England, and afterward became Earl of Limerick.

Dongan, whose sympathies were in unison with the popular desires. The Assembly chose the experienced Matthew Nicolls speaker and John Spragg clerk. They sat three weeks and passed fourteen acts, all of which were assented to by the governor, with the advice of his Council. The first of these acts was entitled "The Charter of Liberties and Privileges, granted by His Royal Highness, to the Inhabitants of New York and its Dependencies." It declared that the supreme legislative power should forever be and reside in the governor, council, and people, met in General Assembly; that every freeholder and freeman should be allowed to vote for representatives without restraint; that no freeman should suffer but by judgment of his peers; that all trials should be by a jury of twelve men; that no tax should be assessed, on any pretence whatever, but by the consent of the Assembly; that no seaman or soldier should be quartered on the inhabitants against their will; that no martial law should exist, and that no person professing faith in God, by Jesus Christ, should at any time be anywise disquieted or questioned for any difference of opinion. Not a feature of the intolerance and bigotry of the New England charters appeared in this first "Charter of Liberties" for the province of New York.

This act was read in front of the City Hall on the morning after its passage in the presence of the governor, his Council, the Assembly, the municipal officers, and the people, the latter having been summoned to the joyous feast by the sounding of trumpets. In this charter was again enunciated the postulate of the Netherlands—"Taxation only by consent."

NEW YORK COUNTY SEAL.

The next act that was passed provided for the division of the province into twelve counties or shires. The names of the twelve are still retained, but their territorial dimensions have been much modified by the erection of new counties from parts of some of them. The names and boundaries of these political divisions as given in the act of 1683 are as follows :*

The *City and County of New York* bear the name of the duke's first title. It included all Manhattan Island, and several adjacent islands.

Westchester County embraced all the territory eastward of Manhattan to the Connecticut line, and northward along the Hudson River to the Highlands.

---

* The seals of the several counties represented on page 99 were of those in use in 1875.

Duchess County was so named in honor of the duke's wife, the Duchess of York.* It extended from Westchester northward to Albany County, and "into the woods twenty miles."

Orange County extended from New Jersey northward along the Hudson River to Murderer's Creek (now Moodna's Creek), above the Highlands near New Windsor, and westward to the Delaware River. It was so named in honor of the duke's son-in-law, the Prince of Orange.

Ulster County derives its name from the duke's Irish earldom. It extended from the northern boundary of Orange County along the river, and "twenty miles into the woods" as far north as Saugerties.

Albany County, bearing the duke's second or Scotch title, extended indefinitely northward from Roeloff Jansen's Kill (Creek) on the east side of the river, and on the west side from Saugerties northward to "the Saraaghtoga."

Richmond County, which included Staten Island and two or three smaller islands, was probably so named in honor of the king's illegitimate son by the Duchess of Portsmouth, the Duke of Richmond.

Kings and *Queens* counties occupied the western portion of Long Island from Oyster Bay and Hempstead, and was named in honor of the monarch and his wife.

Suffolk County embraced the eastern portion of Long Island, and derived its name from that of the most easterly county in England, south of Norfolk.

The duke's possession in Maine (at Pemaquid) was called *Cornwall* County. The islands off the coast of Massachusetts which were included in his charter were constituted *Duke's* County.

Courts of justice were established by the Assembly in the several counties. These consisted of four tribunals—town courts, county courts or Courts of Sessions, a court of Oyer and Terminer, and a court of Chancery to be the Supreme Court of the province. The latter was composed of the governor and his Council. But every inhabitant of the province was allowed the right to appeal to the king from the judg-

---

* When the names of the counties were given, the title of the wife of a duke was spelled with a "t"—du*t*chess—and so continued in the English language until the appearance of Johnson's Dictionary, in 1755. He gave it the orthography of its French derivitive—*duchesse*—omitting the final *e*. The name being spelled with a "t" in the early records of the State, it was not changed when the orthography of the name of the wife of a duke was changed, and through inadvertence and ignorance of its origin, the name of Duchess County has been spelled with a "t" until within a few years, when attention was called to the fact that the county was named in honor of the Duchess of York. It is now universally spelled without a "t" by well-informed people. It is so spelled in the United States Census Reports of 1880.

ment of any court. All the laws passed by this first General Assembly of New York were read to the people in front of the City Hall, and were then sent to England for the consideration of the duke.*

Dongan conducted his "foreign relations" with spirit. He told the pestering Connecticut authorities that if they did not keep quiet and

SEALS OF THE FIRST ORGANIZED COUNTIES IN NEW YORK.

adhere to the boundary agreement of 1650, which was a line twenty miles east of the Hudson River, he should proceed to claim the original territory defined in the duke's patent, eastward to the Connecticut

---

* Late in 1683 the city of New York was divided into six wards, named respectively North Ward, South Ward, East Ward, West Ward, Dock Ward, and Out Ward. James Graham, one of the late aldermen, was commissioned the first recorder of New

River. He renewed the claims of Andros to sovereignty over the Five Nations. At an interview with Mohawk leaders at Albany, in the presence of the Governor of Virginia (Lord Effingham), he enjoined them not to deal with the French without his leave, nor allow any of that nation to live among them excepting the missionaries. The Mohawks readily assented, and so unfriendly did the Iroquois deport themselves toward the French that most of the missionaries, alarmed, went back to Canada. Dongan also warned the French, who had come among the Indians at Pemaquid—especially the Baron de Castin *—to come under the duke's authority or to leave the region. So thoroughly did Dongan win the respect and reverence of the Iroquois that they called Albany their " sixth castle." Four of the nations requested the governor to put the Duke of York's arms on their castles as a protection against the French.

When, in 1682, the Count de la Barré became Governor-General of Canada he resolved to bring the Iroquois into subjection to the French. This design he cherished continually, but he found the energetic Dongan a bar to his ambitious schemes. A crisis came early in 1684. De la Barré was preparing to attack the Senecas. Dongan notified him that *all* the Iroquois nations were subject to the Duke of York; that the duke's territory extended to Lake Ontario and the St. Lawrence River, and that if the French did not come south of those waters the English would not go north of them. Dongan's tone was so firm, yet conciliatory, that De la Barré paused for awhile. In the following summer he made an attempt to carry out his threat with the aid of the Jesuit missionaries, but signally failed. The Intendant of Canada said he was "fooled in the most shameful manner" by Dongan and the Iroquois.

York,* who took a seat on the bench of the Mayor's Court on the right hand of the Mayor. The shipping of the port of New York at that time consisted of three barks, three brigantines, twenty-seven sloops, and forty-six open boats.

* The Baron de Castin, a French nobleman and military leader, established a trading house at the mouth of the Penobscot River, and exhibited hostile movements, at times, toward the duke's possessions in Maine. He married the daughter of an Indian chief. In 1695, accompanied by Iberville, he led about two hundred Indians against Pemaquid, and captured it.

---

* James Graham, the first recorder of the city of New York, was a Scotchman and kinsman of the Earl of Montrose. He was an able lawyer, and practised his profession while conducting a mercantile business in New York. He was an alderman in 1680, and became attorney-general and one of the Council in 1685. He was attorney-general under Andros, in Boston, shared the odium of the governor, and on the downfall of the latter was imprisoned awhile. In 1691 he returned to New York, was elected to the Assembly, and became its Speaker. He was again in the Council in 1699. Graham had been active in urging the execution of Leisler, and shared the fortunes of the anti-Leislerians, which ended his public career in 1701. He died at Morrisania the same year.

The discomfited De la Barré wrote to the French minister that his campaign had been "bloodless!" It had been fruitless as well, and worse.

Early in February, 1685, King Charles II. died at the age of fifty-five years, a worn-out libertine. His brother, the Duke of York, took his place on the throne of Great Britain as James II. He had hesitated about sending the promised "Charter of Liberties" to New York; now, as *king*, he positively refused to confirm what, as *duke*, he had promised. He instantly began to demolish the fair fabric of civil and religious liberty which had been raised with so much hope in New York. A direct tax was ordered without the consent of the people; the printing-press—the right arm of knowledge and freedom—was forbidden a place in the colony; and as he had determined to establish the Roman Catholic faith as the State religion throughout his realm, the provincial offices were largely filled by adherents of the Italian Church.

The liberal-minded Dongan lamented these proceedings; and when the scheming monarch instructed the governor to introduce French missionaries among the Five Nations, he resisted the measure as dangerous to the English power on the American continent. Fortunately the Iroquois Confederacy remained firm in their friendship for the English in after years, and stood as a powerful barrier against the aggressive French when the latter twice attempted to reach the white settlers at Albany with hostile intentions.

The clear-headed and right-hearted Dongan stood by the people and the interests of England with a firmness which finally offended the monarch. Dongan knew that the king had a great love for the French, and when he saw the advantages which he was disposed to give them in America by his unwise acts, he could not but regard his sovereign's conduct as treason toward his country. For his faithfulness he was rewarded with the gratitude of the people of New York and the displeasure of the monarch, who dismissed him from the office of governor. He received a letter from James in the spring of 1688 ordering him to surrender the government into the hands of Andros, who held a vice-regal commission to rule New York and all New England. New York was made a royal British province. It had been a dukedom of a royal English subject for about twenty years. James was proclaimed king, at New York, on April 22d, 1685.

In the mean time, Dongan had experienced more trouble with the French. The Marquis de Nonville had become Governor of Canada. He resolved to build a fort at the mouth of the Niagara River to overawe the Iroquois, and he prepared to attack the Senecas. The Jesuit missionaries united with him. To counteract their influence, Dongan summoned the Five Nations to a conference at Albany in the spring of 1686.* The Indians asked to be relieved of the French priests at their castles, to be replaced by English priests. The governor promised to establish an English church at Saratoga, and to ask the king to send over English priests; at the same time he warned the Iroquois of De Nonville's intention to attack them.

De Nonville now appealed to Dongan as a Roman Catholic to aid him in converting the Indians to Christianity. Dongan was not deceived by this false pretence. He promised to do all he could to protect the missionaries among the barbarians; that was all. The Governor of New York outwitted and outgeneralled the Governor of Canada at every point, though the latter was ably assisted by the venerable Lamberville, the Jesuit priest at the Onondaga Castle. Exasperated beyond measure, the discomfited De Nonville wrote to the French Minister: "I am disposed to go straight to Orange [Albany], storm their fort, and burn the whole concern."

SEAL OF THE CITY OF ALBANY.

In May, 1687, De Nonville, with a force of over two thousand French

---

* In 1686 (July 22d) Governor Dongan incorporated Albany as a city, with large franchises, including the management of the Indian trade, and appointed Peter Schuyler to be its first mayor, Isaac Swinton its recorder, and Robert Livingston its clerk. Dirck Wessels, Jan Jansen Bleecker, David Schuyler, Johannes Wendell, Levinus van Schaick, and Adraien Garritse were appointed aldermen; Joachim Staats, John Lansing, Isaac Ver Planck, Lawrence van Ale, Albert Ryckman, and Elbert Winantse, assistants; Jan Bleecker, chamberlain; Richard Pretty, sheriff; and James Parker, marshal. Such was the first political organization of the city of Albany, the capital of the State of New York.

regulars, Canadians, and Indians, coasted along the southern shores of Lake Ontario and penetrated the Seneca country from Irondequoit Bay. Eight hundred of his regular troops had been sent over from France for this expedition. The invaders desolated the Seneca country, destroying all the stored corn (more than a million bushels), the growing crops, cabins, and a vast number of swine belonging to the natives. Then De Nonville took possession of the country in the name of the French king; but by an act of foul treachery and atrocious cruelty he gave a death-blow to Jesuit missions among the Five Nations, and confirmed their friendship for the English. De Nonville had employed Lamberville, the venerated Jesuit priest at Onondaga Castle, to decoy many Iroquois chiefs into a stronghold under the pretence of holding a conference. There the dusky representatives of their people were seized, put in irons, sent to France, and committed to the chain-galleys at Marseilles. This was done to strike the Five Nations with terror. It had an opposite effect. The missionaries had to flee for their lives before the angered braves, and Lamberville was saved only by the generous protection of the chief of the Onondagas.

In the spring of 1688 the province of New York was "consolidated" with New England under a colonial viceroy (Sir Edmond Andros), and formed a part of the ephemeral political organization known as the "Dominion of New England." At this time the king, as he informed the Pope, was preparing to "set up the Roman Catholic religion in the English Plantations."

The viceroy arrived in New York from Boston in August, and was received by the loyal aristocracy with great parade. In the midst of the rejoicings news came that the young queen (James's second wife) had given birth to a Prince of Wales, heir to the British throne. The event was celebrated by the royalists the same evening by bonfires in the streets and a banquet at the City Hall. At the festive board Mayor Van Cortlandt became so hilarious, it is said, that he made a burnt sacrifice to his loyalty of his hat and periwig, waving the blazing victims over the banquet table on the point of his straight sword.

The Dutch inhabitants of New York (as well as the Protestant republicans) were disappointed. They had looked forward with hope for the accession of James's daughter Mary, the wife of their own Protestant Prince of Orange, to the throne of Great Britain; now it could not be hoped for excepting on the death of the infant Prince of Wales or revolution. The latter alternative was near at hand.

The folly and recklessness of King James in his efforts to establish the Roman Catholic as the State religion of his realm alarmed the Pope, who said to his cardinals : " We must excommunicate this king or he will destroy the little Catholicism which remains in England." Before this remedy could be applied the fate of King James was fixed. His folly and recklessness had aroused the whole English people to a keen sense of the danger impending over their liberties.

The crisis was soon reached. The king unwisely declared that none should serve him but such as would aid him in his designs. There was soon an open rupture between the monarch and the Anglican Church and the great universities, which he sought to control. The royal soldiers in camp, the Churchmen and Dissenters, the Whigs and the Tories coalesced in sentiment, and an invitation was sent secretly to William of Orange to come and "deliver the land from popery and slavery."

William had expected such an invitation for a long time, and was ready to accept it. He gathered a fleet in Holland, for what purpose neither James nor his friend and coreligionist, Louis of France, knew. After accepting the call of a nation for help, William published a declaration that he was bound for England to save the liberties of the people there, and to investigate the alleged birth of a Prince of Wales,* in which matter he and his wife were deeply concerned.

With a strong land and naval force William reached Torbay, on the coast of Devonshire, where he landed on November 5th, 1688. The best men of the country joined his standard. James was forsaken by his army and family; even his son-in-law, Prince George of Denmark, who married the Princess Anne, joined the deliverers. Perceiving that all was lost, James secretly sent his queen and infant son to France, and soon followed them thither. He left his palace a little after midnight in December, and cast his Great Seal into the Thames; but he was brought back. He succeeded in reaching France not long afterward. So ended the Stuart dynasty in Great Britain.

On the flight of the king the government authority was assumed by the House of Lords. They requested William of Orange to take control of public affairs and to call a convention, to assemble on January 22d following. That body declared William and Mary joint sovereigns of Great Britain. James made efforts to recover the throne he had abdicated, but failed.

News of the revolution in England first reached Virginia, whence it

---

* It was alleged that the son of James's Italian wife was only a supposititious child, the offspring of another beside the queen. He was excluded from the succession. In 1715 he laid claim to the crown of Great Britain, and is known in history as "The Old Pretender."

was carried to New York, in February (1689), by a skipper, and communicated to Francis Nicholson at Fort James. He was the lieutenant-governor of the province. He forbade its divulgence among the people, as he wished to prevent any "private tumults" until he could communicate with Andros, who was at Fort Charles at Pemaquid. Andros had departed from Pemaquid for Boston when the express arrived, and reached that place at near the close of March. The people there, suffering from the tyrannies of Andros, were on the verge of open insurrection when, on the 14th of April, a vessel brought to Boston authentic information of the accession of William and Mary. Andros was seized and cast into prison, and soon afterward he, with fifty of his political associates, was sent to England, charged with maladministration of affairs in the colonies.

Meanwhile a crisis in public affairs had been reached at New York. The people there were also on the verge of insurrection when the "great news" was revealed in that city. The authority of Lieutenant-Governor Nicholson was questioned by a large portion of the inhabitants of the city and province. Two parties were formed, one composed of the adherents of James, the other of the friends of William and Mary. The former embraced the aristocratic citizens, including Nicholas Bayard, the commander of the city militia, the members of the council, and the municipal authorities.

SIGNATURE OF FRANCIS NICHOLSON.

The friends of the new monarchs formed a large majority of the citizens. They maintained that the entire fabric of the imperial government, including that of the colonies, had been overthrown by the revolution, and that, as no person was invested with authority in the province, it reverted to the legitimate source of all authority—the *people*—who might delegate their powers to whomsoever they would.

Among the principal supporters of this view was Jacob Leisler, a German by birth, a merchant, the senior captain of one of the five train-bands of the city commanded by Colonel Bayard, and one of the oldest and wealthiest inhabitants. His wife was Alice, daughter of Govert Loockermans. He was a zealous opponent of the Roman Catholics, and a man of great energy and determination. He was kind and benevolent, and was very popular. He had just bought lands in Westchester County to form an asylum for persecuted Huguenots, who had fled from France after the revocation of the Edict of Nantes.* The domain was named New Rochelle, after Rochelle in France, from which place many of them came.

Rumors of terrible things contemplated by the adherents of James spread over the town, and produced great excitement. The five companies of militia and a crowd of citizens gathered at the house of Leisler, and induced him to become their leader and guide in this emergency. Colonel Bayard attempted to disperse them, but he was compelled to fly for his life. A distinct line was now drawn between the *aristocrats*, led by Bayard, Van Cortlandt, Robert Livingston, and others, and the *democrats*—the majority of the people—who regarded Leisler as their leader and champion. At his suggestion a "Committee of Safety" was formed, composed of ten members—Dutch, Huguenot, and English. They constituted Leisler "Captain of the Fort," and invested him with the powers of commander-in-chief—really chief magistrate—until orders should come from the new monarch. This was the

THE BAYARD ARMS.

SIGNATURE OF NICHOLAS BAYARD.

first really republican ruler that ever attained to power in America. He took possession of Fort James and the public funds that were in it, and in June, 1689, he proclaimed, with the sound of trumpets, William and Mary sovereigns of Great Britain and the colonies. Then he sent a

---

* Jacob Leisler was born at Frankfort-on-the-Main, and emigrated to America in 1660. In 1683 he was appointed one of the commissioners of the Court of Admiralty at New York, and was the leader in the popular movement of assuming the functions of government on hearing of the revolution in England. The people chose him to be their governor until the new British sovereigns should send them one. His political enemies finally brought him to the scaffold in 1691.

letter to the king, giving him an account of what he had done. The New Englanders commended Leisler's acts. Lieutenant-Governor Nicholson, lacking spirit, and fast bound by "red tape," perceiving the strong support given to Leisler by the New Yorkers, departed for England after formally giving authority to his councillors to preserve the peace during his absence, and until their Majesties' pleasure should be made known.

At this juncture the northern colonies were thoroughly alarmed by the opening hostilities of the French and Indians on the frontiers. A convention of delegates from the colonies of Massachusetts, Plymouth, Connecticut, and New York assembled at Albany, and there held a conference (September, 1689) with the heads of the Five Nations. The New England delegates tried to persuade the Iroquois to engage in the war against the Eastern Indians, but they wisely declined. They, however, ratified the existing friendship between them and the English colonists.

SIGNATURE AND SEAL OF JACOB LEISLER.

Nicholson's desertion of his post gave Leisler and the Republicans great advantages. He ordered the several counties of the province to elect their civil and military officers. Some counties obeyed, and others did not. The counter influence of Nicholson's councillors was continually and persistently felt, and Leisler and his party became greatly incensed against them, especially against Bayard, who was the chief instigator of the opposition to the "usurper," as he called the Republican leader. So hot became the indignation of Leisler and his friends that Bayard was compelled to fly for his life to Albany. The other councillors, alarmed, soon followed him. At Albany they acknowledged allegiance to William and Mary. They set up an independent government, and claimed to be the true and only rulers of the province. In this position they were sustained by the civil authorities at Albany.

Leisler now sent his son-in-law, Jacob Milborne, an Englishman, with three sloops filled with armed men and ammunition to take possession of Albany, protect the inhabitants against the menaced attack of the French from Canada, and to assert there the supreme power of the people's governor at New York. Milborne was instructed to withhold assistance against the barbarians in case he should be denied admission to the fort.

Milborne, with his force, arrived at Albany early in November, and demanded of Mayor Schuyler, who had been appointed the commander of the fort, admission to it. It was refused. At that time a convention, largely controlled by Robert Livingston, composed of delegates from each ward in the city, was sitting daily in Albany, and exercising executive authority temporarily. A deputation was sent from the convention to meet Milborne. They introduced him to the convention, when he harangued the members for some time, but with little effect. Then he presented his credentials to the recorder, and afterward harangued the populace in front of the City Hall, but they were not responsive.

ROBERT LIVINGSTON.

Milborne now took a bolder step. He flung open the gate of the city near the fort, marched his men out with loaded guns, and drawing them up in front of the stronghold, made a peremptory demand for its surrender. Schuyler refused compliance, and caused a protest of the convention to be read from one of the bastions. Some Mohawk warriors, who had been watching Milborne's movements from a neighboring hill, sent word to Schuyler that if the New Yorkers should attack the fort they would fire on them. Perceiving his peril, Milborne took counsel of prudence, withdrew, dismissed his men in confusion, and hastened back to New York. A letter soon came from the sheriff at Albany reporting treasonable words spoken by Robert Livingston con-

THE LIVINGSTON ARMS.

cerning King William. Leisler ordered Livingston's arrest, but he escaped to New England. Soon after this event a letter arrived at New York by a special messenger from the British Privy Council, directed to "Francis Nicholson, Esq., or, in his absence, to such as, for the time being, take care for preserving the peace and administering the laws in His Majesty's province of New York." Bayard having heard of the document, entered the city in disguise, had a clandestine interview with the bearer of the letter, and claimed the right, as one of Nicholson's councillors, to open the despatch. The messenger refused to let him have it, but delivered it to Leisler, whom he found acting as governor by the grant of the people. Leisler at once caused the arrest and imprisonment of Bayard on a charge of a "high misdemeanor against His Majesty's authority." From this time the opposition to Leisler's government assumed an organized shape, and was sleepless and relentless. Leisler justly regarding himself as invested with supreme power by the people and the spirit of the letter from the Privy Council, at once assumed the title of lieutenant-governor; appointed councillors; made a new provincial seal; established courts, and called an assembly to provide means for carrying on war with Canada. The aggressive old Count Frontenac was again governor of that province, and was making preparations to extend the French dominion southward. The conflict that ensued will be noted presently.

FIRST GREAT SEAL OF THE PROVINCE OF NEW YORK.*

Colonel Henry Sloughter was appointed Governor of New York, but did not arrive until the spring of 1691. Richard Ingoldsby, a captain

---

* The first great seal of the province of New York was sent over by Governor Sloughter from William and Mary in 1691. It bears the full-length effigies of the joint sovereigns, before whom kneel two Indians in the position of offering gifts. The woman presents to the queen a beaver-skin; the man presents to the king a roll of wampum. On the reverse of the seal are the royal arms of Great Britain, with the inscription round the circumference: SIG LUM PROVINC : NOSR : NOV : EBOR : ETC. IN AMERICA. This seal was superseded by ͟ ͟e sent by Queen Anne in 1705.

of foot, arrived early in the year, with a company of regular soldiers, to take possession of and hold the government until the arrival of the governor. He was urged by Leisler's enemies to assume supreme power at once, as he was the highest royal officer in the province. He haughtily demanded of Leisler the surrender of the fort, without deigning to show the governor his credentials. Leisler, of course, refused, and ordered the troops to be quartered in the city. Ingoldsby attempted to take the fort by force, but failed. For several weeks the city was fearfully excited by rival factions—"Leislerians" and "anti-Leislerians."

On the arrival of Governor Sloughter, in March (1691), Leisler at once loyally tendered to him the fort and the province. Under the influence of the enemies of Leisler, the royal governor responded to this meritorious action by ordering the arrest of the lieutenant-governor; also Milborne, and six other "inferior insurgents"—Abraham Gouverneur (Leisler's secretary), Gerardus Beeckman,* Johannes Vermilye, Thomas Williams, Myndert Coerten, and Abraham Brasher — on a

---

* Gerardus Beeckman, son of William Beeckman, was a leading citizen of New York, living at Brooklyn. He was a physician, and took a prominent part in public affairs. He was one of Leisler's warmest adherents, and was a member of his council. After Leisler's death Dr. Beeckman was tried for treason, condemned, and sentenced to be hung, but was pardoned by order of the king in 1694. He was a member of the provincial council under Governors Cornbury, Hunter, and Burnet, and died in 1724.

charge of high treason. The accused were imprisoned. "Bayard's chain was put upon Leisler's leg." The enemies of the latter were resolved on swift revenge.

When the accused were arraigned, Leisler and Milborne refused to plead to the indictment, for they denied the authority of the court which had just been organized for the purpose, and was composed wholly of Bayard's political friends. The judges were all councillors, and the petit jury was composed of "youths and other bitter men," quotes Brodhead. The trial, as had been predetermined, resulted in the conviction of the accused, and they were sentenced to be hanged. All but Leisler and Milborne were afterward pardoned. The excepted prisoners had appealed to the king, but the perfidious councillors did not send their appeal to His Majesty!

THE BEECKMAN ARMS.

Evident enemies of Leisler, in Albany, sent word to Bayard, at whose house Governor Sloughter was staying, that the Mohawks, disgusted with the mismanagement of Leisler, were in treaty with the French, and that it was indispensable that the governor should quickly conciliate the Five Nations. Bayard urged the governor

SIGNATURE OF ABRAHAM GOUVERNEUR.

to act promptly. So urged, he asked the opinion of his Council, in which Bayard was most powerful. That body unanimously resolved, "That, as well for the satisfaction of the Indians as the asserting of the government authority residing in his Excellency, and preventing insurrections and disorders for the future, it is absolutely necessary that the sentence pronounced against the principal offenders be forthwith put into execution." This resolution was communicated to the Assembly, which answered, "that this House, according to their opinion given, do approve of what his Excellency and Council have done."

The governor hesitated; for, though a libertine in morals and an habitual drunkard, he was a just man, and had determined not to sign the death-warrants of the convicted until he should hear from his sovereign, supposing Leisler's appeal had been sent to him.

Meanwhile the people, in large numbers, signed petitions to the governor for the pardon of these prisoners. The council became alarmed, and caused the arrest of some of those who brought the petitions. Fearing the effects of the daily increasing clamor of the people; determined to have the lives of the prisoners, and finding they could not induce the governor to violate justice or his conscience, the councillors conspired to extort from him his signature to the death-warrant by foul means. They invited him to a dinner-party at the house of one of them, on Staten Island, on a beautiful day in May. One of the councillors carried to the banquet a legally drawn death-warrant, and when the governor was sufficiently stupefied by excessive draughts of wine, he was induced to sign the awful paper, unconscious of its purport. It was sent to the sheriff at New York the same evening, and the next morning Leisler and Milborne were summoned to prepare for immediate execution. They sent for their wives and children, and after a sorrowful parting, the two victims were led to the scaffold in a drenching rain. Their enemies, fearing the governor might reprieve the prisoners, kept him drunk, and the victims were hanged before he became sober.* The scaffold stood near the site of the *Tribune* building, on Printing House Square, New York.

An eye-witness of this murder by the form of law wrote that just at the moment of the execution the heavens grew black, the rain fell in torrents, and the screams of women, who were present, were heard on every side. Restrained by the troops, only a few citizens were present. Milborne, seeing among them Livingston, one of the worst

---

* We have observed that six of the friends of Leisler condemned to death were pardoned. On the day of the execution of Leisler and Milborne (May 16th, 1691) the Legislature of New York passed an act for the pardon of all such as had been active "in the late disorders." Twenty-two persons received the benefit of this act. In 1699 an act of indemnity was passed in favor of all these persons excepting Leisler and Milborne.

enemies of Leisler, said, "Robert Livingston, I will implead thee at the bar of Heaven for this deed." Leisler uttered a prayer for blessings upon the province and his family ; and alluding to his enemies, he said, "Father, forgive them ; they know not what they do."

"Thus perished," says Hoffman, "the loyal and noble Captain Leisler of New York ; so loyal to his king, so noble to his compatriots." His enemies extended their malice to his family and that of Milborne. They were attainted, and their property was confiscated. But justice was swift in righting a great wrong. Before four years had passed by their property was restored, and the British Parliament declared that Leisler and Milborne were innocent of the crime of treason.

When the governor became sober, he was appalled at what he had done. He was so keenly stung by remorse and afflicted by *delirium tremens* that he died a few weeks afterward. Calm and impartial judgment, enlightened by truth, now assigns to Jacob Leisler the high position in history of a *patriot* and *martyr*.

CHAPTER IX.

The revolution of 1688 in England produced much suffering in some of the English colonies, for it was the cause of war between Great Britain and France, which extended to their respective American dominions. It continued about seven years, and is known in American history as "King William's War."

In this conflict the Indians bore a conspicuous part, and terrible were many of their achievements. Under the influence of Jesuit priests they became allies of the French.

Hostilities began in the East in the summer of 1689. The Indians attacked the frontier settlements of New England in July, killing and torturing many white people. In August a war-party fell upon the stockade at Pemaquid, in Maine, and captured the garrison. A few months later Governor Frontenac sent an expedition into New York, with the design of seizing Albany. He had gathered at Montreal a large military force of French and barbarians, and in the dead of winter (February, 1670) he despatched over two hundred French and Indians (eighty of the latter were "praying Indians," or Roman Catholic converts), under two lieutenants, with orders to penetrate the Mohawk country and attempt the capture of Albany.

The weather was intensely cold, and the snow was deep. The expedition traversed the wilderness with snow-shoes. It was resolved at a council to first attack Schenectady, a stockaded village containing about eighty comfortable houses, on the bank of the Mohawk River. A few Connecticut soldiers were in it. As the expedition drew near the place they met some Indian women who directed them how to enter the village secretly by one of the two gates, which was always standing open. The villagers, unsuspicious of any danger, felt so secure that a few hours before the attack, when warned by the commander of the soldiers to be vigilant, they set up some snow images in mockery to personate sentinels.

The blow fell upon Schenectady suddenly and with frightful energy at midnight, while the inhabitants were asleep. Sixty-three persons were massacred, twenty-seven were carried into captivity, and the Dutch Church and sixty-three houses were laid in ashes. Nearly all of the little garrison were killed. A few persons escaped to Albany, travelling through the snow in the keen wintry air in their night-clothes. Informed of the strength of Albany, the invaders did not attempt its capture, but hastened back toward Canada with their plunder.

Governor Leisler now proposed a union of New York and New England, in an effort to conquer Canada and expel the French from the Continent. At the suggestion of Massachusetts he called a Colonial Congress, which met in New York in April—the first ever convened in America. An arrangement was made for an invasion of Canada. All the colonies were aroused to a sense of mutual danger, and the Congress resolved to invade Canada by land and sea. It was agreed that New York should provide 400 men; Massachusetts, 160; Connecticut, 135, and Plymouth, 60, while Maryland promised 100, making a total land force of 857.

To stimulate Massachusetts to undertake a naval expedition against the French, Leisler fitted out three war-vessels for the capture of Quebec, commissioned to "attack Canada and take French prisoners at sea." This little squadron—the first war-ships sent out from New York —sailed late in May, with orders to stop at Cape Ann, and going on to Port Royal, Acadia, "entice the Boston fleet" to go with them. The latter, commanded by Sir William Phips, and bearing about eight hundred men, did go to Port Royal (May, 1690), and seized and plundered it. That place was soon afterward plundered again by English privateers from the West Indies.

Encouraged by these successes, another expedition was planned, having for its object an invasion of Canada by land and water. It was arranged for an army to march from Albany by way of Lake Champlain to Montreal, and at the same time a strong naval armament was to sail from Boston, ascend the St. Lawrence, and attack Quebec. The army was placed under the command of General Winthrop, a son of Governor Winthrop, of Connecticut, the cost of the expedition to be borne jointly by that colony and New York. The command of the fleet, which was composed of thirty-four vessels manned by two thousand New Englanders, was given to Sir William Phips, who, as we have observed, had seized and plundered Port Royal a short time before.

The army moved slowly from Albany early in July. The greater portion of the troops had only reached the head of Lake Champlain (now White Hall) early in September, where they remained for want of boats or canoes, while some white troops and Iroquois Indians, commanded by Captain John Schuyler, pushed on toward the St. Lawrence. Old Count Frontenac was in Montreal when he was informed of the approach of the invaders. He called out his Indian allies, and taking a tomahawk in his hand, the aged nobleman danced the war-dance and chanted the war-song in their presence. The excited braves were then led by him against the foe. Schuyler was compelled to withdraw, and the whole army returned to New York. The expedition was a failure, partly from a want of supplies and partly from sickness.

Phips sailed from Boston, and without pilots or charts crawled cautiously around Acadia and up the St. Lawrence for nine weeks. A swift Indian runner, starting from Pemaquid, carried the news of the naval expedition to Frontenac at Montreal in time to enable him to reach Quebec with re-enforcements early enough to strengthen its defences before the arrival of Phips. When the "admiral" appeared before the town and demanded its surrender, Frontenac treated the summons with contempt.* Failing in attempts to take the city, and hearing of the failure of the land expedition, Phips returned to Boston.

Leisler attributed the failure of the land expedition to Winthrop, and even charged him with treachery, and put him under arrest awhile. Winthrop charged the failure chiefly to the incompetency of Milborne, Leisler's son-in-law, who had engaged to furnish boats for transportation and all other supplies, but failed to do so in time.

The French and their barbarian allies in Canada and Acadia were greatly elated by the repulse of their assailants; and so important was the event regarded by French statesmen, that King Louis caused a medal to be struck bearing his likeness on one side and on the other a figure seated on military trophies, symbolizing France, with the legend around it: "FRANCE VICTORIOUS IN NEW ENGLAND." The expedition exhausted the treasury of Massachusetts, and compelled the Government to emit new bills of credit. The first emission was in February, 1690, and was the first paper money ever issued on the continent of America.

On the death of Governor Sloughter (June 16th, 1691) the care of the Government devolved upon Dudley,† the chief-justice and senior

---

* Sir William sent a messenger with a written demand for the surrender of the city. The bearer was taken, blindfolded, before Frontenac, who, after reading the demand, angrily threw the paper in the messenger's face, and gave his answer that "Sir William Phips and those with him were heretics and traitors, and had taken up with that usurper the Prince of Orange, and had made a revolution which, if it had not been made, New England and the French had all been one; and that no other answer was to be expected from him but what should be from the mouth of his cannon."

† Joseph Dudley was born in Roxbury, Mass., in 1647; died there in 1720. He represented his native town in the General Court from 1673 to 1681, and was one of the Commissioners of the United Colonies of New England. In 1682 he was agent of the colony of Massachusetts in England. James II. appointed him President of New England in 1685, and in 1687 he was commissioned Chief-Justice of the Superior Court, and the next year he was sent to England with Andros by the Bostonians, who expelled them from

member of the governor's council. He was then absent at Curaçoa. His associates filled his place temporarily with Captain Ingoldsby, who, as commander of the troops, had more real power than any one else in the province. He held the position until late the next year, when, at the close of August, Colonel Benjamin Fletcher, who had been commissioned Governor of New York, arrived. Fletcher was by profession a soldier, a man of strong passions, inconsiderable ability, aristocratic in his tendencies, opposed to all popular concessions, averse to religious toleration, and very avaricious. Fortunately for himself and the public welfare, he early became acquainted with Major Peter Schuyler, of Albany, who had almost unbounded influence over the Five Nations The governor appointed him one of his council, and his influence there was equally salutary. He so guided the conduct of the governor that he saved the magistrate from becoming intolerably obnoxious to the people, for Fletcher's incessant solicitations for money, his passionate temper, and his bigotry were continually manifested. During the whole

SIGNATURE AND SEAL OF GOVERNOR FLETCHER.

of his administration of seven years, party rancor, kindled by the death of Leisler, burned intensely, and at one time menaced the province with civil war. He adopted the views of the anti-Leislerians, and became their supple instrument.

Although the New York Assembly was filled with bitter opponents of Leisler, they, as boldly as he, asserted the supremacy of the people, and would suffer no encroachments on colonial rights and privileges. They rebuked the interference of the governor in legislation by insisting upon amendments to bills, and drew from him on one occasion the reproachful words which tell of their independence and firmness: "There never was an amendment desired by the Council Board," said Fletcher, "but

---

the colony. Then he was made Chief-Justice of New York (1690), where he served until 1693, when he returned to England and was made Deputy-Governor of the Isle of Wight. He was in Parliament in 1701, and from 1702 until 1715 he was Captain-General and Governor of Massachusetts. Retired to private life at Roxbury.

what it was rejected. It is a sign of a stubborn ill-temper." With that "stubborn ill-temper" of the Assembly the governor was almost continually in conflict, and when he was recalled he seemed as glad to leave the province as the people were to get rid of him.*

From the beginning of Fletcher's administration, Frontenac almost continually gave the province uneasiness by his attempts to win the Five Nations to the French interest by persuasions and threats. Failing to persuade them, he struck the Mohawks a severe blow early in 1693. Colonel Schuyler hastened from Albany with pale and dusky volunteers to the aid of the Iroquois, and drove the invaders back. He re-took about fifty captives from the French.

When Fletcher heard of this invasion, he hastened to Albany with three hundred militia volunteers. The river being free of ice, they ascended it to Albany in sloops, with a fair wind, in three days. This promptness and celerity gained great credit for the governor. The Iroquois called him " The very Swift Arrow."

The restless Frontenac continually disturbed the Five Nations and the English by menaces, until finally, in the summer of 1696, he invaded the heart of the country of the Iroquois with a large army. He had gathered at Montreal all the regulars and militia under his command and a host of Indian warriors ; and in light boats and bark canoes they ascended the St. Lawrence, entered Lake Ontario, and crossed it to the mouth of

---

* To Governor Fletcher was intrusted the large powers of commander-in-chief of the militia of Connecticut and New Jersey. Late in the autumn of 1693 he went to Hartford with Colonel Bayard and others to assert his authority there, which had been questioned. He ordered out the Connecticut militia when the season for parades had ended. The charter of the colony denied Fletcher's jurisdiction. The Assembly, then in session, promptly gave utterance to that denial on this occasion. Fletcher haughtily said to the governor : " I will not set my foot out of this colony until I have seen His Majesty's commission obeyed." The governor yielded so much as to allow Captain Wadsworth to call out the train-bands of Hartford.

When these troops were assembled Fletcher stepped forward to take the command, and ordered Bayard to read his Excellency's commission. At that moment Wadsworth ordered the drums to be beaten.

" Silence !" angrily cried Fletcher, and Bayard began to read again.

" Drum ! drum ! I say !" shouted Wadsworth, and the voice of Bayard was drowned in the sonorous roll that followed. Fletcher, enraged, stamped his foot and cried, " Silence !" and threatened the captain with punishment. Wadsworth instantly stepped in front of the irate governor, and while his hand rested on his sword-belt, he said in a firm voice :

" If my drummers are interrupted again I'll make the sunlight show through you. We deny and defy your authority."

The governor was a coward. He meekly folded up his commission, and with his retinue retired to New York. He complained to the king, but nothing came of it.

the Onondaga River at Oswego. This narrow and rapid stream they ascended (carrying the boats around the falls) to Onondaga Lake, fifty men marching on each side of the river. The Onondagas had sent away their wives and children, and had determined to defend their castle near the shore of the lake; but when they discovered the number of the invaders and the nature of their weapons, they set fire to their village and fled into the deep forest. The old Count Frontenac was carried in an elbow-chair. His only trophy was a venerable sachem about one hundred years old, who saluted him at the castle. With the count's permission the French Indians put the old man to the most exquisite tortures, which he bore with amazing fortitude and defiance.

When the invaders turned their forces toward Canada, the Onondagas pursued them, and annoyed them all the way. This expensive expedition and the continual incursions of the Five Nations into the country near Montreal spread famine in Canada. Frontenac continued to send out scalping parties until the treaty of Ryswyk, in 1697, brought comparative peace to the contending nations. Count Frontenac died the next year.

From the beginning of his administration Fletcher made strenuous efforts to introduce the Anglican Church, with its ritual, into the city and province of New York. He was very intemperate in his zeal to accomplish his purpose, for he was a bigot. A majority of the inhabitants of the province were of Dutch descent, and were members of the Dutch Reformed Church, which they regarded as the established church in New York.

The governor succeeded in procuring from the Assembly, in 1693, an act which he construed as giving him the right to recognize the Anglican instead of the Dutch Reformed Church as the State religion. Under this act Trinity Church was organized, and its first edifice for public worship was completed in 1696.* The first printing-press in the province was set up by William Bradford, a Quaker from Philadelphia, in 1693. He was afterward employed by the city government to print the corporation laws and ordinances. In 1725 Bradford began the publica-

---

* This church corporation still exists. The first vestrymen were: Thomas Wenham and Robert Lusting, *church-wardens;* Caleb Heathcote, William Merritt, John Tudor, James Emott, William Morris, Thomas Clarke, Ebenezer Wilson, Samuel Burt, James Everts, Nathaniel Marston, Michael Howden, John Crooke, William Sharpas, Lawrence Reed, David Jamison, William Huddleston, Gabriel Ludlow, Thomas Burroughs, John Merritt, and William Janeway.

There is no drawing of the first church edifice in existence. The engraving represents the second or enlarged church, erected in 1737. It was destroyed by fire in 1776.

tion of a newspaper in New York, the first ever issued in that province. During Fletcher's administration an organized system of piracy (its name softened to "privateering") grew up and extensively prevailed, especially on the coasts of New York and the middle provinces. Some of these marauders sailed out of the port of New York, and merchant ves-

OLD TRINITY CHURCH.

sels were seized and plundered in sight of that port. The system was then encouraged by governments as a strong arm in fighting their enemies, and by men in high places, who, as shareholders in " privateers," found it profitable. It finally became so odious, so absolutely piratical, and so injurious to commerce, that it was resolved to break up the system.

Fletcher's direct and indirect connection with the pirates, his petty tyranny, his participation in frauds in making grants of land, and his universal unpopularity caused his recall in 1695, when Richard Coote, Earl of Bellomont,* an Irish peer, was appointed his successor. The

---

* Richard Coote was born in the county of Sligo, Ireland, in 1636, and succeeded his father as Baron of Coloony in 1683. He was among the first who espoused the cause of the Prince of Orange in 1688. On the accession of James he went to the Continent, but returned in 1688 and became a member of Parliament. He was made the treasurer of Queen Mary, and was created Earl of Bellomont. Succeeding Fletcher as Governor of New York, his conduct there made him popular. Bellomont died in New York City.

earl was specially charged to investigate the conduct of his predecessor, to enforce the navigation laws, and to suppress piracy. But the earl did not arrive in the province until April, 1698, when he bore the commission of governor not only of New York, but of Massachusetts and New Hampshire. To assist him in his arduous duties, he brought with him his kinsman, John Nanfan, as Lieutenant-Governor of New York. The British Government seemed powerless to suppress the pirates. They infested almost every sea. Before Bellomont left England a stock company was formed for the purpose of attempting the task. It was composed of the king, Governor Bellomont, several noblemen, Robert Livingston, the first "Lord of the Manor of Livingston," and others. They fitted out the galley *Adventure* as a "privateer," well manned, armed, and provisioned.

EARL OF BELLOMONT.

Livingston, who had proposed the scheme, recommended Captain William Kidd, a notable ship-master of New York (then in England), as her commander.* He was commissioned by King William, sailed from Plymouth for New York in April, 1696, and soon did noble service in clearing American waters of pirates. Then he sailed for Eastern seas with a crew of one hundred and fifty-five men to measure strength with the pirates in the Indian Ocean.

SIGNATURE OF EARL OF BELLOMONT.

---

* This privateering company was proposed by Robert Livingston, who offered to be "concerned with Kidd a fifth part in the ship and charges. The king approved the project, raising a tenth share to show that he was concerned in the enterprise." Lord Chancellor Somers, the Duke of Shrewsbury, the Earls of Romney and Oxford, Sir Edward Harrison, and others joined in the scheme to the amount of $30,000. The management of the whole affair was left to Lord Bellomont. Kidd sailed from Plymouth for New York in his own ship in April, 1696.

Kidd was successful as a *privateer*, but soon became a *pirate* himself. At Madagascar he exchanged his ship for another, and swept the seas for booty from Farther India to the coasts of South America, respecting no flag or nationality. Thence he made his way homeward (1698), and on Gardiner's Island, east of Long Island, he buried much treasure, consisting of gold, silver, and precious stones. His piracies were known in England long before the company noticed them. The belief became general that the monarch, the earl, the Lord of the Manor and their noble associates had shared the plunder with Kidd. It became necessary to vindicate their character. They needed a scapegoat, and Kidd was made their victim. After burying his treasures he appeared openly in Boston, for in his pocket was his king's commission, and Governor Bellomont, who was there, was his partner in business. What had he to fear? The earl, expressing a horror of Kidd's crimes, ordered his arrest, and he was brought before his associates a prisoner in irons.

Kidd sought Bellomont's favor by revealing to him the place where the treasures were hidden. It was a critical moment for the earl, for his safety lay in an attitude of immovable firmness. He was deaf to the prayers of the prisoner and the entreaties of his wife for mercy, human and divine, for her erring husband. There was a severe struggle in the breast of the governor between pride and fear and his better nature. The former triumphed. Kidd was sent to England in fetters to be tried on a charge of piracy and murder. He was convicted of the second-named offence, and was hanged in London, in May, 1701. So the penalty of omission, at least, of the associate king and nobles and rich citizens was borne by the poor commoner on the scaffold. The earl secured the buried treasure, and at his coffers its history ends in impenetrable mystery.

Bellomont arrived at New York in the spring of 1698. Before he sailed for America he had learned much concerning public affairs in the province from Robert Livingston, who had been one of the bitterest foes of Leisler. Aware that the new governor had espoused the cause of Leisler and Milborne, and always willing to favor the stronger side in public questions, Livingston now changed his political position. On his return to New York he was found to be a professedly warm friend of the new governor, as he had been of Fletcher. He had shared with the latter the profits of "privateering," and had flourished under his official favor. Now as Bellomont had attached himself to the democratic or Leislerian party, Livingston found himself opposed to his old associates, Bayard, Van Cortlandt, and others, who still held places in the council, and wielded much power. Livingston had become a *patroon*—

the possessor of a manorial estate of many thousand acres on the eastern border of the Hudson River, south of the Van Rensselaer Manor. Active, shrewd, and intelligent, he became one of the most useful men in the province.

The Provincial Assembly convened on the 18th of May, 1698. It comprised nineteen members. In his speech to them the governor alluded to the legacy his predecessor had left him—"a divided people ; an empty purse ; a few miserable, naked, half-starved soldiers, not half the number the king allowed pay for ; the fortifications and even the Government House very much out of repair ; the province a receptacle of pirates, and the Acts of Trade violated by the neglect and connivance of those whose duty it was to have prevented it." It was a severe commentary on the conduct of his predecessor when he added : "I will take care there shall be no misapplication of the public money ; I will pocket none of it myself, nor shall there be any embezzlement by others." Perceiving the danger to be apprehended from so small a body through undue influences, the governor recommended an increase of the number of representatives to thirty.

The Assembly was strongly anti-Leislerian in its composition. The members agreed in a hearty address of thanks to the new governor, but really in nothing else. They wrangled continually. The late elections formed a subject for angry controversy. At the beginning of June six members seceded, when the governor dissolved the Assembly, and soon afterward dismissed two of his council who were specially obnoxious. They were all anti-Leislerians, and friends of Fletcher.*

Bellomont found the province disturbed by the continued hostile attitude of the French in Canada toward the Five Nations. He sent Colonel John Schuyler and Dominie Dellius (April, 1698) to Count Frontenac, at Montreal, with tidings of the treaty of peace at Ryswyk, and a request for an exchange of prisoners, "whether Christians or Indians," who had been taken in wars between the French and the Five Nations and the English. The old count, still claiming for France sovereignty over the Iroquois, refused to give up barbarian prisoners ; and Jesuit priests insisted upon keeping up missionary stations among the Iroquois in defiance of the opposition of the latter. Bellomont finally said to Frontenac : "If it is necessary I will arm every man in the provinces under my government to oppose you, and redress the injury you may perpetrate against our Indians." He added that he

---

* The following gentlemen composed the council : Frederick Philipse, Stephen Van Cortlandt, Nicholas Bayard, Gabriel Mienvielle, William Smith, William Nicoll, Thomas Willett, William Pinhorne, John Lawrence.

would not suffer them to be insulted ; and he threatened to execute the laws of England upon the missionaries "if they continued longer in the Five Cantons." Another war seemed to be impending, but this certainty was averted by the death of Frontenac in the fall of 1698.* During this controversy, Bellomont visited Albany to strengthen the Iroquois by his presence and by material aid. On his return he completed the weeding out of obnoxious members of his council. Pinhorne and Brook had been dismissed from office in June, and now Bayard, Mienvielle, Willett, and Lawrence were suspended, and Philipse resigned. Their respective places were soon filled. Abraham de Peyster, Robert Livingston, Dr. Samuel Staats, and Robert Walters took seats at the Board. They were all Leislerians.

The anti-Leislerians perceived that they had nothing to expect from the new governor. Indeed, he did not conceal his indifference to their praise or censure. He continually opposed and exasperated their leaders. Early in the fall of 1698 he granted to the families of Leisler and Milborne the privilege of exhuming the remains of their murdered kinsmen and giving them Christian burial. They were taken from the soil near the gallows into which they had been almost as rudely thrust seven years before as if they were mere brutes. They were placed in coffins, and at the request of their political friends they were permitted to lie in state in the old City Hall, at Coenties Slip, several days. There was fearful public excitement during the time, for this act was fraught with a significance almost incomprehensible to us. It was a gauntlet of defiance cast by the democracy of the day at the feet of the aristocracy.

The re-interment of the remains of the martyrs was marked by imposing ceremonies. It was late in September, and the autumnal "equinoctial storm" was raging. Fearing a riot, the governor furnished a military guard to the procession of men, women, and children, who were preceded by trumpeters and drummers beating a funeral march. From the City Hall they moved with solemn tread, unmindful of the wind and rain, and deposited the precious burdens in one grave in the burial-ground of the little Dutch Reformed Church, in

---

* On every occasion the French did all in their power to win the alliance and the allegiance of the Iroquois by flattery, by displays of power, and especially by the spectacular ministrations of the Roman Catholic Church, which captivated the barbaric imagination. As an illustration, Dr. Cadwallader Colden mentions the parade made by the French at Montreal on the occasion of the funeral of one of their Indians. "The priest that attended him at his death," says Colden, "declared that he died a true Christian, and as a proof he gave his exclamation on hearing of the crucifixion : ' Oh, had I been there I would have revenged his death and brought away their scalps ! ' "

Garden Street, near Wall Street.* "There was a great concourse of people [twelve hundred 'tis said] at the funeral," wrote Bellomont to the Lords of Trade, "and would, 'tis thought, have been as many more, but that it blew a rank storm for two or three days together, that hindered people from coming down or crossing the rivers."

A new Assembly convened in March, 1699. It was almost entirely Leislerian or democratic in character. The governor, lieutenant-governor, and the council were the same. A great change in public affairs soon appeared. Among the most radical and influential members of the Assembly was Abraham Gouverneur, who had been Leisler's secretary, had been condemned to death but pardoned, and had married the widow of Milborne. He represented Orange County.

Wrongs were righted and wrongs were committed by this reacting Assembly. Righteous indemnifications were granted, and liberal allowances were voted for the governor and lieutenant-governor. Such was the confidence reposed in the integrity and judgment of Bellomont, that a revenue for six years was voted and placed at his absolute disposal.

The most important business of the Assembly was the revocation of most extravagant and fraudulent grants of lands by Governor Fletcher for money considerations which swelled his purse.

DUTCH REFORMED CHURCH IN GARDEN STREET.

These grants were made to favorites. Among others, and the most conspicuous of the receivers of these grants, was Nicholas Bayard, Fletcher's right-hand man, whose acres thus bestowed exceeded in number those of any patroon. He and others attempted to monopolize all the lands on the

---

* This little structure was built of wood, octagonal in form, with a very high, steep roof, and a cupola in the centre of it surmounted by a "weather-cock." It was enlarged and repaired in 1776, and was rebuilt of stone in 1807. It stood upon a lane extending eastward from Broad Street parallel with Wall Street. The grounds on the lane were neatly laid out and well cultivated, and it received the name of "Garden Lane," and finally Garden Street, now Exchange Place. When it was built, in 1693, it was considered rather too far out of town.

upper Hudson and the Mohawk River. Dominie Dellius, of the Dutch Reformed Church, was convicted of obtaining, by fraud, an enormous tract of land from the Indians, while holding an official position among them, which Fletcher had confirmed on receiving a portion of the plunder as a bribe. The timely demolition by the Assembly and the governor of these huge schemes of land monopoly removed a great bar to emigration to the interior of the province of New York. It also

NEW CITY HALL, NEW YORK, 1700.

served to maintain the good-will of the Five Nations, who had been disturbed by the operation of these land robbers under Fletcher.

Earl Bellomont went to Boston in June, 1699, leaving the province of New York in the care of Lieutenant-Governor Nanfan. Little of public importance occurred during his absence, excepting further mischievous meddling with the Iroquois by the French in Canada and the Jesuit missionaries. The earl returned in the summer of 1700, and met the Assembly. Irritated by the conduct of the French, and especially by that of the missionaries, that body, at the earl's suggestion, passed a law for hanging every Roman Catholic priest who should come voluntarily into the province—a law which Chief-Justice Smith, the historian, writing fifty or sixty years afterward, said "ought to be in full force to this day."

Governor Bellomont died in the city of New York on the 5th of

March, 1701. His remains lay in state a day or two, when they were buried with public honors under the chapel of the fort. A few days afterward his arms were carried in state and placed on the front of the new City Hall, then just completed, in Wall Street, at the head of Broad Street. His remains, enclosed in a leaden coffin, were transferred to St. Paul's churchyard nearly a hundred years afterward, where they still lie.

Lord Bellomont had many and bitter enemies and also warm friends. The late Frederick de Peyster, LL.D., wrote on this subject:

"I am convinced that he was persistently maligned and abused solely because he had an eye to the public service and not to individual advancement. Strange to say, his enemies were to be found among all classes—a fact which, to my mind, however, determines his great honesty and independence of character. Those engaged in illegal trade hated him, because he was not to be bribed or cajoled into tolerating the least infraction of laws. The merchants were also his enemies, because he would not violate his obligation of office and wink at their evasions of the Acts of Trade. All opposed to Leisler and Milborne were against him, because he carried out the Acts of Parliament ordering that justice be done their memory. Even a greater part of the clergy were arrayed against him: those of the Dutch Church because he would not tolerate the iniquitous conduct of Dellius [see page 126]; and those of the English Church because he would not alienate a portion of the estate attached to the governor's residence. Thus it will be seen the private interests of a large class were opposed to law; and Bellomont, as the representative of the law and its faithful administrator, was reprobated and vilified by that class."

CHAPTER X.

New political troubles in the province appeared on the death of Governor Bellomont (March, 1701). Lieutenant-Governor Nanfan was then in Barbadoes, and the question arose, Who shall rightfully exercise the powers of government? The Leislerians declared that the power devolved on the Council collectively; the president of the Council, Colonel William Smith, contended that he alone had a right to exercise the supreme provincial power. In this view he was joined by Peter Schuyler and Robert Livingston. The Assembly was perplexed by these opinions, and adjourned in April; and disputes continued with much asperity until the middle of May, when Nanfan returned and lawfully assumed supreme authority. He dissolved the Assembly in June. A new Assembly was chosen, and convened on August 19th.

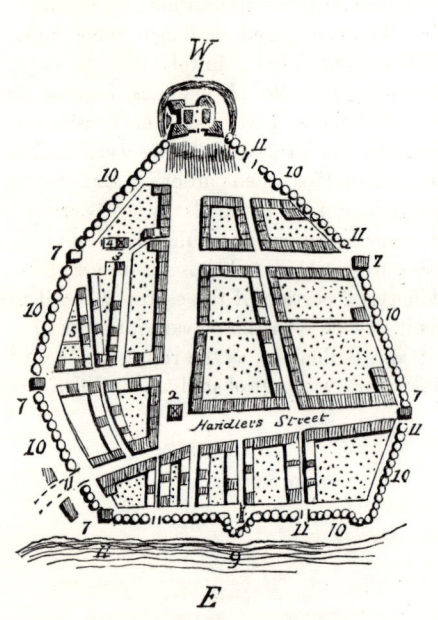

PLAN OF ALBANY IN 1695.

Meanwhile a grant of an immense tract of land had been made (July 19th) by the Five Nations to the British crown to insure protection against the French, and the king had given out of the exchequer $12,500 for strengthening the defences at Albany and Schenectady and to build a fort in the Onondaga country; also $4000 for presents to the Indians. These were wise measures, and strengthened the bond of friendship between the English and the Iroquois.

The government of the province was now under the full control of the

Leislerians or Democrats. A new Court of Chancery was organized, the power of chancellor, as before, being vested in the governor and Council. William Atwood, a zealous Leislerian, was chief-justice of the Supreme Court, with Abraham de Peyster * and Robert Walters as his associates on the bench. In the Assembly the fires of contention blazed fiercely, and Livingston, who had taken sides with Smith in the controversy about the lawful depository of executive power, became the object of bitter persecution by the more radical Leislerians. Indeed, the foundations of most of the public quarrels of the day were laid in personal animosities. Such was largely the case during the twenty years of warfare between the political factions in the province of New York from the death of Leisler. At the same time the seminal idea of republicanism was working powerfully in the public mind, and there

ABRAHAM DE PEYSTER.

was a steady and permanent advance in the direction of popular liberty.

Governor Nanfan's administration was brief. King William died in the spring of 1702 without legitimate issue. His queen, Mary, had died several years before, and her sister Anne now became the sovereign of Great Britain. Anne appointed her uncle, Sir Edward Hyde (a son of Lord Clarendon, and called Lord Cornbury by courtesy), Governor of New York. He was a libertine and a knave, and cursed the province with his presence and misrule about seven years. He was a bigot, and

---

* Abraham de Peyster was a distinguished citizen of New York, and an eminent merchant. He was the eldest son of Johannes de Peyster, born in New York City in 1658, and died there in 1728. He was Mayor of New York between 1691 and 1695 ; was afterward chief-justice of the province and president of the King's Council, in which capacity he performed the duties of governor in 1701, on the death of Lord Bellomont. He was colonel of the military forces of New York, and treasurer of that province and of New Jersey. He and William Penn were intimate friends. His spacious mansion on Pearl Street was the headquarters of Washington in 1776. It existed until 1856, when it was demolished. Colonel de Peyster was considered the most popular man in the city of New York in his day. He married his beautiful cousin, Katharine de Peyster, while on a visit to Holland. His sister Maria married David Provost. After his death she married James Alexander, secretary of the province, and by him became the mother of William Alexander, Lord Sterling.

persecuted all denominations of Christians outside of the Church of England. He embezzled the public money, and on all occasions was the persistent enemy of popular freedom and common justice.

"I know no right which you have as an Assembly," he said to the representatives of the people, "but such as the queen is pleased to allow you."

This was said in 1705, the year when that Assembly won the first substantial victory over absolutism or despotic rule. They obtained from the queen permission to make specific appropriations of incidental grants of money, and to appoint their own treasurer to take charge of extraordinary supplies. This was a bold and important step in the direction of popular independence and sovereignty.

When the news of the appointment of Cornbury reached New York the aristocracy took heart, and their leaders became insolent and defiant; for they felt sure of the friendship of the new governor. Nor were they disappointed. Nicholas Bayard was still the most conspicuous of their leaders for zeal and activity. He promulgated addresses to the king, the Parliament, and to Governor Cornbury, libelling the Leislerians and the administrations of Bellomont and Nanfan in the most scandalous manner. One of these addresses contained thirty-two "Heads of Accusation of the Earl of Bellomont." It was specially untruthful, and was calculated to stir up revolt in the colony. This seditious and dangerous paper Bayard dared not issue over his own signature, but signed it with the fictitious name of "John Key."

THE DE PEYSTER ARMS.

Nanfan was aroused to immediate and energetic action. In the spring of 1691 Bayard had procured the enactment of a law intended for the special punishment of Leisler. That law declared that whoever should attempt to "disturb the peace, good, and quiet of the government should be deemed a rebel and a traitor, and punished accordingly." Into this trap set for Leisler Bayard now fell. Putting this unrepealed law in force, Nanfan caused the arrest of Bayard on a charge of treason. He was tried before Justice Atwood and his associate justices in February (1702), found guilty, and sentenced to be "hanged, drawn, and quartered," in accordance with British law. After a virtual confession of guilt he was reprieved by Nanfan "until His Majesty's pleasure should be known." On the arrival of Cornbury (who had been "hunted out of England by a host of hungry creditors") these proceedings were all reversed, and Bayard was set at liberty. Governor Cornbury espoused the anti-Leislerian party, which immediately arose into power, and then began the flight of some of the Leislerian leaders. This change was of short duration.

New York City was sorely smitten by yellow fever in the summer of 1703. The governor transferred his court to Jamaica, Long Island, where he exercised his bigotry and petty tyranny in the most scandalous manner. One illustrative example will suffice. The best house in the village was the dwelling of the Presbyterian minister, built by his congregation. Cornbury begged the minister to allow his lordship to occupy the parsonage for a while. It was cheerfully done. This hospitality was requited by the seizure of the parsonage, the meetinghouse, and the glebe for the use of the members of the Church of England residing there.* When resistance to this act of robbery was made, the victims were subjected to fines and imprisonments!

GOVERNOR CORNBURY.

SIGNATURE OF GOVERNOR CORNBURY.

And yet this governor, weak-minded, mean-spirited, and vacillating, was so overpowered by the indomitable will of the people—a hardy, mixed race—that he often submitted to reproof, and in the poverty of his soul and purse he humbly thanked the Assembly for simple justice. For three years (1705-08) there was no meeting of that body. Intolerance, licentiousness, and dishonesty were conspicuous traits in this governor's character.†

---

* Lord Cornbury sent an order over his own signature for the minister (Rev. Mr. Hubbard), on July 4th, 1704, to deliver his house and lands to the sheriff, and not to fail at his "perill." On the same day he signed an order for the sheriff to eject the minister from the premises, claiming that the property belonged to the Anglican Church at Jamaica.

† "We never had a governor so universally detested," says Smith, the historian, "nor

He contracted debts everywhere, and refused to pay; and when, in 1708, the queen, yielding to the desires of the people, recalled him, and he left the chair of State, his creditors cast him into prison, and kept him there until the death of his father the next year made him a peer of the realm and a member of the House of Lords. Then the unrighteous law of the kingdom which exempts a member of that body from arrest and imprisonment for debt set him free, and he returned to England.

One of the most distinguished and useful men in the province at this time was Caleb Heathcote, proprietor of the manor of Scarsdale, in Westchester County, a representative of the ancient family of Heathcote of Scarsdale, Derbyshire, England, who came to America in 1692, and became a member of Governor Fletcher's council the next year. He was an earnest adherent of the Church of England, and exercised his authority judiciously as colonel of militia in the maintenance of morality and religion.*

CALEB HEATHCOTE.

SIGNATURE OF CALEB HEATHCOTE.

At about the beginning of Cornbury's administration war between France and England was kindled. It extended to their American colonies. This contest, known as "Queen Anne's War," lasted about eleven years, and

---

any who so richly deserves the public abhorrence. In spite of his noble descent, his behavior was trifling, mean, and extravagant. It was not uncommon for him to dress in a woman's habit, and then to patrol the fort in which he lived. Such freaks of low humor exposed him to the universal contempt of the whole people. Their indignation was kindled by his despotic rule, savage bigotry, insatiable avarice and injustice, not only to the public, but even his private creditors."

* Caleb Heathcote was a son of the wealthy Mayor of Chester, England. His oldest brother, Sir Gilbert Heathcote, was the first President of the Bank of England and Lord Mayor of London. Caleb was affianced to a beautiful maiden, and took his bachelor brother Gilbert to see her. Smitten by her charms, Gilbert supplanted his brother, when Caleb sought relief from the pangs of disappointment, took refuge with his uncle in New York, and afterward married a daughter of William ("Tangier") Smith, of Long Island. He found Westchester County, he wrote in 1704, "the most heathenish country I ever

was ended by the treaty of Utrecht in 1713. Its ravages in the colonies were chiefly felt by the English in New England and farther east. The Five Nations had made a treaty of neutrality with the French in Canada, and they stood as a barrier against incursions of the French and Indians into New York. That province enjoyed peace during the long war.

John, Lord Lovelace, succeeded Cornbury as Governor of New York. He did not reach the province until near the close of 1708, when he found the Assembly and the people strongly democratic in their political views. The very vices of the late governor had disciplined them to the exercise of resistance to oppression and to aspire to self-government, and secured to them the exercise of rights which might have been postponed for many years.

SIGNATURE OF LORD LOVELACE.

The new governor was cordially received by the people, and his course was judicious. He called a new Assembly in April, 1709, who, taught

SIGNATURE OF CAPTAIN INGOLDSBY.

by experience, refused to vote a permanent revenue without appropriation, but resolved to raise an annual revenue and appropriate it specifically. This would make the servants of the crown dependent upon the

---

saw which called themselves Christians," there being not the "least footsteps of religion." Sabbaths were spent in "vain sports and lewd derision." As colonel of militia he ordered his captains to require the men in every town to appoint readers of the Scriptures on Sundays, and if they refused, to call their men under arms on Sundays and spend the day in military exercises. They chose "readers." Heathcote was Mayor of the city of New York from 1711 to 1714; judge of Westchester County; made commander-in-chief of the forces of the colony; surveyor-general of the province for some time, and from 1715 till 1721 was receiver-general of the customs for all North America. Colonel Heathcote's last will was dated February 29th, 1719. He left his large estate to two daughters, one of whom married James de Lancey.

people for their salaries. The Assembly showed a firm disposition to assert and maintain all the popular rights which they had acquired, and now fairly began the contest in the province of New York between democracy and absolutism, which ended in permanent victory for the former at the close of the old war for independence three fourths of a century afterward.

Before the issue concerning the revenue had fairly assumed positive form Lord Lovelace died. His lieutenant, Richard Ingoldsby* (the contestant with Leisler for power in 1691), succeeded him. During Ingoldsby's administration of eleven months another feeble attempt was made to conquer Canada.

In this enterprise the province of New York engaged with great zeal. The Assembly appointed commissioners to procure the materials for war and transportation; issued bills of credit (New York's first paper money), and through the powerful influence of Colonel Peter Schuyler secured the neutrality and warm friendship of the Five Nations.

New York and New Jersey raised an army of about two thousand men, and Francis Nicholson, Andros's lieutenant-governor, was made the chief commander of these forces. The little army moved from Albany for Montreal before the close of June, and early in August they had halted at the southern end of Lake Champlain.

PETER SCHUYLER.

There they waited long for tidings of the departure from Boston of a promised English fleet destined to attack Quebec. No such tidings came, and the sadly disappointed soldiers, as in 1691, were compelled to return to their homes, their ranks thinned by sickness and death. This event

---

* Richard Ingoldsby, who came to New York in 1691 in command of forces sent with Governor Sloughter, had served as a field officer in Holland. We have observed his conduct at New York in preceding pages. He returned to England on furlough in 1696, and was absent several years, leaving his wife and children in New York with scanty means of support. He was commissioned Lieutenant-Governor of New York and New Jersey in 1702, but did not return until 1706. On the death of Governor Lovelace he administered the government until the arrival of Governor Hunter.

caused much irritation in the public mind, and weakened the confidence of the Five Nations in the puissance of Great Britain.

Colonel Schuyler,* mortified and alarmed by the apathy and neglect of the home government, which seemed unconscious of the importance to British interests in America of effecting the conquest of Canada, went to England the next year, at his own expense, to arouse the court and people to vigorous action in support of the momentous cause he had espoused. He persuaded a sachem from each Iroquois nation to accompany him, that the Confederacy might be certified of the immense strength of Great Britain. The presence of these barbarian kings produced a great sensation throughout the realm, especially in London. Multitudes followed the dusky monarchs wherever they went. Their portraits soon appeared in the print-shops. The queen caused them to be covered with scarlet mantles edged with gold. They were feasted at banquets; witnessed military reviews; saw a part of the mighty British navy; in a word, they were shown the glories of the kingdom, and were deeply impressed by the evidences of British power. They were conveyed to the palace of St. James to stand before the queen; and they gave belts of wampum and signed their *totems* to documents as pledges of their friendship and fidelity.

THE SCHUYLER ARMS.

The grand objects of Schuyler's mission were accomplished. The friendship and loyalty of the Five Nations were secured for the English forever, and the Iroquois were made willing to join the latter in an attempt to conquer Canada. The new British ministry authorized a campaign for the purpose. Henry St. John (Lord Boling-

---

* Peter Schuyler was one of the most useful men in the province for a period of almost forty years. He was the first Mayor of Albany, and there led the movement against Leisler. In Governor Fletcher's Council he performed most important public service. He was not only a statesman, but the foremost military leader in the province, as his operations against the French in Canada show. As Commissioner of Indian Affairs, he wielded potential influence over the Iroquois Confederacy, and by his courage, skill, and goodness won the affections of the white people and the Indians. The latter called him "Brother Quedor." When Governor Hunter retired, Schuyler, as President of the Council, became acting governor of the province. As such he displayed great wisdom and energy at a trying period.

broke),* the Secretary of State, planned a naval expedition against Quebec to co-operate with a land force of provincials to proceed from the Hudson River and attack Montreal.

A fleet of war-ships—transports and store-ships—bearing marines and regular troops was sent to Boston early in the summer of 1711 under the command of Admiral Sir Hovenden Walker. He sailed from that port with about seven thousand regulars and provincial troops on the 10th of August. Like Braddock, the haughty commander disdained the opinions and advice of experienced subordinates, and lost eight of his transports and nearly one thousand men among the rocks at the mouth of the St. Lawrence River. The expedition was abandoned.† Meanwhile New York, New Jersey, and Connecticut had formed a provincial army for the capture of Montreal and the holding of the upper waters of the St. Lawrence. These were under the command of Nicholson, who held a general's commission. They marched from Albany, four thousand strong, toward Lake Champlain. Among them were six hundred Iroquois warriors. Hearing of Walker's disaster, these troops also abandoned the expedition and returned home. So ended in failure the third attempt of the English to conquer Canada.

SIGNATURE OF LORD BOLINGBROKE.

Robert Hunter, a Scotchman, succeeded Lord Lovelace as Governor of New York. He had risen in military rank from a private soldier to brigadier-general. His literary accomplishments had gained for him the friendship of Addison and Swift, and his handsome person and

---

* Henry St. John, Lord Bolingbroke, was born in 1678, and became a member of Parliament in 1701. In 1704 he was made Secretary of War, and left office with a change in the ministry in 1708. In 1710 he became Secretary of State for Foreign Affairs, and was the principal negotiator of the treaty of Utrecht in 1713. He had been created Viscount Bolingbroke, and became prime-minister a few weeks before the death of Queen Anne. Being known as a Jacobite, he now fled to France, and entered the service of the Pretender, who appointed him his prime-minister. In 1720 he married a French lady, and was permitted to return to England in 1723. He died in 1751. Bolingbroke was a good writer and brilliant orator. Pope addressed his "Essay on Man" to St. John.

† "According to Harley," says Smith, in his *History of New York*, "this expedition was a contrivance of Bolingbroke, Moore, and the Lord Chancellor Harcourt to cheat the public of twenty thousand pounds. The latter of these was pleased to say, 'No government was worth serving that would not admit of such advantageous jobs.'"

insinuating manners had won the hand of a peeress—Lady Hay. By her influence he obtained the appointment first to the office of Lieutenant-Governor of Virginia, and then Governor of New York and New Jersey.

With Hunter came three thousand German Lutherans, refugees from the Palatinate of the Rhine, who had been driven from their homes by the persecutions of the King of France, and had taken refuge in England. The queen and Parliament sent them to America free of expense. They settled some on Livingston's Manor, some in the valley of the Schoharie, others on the Upper Mohawk at the "German Flats," and some in the city of New York, where they built a Lutheran church. A large portion of these refugees settled in Pennsylvania, and became the ancestors of much of the German population in that State. A few went to North Carolina.

SIGNATURE OF ROBERT HUNTER.

It was during Hunter's administration that the Tuscaroras fled from North Carolina (1712) and joined their Iroquois brethren in New York, as we have observed, and so made the Confederacy a league of Six Nations. In the same year the inhabitants of New York were greatly disturbed by apprehensions of an impending servile insurrection there. The population of the city was then about six thousand, a large proportion of which were negro slaves.

At that time there was a brisk slave-trade carried on at New York, Newport, and Boston, for since the revolution (1688) this trade had been thrown open.* The slaves in New York were held in the most abject bondage, and the masters were forbidden by law to set them free. In 1709 a slave-market was established at the foot of Wall Street, where they were sold and hired. A slave caught out at night

SEAL OF ROBERT HUNTER.

---

* The Stuart kings of England had chartered slave-dealing companies, and Charles II. and his brother, the Duke of York, were shareholders in them. In 1713 an English company obtained the privilege of supplying the Spanish colonies in America with African slaves for thirty years, stipulating to deliver one hundred and forty-four thousand negro slaves within that period. One quarter of the stock of the company was

without a lantern and a lighted candle in it was put in jail and his master was fined; and the authorities pledged themselves that the prisoner should receive thirty-nine lashes at the whipping-post if the master desired it. Other punishments for offences were sometimes very cruel. Human nature revolted, but chiefly under a mask. From time to time the slaves made some resistance. In one case they murdered a white family in revenge.

"Conscience makes cowards of us all." A rumor spread that a plot of the negroes to murder the white people and burn the city had been discovered. A sense of impending peril filled the town with terror. A riot that occurred at that moment, during which a house was burnt and several white people were killed, intensified the alarm. The magistrates acted promptly. The jail and other strong places were immediately filled with suspected slaves. Almost without evidence nineteen suspects were found guilty of conspiracy, and were summarily hanged or burnt alive. A similar scene occurred thirty years afterward.

Hunter's administration was marked by frequent and violent contests between the chief magistrate and the Assembly, the latter boldly asserting that they possessed an inherent right to legislate, not from any commission or grant from the crown, but from the free choice and election of the people, who ought not, nor justly could be divested of their property, by taxation or otherwise, without their consent." The governor could not assent to this republican doctrine, and the Assembly would not recede a line.

Hunter loved ease and quiet. These disputations wearied him. At one time he wrote: "I have spent three years in such torture and vexation that nothing in life can make amends for it." In 1719 failing health compelled him to return to England, when he left the government of the province in the hands of Colonel Peter Schuyler, the senior member of his Council.

William Burnet[*] succeeded Hunter as Governor of New York, and

taken by King Philip V. of Spain, and Queen Anne of England reserved for herself another quarter.

[*] William Burnet, a son of the eminent Bishop Burnet, was born at the Hague in 1688, and had William the Prince of Orange (afterward William III. of England) for his godfather. He had been engaged in public office in London when he was appointed Governor of New York and New Jersey. He reached New York in September, 1720. His administration was popular. On the accession of George II. he was transferred to the government of Massachusetts and New Hampshire, in 1728. He is represented as majestic in stature, frank in manner, witty and brilliant in conversation. He was also a clever writer. Governor Burnet died in Boston in September, 1729.

inherited his political discomforts; but he soon found a cure for them in his own disposition and the exercise of common sense. His administration of about eight years (1720-28) was generally serene and more beneficial to the province than any which had preceded it. Indeed, it was more quiet than any which succeeded it in the colonial period. Toward the last he incurred the enmity of a powerful body of merchants who controlled the Assembly, and his position was made so uncomfortable that he was transferred to the government of Massachusetts at his own request.

Governor Burnet was a scholar, but not a recluse, and soon became very popular. He " was gay and condescending," affected no pomp, but visited every family of reputation, and often diverted himself in free converse with the ladies, by whom he was much admired. He made few changes among public officers. He called Dr. Cadwallader Colden and James Alexander to the Council Board. They were both men of learning and sterling worth. Colden was a philosopher, and was specially familiar with the affairs of the

WILLIAM BURNET.

colony and with matters pertaining to the Indians, and the latter was an able lawyer and man of business. The governor's most trusted confidant was Chief-Justice Lewis Morris.

The Assembly, in response to the governor's first message to them, returned a most cordial address, and voted him a five years' support. Everything was done to promote harmony and good feeling. Such confidence did the governor repose in the integrity, wisdom, and patriotism of the Assembly that he did not dissolve them, but continued them on, session after session, until jealousy was excited by the self-interest of certain merchants.

Since the treaty of Utrecht in 1713 a large and increasing trade had been carried on between merchants in New York and Albany and the French in Canada, in goods salable among the Indians. The Iroquois, who were thus compelled to buy most of these goods from the French, as "middle men," at a high price, complained to the commissioners of

Indian Affairs,* because the trade was injurious to them. Wise men in and out of the Assembly perceived the danger that might ensue to the friendship between the Five Nations and the English by this continual trade intercourse with the French, for the Jesuit missionaries were now more active than ever in their endeavors to alienate the Iroquois from the English and to win them to the French interest. A law was finally passed prohibiting this inter-colonial traffic. The governor also perceived the necessity of acquiring control of Lake Ontario for the benefit of trade and the security of the friendship of the Six Nations, so as to frustrate the designs of the French. Accordingly, in 1722, with the sanction of the Assembly, he caused a trading-house to be erected at Oswego, at the mouth of the Onondaga River. These measures at once created a strong opposition to the provincial government among the merchants engaged in the inter-colonial trade, and excited the indignation and alarm of the French in Canada, for they saw that their trade and their dominion were both in peril. The latter immediately proceeded to erect a strong storehouse at the mouth of the Niagara River, and to repair the fort there. Unable to prevent this work, the governor caused a fort to be built at Oswego, at his own private expense, for the protection of the trading post and trade there. The French were incensed and made threats, but prudently curbed their wrath.

SEAL OF CADWALLADER COLDEN.

This state of things disturbed the political tranquillity of the province. Party spirit grew apace, and there finally arose such a clamor against the " permanent" and " unconstitutional " Assembly that the governor dissolved them. There was great excitement at the ensuing election, and when the new Assembly met, in the spring of 1727, the majority of the

---

* The commissioners of Indian Affairs resided at Albany. They served as such without salaries, but the advantages as traders which their position gave them was ample compensation. For many years William Johnson (made Sir William in 1755) was the sole Commissioner of Indian Affairs and became very wealthy, especially in land. It was the business of the commissioners to maintain the friendship of the Iroquois. They received and distributed the moneys and presents provided for that purpose. A secretary was paid for keeping a record of these transactions. At the breaking out of the Revolution, power wielded by Sir William Johnson alone passed again into the hands of a committee.

members were ill-affected toward the chief magistrate. His removal seemed necessary to insure the public tranquillity, and on April 15th, 1728, Governor Burnet surrendered into the hands of John Montgomery (or Montgomerie), his appointed successor, the great seal of the province.*

Montgomery was a Scotchman. He was bred a soldier, and had held a place at court and also a seat in Parliament. He was much inferior to his predecessor in abilities, and made no pretensions to scholarship. Loving his ease, he allowed public affairs to flow on placidly, and during the three years of his administration nothing of special public importance

FORT IN OSWEGO, IN 1750.
(From a print in Smith's " History of New York.")

occurred in the colony excepting the repeal of the law (1729) prohibiting the trade with the Canadians. This repeal was effected through the influence of the interested merchants. This trade worked mischief.

Governor Montgomery died on July 1st, 1731, when the chief command of the province devolved on Rip Van Dam, the senior member of the Council and an eminent and wealthy merchant. Van Dam filled the office well until August 1st, 1732, when William Cosby arrived bearing a commission as governor of the province of New York.

Just before the death of Montgomery a settlement of the long-continued controversy about the boundary-line between New York and Con-

---

* The provincial seal of New York was changed (as in other provinces) on the accession of successive monarchs. There were two great seals of New York made during the reign of Queen Anne, on which appeared an effigy of a *queen* and Indians making presents, similar to the device on the seal on page 109. The seals of the three Georges each bore the effigy of a *king*, with Indians making presents, but modified in design. The reverse of each seal was similar.

necticut was definitely settled. The partition-line agreed upon in 1664 being considered fraudulent, attempts were afterward made to effect a settlement of the question in a manner mutually satisfactory, but this was not accomplished until May, 1731. In 1725 a partition-line was agreed upon by the commissioners of both colonies, but it was not entirely satisfactory; now a tract of sixty thousand acres, lying on the Connecticut side of the line, and from its figure called the Oblong, was ceded to New York, and an equivalent in territory near Long Island Sound was surrendered to Connecticut. Hence the divergence from a straight line north and south seen in the southern boundary between New York and Connecticut.

RIP VAN DAM.

The Oblong is nearly two miles wide. Through its centre a line was drawn, and the whole tract was divided into lots of five hundred acres each, on both sides, and sold to emigrants, who came chiefly from New England. Governor Cosby was avaricious, unscrupulous, and arbitrary. He had been a colonel in the British army, and came to New York intent upon making a fortune. He could not comprehend the liberal spirit that prevailed in the colony, and he played the part of a petty military tyrant in the most ridiculous manner. As English officials were wont to do at that time, he looked with contempt upon all provincials, treated them accordingly, and soon became one of the most obnoxious governors which had afflicted the colony.

Cosby came in conflict with Van Dam at the outset. He brought with him a royal order for an equal division between himself and the president of the Council of "the salary, emoluments, and perquisites" of the office of governor during the thirteen months the merchant had exercised its functions. Cosby demanded half the salary which the merchant had received; Van Dam claimed one half the perquisites, etc., according to the order. Cosby refused, and brought a suit against Van Dam in the Court of Chancery, over which the governor presided *ex-officio*. Van Dam tried to bring a counter-suit at common law, but failed. Cosby's judges, James De Lancey and Adolph Philipse, were the governor's personal friends and willing instruments. Lewis Morris, the able chief-justice of the province for twenty years, denied the jurisdiction of the court; but the trial went on, and, of course, was decided in favor of the governor. Morris published his *Opinion*, and was punished by the governor by dismissal from the high office of chief-justice, and filling it by the appointment of De Lancey without even the formality of consulting his council.

The sympathies of the people were with Van Dam, and these high-handed proceedings provoked intense public indignation. They led to the establishment of a democratic newspaper and a trial in which popular liberty and the freedom of the press were vindicated. This famous trial was the most conspicuous event of the administration of Governor Cosby.

THE MORRIS ARMS.

William Bradford issued the first newspaper printed in the province of New York, in October, 1725, called the *New York Gazette*. He was the Government printer, and his *Gazette* was controlled by Cosby and his political friends. Bradford had, first as an apprentice and afterward as a business partner for a short time, the son of a widow among the Palatines who came with Governor Hunter, John Peter Zenger.

SIGNATURE OF LEWIS MORRIS.

The opponents of Cosby induced Zenger to establish a newspaper that might be an organ of the democratic party—a tribune of the people. It was first issued in November, 1733, and was named the *New York Weekly Journal*. Van Dam stood at the back of Zenger financially.

The *Journal* made vigorous warfare upon the governor and his official friends, as well as upon public measures. It kept up a continuous fusillade of squibs, lampoons, and satires; and it finally charged the governor and his council with violating the rights of the people, the illegal assumption of power, and the perversion of their official stations for selfish purposes. The Assembly, which was a "permanent" one and very obsequious, received its share of animadversion.*

These attacks were endured by the officials for about a year, when, in the autumn of 1734, the governor and council ordered certain copies of Zenger's paper to be publicly burnt by the common hangman. Then they caused the arrest of the publisher, and he was cast into prison on a charge of libelling the government. The Grand Jury refused to find a bill of indictment for this offence, but he was held by another process—*information.* James Alexander and William Smith, the eminent lawyers, became his counsel. Unable to give bail, he was kept in jail until early in the next August, when he was brought to trial in the City Hall, New York. The case excited intense interest throughout the whole country, for it involved the great subject of liberty of speech and of the press.

THE PHILIPSE ARMS.

"Meanwhile an association called the Sons of Liberty had worked diligently for Zenger. The venerable Andrew Hamilton, of Philadelphia, then eighty years of age and the foremost lawyer in the country, was engaged as the prisoner's counsel. On the hot morning when the trial began the court-room was densely crowded. Chief-Justice De Lancey presided. A jury was impanelled. The prisoner pleaded 'Not guilty,' but boldly admitted the publication of the alleged libel, and offered full proof of its justification. The attorney-general (Bradley) had just risen to oppose the introduction of such proof, when the vener-

---

* Illustrative of the obsequious deference which was then paid in the colonies even to an insignificant scion of nobility, a contemporary writer relates that when the young Lord Augustus Fitzroy, son of the Duke of Grafton, a favorite of the king, arrived in New York, in the fall of 1732, on a visit to the governor (and who was induced to marry his daughter), the corporation of the city waited upon the young man " in a full body, and the recorder addressed his lordship in a speech of congratulation, returning him thanks for the honor of his presence, and presented him the Freedom of the City in a gold box."

Smith, the historian, speaking of the marriage of the young lord to Cosby's daughter, says: "The match was clandestinely brought about by the intrigues of Mrs. Cosby, Lord Augustus being then on his travels through the provinces; and to blind his relations and secure the governor from the wrath of his father, a mock persecution was instituted against Campbell, the parson, who had scaled the wall of the fort and solemnized the nuptials without a written license from the governor or any publication of the banns." The duke refused to acknowledge the wife of his son, and the ambition of her parents was wofully disappointed.

able Hamilton unexpectedly entered the room, his long white hair flowing over his shoulders instead of being made into a queue, in the fashion of the day. The excited audience, most of them in sympathy with the prisoner, arose to their feet, and in spite of the voice and frowns of the chief-justice, waved their hats and shouted loud huzzas. When silence prevailed the attorney-general took the ground that facts in justification of an alleged libel were not admissible in evidence. The court sustained him.*

"When Hamilton arose a murmur of applause ran through the crowd. In a few eloquent sentences he scattered to the winds the sophistries which supported the pernicious doctrine, 'the greater the truth the greater the libel.' He declared that the jury were themselves judges of the facts and the law, and that they were competent to judge of the guilt or innocence of the accused. He reminded them that they were the sworn protectors of the rights, liberties, and privileges of their fellow-citizens, which, in this instance, had been violated by a most outrageous and vindictive series of persecutions. He conjured them to remember that it was for them to interpose between the tyrannical and arbitrary violators of the law and their intended victim, and to assert, by their verdict, in the fullest manner the freedom of speech and of the press, and of the supremacy of the people over their wanton and powerful oppressors.

ANDREW HAMILTON AT MIDDLE LIFE.

---

* Mr. De Lancey exercised much arbitrary power, and was always impatient of any opposition. One illustrative instance may suffice. James Alexander and William Smith were leading lawyers in the province. As counsel for Zenger, they interposed exceptions to the indictment of their client on *information* at the spring term. They also questioned the validity of the commission of the chief-justice. They made a motion that these exceptions should be filed. De Lancey refused to receive the exceptions. "You thought to have gained a great deal of applause and popularity by opposing this court," he said; "but you have brought it to this point, that either we must go from the Bench or you must go from the Bar." He then issued an order excluding them from any further practice in that court. This dissolving Zenger's counsel caused his friends to seek the services of Andrew Hamilton.

"Notwithstanding the charge of the chief-justice was wholly adverse to the doctrines of the great advocate, the jury, after brief deliberation,

HAMILTON AND THE PEOPLE.

returned a verdict of 'Not guilty.' Then a shout of triumph went up from the multitude, and Hamilton was borne out of the court-room upon the shoulders of the people to a grand entertainment which had been prepared for him. On the following day a public dinner was given him by the citizens. At the close of September following, the corporation of the city of New York presented to Mr. Hamilton the Freedom of the City and their thanks in a gold box weighing five and a half ounces, made for the occasion. In this document they cordially thanked him for his 'learned and generous defence of the rights of mankind and the liberties of the press,' and for his signal service which 'he cheerfully undertook, under great indisposition of body, and generously performed, refusing fee or reward.'

"This triumph of the popular cause, this vindication of the freedom of the press, this evidence of a determination of the people to protect their champions, and this success of an organization in its infancy, which appeared in power thirty years later under the same name—'Sons of Liberty'—was a sure prophecy of that political independence of the colonies which was speedily fulfilled. Yet the stupid governor, staggered by the blow, could not understand the meaning of the prophecy, and only his death, a few months after this trial, put an end to his vindictive proceedings." *

Governor Cosby died on March 10th, 1736.

---

* Lossing's *Our Country*, I., 368–70. Gouverneur Morris, it is reported, said: "Instead of dating American liberty from the Stamp Act, I trace it to the persecution of Peter Zenger, because that event revealed the philosophy of freedom both of thought and speech as an inborn human right, so nobly set forth in Milton's *Treatise on Unlicensed Printing.*"

CHAPTER XI.

From the arrival of Governor Cosby, in 1732, to the beginning of the Seven Years' War between France and England (1755-62), which is known in America as the "French and Indian War," the history of the province of New York is little more than a record of the operations of a violent party spirit engendered by selfish men struggling for power. Let us turn for a moment from this unpleasant subject to take a brief glance, through the optics of contemporary writers, at the character of society in the city and province of New York at that period.

The population of the province at the time we are considering did not exceed one hundred thousand. There were many discouragements to settlements. The dread of hostile incursions by the French and Indians on the north; the transportation hither from Great Britain of ship-loads of felons; the oppressive nature of navigation laws; the avarice, bigotry, and tyranny of some of the governors who had been sent to rule the province, and the lavish grants of much of the best land in the colony to their favorites and instruments, were special hindrances to a rapid increase of population. The holders of large estates rated their lands so high that poorer persons could neither buy nor lease farms. The price of labor was so enormously high, because of the sparse population, that the importation of negroes had become a prime industrial necessity, and they were then very numerous in the province. The Dutch language was yet so generally used in some of the counties that sheriffs found it difficult to procure persons sufficiently acquainted with the English tongue to serve as jurors in the courts. The manners of the people were simple and various according to locality and condition. The prevalence of the Dutch, the German, the English, and the French (Huguenots) in certain places modified manners.

In the city of New York, where there was constant intercourse with Europe, particularly with Great Britain, the London fashions, much modified however, were followed; yet these were sometimes disused in England by the time they were adopted here. Among the wealthier classes considerable luxury in table, dress, and furniture was exhibited, yet the people were not so gay as in Boston, where society was almost purely English, and presented greater cultivation. In New York wealth was more equally distributed. There was an aspect of comfort throughout society.

New York City was more social in its character than any other place on the continent. It now had a mixed population, sturdy in individual character and cosmopolitan in feeling. Society presented an almost even surface of equality and independence. It consisted chiefly of merchants, shop-keepers, and tradesmen. Their recreations were simple.

NEW YORK COSTUMES AND FURNITURE IN 1740.

The men enjoyed themselves at a weekly evening club, and the women frequented musical concerts and dancing assemblies with their husbands and brothers. The women were generally comely in person, dressed with taste, were notable housekeepers, managed their households with neatness and thrift, and made happy homes. They seldom or never engaged in gaming, as was the habit of fashionable women in England at that time.

Both sexes were very neglectful of intellectual cultivation. They read very little. The schools were of a low order. "The instructors want instruction," wrote a contemporary. "Through long and shameful neglect of all the arts and sciences, our common speech is extremely corrupt, and the evidences of a bad taste, both as to thought and language, are visible in all our proceedings, private and public." Virtue was predominant. The women were modest, sprightly, and good-humored; and there was diffused throughout society an uncommon

MILKING-TIME AT ALBANY.

degree of domestic felicity, both in the city and province. The merchants and traders had a high reputation for honesty and fair-dealing, and the people everywhere, in town and country, were sober, industrious, and hospitable, yet eagerly intent upon gain.

The people were generally religious. The principal church organizations were the Dutch Reformed, the Lutheran, the English Episcopal, and the Presbyterian. There was much latitudinarianism, much freedom of thought and action among the people, that fostered a spirit of independence. They were not bound hand and foot by rigid religious and political creeds, as were the people of New England, but were thoroughly imbued with the toleration inherited from the first Dutch settlers, and theological disputes were seldom indulged in.

New York society possessed the elements of a noble State. These elements entered into the political and social structure of the commonwealth after the Declaration of Independence with the grand result now manifested to the world.*

On the death of Governor Cosby, Rip Van Dam, the senior councillor, again prepared to assume the functions of governor. When he called for the seals of office, etc., he was informed that Cosby had suspended him from the Council Board several months before. This had been

---

* Mrs. Grant, of Laggan, in her *Memoirs of an American Lady*, has left us some charming pictures of social life at Albany, where the population was chiefly of Dutch descent, and the habits of the people were more simple than at New York. She tarried among them awhile at the time we are considering. She says the houses were very neat within and without, and were built chiefly of stone or brick. The streets were broad and lined with shade trees. Each house had its garden, and before each door a tree was planted and shaded the "stoops" or porches, which were furnished with spacious seats on which domestic groups were seated on summer evenings. Each family had a cow, fed in a common pasture at the end of the town. At evening the herd returned altogether of their own accord, with their tinkling bells hung at their necks, along the wide and grassy street, to their wonted sheltering trees, to be milked at their masters' doors.

On pleasant evenings the "stoops" were filled with groups of old and young of both sexes discussing grave questions or gayly chatting and singing together. The mischievous gossip was unknown, for intercourse was so free and friendship so real that there was no place for such a creature; and politicians seldom disturbed these social gatherings. A peculiar social custom arranged the young people in congenial companies, composed of an equal number of both sexes, quite small children being admitted, and the association continued until maturity. The result was a perfect knowledge of each other, and happy and suitable marriages prevailed.

The summer amusements of the young were simple, the principal one being what we call *picnics*, often held upon the pretty islands near Albany, or in "the bush." These were days of pure enjoyment, for everybody was unrestrained by conventionalities. In winter the frozen bosom of the Hudson would be alive with merry skaters of both sexes. Small evening parties were frequent, and were generally the sequel of quilting parties. The young men sometimes enjoyed convivial parties at taverns, but habitual drunkenness was extremely rare.

African slavery was seen at Albany and vicinity in its mildest form. It was softened by gentleness and mutual attachments. It appeared patriarchal, and a real blessing to the negroes. Master and slave stood in the relation of friends. Immoralities were rare. There was no hatred engendered by neglect, cruelty, or injustice; and such excitements as the "Negro Plots" of 1712 and 1741 in New York City were impossible. Industry and frugality ranked among the cardinal virtues of the people.

done secretly, that George Clarke, an English adventurer and one of Cosby's tools, might become president of the Council. Clarke, as such, now assumed the office of lieutenant-governor. Van Dam would not yield, and the "rival governors" proceeded to act independently of each other. This state of things involved the Assembly and the corporation of New York City in fierce contentions, and the public excitement became so intense that open insurrection was threatened. It was finally allayed by the confirmation of Clarke's claim by the home government. His administration was marked by continual contests with the Assembly. It terminated in September, 1743, by the arrival of Sir George Clinton as governor of the province,* a younger son of the Earl of Lincoln and the father of Sir Henry Clinton, the commander-in-chief of the British forces in America during a portion of the old war for independence.

The most conspicuous event of Clarke's administration was that known as the "Negro Plot," in 1741. Causes similar to those which made the inhabitants of the city dread a servile insurrection in 1712 (see page 138) excited them at this time. As before, the tongue of rumor sounded an alarm which produced a panic. A bold robbery, almost simultaneous fires in different parts of the city (though in the day-time), idle words spoken by negroes, and the grumbling of some black people who had been brought into the port in a Spanish prize-ship and sold into slavery, combined in suggesting to the excited minds of the

CLARKE'S MONUMENT AT CHESHIRE.

---

* Sir George Clarke was a prominent man in New York for nearly half a century. He was a native of England, was a lawyer, married Miss Hyde, a relative of Governor Cornbury, and was appointed secretary of the province of New York in 1703. He was a shrewd, thrifty man, and left America with a large fortune, like that of Cosby mysteriously gathered. He sailed for England in 1745. On his passage he was captured by a French cruiser, but was soon released, when the British Government indemnified him for his losses. Retiring to a handsome estate near Cheshire, he died there at an advanced age in 1760. His wife, a woman of fine accomplishments, died in New York.

people suspicions of a conspiracy, and creating a fearful panic. The people were deaf to reason. The magistrates and lawyers "lost their heads," and by their acts increased the public alarm.

False accusers charged negroes with incendiarism, robbery, and conspiracy to burn the city and murder the white people. Very soon the jail and apartments in the City Hall were crowded with the accused. The keeper of a low tavern and brothel (John Hughson), his wife, and a strumpet who lived with them were accused by an indented servant girl of sixteen (Mary Burton) of complicity, with negroes named, in the robbery and in a conspiracy to burn the town and destroy the inhabitants. She had been tempted by fear and selfishness, by threats, and by promises of money and freedom from her master (Hughson) to "tell all she knew"—in other words, to make false accusations and to bear false testimony. She declared that her master and mistress received and concealed the stolen property from negroes whom she named, conferred with some of the slaves about burning the city and killing the inhabitants, and that her master threatened to poison her if she exposed him; while the negroes swore they would burn her alive if she revealed their secret. She said her master and mistress and the bawd whom they harbored were the only white persons present at the plotting with the negroes. The excited and credulous magistrates received this absurd story and others uttered by the lying servant girl as truth.

Without the semblance of justice or of common sense, and moved by the unsupported assertions of Mary Burton, the magistrates committed persons to the jail. The excited lawyers perplexed and terrified the poor prisoners, and the half-dazed jurors found the tavern-keeper, his wife, and their wretched boarder guilty. They were hanged. Eighteen negroes were also hung in a green vale, the site of the modern Five Points; eleven were burned alive, and fifty were sold into slavery in the West Indies. Three of the colored people were burnt on the site of the (present) City Hall, one of whom was a woman. All who suffered at that time were undoubtedly innocent victims of groundless fright created by imaginary danger. This "reign of terror" continued about six months, when a day was set apart for public thanksgiving for the "great deliverance."

The "Negro Plot" may be classed among the conspicuous delusions of modern times. It is a counterpart in wickedness and absurdity to the "Salem Witchcraft" delusion in the preceding century.

There was another and a peculiar sufferer at this time—a victim of false accusations, perjury, and bigotry. His name was John Ury, his profession a schoolmaster and a nonjuring minister of the Church of

England. He was charged with being a Jesuit priest in disguise, and was accused of inciting the negroes to burn the governor's house, which was the first of the almost simultaneous fires already alluded to. The only witnesses against him were the perjured Mary Burton and a daughter of the tavern-keeper just hanged. The latter was brought from a felon's cell and pardoned on the condition that she should give certain testimony against the accused. She swore that Ury had counselled negroes to burn the governor's house (which the governor himself declared had been accidentally set on fire through the carelessness of a plumber while soldering a tin gutter); that he had practised the rites of the Roman Catholic Church among the negroes in her presence at her father's house, and that he received confessions, etc.

Competent testimony of respectable citizens to the contrary—that he was a schoolmaster and a clergyman of the Church of England—was clearly given, but was not heeded. The charge of the chief-justice (De Lancey) and the speech of the attorney-general (Bradley) were largely mere tirades against popery and warnings against its secret emissaries. The misled jury were easily persuaded to pronounce poor Ury guilty, and the bigoted court, taking advantage of an unrepealed statute against priests, sentenced him to be hanged. Ury protested his innocence to the last moment. The chief instrument in bringing this evidently innocent man to the scaffold was the disgraceful statute which condemned to death every Roman Catholic priest who should voluntarily come into the province. (See p. 126.)

SIGNATURE AND ARMS OF GEORGE CLINTON.

In the whole of the wretched business of the "Negro Plot" not a single charge of conspiracy was proven by a competent witness.

Sir George Clinton* published his commission as Governor of New

---

* Sir George Clinton was the youngest son of the sixth Earl of Lincoln, and rose to distinction in the British navy. He was commissioned a commodore, and made Governor

York on the day of his arrival, September 20th, 1743. He held the office ten years. Clinton was wholly unfitted by his training and disposition for the chief magistracy of a people like those of New York—sturdy, independent, and courageous; free-thinkers in politics and irrepressible aspirants for self-government.

After a peace between France and Great Britain for more than thirty years, during which time the American colonists enjoyed comparative repose, war was again kindled. It was declared in March, 1744. The colonists promptly rose in their might and donned their armor. The struggle that ensued continued about four years, and is known in American history as *King George's War*, because George II. of England espoused the cause of the Empress of Austria, the celebrated Maria Theresa. In Europe it was known as the War of the Austrian Succession.

This war was not distinguished by many stirring events in America. The most important was the capture of Louisburg and its strong fortress, on the island of Cape Breton, which the French had constructed after the treaty of Utrecht at a cost of $5,500,000. William Shirley,* a good soldier and energetic statesman, was then Governor of Massachusetts. He perceived the importance of Louisburg in the coming contest, and plans for its capture were soon perfected by the Legislature of Massachusetts. He asked England for aid in the enterprise, and Admiral Warren was ordered to Boston from the West Indies with a fleet and troops. Rhode Island, New Hampshire, and Connecticut furnished their proper quota of men. New York sent artillery, and Pennsylvania sent provisions. Thus common danger was teaching the necessity for a

---

of Newfoundland in 1732. In 1743 he was appointed Governor of New York, and had a tumultuous administration for ten years. He was unlettered, and of irritable temperament. In all his controversies with the New York Assembly he was ably assisted by the mind and pen of Dr. Cadwallader Colden. His chief opponent was Daniel Horsmanden, at one time chief-justice of the colony. He quarrelled with all the political factions in the colony, and returned home in 1753, when he was given the sinecure of Governor of Greenwich Hospital. In 1745 he was appointed vice-admiral of the Red, and in 1757 admiral of the Fleet. Again Governor of Newfoundland, he died there in 1761.

* William Shirley was born in Sussex, England, in 1693, and died at Roxbury, Mass., in 1771. He came to Boston in 1734, and practised the profession of a lawyer there. Active in public affairs, he was appointed Governor of Massachusetts in 1741, and became a skilful military leader in the French and Indian War. He was also a skilful diplomatist. For a while he was commander-in-chief of the British forces in America. In 1759 he was commissioned lieutenant-general and governor of one of the Bahama Islands, but returned to Boston in 1770. He built a fine mansion at Roxbury, bu never occupied it.

political union of the English American colonies fully thirty years before such union was effected.

The colonial forces, commanded by General William Pepperell,* thirty-two hundred strong, sailed from Boston in the spring of 1745, and were joined by Warren at Canseau with ships and troops. The combined forces, four thousand in number, landed not far from Louisburg at the close of April, took the French by surprise, and speedily began a vigorous siege of the strong fortress. Finally a combined attack by sea and land, at the close of June, compelled the French to surrender the fortress, the city of Louisburg, and the island of Cape Breton to the English. The mortified French ministry sent the Duke d'Anville the next year with a powerful naval armament to recover what had been lost, and to desolate the English settlements along the New England coasts. Storms wrecked many of his vessels, and disease soon wasted hundreds of his men. The duke was compelled to abandon the enterprise without striking a blow. The New England people regarded these misfortunes of the enemy as a providential interference in their favor.

Meanwhile New York had been vigilant and active. Its immense frontier on the north exposed it to easy inroads of the common enemy. The Iroquois formed a trustworthy but not an omnipotent defence. The garrisons at Albany, Schenectady, and Oswego were strengthened, and the erection of block-houses was begun on the upper Hudson.

Notwithstanding these precautions five hundred French Canadians and Huron Indians and a few disaffected Iroquois warriors swept down the upper valley of the Hudson late in the fall of 1745, as far as Saratoga, leaving there a horrible record, and spreading the wildest alarm among the frontier settlements far and near. The invaders were commanded by M. Marin, an active French officer. They had rendezvoused at Crown Point, on Lake Champlain, where, at the suggestion of Father Piquet, the French Prefect Apostolique to Canada, it was resolved to sweep down toward Albany and cut off the advancing English settlements.

Saratoga was a scattered village on the flats at the junction of the Fish Creek and the Hudson River, near (present) Schuylerville. It com-

---

* William Pepperell was born in Maine in 1696, and died there in 1759. His father was a Welshman, and was made an apprentice to a fisherman when he came to New England. His son became a merchant. Liking military life, he was frequently engaged in fighting Indians. In 1727 he was appointed one of the king's Council, in Massachusetts, and held the office thirty-two consecutive years. He became an eminent jurist, and was made chief-justice of the Common Pleas in 1730. After his successful expedition against Louisburg he was knighted (1745), and was appointed colonel in the royal army; then a major-general, and lieutenant-general in 1759. For two years (1756-58) he was Acting-Governor of Massachusetts.

prised about thirty families, many of them tenants of Philip Schuyler, brother of the Mayor of Albany, and owner of all the lands in the vicinity. The invaders murdered Mr. Schuyler, plundered and burnt the village, and carried away over one hundred men, women, and children, including negroes, as captives. Mr. Schuyler's house, with his body in it, was burned. On the following morning the invaders, after chanting the *Te Deum*, departed for Canada with their plunder and prisoners.

The energetic Governor Shirley, flushed with the victory in the east, contemplated the conquest of the entire French dominions in America. His general plan of operations was similar to that of former expeditions for the capture of Quebec and Montreal.

Governor Clinton favored the project, and the Assembly voted aid. The erection of block-houses on the northern frontiers was authorized, also a new emission of bills of credit. Bounties were raised for volunteers, and provision was made for supplies of all kinds. The Six Nations were invited to meet the governor at a conference at Albany, at which appeared representatives of other colonies. The object of the conference was to engage the Iroquois to fight for the English in the conflict supposed to be impending. This conference was held in the summer of 1746.

William Johnson, a nephew of Admiral Warren, and then in the prime of young manhood, had been appointed Indian commissioner in place of Colonel Schuyler, who had long performed the duties of that office most efficiently. Johnson had made great efforts to arouse the Mohawks, among whom he lived, to make war on the French. At the time appointed for the conference he appeared on the hills overlooking Albany at the head of a large number of the Iroquois chiefs, habited and painted like the barbarians. Among these were leaders from the Delawares, the Susquehannas, the River Indians, and the Mohegans of Connecticut, all eager to raise the hatchet against the French. The conference was satisfactory. The Indians were dismissed with presents, and Johnson was furnished with arms and with instructions to send out war parties from the Mohawk Valley to annoy their enemies on the border.

The British ministry failed to send promised assistance to the colonies, and Shirley's grand project was abandoned. From this time no actual hostilities of importance occurred within the province of New York or on its frontiers in several years; but the annals of New Hampshire, on its eastern border, for two years thereafter present a long and mournful catalogue of plantations laid waste and colonists slain or carried into captivity by the French and Indians. The treaty of peace concluded at

Aix-la-Chapelle, in October, 1748, ended hostilities between France and England and the American colonies for a time.

During the whole administration of Governor Clinton rancorous party spirit cursed the province. He had passed a greater portion of his life in the royal navy, and had learned and practised its imperious ways. These ways were, of course, often offensive. He loved his ease and good cheer, was kind-hearted and good-humored, and tried to control the storms of passion around him. Unfortunately, the surviving politicians who had quarrelled throughout the administrations of Cosby and Clarke were as rancorous and active as ever. He tried to propitiate both parties, and failed, of course. The Assembly persistently refused to yield an iota of their rights and privileges, and their independence vexed and worried Clinton.

SIGNATURE OF JAMES DE LANCEY.

Unfortunately for the governor and the province, Clinton made Chief-Justice De Lancey his confidant and guide. De Lancey was a politician of exquisite mould, and then wielded almost absolute sway over the Assembly and the people. At length the governor and the chief-justice quarrelled over their cups at a banquet. The latter swore he would be revenged; and from that time Clinton found no peace in public life. De Lancey was implacable. He pursued the governor as a personal and political enemy with the tenacity of a hound, and stirred up opposition to Clinton's authority and his measures everywhere. Wielding power, the governor dealt some hard blows in return.*

SEAL OF JAMES DE LANCEY.

An open rupture between the governor and the Assembly occurred in 1749. Under instructions from the king, Clinton demanded from the

---

* James De Lancey was born in New York City in 1703, and died there, 1760. He was educated in England, studied law there, and soon after his return (1729) was made a justice of the Supreme Court of the province. He became chief-justice in 1733. He was lieutenant-governor and acting-governor of the province for several years, and was one of the most influential men in the province in politics and legislation. Mr. De Lancey was one of the founders of King's (now Columbia) College. His wife was Anne, eldest daughter of Colonel Caleb Heathcote.

SELF-DESTRUCTION OF A GOVERNOR.

Assembly the grant of a permanent revenue for five years, that he might be independent of the people. As in times past, the Assembly refused to grant it. The governor unwisely told them that their authority to act at all, and the political rights and privileges which they enjoyed depended upon the breath of the monarch whom he represented, and he threatened to punish them if they did not comply with his wishes. The Assembly boldly said in substance:

"Your conduct is arbitrary, illegal, and in violation of our privileges, and we will not comply with your demands."

In this quarrel, which continued until the end of Clinton's administration, the unfortunate governor was placed in a delicate and even a false position. He was bound to obey his instructions in making the demand, at the same time he felt that the attitude of the Assembly was essentially right, and he urged upon the home government the propriety of making concessions to the popular leaders. Strangely enough, at about this period the chief leaders of the aristocratic faction, led by the chief-justice, became the popular leaders opposed to the governor and the crown.

Wearied, worried, and disgusted, Governor Clinton resigned his office in the summer of 1753, and on September 7th he gave into the hands of his successor, Sir Danvers Osborne, the great seal of the province. Chief-Justice De Lancey had been appointed lieutenant-governor.

Osborne's administration was exceedingly short. He was received with demonstrations of joy by the people, and was magnificently entertained by the corporation of the city of New York. But he bore royal instructions more arbitrary and tyrannical than those which, attempted to be enforced, had made his predecessor odious to the people. He learned by conversation with those who feasted him that the course he was instructed to pursue would be highly displeasing to the people and render him odious in their estimation.

Having been greatly depressed in spirits by the recent death of his wife, Sir Danvers was made more melancholy by the gloomy prospects before him—continual disputes with the representatives of the people, the sport of factions, and a tarnished reputation. He said to De Lancey in a plaintive voice:

"What am I here for? I shall soon leave you the government. I am unable to bear the burden."

Brooding over his situation, his disturbed reason became unseated, and five days after his arrival his lifeless body was found, early on the morning of the 12th, suspended by a pocket-handkerchief around his neck to the fence of the garden of Mr. Murray, one of the Council, whose hospitality he was enjoying.

De Lancey again became acting Governor of New York. He was now placed in a delicate situation, but he was equal to the occasion. He had recently been a leader of the opposition in the Assembly in his persecution of Clinton ; now he was compelled to wear the mask of Janus and rebuke the Assembly *publicly* for not obeying the royal instructions in granting supplies, while he secretly confederated in the promotion of measures directly opposed to the expressed will of the crown. The Assembly were equal dissemblers. They lauded De Lancey, boasted of their loyalty, and declared that nothing should be wanting to promote the king's service. At the same time they firmly resisted taxation without their consent. With well-dissembled zeal De Lancey joined the other royal governors in urging the British Government to put in action a scheme of general taxation in America.

De Lancey remained the political head of the province two years, when Sir Charles Hardy, a captain in the British navy, ignorant of the country, the people, and the government he was to administer, arrived at New York (September, 1755) bearing the commission of governor.* De Lancey really continued to govern the province for about five years. Sir Charles was a plastic instrument in De Lancey's hands.

The treaty of Aix-la-Chapelle was, practically, only a contract for a truce. The traditional enmity between France and England only slumbered. The Jesuits, bearing the Cross and the Lily, had discovered the magnificent country around the great lakes and in the Mississippi Valley, and revealed its riches to the French court. French missionary stations and trading-posts were established deep in the wilderness, but these did not attract the serious attention of the English until after the capture of Louisburg, when the French began the building of strong vessels at Fort Frontenac at the foot of Lake Ontario, and the erection of more than sixty forts between Montreal and the site of New Orleans. In 1753 the Governor of Canada sent twelve hundred French soldiers to occupy the Ohio Valley to the exclusion of the English.

At the time we are considering the French in America were not over one hundred thousand in number, and were scattered in trading settlements for almost one thousand miles along the St. Lawrence River and our immense inland seas ; also at points on the Mississippi River and its

---

* Sir Charles was a grandson of Sir Thomas Hardy, a distinguished naval commander in the reign of Queen Anne. He was himself a naval commander. After leaving New York, he was appointed (1757) rear-admiral of the Blue, and commanded in the expedition against Louisburg. He was promoted to vice-admiral, and in 1764 was a member of Parliament. He became admiral in 1770, and commanded a large squadron. Sir Charles died in England in 1780, aged about sixty-seven years.

tributaries. The English numbered more than a million, and occupied a line of territory more than a thousand miles in extent along the Atlantic seaboard, in the form of agricultural communities. The French, through the influence of the Jesuit priests and kind treatment, had won the friendship of the barbarians around them.

The French, on the English plea of discovery and priority of occupation, claimed jurisdiction over the region of the Ohio River and its tributaries. The King of England, on the same plea, claimed that region, and granted to a company of London merchants and Virginia speculators a tract of six hundred thousand acres of land there. This company began the establishment of trading-posts on this domain. The French regarded them as intruders. The Indians properly said:

"The English claim all the land on one side of the river, and the French claim all the land on the other side of the river. Where is the Indian's land?" Echo answered, "Where?" etc. The rightful claim of the first occupants of the soil was not considered by the voracious European robbers.

Apprehending the loss of their trade and their dominion, the French built a fort on the southern shore of Lake Erie ; also others near the domain of the English company. The Governor of Virginia sent a remonstrance to the French commander in that region (St. Pierre). The bearer of the despatch was young George Washington, then less than twenty-two years of age. He made the perilous journey with two or three attendants. The Indians were hostile to the English, and the French were their traditional enemies ; but the dangerous journey was performed in safety, and the mission was executed with skill and judgment. Washington returned in January, 1754, with an unsatisfactory response to the message he had delivered, but with much valuable information. When wine was in and wit was out of the heads of the French officers at their commander's table, they had revealed many important secrets to their sober young visitor.

Satisfied that the French in Canada were contemplating aggressive war upon the English colonies, the latter prepared to meet the blow. In the summer of 1754 twenty-five delegates, representing seven English-American colonies—New Hampshire, Massachusetts, Rhode Island, Connecticut, New York, Pennsylvania, and Maryland—met in convention at Albany to renew treaties with the Six Nations and to consider the important subject of the formation of a colonial confederacy. Lieutenant-Governor De Lancey presided over the convention. The treaty was renewed, and in July Dr. Franklin, a delegate from Pennsylvania, presented to the convention a plan of union having many of the features of our national Constitution. It was adopted, and copies were sent to the several colonial Assemblies and to the imperial Board of Trade for ratification.

The history of this plan is singular. The Assemblies refused their assent because it seemed too *aristocratic*—giving the governor to be appointed by the king too much power. The Board of Trade rejected it because it was too *democratic*—gave too much power to the people.*

Meanwhile war had actually been begun near the upper waters of the Ohio River. The English Land Company had begun the erection of a fort on the site of (present) Pittsburg. The workmen were driven away by French soldiers, who finished the work and named it Fort Duquesne in honor of the Governor of Canada. The Governor of Virginia (Dinwiddie) sent six hundred troops under Colonel Joshua Fry, with Washington, commissioned a major, as his lieutenant, to expel the French. The advanced corps under Major Washington, when about fifty miles from Fort Duquesne, was compelled to halt and construct a stockade (which was called Fort Necessity) and prepare for resisting a detachment of French troops which had been sent to intercept them. Before the fort was completed a party was sent out to attack the approaching foe. This was done at the dead of night. The commander of the French (Jumonville) was slain, and only fifteen of his fifty men escaped. A larger French force soon invested Fort Necessity, and notwithstanding it had been re-enforced by troops from New York, Washington was compelled to surrender on the morning of July 4th and return to Virginia. So the French and Indian War was begun in the colonies about two years before the War of the Austrian Succession, of which it was a part, was proclaimed by France and Great Britain.

The British Government, though it perceived that a conflict in America was impending more serious than any which had yet occurred, gave a very small amount of aid to the English-American colonies. It contributed only $50,000 and a commission for Governor Sharpe, of

---

* It proposed a general government to be administered by one chief magistrate appointed by the crown and a council of forty-eight members chosen by the several legislatures. This council, answering to our Senate, was to have power to declare war, levy troops, raise money, regulate trade, conclude peace, and do many other things necessary for the general good. The Board of Trade had proposed a plan which contained all the elements of a system for the utter enslavement and dependence of the Americans. They proposed a general government composed of the governors of the several colonies and certain select members of the general councils. These were to have power to draw on the British Treasury for money to carry on the impending war, the sum to be reimbursed by taxes imposed by Parliament on the colonists. The latter preferred to do their own fighting and levy their own taxes independent of Great Britain.

MILITARY EXPEDITIONS PLANNED.

Maryland, as commander-in-chief of the colonial forces. Sharpe did not serve. Shirley put forth energetic efforts in Massachusetts; New York voted $25,000 for military purposes, and Maryland voted $30,000 for the same purpose.

The war that ensued forms an important part of the history of our Republic, but the plan and scope of this work precludes the possibility of giving an account of even important events, civil and military, which have occurred outside of the province and State of New York, excepting such connected with its history as may be necessary to elucidate our subject.

General Edward Braddock was sent to America early in 1755 as commander-in-chief of all the provincial forces. In April he met in conference, at Alexandria, Va., six colonial governors—namely, Shirley, of Massachusetts; Dinwiddie, of Virginia; De Lancey, of New York; Sharpe, of Maryland; Morris, of Pennsylvania; and Dobbs, of North Carolina. They planned three expeditions—one against Fort Duquesne, to be commanded by Braddock; a second against Forts Niagara and Frontenac (Kingston, U. C.), to be commanded by Governor Shirley; and a third against Crown Point, on Lake Champlain, to be led by William Johnson, the Indian commissioner. A fourth expedition had already been arranged by Governor Shirley, of Massachusetts, and Governor Lawrence, of Nova Scotia, for the purpose of driving the French Neutrals, or Acadians, out of the peninsula. It was led by General Winslow, of Boston.

The expedition against the Acadians was successful, but the cruel circumstances and the result of their expulsion justly places it among the great crimes of history. The expedition against Fort Duquesne was a disastrous failure. Braddock was defeated and mortally wounded in the battle of the Monongahela in July. Colonel Washington was the only officer of his staff who remained unhurt, and he saved the remnant of the army from annihilation by conducting a masterly retreat. The expeditions of Shirley and Johnson within the State of New York will be noticed presently.

CHAPTER XII.

While politicians of the baser sort, in and out of the New York Assembly, were playing disreputable games in which the best interests of the commonwealth were more or less involved, the people at large, alarmed by the evidences that a war was a-kindling at their very doors, became clamorous for the adoption of measures of defence against their implacable foe. Heeding these clamors, De Lancey convened the Assembly early in February (1755), and in his message to them he desired that body to make proper provisions for putting the province in a state of suitable defence, to secure Albany against the French and Indians, and to authorize the building of a strong fortification farther up the Hudson River.

The Assembly took prompt action. Utterly disregarding the royal instructions which prohibited the further issue of paper money by the colony unless authorized to do so by the crown, they ordered the emission of over $100,000 in bills of credit. They authorized the levy of eight hundred men and the impressment of artificers, prohibited the exportation of provisions to the French colonies, and provided funds for arming the troops and for making presents to the Indians to secure their co-operation.

It was at this juncture that active preparations for the expeditions against Forts Niagara and Frontenac, under Shirley, and Crown Point, under William Johnson, were begun. The call for volunteers and levies was cheerfully responded to. The troops destined for these expeditions were ordered to assemble at Albany, and were gathered there at the close of June. Those who were to follow Shirley consisted of certain regiments of regulars from New England, New York, and New Jersey, and a band of Indian auxiliaries. Those who were to follow Johnson were chiefly New England and New York militia, nearly six thousand in number. Ship-carpenters were sent to Oswego to prepare vessels to cope with the French on Lake Ontario. The first armed schooner, carrying a dozen swivel-guns, was launched there at the close of June.

Johnson's second in command was Colonel Lyman, of Connecticut,[*] who

---

[*] Phineas Lyman was born at Durham, Conn., about 1716; died in West Florida in 1775. He was a graduate of Yale College, and was a tutor there. He was first a merchant and then a lawyer in Suffield, where he was a magistrate several years. He was

bore the commission of major-general when he arrived at Albany at the middle of June. He was much superior in military ability to his chief, and should have held his place. He arranged the expedition for Johnson with skill and energy, and then, with the main body of the little army, he pressed forward during the hot days of midsummer to the "great carrying-place" between the Hudson and Lake Champlain, fifty miles from Albany. He was accompanied by three hundred Mohawk warriors under the famous Mohawk chief King Hendrick.* While waiting for the tardy Johnson to arrive with artillery and stores, Lyman caused his men to construct a strong fortification of timber and earth, which was named Fort Lyman; but Johnson afterward ungenerously changed the name to Fort Edward, that he might pay successful court to a young scion of royalty.

When Johnson arrived at Fort Edward he took command of the army. News of Braddock's defeat dispirited him, and he would have abandoned the expedition had not Lyman urged him to go forward. It was determined to proceed against Crown Point by way of Lake St. Sacrament,

---

commander-in-chief of the Connecticut forces at the breaking out of the French and Indian War, and performed admirable service at Lake George and its vicinity, as mentioned in the text. He was with Lord Howe when he was killed in 1758; was at the capture of Crown Point and Montreal, and in 1762 he led troops against Havana, Cuba. In 1763 General Lyman went to England to secure prize-money for himself and soldiers, and a grant of land near Natchez, on the Mississippi. The region was called West Florida, and there he died soon after reaching it.

* Hendrick was a famous Mohawk sachem as well as a warrior, and was sometimes called "King Hendrick." When Johnson encamped at Lake George and proposed to send out a small party to meet an approaching French force, Hendrick, who was wise and sagacious, said, "If they are to fight, they are too few; if they are to be killed, they are too many." Johnson deferred to Hendrick's judgment, and sent out twelve hundred men. Hendrick was one of the most sagacious Indian statesmen of his time, but Johnson outwitted him once. Being at Johnson Hall, Hendrick saw and coveted a richly embroidered scarlet coat. He tarried all night at the Hall. The next morning Hendrick said to Johnson, "Brother, me dream last night." "Indeed," answered Johnson. "What did my red brother dream?" "Me dream that coat be mine." "It is yours," said the shrewd Indian agent. Not long afterward Johnson visited Hendrick, and said, "Brother, I dreamed last night." "What did you dream?" asked Hendrick. "I dreamed that this tract of land was mine," describing a boundary which included nearly one hundred thousand acres of land. Hendrick was astounded, but would not be outdone in generosity. Pondering a few moments, he said, "Brother, the land is yours; but you must not dream again." The title was conferred by the British Government, and the tract was called "The Royal Grant." The portrait on page 166 is copied from a colored print made in London while Hendrick was on a visit there, about 1750. He appears in a full court dress presented to him by the king. His signature and *totem* may be seen among totemic signatures on page 6. Hendrick was born about 1680, and was killed in battle near Lake George in 1755.

which Johnson now named Lake George in honor of his king. At the head of that lake the commander established an open camp, utterly neglecting to intrench it. Suddenly scouts brought the alarming intelligence that the forest between Fort Edward and the head of Lake Champlain was swarming with French regulars, Canadian militia, and Indians. Johnson immediately sent out Colonel Ephraim Williams (September 8th, 1755) with a thousand provincials and two hundred Mohawks under Hendrick to the relief of Fort Edward. The foe had changed their destination, and were approaching Johnson's camp. The detachment fell into an ambuscade. Williams and Hendrick and many of their followers were slain. The remainder fled back to the camp hotly pursued by the victors, two thousand strong, led by General the Baron Dieskau.

KING HENDRICK.

Johnson was apprised of this disaster before the arrival of the fugitives, and hastily threw up a breastwork of trees, upon which he planted two cannons received the day before from Fort Edward. As the motley foe rushed upon the camp, discharges from these great guns terrified the Indians, and they fled to the woods. At that moment Lyman, who had hastened from Fort Edward to Johnson's relief, appeared, when the Canadian militia also fled.

Johnson had been wounded by a musket-ball in the fleshy part of the thigh at the beginning of the action, and Lyman took the command. The French regulars continued the fight for about four hours, when, their commander being fatally wounded, they also fled and hastened back to Crown Point. General Lyman had won the victory and saved the army.

Learning that the French were strengthening Crown Point, Johnson, contrary to the opinions and wishes of his officers and troops, abandoned the enterprise and lingered long in his camp—long enough to build a fort at the head of the lake, which he named William Henry. Having garrisoned it and Fort Edward, he returned to Albany with the remainder of his forces in October. He was rewarded for his services in the campaign with the honors of knighthood and $25,000 to support the dignity. This honor and emolument properly belonged to General Phineas Lyman.*

The expedition of Governor Shirley against Forts Niagara and Frontenac was unsuccessful. It was late in August before the main body of his troops were gathered at Oswego, twenty-five hundred in number. Storms on the lake, sickness in his camp, and the desertion of his Indian allies (warriors of the Six Nations) compelled Shirley to abandon the expedition. Leaving a sufficient garrison at Oswego under Colonel Mercer, the remainder of the troops were marched back to Albany and disbanded. So ended the campaign of 1755.

The home government now took up the quarrel. Great Britain declared war against France in May, 1756, and France reciprocated it by a similar declaration in June. The plan of the campaign for that year submitted by Shirley, the successor of Braddock—a splendid theorist, but with little practical knowledge of military matters—had already been adopted at a convention of colonial governors held at Albany in December, 1755. It was arranged that ten thousand men should proceed against Crown Point; six thousand against Niagara; three thousand against Fort Duquesne, and two thousand to cross the wilderness between the Kennebec and Chaudière rivers and menace Quebec by attacking the French settlers in that region of Canada.

Lord Loudoun,† a very lazy and most inefficient man, was appointed Shirley's successor as commander-in-chief of the British forces in America. He sent his lieutenant, General Abercrombie (by no means a brilliant man), to America in the spring of 1756. He arrived at New

---

* After the victory at Lake George Lyman vehemently urged Johnson to push forward immediately and take possession of Ticonderoga and Crown Point, which he might easily have done while the French were panic-stricken by their defeat. But Johnson had none of the qualities of a good general, not even sufficient moral courage, and did know how to profit by success. Shirley and others, and a council of war of his own officers, urged him to advance, but he spent weeks in his camp instead in building Fort William Henry. Jealous of General Lyman, whose superiority he felt, and with meanness only equalled by his incapacity, he did not even mention Lyman's name in his report of the battle to the Lords of Trade; and immediately after the battle he changed the name of Fort Lyman to Fort Edward, as we have observed. The influence of friends at court secured to Johnson the honors and emoluments mentioned in the text. They were unworthily bestowed upon an avaricious and immoral man and an unskilful general, while a noble, pure, and brave officer was suffered to go unnoticed either by his commander or the king whom he faithfully served. The pen of history will not neglect him.

† John Campbell, fourth Earl of Loudoun, was born in Scotland in 1705. He was appointed Governor of Virginia in 1756, but leaving the province in charge of his lieutenant, Dinwiddie, he engaged in military affairs, in which his indolence and inefficiency worked much mischief. He was recalled from the colonies in 1757, and was made lieutenant-general the next year. He was created general in 1770, and died in 1782.

York in June with some regular soldiers, and after loitering awhile near the sea he ascended the Hudson to Albany, where he found General Winslow at the head of seven thousand provincial troops. Winslow had been commissioned by Shirley to command the expedition against Crown Point. These troops were anxious to press forward, for the whole frontier of New York was menaced by the French and Indians. The enthusiasm and patriotism of the soldiers were repressed by Abercrombie, who cast a firebrand among them and the people by insisting upon the right of regular officers to command provincial officers of the same rank, and also the propriety of quartering the regular officers on the inhabitants. These assumptions, haughtily presented, caused serious disputes and mutual dislikes. Van Schaick, Mayor of Albany, disgusted with the superciliousness of the regular officers, said to them : " Go back again ; go back, for we can defend our frontiers ourselves."

But Abercrombie would not allow the troops to move either way. He kept at least ten thousand men, regulars and provincials, at Albany until near the close of summer waiting for Loudoun, when the French had gained advantages that disconcerted the whole plan of the campaign.

An energetic provincial officer—Colonel John Bradstreet—had performed a signal service in the interior with a handful of men, and rebuked his superiors by his activity. It was necessary to send provisions to the garrison at Oswego. Bradstreet was appointed to undertake the perilous task—perilous because it was known that the French and Indians were hovering around Oswego. With only two hundred provincials Bradstreet traversed the wilderness by way of the Mohawk River, Wood Creek, and Oneida Lake, and passing down the Oswego River, put into the forts at Oswego provisions for five thousand men for six months. He returned in safety after suffering incredible hardships.

The Marquis de Montcalm, a field-marshal of France, had succeeded the Baron Dieskau in command of the French troops in America. Profiting by the delays of the English at Albany, and aware of the weakness of the British commanders, Montcalm proceeded to attack the post at Oswego. He gathered five thousand Frenchmen, Canadians, and Indians at Fort Frontenac (Kingston), crossed Lake Ontario, and on August 11th appeared before Fort Ontario, on the east side of the river at Oswego, and demanded the surrender of the garrison. That fort had been built recently. Colonel Mercer, in command, refused compliance, when the French began a regular siege. An attack at midnight was bravely resisted, when Colonel Mercer spiked his guns and withdrew the garrison to an older fort (built by Governor Burnet) on the west side of the river. Montcalm brought his cannon to bear upon this fort.

Colonel Mercer was killed, and on the 14th the garrison, sixteen hundred strong, surrendered. The forts were demolished, Oswego was made desolate, and the country of the Six Nations was laid open to easy incursions by the enemy.

The sluggish Lord Loudoun had just arrived, and was temporarily alarmed. After loitering at Albany a few weeks longer, recalling troops which had been sent toward Ticonderoga, and making wicked, unjust, and ungenerous complaints against the provincials, expecting thereby to conceal his own imbecility, he dismissed them and ordered the regulars into winter quarters. He took a thousand of the latter to New York City, and haughtily demanded the billeting of their officers upon the inhabitants free of charge. The mayor, in behalf of the people, questioned the righteousness of the demand, when Loudoun, uttering a coarse oath, said:

"If you do not billet my officers upon free quarters this day I'll order all the troops in North America under my command, and billet them myself upon the city."

Loudoun's demand was sustained by an Order in Council * passed a few months before, that troops might be kept in the colonies and quartered on the people without the consent of colonial legislatures. The authorities at New York yielded to Loudoun's demand under a silent but most solemn protest. This was the earl's only victory in America. That order, virtually authorizing a standing army in the colonies to be maintained, in a great measure, by the people, was the magnetic touch that gave vitality to the sentiment of resistance which soon sounded the tocsin of revolution.

Military operations under Loudoun's command were quite as inefficient elsewhere as in the province of New York. Colonel Washington was at the head of fifteen hundred volunteers and drafted militia, and was anxious to act against Fort Duquesne; but he was made powerless by official interference and incapacity.

Loudoun called a military council at Boston in January, 1757. He proposed to confine the operations of that year to an expedition against Louisburg (which had been restored to the French by the treaty of Aix-la-Chapelle), and to a defence of the northern frontiers. The colonists of New York and New England desired to expel the French from the

---

* The British Privy Council is an assembly of advisers in matters of State appointed by the sovereign. It was first established by King Alfred in 895, and consisted of only twelve members, and was a permanent committee. Now it is composed of the chief magnates of the nation, including the ministry. A Privy Councillor must be a native of Great Britain. The authority of Parliament is delegated to this body in the regulation of public affairs. "Orders in council" have the force of constitutional commands.

region south of the St. Lawrence and to recover Oswego. They were grievously disappointed by Loudoun's perverseness; yet their ardor and patriotism were not much abated, for at the opening of summer six thousand provincials were under arms. Members of the military council had mildly remonstrated, but in vain. Loudoun was imperious, and had very little respect for the opinions of provincials; and wiser and better men than he were compelled to acquiesce.

Loudoun determined to go to Louisburg himself. After impressing into the British service four hundred men at New York, he sailed for Halifax in June, where he found himself at the head of a well-appointed army of ten thousand men and a fleet of sixteen ships of the line and several frigates. Instead of going to Cape Breton at once and attacking the strong fortress there, Loudoun employed his men in laying out a parade, planting a vegetable garden for their use, and exercising them in sham battles. So he wasted the precious summer-time. At last when, in August, he prepared to sail for Louisburg, he was informed that the garrison there had been re-enforced, and that the French had one more ship than he. Alarmed, this absurd leader, who was always in a hurry but always unready—"like St. George on a tavern sign, always on horseback but never going forward"—abandoned the enterprise and sailed for New York to hear of military disasters in that province. These will be noticed presently.

For more than a year the English in America had acted so much "like women" that the Indians were disgusted, while the activity of the French won their admiration and alliance. At the beginning of the summer of 1757 warriors from "more than thirty nations" were at Montreal. Governor Vaudreuil told them of glory and plunder surely to be obtained by alliance with the French. Montcalm danced their wild war-dances with them and sung their fierce war-songs with them until their affection for him and enthusiasm for the French cause became intense. They went in a wild, tumultuous march for St. John's, on the Sorel (the outlet of Lake Champlain), accompanied by priests who chanted hymns and anthems in almost every Indian dialect. In canoes and bateaux the French and their dusky allies went up Lake Champlain and landed at Ticonderoga in hot July. Thence Montcalm sent marauding parties almost to Fort Edward under Marin, who had destroyed the hamlet of Saratoga more than a dozen years before.

Very soon Montcalm* appeared on Lake George with eight thousand

---

* The Marquis de Montcalm was born in France in 1712, and was of noble descent. He entered the army while he was yet a lad, and soon distinguished himself. In 1756 he

men (two thousand of them Indians) and a train of artillery, and laid siege (August 2d) to Fort William Henry,* then garrisoned by less than five hundred men under Colonel Munro, supported by almost ten thousand provincials in an entrenched camp upon a gentle rocky eminence, where may now be seen the dim ruins of the citadel of Fort George. A little more than a dozen miles distant was Fort Edward, where lay the timid General Webb with about four thousand troops.

Munro was surprised. General Webb had learned from scouts of the approach of the foe, but more willing to have them fall upon Fort William Henry than upon Fort Edward, he concealed the fact from Munro. When Montcalm appeared the latter sent an express to Webb imploring succor. Not doubting it would be sent, he promptly refused compliance with Montcalm's summons to surrender the fort, and bravely sustained a siege for several days, continually expecting aid from Fort Edward in response to several expresses sent to Webb. But no succor came. Webb would not spare a man. He finally sent a letter to Munro filled with exaggerations, and advising him to surrender. The letter fell into the hands of Montcalm at a moment when he was about to abandon the siege and retire. The French leader immediately made a peremptory demand for a surrender. Despairing of succor, Munro yielded, and on the morning of August 9th (1757) the garrison marched out to the intrenched camp under a promise of protection and other honorable conditions. They were promised that they should proceed in safety to Fort Edward on parole.

Montcalm had kept intoxicating liquors from his Indians, but the English settlers supplied them with rum. After a night's carousal the barbarians, inflamed with intoxication and a desire for plunder, were ready for any mischief, and when the prisoners left the camp for Fort Edward

---

was sent to Canada, with the rank of major-general, to take the chief military command there. After serving with skill and bravery in America for about three years, he was killed in battle at Quebec in September, 1759.

* During the previous winter fifteen hundred French regulars and Canadian militia went down from the St. Lawrence to Lake George, travelling much of the way with snow-shoes, and attempted to take Fort William Henry by surprise. Their provisions were carried on small sledges drawn by dogs, and their beds were bear-skins spread on the snow. Stealthily they went over the frozen lake and appeared before the fort at midnight (March 16th, 1757). The garrison were on the alert. The invaders set fire to three vessels frozen in the ice there, a storehouse, and some huts, and escaped by the light of the conflagration. Rogers's Rangers were at the fort, and were noted for their aggressive movements that winter. One of their bravest men was Lieutenant Stark (afterward the hero of Bennington), who commanded the Rangers in the absence of Rogers. Under Stark they were often found attacking parties of the foe in the vicinity of Ticonderoga and Crown Point.

the crazed Indians, defying Montcalm's efforts to restrain them, fell upon the defenceless captives, when a fearful scene of slaughter, plunder, and devastation ensued. The fort and its appendages were laid in ruins, and for nearly one hundred years nothing marked its site but some half-concealed mounds. Now a large summer hotel stands upon its site. This sad event was the closing one of the campaign of 1757, and, happily, ended the leadership of the Earl of Loudoun on this side of the Atlantic.

Montcalm did not attempt further conquests at that time, but returned to Ticonderoga, strengthened the works there, and sent out scouting parties to annoy the British and capture their foragers. These enterprises were fruitful of exciting scenes.*

The position of affairs in America now alarmed the English people. The Americans were brave and high-spirited, and recent events had manifested strength and their ability to support themselves. With a sense of their independence of Great Britain there was danger of their alienation. Some of the royal governors were rapacious; others were incompetent; all were, as a rule, haughty in their demeanor. The arrogant assumption of superiority by the British military officers disgusted the provincial troops and often cooled the ardor of whole regiments.

Perceiving the incompetency of the government of the aristocracy, the people of Great Britain yearned for a change in the administration of public affairs. The popular will prevailed. William Pitt was called to the premiership in June, 1757. "Give me your confidence," said the great commoner to the king, "and I will deserve it." "Deserve my confidence," the king replied, "and you shall have it."

Pitt would not listen to the pernicious twaddle about enforcing royal authority in America that fell from the lips of the Lords of Trade. "We want the co-operation of the Americans," he said, "and to have it we must be just and allow them freedom." These words ran like an

---

* These scouting parties were watched by Major Rogers and his Rangers of New Hampshire. The afterward famous Israel Putnam was his lieutenant. On one occasion a party of French and Indians led by Captain Molang captured a convoy of English wagoners. Rogers and Putnam attempted to intercept the French on their return, but fell into an ambush, and Putnam and a few followers, separated from the rest, were captured. His comrades were killed and scalped, but he was reserved for torture. He passed the night bound to a tree, where his clothes were riddled with bullets by the cross firing of the combatants. He was taken deeper into the forest, fast bound to a tree, and a fire was built around him, when a sudden thunder-shower nearly extinguished the flames. They soon began to blaze fiercely again, when Molang, who had heard of these proceedings, rushed through the band of Indians, released Putnam, and carried him to Ticonderoga.

electric thrill through the hearts of the colonists, and men and money were freely offered for the cause. The French in Canada were growing weaker, for they received scanty aid from France. "The king relies on your zeal and obstinacy of courage," wrote the French Minister to Montcalm in 1758. "Without unexpected good fortune or blunders on the part of the English," the candid general replied, "Canada must be lost this campaign, or certainly the next."

Pitt soon diffused his own energy and wisdom into every department of the government. He did not *demand* anything of the colonies, but *asked* them to raise and clothe twenty thousand men, promising them, in the name of Parliament, to furnish arms, tents, and provisions for such levies, and also to reimburse the several colonies all the money they should expend in raising and clothing these troops. A large naval armament for American waters was placed under the command of Admiral Boscawen, and twelve thousand British troops were allotted for service in America. This liberal policy had a magical effect. New England alone raised fifteen thousand of the required levies; New York furnished about three thousand; New Jersey, one thousand; Pennsylvania, three thousand, and Virginia two thousand.

The scheme for the campaign of 1758 was extensive in its intended operations. Shirley's plan of 1756 was revived and its general outlines were adopted. The chief points of assault were designated—Louisburg, Ticonderoga, and Duquesne. Twelve thousand men under General Amherst were to attack Louisburg, and possibly Quebec. Another army was to be led from Albany by Abercrombie and young Lord Howe to attack Ticonderoga, and General Joseph Forbes was appointed to lead another army over the Alleghany Mountains to attack Fort Duquesne.

Louisburg received the first blow. Boscawen with forty armed vessels, bearing Amherst with a land force of twelve thousand men, and having General Wolfe as his lieutenant, left Halifax at near the close of May, and on June 8th the troops landed near Louisburg. The French, after a vigorous resistance of about fifty days, surrendered the fort and city and the islands of Cape Breton and Prince Edward to the British. When Louisburg fell the French dominion in America began to wane, and from that time its decline was rapid.

While Amherst and Wolfe were conquering in the east, Abercrombie and young Lord Howe were leading seven thousand regulars, nine thousand provincials, and a large train of artillery against Ticonderoga, then occupied by Montcalm with about four thousand soldiers. Howe was "the soul of the expedition." He was a "Lycurgus of the camp," introducing stern rules and radical reforms, and adapting everything to the absolute needs of the service.

Through the activity of Colonel John Bradstreet,* ably assisted by Major Philip Schuyler, bateaux for carrying troops over Lake George were ready by the time the necessary stores arrived from England, and before the end of June Howe led the first division of the troops to the head of the lake. Abercrombie arrived there with the remainder at the beginning of July. The provincial troops were chiefly from New England and New York. Among the officers were Captains Stark, of New Hampshire, and Putnam, of Connecticut.

The whole armament went down the lake on a beautiful Sabbath afternoon (July 5th, 1758), led by Lord Howe in a large boat, and landed at

SIGNATURE OF JOHN BRADSTREET.

dawn the next morning at its northern extremity between four and five miles from Fort Ticonderoga. The occupants of a French outpost there fled. The first intimation they had of the proximity of an enemy was the blaze of the scarlet uniforms of the British in the morning sun.

The country between the lake and Ticonderoga was covered with a dense forest and tangled morasses. The British immediately pressed forward, Lord Howe leading the advanced guard. Following incompetent guides, they became bewildered, and while in that condition they suddenly encountered a French scouting party. A sharp skirmish ensued, and the French troops were defeated; but Lord Howe was slain in the first fire. He was pierced by a bullet and expired immediately.

---

* John Bradstreet was born in 1711; died in the city of New York September 25th, 1774. He was a lieutenant-colonel of Pepperell's provincial regiment at the siege of Louisburg in 1745, and in the autumn was commissioned captain in a regular regiment. In 1746 he was appointed Lieutenant-Governor of St. John's, Newfoundland. He was General Shirley's adjutant at Oswego in 1755, and in 1756 conveyed supplies to that post through great perils. He was quartermaster-general of the provincial forces under General Abercrombie, and after the repulse at Ticonderoga led a successful expedition against Fort Frontenac. He was an efficient officer under Amherst in 1759, was commissioned colonel in 1762, major-general in 1764, and commanded an expedition against the Western Indians, and negotiated a treaty of peace.

His followers, dismayed, retreated in wild confusion to the landing-place and bivouacked for the night.*

Abercrombie advanced about half way to Ticonderoga the next day, and sent his chief engineer, with some rangers under Captain Stark, to reconnoitre the French works. The engineer reported the works very weak. Stark, instructed by his practised eye, declared they were very strong. Abercrombie, with his usual contempt for provincials, rejected Stark's testimony, and on the morning of the 8th, having been joined by Sir William Johnson with more than four hundred Indians, he ordered his men forward to scale the breastworks of the French lines, while he, like a coward, remained behind.

LORD HOWE.

The assailants soon found that Stark was right. The breastworks were strong, and after a most sanguinary struggle for about four hours the British were repulsed with fearful loss. They fled with precipitation back to Lake George, leaving almost two thousand of their comrades dead or wounded in the forest. Abercrombie had preceded them in their flight, in "extremest fright;" and all hurried to their old camp at the head of the lake. Abercrombie felt safer when he had put that little sea, thirty-eight miles in length, between himself and Montcalm.

Colonel Bradstreet, burning with indignation because of the shameful defeat, urged upon a council of war held at the head of the lake the importance of capturing Fort Frontenac, and offered to lead an expedition against it. After much hesitation Abercrombie commissioned him to undertake the enterprise with three thousand men. Bradstreet hastened with them to Albany, where he was joined by Major Philip

---

* George, Lord-Viscount Howe, was the eldest son of Sir E. Scrope, second Viscount Howe of Ireland. He commanded five thousand British troops who arrived at Halifax in 1757, and the next year, as we have observed in the text, he accompanied Abercrombie on his expedition against Ticonderoga. He was the idol of his soldiers. Mante observes: "With him the soul of the army seemed to expire." He was thirty-four years of age at his death. The General Court of Massachusetts Bay appropriated $1250 for the erection of a monument to his memory in Westminster Abbey.

Schuyler, and then "almost flew" up the valley of the Mohawk and on to Oswego. Schuyler and some men had reached that post earlier and prepared vessels wherewith to cross the lake with men, cannons, and stores. The expedition landed near Frontenac on the evening of August 25th. The French were taken completely by surprise. The fort mounted sixty cannons, but the garrison was very small. The commander sent to Montreal for aid, but before it could reach him he was compelled to surrender the fort and its dependencies, with immense spoil, particularly in stores destined for Fort Duquesne; also nine armed vessels carrying from eight to eighteen guns each.

The capture of Frontenac, the result of a brilliant expedition, was one of the most important events of the war. It facilitated the fall of Duquesne, discouraged the French, gave joy to the English, and reflected honor on the provincials. It raised a cry for peace throughout Canada, the resources of which were almost exhausted. "I am not discouraged," wrote Montcalm, in evident disappointment, "nor are my troops. We are resolved to find our graves under the ruins of the colony." *

COLONEL GEORGE WASHINGTON.†

The expedition against Fort Duquesne, led by General Forbes, was finally successful in spite of him. He set out with about six thousand men in July. He was a Scotchman and a "regular" British officer; perverse in will and judgment, and indecisive in action. Sickness and inefficiency and a persistence in constructing a new military road over the mountains pro-

---

* Bradstreet lost only four or five men before the capture of Frontenac. Then a fearful sickness—dysentery—broke out among his troops, and five hundred of them were swept away. With the remainder he slowly retraced his steps, and on the Mohawk River, at the site of the (present) village of Rome, his troops assisted in building Fort Stanwix under the direction of General Stanwix.

† The pen-and-ink sketch above given was made from a photograph of the original study made by Charles Willson Peale for his three-quarter length portrait of Washington in the uniform of a Virginia colonel. It was made at Mount Vernon in 1772, when Colonel Washington was forty years of age.

duced such almost interminable delays that on November 1st the army was fifty miles from Fort Duquesne. At length the impatient Colonel Washington was sent forward with a detachment of Virginians, and very soon accomplished the object of the expedition. Indian scouts employed by the French discovered Washington's approach, and their report so greatly exaggerated the number of his men that the frightened garrison, five hundred strong, set fire to the fort in the evening (November 24th, 1758) and fled in confusion down the Ohio in boats by the light of the flames, leaving everything behind them. The Virginians took possession of the fort the next day, and the name of Fort Duquesne was changed to Fort Pitt in honor of the British Prime-Minister.

With the close of this expedition ended the campaign of 1758. It had, on the whole, resulted favorably to Great Britain, and Pitt made vast preparations for the campaign of the next year. The attachment of some of the Indian allies of the French had been much weakened, and at a great council held at Easton, in Pennsylvania, in the summer of 1758, six tribes had, with the Six Nations, made treaties of friendship and neutrality with the English.

CHAPTER XIII.

The final struggle between the French and English for mastery in North America was now at hand. Pitt, with wonderful sagacity and with as wonderful knowledge of the theatre of conflict in America, conceived a magnificent plan for the conquest of Canada and the destruction, at one blow, of the French dominion beyond the Atlantic. That dominion now did not really extend beyond the region of the St. Lawrence, for the settlements or stations in the far west and south were like distant, isolated, and weak colonies cut off from the parent country. The French in America were then comparatively few in number and weak in supplies of every kind. Montcalm was then chief military commander; but in all Canada he could not muster seven thousand men into active service, and very few Indians.

Pitt had the rare good fortune to possess the confidence of Parliament and the English-American colonies. The former were dazzled by his greatness, the latter were impressed with his justice. He had promptly reimbursed the expenses of the colonists in raising and clothing troops, a sum amounting to at least $1,000,000; and they cordially seconded his scheme of conquest, which had been communicated to their chief men under an oath of secrecy. The Parliament voted $60,000,000 for the American service, and forces by land and sea such as had never before been known in England. "This is Pitt's work," said the Earl of Chesterfield, "and it is marvellous in our eyes!" The inefficient Abercrombie was superseded in the chief command in America by Sir Jeffrey Amherst,[*] with General James Wolfe as his lieutenant.

The plan of operations was simple. General Wolfe, with a strong

---

[*] Sir Jeffrey Amherst was born in Kent, England, January 29th, 1717; died August 3d, 1797. He entered the royal army as ensign in 1731, and was aide to Lord Ligonier and the Duke of Cumberland. He was promoted to major-general in 1756, and was in chief command of the English forces sent against Louisburg in 1758. In September that year he was appointed commander-in-chief of the British forces in America, and led the troops that drove the French from Lake Champlain in 1759. The next year he captured Montreal and completed the conquest of Canada. For these acts he was rewarded with thanks and knighthood. In 1763 he was appointed Governor of Virginia. In 1771 he was Governor of Guernsey, and was created a baron in 1776. He was commander-in-chief of the British forces from 1778 until 1795, and was created a field marshal in 1796.

land force and a well-manned fleet under Admiral Saunders, was to ascend the St. Lawrence River and attack Quebec. Another force under General Amherst was to drive the French from Lake Champlain, seize Montreal, and join Wolfe at Quebec; while a third expedition, led by General Prideaux, was to attempt the capture of Fort Niagara, and, if successful, to go down Lake Ontario and the St. Lawrence to Montreal.

When, at the close of summer (1758), Amherst, at Cape Breton, heard of the disaster at Ticonderoga he sailed for Boston with four regiments and a battalion, and made a forced march across New England to Albany to re-enforce the defeated Abercrombie. He arrived at Lake George early in October, but too late for further action in the field that season.

SIR JEFFREY AMHERST.

He went to New York, and in November he received his commission as commander-in-chief. He spent the winter in New York City making preparations for the next campaign. In the spring he made his head-quarters at Albany; appointed Colonel Bradstreet quartermaster-general of his army; collected his forces, and at the close of May found himself at the head of twelve thousand men, chiefly of New York and New England. The Assembly of New York had authorized the emission of half a million dollars in bills of credit, and a loan to the crown of a large sum, to be reimbursed before the close of the year.

Prideaux collected his forces, chiefly provincials, at Oswego. From that point, accompanied by Sir William Johnson and some Mohawks, he sailed for Niagara, and landed there without much opposition on July 15th. A siege was immediately begun, and on the same day Prideaux was killed by the bursting of one of his cannons, when Johnson assumed the chief command. He demanded the surrender of the fort. The commander was in hourly expectation of re-enforcements and refused compliance, and for several days the garrison made a brave resistance.

On the 24th about fifteen hundred French regulars and many Creek and Cherokee warriors, drawn from Detroit and elsewhere, appeared, commanded by Colonel D'Aubrey, when a sharp battle ensued. The

French and their allies were soon effectually routed and dispersed. The next day (July 25th) the fort and its dependencies were surrendered to the British. The French dominion in that region was fairly annihilated, and the connecting link of military power between Canada and Louisiana was broken never to be restored. Lieutenant-Governor De Lancey wrote to the Lords of Trade : " His Majesty is now in possession of the most important pass in all the Indian countries."

Johnson was so encumbered with prisoners that he could not provide a sufficiency of vessels to convey him and his troops, with the captives, to Montreal, so he garrisoned Fort Niagara and returned to Albany.

Late in June Amherst was at the head of Lake George with about twelve thousand troops, regulars and provincials in equal numbers ; and on July 22d he appeared before the lines at Ticonderoga with about eleven thousand men. The French, conscious of their own weakness and peril, fled down the lake to Crown Point, and almost immediately abandoned that post also and took a longer flight, halting at Isle aux Noix, at the foot of the lake, or rather in the Sorel River, its outlet. Amherst took possession of Crown Point without opposition, and was about to follow the French with a detachment of his army, when he was informed that the allies were three thousand strong and that the lake was guarded by four vessels carrying heavy guns numerously manned, under the command of a skilful French naval officer.

Amherst paused, and ordered the construction of several vessels of war at Crown Point. Upon these he embarked his whole army at the middle of October, for the purpose of driving the French beyond the St. Lawrence. Heavy tempests drove him back to Crown Point, where he went into winter quarters, and then set his troops at work in the construction of a strong and costly fort, the picturesque ruins of which are seen by tourists on Lake Champlain. The fort and its appurtenances cost the British Government several million dollars. It remained in their possession until 1775.

Meanwhile a more successful expedition was consummated. The fleet of Admiral Saunders, consisting of twenty-two line-of-battle ships, many frigates and smaller vessels, bore General Wolfe and eight thousand troops up the St. Lawrence River in June (1759). These landed on the Island of Orleans, a few miles below Quebec, on the 27th.

Quebec, then as now, consisted of an Upper and Lower Town, the former being surrounded by a strongly fortified wall pierced by five gates. An elevated plateau three hundred feet above the river and extending from the rear of the city some distance up the St. Lawrence is called the Plains of Abraham, a locality made famous in history by the events of this expedition. At the junction of the St. Charles River with the St. Lawrence, at the foot of the rocky promontory on which lies the Upper Town, the French had armed vessels and floating batteries. The city was strongly garrisoned by French regulars, and along the river from Quebec to the Montmorenci River, a distance of seven miles, lay the army of Montcalm, consisting chiefly of Canadians and Indians, in an intrenched camp.*

With amazing skill and vigor Wolfe prepared for the siege of Quebec. He took possession of Point Levi, nearly opposite the city, a mile distant, on July 30th, where he erected batteries and whence he hurled blazing bombshells upon the Lower Town, setting on fire fifty houses in one night. The citadel was beyond their reach. The French sent down fire-rafts to burn the British fleet anchored below, but without success.

Wolfe, eager to gain a victory speedily, had landed a large force (July 10th, 1759) under Generals Townshend and Murray below the Montmorenci, and formed a camp there. Wolfe was in possession of the river, but the large fleet could do little more than reconnoitre, transport troops, and guard the channels. It seemed impossible to force a passage across the Montmorenci above the cataract. The only way was to cross it at its mouth at low tide.

Finally, at near the close of July, General Monckton, with grenadiers and other troops, was sent over from Point Levi, and landed on the beach above the mouth of the Montmorenci. Without waiting for troops from the British camp below to join him, Monckton, with his grenadiers, rushed up the steep acclivity to attack Montcalm's lines, when they were driven back to the beach, while a fierce thunder-storm was raging. Darkness came on. The roar of the rising tide admonished them to take to their boats, which they did, but with a loss of nearly five hundred of their comrades, who had perished.

Wolfe sent Murray above the town with twelve hundred men to destroy French ships there, and to open the way for Amherst. But alas! Amherst did not come. Murray heard of the fall of Fort Niagara and of the expedition of the French from Lake Champlain, but received no direct tidings from Amherst.

Two months had passed away since the landing on Orleans, and yet no important advance had been made. In vain Wolfe listened for the drums of Amherst. Not even a message came from him, for reasons already given. Exposure, anxiety, and fatigue prostrated the commander

---

* Montcalm had his headquarters in a stone building not far from Beauport Mills. It commanded a view of Quebec and its immediate vicinity.

early in September. He called a council of war at his bedside, when it was determined to scale the Heights of Abraham and assail the city in the rear. Feeble as he was, Wolfe resolved to lead the attack in person. The camp at the Montmorenci was broken up (September 8th), and the attention of Montcalm was diverted from the real designs of the British by seeming preparations to attack his lines. The affair was managed so secretly and skilfully that even De Bougainville, a French officer with fifteen hundred men who had been sent up the river to watch the movements of the British, did not suspect their design.

On the evening of the 12th the whole army destined for the assault moved up the river from Point Levi in transports, several leagues above the chosen landing-place. At midnight they left the ships, and embarking in flat-boats, floated noiselessly down the stream with the ebbing tide.* Black clouds obscured the sky, but the voyagers reached their destination in good order, and landed without being discovered. The place where they disembarked is still known as Wolfe's Cove. They at once clambered up the tangled ravine that led to the Plains of Abraham, and at dawn on the 13th about five thousand British troops stood upon the heights, a fearful apparition to the French sentinels and the sergeants' guard at the brow of the acclivity, who, in hot haste, carried the alarming news first to the garrison in Quebec and then to Montcalm at Beauport, beyond the St. Charles River. "It can only be a small party come to burn a few houses and return," said the incredulous commander.

Montcalm was soon undeceived. He immediately sent orders for De Levi and De Bougainville to return with their troops. Abandoning his intrenchments, he led a greater portion of his army across the St. Charles, and at ten o'clock in the morning they stood in battle array on the Plains

---

* Wolfe appeared to be in good spirits, yet there was evidently a brooding shadow of a presentiment of evil. At the evening mess he sang the little campaign song beginning,

"Why, soldiers, why
Should we be melancholy boys?
Why, soldiers, why,
Whose business 'tis to die," etc.

And as he sat among his officers and floated softly down the river in the gloom, he repeated, in his musing tones, that stanza from Gray's "Elegy in a Country Churchyard"—

"The boast of heraldry, the pomp of power,
And all that beauty, all that wealth e'er gave,
Await alike th' inevitable hour—
The path of glory leads but to the grave."

At the close he said, "Now, gentlemen, I would prefer being the author of that poem to the glory of beating the French to-morrow."

of Abraham, near the town. Both parties lacked heavy guns. The French had three field-pieces, the English only one — a light six-pounder which some sailors had dragged up the ravine. The two commanders, at the head of their respective troops, faced each other.

A general, fierce, and sanguinary battle now ensued. The British muskets were double-shotted, and the soldiers reserved their fire until within forty yards of their foes, when they poured upon the French such destructive volleys that the latter were thrown into utter confusion. The terrible English bayonet completed the work and secured the victory. Wolfe and Montcalm had both been mortally wounded. Wolfe, leaning on the shoulder of an officer, was borne to the rear. His ear caught the exclamation, "See! they run! they run!"

"Who runs?" asked the dying hero in a whisper.

"The enemy, sir; they give way everywhere!" was the reply. Wolfe then gave an order to cut off their retreat, and then said, in an almost inaudible whisper:

"Now, God be praised, I die happy!" and expired.

Montcalm's surgeon said to his wounded general, "Death is certain."

"I am glad of it," said the marquis. "How long have I to live?"

"Ten or twelve hours; perhaps less."

"So much the better; I shall not live to see the surrender of Quebec!"

About seventy years after this event an English governor of Canada caused a modest granite column to be erected on the spot where Wolfe fell, with the inscription, "Here died Wolfe, victorious September 13th, 1759." In its place now stands a beautiful Doric column of granite dedicated to the memory of both Wolfe and Montcalm. It also bears the former inscription. It was erected by the British army in Canada in 1849.

General Townshend assumed the command of the British army, and five days after the battle he received the formal surrender of the city of Quebec. The remainder of Montcalm's army, under De Levi, fled to Montreal. So, brilliantly for the English, ended the campaign of 1759. Yet Canada was not conquered. Five thousand troops under General Murray took possession of the great prize. The fleet, with French prisoners, sailed for Halifax.

The final struggle for the mastery in Canada was begun early in the spring of 1760, when Vaudreuil, the governor-general, sent De Levi, with ten thousand regulars, Canadians, and Indians in six frigates to attempt the recovery of Quebec. De Levi appeared before the city at the close of March, when the brave Murray went out with his whole force—less than three thousand—to attack him. At Sillery, three miles above Quebec, one of the most sanguinary battles of the war was fought.

Murray was defeated. He lost all his artillery and a thousand men, but managed to get back into the city with the remainder. De Levi then began a siege, and Murray's condition was becoming desperate when a British squadron, with re-enforcements and supplies, appeared. Supposing it to be the whole British fleet, De Levi withdrew and fled to Montreal, after losing most of his shipping. Vaudreuil gathered all his forces at Montreal, the last stronghold of French dominion in America. Amherst spent the whole summer in preparations for an attack upon that city. His movements were slow but sure. With almost ten thousand men and one thousand Indians under Sir William Johnson he proceeded to Oswego, crossed Lake Ontario, went down the St. Lawrence, and appeared before Montreal on September 6th. He had captured Fort Presentation, at the mouth of the Oswegatchie River (now Ogdensburg), on his way. Murray arrived from Quebec at noon the same day with four thousand troops, and before night Colonel Haviland, who had proceeded from Crown Point and had driven the French from Isle aux Noix, arrived there with three thousand men.

Surrounded by almost seventeen thousand foes, Vaudreuil at once capitulated, and on the 8th Montreal and all Canada passed into the possession of the British crown. General Gage was appointed governor-general at Montreal, and Murray, with his four thousand troops, garrisoned Quebec. Fort Detroit was yet in possession of the French. Major Robert Rogers* was sent with some rangers

---

* Robert Rogers, a famous partisan soldier in the French and Indian War, was born at Dumbarton, N. H., about 1730, and died in England in 1780. His father was from Ireland, and an early settler of Dumbarton. Robert was in command of a corps of rangers during the French and Indian War, and did gallant service. In 1758 he fought a bloody battle with the French and their Indian allies in Northern New York. He had 170 men; the French, 700, including 600 Indians. After losing 150 men he retreated, leaving 150 of his enemies dead on the field. In 1759 General Amherst sent him to destroy the Indian village of St. Francis, which he did, killing 200 of the barbarians. In 1760 he was sent to take possession of Detroit and other Western forts ceded to Great Britain. It was done. Then he went to England, and in 1765 was appointed governor of Mackinaw. Accused of treasonable designs, he was sent to Montreal in irons, tried by a court-martial, and was acquitted. In 1769 he again went to England, and was graciously received by the king. Becoming financially embarrassed, he went to Algiers, where he fought two battles for the Dey. He returned to America, and at the opening of the war for independence his course was so suspicious that he was arrested by order of Congress, and released on parole. In 1776 Washington, suspecting him of being a spy, arrested him. Congress soon released him, when he openly took up arms for the crown, and raised a corp of Loyalists, which he called the "Queen's Rangers." He soon went to England, leaving them in command of Lieutenant-Colonel Simcoe, under whom they became a famous partisan corps. In 1776 Major Rogers published, in London, "Journals of the French War."

to take possession of it, which was accomplished at the close of November.

This conquest and the treaty signed at Paris early in 1763 deprived France of all her territorial possessions in North America. Great Britain soon became the sole possessor of the Continent from the Gulf of Mexico to the Arctic seas and from ocean to ocean, but at a cost during her several struggles of fully $500,000,000 and many thousand precious lives.

During many long and gloomy years the colonists had struggled up, unaided and alone, from feebleness to strength. They had erected forts, raised armies, and fought battles cheerfully for England's glory and their own preservation without England's aid and often without her sympathy.* During the French and Indian War, the turmoil of which in America was now ended, did they cheerfully tax themselves and contribute men, money, and provisions. They lost during that war 25,000 robust men on land, and many seamen. That war cost the colonists, in the aggregate, fully $20,000,000, besides the flower of their youths; and in return Parliament granted them, at different times during the contest, only about $5,500,000. And yet the British Ministry, in 1760, while the colonists were so generously supporting the power and dignity of the realm, regarded them as mere servile subjects to the king, and imposed a tax upon them to replenish the exhausted British Treasury.

MAJOR ROBERT ROGERS.
(From a print published in London in 1776.)

A dangerous movement, known as "Pontiac's Conspiracy," immediately followed the war—a conspiracy planned by Pontiac, a powerful,

---

* When, on the floor of the British House of Commons, Charles Townshend, speaking of the English-American colonists, said : "They have been planted by our care, nourished by our indulgence, and protected by our arms," Colonel Barré retorted : "No ; *your oppression* planted them in America ; they grew by *your neglect* ; and they have nobly taken up arms in *your defence*."

sagacious, and ambitious Ottowa chief, who succeeded in confederating several Algonquin tribes for the purpose of crushing the newly-acquired British power westward of the Niagara River.* It was an echo of the French and Indian War. It was ripe before its growth was even suspected. Within a fortnight, in the summer of 1763, all military posts in possession of the British west of Oswego to Lake Michigan fell into the possession of Pontiac by treachery or surprise, excepting Forts Niagara, Pitt, and Detroit. The conspiracy was soon subdued, and the power of the hostile tribes was broken. Pontiac would not yield, but took refuge in the country of the Illinois, where he was treacherously murdered by one of his own race.

Lieutenant-Governor De Lancey managed the civil affairs of the province of New York with wisdom and energy from the death of Sir Danvers Osborne, in 1753, until his own sudden death from apoplexy in the summer of 1760,† a period of about seven years. As we have observed, Sir Charles Hardy, a naval officer, came to New York as governor in 1755, but, more incompetent than Clinton as a civil ruler, he was completely dominated by De Lancey. He received his salary, and allowed the lieutenant-governor to hold the helm of the ship of State. Sir Charles left the province in the summer of 1757, when he hoisted his flag over a naval vessel in the harbor of New York as Rear-Admiral of the Blue, and took command in the expedition against Louisburg. He never returned to the executive chair.

During the administration of De Lancey important social movements had occurred in the city of New York. Allusion has been made to the

---

* In April, 1763, Pontiac called a council near Detroit of representatives of many North-Western tribes, and the Senecas of Western New York. That council presented a gay scene. The chiefs were attended by their families, dressed in their gaudiest apparel. They gathered in groups to feast, smoke, gamble, and tell stories; many of them were bedizened with feathers, beads, and other tokens of pride—"young maidens," says Parkman, "radiant with bear's oil and ruddy with vermilion, and versed in all the arts of forest coquetry." The grave men were seated on the ground in council in consecutive rows, and after the pipe had gone round from hand to hand, Pontiac, painted and plumed, arose and delivered an impassioned speech. He displayed in one hand a broad belt of wampum, and assured his hearers that it came from the French, who would soon come with ships and armies to reconquer Canada.

† De Lancey was found by one of his children, on the morning of July 30th, 1760, dying, in his chair, in his study, in which he had probably sat all night, as he frequently did, on account of chronic asthma. He had dined the day before, with a number of leading men of the province, on Staten Island, where he indulged, as was common on such occasions, in excessive eating and drinking. He returned to his home in the Bowery in the evening and retired to his study, from which he never emerged alive. There was an ostentatious funeral. His body was buried beneath the middle aisle of Trinity Church, the Rev. Mr. Barclay conducting the funeral services.

neglect of intellectual cultivation in the province. Leading men had long deplored this state of things, and perceived the danger to society which might be evolved by such neglect as population and wealth increased. Finally, in 1754, Dr. Cadwallader Colden,* James de Lancey, Philip Livingston, Peter Schuyler, Abraham de Peyster, Frederick Philipse, William Smith, and others founded the New York Society Library, now one of the noblest of the literary institutions of the city. A neglected germ of such an institution had existed about fifty years. The chaplain of Governor Bellomont (Jacob Sharp) gave to the city, in 1700, a collection of books to which was afterward added many more by the Rev. John Millington, of England. It formed the Corporation Library; but the books were neglected and nearly forgotten. When the Society Library was formed, these books were added to it.

CADWALLADER COLDEN.

At the same period an effectual movement was made for the foundation of a college in the city of New York. There were then few collegians in the province. For many years Mr. De Lancey and William Smith, the elder, were the only "academics," excepting those in holy orders; and at the time in question there were only thirteen others, the youngest of whom had his

SIGNATURE OF CADWALLADER COLDEN.

---

* Cadwallader Colden was a physician and a native of Scotland, where he was born in 1688. He emigrated to Pennsylvania in 1708, returned to Scotland, and came back to America in 1716. Two years later he made the province of New York his residence at the request of Governor Hunter, and was appointed surveyor-general of the colony. In 1720 he became a member of Governor Burnet's Council, and made his residence in Orange County. He became lieutenant-governor of the province in 1761, which position he occupied during the remainder of his life. He died on Long Island in 1776. Throughout the troublous times preceding the Revolution, he managed public affairs with great sagacity.

bachelor's degree at the age of seventeen.* In 1746 the Assembly authorized a lottery to raise funds for the establishment of a college. Nearly $6000 were thus raised. It was increased in 1754, and King's (now Columbia) College was founded and chartered.

At that time sectarianism was rampant in the province, and there was a bitter strife between the Episcopalians, or those of the Church of England, and the Presbyterians, for the control of the college. The aristocracy were generally members of the Episcopal Church, and in the contest for the control of the college they were victorious. Trinity Church offered a site for the college building on the condition that the president should always be an Episcopalian, and that the prayers of the Church should always be used in it. Governor De Lancey gave it a charter on these conditions in 1754, but there was a liberal distribution of the trusteeship among other denominations. Rev. William Samuel Johnson, D.D., was appointed the first president.†

New York City at that time had a population of about fourteen thousand, and contained an Episcopal, a Presbyterian, and a French church, two German Lutheran churches, a Quaker and an Anabaptist meetinghouse, a Jewish synagogue, and a Moravian congregation. The Jews were disfranchised, and the Moravians were persecuted as Jesuits in disguise.

The sectarian controversy at that time was a consequence of a discovered scheme of Dr. Secker, Archbishop of Canterbury, for the establishment of Episcopacy in the colonies, largely for the purpose of curbing the Puritan spirit in political and religious affairs. The throne and the hierarchy were, in a sense, mutually dependent, and Dr. Secker's proposition was warmly supported by the British Cabinet. It was as warmly opposed by the Dissenters and all independent thinkers in the colonies.

---

* These collegians were Peter van Brugh Livingston, John Livingston, Philip Livingston, William Livingston, William Nicoll, Benjamin Nicoll, Henry Hansen, William Peartree Smith, Benjamin Woolsey, William Smith, Jr. (the historian), John McEvers, and John van Horner.

† William Samuel Johnson, D.D., was born in Guilford, Conn., in 1696, and was sixty years of age when he became president of King's College. He was a graduate of Yale in 1714, and was a tutor there for a while. In 1720 he became a preacher at West Haven, and went to England in 1722 to receive Episcopal ordination. He returned in 1723 with the honor of the degree of M.A., conferred at Oxford. He settled in Stratford, but was persecuted by the other sects there. He left the place, and was absent several years; engaged much in literary pursuits, preparing, among other useful works, a *System of Morality*, which Dr. Franklin published as a text-book for the University of Pennsylvania. Dr. Johnson was a man of great learning. He resigned in 1763, and returned to Stratford the same year. There, resuming the charge of his old parish, he lived until his death in January, 1772.

The latter regarded the scheme as a weapon of contemplated tyranny. Then was kindled the flame of desire in the hearts of a vast number of English-Americans to have

> " A Church without a Bishop,
> A Throne without a King,"

which burned so fiercely a few years later.*

Dr. Colden, the President of the Council, and then seventy-three years of age, became acting governor on the death of De Lancey, and soon received the appointment of lieutenant-governor. He was continued in that office about sixteen years, and, in consequence of the frequent absence of the governors, was repeatedly at the head of public affairs.

On the death of De Lancey the office of chief-justice became vacant. Colden was urged to appoint an incumbent at once. Wishing to compliment the Earl of Halifax, the Secretary of State for the colonies, Colden asked him to nominate a candidate for chief-justice. To the amazement and indignation of the New York Assembly and the people, instead of a *nomination* there came an *appointment* to the office by the king of a Boston lawyer named Pratt. He was not appointed, as formerly, to hold the office " during good behavior," but " at the pleasure of the king." This was one of the first of the arbitrary acts of young George III., who had just ascended the throne, which drove the colonies to rebellion. Indeed, the New York Assembly rebelled at that time. They resolved that while judges held office by such a tenure, and were mere instruments of the royal will, they would grant them no salaries. Colden found himself in trouble at the very beginning.

The authorities of New York had a long and serious quarrel with the inhabitants of the territory of the (present) State of Vermont at this period. After the settlement of the boundary-line between New York and Connecticut mentioned in a former chapter, the boundary between New York and Massachusetts was tacitly fixed on a line parallel to that of the former, and permanently so in 1764. Governor Benning Wentworth assumed that a line parallel to that of the western boundary of Connecticut was the true boundary of his own province. Having

---

* The chief controversialist on the side of the Dissenters was William Livingston, afterward Governor of New Jersey, and then a young lawyer of much repute. He dealt heavy blows against Episcopacy and in favor of Presbyterianism in a weekly publication called the *Independent Reflector*, first issued late in 1752. He began his assaults on Episcopacy in 1753 behind the veil of anonymity. His language was bold and defiant, but dignified and unexceptionable. The influence of the civil authority, the Episcopal clergy, and the aristocracy at length induced the printer to cease printing the *Reflector*, and with its fifty-second number (November, 1753) it was discontinued.

authority to issue grants of unoccupied lands within his province, he gave many patents to settlers west of the Connecticut River.

The New York authorities, who had acquiesced in the boundaries of Connecticut and Massachusetts, now claimed territorial jurisdiction north of Massachusetts, eastward to the Connecticut River, by virtue of the original grant given to the Duke of York. Regardless of this claim, Wentworth issued a patent for a township six miles square, which was named Bennington. This brought the question of jurisdiction to an issue. New York vehemently asserted its claim; Wentworth paid no attention to it; and when the French and Indian War broke out, he had issued patents for fourteen townships west of the Connecticut River.

The dispute was renewed after the war, and when, in 1763, Lieutenant-Governor Colden sent a proclamation among the people in that region declaring the Connecticut River to be the eastern boundary of the province of New York, Wentworth had created one hundred and thirty-eight townships the size of Bennington west of the Connecticut. They occupied a greater portion of the area of the (present) State of Vermont, and were called "The New Hampshire Grants" from that time.

The authorities of New York, inspired by grasping land speculators, not content with asserting territorial jurisdiction, claimed the right of property in the soil of that territory, and declared Wentworth's patents to settlers invalid. The crown confirmed these claims, and orders were issued for the survey and sale of farms in the possession of settlers who had paid for and improved them. This act of oppression was like sowing dragons' teeth to see them produce a crop of armed men. The settlers cared not who were their political masters so long as their private rights were respected. But this act of injustice converted them into rebellious foes, determined and defiant. There appeared at once an opposition not only of words, but of sinews and muskets, supported by indomitable courage and inflexible wills—the spirit of true English liberty coming down to them through their Puritan ancestors. Foremost among those who took a firm stand in opposition to the oppressors was Ethan Allen, the boldest of the bold.

Finally the governor and Council of New York summoned all the claimants under the grants of New Hampshire to appear before them at Albany, with their deeds, on a certain day. No attention was paid to the summons. Writs were issued for the ejectment of the settlers from their estates, and surveyors were sent to resurvey the lands. This movement brought on a crisis, and for several years the New Hampshire grants formed a theatre where all the elements of civil war excepting actual carnage were in exercise. Magistrates, police, and armed citizens were constantly vigilant, and when an officer of the Government or of the land speculators of New York appeared he was seized and punished by whipping or other severity, and was driven out of the domain. No legal process could be served, nor the sentence of any court established there by New York be carried out. The settlers effectively spurned the bribes and the threats of the New Yorkers.

The settlers sent an agent to London to lay their case before the crown. He returned in 1767 with a royal order directing the government of New York to suspend all proceedings against the people of the "Grants;" but very little attention was paid to the royal mandate. In 1770 the settlers appointed a Committee of Safety to manage public affairs. They commissioned Ethan Allen colonel commandant, and in 1771 they passed a resolution that no officer from New York should be allowed to exercise any jurisdiction over the people of the "Grants" in any capacity without permission from the committee.

In 1772 Governor Tryon attempted conciliation, but failed. The Legislature of New York passed a law that any offender against its authority on the "Grants" who should not surrender on the order of the governor within a specified time should be deemed guilty of a felony and punished with death, "without benefit of clergy," such culprit to be tried for the crime in the county of Albany. A reward was offered for the apprehension of Allen and other leaders.

This harsh legislation did not alarm the settlers, and the struggle continued sharply until the beginning of the old war for independence. It was kept up in a mild form during that war, and afterward until the admission of Vermont into the Union, in 1791, a period of forty years. The defenders of the rights of the people of the "Grants" acquired the name of "Green Mountain Boys." * Allen and other leaders, as well as the "rank and file," played a conspicuous part in the war for independence.

The story of the conflict between the government of a powerful province against a few settlers on disputed territory forms one of the most interesting chapters in our national history.

---

* On account of the loftiest hills in that region being covered with verdure, the name of Vert Mont—Green Mountain—was given to it. In the conflicts with the "Yorkers," some of the settlers were driven from the Champlain slope into the mountains, from which they issued for purposes of resistance, and were called "Green Mountain Boys."

CHAPTER XIV.

On the morning of October 25th, 1760, Prince George, heir-apparent to the throne of Great Britain, and then about twenty-three years of age, was riding on horseback near Kew Palace with his tutor the Earl of Bute, when a messenger informed him that his grandfather, King George II., had been found dead in a closet. Pitt called upon him the next day at the palace of St. James and presented him with a copy of an address to be read to the Privy Council. The minister was politely informed that a speech had already been prepared and every preliminary arranged. Pitt perceived that the courtier, Bute, had made the arrangements, and he withdrew. This circumstance had an important relation to the future destiny of the English-American colonies, and particularly of that of New York, as we shall observe presently.

SEAL OF GOV. MONCKTON.

Robert Monckton, son of Viscount Galway and a major-general in the British army, was appointed Governor of New York, but did not occupy the chair long. He arrived in November, 1761, and in February following he took command of an expedition destined for the capture of the

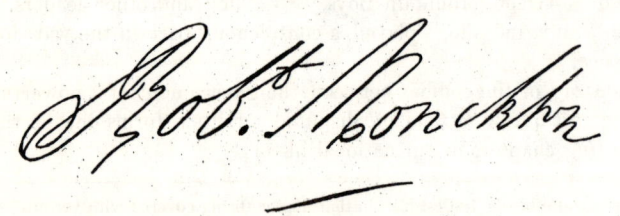

SIGNATURE OF GOVERNOR MONCKTON.

island of Martinique. He sailed from New York with twelve thousand men, was successful, returned to New York the next June, and "began his administration," says Smith, "with a splendor and magnificence equal to his birth."

General Monckton remained in New York awhile, and then left the government to Colden. Monckton was succeeded in office early in 1764 by Sir Henry Moore, a gay, affable, good-natured, and well-bred gentleman. Moore's administration did not begin until late in 1765. It covered a large portion of a stormy period in the history of New York. Sir Henry left the province in 1769, when Colden again assumed the reins of government.

The young king on his accession had parted with Pitt as his chief adviser, and, as we have just observed, made the Earl of Bute, a Scotch adventurer and a special favorite of the sovereign's mother, prime-minister of the realm. Bute proposed to bring the American colonies into absolute subjection to the crown and Parliament. To do this effectually it was resolved, in accordance with the recommendation of the Board of Trade and Plantations, to annul the American charter, to reduce all the American provinces to royal governments, and to gain a revenue by collecting duties to be imposed upon goods imported into the colonies.

SEAL OF GOVERNOR MOORE.

Among the first movements toward this end was making the judiciary of New York dependent upon the crown, to which allusion has been made. As we have observed, this act created much alarm and indignation in the public mind. "To make the king's will the tenure of office," said a representative of the people, "is to make the bench of judges the instrument of the royal prerogative." William Livingston, John Morin Scott, and William Smith, three eminent lawyers of New York, expressed their opinions freely and protested boldly in the newspapers against the measure; and the New York Assembly resolutely refused to grant a salary to Chief-Justice Pratt, who finally received it from the crown. Governor Moore disapproved the obnoxious measure, and even Governor Colden advised against it; but it was persisted in, and the crown continued to appoint judges, paying their salaries and making them independent of the people.

SIGNATURE OF GOVERNOR MOORE.

Another cause of popular irritation and resistance was the practical assertion of Parliament of its right to tax the colonists without their consent. Duties were imposed upon goods imported into the colonies, and collectors of customs were sent to enforce the revenue laws. These laws were frequently resisted or evaded, especially at Boston. The Superior Court of Massachusetts gave the collectors warrants, called "Writs of Assistance," which authorized the holders to search for smuggled goods when and where they pleased, and to demand assistance from others. "The meanest deputy of a deputy's deputy" might enter the house of a citizen unchallenged. The people regarded the matter as a violation of their liberties—a violation of the English maxim, "Every man's house is his castle." A solemn protest produced an argument before a crowded meeting of citizens in Boston, when the fiery James Otis vehemently denounced the writs, and said :

"I have determined to sacrifice estate, ease, health, applause, and even my life to the sacred call of my country in opposition to a kind of power, the exercise of which cost one king his head and another his throne." "On that day," said a contemporary, "the trumpet of the Revolution was sounded."

Then followed the fearful popular agitation in the colonies caused by the famous Stamp Act, in which New York appeared conspicuous—an act which declared that no legal instrument used in the colonies should be valid, after a prescribed date, unless it bore a government stamp, for each of which a prescribed sum of money, varying in amount from three cents to thirty dollars, was demanded. With greater boldness or recklessness than any former minister had exhibited, George Grenville, at the head of the Treasury and the ablest man in the House of Commons, submitted a bill authorizing stamp duties early in 1764. Even the great minister, Walpole, had said, many years before, "I will leave the taxation of America to some of my successors who have more courage than I have ;" and the greater Pitt said, in 1759, "I will never burn my fingers with an American Stamp Act."

This proposed measure caused universal excitement in the colonies. The people were divided. The old English titles of "Whig" and "Tory" now first came into use in America. The great question was freely discussed at public gatherings. The pulpit sometimes sounded an alarm. The newspaper press spoke out boldly. "If the colonist is taxed without his consent, he will, perhaps, seek a change," said Holt's *New York Gazette*, significantly.

Nowhere did the flame of resentment burn more fiercely than in New York, and nowhere were its manifestations more emphatic. Colden, the acting governor, then seventy-seven years of age, true to his sovereign, endeavored to suppress all opposition to the acts of the imperial legislature; but his efforts were like a breath against a gale. The association of the Sons of Liberty, which had appeared thirty years before, was revived with great vigor,* and a Committee of Correspondence to communicate with the agent of the colony in England and with

FORT GEORGE, BATTERY, AND BOWLING GREEN.†

the several colonial assemblies on the subject of the oppressive measures of Parliament was appointed.

When, in the spring of 1765, the Stamp Act became a law, words of defiance were uttered everywhere in the colonies. Energetic action soon followed. Public sentiment took a more dignified form than popular

---

* The principal members of the Association in the province of New York at that time were Isaac Sears, John Lamb, Alexander MacDougal, Marinus Willett, William Wiley, Edward Laight, Thomas Robinson, Hugh Hughes, Floris Bancker, Charles Nicoll, Joseph Allcock, and Gershom Mott, of New York City; Jeremiah van Rensselaer, Myndert Rosenbaum, Robert Henry, Volkert P. Douw, Jelles Fonda, and Thomas Young, of Albany and Tryon counties; John Sloss Hobart, Gilbert Potter, Thomas Brush, Cornelius Conklin, and Nathan Williams, of Huntington, L. I.; George Townsend, Baruk Sneething, Benjamin Townsend, George and Michael Weekes, and Rowland Chambers, of Oyster Bay, L. I.

† From an engraving by Tiebout in 1792. Within the Bowling Green is seen the pedestal on which stood the equestrian statue of King George III. The spear-heads of the pickets, as may now (1887) be seen, were all broken off. On the right is No. 1 Broadway, the headquarters of General Sir Henry Clinton. On the left is seen a point of Governor's Island; on the right, in the distance, is Staten Island, and in the extreme distance the Narrows, the open gateway from the harbor to the ocean.

harangues and heated discussions. At the suggestion of the Massachusetts Assembly a colonial convention of delegates assembled at the city of New York on October 7th, 1765. Nine colonies were represented by twenty-seven delegates. Those of New York were Robert R. Livingston, John Cruger, Philip Livingston, William Bayard, and Leonard Lispenard. Timothy Ruggles, of Massachusetts, presided. They were in session fourteen days, and sent forth three able State papers—namely, a " Declaration of Rights," written by John Cruger, of New York ; a " Memorial to both Houses of Parliament," by Robert R. Livingston, also of New York ; and a " Petition to the King," written by James Otis, of Massachusetts. The proceedings of this Stamp Act Congress were approved and signed by all the members excepting Timothy Ruggles, of Massachusetts, and Robert Ogden, of New Jersey, who espoused the cause of the crown in the great struggle that ensued.

The first day of November (1765) was the time appointed for the Stamp Act to go into operation. Stamp-distributors for their sale were appointed. James McEvers had been chosen the agent for New York.

The Sons of Liberty demanded his resignation. Colden promised him protection ; but when the stamps arrived, late in November, McEvers was so alarmed by the manifestations of opposition that he refused to receive them, and they were taken into the fort for safety, where the venerable Colden resided. The people were exasperated, and appearing in large numbers before the fort, demanded the delivery of the stamps to them. A refusal was answered by defiant shouts by the Sons of Liberty, who were not dismayed by the presence of British ships of war in the harbor and the pointing of the cannons of the fort upon them and upon the town.

An orderly procession was formed. It soon became a roaring mob. Half an hour after the governor's refusal he was hung in effigy on the spot where Leisler, the democrat, was executed seventy-five years before. Then the mob went back to the fort, dragged Colden's fine coach * to the open space in front of it, and tearing down the wooden railing that surrounded the Bowling Green, piled it upon the vehicle and made a bonfire of the whole. After committing some other excesses,† the

---

* Colden's coach-house and stable were outside the fort and easy of access. There were only three or four coaches in the city at that time, and as they belonged to wealthy friends of Government, they were considered by the people as evidences of aristocratic pride.

† The mob rushed out to the beautiful seat of Major James, at the intersection of (present) Worth Street and West Broadway, where they destroyed his fine library, works of art and rich furniture, and desolated his charming garden. His seat was named

excited populace paraded the streets with the Stamp Act printed on large sheets and raised upon poles, with the words, "ENGLAND'S FOLLY AND AMERICA'S RUIN."

Colden, clearly perceiving that further resistance to the popular will would be futile, ordered the stamps to be delivered to the mayor (Cruger) and the Common Council, on condition that any that should be destroyed or lost should be paid for. Quiet was restored. Soon afterward a brig brought to New York ten boxes of stamps. They were seized by some citizens and burnt at the shipyard at the foot of (present) Catharine Street.

The first of November was Friday—a truly "black Friday" in America. It was ushered in by the tolling of bells and the display of flags at half-mast, as if a national calamity had occurred. Minute guns were fired. There were orations and sermons adapted to the occasion. As none but stamped paper could be legally used, and as the people were determined not to use it, all business was suspended. The courts were closed, marriages ceased, and social and commercial operations in America were paralyzed. Yet the people did not despair, nor even despond. They felt conscious of rectitude and of inherent strength. They held in their own hands a remedy, and very soon applied it effectually.

On the day before the Stamp Act was to take effect many merchants in New York City, at a meeting held there, entered into a solemn agreement not to import from England certain enumerated articles after the first of January next ensuing. The chairman of an active committee of correspondence (John Lamb) addressed a circular letter to the merchants in other cities, inviting their co-operation in the non-importation policy. It was cheerfully acceded to, and merchants great and small followed the example of New York traders. The patriotic people co-operated with the merchants, and began domestic manufactures. The wealthiest vied with the middling classes in wearing clothing of their own manufacture. That wool might not become scarce, the use of sheep flesh for food was discouraged.

The mighty forces for defence against oppression, which for years worked so potentially in favor of liberty in America, thus put in motion in New York, hurled back upon England with great power the commercial miseries which she had inflicted upon her colonies. The most sensitive nerve of her political and social organism was so rudely touched that

---

Ranelagh. A few months afterward it was converted into a place of public resort, and called the Ranelagh Garden. James was a British officer who had become obnoxious to the people.

the British merchants and manufacturers earnestly joined the Americans in efforts to compel the Government to repeal the obnoxious act. They were successful. The Stamp Act was repealed early in 1766, having existed in a helpless state one year. In the words of a couplet upon the tombstone of a little baby, it might have asked,

> "If I so soon am done for,
> I wonder what I was begun for?"

To New York merchants is due the honor of having invented those two powerful engines of resistance to obnoxious acts of the British

BURNS'S COFFEE-HOUSE.*

Parliament, and which worked with so much potency at the beginning of the old war for independence—namely, the Committee of Correspondence and the Non-importation League. The repeal of the Stamp Act caused great rejoicings on both sides of the Atlantic. The city of New York was filled with delight on the beautiful May day when

---

* This was a famous place of resort for the Sons of Liberty in New York for several years before the old war for independence. It was a coffee-house kept by George Burns, at No. 9 Broadway. There the first non-importation league of the merchants of New York was formed, on October 31st, 1765—a consequence of the obnoxious Stamp Act. The league was signed by more than two hundred merchants. The above engraving shows the house as it appeared at the time of that occurrence. It remained a place of public resort until about 1860. Broadway slopes a little at that point.

the glad tidings arrived. Cannons thundered a royal salute, bells rang out merry peals, and the Sons of Liberty feasted together. A month later, on the king's birthday (June 4th), there was another public celebration, given under the auspices of Governor Moore, when royal salutes were again fired. There was a banquet at the King's Arms Tavern, near the Bowling Green, in which all the magnates of the city participated. Again the Sons of Liberty feasted together; and in the Fields (now the City Hall Park) an ox was roasted whole, and twenty-five barrels of beer and a hogshead of rum were provided for the people. The town was illuminated in the evening, and bonfires blazed, while the heavens were made brilliant with fireworks. The people erected a tall mast and unfurled a banner, upon it inscribed, "THE KING, PITT, AND LIBERTY," and called it Liberty Pole.

Pitt, who had been the chief instrument in Parliament in securing the repeal, was idolized by the people. At a meeting of citizens (June 23d) a petition was unanimously signed praying the Provincial Assembly to erect a statue in honor of the "Great Commoner" in the city of New York. The Assembly complied, and at the same time voted an equestrian statue of the king. Both were set up in 1770, that of Pitt being of marble, and that of the king lead. Pitt's statue was erected at the junction of Wall and William (then Smith) streets; the king's was set up in the centre of the Bowling Green.* Six years afterward the statue of the king was pulled down by an indignant populace, and a little later British soldiers mutilated the statue of Pitt.

EQUESTRIAN STATUE OF GEORGE III.

---

* By a singular oversight the artist omitted to give the king's saddle stirrups, as will be seen in the sketch. The Whigs of New York said, in 1776, " Good enough for him; he ought to ride a hard-trotting horse without stirrups."

Popular discontent soon followed the hallelujahs of joy, for the repeal act was accompanied by another which declared that the British Parliament had the right to "bind the colonies in all cases whatsoever." Sagacious men clearly saw in this declaratory act an egg of tyranny concealed, out of which might proceed untold evils. Events soon justified their forecast. The incubation was not protracted.

Almost at the moment when the people were celebrating the king's birthday in a spirit of hearty loyalty, Governor Moore informed the New York Assembly, then in session, that he hourly expected troops from England to garrison the fort there, and desired them to make immediate provision for them, in accordance with the requirements of the British Mutiny Act, which commanded citizens to billet troops upon themselves when necessity called for the measure. The Assembly declared that the power of the act did not extend to the colonies, and that there was no necessity for more troops at New York. The governor persisted, but the Assembly were firm in their refusal to comply with his requisition.

The troops came with authority to break into houses in searching for deserters, and to do other arbitrary things. The people were indignant. The Sons of Liberty were aroused to vigorous action. They rallied around the Liberty Pole which they had erected under the inspiration of true loyalty to their sovereign. The insolent soldiers cut down the symbol of liberty, and when, the next day, the citizens were setting it up again they were attacked by the troops. Still another pole was erected, and Governor Moore forbade the soldiers to touch it.

In January, 1770, soldiers went out from the barracks at midnight, prostrated the Liberty Pole, sawed it into pieces, and piled them before the headquarters of the Sons of Liberty. The bells of St. George's Chapel in Beekman Street rang an alarm, and very soon fully three thousand indignant citizens stood around the mutilated flag-staff. The city was fearfully agitated for several days, and affrays between the citizens and soldiers occurred. Finally they had a severe encounter on Golden Hill (between Cliff and William, John and Fulton streets), in which the soldiers were worsted and several of them were disarmed. The citizens were armed with various missiles. The conflict on Golden Hill in New York City may be regarded as the initial battle of the old war for independence.

The New York Assembly steadily refused to comply with the requirements of the Mutiny Act. The press spoke out boldly. William Livingston wrote prophetically in a New York newspaper:

"Courage, Americans! Liberty, religion, and science are on the wing to these shores. The finger of God points out a mighty empire to your sons. The savages of the wilderness were never expelled to make room for idolaters and slaves. The land we possess is the gift of Heaven to our fathers, and Divine Providence seems to have decreed it to our latest posterity. The day dawns in which the foundation of this mighty empire is to be laid, by the establishment of a regular American Constitution. All that has hitherto been done seems little beside the collection of materials for this glorious fabric. 'Tis time to put them together. The transfer of the European family is so vast, and our growth so swift, that before seven years will roll over our heads the first stone must be laid."

Seven years afterward the first Continental Congress assembled at Philadelphia.

The rebellious spirit manifested by the New Yorkers amazed and incensed the British Ministry, and they resolved to bring the refractory Assembly into humble obedience. Parliament forbade (1767) the "governor, Council, and Assembly of New York passing any legislative act for any purpose whatever" until they should comply with the requirements of the Mutiny Act. Parliament levied duties upon certain necessary articles imported into the colonies with the avowed purpose of drawing a revenue from them, and authorized the establishment of a Board of Trade, or Commissioners of Customs, to regulate and collect the revenue thus ordered. They also attempted to suppress free discussion in the colonies by means of Committees of Correspondence.

This last act aroused the free spirit of the people to instant resistance. When Governor Moore transmitted to the New York Assembly instructions from Lord Hillsborough against "holding seditious correspondence with other colonies," and called upon the Legislature to yield obedience, they boldly remonstrated against this ministerial interference with the inalienable right of a subject, and refused to obey.

On the death of Governor Moore, in September, 1769, Colden again became acting governor, when he coalesced politically with the De Lancey party. Very soon a gradual change in the political complexion of the Provincial Assembly was apparent. The leaven of aristocracy had begun a transformation, and a game for political power, based upon a proposed financial scheme, was begun.* It was a scheme which menaced the liberties of the people.

---

* This was issuing bills of credit, on the security of the province, to the amount of $300,000, to be loaned to the people, the interest to be applied to defraying the expenses of the colonial government. It was really a proposition for a monster bank without checks, and intended to cheat the people into a compliance with the requirements of the Mutiny Act by the indirect method of applying the profits to that purpose.

The popular leaders, discerning the danger, sounded the alarm. An incendiary hand-bill, signed "A Son of Liberty," was posted throughout the city, calling a meeting of the "betrayed inhabitants" in the Fields. It denounced the money scheme and the Assembly, and pointed to the political coalition as an omen of danger. Obedient to the call, a very large concourse of citizens gathered around the Liberty Pole on a cold December day, who, after a harangue by John Lamb, by unanimous vote condemned the proceedings of the Assembly. Another hand-bill from the same pen appeared the next day, and more severely denounced the Assembly in terms which were deemed libellous. A reward was offered for the name of the author. He was soon found to be Alexander McDougal, a seaman, who was afterward a major-general in the Continental Army. He was arrested, and refusing to plead or give bail, was sent to prison. On his way to jail he said:

"I rejoice that I am the first to suffer for liberty since the commencement of our glorious struggle."

Being a sailor, McDougal was regarded as the "true type of imprisoned commerce;" also as a martyr to the cause of liberty. His prison was daily the scene of a public reception. The most respectable citizens visited him. He was toasted at a banquet of the Sons of Liberty, who went in a procession to the jail to visit him. Ladies of distinction daily thronged there. Popular songs were written and sung below his prison-bars, and emblematic swords were worn. He was finally released on bail, and he was never tried.

Open rebellion in the colonies now seemed imminent. British soldiers were stationed in New York and Boston to overawe the people. Their insolence in words and manner produced continual irritation. There was a collision in Boston on March 5th (1770) between the citizens and soldiers, which aroused the indignation of all the colonies. Three persons were killed by the soldiers, and five were dangerously wounded. This event is known in history as the Boston Massacre.

On the day of the massacre the British prime-minister (Lord North) introduced into Parliament his famous Tea Act, which repealed all duties imposed upon articles imported into the American colonies, excepting upon tea. This one article was excepted as a practical assertion that Parliament had a right to tax the Americans without their consent. But this was the substance of the vital principle involved in the dispute, and the grand political postulate, "Taxation without representation is tyranny," was vehemently asserted. The non-importation power was set in motion, and the people warmly co-operated by refusing to use tea.* The stubborn king and the stupid ministry could not comprehend the idea involved, that a tax upon a single article, however small, was as much a violation of the spirit and letter of the postulate as if laid, in oppressive measure, upon a dozen articles.

Meanwhile the leaven of Toryism in the Assembly had extended its influence among the people. The Sons of Liberty in New York had formed a General Committee of One Hundred and a Vigilance Committee of Fifty, charged with the duty of watching the movements of the Whigs and Tories, and preventing, if possible, violations of the non-importation agreement. The Committee of One Hundred became widely disaffected by Toryism. The Vigilance Committee, more radical, denounced them, and the patriotic citizens of New England uttered indignant protests, but in vain. The New York merchants at large became disaffected, and at midsummer, 1770, the Committee of One Hundred, composed largely of merchants, resolved upon a resumption of importations of everything but tea. They issued a circular letter justifying their course. It was indignantly torn and scattered to the winds in Boston. The merchants of Philadelphia received it with scorn, and the sturdier patriots of that city said: "The old Liberty Pole of New York ought to be transferred to this city, as it is no longer a rallying-point for the votaries of freedom at home." The students at Princeton College, with James Madison at their head, burned the letter on the campus.

SEAL OF GOVERNOR DUNMORE.

SIGNATURE OF GOV. DUNMORE.

In October (1770) John Murray, Earl of Dunmore, succeeded Sir Henry Moore as Governor of New York. He remained such for only about nine months, when he was succeeded by Sir William Tryon, an Irish baronet, who had misruled North Carolina and stirred up a rebellion there. The Assembly, now thoroughly imbued with Tory-

---

* In Boston the mistresses of three hundred families subscribed their names to a league, binding themselves not to drink any tea until the Revenue Act was repealed. Three days afterward the young women followed their example. It was imitated in New York and Philadelphia.

ism, complimented the retiring governor, who was transferred to Virginia, and in a most cringing address, written by Captain Oliver de Lancey, replied to Tryon's opening message, at the beginning of 1772.

The state of political society in New York at this time was peculiar. Social differences had produced two distinct parties among the professed republicans, which were designated respectively Patricians and Tribunes. The former consisted chiefly of the merchants and gentry, and the latter were mostly mechanics. The latter were radicals, the former were conservatives, and joined the Loyalists or Tories, who were trying to check the influence of the more zealous democrats.

SEAL OF GOVERNOR TRYON.

Comparative quiet had prevailed in New York for nearly three years, when an attempt to enforce North's Tea Act set the colonies in a blaze again.* The East India Company, who had the monopoly of the tea trade, having lost their valuable customers in America by the operations of the non-importation measures, asked Parliament to take off three pence a pound levied upon its importation into America, and agreed to pay the Government more than an equal amount in export duty, in case the change should be made.

SIGNATURE OF GOVERNOR TRYON.

Here was an excellent opportunity for the Government to act justly and wisely and to produce a reconciliation;

---

* An event occurred in Narraganset Bay in the summer of 1772 which produced widespread excitement and widened the breach between the mother country and the colonies. The armed schooner *Gaspé* was stationed in the bay to enforce the revenue laws. Her commander haughtily ordered every American vessel when passing his schooner to lower its colors, in token of obedience. The master of a Providence sloop refused to bow to this nautical Gesler's cap, and was fired at and chased by the *Gaspé*. The latter grounded upon a sand-bar. That night Abraham Whipple (who was a naval commander during the Revolution), with sixty armed men, went down the bay in boats, captured the people on the schooner and burned her. Although a large reward was offered for the apprehension of the perpetrators they were not betrayed. Four years afterward, when Captain Wallace, a British naval commander near Newport, heard that Whipple was the leader of the offenders, he wrote to him, saying:

"On June 9th, 1772, you burned His Majesty's vessel the *Gaspé*, and I will hang you at the yard-arm!"

To this Whipple instantly replied: "Sir, always catch a man before you hang him!"

but the stupid ministry, fearing it might be considered a submission to "rebellious subjects," refused this olive branch. They allowed the company to send their tea free of export duty, but retained the import duty.

This concession to a great commercial monopoly, while spurning the appeals of subjects governed by a great principle, created indignation and contempt throughout the colonies. As this would make tea cheaper in America than in England, the Government and the East India Company unwisely concluded that the Americans would not object to paying the small duty. They were mistaken, as they very soon learned. Assured that Governor Tryon at New York would enforce the law, the company sent several ships laden with tea to that and other American ports early in 1773.

Already the Americans had resolved not to allow a pound of tea to be landed in any of the seaports. At a meeting held at New York on October 20th (1773), it was declared that the tea consignees and stamp distributors were equally obnoxious. The consignees, alarmed, promised not to receive the tea, notwithstanding Governor Tryon had promised them ample protection. The governor declared the tea should be delivered to the consignees, even if it should be "sprinkled with blood."

JOHN LAMB.

SIGNATURE OF JOHN LAMB.

John Lamb (afterward a commander of artillery in the war for independence, and one of the foremost of the Sons of Liberty) said to his informer of these words: "Tell Tryon, for me, that the tea shall *not* be landed; and if force is attempted to effect it, his blood will be the first shed in the conflict. The people of the city are firmly resolved on that head." Tryon took counsel of prudence.

At the middle of December the famous Boston Tea Party occurred, when three hundred and forty-three chests of tea were taken from ships moored at the wharves, broken open, and their contents cast into the waters of the harbor in the space of two hours, by men disguised as

Indians. The next day a meeting was held in the Fields at New York, which was addressed by John Lamb.* Strong resolutions in favor of resistance were passed; a Committee of Fifteen to carry on correspondence with the Sons of Liberty elsewhere was appointed, and the meeting was adjourned " till the arrival of the tea ships."

The ships did not arrive until April following, when the *Nancy*, Captain Lockyer, appeared at Sandy Hook with a cargo of tea. Apprised of the state of feeling in the city, and heeding the advice of the consignee, Lockyer prudently concluded to return to England with his cargo. A merchant vessel arrived at about the same time with several chests of tea concealed among her cargo. They were discovered, seized, and their contents were thrown into the waters of New York Harbor. The captain took refuge from the hands of the indignant people on board the *Nancy*, and sailed away in her.

At about this time a new Committee of One Hundred, also a Vigilance Committee, composed of the most substantial citizens, who were wise, watchful, and active, was created. The governor and a majority of the Assembly, being in political accord, needed watching; hence the formation of these two committees.

A misfortune befell the governor at this juncture which won for him public sympathy. At near the close of 1773 his house, with all his personal property, was accidentally burned. The Assembly voted him $20,000 in consideration of his loss, and with this money he left the province in charge of Dr. Colden, and went to England in the spring of 1774.

The destruction of tea in Boston Harbor created intense excitement in Great Britain. The exasperated ministry conceived several retaliatory measures, which were authorized by Parliament, the most conspicuous of which was an order for the closing of the port of Boston against all commercial transactions whatever, and the removal of all public offices thence to Salem. This prostration of all kinds of business occasioned widespread distress and created more widespread sympathy. Even the

---

* John Lamb, an artillery officer of the Revolution, was born in New York City January 1st, 1735; died there May 31st, 1800. He was one of the most active Sons of Liberty, and when the old war for independence began he entered the military service. He was in command of the artillery under General Montgomery at the siege of Quebec, where he was wounded and made prisoner. With the rank of major he served in the regiment of Colonel Knox the next summer, and on January 1st, 1777, he was commissioned a colonel of New York artillery. Lamb performed good service throughout the war, and ended his military career at the siege of Yorktown. He afterward became a member of the New York Assembly. President Washington appointed him (1789) collector of the customs at the port of New York.

city of London, in its corporate capacity, sent aid to the sufferers at Boston of the money value of fully $150,000. Another measure levelled a deadly blow at the charter of Massachusetts; another provided for the trial, in England, of all persons charged in the colonies with murder committed in support of the Government, giving, as Colonel Barré said on the floor of Parliament, "encouragement to military insolence already insupportable." A fourth provided for the quartering of troops at the expense of the colonies. The port of Boston was to be closed in June, and in May General Gage was sent to enforce the measure.

The people were intensely excited by these cruel measures. They despaired of justice at the hands of the British ministry. They began to feel that war was inevitable, and proceeded to arm and discipline themselves, and to manufacture guns and gunpowder. Every man capable of bearing arms enrolled himself in a company pledged to be ready to take the field at a minute's warning. So was created the vast army of Minute Men. Its headquarters was under every roof. It bivouacked in every church and household; and mothers, wives, sisters, and sweethearts made cartridges for its muskets and supplied its commissariat.

A crowded meeting in Faneuil Hall, in Boston, resolved to resume the non-importation measures with all their stringency. They sent Paul Revere with their resolutions to the Sons of Liberty in New York, whom the Loyalists called "Presbyterian Jesuits." The Committee of Fifty-One did not approve the resolutions, but favored the assembling of a general congress of deputies. In their reply to the communication from Boston they said:

"The cause is general, and concerns a whole continent, who are equally interested with you and us; and we foresee that no remedy can be of avail unless it proceeds from their joint acts and approbation. From a virtuous and spirited union much may be expected, while the feeble efforts of a few will only be attended with mischief and disappointment to themselves, and triumph to the adversaries of liberty. Upon these reasons we conclude that a CONGRESS OF DEPUTIES FROM THE COLONIES IN GENERAL is of the utmost importance; that it ought to be assembled without delay, and some unanimous resolutions formed in this fatal emergency, not only respecting your deplorable circumstances [the destruction of all commercial business by the closing of the port], but for the security of our common rights."

This recommendation for a General Congress, written, it is believed, by John Jay, found a hearty response everywhere. While the Bostonians approved the measure and suggested the time for holding the Congress, they adopted stringent non-importation measures. The people in other colonies did the same, and New York stood almost alone in refusing to acquiesce. At this the Loyalists rejoiced, and Rivington, the King's Printer, published the following lines in his *Gazetteer:*

> "And so, my good masters, I find it no joke,
> For YORK has stepped forward and thrown off the yoke
> Of Congress, committees, and even King Sears,*
> Who shows you good-nature by showing his ears."

At this time there were two prominent political committees in New York—namely, the old Vigilance Committee of Fifty and a newly-organized Committee of Fifty-One. The former was composed of radicals, Sons of Liberty, led by McDougall, Sears, and Lamb, and favored non-importation measures; the latter consisted of conservatives, and favored a General Congress rather than non-importation measures. Adherents of the former called a meeting in the Fields on July 6th (1774), which, on account of its numbers, was known as "The Great Meeting." On that occasion a student of King's (now Columbia) College, known as the "Young West Indian," a delicate boy, girl-like in personal grace and stature, only seventeen years of age, made a speech, and astonished the multitude by his eloquence and logic. He was Alexander Hamilton, from the island of Nevis, who was destined to play an important part in the drama of our national history.

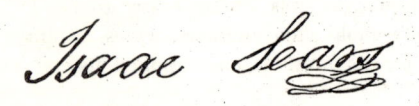

SIGNATURE OF ISAAC SEARS.

The Great Meeting denounced the Boston Port Bill and declared that an attack upon the liberties of one colony concerned the whole. The meeting pledged New York to join with others in a non-importation league, and to be governed by the action of the contemplated General Congress. The Committee of Fifty-One denounced these proceedings

---

* Isaac Sears was one of the most active and energetic of the Sons of Liberty. He was a native of Norwalk, Conn., where he was born in 1729; he died in Canton, China, in 1786. He was a successful merchant in New York, engaged in the European and West India trade. Having commanded a merchant vessel, he was generally known as Captain Sears, and because of his valiant leadership in opposition to the Government he was called "King Sears." He was thoroughly hated, maligned, caricatured, and satirized by his political enemies. Rivington, the King's Printer, abused him shamefully, and in retaliation Sears entered the city in 1775 with some Connecticut light horsemen and destroyed his maligner's printing establishment. At the end of the war his business and fortune were gone. In 1785 he went, as supercargo, to China, and died soon after his arrival at Canton.

as "seditious and incendiary." This offended a dozen of their members, who withdrew from the committee. But these feuds were soon healed by the exigencies of the occasion, and the patriots of New York, early in July (1774), chose delegates to represent the province in the General Congress to be convened at Philadelphia on the 5th day of September. They chose as representatives of the city of New York: Philip Livingston, John Alsop, Isaac Low, James Duane, and John Jay. Suffolk County, on Long Island, elected William Floyd; Orange County, Henry Wisner and John Herring; and King's County, Simon Boerum. Duchess and Westchester counties adopted the New York City delegates as their representatives; so also did the city and county of Albany.*

---

* The people of Albany County were anxious to send Colonel Philip Schuyler as their deputy, but he was too severely afflicted with rheumatism and hereditary gout to allow him to serve them. Toward the close of July his friend, Councillor William Smith, wrote to him from New York: "The colonies are preparing for the grand *Wittenagemote* [Great Assembly] with great spirit. At Philadelphia a plan is digesting for an American Constitution. I know not the outlines of it. I hope it is for a Parliament to meet annually. Our people will be the last of all in the appointment of delegates. I wish your county would assist in the choice. Expresses will be sent through the whole colony to call upon the counties for the purpose. . . . The people of England begin to call out for an American Parliament."

CHAPTER XV.

Committees of Correspondence, which had been formed in every colony in 1773, had been busy in the interchange of sentiments and opinions, and throughout the entire community of British-Americans from Maine to Georgia there was evidently a consonance of feeling favorable to united efforts in opposing the augmenting oppression of the mother country. And yet they hesitated, and resolved to deliberate in solemn council before they should appeal to arms—"the last argument of kings."

To this end deputies representing twelve British-American colonies met in Carpenter's Hall, at Philadelphia, on September 5th, 1774, and chose Peyton Randolph* president and Charles Thomson secretary of that body. There were forty-four delegates present on that day. Those from the province of New York were James Duane, John Jay, Philip Livingston, Isaac Low and William Floyd.

PEYTON RANDOLPH.

That first Continental Congress remained in session until October 26th, during which time they matured measures for future action. One of the most important of these measures was the formation of a league

---

* Peyton Randolph was born in 1723, in Virginia, and, like other young men of wealthy parents in the colonies, was educated in England. He became a lawyer, and at the age of twenty-seven years was appointed attorney-general of the province. He went with a band of volunteers against the Indians on the Virginia frontier in 1756. A member of the House of Burgesses several years, he was its Speaker at one time. He was chairman of a committee to revise the laws of Virginia; went to England to seek redress of grievances; framed the remonstrance of the House of Burgesses against the Stamp Act; presided over the Virginia Provincial Convention at Williamsburg in 1774, and the first Continental Congress the same year; presided over the second Virginia Convention in March, 1775; was in the Continental Congress a short time that year, and died of apoplexy at Philadelphia, October 22d, 1775. His portrait here given was copied from a miniature by Charles Willson Beale.

for a general commercial non-intercourse with Great Britain and her West India possessions. It was named the American Association. In addition to its non-intercourse provisions, it recommended the abandonment of the slave-trade, the improvement in the breed of sheep, abstention from all extravagance in living, indulgence in horse-racing, etc., and the appointment of a sort of vigilance committee in every town to promote conformity to the requirements of the Association. It was signed by the fifty-two members who were present at its adoption.

This first Continental Congress put forth several able State papers—a Bill of Rights; an Address to the People of Great Britain; another to the several British-American colonies; another to the Inhabitants of the Province of Quebec, and a petition to the king. One of the most significant acts of the Congress, the most offensive to Great Britain, and which constituted the whole business of the day, was the passage of the following resolution on October 8th:

"*Resolved*, That this Congress approve the opposition of the inhabitants of Massachusetts Bay to the execution of the late acts of Parliament; and if the same shall be attempted to be carried into execution by force, in such case all America ought to support them in their opposition."

SIGNATURE OF PEYTON RANDOLPH.

Thus defiantly was the gauntlet cast down at the feet of the king and Parliament. The Congress adjourned eighteen days afterward to meet at the same place on May 10th following, unless the desired redress of grievances should be obtained.

The public press in the colonies almost unanimously supported the attitude assumed by the Congress. There were only four newspapers then published in the province of New York, and these were sent forth from the city. They were Hugh Gaines's *New York Mercury*, John Holt's *New York Journal*, John Anderson's *Constitutional Gazette*, and James Rivington's *New York Gazette*. The first three named were in sympathy with the patriots. The latter favored the royal side in political discussions.* The Whig papers everywhere abounded in

---

* Holt's *Journal* was the most outspoken of any of the Whig newspapers. Before the meeting of the first Continental Congress it contained at its head the device of a snake disjointed, each piece having the initials of one of the English-American colonies. He pleaded for its union. In December, after the session of that Congress was ended, it contained another significant device. It represented a column, its base resting upon Magna Charta and upheld by thirteen strong arms reaching out of clouds. The column

pointed epigrams, squibs, keen satirical sonnets, and sententious arguments and logic, like the following:

THE QUARREL WITH AMERICA FAIRLY STATED.

"Rudely forced to drink tea, Massachusetts, in anger,
Spilt the tea on John Bull—John fell on to bang her;
Massachusetts, enraged, calls her neighbors to aid,
And give Master John a severe bastinade.
Now, good men of the law, pray who is at fault,
The one who begins or resists the assault?"

The proceedings of the Continental Congress produced a most profound sensation in Great Britain. When Parliament reassembled after the holidays (January 20th, 1775) the king denounced the American colonists as "rebels," and promised ample means to bring them into subjection. William Pitt (now become Earl of Chatham) made a powerful speech in the House of Lords in favor of the Americans, which drew from that House a severe reprimand by a decided majority. Thus supported by the king and lords, the ministry proceeded to put the engine of coercion into swift operation. Restrictive and other oppressive acts were passed, and war was virtually declared against the British-American colonists.

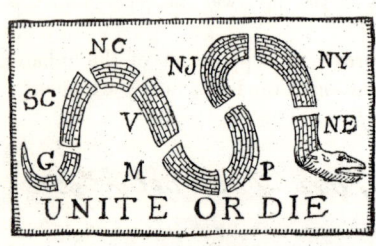

SNAKE DEVICE.

Meanwhile the several colonies had expressed their approval of the proceedings of the Continental Congress. New York alone refused to do so, but finally yielded. In November, 1774, the Committee of Fifty-One was dissolved, and at a meeting of "freeholders and freemen," held at the City Hall on the 22d of that month, a committee of sixty persons were chosen "for carrying into execution the Association entered into by the Continental Congress."

So soon as the Congress adjourned the Loyalists and the High Church party in New York undertook to weaken the force of the American

---

was surmounted by the cap of Liberty. The whole was encircled by a snake in two coils, upon which were the words:

"United now, alone and free,
Firm on this basis Liberty shall stand,
And thus supported, ever bless our land,
Till Time becomes Eternity."

Association by inducing violations of its requirements. To this end scholars and divines who had been engaged in the controversy concerning an American episcopate now resumed their pens. Among the most eminent of these writers on the Tory side were Rev. Myles Cooper, D.D., President of King's College, and Drs. Inglis, Seabury and Chandler, of the Anglican Church. They were ably answered by William Livingston, John Jay, young Alexander Hamilton, and others. It was at this time that the last named entered the list of political writers, and soon became their peer and leader.

The first session of the New York Assembly after the adjournment of the Continental Congress began on January 10th, 1775. In it was a

SIGNATURE OF OLIVER DE LANCEY.

clear working majority of Tories. Colonel Philip Schuyler was the acknowledged leader of the opposition. He was ably supported by George Clinton and others, and they resolved to have the political issues between the people and the Government distinctly drawn and specifically considered.

The venerable Colden, now at the head of the provincial government, called the attention of the Legislature, in his message, to the "alarming crisis," and admonished them that the country looked to them for wise counsel. He was a Loyalist, but was now conservative in feeling. He exhorted the Assembly to discontinue all measures calculated to increase the public distress, and promised them his aid. The response to the message was drawn by Oliver de Lancey,* and took conservative ground.

---

* Oliver de Lancey, a brother of Lieutenant-Governor James de Lancey, was born in 1717; died in England in 1785. He possessed large wealth and great influence. He adhered to the crown when the war for independence began; was commissioned a brigadier-general, and raised and commanded three battalions of Loyalists. His son, Oliver, became a captain of cavalry, and succeeded Major André as adjutant-general under General Clinton. The De Lanceys performed efficient service for the royal cause in Westchester County, N. Y. At the close of the war the general, accompanied by his son, went to England, where the latter rose to the rank of major-general, and at the time of his death was almost at the head of the British army list. The elder General De Lancey became a member of Parliament. His nephew, James de Lancey, commanded a battalion of horse in Westchester County, and because of his zeal in supplying the British army with cattle from the farms of that county, his troopers were called *cow-boys*. Confiscation acts swept away the larger portion of the De Lancey estate in America.

At length a question came up (January 26th, 1775) which tested the political character of the Assembly. Abraham Tenbroeck moved that the House should "take into consideration the proceedings of the Continental Congress," etc. The motion was negatived by a majority of only one. Notwithstanding the meagreness of this majority, the result gave great joy to the Tories. One of them wrote to a gentleman in Boston: "Worthy old Silver Locks (Lieutenant-Governor Colden), when he heard that the Assembly had acted right, cried out, 'Lord, now lettest thy servant depart in peace.'"

Soon after these efforts were made in the Assembly to bring it into sympathetic action with those of the other colonies, Colonel Schuyler moved that certain letters which had passed between the Committees of Correspondence of New York and Connecticut, and a certain letter to Edmund Burke (the agent in England of the colony of New York), in June, 1774, on the subject of a general Congress, "be forthwith entered upon the journals of the House and supplied to the newspapers for publication." It was rejected by a vote of 16 to 9. Colonel Nathaniel Woodhull moved that the thanks of the House should be given to the delegates in the late Continental Congress "for their faithful discharge of the trust reposed in them." This was negatived—15 to 9. By the same vote a motion to thank the merchants and others who had adhered to the non-importation and non-intercourse league was negatived. A motion to appoint delegates to the proposed second Continental Congress was lost by a vote of 17 to 9.

The Assembly agreed, by a majority vote, that Parliament had a right to tax the colonies without their consent. Late in February a petition to the king was presented for consideration. It was so cringing in tone —speaking of the monarch as "an indulgent father" and the colonists as "infants" who had "submitted hitherto without repining" to the authority of "the parent"—that the manliness, the patriotism, and the indignation of Schuyler and his friends were thoroughly aroused to most vigorous opposition. Schuyler offered several amendments; but these, with resolutions presented by him, were voted down. Amendments offered to a memorial to the House of Lords met with similar treatment. Finally the several papers adopted by the Assembly, though they did not express the sentiments of the people of the province, were ordered to be sent to Mr. Burke. The Assembly had been induced to send a remonstrance to Parliament against its harsh treatment of the colonists. Its terms, though mild, were so distasteful that it was not received by Parliament.

On April 3d, 1775, the Provincial Assembly of New York—a legislative body which had existed more than one hundred years—was adjourned never to meet again. The people now took public matters into their own hands. The whole continent was moving rapidly toward an attitude of rebellion and self-government. The newspapers, as we have observed, were filled with exciting matter, and warlike preparations were observed on every side. General Gage, in command of troops at Boston, became alarmed, and began fortifying Boston Neck. He seized and conveyed to that town quantities of gunpowder found in neighboring villages, and he adopted stringent measures to prevent intercourse between citizens of the town and the country.

Fierce exasperation followed these impolitic measures, and it was not long before hundreds of armed men assembled at Cambridge. At Charlestown, near Boston, the people took possession of the Arsenal after Gage had carried off the powder. The people also captured the fort at Portsmouth, N. H., and carried off the powder. The people of Rhode Island seized the powder and forty cannons at the entrance of Newport Harbor. Similar defensive measures were taken at Philadelphia, Annapolis, Williamsburg, Charleston, and Savannah.

The Republicans of New York having failed in their efforts in the Assembly to procure the appointment of delegates to the second Continental Congress, which was to convene on May 10th, nothing was left for them but to appeal to the people. The new general Committee of Sixty, temporarily exercising governmental functions and yielding to the pressure of popular sentiment, took measures for assembling a convention of representatives of the several counties in the province for the purpose of choosing deputies to the General Congress. The Loyalists opposed the measure as disrespectful to the Assembly, which had refused to appoint delegates.

The people, wearied of the Legislature, were now driven to a point where respect for authorities whose views were not in consonance with the spirit of liberty and free discussion was almost wholly unknown.

They first rallied around the Liberty Pole (April 6th, 1775), beneath a banner inscribed "Constitutional Liberty," and marching to the Exchange, were met there by large numbers of Loyalists, led by members of the Council and the Assembly, with officers of the army and navy, who came to overawe the people. They failed. A Provincial Convention was called, and assembled at the Exchange, forty-two in number, on April 20th, and chose Philip Livingston, James Duane, John Alsop, John Jay, Simon Boerum, William Floyd, Henry Wisner, Philip Schuyler, George Clinton, Lewis Morris, Francis Lewis, and Robert R.

Livingston deputies to represent the province of New York in the Continental Congress.

On May 22d (1775) deputies from the several counties assembled in New York and organized a Provincial Congress, with Peter van Brugh Livingston, president; Volkert P. Douw, vice-president; and John McKesson and Robert Benson, secretaries.* That body assumed the functions of a provincial government, and utterly ignored the royal governor and his Council.

The great crisis was now approaching. When, just after the adjournment of the Provincial Convention (April 24th), news came of the tragedy at Lexington and Concord the public mind at New York was fearfully excited by that intelligence, and by the arrest of Captain Isaac Sears, the bold leader of the Sons of Liberty, on a charge of seditious utterances. On his way to jail he was taken from the officers by his friends and borne in triumph through the streets, preceded by a band of music and a banner. That night Sears addressed the people in "The Fields,"

---

* Members of the first Provincial Congress of New York, which met in the city of New York on May 23d, 1775:

For the City and County of New York.—Isaac Low, L. Lispenard, Abraham Walton, Isaac Roosevelt, Abraham Brasher, Alexander McDougal, P. van Brugh Livingston, James Beekman, John Morin Scott, Thomas Smith, Benjamin Kissam, Samuel Verplanck, David Clarkson, George Folliot, Joseph Hallet, John van Cortlandt, John de Lancey, Richard Yates, John Marston, Walter Franklin, Jacobus van Zandt.

For the City and County of Albany.—Volkert P. Douw, Abraham Yates, Robert Yates, Jacob Cuyler, Peter Sylvester, Dirck Swart, Walter Livingston, Robert van Rensselaer, Henry Glenn, Abraham Tenbroeck, Francis Nicoll.

For Duchess County.—Dirck Brinkerhoff, Andrew Hoffman, Zephaniah Platt, Richard Montgomery, Ephraim Paine, Gilbert Livingston, Jonathan Langdon, Gysbert Schenck, Melancton Smith, Nathaniel Sackett.

For Ulster County.—Colonel John Hardenburg, Egbert Dumond, Christopher Tappan, James Clinton, Dr. Charles Clinton, John Nicholson, Jacob Hornbeck.

For Orange County.—John Coe, David Pye, Michael Jackson, Benjamin Tustin, Peter Clowes, William Allison, Abraham Lent, John Haring.

For Suffolk County.—Nathaniel Woodhull, John Sloss Hobart, Ezra L'Hommedieu, Thomas Wickham, Thomas Treadwell, John Foster, James Haven, Selah Strong.

For Richmond County.—Paul Micheau, John Journey, Richard Conner, Richard Lawrence, Aaron Cortelyou.

For Westchester County.—Gouverneur Morris, Lewis Graham, James van Cortlandt, Stephen Ward, Joseph Drake, Philip van Cortlandt, John Thomas, Jr., Robert Graham, William Paulding.

For Kings County.—John E. Lott, Henry Williams, J. Remsen, Richard Stillwill, Theodore Polhemus, John Lefferts, Nicholas Covenhoven, John Vanderbilt.

For Queens County.—Jacob Blackwell, Joseph Lawrence, Daniel Rapelje, Zebulon Williams, Samuel Townsend, Joseph Trench, Joseph Robinson, Nathaniel Tom, Thomas Hicks, Richard Thone.

For Charlotte.—Dr. John Williams, William Marston.

and a few days afterward he was elected a member of the Provincial Congress.

The aroused Sons of Liberty embargoed all vessels in the harbor laden with provisions for the British troops in Boston. They did more; they demanded and received the keys of the Custom House, dismissed the employés, and closed it. They also seized public arms, and placed a guard at the arsenal. Then they boldly proclaimed this overt act of treason to their brethren in other cities. General alarm prevailed, especially among the Tories. A Grand Committee of Safety, consisting of one hundred of the most respectable citizens,* was organized, and a military association for practice in the use of fire-arms was formed. The Committee of One Hundred assumed the functions of municipal government.

When the Provincial Congress assembled its complexion disappointed the people. Toryism and timidity prevailed in that body, and schemes for conciliation instead of measures for defence occupied the majority. Family influence was very powerful in the colony in every department of social life, and through it the Provincial Assembly and the Provincial Congress were loyally inclined. The masses of the people were chiefly Republican in feeling, and Toryism in the Provincial Congress, hard pressed by popular sentiment and the influence of important events daily occurring, was soon compelled to yield. When it was finally crushed out, no province or State was more patriotic and more active in the cause of liberty than New York. With a population of only 164,000 in 1780,

---

* The following are the names of the Committee of One Hundred: Isaac Low, chairman; John Jay, Francis Lewis, John Alsop, Philip Livingston, James Duane, Evert Duyckman, William Seton, William W. Ludlow, Cornelius Clopper, Abraham Brinkerhoff, Henry Remsen, Robert Ray, Evert Bancker, Joseph Totten, Abraham P. Lott, David Beekman, Isaac Roosevelt, Gabriel H. Ludlow, William Walton, Daniel Phœnix, Frederick Jay, Samuel Broome, John de Lancey, Augustus van Horne, Abraham Duryée, Samuel Verplanck, Rudolphus Ritzema, John Morton, Joseph Hallet, Robert Benson, Abraham Brasher, Leonard Lispenard, Nicholas Hoffman, Peter van Brugh Livingston, Thomas Marsten, Lewis Pintard, John Imlay, Eleazer Miller, Jr., John Broome, John B. Moore, Nicholas Bogart, John Anthony, Victor Bicker, William Goforth, Hercules Mulligan, Alexander McDougal, John Reade, Joseph Ball, George Janeway, John White, Gabriel W. Ludlow, John Lasher, Theophilus Anthony, Thomas Smith, Richard Yates, Oliver Templeton, Jacobus van Landby, Jeremiah Platt, Peter S. Curtenius, Thomas Randall, Lancaster Burling, Benjamin Kissam, Jacob Lefferts, Anthony van Dam, Abraham Walton, Hamilton Young, Nicholas Roosevelt, Cornelius P. Low, Francis Bassett, James Beekman, Thomas Ivers, William Dunning, John Berrien, Benjamin Helme, William W. Gilbert, Daniel Dunscombe, John Lamb, Richard Sharp, John Morin Scott, Jacob van Voorhis, Comfort Sands, Edward Flemming, Peter Goelet, Gerrit Kettletas, Thomas Buchanan, James Desbrosses, Petrus Byvanck, and Lott Embree.

of whom 32,500 were liable to military duty, New York had furnished 17,780 soldiers for the Continental Army, or over 3000 more than Congress required. Even at the juncture we are considering, the Provincial Congress authorized the raising and furnishing of four regiments, the construction of fortifications at the northern end of Manhattan Island, and fortifications in the Hudson Highlands.

Already the first military conquest made by the Americans in the old war for independence had been achieved within the province of New York. It was done chiefly by the prowess of Green Mountain Boys, who had so long and so successfully defied the authorities and the land speculators of New York. Benedict Arnold, of Connecticut, who had hastened to Cambridge with a military company on hearing of the affrays at Lexington and Concord, proposed to the Massachusetts Provincial Congress the seizure of the stronghold of Ticonderoga, on Lake Champlain. He was commissioned a colonel, and authorized to raise men for the enterprise. Meanwhile some Connecticut people, bent on a similar enterprise, had repaired to Pittsfield, in Western Massachusetts, where they were joined by Colonels Eaton and Brown and some of their followers. They all went to Bennington, where Colonel Ethan Allen and a considerable force of Green Mountain Boys joined them. The whole force rendezvoused at Castleton, where they chose Allen as commander-in-chief of the expedition. There Arnold joined the little host with a few followers, and, by virtue of his commission, claimed the right to supreme command. The Green Mountain Boys objected. Arnold yielded. On the night of May 9th (1775) most of the little army crossed Lake Champlain near Ticonderoga, and at early dawn on the 10th Allen and Arnold, with a considerable force, having seized the sentinel at the sallyport, passed through a covered way, and before they were discovered were on the parade within the fort. They had taken the garrison by surprise. Allen proceeded to the quarters of the commandant, who had just been awakened from his slumbers, and demanded the surrender of the fort.

"By what authority do *you* make such a demand?" asked the commandant, who knew Allen.

"By the authority of the Great Jehovah and the Continental Congress!" said Allen, in a loud voice. Dubious about Allen's divine authority, the commandant nevertheless yielded, although the Continental Congress did not exist until some hours later on that day. The spoils of victory comprised 120 iron cannons, 50 swivels, 2 mortars, and a large amount of ammunition and stores, which were used in the siege of Boston a few months afterward. Two days later Colonel Seth

Warner and some Green Mountain Boys took possession of Crown Point, a few miles from Ticonderoga. Thus, at the outset of the war, the Republicans gained possession of Lake Champlain and the key to Canada.

On the day of the capture of Ticonderoga (May 10th, 1775) the second Continental Congress assembled at Philadelphia, and chose Peyton Randolph president and Charles Thomson secretary. The grave questions arose, What are we here for? and What are our powers? They simply composed a large Committee of Conference like the Congress of 1774,

RUINS OF FORT TICONDEROGA.*

without specifically delegated legislative or executive powers; yet the common-sense of the inhabitants of the colonies represented there at that perilous hour, regarded them as fully invested with supreme legislative and executive functions. The deference paid by the provincial authorities of Massachusetts and New York in asking the advice of Congress about public affairs was a tacit acknowledgment of the supremacy of the Continental Congress, and action was taken accordingly. That body proceeded to issue bills of credit, create an army and navy, establish a postal service, and to do all other acts of sovereignty.

---

* This is a view of the ruins of the famous old fort as it appeared in 1848, taken from the bank of the lake. The place of the covered way through which Allen and his followers entered the fort was at the left corner of the picture near the sheep in the foreground.

Meanwhile the patriots of New England had gathered in large numbers around Boston, determined to confine the British troops that occupied the town within the bounds of the peninsula. The battle of Bunker (Breed's) Hill was fought on June 17th; a Continental Army had just been organized, and George Washington, of Virginia, appointed its commander-in-chief; and the Continental Congress made vigorous preparations for the defence of liberty in America.

Rumors reached the Provincial Congress of New York that British troops were coming from Ireland to occupy the city. That body, now somewhat purged of its Toryism by intelligence from the East, invited General Wooster, who was in command of a body of militia at Greenwich, in Connecticut, for the defence of the shores of that colony, to come to the protection of New York. He encamped at Harlem for several weeks, and sent detachments to drive off marauders on Long Island, who were stealing cattle for the use of the British Army at Boston. His presence so emboldened the patriots at New York that at midnight late in July they captured British stores on the eastern verge of Manhattan Island (foot of present Forty-seventh Street), and sent part of them to the American army before Boston and a part to the garrison at Ticonderoga. They also seized a tender belonging to the *Asia*, a British man-of-war lying in New York Harbor.

Governor Tryon had returned to New York in the *Asia* late in June, and was received with much respect; but he soon offended the Republicans. The energetic action of the Committee of One Hundred soon taught him to be circumspect in public, but he was continually engaged in private intrigues in fostering the spirit of Toryism in the Provincial Congress.

Washington arrived at New York on his way to take command of the army at Cambridge on the same day when Tryon arrived at Sandy Hook (June 25th, 1775). This coincidence embarrassed the Provincial Congress and the municipal authorities. The public functions of the two men were seriously antagonistic, and their respective political friends were fiercely hostile. To avoid offence honors must be given to both. What was to be done? Fortunately, these magnates did not reach the city simultaneously. Washington and his party, to avoid British vessels in the harbor, were landed at the seat of Colonel Lispenard, on the Hudson, about a mile above the town, in the afternoon, and were conducted into the city by nine companies of foot and a great multitude of citizens, where they were received by the civil authorities. The President of the Congress (Philip Livingston) pronounced a cautious and conservative address, to which the general replied. Governor Tryon arrived four hours later, and was conducted to the house of Hugh Wallace, Esq. The civic and military ceremonies were partially repeated in the evening, and all parties were satisfied. It was a memorable Sabbath day in New York.

The province of New York at this crisis presented three dangerous elements of weakness—namely, an exposed frontier, a wily and powerful internal foe (Indians and Tories), and a demoralizing loyalty. On its northern border was Canada with a population practically neutral on the great question at issue, and prone to be hostile to the patriots. The central and western regions of the province were swarming with the Six Nations of Iroquois, whose almost universal loyalty had now been secured by the influence of Sir William Johnson and his family, while nearer the seaboard and in the metropolis, family compacts and commercial interests were powerfully swayed by traditional and natural attachments to the crown. These neutralized, to a great extent,

PHILIP LIVINGSTON.*

* Philip Livingston was one of the most energetic, upright, public-spirited, and esteemed business men in the province of New York at the period immediately preceding the Revolution ; and he was one of the most trustworthy and efficient of the supporters of the cause of the American patriots. He was a grandson of Robert Livingston, the first "Lord of the Manor." He was born in Albany in 1716, the year when the manor was first accorded the privilege of a representative in the Colonial Assembly. He became a merchant, and a most energetic and thrifty one ; and he entered vigorously into the heated political discussions before the old war for independence began. His business was in New York City, where he was alderman nine years. He represented the manor in the Assembly during the French and Indian War, where he had great influence as a leader of the patriotic party in that body, with Colonel Schuyler, Pierre van Cortlandt, Charles De Witt, etc. ; and corresponded much with Edmund Burke. Mr. Livingston represented New York in the first Continental Congress, and was on the committee that prepared the remarkable "Address to the People of Great Britain," which drew forth warm encomiums from William Pitt (Lord Chatham). He was an active member of the New York Provincial Congress in 1775, and earnestly supported the proposition for independence, signing the great Declaration. Mr. Livingston was a member of the first Senate of the *State* of New York, and also a delegate in the General Congress. When the sessions of that body were held at Lancaster and York his health rapidly failed, and he died at York on June 11th, 1778. He was one of the founders of the New York Society Library, of King's (now Columbia) College, and of the Chamber of Commerce.

the influence of the few sturdy patriots who, in the face of frowns and menaces and the fears of the timid, kept the fires of the Revolution burning with continually increasing brightness.

The whole province of New York constituted the "Northern Department" of the Continental Army. Washington placed it under the charge of Philip Schuyler, one of his four major-generals, whose sleepless vigilance caused him to be designated the "Great Eye" of the department. In his instructions to Schuyler, given at New York, Washington admonished him to "keep a watchful eye upon Governor Tryon," and to use every means in his power to frustrate his designs "inimical to the common cause."

Affairs on Lake Champlain demanded Schuyler's first and most earnest attention, for the possession of Canada by an alliance or by conquest was a consideration of the greatest consequence. As the inhabitants were French Roman Catholics, having no sympathy in religion or nationality with either party, they were objects of great solicitude to both. Friendly overtures were made to them by the colonies then in league, but imprudent language interfered. Had wise words and measures been adopted at the outset the Canadians might have been easily won to an alliance, for a traditional feud between the French and English had existed for a thousand years, and the recent conquest of Canada by the English was yet a cause for much irritation ; or had Congress acted promptly upon the suggestions of Colonels Allen and Arnold soon after the capture of Ticonderoga, Canada might have been easily won by conquest. The New York Provincial Congress thought it an "impertinent proposal coming from Allen, a man who had been outlawed by the authorities of New York."

The two heroes (Allen and Arnold) had already on their own responsibility taken preliminary steps toward such conquest. They went down the lake in a schooner and bateaux with armed men, and Arnold captured St. Johns, on the Sorel (the outlet of the lake), but could not hold the prize. Again, when Arnold heard that the Governor of Canada had sent an armed force to St. Johns for the purpose of attempting the recapture of the lake forts, he proceeded without authority to fit out, arm, and man with one hundred and fifty persons all the vessels he could lay his hands upon, and, as self-constituted commodore, he took post at Crown Point and awaited the coming of the foes. They did not come. This was the first Continental Navy. It was put afloat in New York waters before the middle of June, 1775.

Colonel Allen and his lieutenant, Seth Warner, appeared before the Continental Congress at Philadelphia, and on the floor of the House he revealed to the members, in quaint phrases and with slow speech, the state of affairs on the northern frontier, and urged the importance of an immediate invasion of Canada before the small British force there should be increased. He asked for authority to raise a new regiment of Green Mountain Boys for that service. His words so deeply impressed the members that on June 17th they

"*Resolved*, That it be recommended to the Convention of New York that they, consulting with General Schuyler, employ in the army to be raised for the defence of America those called 'Green Mountain Boys,' under such officers as the said Green Mountain Boys shall choose."

Allen and Warner soon appeared in New York and craved an audience with the Provincial Congress. Their errand produced much embarrassment. How could members treat with men who had recently been proclaimed outlaws? Debates ran high, when Captain Sears moved that "Ethan Allen be admitted to the floor of the House." The motion was adopted by a large majority. The old feud was instantly healed, and the Congress decreed that a regiment of Green Mountain Boys, five hundred strong, should be raised.

Already Governor Trumbull, of Connecticut, had sent troops to Ticonderoga, under Colonel Hinman, who held the chief command there until superseded by General Schuyler. The military force then in the province did not exceed three thousand men fit for duty, and yet preparations were made in New York for an invasion of Canada. The visit of Allen and Warner had quickened the perceptions of the Continental Congress of the necessity of such an invasion, and on June 27th that body ordered General Schuyler, if he should "find it practicable and not disagreeable to the Canadians, immediately to take possession of St. Johns and Montreal, and pursue such other measures in Canada as might have a tendency to promote the peace and security of these provinces"—in other words, to undertake an armed invasion of Canada.

CHAPTER XVI.

GENERAL SCHUYLER had accompanied Washington from Philadelphia to New York. When he arrived at Albany early in July he found the aspect of affairs in Northern New York dark and unpromising to the Republican cause.

Sir William Johnson,* who had taken sides with the crown in the political movements of the time, had died the previous autumn. His mantle of almost unbounded influence over the Indians of the Mohawk Valley and beyond had fallen upon his energetic son-in-law, Colonel Guy Johnson, who succeeded him as Superintendent of Indian Affairs. Sir William's son John inherited the title and estates of the baronet, and was at that time earnestly engaged in keeping Toryism actively alive in the Mohawk Valley. He had been appointed, in 1774, brigadier-general of the militia of Tryon County, which extended west of Albany County almost indefinitely.

SIR WILLIAM JOHNSON.

These successors of Sir William, especially Guy, professed peaceable

---

* Sir William Johnson was a conspicuous character in the later period of the colonial history of New York. He was a native of Ireland, where he was born in 1715. Educated for a merchant, an unfortunate love affair changed the tenor of his life. He came to America to take charge of landed property in the region of the Mohawk Valley belonging to his uncle, Admiral Sir Peter Warren. His good treatment of the Indians made him a favorite with them. He built a fine mansion (yet standing), which he called "Johnson Hall," and there the village of Johnstown, in Fulton County, now flourishes. He married a pretty German girl, by whom he had two children, a son (afterward Sir John Johnson) and a daughter. By his housekeeper, Mary Brant, the sister of Brant, the celebrated Mohawk chief, he had eight children. She lived with him until his death in 1774. When the French and Indian War broke out Johnson was appointed sole agent of Indian affairs in the province of New York, and managed the business most judiciously. The king granted him 100,000 acres of land in the Mohawk Valley. He lived on his domain in his fine mansion in rude baronial splendor.

intentions, but the movements of the latter had been so suspicious for some time that the patriotic citizens of Tryon County were filled with apprehensions.

Guy Johnson was holding a council, in the spring of 1775, with the Indians at his house* (near the present village of Amsterdam), on the Mohawk, when news from Lexington and intimations that he was about to be arrested so alarmed him that he hastily adjourned the council, first to the German Flats and then to Fort Stanwix, now

SIGNATURE OF SIR WILLIAM JOHNSON.

Rome. He had taken his family with him. He soon pushed onward to the heart of the country of the fierce Cayugas and Senecas, and at Ontario (according to tradition) he called a great council of the Six

GUY JOHNSON'S HOUSE.

Nations. He was accompanied by Brant (whose sister had been the concubine—the wife, according to Indian customs—of Sir William) as

---

* This house, substantially built of stone, is yet standing on the north side of the Mohawk River, a mile from the village of Amsterdam, in Montgomery County. Sir William Johnson had an equally strong mansion, two stories in height, with a high peaked roof, wherein he resided twenty years before he built Johnson Hall. It is yet standing, about three miles west of Amsterdam. It was fortified and called "Fort Johnson."

his secretary; also by Colonel John Butler and his son Walter, who was afterward engaged in bloody forays upon the defenceless white inhabitants of the Mohawk region.

The council at Ontario, at which about fourteen hundred barbarians were assembled, was satisfactory to Colonel Johnson. Thence he went to Oswego and invited representatives of the Six Nations to meet him in

JOHNSON HALL.†
(From a sketch made in 1848.)

council there, to "feast on a Bostonian and to drink his blood"—in other words, to eat a roasted ox and to drink a pipe of wine.* The council was held; and at the conclusion Johnson, with a large number of Iroquois chiefs and warriors, crossed Lake Ontario, went down the St. Lawrence to Montreal, and entered the British military service. They were chiefly Mohawks under Brant.

---

* Some doubt has been expressed by a late investigator (Mr. A. McF. Davis) as to *two* conferences in the summer of 1775, as Ontario and Oswego were names sometimes applied to the same place at the mouth of the Oswego River by writers at that day. There was a place in the Seneca country on the borders of Lake Ontario called "Ontario," where a conference *may* have been held, as stated in the text.

† Johnson Hall, yet standing upon a gentle eminence about three fourths of a mile north of the court-house in the village of Johnstown, Fulton County, was built about the year 1760 by Sir William Johnson, and was, probably, the finest mansion in the province of New York at that time. The main building is of wood, clapboarded in a manner to represent blocks of stone. It is forty feet wide, sixty feet long, and two stories high. The detached wings, built for flanking block-houses, are of stone. The walls are very thick, and pierced near the eaves for musketry. One of these was recently removed.

While Guy Johnson was thus forming an active alliance of many of the tribes of the Six Nations (and especially the Mohawks) with the British in Canada, Sir John Johnson remained at Johnson Hall, the seat of Sir William, which he had fortified, exerting an equally powerful influence in a more quiet way in favor of the crown as a military leader and as a manorial proprietor over a large number of Scotch retainers, who were all Loyalists.

So was inaugurated the coalition with the British of Indians and Tories in New York, whose atrocious deeds in the Mohawk region gave it the name of "The Dark and Bloody Ground."

The Continental Congress now perceiving the necessity of securing the neutrality if not the alliance of the Indians, established a Board of Commissioners of Indian Affairs in three departments. General Schuyler, Major Joseph Hawley, Turbutt Francis, Oliver Wolcott, and Volkert P. Douw were appointed commissioners for the Northern Department. Through this Board Congress addressed earnest and friendly "talks" to the Six Nations, entreating them not to engage in the contest. "This is a family quarrel between us and Old England," they said. "You Indians are not concerned in it. We do not wish you to take up the hatchet against the king's troops. We desire you to remain at home and not join on either side."

Had a like humane and discreet policy governed the councils of the British Ministry many a horrible deed the record of which stains the annals of the period might never have been committed.

Tionderoga, or Ticonderoga, was made the point of rendezvous for the troops designed for the invasion of Canada. Schuyler was there at the middle of July. Only a handful of meanly-clad and poorly-fed armed men were there, under the command of Colonel Hinman, among whom insubordination was the rule. Brigadier-General Richard Montgomery, Schuyler's second in command, had been left at Albany to receive and discipline troops that might arrive until the commissariat at Ticonderoga should be in an efficient condition.

It had been agreed that Connecticut should furnish *men* and New York *supplies*. Both were tardy in performance, and the summer was almost ended before there was a sufficient force fairly equipped at Ticonderoga to warrant Schuyler in ordering an advance toward Canada. Washington, in command of the Continental troops before Boston, gave all aid to the enterprise in his power, and when the movement began he sent Colonel Arnold with over a thousand men across the wilderness of Western Maine to co-operate in efforts to seize Quebec.

The Provincial Congress of New York was almost powerless to act.

"You cannot conceive," wrote its president to General Schuyler in August, "the trouble we have with our troops for want of money. To this hour we have not received a shilling of the public money. Two of our members have been at Philadelphia almost a fortnight waiting for the cash. Our men insist on being paid before they march, not their subsistence only, but also their billeting money. Perhaps no men have been more embarrassed than we."

This inability was called indifference by some and disaffection by others, and drew forth ungenerous reflections. "That Congress," wrote Samuel Mott to Governor Trumbull from Ticonderoga, "are still unsound at heart. They make a great noise and send forward a few officers to command ; but as to soldiers in the service, I believe they are not more than one hundred and fifty strong at all the posts this side of Albany." And Major Brown, then on a mission in Canada, wrote to the same gentleman : "The New Yorkers have acted a droll part, and are determined to defeat us if they can."

Schuyler had sent Major Brown, an American and a resident on the Sorel, into Canada for information. At the middle of August he reported that there were seven hundred regular troops in Canada, of whom three hundred were at St. Johns ; that five hundred Tories and Indians under Sir John Johnson were near Montreal trying to persuade the Caughnawagas to join them ; that the French Canadians, restive under British rule, were generally disposed to remain neutral, and that he believed the conquest of Canada, if undertaken at once, might easily be achieved.

Schuyler now resolved to push forward as speedily as possible. Troops and supplies were coming forward. The Provincial Congress of New York was using every effort to furnish its one thousand men. Four regiments were organized under the respective commands of Colonels McDougal, Van Schaick, Clinton, and Holmes, and Captain John Lamb was authorized to raise a company of artillery one hundred strong, to be attached to McDougal's regiment. The Committee of Safety of New Hampshire sent to the gathering army on the lake three companies, under Colonel Bedel, who were accustomed to the woods and well acquainted with Canada. But the Green Mountain Boys were tardy in forming their regiment.

Toward the close of August the troops at Ticonderoga moved down the lake under the command of Generals Montgomery* and Wooster,

---

* Richard Montgomery was born in the north of Ireland in 1736 ; entered the British Army ; assisted in the capture of Quebec in 1759 ; was in the campaign against Havana with General Lyman, and, returning to New York, he made that city his residence. He went to England, sold his commission in 1772, came back, and bought a beautiful estate

and took post at Isle aux Noix, on the Sorel, a few miles above St. Johns. There Schuyler joined them. He had been in attendance upon his duty as Commissioner of Indian Affairs in holding a conference with representatives of the Six Nations at Albany. The troops remained at Isle aux Noix until the middle of September, when Schuyler, prostrated by illness, transferred the chief command to Montgomery and returned to Ticonderoga.

On the day of Schuyler's departure (September 25th) Montgomery advanced upon the fort at St. Johns with about a thousand men without artillery, and began a siege on the 18th. The garrison, commanded by Colonel Preston, maintained a vigorous resistance for more than a month. The fort was surrendered to Montgomery on November 3d, 1775.

GENERAL RICHARD MONTGOMERY.

During the siege small detachments from Montgomery's force went out upon daring enterprises. Colonel Ethan Allen had joined the little patriot army. At the head of eighty men, at the suggestion of Colonel John Brown, who was to co-operate with him, he pushed across the St. Lawrence to attack Montreal. Brown failed to co-operate. Allen was defeated, made prisoner, and was sent to England to be tried for treason, but was exchanged in May, 1778. Montgomery took Montreal.

General Montgomery wrote to the Continental Congress: "Until Quebec is taken Canada remains unconquered." Impressed with this idea, he lost no time in pressing toward Quebec in the face of terrible discouragements—inclement weather, the desertion of troops, hostility of the Canadians, and a lean commissariat. Frost was binding the waters, snow was mantling the whole country, and the rigors of a Canadian winter menaced him.

---

on the east bank of the Hudson, in Duchess County, and soon afterward married a daughter of Robert Livingston. He espoused the patriot cause; was commissioned a brigadier-general, and joined General Schuyler in the expedition to conquer Canada in 1775. He was in chief command of the troops that captured St. Johns and Montreal, and laid siege to Quebec. In an attack upon that city he was killed. There is a fine memorial monument to his memory on the front of St. Paul's Church, New York City.

Twenty miles above Quebec Montgomery met Arnold (December 11th) with a shattered remnant of his followers, tattered and torn, who had been driven from before the city, when woollen suits brought from Montreal were placed upon their shivering limbs. The united forces stood upon the Plains of Abraham, before Quebec, on December 1st, and demanded the surrender of the city. A scornful refusal was followed by a siege which lasted three weeks. It was carried on with a few light cannons and mortars mounted upon brittle ice redoubts, the men exposed to almost daily snow-storms in the open fields.

On the early morning of the last day of the year 1775 the little besieging army attempted to take Quebec by storm. The force was divided. One portion was led by Montgomery on the St. Lawrence side of the town; the other portion was led by Arnold on the St. Charles side. They were to meet and attempt a forced entrance into the city through Prescott Gate at Mountain Street. Just before dawn, while he was pressing forward at the head of the New York troops in the face of a blinding snow-storm, Montgomery was killed by a grape-shot from a masked battery at the foot of Cape Diamond.

DAVID WOOSTER IN 1758.

Arnold had been wounded and sent to a hospital. After a further struggle the British made a sortie through Palace Gate and captured the whole of Arnold's division. Arnold, now in chief command, retreated a few miles up the St. Lawrence, and for a while blockaded the garrison at Quebec. He was soon succeeded in command by General Wooster,[*] who came down from Montreal.

---

[*] David Wooster was born at Stratford, Conn., March 2d, 1710, and was educated at Yale College. He performed excellent military service among provincial forces before the Revolution. He was colonel of a Connecticut regiment, and became a brigadier-general in the French and Indian War. He was with Allen and Arnold at the capture of Ticonderoga in 1775; was in command in Canada, with the commission of a brigadier-general, in the spring of 1776, and on his return was made first major-general of Connecticut militia. Opposing the invasion of his State in the spring of 1777, he was fatally wounded in a skirmish at Ridgefield, and died on May 2d.

General Schuyler had just heard of the death of Montgomery, when he was called up the Mohawk Valley to disarm the Tories of Tryon County. It was evident that Sir John Johnson and his retainers were preparing for an active armed alliance with the British in Canada. Schuyler, acting under instructions from the Continental Congress, called for seven hundred militia to assist him. The response was marvellous. Before he reached Caughnawaga on the Mohawk, a few miles from Johnson Hall, he had three thousand armed followers, including nine hundred of the Tryon County militia.

By appointment Schuyler met the baronet at the late residence of Guy Johnson, on the Mohawk, from whom he demanded, as terms of peace, the immediate cessation of all hostile demonstrations; the surrender of all arms, ammunition, and stores in the possession of Johnson; the delivery to him of all the arms and accoutrements held by the Tories and Indians, and Sir John's parole of honor not to act inimically to the patriot cause.

SIR JOHN JOHNSON.

Sir John was compelled to comply with the terms, and gave his pledge.*

On January 19th (1776) the expedition under Schuyler was at Johnstown, where the arms and military stores were delivered up, and at noon the next day nearly three hundred Scotch Highlanders laid down their arms before a line of armed militia in the streets of Johnstown. The Mohawks meanwhile had remained neutral. With six Scottish chiefs and more than one hundred Tory prisoners, and some heavy guns as trophies, Schuyler marched back to Albany. He had disarmed between six and seven hundred Tories, conciliated the Mohawks, and diluted

---

* Sir John Johnson was born in 1742; died at Montreal June 4th, 1830. In 1774 he was appointed major-general of the New York militia. He was an active Tory and British partisan during the old war for independence, and produced great distress among the patriotic inhabitants of the Mohawk Valley by participation with the Indians on their destructive forays with his "Royal Greens," a partisan corps. He went to England, but returned in 1785 and resided in Canada, where he was made Superintendent of Indian Affairs. He was also a member of the Legislative Council of Canada. To compensate him for his losses, the British Government made him grants of land in Canada.

the loyalty of some of the most prominent leaders among the Six Nations.

During the summer and fall of 1775 stirring events occurred in the city of New York. The course of Governor Tryon was so evidently hostile to the Republican cause that the Provincial Congress, now governed by the popular will, and perceiving a resort to arms to be inevitable, ordered Captain John Lamb, then recruiting an artillery company, to take the cannons from the fort and the grand battery to a place of safety. With a small military force and a body of citizens led by Captain Sears, he went to the Battery at nine o'clock in the evening (August 25th) and began the task. A bullet was sent among the people from a barge filled with armed men from the *Asia*, which was concealed near by. A volley was returned, and the barge, bearing several men killed and wounded, hastened back to the *Asia*. That vessel immediately hurled three cannon shots ashore in quick succession. Lamb ordered the drums to beat to arms. The church-bells rang out an alarum; and while all was confusion and fear broadside after broadside of grape-shot from the *Asia* was fired upon the town, injuring several houses;[*] but no life was sacrificed. Believing that the town was to be sacked and burnt, hundreds of men, women, and children were seen at midnight hurrying away with their light effects to places of safety in the suburbs. Yet the patriots at the Battery stood firm, and in the face of the cannonade from the *Asia* every gun was removed. There were twenty-one iron 18-pounders and some smaller cannons.

The conduct of the commander of the *Asia* caused intense exasperation among the patriots, and Governor Tryon, taking counsel of prudence and his fears, sought refuge from the wrath of the people on board a British ship-of-war in the harbor. From that aquatic "palace" he attempted to rule the province. There his Council joined him.[†] But royal authority was at an end at New York forever.

Rivington, the loyal printer, had changed the name of his newspaper to the *Royal Gazette*, and was using his great influence as a journalist in

---

[*] Among the houses injured at that time was the tavern of Samuel Fraunce, a West Indian by birth, and of such a dark complexion that he was familiarly known as "Black Sam." His house was on the corner of Broad and Pearl streets. Freneau, in his "Petition of Hugh Gains," makes that time-serving journalist say, in alluding to the cannonade of the *Asia*:

> "At first we supposed it was only a sham,
> Till he drove a round ball through the roof of Black Sam."

[†] The members of his Council who joined him were: Oliver de Lancey, Hugh Wallace, William Axtelle, John Harris Cruger, and James Jauncey.

fostering Toryism in the province. He abused the Sons of Liberty (especially Captain Sears) in his paper without stint. Fired by personal insult and patriotic zeal, Sears went to Connecticut, and at noon on a bright day in November (25th) he entered the city at the head of seventy-five light horsemen, proceeded to the printing establishment of Rivington* at the foot of Wall Street, placed a guard around it, put the type into bags, destroyed the press and other appurtenances, and then rode out of the city amid the shouts of the populace and to the tune of Yankee Doodle. The type was cast into bullets Rivington finding New York too hot for him, fled to England, but returned the next year, when British troops held possession of the city, and resumed the publication of his *Gazetteer*.

Notwithstanding this action and the aggressive zeal of the Republicans, disaffection to their cause extensively prevailed throughout the province of New York during the winter of 1775–76. In Queens County, on Long Island, many of the people began to arm in favor of the crown, and from his floating refuge in the harbor Governor Tryon kept up a continual correspondence with Mayor Matthews, Oliver de Lancey, and other Loyalists on shore. The Continental Congress as vigorously opposed his influence, and took measures to disarm the Tories everywhere, while Washington, besieging Boston, kept a vigilant eye upon all that might harm the colony of New York.

JAMES RIVINGTON.

* James Rivington, the "King's printer" in New York, was a native of England. Failing in business as a bookseller in London, he came to America in 1760 and opened a book-store in Philadelphia. He opened another the following year at the foot of Wall Street, in New York. He printed books, and in 1773 he began the publication of the *Royal Gazetteer*, a weekly newspaper. After the Revolutionary War began he took strong ground in favor of the crown, and so continued until the close of the contest. It seems to be a well-attested fact that Rivington played false to the Royalists, and furnished much information to Washington. He, an apparent Anti-Loyalist, was permitted to remain in the city unmolested when, at the evacuation in 1783, hundreds of lesser sinners were compelled to flee. He died in July, 1802, at the age of seventy-eight years.

When, in January, 1776, Sir Henry Clinton, with a considerable force, sailed from Boston, Washington, believing New York to be his destination, sent General Charles Lee thither, instructed to gather a force on his way and take a position to defend that city. With marvellous rapidity Lee collected about twelve hundred men and encamped with

SIGNATURE OF JAMES RIVINGTON.

them in "The Fields" on the verge of the city, in spite of the protests of the Committee of Safety, who had been made timid by a threat of the commander of the *Asia* that he would bombard the town if "rebel troops" were allowed to enter it. Lee made his headquarters at No. 1 Broadway and issued a proclamation, in which he said:

"I come to prevent the occupation of Long Island and the city by the enemies of liberty. If the ships-of-war are quiet I shall be quiet; if they make my presence a pretext for firing upon the town, the first house set in flames by their guns shall be the funeral-pile of some of their best friends."

At these brave words the Tories shrunk into inactivity; the Provincial Congress felt a glow of patriotism, and measures were immediately adopted for fortifying the city and the approaches to it, and garrisoning it with two thousand men.* Sir Henry Clinton arrived at Sandy Hook on the day when Lee entered the city. Informed of Lee's presence, he sailed southward. Lee followed by land, leaving the little army at New York in charge of Lord Stirling. In June following Lee and Clinton were in conflict in Charleston Harbor.

Washington prosecuted the siege of Boston with as much vigor as circumstances would allow, and in March, 1776, he drove General Howe and his troops from the town literally into the sea. He allowed them to evacuate Boston (March 17th) and to sail away quietly and unmolested, accompanied by a large number of Loyalists, who fled before the indignation of a multitude of Whigs whom they had persecuted for months.

---

* For a description of the fortifications thus erected, see Lossing's *Pictorial Field Book of the Revolution*, Vol. II., p. 593, *note*.

Howe sailed for Halifax, Nova Scotia, and the following summer he appeared with a large armed force before New York City, borne thither in a fleet commanded by his brother, Lord Howe, and took possession of Staten Island.

Suspecting Howe had sailed for New York, Washington, with a larger part of his army, hastened to that city immediately after the evacuation of Boston, and held it until September.

During the heats of the summer Washington made his headquarters at Richmond Hill, far "out of town," with the bulk of his army encamped near by. Tryon was yet at his floating headquarters in the *Duchess of Gordon* war-ship plotting, plotting, plotting with his friends on shore for the ruin of the Republican cause. He formed a plan for the murder of Washington and his principal officers, or for their arrest and transportation to England to be tried for treason, and the capture of the troops on Manhattan Island. He sent money ashore freely for purposes of bribery. The Life Guard of Washington* was tampered with, and two of them were seduced from their fidelity. To one of them, an Irishman named Hickey, was intrusted the task of destroying Washington. He knew that his commander was very fond of green peas, and he resolved to

UZAL KNAPP.

---

* Washington's Life Guard was organized in the autumn of 1776 on Harlem Heights, and consisted of one hundred and eighty picked men, first commanded by Caleb Gibbs, of Rhode Island, with the rank of captain. William Colfax was the last commander. The special service of the Life Guard was to guard the headquarters of the commander-in-chief, but they were never spared in battle. The last survivor of Washington's Life Guard was Uzal Knapp, who died in the town of New Windsor, Orange County, N. Y., in January, 1857, when he was a little more than ninety-seven years of age. He was a native of Stamford, Conn., and was a sergeant in the Guard. Over his grave near Washington's Headquarters at Newburgh is a handsome mausoleum of brown freestone, made from designs by H. K. Brown, the sculptor.

The sketch on the following page of the banner of the Guard was copied from one in the museum at Alexandria, Va., in 1848, deposited there by George Washington Parke Custis. The figure of the guardsman shows the uniform of the Guard. It consists of a blue coat with white facings, white waistcoat and breeches, black half gaiters, a cocked hat with a blue and white feather. The banner was white silk.

slay him by poison mixed in a dish of them to be set before him at dinner.

Hickey tried to make the general's housekeeper, a faithful maiden, an accomplice in the deed by placing the poison in the peas. She pretended to favor his plans. At the appointed time for placing the savory dish before the general Hickey watched her movements through a half-opened door. The general made some excuse for ordering the dish away without tasting the peas. The girl had forewarned him. Hickey was arrested, found guilty, and hanged on a tree (June 28th, 1776) in the presence of fully twenty thousand people. It was the first military execution in the Continental Army. Mayor Matthews and more than twenty others were arrested on suspicion of complicity in the plot, but only Hickey suffered. The plot was traced directly to Tryon as its author.

At this juncture the Continental Congress, now become a permanent body, sitting at Philadelphia, were engaged in the discussion of a most important matter. The people in general until lately had not expressed a desire for political independence of Great Britain. There were a few who had warmly advocated it for some time. At the beginning of 1776 Thomas Paine, an English radical living in Philadelphia, put forth a powerful pamphlet, at the suggestion of Dr. Rush, in which he pleaded earnestly for independence. It was termed *Common Sense*. In terse, sharp, incisive, and vigorous sentences bristling with logic, he embodied the sentiments of reflecting men and women throughout the colonies.

BANNER OF WASHINGTON'S LIFE GUARD.

"Independence," he said, "is now the only bond that will keep us together. We shall then be on a proper footing to treat with Great Britain. . . . Every quiet method for peace hath been ineffectual. Our prayers have been rejected with disdain. Reconciliation is now a fallacious dream. Bring the doctrine of reconciliation to the touchstone of nature ; can you hereafter love, honor, and faithfully serve the power that hath carried fire and sword into your land ? Ye that tell us of harmony, can you restore us to the time that is past ? The blood of the slain, the weeping voice of nature cries, ' 'Tis time to part.' The last chord is now broken ; the people of England are now presenting addresses against us. A government of our own is a natural right. Ye that love mankind, that dare oppose not only tyranny but the tyrant, stand forth ! Every spot of the old world is overrun with oppression. Freedom hath been hunted round the globe. Asia and Africa hath long expelled her ; Europe regards her like a stranger ; and England hath given her warning to depart. Oh, receive the fugitive and prepare an asylum for mankind !"

The effect of this pamphlet was marvellous. It carried dismay into the enemy's camp. One hundred thousand copies were sent broadcast over the land, and produced an almost universal desire for independence among the people, for its trumpet tones awakened the continent and made every patriotic heart thrill with joy. It gave expression to a feeling that already filled the hearts of the people and was waiting for a voice.

Very soon legislative bodies began to move in the matter. North Carolina was the first colony that took positive action. It authorized its delegates in Congress to " concur with those of other colonies in declaring independence." Other colonies did the same. Others *permitted* their deputies to do so, and still others refused assent and were silent. Among the latter were New York, South Carolina, and Georgia.

At length the Continental Congress moved in favor of independence, satisfied that the people were ripe for it. In April they recommended the several provincial assemblies to form State governments. General letters of marque and reprisal were granted, and the American ports were opened to all nations excepting the British. Finally on June 7th, on motion of Richard Henry Lee, of Virginia (seconded by John Adams, of Massachusetts), the Congress resolved that the colonies were, and of right ought to be, free and independent States, and that all political connection between them and the State of Great Britain was, and ought to be, dissolved.

The consideration of this resolution was deferred, and a committee was appointed to draw up a formal declaration of causes for the action. The resolution was debated from time to time for nearly a month. It was adopted on July 2d by the unanimous vote of the colonies (not of the representatives), and on July 4th the Declaration, written by Thomas

Jefferson, was adopted by the same vote. The Declaration was signed on the same day by all the members who voted for it, when it was printed and sent out in every direction bearing the signatures of only John Hancock, president, and Charles Thomson, secretary. It was engrossed on parchment and signed afterward.

Toward evening on July 9th the Declaration of Independence was read to a brigade of the Continental Army in New York City, which was drawn up in a hollow square on the site of the City Hall. Washington was present. The Declaration was read in a clear voice by one of his aides. At early twilight the excited populace, citizens and soldiers, were led to the Bowling Green, where they attached ropes to the equestrian statue of George III. erected there, as we have observed, in 1770 (see page 199), and man and horse were pulled headlong to the ground. The statue, made of lead, was broken into fragments, and a large portion of it was cast into bullets which were afterward used by the Continental soldiers. "So," wrote a contemporary, "the British had melted majesty hurled at them."

A sudden change in action now appeared in the newly-elected Provincial Congress of New York. A large British force, just landed on Staten Island, was menacing the city. The Congress adjourned to White Plains, in Westchester County, and reassembled there on July 9th. They emphatically approved the Declaration of Independence,* and changed the title of their body to "Convention of Representatives of the State of New York," though the State was not yet organized. That measure was then under consideration.

It was now clearly manifest that the province of New York was to be the theatre of the first great effort to crush the "rebellion" in accordance with a plan devised by the British Ministry the year before, and which had been partially revealed. It contemplated the seizure of New York and Albany, and to strongly garrison both cities; to declare all persons "rebels" who should oppose the royal troops; to take possession of the Hudson and East rivers with small armed vessels, and so to form a strong line of military power between New England and the rest of the colonies, extending from Manhattan Island through the valleys of

---

* The Declaration was referred to a committee, of which John Jay was chairman. He almost instantly reported the following resolution, which was adopted:

"*Resolved, unanimously,* That the reasons assigned by the Continental Congress for declaring these united colonies free and independent States are cogent and conclusive, and that, while we lament the cruel necessity which has rendered the measure unavoidable, we approve the same, and will, at the risk of our lives and fortunes, join with the other colonies in supporting it."

the Hudson to Canada; to retake the forts on Lake Champlain, and with regulars, Canadians, Tories, and Indians, easily make destructive irruptions into New England and Pennsylvania. This would secure a safe communication between Quebec and New York, separate and weaken the most important colonies, and make the subjugation of all the colonies an easy task. This plan was devised by the ministry after the battle of Bunker (Breed's) Hill, and was made known to members of

SAMUEL CHASE. BENJAMIN FRANKLIN. CHARLES CARROLL.

the New York Provincial Congress by a letter from London during that summer.

The Continental Congress, satisfied that such a plan of subjugation was to be attempted, perceived the necessity of forming an alliance with Canada or achieving its conquest, and in the spring of 1776 Dr. Franklin, Samuel Chase, and Charles Carroll, of Carrollton, were sent into that province invested with extraordinary powers. They were accompanied by Rev. John Carroll, a Roman Catholic priest. They were authorized to regulate all military matters in the Republican army there; to treat with the Canadians as friends and brethren; to organize a republic there, and to admit Canada into union with the colonies they represented.

The commissioners were cordially received at Montreal,* but circum-

* The commissioners were entertained at New York by Lord Stirling, and set sail up the Hudson in a sloop furnished by him for the purpose at five o'clock P.M., April 2d, 1776. They came to anchor off the upper end of Manhattan Island, and lay there twenty-four hours because of a heavy north-east storm. They proceeded, and had a perilous voyage

stances rendered their mission futile. The British Government had hired thousands of soldiers from petty German princes to assist in enslaving its subjects in America. Some of these, under the command of General de Riedesel, with British re-enforcements commanded by Sir John Burgoyne, arrived at Quebec early in May (1776), and very soon the little Republican army in Canada, sorely smitten with the scourge of small-pox, was driven out of that province.

General John Thomas, a brave and skilful officer, had been sent by Washington to take command of the Republican troops in Canada and attempt a retrieval of losses there. He reached the camp near Quebec late in April (1776). The arrival of British re-enforcements there compelled him to retreat up the St. Lawrence. He continued his retreat to the Sorel, where he died of small-pox, when the command devolved upon General Sullivan. That officer struggled bravely with fate, but was compelled to yield to a superior force. With the shattered remnant of the Republican army he retreated to Crown Point. Of five thousand troops gathered there, poorly clad, fed, and sheltered, fully one half were sick early in July. The Northern army had lost, by death and desertion, fully five thousand men.

So ended in disaster that remarkable invasion. The incidents of its execution rank among the most startling and romantic in the annals of war.*

We have observed that Sir John Johnson gave his parole of honor to remain quiet. Early in May (1776) Schuyler was informed that Sir John, with Brant and others, was holding conferences with the Indians and inciting them to war, and that the baronet was preparing to make hostile movements in Tryon County with his Scotch retainers and the barbarians. Colonel Elias Dayton, a judicious officer, was sent with a competent force to Johnstown to arrest the baronet and take him to Albany, with his Scotch retainers and their families. When Dayton

---

through the Highlands, for the storm continued. When it abated they sailed with a fair wind and pleasant weather to Albany, where they were hospitably entertained by General Schuyler. Charles Carroll wrote : " He lives in pretty style ; has two daughters (Betsy and Peggy), lively, agreeable, black-eyed gals." " Peggy" became Mrs. (Patroon) Van Rensselaer, and "Betsy" Mrs. General Hamilton. The general conveyed them first to his country-seat at Saratoga, and thence to Lake George, where he had prepared for them a stout bateau. They crossed the lake among floating ice. Their bateau was drawn over to Lake Champlain (four miles) by six yoke of oxen. There the commissioners embarked on it and voyaged to St. Johns, at the foot of the lake, and thence, by land, to Montreal in *calèches*—two-wheeled vehicles.

* For a more minute account of this invasion, see Lossing's *Life and Times of Philip Schuyler*.

arrived the baronet had fled to the forest, and Lady Johnson assured him that her husband was on his way to Niagara with his retainers, and that his enemies would "soon hear where he was."

Lady Johnson was a spirited woman, a daughter of John Watts, one of the king's provincial councillors. Dayton informed her that measures would be taken to frustrate her husband's designs, and that she must accompany him to Albany. She was then conveyed thither, where she was treated with all the delicacy due to her sex and her social position. She was retained there some time as a hostage for the good behavior of her husband.

Sir John and his followers did not go to Niagara, but started for the St. Lawrence. They suffered intensely from weariness and starvation on the way, and reached that river in a wretched plight some distance above Montreal. The baronet was immediately commissioned a brigadier-general in the British service. He raised two battalions—a total of one thousand men—composed of his immediate followers and other American loyalists who followed his example in deserting their country, and these formed that active and formidable corps known in the frontier warfare of that period in Northern and Central New York as the "Royal Greens."

CHAPTER XVII.

An arrangement had been made by the British Cabinet to attack the Americans in 1776 simultaneously at three points. Sir Henry Clinton was to invade the Southern colonies; General Sir John Burgoyne was to clear Canada of the "rebels;" and General Howe, with the main army of thirty thousand men, including twelve thousand Germans, was to seize and occupy New York City, and thence form a junction with Burgoyne at Albany.

At the close of June General Howe arrived at Sandy Hook from Halifax with a large army, in transports, and on July 8th landed nine thousand troops on Staten Island, where he awaited the arrival of his brother, Admiral Lord Howe, with British regulars and some of the German hirelings.

Sir Henry Clinton joined Howe on the 11th with troops from Charleston, S. C., where they had co-operated with Admiral Sir Peter Parker's fleet in an unsuccessful attack upon Fort Moultrie, on June 28th. That conflict raged furiously about ten hours, when the terribly shattered fleet withdrew, and the seaworthy vessels sailed with the army for Sandy Hook.

Admiral Howe arrived at Sandy Hook on the 12th, and very soon other vessels came with German mercenaries. When August arrived nearly thirty thousand veteran soldiers stood ready to fall upon the Republican army (who were mostly militia, and nearly one fourth of them sick and unfit for duty), then occupying the city of New York, under the immediate command of Washington.

General Howe and his brother appeared in the twofold character of peace commissioners and as military commanders empowered to make war. They were authorized to treat for peace, but only on the condition of absolute submission on the part of the Americans. They were also authorized to grant pardons and amnesty to penitents. They made a most silly blunder at the outset in endeavoring to open negotiations with Washington by sending him a letter addressed to "George Washington, Esq." The general refused to receive it unless addressed to him by his military title. This the commissioners were instructed not to do; also not to recognize the Congress in an official capacity. Howe's adjutant-general (Major Patterson) was sent with another communication. It was not received, but he was admitted to the presence of Washington. He expressed a hope that reconciliation might be effected, and said the commissioners had large powers. "They have power only to grant pardon," said Washington. "The Americans are only defending their rights as British subjects, and have been guilty of no act requiring pardon," he continued. Here ended the interview.

Admiral Howe, who was personally acquainted with Dr. Franklin and most sincerely desired reconciliation, wrote to that gentleman on his first arrival. The doctor's reply satisfied the earl that his Government misapprehended the temper of the American people, and that Franklin expressed the sentiments of the Continental Congress when he wrote at the conclusion of his letter : "This war against us is both unjust and unwise ; posterity will condemn to infamy those who advised it ; and even success will not save from some degree of dishonor those who voluntarily engage in it." Here the commissioners paused in efforts to negotiate, and prepared immediately to strike the "rebellion" an effectual blow.

Already British ships-of-war had run up the Hudson River past American batteries, and were menacing the country in the rear of Manhattan Island with the intention of keeping open a free communication with Canada and facilities for furnishing arms to Tories in the interior. In the city of New York a majority of the influential inhabitants were active or passive Tories. The provincial authorities were yet acting timidly. In this exigency Washington appealed to the country. It was nobly responded to by the farmers of Connecticut, New York, Pennsylvania, Delaware, and Maryland, where harvest-fields needed them, and very soon they swelled the army at New York to about seventeen thousand effective men.

Both parties now prepared for an inevitable conflict. Hulks of vessels were sunk in the channel of the Hudson opposite the height on which Fort Washington was built. Fort Lee was erected on the Palisades beyond the river. Batteries were constructed at various points on Manhattan Island, and troops under the command of General Greene were sent over the East River to erect fortifications on Long Island back of Brooklyn. Greene was soon prostrated by fever, and resigned the command to General Sullivan, who had lately come from Lake Champlain. Small detachments were placed on Governor's Island and at Paulus's Hook (now Jersey City), and some militia were posted in lower Westchester County under General James Clinton to oppose the landing of British troops on the shores of Long Island Sound. Sullivan placed guards at several passes through a range of wooded hills on Long Island extending from the Narrows to Jamaica. Late in August the Americans had a line of defences extending from (present) Greenwood Cemetery to the Navy Yard, a distance of nearly two miles. These were armed with twenty cannons, and there was a strong redoubt with seven great guns on Brooklyn Heights.

On August 26th from twelve to fifteen thousand British troops were landed at the western end of Long Island. Washington immediately sent over a small re-enforcement to the Americans near Brooklyn, placed General Putnam in chief command on Long Island, and ordered General Sullivan to command the troops outside the lines. On that evening the British began an advance in three divisions. Their left, under General Grant, moved along the road nearest New York Bay; their right, under Sir Henry Clinton and Earl Cornwallis, accompanied by Howe, moved toward the interior of the island, and their centre, composed of Germans and led by General De Heister, advanced by Flatbush. The British had then afloat in adjacent waters ten ships of the line, twenty frigates, some bomb-ketches, and almost three hundred and fifty transports. The American troops on Long Island did not exceed eight thousand in number.

Informed that his pickets at the lower pass below Greenwood had been driven in, Putnam sent General Lord Stirling with some Delaware and Maryland troops to confront the enemy. He unexpectedly met a large force. Planting his only two cannons upon a wooded height ("Battle Hill" in Greenwood), he waited for the coming enemy, to give battle.

Meanwhile the Germans were pushing forward to force their way through the Flatbush Pass (now in Prospect Park, its place marked by an inscription), while Clinton and Cornwallis were eagerly pressing on to gain the Bedford and Jamaica passes. The latter had been neglected by Putnam, and having no defenders, Clinton easily seized it. While Sullivan was defending the Flatbush Pass against De Heister, the baronet with a strong force descended from the woods and attacked the Americans there on flank and rear. Sullivan attempted to retreat to the American lines, but failed, and with a large portion of his men he was made a prisoner.

Stirling and his party were now the only Americans in the field with unbroken ranks. They fought Grant's column with spirit for four hours. Then Cornwallis descended the Port or Mill Road with the bulk of Clinton's column and fell upon Stirling. The latter ordered a retreat, but the bridge over Gowanus Creek was in flames and the tide was rising. There was no alternative but to wade the creek. He ordered one half of his troops, with some German prisoners, to cross the muddy channel, while he and the rest should fight Cornwallis. Stirling was finally overcome and was made a prisoner.* By noon the victory for the British was complete. The Americans had lost about five hundred men killed and wounded, and one hundred and eleven made prisoners. The victors encamped in front of the American lines and prepared to besiege them.

Washington, who had beheld these movements with great anxiety, crossed the river on the morning of the 28th, and was rejoiced to find the British encamped and delaying an attack until their fleet should co-operate with them. He at once conceived a plan for the salvation of his imperilled little army. He resolved to attempt a retreat across the river to New York under the shadow of the ensuing night. Providentially a dense fog which overspread both armies at midnight and covered the whole region gave him essential aid. It did not disperse until after sunrise the next morning, when, under its sheltering wing and unsuspected by the British, the whole American army had passed the stream in boats and bateaux, carrying everything with them excepting heavy cannons. Washington and his staff, who had been in the saddle all night, remained on the Brooklyn side of the river until the last boat-load had departed.

LORD STIRLING.

Immediately after the battle General Howe again proposed to treat for peace. This was a reason for his delay in attacking the American camp. He sent a verbal message to the Continental Congress, whose

---

* William Alexander (Lord Stirling) was born in New York City in 1720, a son of Secretary Alexander, of New Jersey. Attached to the commissariat of the British Army in America, he attracted the notice of General Shirley, who made him his private secretary. He went to Scotland in 1755, and unsuccessfully presented his claim to the Earldom of Stirling. It was generally believed that his claim was just, and he ever afterward bore the empty title of "Lord Stirling," in America. In 1776 he was commissioned a brigadier-general in the Continental Army, and served with distinction during the war then begun. He married a daughter of William Livingston, of New Jersey. He was one of the founders of the New York Society Library and King's (now Columbia) College. Lord Stirling died June 15th, 1783.

authority he had been instructed not to recognize, proposing an informal conference with any persons whom that body might appoint. Congress consented, and early in September Dr. Franklin, John Adams, and Edward Rutledge met Howe at a house on Staten Island opposite Amboy, known as the "Billop House."* The meeting was friendly, but barren of expected fruit. Howe could not meet the three gentlemen as members of Congress, but only as private citizens; and he informed them that the independence of the colonies would not be considered for a moment. The gulf between them was impassable, and the conference soon ended.

The disaster on Long Island disheartened the American army, and

THE BILLOP HOUSE.

hundreds deserted and went home. General insubordination prevailed, and the army was weakened by the practice of many vices. Drunkenness was very common, and licentiousness poisoned the regiments. The outlook was extremely gloomy, and it was determined to take the sick and wounded to New Jersey, the military stores up the Hudson to Dobbs Ferry, abandon the city, and establish a fortified camp on Harlem Heights, near Fort Washington, toward the upper part of Manhattan Island.†

---

* This house was the residence of Captain Christopher Billop, formerly of the British Navy. It was now abandoned by the family. It stood upon high ground opposite Perth Amboy.

† Washington, in his retreat from the city to Harlem Heights, made his headquarters for a day or two at the home of Robert Murray on (present) Murray Hill, where he gave instructions to Captain Nathan Hale, who had volunteered to visit the British camp on Long Island, in disguise, and obtain information. While on that business Hale was recognized and exposed. He was arrested, sent to Howe's headquarters at Turtle Bay, East River (at Forty-seventh Street), and hanged as a spy by the notorious provost-marshal,

General Howe was indolent and fond of sensual pleasures. Procrastination marred many of his plans. When he found the Americans had escaped he leisurely prepared to invade Manhattan Island in the rear of the American army there. Before he was ready to do so that army was so strongly intrenched upon Harlem Heights that they defied him. Washington made his headquarters at the home of his companion-in-arms on the field of Monongahela, Roger Morris, which is yet standing.

After various menacing movements had been made, a strong British force crossed the East River (September 15th) from Long Island and landed at Kip's Bay, at the foot of (present) Thirty-fourth Street, under cover of a cannonade. The American guard there fled, but were soon rallied. So long delayed were the movements of the British toward the Hudson River that Putnam, who had been left in the city with a few troops, was enabled to escape to Harlem Heights.

On the following day some British infantry and Scotch Highlanders, led by General Leslie, encountered some Connecticut Rangers and a force of Virginians, under Colonel Knowlton and Major Leitch, on Harlem Plains. They fought desperately until Washington sent some re-enforcements, when the enemy was forced back to the high rocky ground at the upper end of Central Park. This affair greatly inspirited the Americans, though they were compelled to mourn the loss of Colonel Knowlton and Major Leitch.

General Robertson was now sent with a considerable force to take possession of the city, where the British intended to make their comfortable winter quarters. While his forces were reposing in their tents on the hills not far northward of the town, at midnight (September 20th–21st) huge columns of lurid smoke arose above the houses. It was soon followed by arrows of flame that shot upward. A terrible conflagration was begun. It broke out, by accident, in a low groggery and brothel at Whitehall, and as most of the Whig inhabitants had fled from the city, there were few to check the flames excepting the soldiers and the sailors from the ships in the harbor. About five hundred buildings were consumed, including Trinity Church, on Broadway.

Howe, re-enforced by troops from Great Britain and more Germans, under the command of General Knyphausen, resolved to gain the rear of Washington's army, which he dared not attack in front. The

---

Cunningham, who exercised the greatest cruelty toward the unfortunate young man. His last words were, as he stood under the tree upon which he was hanged, with a rope around his neck: "I only regret that I have but one life to give to my country." Hale is justly regarded as a martyr to human liberty. André, who suffered for the same offence, was the victim of his own ambition.

Germans had come in seventy vessels, and numbered about ten thousand men, swelling Howe's forces to about thirty-five thousand. On October 12th Howe embarked a large portion of his army in ninety flat-boats and landed them on a low peninsula of the main of Westchester County. Washington sent General Heath to confront the invaders and check their movements toward his rear.

Perceiving his peril, Washington called a council of war, when it was resolved to evacuate Manhattan Island and take position on the Bronx River in Westchester, to meet the invaders face to face, or secure a safe retreat to the Hudson Highlands. Leaving a garrison of nearly three thousand men in Fort Washington, under Colonel Magaw, the army withdrew, and, marching up the valley of the Bronx, formed intrenched camps from the heights of Fordham to White Plains. Washington made his headquarters near White Plains village on the 21st. General Greene commanded a small force which garrisoned Fort Lee, on the west side of the Hudson.

After almost daily skirmishing the two armies, each about thirteen thousand strong, met in battle array near the village of White Plains on October 28th. The strongest position of the Americans was behind breastworks upon Chatterton's Hill, a lofty eminence on the right side of the Bronx opposite the village.

Howe's army advanced in two divisions, one led by Sir Henry Clinton, and the other by Generals De Heister and Erskine. Howe was with the latter. A hurried council of war was held by these officers on horseback, when some troops, under cover of a heavy cannonade, proceeded to build a rude bridge over the Bronx. Over this British troops crossed and drove the Americans from Chatterton's Hill. The Republicans retreated to their intrenched camp nearer the village, where they remained unmolested until the night of the 31st. Howe dared not attack the apparently formidable breastworks of Washington's intrenchments, which were really composed chiefly of cornstalks slightly covered with earth. The Americans withdrew in the night to a strong position on the heights of North Castle, five miles farther north. The British did not pursue. Washington with his main army crossed the Hudson and encamped between Fort Lee and Hackensack, in New Jersey. He left General Lee in command of a strong force at North Castle, with instructions to follow him into New Jersey if necessary, and he put Heath in command in the Hudson Highlands.

Isolated Fort Washington, standing upon the highest land on the island, overlooking and commanding the Hudson River, between One Hundred and Eighty-first Street and One Hundred and Eighty-sixth

Street, was the next point of attack by the British under Howe. It was a five-sided earthwork, two hundred and thirty feet above tide-water, a mile north of Washington's former headquarters at the Roger Morris home. It mounted thirty-four great guns, and it was defended by several outlying redoubts and batteries on the north and south, extending across the island between the Hudson and Harlem rivers.

Howe procrastinated as usual, and it was the middle of November before he attacked Fort Washington. On the morning of the 16th he put troops in motion for a simultaneous assault at four different points.

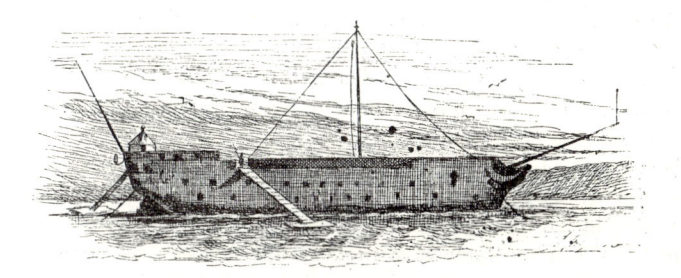

THE JERSEY PRISON-SHIP.

They crossed the Harlem River under cover of a cannonade. The troops were led, respectively, by General Knyphausen (who commanded the Germans), Lords Percy and Cornwallis, General Mathews, and others. Before noon the occupants of supporting redoubts and batteries were driven into the fort. At one o'clock in the afternoon it had been surrendered, and the British flag was waving over it. Its name was changed to Fort Knyphausen.* Twenty-six hundred men became prisoners of war, and many of them were long sufferers in the loathsome prisons of New York and the more loathsome prison-ships afloat in the surrounding waters.†

---

* On the day of the final attack, Washington, with Generals Putnam, Greene, and Mercer, crossed the river, ascended the heights, and went to the abandoned mansion of Roger Morris, where the commander-in-chief had established his headquarters on Harlem Heights. From that point they took a hasty view of the scene of operations, and hastily departed. Within fifteen minutes after they left the mansion the British Colonel Sterling with his victorious troops took possession of it.

† Among the most notable of these prison-ships was the hulk of the *Jersey*, which was moored at the Wallabout, now the site of the Navy Yard at Brooklyn. It was called "hell afloat." A greater portion of its inmates were captive American sailors. The most wanton outrages were suffered by the poor victims. The number of deaths in this

Washington, satisfied that Howe would now turn his attention to the Federal City (Philadelphia), where Congress was sitting, prepared to hasten to its defence. Fort Lee was abandoned, but before its stores could be removed Cornwallis had crossed the Hudson with six thousand men, and was rapidly approaching it. The garrison fled to the camp near Hackensack, and then began Washington's famous retreat across New Jersey, pursued by Cornwallis, to the Delaware River.

The British were now in full possession of the city of New York and Manhattan Island, and held them more than seven years. The Provincial Congress of New York became migratory. Driven from the city in August (1776), they sat a short time at Harlem, then at Kingsbridge, White Plains, the Philipse Manor, Fishkill, Poughkeepsie, and finally at Kingston, in Ulster County. There they remained until their final dissolution on the establishment of a State Government, in the spring and summer of 1777.

While the important military events just recorded were occurring in Southern New York near the sea, others of great importance were occurring in Northern New York near the borders of Canada. A large British and German force were in the latter province under the general command of Sir John Burgoyne, and were united with troops under General Guy Carleton, the Governor of Canada, in preparation for executing the plan for the severance of New England from the other colonies, already mentioned. This gave the Continental Congress and their constituents great anxiety, and in June the Congress sent General Horatio Gates to take command of the Republican army in Canada, independent of General Schuyler's control.

When Gates arrived in Albany he was thus first informed that the army was *out* of Canada, and the remnant of it was at Crown Point. He hastened thither, took command of that remnant, and proceeded to

---

"hell" was frightful. Starvation, fever, and even suffocation in the pent-up air at night made a fearful daily sacrifice of human creatures. Every morning there went down the hatchway from the deck the terrible cry, "Rebels, turn out your dead!" Then a score of dead bodies covered with vermin would be carried up by tottering half skeletons, their suffering companions, when they were taken to the shore and lightly buried in the sands of the beach. Such was the fate of eleven thousand American prisoners during the war.

The cruelties inflicted by Cunningham, the brutal provost-marshal, who had the general supervision of American prisoners in New York City, were terrible. He seemed to be acting independent of the military officers. In his confession before his execution in England for a capital crime, he said: "I shudder to think of the murders I have been accessory to, with and without orders from Government, especially while in New York, during which time there were more than two thousand prisoners starved in the different buildings used as prisons, by stopping their rations, which I sold!"

construct a flotilla of armed vessels to oppose the advance of the British. General Arnold was appointed commander-in-chief of the flotilla, and by the middle of August (1776) ten vessels, large and small, were ready for service. Meanwhile the British were busy in the construction of an armed flotilla at St. Johns, on the Sorel.

Toward the close of August the impatient and impetuous Arnold was permitted to go down the lake to meet the foe, but instructed not to go beyond (present) Rouse's Point, on the boundary-line between New York and Canada. He soon found himself in a perilous position, and fell back some distance. In the course of a few weeks his flotilla was increased, and early in October he was in command of a fleet composed of three schooners, two sloops, three galleys, eight gondolas, and twenty-one gun-boats, bearing an aggregate armament of sixty-seven cannons and ninety-four mortars, and manned by about five hundred men.

Ignorant of the strength of the naval armament preparing at St. Johns, and unwilling to meet a superior force on the broad lake, Arnold committed the foolish blunder of arranging his vessels in a line across the comparatively narrow channel between Valcour Island and the western shore of the lake, a few miles below Plattsburg. His flag-ship was the schooner *Royal Savage*, twelve guns. There he was attacked by a formidable flotilla, manned by many veterans of the Royal Navy, on the morning of October 11th. It was commanded by Captain Pringle in the *Inflexible*, though the expedition was under the supreme command of General Carleton, who was with the fleet, with British and German officers and troops. A severe action ensued, which continued almost five hours. Arnold and his men fought desperately. His vessel grounded and was burned by the enemy, but the crew were saved. Night closed upon the scene, when neither party was victorious.

The two fleets anchored within a few hundred yards of each other.

THE (ROYAL) SAVAGE.[*]

---

[*] Copied from a water-color sketch found by the writer among the papers of General Philip Schuyler in 1856. It settled the important question, What was the device on the "Union flag" hoisted over the American camp at Cambridge on January 1st, 1776?

Arnold determined to retreat to Crown Point that night. Anticipating such a movement, the British flotilla was anchored in a line across the lake to intercept his vessels. The night was intensely dark, heavy clouds having gathered over the sky. At ten o'clock the Americans weighed anchor, and with a stiff breeze from the north the whole flotilla passed through the British line unobserved. The astonished enemy gave chase the next morning. Calms and head winds ensued, and it was not until the morning of the 13th that the fugitives were overtaken. Then another desperate fight ensued for several hours. One of the American vessels (the *Washington*) was captured, and General Waterbury and her crew were made prisoners. Arnold was on the *Congress*. When she became shattered almost to a wreck he ran her ashore, with other vessels, a few miles below Crown Point, set them on fire, and escaped.

General Carleton, with Generals Burgoyne and Riedesel (the latter the commander of the Germans), who accompanied the expedition, took possession of Crown Point and held it about a fortnight, but refused to attempt to recapture Ticonderoga. The whole British force sailed down the lake early in November, and went into winter quarters in Canada. Burgoyne soon afterward returned to England. At the end of 1776 Lake Champlain was really at the mercy of the British, and the Americans had lost all territory acquired since Allen took Ticonderoga.

Early in the struggle British cruisers kept the people on the New England coasts in a state of continual alarm. One of them bombarded and burnt Falmouth (now Portland), in Maine, and other depredations were committed by British armed vessels. The Continental Congress, perceiving the necessity for meeting this exigency, took measures for creating a navy. At near the close of the year they ordered a considerable number of armed vessels to be built. Esek Hopkins, of Rhode Island, was appointed the chief naval commander, and in February (1776) he sailed from the Delaware with a little squadron to oppose Lord Dunmore, the fugitive royal governor of Virginia, who was devastating the shores of that province. On January 1st (1776) he had burned Norfolk. Hopkins went on to the Bahama Islands, seized Nassau, and carried off one hundred cannons and a large quantity of stores. The Continental Navy was never powerful, but numerous privateers authorized by Congress performed efficient service.

Two of the vessels of war ordered by Congress were built at Poughkeepsie, on the Hudson, by Van Zandt, Lawrence & Tudor, who established a "Continental Ship Yard" there. These were the *Congress*, twenty-eight guns, and the *Montgomery*, twenty-four guns. These naval constructors were also employed in building the boom composed of timbers and iron chains across the Hudson at Anthony's Nose, at the southern entrance of the Highlands. It was constructed by command of the Committee of Safety appointed by the Provincial Congress. It was completed in the spring of 1777.*

The military disasters in different parts of New York were partially counterbalanced by brilliant achievements of American soldiers in New Jersey, in the early winter of 1776-77. In the race for the Delaware River between Washington and Cornwallis the former won; but important places—Newark, Brunswick, Princeton, and Trenton—fell into the hands of the invader. The little army of Washington continually

LINKS OF THE CHAIN AT WEST POINT.

diminished during his flight across New Jersey, and when he reached the Delaware and crossed the river into Pennsylvania he had scarcely three thousand soldiers left. Republicans in New Jersey seemed paralyzed in the presence of the British army. Washington had urged Lee to join him with the troops left at North Castle, but he would not do so; and after the little army had crossed the Delaware that officer, who, it is now known, was a traitor to the cause, allowed himself to be made a prisoner in New Jersey and taken to New York.

The procrastinating Howe, feeling sure that he could now capture Philadelphia at any time, ordered Cornwallis to defer the crossing of the river until it should be sufficiently frozen to allow the troops to move

---

* The boom consisted of a heavy iron chain borne by strong floats. A more powerful boom was stretched across the river from West Point to Constitution Island. The chain was buoyed by logs about sixteen feet in length sharpened at each end, so as to offer little resistance to the tides. To these logs the chain was firmly fastened. Several links of the chain may be seen at West Point surrounding a mortar. The links are made of **iron bars** two inches and a half square and a little more than three feet in length. Each weighed about one hundred and sixty pounds.

over upon the ice. They were cantoned along the New Jersey side of the river from Trenton to Burlington. A detachment of Germans under Colonel Rall and some British light horse were stationed at Trenton; and so confident were the British that the inchoate republic was ruined, that Cornwallis prepared to return to England. When Rall sent to General Grant for re-enforcements, the latter said to the messenger: "Tell the colonel he is very safe. I will undertake to keep the peace in New Jersey with a corporal's guard."

Dark, indeed, was the aspect of public affairs for the Republicans at that moment. The frightened Congress had fled from Philadelphia to Baltimore. The public mind was despondent. Recruiting for the army seemed impossible. Terms of service of the soldiers were about to expire, and the army was reduced to seventeen hundred men. Yet Washington, knowing the cause to be just, and relying upon Omnipotence, never lost hope. At that gloomy hour he conceived a masterly stroke of military skill. Liberal bounties were offered for recruits, and brought them. Lee's division, under Sullivan, joined him. So, also, did regiments from Ticonderoga. The Pennsylvania militia turned out with considerable alacrity, and the spell-bound people of New Jersey began to recover their senses.

Thus strengthened, Washington resolved to recross the Delaware and smite the enemy at Trenton. He chose Christmas night for the enterprise, knowing that a large portion of the Germans would probably be disabled by their holiday indulgences.

In a storm of sleet the Americans, two thousand strong, with twenty cannons, crossed the Delaware at night on flat-boats amid thin floating ice, and hoped to reach Trenton before daylight. They could not. The German guards at the outskirts of the village, surprised, were driven in, and gave an alarm. The drums beat to arms, and very soon Colonel Rall and his disordered troops were in the streets. In the sharp skirmish that ensued Rall fell, mortally wounded. His troops, panic-stricken, broke and fled in confusion, but were intercepted by some Pennsylvania riflemen under Colonel Hand and made prisoners. The light horse escaped. The victory was complete. As a prudential measure Washington immediately recrossed the river with his captives and spoils.

The British were astounded, and fell back from the Delaware. Washington's ranks were rapidly filled. Congress had clothed him with the powers of a dictator. He recrossed the Delaware (December 30th), took post at Trenton with about five thousand men, and resolved to act on the offensive. Cornwallis returned to New Jersey, and the British and German troops were concentrated at Princeton, only ten miles distant.

On January 2d (1777) Cornwallis, with a strong force, moved against Washington from Princeton. At Trenton they had some skirmishing, when each party encamped for the night upon opposite sides of a small stream. Expecting re-enforcements in the morning, Cornwallis felt sure of his prey. But Washington, with his troops, moved secretly away after midnight, and before sunrise he was engaged in battle near Princeton with the reserved troops who had started to re-enforce Cornwallis. The battle was short, sharp, and decisive. The brave General Hugh Mercer was mortally wounded, and many other American officers were slain on that snowy field.

When the astonished Cornwallis found that his anticipated prey had escaped, and he heard the booming of cannon at Princeton, he hastened back; but not a "rebel" was found there. They had won a victory and passed on, and made their way to Morristown, in the hill country of East Jersey, where Washington established his winter quarters.

CHAPTER XVIII.

Two very important events occurred within the domain of New York during the year 1777, namely: (1) The framing of a constitution for the government of the Commonwealth and the establishment and organization of an independent State government; (2) A formidable invasion of the State by British troops from Canada, under the command of Lieutenant-General Sir John Burgoyne.

The final movement in their migrations by the Provincial Congress, or, rather, the "Convention of Representatives of the State of New York," as that body was now called, occurred in February, 1777, when they adjourned from Poughkeepsie to Kingston. In April, the previous year, the Continental Congress resolved, "That it be recommended to the several Assemblies and Conventions of the United Colonies, where no government sufficient to the exigencies of their affairs hath hitherto been established, to adopt such a government as shall, in the opinion of the representatives of the people, best conduce to the happiness and safety of their constituents in particular, and of America in general."

This was a bold but cautious step in the direction of independence. The people of New York, though Toryism was yet rife among them, favored the recommendation of Congress by a large majority, and proceeded to elect a new Convention.* It assembled at White Plains in

---

* At that time the State was divided into fourteen counties—namely, New York, Richmond, Kings, Queens, Suffolk, Westchester, Duchess, Orange, Ulster, Albany, Tryon, Charlotte, Cumberland, and Gloucester. The last two counties formed a part of the (present) State of Vermont. The following are the names of the members who were present at the session at Kingston and assisted in the formation of a State government for New York:

New York City.—John Jay, James Duane, John Morin Scott, James Beekman, Daniel Dunscomb, Robert Harper, Philip Livingston, Abraham P. Lott, Peter van Zandt, Anthony Rutgers, Evert Bancker, Isaac Stoutenburgh, Isaac Roosevelt, John van Cortlandt, William Denning.

Albany.—Abraham Ten Broeck, Robert Yates, Leonard Gansevoort, Abraham Yates, Jr., John Ten Broeck, John Taylor, Peter R. Livingston, Robert van Rensselaer, Matthew Adgate, John I. Bleecker, Jacob Cuyler.

Duchess.—Robert R. Livingston, Zephaniah Platt, John Schenck, Jonathan Landon, Gilbert Livingston, James Livingston, Henry Schenck.

Ulster.—Christopher Tappen, Matthew Rea, Matthew Cantine, Charles De Witt, Arthur Parks.

July, for the double purpose of framing a State Constitution and of exercising all the powers of government until that duty should be performed.

On August 1st (1776) the Convention appointed a committee to prepare a Constitution. Mr. Jay was made chairman of the committee. The exigencies of public affairs, in which he was deeply engaged, caused considerable delay in their work, for almost the entire labor devolved upon him. The draft, in the handwriting of Mr. Jay, was submitted to the Convention on March 12th, 1777. That body were then sitting at Kingston, in a substantial house built of blue limestone, on the corner of Main and Fair streets, which is yet (1886) standing. It was one of the few houses spared by the torches of British incendiaries who burned Kingston in the autumn of the same year.

JOHN JAY.*

Westchester.—Pierre van Cortlandt, Gouverneur Morris, Gilbert Drake, Lewis Graham, Ezra Lockwood, Zebediah Mills, Jonathan Platt, Jonathan G. Tompkins.

Orange.—William Allison, Henry Wisner, Jeremiah Clarke, Isaac Sherwood, Joshua H. Smith.

Suffolk.—William Smith, Thomas Treadwell, John Sloss Hobart, Matthias Burnet Miller, Ezra L'Hommedieu.

Queens.—Jonathan Lawrence.

Tryon.—William Harper, Isaac Paris, Mr. Vedder, John Morse, Benjamin Newkirk.

Charlotte.—John Williams, Alexander Webster, William Duer.

Cumberland.—Simon Stephens.

Kings, Richmond, and *Gloucester* were not represented.

* John Jay was born in the city of New York on December 12th, 1745. He entered King's (now Columbia) College when he was fourteen years old, and gave early promise of a brilliant career. He was admitted to the bar in 1768 ; soon became an eminent lawyer ; married a daughter of William Livingston, of New Jersey, in 1774, and joined vigorously in opposition to the measures of the British ministry as a champion of popular rights. He was the youngest member of the first Continental Congress, and was one of the most efficient men in that body. After assisting in the organization of the *State* of New York, he became president of the Continental Congress, and in 1779 was sent as minister at the Spanish court. He was one of the commissioners to negotiate the Preliminary Treaty of Peace in 1782, and the following year he affixed his signature to the definite Treaty. On his return he assumed the duties of chief of the Foreign Depart-

The Constitution was under consideration for more than a month. Mr. Jay, on reflecting upon the character and feelings of the members of the Convention, had omitted several important provisions, which he proposed to offer separately as amendments before it should be finally acted upon. That action was taken, in a precipitate manner, on April 20th.* Mr. Jay was then absent in attendance upon his dying mother. Before his return the instrument was adopted, with some additions and

HOUSE IN WHICH THE CONSTITUTION WAS ADOPTED.

omissions, which he regretted. In a letter penned a few days afterward concerning the hurried manner in which this important business had been concluded, Mr. Jay wrote, after pointing out his objections:

"The other parts of the Constitution I approve, and only regret that, like a harvest cut before it was well ripe, some of the grains have shrunk. Exclusive of the clauses which I have mentioned, and which

---

ment of the Federal Government, and so remained until the National Government was established, in 1789, when he was appointed the first Chief-Justice of the United States. In 1794 he negotiated a new treaty with Great Britain. During his absence he was elected Governor of the State of New York, and held that office until 1801. Governor Jay died May 17th, 1829.

* On April 22d the Constitution was published by the reading of it to the members of the Convention and the people by Robert Benson, the secretary, in front of the court-house in Kingston. Benson stood upon a barrel, and his clear voice was distinctly heard by the multitude. Three thousand copies of the document were printed by John Holt, at Fishkill, for distribution.

I wish had been added, another material one has been omitted—namely, a direction that all persons holding office under the government should swear allegiance to it, and renounce all allegiance and subjection to foreign kings, princes, and States, in all matters, ecclesiastical as well as civil. I should also have been for a clause against the continuance of domestic slavery, and for the support and encouragement of literature." Because of Mr. Jay's temporary absence from the Convention it is probable that the State of New York was deprived of the honor of

PUBLISHING THE CONSTITUTION.

setting the first example in America of the voluntary abolition of slavery. Among the most prominent features of the Constitution, and which were subsequently eliminated from it by revisions and amendments, were (1) a provision for a Council of Appointment, composed of the governor and four Senators, the latter chosen by the Assembly to serve for two years. This Council appointed nearly all officers, excepting the chancellor and Supreme Court judges. The term of office of their appointees depended upon the will of the Council; (2) a Council of

Revision, composed of the governor, the chancellor, and Supreme Court judges, whose duty it was to revise all bills about to be passed into laws by the Legislature; (3) a property qualification to enable a citizen to exercise the right of the elective franchise, and requiring Senators to be freeholders; giving power to the governor to prorogue the Legislature.

Unlike the more democratic usage of to-day, no provision was made for the submission of the Constitution to the judgment of the people, and the latter had no opportunity to discuss its provisions or form an opinion of it until it was too late to do so. The Convention was urged by the "Union Mechanics," of New York City, to submit it to the people; but as the members of the Convention were anxious to return home, and public affairs required a speedy organization of a State government, this fundamental law of the State was put forth, the product of the *representatives* only of the people.

In the full history of these movements toward the perfecting the Constitution of the State of New York is developed much of the philosophy of that progress which marks so distinctly the onward career of our Commonwealth. From the old Dutch laws, sometimes narrow and despotic, but usually marked by a sound and expansive policy, have evolved, by degrees, the enlightened features of the present Constitution of the State. In it we may trace the growth of the benevolent principles of human equality and the correct appreciation in the public mind of the rights of man.

Provision was made for putting the State Government into active operation immediately.* Robert R. Livingston was appointed by the Convention, Chancellor; John Jay, Chief-Justice; Robert Yates, Jr., and John Sloss Hobart, puisne justices, and Egbert Benson, Attorney-General. The benches of the courts of the several counties were filled. A Council of Safety was appointed, composed of John Morin Scott, Robert R. Livingston, Charles Tappen, Abraham Yates, Jr., Gouverneur Morris, Zephaniah Platt, John Jay, Charles De Witt, Robert Harper, Jacob Cuyler, Thomas Treadwell, J. Sloss Hobart, and Jonathan G. Tompkins. To this Council were confided all the powers of the State, to be exercised without control, until superseded by the regularly constituted authorities.

The Convention also appointed a sort of Vigilance Committee, for

---

* A committee composed of John Jay, Robert R. Livingston, Gouverneur Morris, John Morin Scott, Abraham Yates, and John Sloss Hobart was appointed to report a plan for organizing the State Government. Fifteen of the members of the Convention were empowered to govern the State until an election could be held for the State officers. They constituted a board called the Council of Safety.

"inquiring into and detecting and defeating all conspiracies that may be formed in the State against the liberties of America." John Jay was the first chairman. They were empowered to send for persons and papers; to call out the militia in the several counties for suppressing insurrection; to apprehend, secure, or remove persons whom they might judge dangerous to the State; to make the necessary drafts upon the treasury; to enjoin secrecy upon their members and the persons they employed. They were empowered to raise and officer two hundred and twenty men, and to avail themselves of their service whenever the committee might see fit.

This formidable committee was kept in active existence during the war, and its powers were employed with energy. A vast number of arrests, imprisonments, and banishments from the State or to within the British lines at New York were made by it. Many Tories and their families were sent into the city of New York from the rural districts; others were expelled from the State, and others were required to give security to a pledge to reside within prescribed limits. Occasionally the jails and even the churches were crowded with prisoners, and many were sent to jails in Connecticut for safe keeping. Among the latter was the Mayor of New York.*

The Convention defined the crime of treason against the State, and imposed the penalty of death upon the offender. They established a system of confiscation; and soon after the Constitution was adopted a law was passed requiring an oath of allegiance to the State. All persons refusing to take such oath were sent within the British lines or were exchanged for prisoners of war. An act of attainder was passed, together with an act for the "forfeiture and sale of the estates of persons

---

* This committee was timely, for the southern portion of the State was so strongly Tory in sentiment that at one time the inhabitants were on the point of open opposition to Congress before the entry of the British troops into New York City. Governor Tryon resumed his authority as supreme ruler. He received the congratulations of the loyal inhabitants signed by Daniel Hommanden, Oliver de Lancey, and nine hundred and forty-six others. They also addressed the brothers Howe, as peace commissioners, praying that reconciliation and general loyalty might be restored. A similar address was made to the governor and the commissioners in October, signed by David Colden and two thousand one hundred and eighty-four inhabitants of Queens County. On the 20th of the same month the committee of Suffolk County dissolved, disclaimed and rejected the orders of Congress, and declared themselves "desirous to obey the legal authority of government, hoping that the governor would pass by their former misconduct and be graciously pleased to protect them, agreeably to the laws of the province." The disaffected everywhere began to correspond with the enemy, and authority was given to county committees to arrest and punish them.

who had adhered to the enemy, and for declaring the sovereignty of the State in respect to all property within it."*

The Convention adjourned in May. The Council of Safety immediately ordered an election of a Legislature and State officers. The returns were made to the Council early in July. General George Clinton was chosen governor, and Pierre van Cortlandt lieutenant-governor. Clinton held the position by successive elections until 1795, when he was succeeded by John Jay. He was installed in office on July 30th, at Kingston. Being then actively engaged in command of the New York militia, he did not quit the field until the defeat of Burgoyne, in the fall, but discharged his civil duties by correspondence with the Council of Safety, which body was continued until the full organization of the State Government, in the spring of 1778.

The first meeting of the Legislature of New York took place at Kingston,[†] when Walter Livingston was chosen Speaker of the Assembly. Pierre van Cortlandt, the lieutenant-governor, presided over the Senate. John Morin Scott was chosen Secretary of State, and Comfort Sands Auditor-General.

Thus was completed by the process of evolution the transformation of the alternate Dutch and English province of New York into an independent commonwealth. It formed a constituent of the then inchoate nation which has become the mightiest power on the earth. New York

---

* The persons subjected to special attention under this law were: John Murray, Earl of Dunmore; William Tryon, governor; John Watts, Oliver de Lancey, Hugh Wallace, Henry White, John Harris Cruger, William Axtell, Roger Morris, late members of the Council; George Duncan Ludlow and Thomas James, late justices of the Supreme Court; John Taber Kempe, late attorney-general; William Bayard, Robert Bayard, James de Lancey, David Matthews (late Mayor of New York), James Jauncey, George Folliot, Thomas White, William McAdam, Isaac Low, Miles Sherbrooke, Alexander Wallace, John Weatherhead, Rev. Charles Inglis, rector of Trinity Church, and Margaretta, his wife; Sir John Johnson, Guy Johnson, Daniel Claas (son-in-law of Sir William Johnson), John Butler, John Joost Herkimer, Frederick Philipse, Senior and Junior; David Colden, Daniel Kissam, Gabriel Ludlow, Philip Skene, Andrew P. Skene, Benjamin Seaman, Christopher Billop, Beverly Robinson, Senior and Junior; Malcomn Morrison, John Kane, Abraham C. Cuyler, Robert Leake, Edward Jesup, Ebenezer Jesup, Peter Dubois, Thomas H. Barclay, Susannah Robinson and her sister, May Morris, John Rapelje, George Morrison, Richard Floyd, Parker Wyckham, Henry Lloyd, and Sir Henry Clinton.

† Kingston was then a pretty, thriving village situated on a plain a short distance west of the river. It was one of the earliest Dutch settlements in the State. It was originally named Esopus, and that region was the theatre of a tragedy, already noticed, in which the Indians took a conspicuous part in Stuyvesant's time. There were Dutch trading settlers there so early as 1616. At the time in question it was one of the larger villages in New York.

is a peerless member of the Thirty-eight United States which form the Great Republic of the West.

While these civil matters were occupying the earnest attention of the people of New York, a most imposing military spectacle was seen within its borders, and filled the minds of every patriot with anxiety and alarm.

We have observed that General Burgoyne was in Canada at the close of 1776 with a large British force. He went to England early in 1777, but returned to Quebec on May 5th following. He came bearing the commission of lieutenant-general and invested with the chief command of the troops in Canada, superseding Governor Carleton. To soothe the feelings of the governor, Burgoyne bore to Carleton tokens of knighthood which had just been bestowed upon him, and thenceforth he was known as Sir Guy Carleton.

Burgoyne was instructed to attempt the execution of the ministerial plan for the severance of New England from the other States then in revolt. He at once made preparations to invade Northern New York by the way of Lake Champlain, with a large force of Britons, Germans, Canadians, and Indians.

The vigilant Schuyler, anticipating such an invasion, had written to Washington early in the year that at least ten thousand troops, well supplied, would be required at Ticonderoga, and two thousand at Fort Stanwix (now Rome) and at other points on the Mohawk River. Schuyler also engaged two trustworthy residents of Canada to furnish him with the best intelligence of affairs there, from time to time.

Washington made strenuous efforts to strengthen the northern army. Some New York and New England troops had joined the garrison at Ticonderoga ; but when, so late as June 20th, Schuyler visited that post, he was deeply concerned to learn from General St. Clair that the garrison was still very weak, the soldiers miserably clad and fed, and that there was almost nothing in store for them. A strong redoubt had been built on Mount Independence on the opposite shore of the here narrow lake, but there were not men enough to properly man it.

At dawn on the very day when Schuyler arrived at Ticonderoga (June 20th), the drums in the British camp at St. Johns, on the Sorel, beat the *generale*, and very soon the army which Burgoyne * had

---

* Sir John Burgoyne was born in England about 1730, and entered the army in his youth. He married a daughter of the Earl of Derby. He became distinguished as a soldier, served with honor in Portugal in 1762, and became a member of Parliament. With the commission of brigadier-general he arrived in Boston late in May, 1775. He returned to England late in 1776, and came back to America in the spring of 1777, and undertook the invasion of the State of New York. He and his whole army were made

gathered there were upon vessels bound up the lake. The wives of many of the officers accompanied their husbands, for they expected a pleasant summer journey over the country to New York, the lieutenant-general having written to General Howe that he should very soon join him on the navigable waters of the Hudson. The Indians were to spread terror over Northern New York by their atrocities, and so make conquest easy, and the voyage up the lake and the march to Albany almost a pleasure excursion.

At the same time an expedition under Colonel St. Leger, composed of regulars, Canadians, and Indians, was despatched to Lake Ontario with orders to cross it, land at Oswego, penetrate and desolate the Mohawk Valley, and join the victorious troops which might sweep down from the north into the valley of the Hudson. The Canadians and Indians were led by Sir John Johnson. At the same time a British force was to ascend the Hudson, seize the American fortifications in the Highlands, waste the country above in case of resistance, and form a junction with Burgoyne at Albany.

To alarm and distract the inhabitants in the lower valley of the Hudson and on the seaboard, marauding expeditions were sent out from New York. Late in April a strong British force went up the Hudson to destroy American stores at Peekskill, at the lower entrance to the Highlands. Too weak to defend them, the Americans, under General McDougal, set them on fire and retreated to the hills in the rear. A little later Governor Tryon, with about two thousand British and Tories, landed on the shores of Connecticut, penetrated the country, destroyed the stores at Danbury, and plundered and burnt that village.

With much display Burgoyne went on board the schooner *Lady Mary*, at St. Johns, when a discharge of cannons from her deck gave a signal for the fleet to move. His second in command was General William Phillips. The Baron de Riedesel * was the commander-in-chief

---

prisoners at Saratoga, when he returned to England and resumed his seat in Parliament. He became a Privy Councillor, commander-in-chief in Ireland, and retired from public life in 1784. He died in London in 1792.

* Baron de Riedesel was a German officer, born in 1738, and died in Brunswick in 1800. He served in the English army in the Seven Years' War in Europe under Prince Ferdinand, and became captain of Hessian Hussars in 1760. In 1767 he became adjutant-general of the Brunswick army. With the rank of major-general he commanded the Brunswickers hired by George III. of England for service in America, and landed with Burgoyne in Canada in the spring of 1775. He assisted that general in his invasion of New York, and was made a prisoner of war. His charming wife accompanied him, and after-

of the Germans. At the mouth of the Boquet River (site of Willsborough, in Essex County) Burgoyne feasted about four hundred Indians, to whom he made a speech, praising them for their fidelity to the king, and exhorting them to "strike at the common enemy of their sovereign and America." He forbade them to kill any excepting in battle, or to take scalps from any but the dead. The whole invading army arrived at Crown Point on June 26th. They then numbered something less than nine thousand men, with a powerful train of artillery.

The garrisons at Ticonderoga and Mount Independence had an aggregate force of not more than thirty-five hundred men, and only one in ten of them possessing a bayonet. Schuyler, who was at Albany making provision to meet the invasion of the Mohawk region, had too few troops to spare a reenforcement for St. Clair without uncovering points which, left unprotected, might allow the invaders to gain the rear of the lake fortresses. There were strong outposts around Ticonderoga, but there were not troops enough to man them; and there were eminences that commanded the fort that were left unguarded for the same reason. Between Ticonderoga and Mount Independence was a boom which the Americans thought would effectually bar the way of British vessels ascending the lake; but it utterly failed in the hour of need.

BARONESS DE RIEDESEL.

At Crown Point Burgoyne issued a pompous proclamation to the inhabitants of the upper Hudson Valley, which he prefaced with a list of his titles, followed by terrible threats in allusion to what the Indians might do if unrestrained. It did not frighten the people at all. They knew the character of the Indians, and regarded the proclama-

---

ward published an interesting account of her experience in America. The baron was exchanged in 1780 and was made lieutenant-general. His wife was a daughter of the Prussian Minister Massow. She died in Berlin in 1808. The baron's Memoirs and his wife's Letters and Journal have been translated into English and published by W. L. Stone, Esq.

tion with contempt.* St. Clair also indulged in hopes and a little boasting.

On July 1st, a bright, hot day, the invading army moved in two divisions from Crown Point to attack Forts Ticonderoga and Independence. The right wing, led by General Phillips, moved up the west side of the lake, and the left wing, composed of the Germans commanded by General Riedesel, moved up the east side. The dragoons formed the advance guard. General Burgoyne and his staff were on the schooner *Royal George*, from which he could watch the movements of each division. The whole force halted within three miles of Forts Ticonderoga and Independence.

A detachment of the right wing of the army seized an eminence that commanded the road to Lake George and some mills, and they soon took possession of the crest of Mount Defiance, and planted a battery upon it, whence plunging shot might be hurled into Fort Ticonderoga from a point several hundred feet above it. This was done so secretly that the first intimation St. Clair had of it was the startling sight, at dawn on July 5th. It seemed to the Americans more like the lingering apparitions of a night vision than the terrible reality they were compelled to acknowledge it to be.

The fort was now clearly untenable. A council of war determined that only in secret flight might the garrison hope for salvation from destruction or capture. The flight was undertaken the same night. The invalids and convalescents, stores and baggage, were sent up the lake that evening to Skenesborough (now Whitehall) on bateaux; and at about two o'clock in the morning (Sunday, July 6th) the garrison

---

* The following poetical paraphrase of the proclamation was attributed to Francis Hopkinson, author of "The Battle of the Kegs:"

> " I will let loose the dogs of hell,
> Five thousand Indians, who shall yell,
> And foam and tear, and grin and roar,
> And drench their moccasins in gore;
> To these I'll give full scope and play,
> From Ticonderog' to Florida.
> They'll scalp your heads and kick your shins,
> And rip your — and flay your skins;
> And of your ears be nimble croppers,
> And make your thumbs tobacco-stoppers.
> If after all these loving warnings,
> My wishes and my bowels' yearnings,
> You shall remain as deaf as adder,
> Or grow with hostile rage the madder,
> I swear by St. George and by St. Paul,
> I will exterminate you all.
> Subscribéd with my manual sign,
> To test these presents—JOHN BURGOYNE."

crossed a floating bridge at the boom to Fort Independence, leaving almost two hundred cannons behind them. With the garrison of the latter they fled southward through the forests of Vermont, hotly pursued by the grenadier brigade of General Fraser and some of the Germans. Overtaken at Hubbardton, the Americans, after a short and sharp battle, were defeated and dispersed. St. Clair finally rallied about two thousand men, and with these reached Fort Edward, on the upper Hudson, in safety.

In the mean time Burgoyne had ordered his gun-boats and other vessels to pursue the fugitive bateaux. Before sunrise these vessels had burst asunder the boom on which the Americans relied, and the whole British flotilla engaged in the chase. The bateaux were overtaken near Skenesborough and destroyed, with all their contents, but the men escaped.

General Schuyler, who was constantly engaged in the oversight of everything in the Northern Department, was severely censured for the evacuation of Ticonderoga, when he had no connection with the event. The evacuation was done without his orders or his knowledge, for he was then at Saratoga on important public business. He was tried for the offence by a court-martial, and most honorably acquitted.*

From Skenesborough Burgoyne sent out a boastful and arrogant proclamation, in which he demanded the instant submission of the people, and required them to send deputies from the several townships to meet Colonel Philip Skene † in conference at Castleton, on July 15th. He threatened them with "military executions" if they refused to obey his commands. At the same time he promised them ample protection if they should be obedient.

General Schuyler, who had hastened to Fort Edward, issued a stirring counter-proclamation, warning the people against the wiles of the enemy, whose sole object was by threats and promises to induce the inhabitants to forsake the cause of their injured country, and to assist the enemy in

---

* For minute particulars concerning the eminent public services of General Schuyler from 1760 until his death in 1804, see Lossing's *Life and Times of Philip Schuyler*, published by Henry Holt & Co., New York.

† Philip Skene came to America with British troops in 1756, and was wounded in the attack on Ticonderoga under Abercrombie. He had entered the army in 1739. He was in command of Crown Point for a while. He planted a settlement at the head of Lake Champlain (now Whitehall) which was called Skenesborough, and there he made his residence in 1770. Adhering to the British crown, he was arrested in Philadelphia, but was exchanged in 1776, and accompanied Burgoyne in his invasion of New York. He was with the British detachment defeated at Bennington, and was taken prisoner at Saratoga. The Legislature of New York confiscated his property in 1779, when he returned to England, and died there in 1810.

forcing slavery upon the people of the United States. He warned his fellow-citizens that the invaders would bring upon them that misery which similar promises brought upon "the deluded inhabitants of New Jersey who were weak enough to confide in them, but soon experienced their fallacy by being treated indiscriminately with those virtuous citizens who came forth in defence of their country, with the most wanton barbarities, and such as hitherto hath not even disgraced barbarians. They cruelly butchered without distinction to age or sex," Schuyler continued. "They ravished children from ten to women of eighty years of age ! they burnt, pillaged, and destroyed whatever came into their power, nor did those edifices dedicated to the worship of Almighty God escape their sacrilegious fury."

Schuyler warned the people of Northern New York that this would be their fate if they heeded Burgoyne's proclamation ; and he told them distinctly that any persons holding any correspondence with the invaders, or who should accept protection from them, would be regarded and punished as traitors to their country.

Burgoyne pushed on from Skenesborough toward Fort Edward, on the upper Hudson, but met with obstructions at almost every step, which had been cast in his way by General Schuyler, who destroyed bridges and felled trees across the roads. Schuyler was then in command of not more than four thousand effective men, a number entirely inadequate to combat a foe twice as strong in numbers and flushed with victory ; but so effectually did he employ his troops in impeding the march of the invading army that they did not arrive at Fort Edward before the close of July. Then occurred there the sad tragedy of the death of Jane McCrea, the story of which, as set afloat at that time, is familiar to all readers of American history ; but truth changed its features many years ago, and gave the story as follows :

Jane McCrea, a daughter of a clergyman in New Jersey, was visiting friends at Fort Edward at the time of the invasion. She was betrothed to a young man living near there, who was then in Burgoyne's army. When that army approached Fort Edward some prowling Indians seized Miss McCrea and her feminine friend with whom she was staying, and attempted to convey them to the British camp at Sandy Hill. They had placed them upon horses (probably by direction of the lover) and were ascending a hill when a detachment of Americans, who were sent to rescue the captives, fired upon the dusky kidnappers. One of the bullets pierced the brain of the maiden, and she fell dead from the horse. Her captors scalped her and carried her glossy tresses into the camp as a trophy. Her lover, shocked by the event, left the army and retired to Canada, carrying with him the precious locks of his affianced. He lived, a moody bachelor, until he was an old man.

The body of Miss McCrea was recovered by her friends, and was buried at Fort Edward. A tale of romance and horror concerning the manner of her death went abroad. In September an open letter of General Gates (who had superseded Schuyler in command) to Burgoyne, full of exaggerations and holding the latter responsible for the death of the maiden, gave great currency to the story; and hundreds, perhaps thousands, of young men, burning with indignation and a spirit of vengeance because of the outrage, flocked to the American camp.

Schuyler continually fell back before the pressure of Burgoyne's superior numbers, made stronger by discipline, until, in August, he resolved to make a stand near Stillwater, on the Hudson, and there establish a fortified camp for recruits, who were coming in rapidly. Burgoyne was evidently becoming weaker as he departed farther from his now precarious supplies. His army was soon in an almost starving condition, and menaced on every side by constantly increasing enemies.

Necessity now compelled Burgoyne to make a bold stroke for food, forage, and conquest. He was informed that the Americans had a large quantity of stores at Bennington, in Vermont. He sent a detachment of Germans, Canadians, Tories, and Indians, under Lieutenant-Colonel Breyman, to seize these supplies, procure horses, and organize the Tories in that region. This force was met by New Hampshire militia and others under General John Starke a short distance from Bennington, and on August 16th (1777) a severe battle occurred. The invaders were defeated and dispersed, and about seven hundred of them became prisoners. Many of the Canadians and Indians deserted, and the survivors marched back in most melancholy mood.

This was a disastrous expedition for the invaders. It greatly inspirited the patriots, disheartened the Tories, and depressed the spirits of the whole of Burgoyne's army. It crippled his movements when it was all-important that he should go forward with celerity, for St. Leger, whom he had sent by way of Lake Ontario and Oswego to invade the Mohawk Valley, was then besieging Fort Stanwix (then called Fort Schuyler), with the expectation of soon meeting the lieutenant-general at Albany. His plans were frustrated. It was perilous for him to remain where he was; it would be perilous to move forward. His troops had to be fed with provisions brought from England by way of Canada and Lakes Champlain and George and a land journey through the forests. Let us leave Burgoyne in this dilemma and take a glance at passing events in the Mohawk Valley.

CHAPTER XIX.

In order to moderate the zeal of the Tories and to encourage and support the Whigs of Tryon County, Fort Schuyler (on the site of Rome, N. Y.) had been garrisoned by seven hundred and fifty men, commanded by Colonel Peter Gansevoort. In July (1777) Colonel Marinus Willett, an active and judicious officer, joined the garrison with his regiment. Another re-enforcement arrived soon afterward with provisions sufficient to subsist the garrison for at least six weeks.

Brigadier-General Nicholas Herkimer, a venerable citizen sixty-five years old, was then in command of the Tryon County militia. The Mohawk chief, Brant,* had returned from Canada in the spring and placed himself at the head of a band of Indian marauders in the vicinity of the head-waters of the Susquehanna River, and the brigadier had watched him for several weeks with sleepless vigilance.

JOSEPH BRANT.

At the beginning of August Colonel St. Leger, with a motley host of Tories and Canadians—the "Johnson (or Royal) Greens"—commanded by Colonels Sir John Johnson, Claas, and Butler, and Indians led by

---

* Joseph Brant (Thay-en-da-ne-gea) was an eminent Mohawk chief, born about 1752, and died at the western end of Lake Ontario, in Canada, in 1807. Sir William Johnson had him educated by Dr. Wheelock at Hanover, N. H. He engaged in the war against Pontiac in 1763. He became secretary to Guy Johnson. In 1776 he went to England and offered his own and his people's services in suppressing the rebellion in the colonies. He and most of the Mohawks remained friends of the crown throughout the war. After the war he prevailed on the Six Nations to make a permanent peace with the new government. He went to England a second time, in 1786, in the interest of his people, who were settled on a reservation on the Grand River, in Canada. His remains rest beneath a

Brant, arrived before Fort Schuyler from Oswego, and began a close siege.* Herkimer with his militia, eight hundred strong, hastened to the assistance of the garrison, sending them word that he was coming. Encouraged by this news, Colonel Willett made a sortie with a part of two regiments. He fell upon the "Greens" so suddenly and furiously that they were compelled to fly in confusion. Sir John had not time to put on his coat. His papers, baggage, clothing, blankets, and camp equipage, sufficient in bulk to fill twenty wagons, were the spoils of victory. The trophies were five British flags. A portion of the "Greens" had gone to meet Herkimer and his men.

On the morning of August 6th Herkimer and his little force were marching, in fancied security, at Oriskany, a few miles west of Utica, when they fell into an ambush of Tories and Indians. They were assailed at all points by pikes, hatchets, and rifle-balls. Herkimer's rear-guard broke and fled; the remainder sustained a fierce conflict for more than an hour, interrupted about fifteen minutes by a sudden thunder-storm. A bullet shattered the leg of the brave old commander,† and

---

handsome mausoleum near a church built on the reservation. His son John was active on the side of the British in the Eastern movements of the War of 1812.

In October, 1886, a slightly colossal statue of Brant, nine feet in height, in Indian costume, was unveiled on the Mohawk reservation at Brantford, on the Grand River, Ontario, Canada. The likeness we give of the chief is from a miniature, exquisitely painted on ivory, from life, when Brant was in London in 1785-86. It is in possession of the Brant family, and has ever been considered the best likeness of him ever painted.

Colonel William L. Stone, the eminent journalist of New York fifty or sixty years ago, has made the students of the history of our Commonwealth his debtors by his elaborate biographies of both Brant and the great Seneca chief, Red Jacket, the most conspicuous representatives of the Iroquois Confederacy.

* The garrison was without a flag when the invaders appeared. One was soon supplied, in pattern that was uniform with the prescription of the Continental Congress, by resolution, adopted a few weeks before—"thirteen stripes, alternate red and white, and thirteen stars displayed upon a blue field." Shirts were cut up to form the white stripes; bits of scarlet cloth were joined for the red stripes, and the blue ground for the stars was composed of a portion of a cloth cloak belonging to Captain Abraham Swartwout, of Duchess County, N. Y., who was then in the fort. It is believed this was the first garrison flag displayed after the passage of the resolution of Congress on June 14th, 1777.

† Nicholas Herkimer (Herkheimer) was born about 1727, and died in 1777. He was a son of a Palatine who settled below Little Falls, in the Mohawk Valley, in the reign of Queen Anne, and was one of the patentees of present Herkimer County. In 1758 Nicholas was made a lieutenant of provincials, and was in command of Fort Herkimer in that year. He was appointed colonel of the first battalion of Tryon County militia in 1775; also chairman of the County Committee of Safety, and in September, 1776, was made a brigadier-general by the Provincial Convention of New York. He died at his home ten days after he was wounded at the battle of Oriskany. The Continental Congress voted to erect a monument to his memory of the value of $500, but it has never been done.

killed the horse upon which he was riding. Seated upon his saddle at the foot of a tree, he calmly gave orders. At length the Indians, hearing the firing occasioned by Willett's sortie, fled to the deep woods in a panic, and were soon followed by the equally alarmed Tories, leaving the patriots masters of the field. Herkimer was taken to his home below the Little Falls of the Mohawk, where he soon afterward died from excessive bleeding from his wound, the result of bad surgery.

MARINUS WILLETT.

The siege of Fort Schuyler was vigorously pressed by St. Leger. On August 9th he made a formal demand for the surrender of the fort. It was refused. Fearing the assailants might be re-enforced, and that his own provisions might fail, Gansevoort sent Lieutenant-Colonel Willett * to Schuyler to ask him to furnish relief. Willett, with a single companion, who was an expert in woodcraft, left the fort stealthily during a series of heavy thunder-storms. He reached the quarters of Schuyler at Stillwater on the 12th, and revealed the urgency of the case to the general.

Schuyler, fully comprehending the importance of checking the advance of St. Leger in the west while endeavoring to roll back the invasion from the north, called a council of officers and proposed to send a detachment to the relief of Fort Schuyler. The council objected because of the pressing need of men for the army confronting Burgoyne.

---

* Marinus Willett was born at Jamaica, L. I., in 1740, and died in New York City in 1830. He was graduated at King's (now Columbia) College, and soon afterward served with Abercrombie in the attack on Ticonderoga in 1758. He was with Bradstreet against Fort Frontenac. Willett was one of the most eminent of the "Sons of Liberty," and became a captain in McDougal's regiment in the invasion of Canada in 1775. He was promoted to lieutenant-colonel of the Third New York Regiment. In 1777 he was in Fort Stanwix and assisted in its defence. In August he bore a message by stealth to General Schuyler asking for relief, which was sent. He was in the battle of Monmouth in 1778, was with Sullivan in his campaign against the Indians in 1779, and in 1784 became sheriff of New York City, in which position he served ten years. In 1807 he was elected mayor of the city. He had been appointed a brigadier-general in the army to act against the Indians in the North-west in 1792, but declined the honor.

Schuyler heard one of the officers say in a half-suppressed whisper, "He means to weaken the army." This was an echo—an epitome—of the slanders with which the general had been assailed since the evacuation of Ticonderoga. With hot indignation he turned upon the slanderer, and unconsciously biting in pieces a clay pipe that he was smoking, exclaimed in a voice that awed the whole company into silence :

"Gentlemen, I shall take the responsibility upon myself; where is the brigadier who will take command of the relief? I shall beat up for volunteers to-morrow."

The brave Benedict Arnold, one of the council, who knew how unjust was the thought that there could be treason in the heart of General Schuyler, immediately stepped forward and offered his services. The drums beat for volunteers the next morning, and before noon (August 13th) eight hundred stalwart men were enrolled for the relief expedition. They were chiefly from the Massachusetts brigade of General Larned.

With such followers—men who had implicit confidence in him—General Arnold pushed rapidly up the Mohawk Valley. By stratagem, audacity, and prowess Arnold impressed the followers of St. Leger with the startling idea that the Americans advancing upon them were overwhelming in numbers.* So impressed, the Indians resolved to fly. No persuasions could hold them. Away they went, as fast as their legs could carry them, toward Oswego and the more western forests. They were followed by their pale-faced *confrères*, pell-mell, helter-skelter, in a race for safety to be found on the bosom of Lake Ontario.

So was suddenly raised the siege of Fort Schuyler, and so ended the really formidable invasion from the west.

The failure of the expedition of St. Leger † was a stunning blow to the hopes of Burgoyne. This disaster, following so closely upon that

---

* At the German Flats Arnold found a half idiotic Tory under sentence of death for some crime he had committed. His mother begged Arnold to pardon him. Her prayer was granted on the condition that he should accompany a friendly Oneida chief among the barbarians into St. Leger's camp, and by representing the oncoming Americans, from whom they had just escaped, as very numerous, frighten them away. The prisoner consented. The Tory had several shots fired through his coat, and with these evidences of a "terrible engagement with the enemy," he ran, almost out of breath, into the Indian camp. Pointing toward the trees and the sky he said : "They are as many as the leaves and the stars at night." Very soon his companion, the Oneida, came running from another direction with the same story, when, as we have seen above, the Indians fled.

† Colonel Barry St. Leger entered the British army in 1749 ; came to America with his regiment in 1757, and was with Wolfe at Quebec. He became lieutenant-colonel in 1772, and was sent to Canada in 1775. After his failure in the Mohawk Valley he disappears from history. He died in 1789.

near Bennington, staggered him. His visions of conquest, "orders," and perhaps a peerage for himself vanished. His army was already conquered. The sad news thoroughly disheartened his troops. The fidelity of the Indians, always fair-weather warriors, waned, and these and Canadians and timid Tories became lukewarm, and they deserted by hundreds.

Burgoyne's perplexity was great. To proceed would be madness; to retreat would give hosts of friends to the Republicans and dissipate the idea of British invincibility. He complained to the ministry that Howe had not co-operated in his favor by movements below, and consequently troops from above the Highlands had swelled the Northern army of the Americans. He resolved to remain where he was (on the heights of Saratoga, where Schuylerville now stands) until the panic in his army should subside and he should receive supplies from posts on Lakes Champlain and George. By great diligence he soon afterward had sufficient provisions brought from Lake George to last his army a month.

At this juncture, when Schuyler, who for weeks had retarded the invasion of Burgoyne with a handful of men ; when his wisdom, prowess, and patriotism were inducing recruits to flock to his standard, now that their summer crops were generally gathered and he was ready to strike a blow for victory, he was superseded in the command of the Northern Department by General Gates. This change had been effected by intrigues, a faction in Congress, and widely circulated slanders. That Schuyler was the victim of a conspiracy no careful student of our history can reasonably doubt. Yet he patriotically acquiesced, and generously offered to give Gates all the aid in his power. Had Gates wisely accepted the generous offer and acted with a proper spirit at that time, he might have gained an early victory over the invaders. But he did not act wisely, generously, nor efficiently, and when a victory was finally won in spite of him, he was not entitled to the honor of achieving it.

Burgoyne established an intrenched camp on the heights of Saratoga. Early in September Gates found himself in command of an army stronger in numbers than the whole British force opposing him. The American forces were well posted on Bemis's Heights, two miles above Stillwater, the right wing resting upon the Hudson River below the Heights, and their left upon gentle hills. Upon their front was a well-constructed line of fortifications.

Imperious necessity compelled Burgoyne to move forward. He took a position within two miles of the American lines, and on the morning of September 19th he advanced to offer battle. He had no alternative but to fight or surrender, for he had been informed that General Lincoln, with two thousand New England militia, had gotten in his rear and had cut off his communication with Canada. On the day before, Colonel John Brown, despatched by General Lincoln with a few troops and some heavy guns, had surprised an outpost between Ticonderoga and Lake George; had taken possession of Mount Defiance; cannonaded Ticonderoga and Fort Independence; destroyed two hundred vessels, including seventeen gun-boats and an armed sloop, at the outlet of Lake George; seized a large quantity of stores; released one hundred American prisoners, and captured about three hundred British soldiers.

Burgoyne's left wing, with an immense artillery train, commanded by Generals Phillips and Riedesel, kept upon the plain near the river. The centre and right, composed largely of Germans, extended across the rolling country on the Heights, and were commanded by Burgoyne in person. Upon the hills on the extreme right General Fraser with grenadiers and Colonel Breyman with riflemen were posted for the purpose of outflanking the Americans. On the front and right flank was a body of Canadians, Tories, and Indians designed to attack the central outposts of the Americans.

During the morning General Arnold, who commanded a division, had observed through vistas in screening woods preparations of the foe for an attack, and urged General Gates to send out a detachment to confront them. But Gates had determined to act on the defensive within his lines, and hesitated. At length he permitted Colonel Morgan and his riflemen, and some infantry under Colonels Dearborn and Scammell, to make an attack upon the Canadians and Tories. After severe skirmishing the parties retired to their respective lines.

At eleven o'clock Burgoyne gave a signal for his whole army to move forward. Gates seemed indisposed to fight, and remained in his tent. General Fraser began the battle by making a rapid movement to turn the American left commanded by Arnold. At the same time Arnold, with equal celerity of movement, attempted to turn the British right. He was frustrated by the refusal of Gates to send him re-enforcements. He was forced back, when Fraser, by a quick movement, called up to his aid some German and other troops from Burgoyne's centre column. Arnold brought his whole division (chiefly New Englanders) into action and called for re-enforcements. They were not supplied; yet he smote the enemy so lustily that their line began to waver, and it soon fell into confusion.

General Phillips, below the Heights, hearing the din of battle, hurried over the hills with fresh troops and artillery, followed by German dragoons under Riedesel, and appeared upon the ground just as victory seemed about to rest with the Americans. Still the battle raged. The ranks of the British were becoming fearfully thinned, when Riedesel made a furious attack upon the flank of the Americans with cannon and musketry, which compelled them to give way. So the Germans saved the British army from ruin.

At the middle of the afternoon there was a lull in the tempest of battle. It was soon succeeded by a more violent outburst of fury. Burgoyne opened a heavy cannonade upon the Americans, who made no response. Then he ordered a bayonet charge. As the invaders rushed forward to the assault their silent antagonists sprang forward from their intrenchments like tigers, and attacked the British so furiously with ball and bayonet that they soon recoiled and were pushed far back.

At that moment Arnold was at headquarters seated on his powerful horse, vainly begging for re-enforcements. The sounds of battle made him exceedingly impatient, and when it was announced that the conflict was indecisive he could no longer brook delay, but turning his horse's head in the direction of the storm, exclaimed, "I'll soon put an end to it!" Putting spurs to his charger, he dashed away on a wild gallop, followed by a young staff officer (Wilkinson), who was sent by Gates to order the impetuous general back. The subaltern could not overtake Arnold before he reached the scene of conflict, where, by words and deeds, the gallant general animated his troops.

For three hours more the battle raged. The Americans had almost turned the British flank when Colonel Breyman with his German riflemen, fighting bravely, averted the blow that might have been fatal to the British army. The combatants had surged in doubt backward and forward across the fields like the ebb and flow of the tide. Darkness fell upon the scene and ended the conflict. The British slept that night upon their arms, and the Americans slumbered within their lines. The American forces much outnumbered those of the British.

Petty jealousies marked the conduct of the opposing chief commanders in this conflict. Twice the German troops had saved the British army during the battle. Burgoyne, regarding Riedesel with envy, withheld the honor due him in his official report. Had Arnold been furnished with re-enforcements when he asked for them, no doubt he would have won a victory in the morning. Gates was not seen on the field during the day,* nor any other general officer besides Arnold but Learned; and

---

* The concurrent testimony of contemporaries plainly shows that Gates scarcely left his tent during the day of the battle, and that under its shelter he freely indulged in strong drinks and in unbecoming remarks concerning officers of whom he was jealous.

but for the prowess and skill of the former, all candid historians admit that Burgoyne would undoubtedly have entered Albany in triumph as a victor at the autumnal equinox. Gates, angry because the army praised Arnold and Morgan, did not mention their names in his official report of the battle!

The wretched condition of his army was revealed to Burgoyne on the morning of the 20th. He had lost about six hundred men. He expected an immediate renewal of the battle by the Americans. With that impression he hastily buried his dead in holes and trenches, and withdrew to high ground about two miles from the American lines. The latter had good reason for removing within their lines, for their ammunition was exhausted. This fact was known only to Gates. He was justified in not acceding to Arnold's urgent request to attack the enemy on that morning.

Burgoyne and the whole army were greatly depressed in spirits by the events of the 19th, yet, hourly expecting good news from Howe or Clinton below, he addressed his troops in a cheerful tone, and declared that he would either leave his dead body on the field or push his way to Albany. On the following day he received a despatch from Clinton, who was in command at New York, promising aid by attacking the forts or the Hudson Highlands. He also gave him the cheering news of Howe's victory on the Brandywine Creek. Burgoyne assured Clinton that he could maintain his position until October 12th.

Burgoyne waited many days for more tidings from Clinton. None came, and on the evening of October 4th he called a council of officers. Phillips proposed an attempt to turn the American left flank by a swift circuitous march. Riedesel favored a rapid retreat to Fort Edward. Fraser was willing to fight then and there. The latter course was agreed upon, and on the morning of the 7th, after liquors and rations for four days had been distributed to the whole army, Burgoyne moved toward the American left with fifteen hundred picked men, eight brass cannons, and two howitzers. He formed a battle-line behind a forest screen three fourths of a mile from the American intrenchments. Generals Riedesel, Phillips, and Fraser were with the lieutenant-general, who sent out a party composed of Canadians, Tories, and Indians to make a circuit through the woods, and, hanging upon the American rear, keep them in check while he should attack them in front.

Burgoyne was discovered before he was ready for battle. The drums of the Americans beat to arms, and an alarm was sent all along the lines. They had been re-enforced by Lincoln, and their army now numbered about ten thousand men—nearly double the number of the British force.

Gates inquired the cause of the disturbance, and when he ascertained the truth he sent out Colonel Morgan with his riflemen and some infantry to secure a position to attack the flank and rear of the British right and to "begin the game." At the same time New Hampshire militia under General Poor and New York militia under General Tenbroeck advanced against the British left.

Meanwhile the Canadians and Tories had turned the flank of the Americans and attacked their pickets in the rear. The British grenadiers soon joined these assailants and drove the Americans back to their lines, where a hot contest ensued, lasting half an hour. In that fight Morgan and his men assailed the foe so vigorously that they were driven back in confusion to the British line, which then stood in battle order in an open field. Grenadiers under Major Acland and artillery commanded by Major Williams formed the left of the line upon rising ground. The centre was composed of Britons and Germans led by Phillips and Riedesel, and the extreme left of infantry under Earl Balcarras. General Fraser at the head of five hundred picked men was a short distance in advance of the British right ready to fall upon the left front of the Americans.

Just as Burgoyne was about to advance, at three o'clock in the afternoon, he was astounded by the thunder of cannons on his left and the rattle of small arms on his right. New Englanders under General Poor had moved stealthily up the slope, upon the crown of which were the troops of Acland and Williams, and pressed through the thick wood toward the batteries of the latter. When the Republicans were discovered the British opened upon them a heavy storm of musket-balls and grape-shot with very little effect, for the missiles passed over their heads. The Americans then sprang forward with a shout and fired rapid volleys, when a fierce conflict ensued. The Republicans rushed up to the mouths of the cannons and engaged in a hand-to-hand struggle for victory among the carriages of the field-pieces. Five times one of the cannons was taken and retaken. It finally remained with the Americans, and as the British fell back Colonel Cilley mounted the gun, waved his sword high in air, and dedicated the weapon to "the American cause."

In this fierce combat Major Acland was seriously wounded [*] and Major Williams was made a prisoner. Their men, panic-stricken, fled in con-

---

[*] The wives of General Riedesel, Major Acland, and others were with their husbands. When Mrs. Acland, a daughter of the Earl of Ilchester, heard of her husband's condition—wounded and a prisoner within the American lines—she obtained permission from Burgoyne to go to him. She was admitted, and was at her husband's bedside at a house on Bemis's Heights until he recovered sufficiently to proceed to New York.

fusion, and the whole eight brass cannons and the field remained in possession of the Americans.

Morgan in the mean time led an attack upon General Fraser and drove him back upon the British lines ; then falling upon their right flank, he broke their ranks and put them in confusion. Colonel Dearborn attacked their front with fresh troops and broke their line, but it was soon rallied.

It was at this moment that General Arnold reappeared upon the scene. Gates's treatment of him had so greatly irritated him that he had demanded a pass to go to Washington's headquarters. It was readily granted, for Gates, now feeling sure of success, did not wish the brave general to have a share in the glory of the achievement. He did not thereby actually take the command of the division from Arnold, but he assigned its control to General Lincoln, who tried to reconcile the differences between the two generals. The officers of the latter, by personal entreaties and a written address, persuaded him to remain, but Gates refused to give him any command. Arnold had no authority even to *fight*, much less to *order*. He was eager to join in the combat at the beginning.

"No man," he exclaimed to his aides, "shall keep me from the field to-day. If I am without command I will fight in the ranks ; but the soldiers, God bless them ! will follow my lead."

Thoroughly aroused by the din of battle at the moment just alluded to, Arnold leaped into his saddle and dashed away to the point of conflict in which his division was engaged, again followed by one of Gates's aides (Armstrong) with instructions to order him back. The chase was in vain. Arnold plunged into the thickest of the fight, where the subaltern dared not follow. His troops welcomed him with shouts. He immediately led them against the British centre, riding along the lines, giving orders, and exposed to imminent peril every moment.

The Germans received the first furious assault from Arnold's troops. They made a brave resistance and flung the assailants back at first, but when at a second charge Arnold dashed among them at the head of his troops, they broke and fled in dismay.

And now the battle became general all along the line. Arnold and Morgan were the ruling spirits that controlled the storm on the part of the Americans. The gallant Fraser was the directing soul of the British troops in action. His skill and courage were everywhere conspicuous. When the lines gave way he brought order out of confusion ; when regiments began to waver he infused courage into them by voice and example. The fate of the battle evidently depended upon him.

Arnold perceived this, and said to Morgan, "That officer in full uniform is General Fraser. It is essential to our success that he be disposed of. Direct the attention of some of the sharpshooters of your riflemen to him." The order was obeyed, and very soon Fraser fell from his horse mortally wounded. It is difficult for a humane and generous mind to accept any excuse for this cruel order and the deed that ensued.*

When the gallant Fraser fell a panic ran along the British line. At that moment three thousand New York militia under General Tenbroeck appeared, when the wavering line gave way and the British troops, covered by Phillips and Riedesel, fled to their intrenchments. Up to these works, in the face of a terrible tempest of bullets and grape-shot, the Americans eagerly pressed, with Arnold at their head, who was seen at all points, through the sulphurous smoke, encouraging his men. His voice could be heard above the din of battle. With a part of the brigades of Generals Paterson and Glover he drove the troops of Earl Balcarras from an *abatis* at the point of the bayonet, and attempted to force his way into the British camp. Failing in this, he led Learned's brigade against the British right. For a while the result was doubtful, but at length the Britons gave way, leaving the Germans under General Specht entirely exposed.

At this moment Arnold ordered up from the left the New York regiments of Colonels Wessen and Livingston and Morgan's riflemen to make a general assault, while he, with the Massachusetts regiment of Colonel Brooks, attacked the Germans commanded by Colonel Breyman. He rushed into the sally-port on his horse and spread terror among them. They had seen him for two hours in the thickest of the fight unhurt, and they regarded him with superstitious awe as a charmed character. They broke and fled. A bullet from a parting volley which they gave on their retreat killed Arnold's horse and wounded him in the same leg that was badly hurt at Quebec. Just then Gates's subaltern overtook the wounded and victorious Arnold and gave his commander's order to return to camp ! Gates had expressed a fear that Arnold might " do some rash thing." He had done a " rash thing" in achieving a decisive victory which Gates was incompetent to win. Yet the latter claimed and received the honors of the achievement

---

* General Fraser died on the morning after the battle. His body was buried at the evening twilight of the same day within a redoubt upon a gentle eminence, which the dying hero designated as the place of his sepulture. It was followed to the grave by Burgoyne and a large number of officers. As soon as the solemn character of the procession was recognized by the Americans a cannonade which they had begun ceased, and they fired minute-guns in honor of the memory of the brave soldier.

The rout of the Germans was complete. They threw down their arms and ran, and could not be rallied. Colonel Breyman was mortally wounded. Darkness ended the conflict.

Burgoyne, resolved to retreat, withdrew his whole force a mile north of his intrenchments, and on the night of the 8th he marched, in a cold rain-storm, for the heights of Saratoga, where the troops arrived, in a most wretched plight, on the morning of the 10th. They had burned the mansion, mills, and other property of General Schuyler on their way.

The American army also moved northward, and a part of it took a position on the hills on the east side of the Hudson directly opposite Burgoyne's camp and within cannon-shot of it. Satisfied that he could neither fight nor retreat with safety, Burgoyne opened negotiations with Gates for a surrender upon honorable terms. A capitulation was signed, and on October 17th, 1777, his troops laid down their arms in submission on the plain, near the Hudson, in front of (present) Schuylerville. Burgoyne surrendered his sword to Gates at the headquarters of the latter, not far from the ruins of General Schuyler's property.*

PHILIP SCHUYLER.

The whole number of troops surrendered to the Americans at Saratoga was five thousand seven hundred and ninety-nine, of whom two thousand four hundred and twelve were Germans. Besides these there were eighteen hundred prisoners of war, including sick and wounded. The entire loss of the British army after they entered the State of New York, including those under St. Leger, who were disabled or captured at Fort Schuyler and Oriskany, was almost ten thousand men. On Burgoyne's

---

* The value of the property destroyed was fully $50,000. When General Schuyler heard of his loss he wrote to Colonel Varick: "The event [the victory] that has taken place makes the heavy loss I have sustained sit quite easy upon me. Britain will probably see how fruitless her attempts to enslave us will be."

After the surrender of Burgoyne, Schuyler entertained the captive general at his house in Albany. The latter spoke feelingly of the injury his troops had done to the private property of General Schuyler. "Say nothing about it," responded Schuyler; "it was the fortune of war."

staff were six members of Parliament. Among the spoils were forty-two pieces of the best brass cannon then known, forty-six hundred muskets and rifles, and a large quantity of munitions of war. Congress awarded thanks and a gold medal to Gates.

Very generous terms were granted to Burgoyne by the capitulation. The troops were held as prisoners of war, but allowed a free passage to Europe for those who wished to go there, and free permission for the Canadians to return to their homes on the condition that none of the troops surrendered should serve against the Americans. The captives were marched to Cambridge, near Boston, expecting to embark for England. Congress ratified the generous terms, but Washington and that body were soon convinced by circumstances that Burgoyne and his officers intended to violate the agreement at the first opportunity. It was therefore resolved not to let the captives go until the British Government should ratify the terms of the capitulation. Here was a dilemma. That Government could not recognize the authority of Congress. So the "convention troops," as the captives were called, were sent to Virginia, and they remained idle in America four or five years. Burgoyne and his chief officers were allowed to depart for home.

THE GATES MEDAL.

The surrender of Burgoyne was a turning-point in the war in favor of the Americans. It inspirited the patriots; revived the credit of the Continental Government; the armies were rapidly recruited, and public opinion in Europe set strongly in favor of the struggling patriots. In less than four months after this event France had formed a treaty of alliance with the United States and acknowledged their independence.

CHAPTER XX.

WHILE General Burgoyne was struggling for victory and conquest in the upper valley of the Hudson, General Sir Henry Clinton, whom Howe had left in command at New York, was making earnest endeavors to aid him and to gain possession of the country between Albany and the sea.

At the lower entrance to the Highlands the Americans had erected two forts—"Clinton" and "Montgomery"—on the west side of the Hudson. They were upon a high, rocky shore, one on each side of a small stream. Between these forts and Anthony's Nose (a lofty hill) opposite they had stretched a boom and chain, as we have observed, to check British vessels ascending the river. These forts were under the immediate command of Generals George and James Clinton, the former then Governor of the State of New York. There was another fort ("Constitution") upon an island opposite West Point. They were all under the chief command of the veteran General Israel Putnam, whose headquarters was at Peekskill, just below the Highlands. The garrisons of these posts were weak at the beginning of October (1777), the aggregate number of troops not exceeding two thousand.

Sir Henry Clinton had waited at New York very impatiently for the arrival of re-enforcements. They came at the beginning of October, after floating upon the bosom of the Atlantic Ocean about three months. On the morning of the 4th he went up the Hudson with between three and four thousand troops, in many armed and unarmed vessels commanded by Commodore Hotham, and landed his men at Verplanck's Point, a few miles below Peekskill, feigning an attack upon the latter post. This feint deceived Putnam, and he sent to the Highland forts for re-enforcements. But Governor Clinton was not deceived, and held back all the forces in the Highlands.

At dawn on the morning of October 6th, under cover of a dense fog, Sir Henry crossed the river to Stony Point with a little more than two thousand men. He there divided his forces. One party under General Vaughan, accompanied by the baronet, pushed on through a defile in the rear of the lofty Donderberg to fall upon Fort Clinton. The party numbered about twelve hundred. Another party nine hundred strong, under Lieutenant-Colonel Campbell, made a longer march around Bear

Mountain, to fall upon Fort Montgomery at the same time. Sir Henry had ordered his war vessels to anchor within point-blank cannon-shot of the forts to co-operate in an attack upon them. On the borders of Lake Sinnipink, at the foot of Bear Mountain, Vaughan encountered some troops sent out by Governor Clinton, and a severe but short battle ensued. The Americans fell back to the fort. Lieutenant-Colonel Campbell appeared before Fort Montgomery toward evening, when a peremptory demand for the surrender of both posts was made. It was refused with words of scorn, when a simultaneous attack was made upon both forts by the forces on land and water. The garrisons, mostly militia, held out bravely until dark, when they sought safety in the adjacent mountains. Many were slain or made prisoners. Governor Clinton escaped across the river, and at midnight was in Putnam's camp at Peekskill. His brother (General James Clinton), badly wounded, made his way over the mountains to his home at New Windsor. The frigate *Montgomery*, a ten-gun sloop, and a row-galley lying above the boom attempted to escape, but could not for want of wind, so their crews set them on fire and abandoned them. The conflagration was a magnificent spectacle. A British officer wrote concerning it:

JAMES CLINTON.*

"The flames suddenly broke forth, and as every sail was set the vessels soon became magnificent pyramids of fire. The reflection on the steep face of the opposite mountain, and the long train of ruddy light which shone upon the waters for a prodigious distance, had a

---

* General James Clinton was born in Orange County, N. Y., in 1736, and died there in 1812. He was fond of military life. At the age of twenty-two he was a captain under Bradstreet in the capture of Fort Frontenac. He was afterward in command of four regiments for the protection of the frontiers of Ulster and Orange counties. When the war for independence began he was appointed colonel of the Third New York Regiment, and accompanied Montgomery to Quebec. He was make a brigadier-general in August, 1776, and was active in the service during a greater part of the war. He joined Sullivan's expedition against the Indians in 1779, and was stationed at Albany most of the time afterward; yet he was present at the surrender of Cornwallis. He held civil offices after the war. General Clinton was the father of De Witt Clinton.

wonderful effect; while the ear was awfully filled with the continued echoes from the rocky shores as the flames gradually reached the loaded cannon. The whole was sublimely terminated by the explosion, which left all again in darkness."

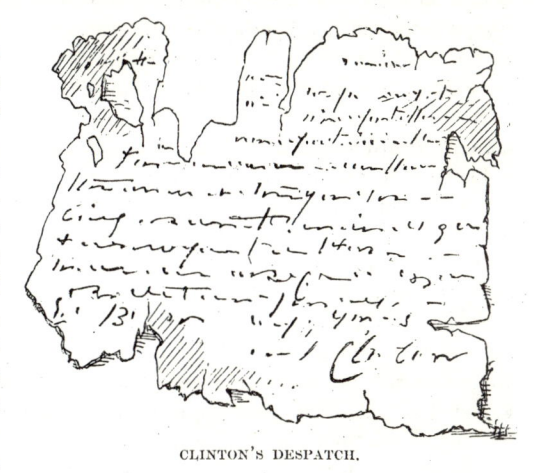

The boom and chain were broken by the British early on the morning of the 7th, and a flying squadron of light vessels commanded by Sir James Wallace, bearing the whole land force of Sir Henry Clinton, went up the Hudson to devastate its shores and keep the militia from joining Gates. They took possession of Fort Constitution

CLINTON'S DESPATCH.

on the way. At the same time Sir Henry despatched a messenger with a note to Burgoyne, as follows:

"*Nous y voici* [Here I am], and nothing between me and Gates. I sincerely hope this little success of ours may facilitate your operations. In answer to your letter of September 28th by C. C., I shall only say I cannot presume to order, or even to advise, for reasons obvious. I wish you success.—H. CLINTON."

SILVER BULLET.

This despatch was written on tissue paper and enclosed in an elliptical hollow silver bullet made so as to be opened at the middle, and of a size to be swallowed conveniently. The messenger was sent up the west side of the river, and while in the camp of Governor Clinton, near New Windsor, he was suspected of being a spy. He was arrested, and was seen to suddenly put something in his mouth and swallow it. An emetic was administered, when the silver bullet was discovered and its contents were revealed. He was hanged as a spy not far from Kingston while that village was in flames, kindled by the hands of British incendiaries.

The British troops in the marauding expedition, thirty-six hundred strong, were commanded by General Vaughan. Every vessel found on the river was burned or otherwise destroyed. The houses of known Whigs on the shores were fired upon, and small parties landing from the vessels desolated neighborhoods with fire and sword. They penetrated as far north as Kingston (Ulster County), then the political capital of the State, and applying the torch (October 13th), laid almost every house in the village in ashes. The Legislature fled to Duchess County, and soon afterward resumed their sittings at Poughkeepsie.

Leaving Kingston, the marauders went up the river as far as Livingston's Manor, destroying much property at Rhinebeck on the way. They had begun to desolate Livingston's estate when they were arrested by the alarming intelligence of Burgoyne's defeat. Then they made a hasty retreat to New York.

So ended the efforts of the British Ministry for taking possession of the valleys of the Hudson and Lake Champlain. On the surrender of Burgoyne the invaders were compelled to evacuate Ticonderoga and Crown Point. British power was now prostrated in the northern section of New York, and the Americans were masters of the territory of the commonwealth from the borders of Canada almost to the sea.

While the events just recorded were occurring in the vicinity of the Hudson or North River, very important events were occurring beyond the Delaware or the South River. For several weeks Washington and Howe confronted each other in hostile movements in New Jersey, each doubtful of the intentions of the other. Finally, at the close of June, the British troops left New Jersey and passed over to Staten Island; and on July 23d Howe, leaving Sir Henry Clinton in command at New York, embarked with eighteen thousand troops for more southern waters.

Suspecting Howe's destination to be the Continental seat of government, Washington, leaving a strong force on the Hudson, hastened to Philadelphia, where he was joined by the young Marquis de Lafayette as a volunteer. Hearing that the British army had landed at the head of Chesapeake Bay, he pushed on to meet Howe. They came in collision on the banks of the Brandywine Creek on September 11th, when a very severe battle was fought. The Americans were defeated, and their shattered battalions retreated to Philadelphia.

So soon as his troops were rested Washington recrossed the Schuylkill and proceeded to confront Howe, who was slowly moving toward the Continental capital. Some skirmishing occurred, and on the night of September 20th a detachment under General Wayne was surprised near the Paoli Tavern and lost about three hundred men.

CONSPIRACY AGAINST WASHINGTON.

While Washington was engaged in securing his stores at Reading, Howe suddenly crossed the Schuylkill and took possession of Philadelphia (September 26th, 1777) without opposition. The Continental Congress fled at his approach, first to Lancaster and then to York, beyond the Susquehanna. It reassembled at York on September 30th, and continued its sessions there until the following summer. The British army encamped at Germantown, about four miles from Philadelphia.

Howe's troops had landed at the head of Chesapeake Bay. While they were pressing on toward Philadelphia the fleet that bore them sailed round to the Delaware, but could not pass obstructions which had been placed in the river just below the city. Above these obstructions were two forts, Mifflin, upon an island, and Mercer, upon the New Jersey shore. These were captured by Britons and Germans sent from Howe's camp, after stout resistance. They took possession of the forts before the middle of November. This conquest greatly strengthened Howe's position.

Meanwhile the British camp at Germantown had been attacked early on the morning of October 4th. A severe battle ensued, which continued nearly three hours. The Americans, who became confused by a dense fog that began to rise at dawn, were defeated, and retired to their camp on Skippack Creek. Washington soon prepared to put them into winter quarters at Whitemarsh, only fourteen miles from Philadelphia. Howe broke up his encampment at Germantown, and made Philadelphia the winter quarters of his army.

Washington did not remain long at Whitemarsh, for he found a more eligible position. He broke up the camp toward the middle of December and removed to Valley Forge, where he was at a greater distance from his foe and could more easily protect the Congress, and his stores at Reading. For about six months the American army lay at Valley Forge, and suffered intensely for want of sufficient food, clothing, and shelter during the first half of that period. It was the severest ordeal in which the patriotism of the soldiers was tried during the long war for independence.

It was at this period that the conspiracy of General Gates and others to deprive Washington of the chief command of the American armies was in active operation—a conspiracy known in history as "Conway's Cabal."* Gates was then president of the Board of War, sitting at

---

* Count de Conway, of Irish birth, was among the French brigadiers in the Continental service. He never won the confidence of Washington, and when it was proposed to promote him to an important command the commander-in-chief strenuously opposed

York, the residence of Congress. That Board planned a winter campaign against Canada. So feasible seemed the plan and so glorious were the results to be obtained, as set forth by Gates and his friends, that Congress approved. The ardent Lafayette was captivated, and strongly urged its prosecution. Washington was not consulted. He, however, obtained such valuable information from General Schuyler, showing the absurdity of the undertaking, that he not only perceived the plan to be a part of the scheme to deprive him of the chief command, but he was enabled to defeat the project and thus save his country from a most perilous, if not ruinous undertaking.

The Board of War, evidently hoping to win Lafayette to the support of their schemes by conferring honors upon him, appointed him commander of the expedition. This also was done without consulting Washington. The shrewd young marquis very soon suspected his appointment was a part of the scheme to injure his revered friend, and he resolved to show his colors at the first opportunity. His suspicions were confirmed while on a visit to York to receive his instructions. At table, with Gates and other members of the Board of War, wine flowed freely and many toasts were given. Lafayette finally arose and said:

"Gentlemen, one toast, I perceive, has been omitted, and which I will now give." They filled their glasses, when he gave, "The commander-in-chief of the American armies." The coldness with which the sentiment was received confirmed the marquis's worst opinions of the men around him.

Lafayette, with General Conway, who was appointed third in command, proceeded to Albany, where he was cordially received by General Schuyler, and became his guest. It was evident that with materials at hand a successful expedition into Canada was impossible. The marquis had been promised three thousand men well supplied. There were not twelve hundred men at Albany fit for duty, and one fourth of these were too naked even for a summer campaign. Gates had assured him that General Stark with New England troops would be at Ticonderoga awaiting his coming, and that he would have burned the British fleet on Lake Champlain before his arrival. He only found a letter from Stark inquiring what number of men, from where, and at what rendezvous he desired him to raise.

The marquis now fully comprehended the vile trick of which he had

---

the measure. Conway was offended, and became a willing instrument of Gates in his conspiracy. The prominent part which he took in that movement caused it to be called "Conway's Cabal."

been made the victim. He had been utterly deceived by the false utterances of Gates. "I fancy," he wrote, "the actual scheme is to have me out of this part of the country and General Conway as chief under the immediate command of Gates." The conspirators found they could not use Lafayette. Congress abandoned the enterprise, and the marquis, disgusted with the whole affair, returned to Washington's camp at Valley Forge.

The British held possession of Fort Niagara and exercised a powerful influence over the Six Nations, especially the more western tribes. They had nearly all become more or less disaffected toward the American cause, and at the close of 1777, so threatening became their aspect, that Congress recommended the Commissioners of Indian Affairs of New York to hold a treaty with them, defining the chief objects to be (1) to induce the Indians to make war upon their enemies, who were then desolating the frontier settlements of Pennsylvania and Virginia, and (2) to induce them to surprise and capture the British post of Niagara.

The commissioners complied. A council was opened at Johnstown early in March (1778), at which about seven hundred barbarian delegates appeared. Lafayette accompanied the commissioners. James Deane, an Indian agent living among the Oneidas, was the interpreter of a speech sent by Congress and read by General Schuyler, in which the power of the United States was asserted most emphatically, and the magnanimous manner in which they had always treated the Six Nations was recounted. The speech charged the Indians with ingratitude, cruelty, and treachery, and demanded reparation for their crimes. From these charges the Oneidas and Tuscaroras were exempted.

The council was not satisfactory. The Mohawks and Cayugas were sullen; the Senecas refused to send delegates. An Oneida sachem, conscious of the faithfulness of his people (and also of the Tuscaroras) to their pledges of neutrality, spoke eloquently in behalf of both, and these two nations renewed their pledges. It was clearly evident, however, that the more powerful of the Six Nations, with Brant at their head, were devising schemes for avenging their losses at Oriskany, and that war was inevitable. "It is strange," said the Senecas, by a messenger sent to announce their refusal to attend the conference, "that while your tomahawks are sticking in our heads [referring to the battle of Oriskany], our wounds bleeding, and our eyes streaming with tears for the loss of our friends, the commissioners should think of inviting us to a treaty."

Earnest efforts were made to avert war with the Indians. Attempts to recruit four hundred warriors of the Six Nations for the Continental service were only partially successful. When the news of the alliance with France was received, early in May, it was circulated as widely as possible among the Iroquois tribes. But little impression seemed to have been made upon the barbarians, and the white people began at once to make preparations to meet hostility. At Cherry Valley the house of Samuel Campbell, the strongest in the settlement, was fortified; and in the Schoharie Valley three buildings were intrenched with breastworks and block-houses and stockaded, by order of Lafayette. Each was garrisoned and armed with a small brass field-piece. These were called respectively the Upper, the Middle, and the Lower Fort. To these strongholds the women and children might fly for safety. Forts Schuyler and Dayton (the latter on the site of the village of Herkimer) were strengthened, and Fort Plain, lower down the Mohawk Valley, was enlarged and better armed.

These precautionary movements were not made too soon. They were keenly watched by Sir John Johnson and his kinsmen and friends. Among them the most active were Colonels John Butler, Guy Johnson, and Daniel Claas, the latter Sir John's brother-in-law. At the same time a nephew of Sir Guy Carleton was lurking near Johnson Hall for the same purpose.

We have observed that Brant returned from Canada in the spring of 1777 with a large band of Mohawk warriors. After the dispersion of St. Leger's invading force, in August, Brant and his followers retired to Fort Niagara, and there during the ensuing winter and spring they made preparations for war.

Early in the spring of 1778 Brant and his warriors appeared at Oghkwaga, their place of rendezvous the previous year. There he organized scalping parties and sent them out upon the borderers, cutting them off in detail. They fell like thunderbolts upon isolated families. Very soon the hills and valleys were nightly illuminated by the blaze of burning dwellings and made hideous by the shrieks of women and children. The inhabitants stood continually on the defensive. Men cultivated the fields with loaded muskets slung upon their backs. Women were taught the use of fire-arms, and half-grown children became expert scouts and discerners of Indian trails. Such was the condition of the settlers in the Mohawk region and the country south of it during a greater portion of the war.

In May (1778) Brant desolated Springfield, at the head of Otsego Lake, ten miles from Cherry Valley. Every house was laid in ashes. At the beginning of June he was in the Schoharie Valley with about three hundred and fifty Indian followers, and on the upper waters of the Cobleskill he had a severe encounter with some regulars and militia commanded by Captains Brown and Patrick. Twenty-two of the Republicans were killed and several were wounded. The houses in that region were plundered and burnt. A month later the terrible tragedy in the Wyoming Valley (to be noticed presently) occurred.

The Johnsons and their Tory followers were the allies of the barbarians in their bloody work south of the Mohawk River. The most savage of these Tories was Walter N. Butler, son of Colonel John Butler, who was in command of a detachment of his father's *Rangers* and had joined Brant. The latter, who was humane and even generous toward women and children placed at his mercy,* detested young Butler for his cruelties, and at first refused to serve with him. The matter was finally adjusted, and at near the middle of November (1778), during a heavy storm of sleet, the two leaders and their followers fell upon Cherry Valley, the wealthiest and most important settlement on the head-waters of the Susquehanna River, in New York.

A fort had been erected at Cherry Valley around a church by order of Lafayette, and was garrisoned by some Continental troops commanded by Colonel Ichabod Alden. He was forewarned by reports of approaching danger, but would not believe the messengers. He was therefore unprepared for an attack when, early in the morning of November 11th, snow, rain, and hail falling copiously, the motley hosts of Brant and Butler burst upon the settlement. They murdered, plundered, and destroyed without stint. Butler was the arch-fiend on that occasion, and would listen to no appeals from Brant for mercy to their victims.

The invaders first entered the house of Mr. Wells, whose wife was a daughter of the venerable minister, Mr. Dunlap. They massacred the whole family. Only his son John, afterward the eminent lawyer of New York, who was then at school in Schenectady, was saved. The family consisted of Mr. Wells, his wife and four children, his mother, brother, sister, and three servants. Colonel Alden, who was in the house at the time, was tomahawked and scalped. The savages then rushed to the dwelling of Rev. Mr. Dunlap and slew his wife before his

---

* Many instances of Brant's humanity are related. When, in 1780, he and Sir John Johnson desolated the Mohawk and Schoharie valleys an infant was carried off. The frantic mother pursued, but could not recover her babe. A day or two afterward General Van Rensselaer, in command of Fort Hunter, received a visit from a young Indian bearing the infant in his arms, and a letter from Brant, who wrote: "SIR: I send you by one of my runners the child which he will deliver, that you may know that whatever others may do, *I* do not make war upon women and children. I am sorry to say that I have those engaged with me who are more savage than the savages themselves." He named the Butlers and others.

eyes. His own life and that of his daughter were saved by the interposition of a Mohawk chief.*

Thirty-two of the inhabitants of Cherry Valley, mostly women and children, were murdered; also sixteen soldiers of the garrison there. Nearly forty men, women, and children were led away captives, marching down the valley that night in the cold storm, huddled together, half naked, with no shelter but the leafless trees, and no resting-place but the cold, wet ground.† With the destruction of Cherry Valley all hostile movements ceased in Tryon County, and were not resumed until the following spring.

A few months before this event the dreadful tragedy in the Wyoming Valley occurred, in which the chief actors were Tories and Iroquois Indians from New York. That valley is a beautiful and picturesque region of Pennsylvania, lying between lofty ranges of mountains and watered by the Susquehanna River, which flows through it. Its inhabitants were mostly from Connecticut. At the close of June (1778) Colonel John Butler, with over a thousand Tories and Indians, entered the valley from the north and made his headquarters at the house of Wintermoot, a Tory. He had been guided by some Tories of the valley, who had joined them. Butler had captured a little fort in the upper part of the valley.

---

* Unfortunately, Brant was not in chief command of the expedition. Walter Butler was the commander. Brant did all in his power to prevent the shedding of innocent blood. On the morning of the attack he left the Indians and endeavored to reach the families of Mr. Wells, Mr. Dunlap, and others, to give them warning, but could not do it in time. He entered dwellings to give the women warning. In one the woman engaged in household duties replied to his advice to fly to some place of safety: "I am in favor of the king, and the Indians won't hurt me."

"That plea will not save you," Brant replied.

"There is one, Joseph Brant," said the woman; "he will protect me."

"I am Joseph Brant, but I have not the command, and I may not be able to save you," he replied.

At that moment he saw the Senecas approaching. "Get into bed quick," he said, "and feign yourself sick."

The woman did so, and so he saved her. Then he gave a shrill signal, which rallied the Mohawks, when he directed them to paint his mark upon the woman and her children.

"You are now probably safe," said Brant, and departed.

† Among the captives were the wife and four children of Colonel Samuel Campbell, whose house had been fortified. He was absent at the time, and on his return he found his property laid waste and his family carried into captivity. They were taken through the wilderness to Fort Niagara. They were treated kindly by the Senecas, and were held as hostages for the safety and exchange of the family of Colonel John Butler, who were then in the custody of the Committee of Safety at Albany.

The whole military force to oppose this invasion was composed of a small company of regulars and a few militia. When the alarm was given the whole population flew to arms. Aged men, boys, and even women seized such weapons as were at hand and joined the soldiery. Colonel Zebulon Butler, an officer of the Continental Army, happened to be at home, and by common consent he was made commander-in-chief of the defenders. Forty Fort, a short distance above Wilkesbarre, was the place of general rendezvous, and in it were gathered the women and children of the valley.

On July 3d Colonel Butler led his little band of patriots—citizens and soldiers—to attempt a surprise of the camp of the invaders at Wintermoot's. The latter, informed of the movement, were ready to receive them. The Tories formed the right of the line of the intruders, resting on the river; the Indians, led by Gi-en-gwa-tah, a Seneca chief,[*] were on the left on a line that extended to a swamp at the foot of the mountain. Upon the latter the defenders struck the first blow, when a general battle ensued. For half an hour it raged furiously, when, just as the Indians were about to give way, a mistaken order caused the Republicans to retreat in much confusion. The infuriated barbarians sprang forward like wounded tigers and gave no quarter. The patriots were slaughtered by scores. Only a few of them escaped to the mountains and were saved. In less than an hour after the battle began two hundred and twenty-five scalps were in the hands of the Seneca braves.

Terror now reigned at Forty Fort, to which the women and children had fled. They had heard the fearful yells of triumph of the Indians. Colonel Dennison, who had reached the valley that morning, had escaped to the fort and prepared to defend its inmates to the last extremity. Colonel Zebulon Butler had reached Wilkesbarre fort in safety.

---

[*] The earlier historians of this event asserted (and believed) that Brant and the Mohawks were the chief actors in this dreadful tragedy. Brant denied it, but the testimony of history was against him. Campbell, in his poem, "Gertrude of Wyoming," published in 1809, misled by the historians, makes an Oneida chief say:

> " 'Gainst Brant himself I went to battle forth;
> Accursed Brant! he left, of all my tribe,
> Nor man, nor child, nor thing of living birth—
> No! not the dog that watched my household hearth
> Escaped that night of blood upon the plains."

In 1823 John Brant, son of the chief, being in England, opened a correspondence with Campbell on the subject of the injustice done to his father in the poem. Partial justice was accorded in the next edition of "Gertrude of Wyoming." The poet, after noting in a note the proofs of error which had been furnished him, said: "The name of Brant, therefore, remains in my poem a pure and declared character of fiction." He did not alter the poem, however, and so it remains.

Darkness put an end to the conflict, but increased the horrors of the scene. Prisoners were tortured and murdered. Sixteen of them were arranged around a low rock, and while held by strong men were nearly all murdered by a tomahawk and club used alternately by a half-blood woman called Queen Esther. Two of them threw off the barbarians who held them and escaped to the mountains.

On the following morning Forty Fort was surrendered. Colonel John Butler promised the inmates protection of their persons and property, and they went back to their homes; but so soon as the Tory leader left the valley the Indians who lingered spread over the plain, and with torch, tomahawk, and scalping-knife soon made it an absolute desolation. Scarcely a dwelling or an outbuilding was left unconsumed. Not a field of grain was left standing; not a life was spared which the barbarians could reach. The inhabitants who had not fled during the previous night were slaughtered or narrowly escaped. Those who departed made their way toward Connecticut. Many perished in the great swamp on Pocono Mountains, ever since known as "The Shades of Death."

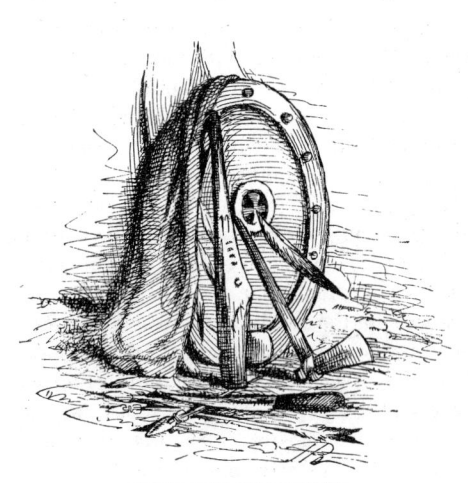

INDIAN WAR IMPLEMENTS.

The details of the desolation of the beautiful Wyoming Valley and of the horrors of the flight of the survivors of the massacre form one of the darkest chapters in human history. The British secretary for the colonies (Lord George Germaine) praised the barbarians for their prowess and humanity, and resolved to direct a succession of similar raids upon the frontiers, and to devastate the older American settlements. "Afterward among the extraordinaries of the army," said a bishop in the House of Lords, "was an order for scalping-knives."

Very important events outside of the State of New York occurred during the year 1778. In general interest the most important was the arrival, at the beginning of May, of the cheering news that a treaty of alliance between France and the United States had been signed at Paris on February 6th. The glad tidings greatly inspirited the Americans. Almost simultaneously appeared a gleam of hope emanating from the British throne and Parliament. The general failure of the campaign of 1777, ending in the capture of Burgoyne's army, made the English people and a powerful minority in Parliament clamorous for peace. Commissioners were sent to America to attempt a settlement of the dispute. They were authorized to treat with Congress as a competent body; but the conciliatory measures they were empowered to agree to did not include a proposition for the independence of the United States. Their mission was therefore a failure.

The English ministry, regarding the alliance with France as equivalent to a declaration of war on the part of that country, felt much anxiety for the safety of their army at Philadelphia and their navy on the Delaware River, especially when informed that the French were fitting out a fleet for American waters. Orders were sent to Howe to evacuate Philadelphia, and to his brother (the admiral) to leave the Delaware and proceed to New York. The land and naval forces were ordered to concentrate there. The French Government sent twelve ships of the line and four frigates, under the Count d'Estaing, to blockade the British fleet on the Delaware. The latter had escaped to sea a few days before the arrival of D'Estaing at the mouth of that river, and found safety on the waters of Amboy or Raritan Bay, into which the heavy French vessels could not enter.

General Sir Henry Clinton had succeeded General Sir William Howe in command of the army at Philadelphia when the order came for the evacuation of that city. He instantly obeyed the order, and on June 18th (1778) passed the Delaware with eleven thousand troops, and attempted a flight across New Jersey to New York by way of New Brunswick and Amboy. His design was frustrated by Washington, who left Valley Forge with a renovated army stronger in numbers than that of his foe, crossed the Delaware, and compelled Clinton to turn his face toward Sandy Hook.

Washington pushed on vigorously in pursuit of the fugitive army. He overtook the British near Monmouth Court-House, and there a sanguinary battle was fought on Sunday, June 28th—an exceedingly hot day. Darkness ended the conflict without any decisive result. The Americans slept on their arms, determined to renew the struggle the next morning; but Clinton stole away silently in the darkness at midnight unobserved by the wearied Americans, reached Sandy Hook in safety, and proceeded to New York by water. Washington did not pursue. He marched to the Hudson River, crossed into Westchester

County, remained there until the autumn, and then recrossed into New Jersey, and made his winter quarters at Middlebrook, on the Raritan. Clinton lost about six hundred men by desertion during his flight across New Jersey.

At this time the British were in possession of Rhode Island. At the request of Washington, D'Estaing proceeded to Newport to assist Generals Sullivan and Lafayette in driving them from the island. On the arrival of the fleet the Americans crossed over from the main to Rhode Island and pressed on toward the British camp. At that moment Howe, with a strongly re-enforced fleet, appeared. D'Estaing went out to meet him. A terrible storm dispersed and shattered both fleets. The French vessels hastened to Boston for repairs, leaving the Americans, who had been promised four thousand troops from the Gallic ships, in a perilous situation. They fell back to the northern end of the island pursued by the British. A severe battle was fought upon Quaker Hill (August 29th), in which the Americans were victorious. The next morning the latter withdrew to the main, leaving the British still in possession of Rhode Island ; but they were in the real position of prisoners. Such also was their position at New York until D'Estaing sailed for the West Indies late in the autumn, when Sir Henry Clinton sent two thousand troops, under Colonel Campbell, to invade Georgia, then the weakest member of the Confederacy. After some resistance the British took possession of Savannah, and it became the headquarters of the British army in the South for some time.

CHAPTER XXI.

SIR HENRY CLINTON * was in command of a force of over sixteen thousand men in the spring of 1779, yet his instructions confined him to a predatory warfare upon the coasts. In May a squadron commanded by Sir George Collier conveyed transports and galleys bearing twenty-five hundred troops, under General Matthews, to the waters in South-eastern Virginia. The commanders sent out parties against Norfolk and other places on the Elizabeth River and the neighborhood, to seize or destroy an immense quantity of naval and military stores and other property gathered there. That whole region was ravaged and made a scene of plunder and conflagration. Soon afterward these forces appeared at New York to join Sir Henry Clinton in an expedition up the Hudson River.

After the capture of Forts Clinton and Montgomery in the Highlands, West Point and Constitution Island opposite were strengthened by fortifications, and forts were erected upon Stony Point and Verplanck's Point opposite, a few miles below the Highlands. Fort Fayette, upon Verplanck's Point, was completed in the early summer of 1779, but that on Stony Point was then unfinished. These forts were to serve the double purpose of protecting the King's Ferry, on the Hudson, the most direct and convenient communication between the Eastern and Middle States, and of disputing the passage of British vessels through the Highlands.

At the close of May, Collier's vessels, seventy in number, great and small (and one hundred and fifty flat-boats), bore Sir Henry Clinton and a land force, under General Vaughan, up the Hudson, to attempt the capture of the two posts last mentioned. The troops were landed before dawn on May 31st, a part of them, under Vaughan, a few miles below Verplanck's Point, and the remainder, led by the baronet, a little below Stony Point. The handful of men at the latter place set fire to the

---

* Sir Henry Clinton was a son of Admiral Sir George Clinton, colonial Governor of New York, and born in 1738. He died in 1795. He entered the army when quite young, and rose to the rank of major-general in 1775, when he was sent to America with Howe and Burgoyne. He was active during the war with the American colonies until 1782, when he returned to England. He had succeeded Sir William Howe as commander-in-chief of the British forces in America in 1778.

block-house there, abandoned the unfinished fort, and fled to the mountains. Heavy artillery was dragged to the crest of the rocky promontory and turned upon Fort Fayette, while Vaughan's troops and the vessels joined in an attack upon that post. The little garrison of seventy men were compelled to surrender. Sir Henry garrisoned both posts, and proceeded to finish, arm, and man the fort at Stony Point.

Meanwhile Washington, believing Sir Henry's object to be the seizure of the Highland forts, had advanced his army toward the river mountains, and made his headquarters at New Windsor, above the Highlands. This movement checked Sir Henry's designs. He soon returned to New York, and sent Collier's vessels on a marauding expedition to the shores of Connecticut. They bore about twenty-five hundred British and Hessian (as the Germans were called) marauders, commanded by ex-Governor Tryon, who seemed to find the errand congenial to his nature. He made the Hessians his incendiaries and executors of his most cruel work.

The expedition left New York on the night of July 3d (1779), and in the space of a week laid waste and carried away a vast amount of private property, and cruelly abused the inhabitants. They plundered New Haven on the 5th; laid East Haven in ashes on the 6th; destroyed Fairfield by fire on the 8th, and plundered and burned Norwalk on the 12th. The soldiers were given free license to abuse and oppress the defenceless inhabitants. While Norwalk was in flames Tryon sat in a rocking-chair upon a hill in the neighborhood, a delighted spectator of the ruin wrought by his orders. In allusion to this and kindred expeditions Trumbull, in his "McFingal," makes Malcolm say:

> "Behold! like whelp of British lion,
> Our warriors, Clinton, Vaughan, and Tryon,
> March forth with patriotic joy
> To ravish, plunder, and destroy.
> Great generals, foremost in their nation,
> The journeymen of Desolation,
> Like Samson's foxes, each assails,
> Let loose with firebrands in their tails,
> And spread destruction more forlorn
> Than they among Philistines' corn."

The British finished, armed, and garrisoned the fort on Stony Point early in July. The Americans resolved to capture it. The impetuous General Wayne * was then in command of some infantry in the High-

---

* Anthony Wayne was born in Chester County, Penn., January 1st, 1745; died at Presque Isle (now Erie), Penn., December 15th, 1796. His father was commander of a

lands. He proposed to surprise the garrison and take the fort by storm. "Can you do it?" asked Washington.

"I'll storm hell if you'll plan it," said Wayne.

Washington gave him permission to undertake Stony Point first. Leading a few hundred men secretly through a mountain pass, Wayne was within half a mile of the rocky promontory on the evening of July 15th. They stealthily approached the only accessible way to the fort, across a marshy strait by a narrow causeway in the rear. They reached that point at midnight. After passing the causeway the little force was divided into two columns to make the attack at different points. With loaded muskets and fixed bayonets they marched up to the attack, preceded by a "forlorn hope" of picked men to make openings in an *abatis* at designated points of assault.

The assailants had nearly reached the *abatis* before they were discovered. The alarmed sentinels fired their muskets, when the startled

GENERAL ANTHONY WAYNE.

garrison flew to arms. The stillness of that hot summer night was suddenly broken by the rattle of musketry and the roar of cannons from the ramparts. In the face of a terrible tempest of bullets and grape-shot the assailants forced their way into the fort at the point of the bayonet. Wayne, who led one of the divisions in person, had been brought to his knees by a stunning blow from a musket-ball that grazed his head.

---

squadron of dragoons under William III. of England at the battle of the Boyne. After his marriage Anthony became a farmer and a surveyor. He was a member of the Pennsylvania Legislature in 1774–75; became a colonel in the Continental army in 1776; went with his regiment to Canada in that year; was wounded in battle, and early in 1777 was commissioned a brigadier. He was in the battle of Brandywine, September 11th, 1776, and a few nights afterward his camp, near the Paoli Tavern, on the road between Philadelphia and Lancaster, was assailed by a British force, and many of his men were slain. He was in the battles of Germantown and Monmouth, and he captured Stony Point, on the Hudson, in July, 1779. Wayne did admirable service in the Southern States during the remainder of the war. In 1792 he became general-in-chief of the armies of the United States. He brought the Indians in the North-west to peaceful relations, and was stationed at Presque Isle at the time of his death. Brave almost to rashness, he received the title of "Mad Anthony."

Believing himself mortally wounded, he exclaimed: "March on! Carry me into the fort, for I will die at the head of my column." He soon recovered, and at two o'clock in the morning he wrote to Washington:

"The fort and garrison, with General Johnston, are ours. Our officers and men behaved like men determined to be free." Wayne also wrote in a subsequent despatch: "The humanity of our brave soldiers,

FAC-SIMILE OF WAYNE'S DESPATCH.

who scorned to take the lives of a vanquished foe when calling for mercy, reflects the highest honor on them, and accounts for the few of the enemy killed on the occasion."

Johnston, the commander of the fort, and five hundred and forty-three men were made prisoners. He had sixty-three killed. The Americans lost one hundred men killed and wounded. The British shipping lying in the river near by slipped their cables and moved down the stream. The Americans attempted to capture Fort Fayette, but failed. Unable to hold and garrison the fort in Stony Point, they removed the heavy ordnance and stores to West Point and abandoned the post. The British repossessed it a few days afterward.

The terrible atrocities of bands of the Six Nations in 1778 around the head-waters of the Susquehanna and their vicinity and in the valley of Wyoming impelled the Americans to the exercise of vengeance against them in the most effectual manner. All of these nations, excepting the Oneidas and Tuscaroras, had been won over to the side of the crown by British emissaries among them, employed by the Johnson family, and the task of chastising them would be hard and perilous. A question of life or death of the frontier settlements was involved, and the people did not hesitate. They cheerfully joined in an expedition to penetrate the heart of the Iroquois country, for the purpose of spreading desolation with fire and sword, and conquering and securing peace by the force of terror.

In the spring of 1779 some preliminary movements to this end were undertaken. The first was against the Onondagas. Between five and six hundred troops, led by Colonels Goose Van Schaick and Marinus Willett, left Fort Schuyler on April 19th, and penetrated the heart of the Onondaga nation south of (present) Syracuse. They took the barbarians by surprise, destroyed three of their villages, burned their provisions, and slaughtered their live-stock. It was an unfortunate expedition, for it exasperated the Indians and did not spread terror among them, as was anticipated. Three hundred Onondaga braves were immediately sent out upon the war-path charged with the vengeance of the nation. They spread terror and desolation far and near in conjunction with other members of the Confederacy. They pushed southward to the waters of the Delaware and the borders of Ulster County.

On the night of July 19th, Brant, with sixty Mohawks and a band of Tories disguised as Indians, fell upon the settlement of Minisink, on the Neversink River, in the western part of Orange County, at the foot of the Shawangunk Mountains. They destroyed the growing crops, burned the church and ten houses, mills, and barns in the neighborhood, and retired with considerable plunder without attempting further violence.

When Colonel Tusten, at Goshen, heard of this raid he hastened with one hundred and fifty men (many of them volunteers) to the scene of desolation. They held a council, when it was concluded to pursue the marauders. Colonel Hathorn had arrived with a few recruits, and took command of the pursuing party. They overtook the main body of them near the mouth of Lackawaxen Creek (July 22d), when Brant by a quick movement threw his force in Hathorn's rear, placing the republicans in an ambush. More than fifty men were separated from the main body, leaving the remainder to sustain the shock of a furious attack. A severe conflict ensued, lasting from eleven o'clock in the morning until sunset. The republicans were beaten, and were murdered after they were made prisoners. Only thirty of the nearly three hundred pursuers survived to tell the sad story of the massacre. Forty-three years afterward the citizens of Orange County caused the bones of the slain to be gathered and buried near the centre of the Green in the village of Goshen, and over them a neat white marble monument was erected, bearing the names of the slain. A more elegant monument commemorative of the event was erected by order of the supervisors of Orange County in 1862. It was the gift of the late Dr. M. H. Cash.

MONUMENT AT GOSHEN.

A more powerful instrument for the chastisement of the offending Iroquois was formed in the summer of 1779. General Washington placed General John Sullivan *

---

* John Sullivan was born at Berwick, Me., February 17th, 1740; died at Durham, N. H., January 23d, 1795. He was a lawyer, a member of the first Continental Congress, and in December, 1774, with John Langdon, led a patriot force against Fort William and Mary, at Portsmouth, N. H., and took from it one hundred barrels of gunpowder, fifteen cannons, many small-arms and stores. In June, 1775, Sullivan was appointed one of the four brigadier-generals of the Continental army; commanded a portion of the troops that besieged Boston, and after the evacuation, in the spring of 1776, he went with troops to re-enforce the patriot army in Canada. On the death of General Thomas there he took the command of the army; skilfully effected a retreat from that province; was made prisoner in the battle on Long Island in August; was exchanged, and joined Washington in Westchester County; did good service in the battles at Trenton and Princeton, at Brandywine and Germantown, and in Rhode Island. After his expedition against the Indians in the State of New York he left the army on account of shattered health, and took a seat in Congress late in 1780. He was attorney-general of New Hampshire from 1782 to 1786, and president of that commonwealth from 1786 to 1789. From the latter date until his death he was United States Judge of New Hampshire.

in command of a force of Continental soldiers gathered in the Wyoming Valley, where the horrible massacre occurred the previous year. He was instructed to penetrate the heart of the Iroquois country and desolate it.

Sullivan left the valley with three thousand men at the close of July, marched up the Susquehanna River, and arrived at Tioga Point on August 22d. There he was joined by General James Clinton with about sixteen hundred men, who came down from Canajoharie, on the Mohawk River, by way of Otsego Lake, debarking on the site of Cooperstown. The combined forces numbered about five thousand, consisting of the brigades of Generals Clinton, Hand, Maxwell, and Poor, with Proctor's artillery and a corps of riflemen. So tardily had the expedition moved that the British authorities had time to send regulars and Tories from Canada and Niagara to assist the Indians in opposing it.

Marching up the eastern bank of the Chemung River on the morning of August 29th, the invaders destroyed the growing crops, and at length encountered a force of regulars, Tories, and Indians, strongly fortified, not far from the site of (present) Elmira. The Indians were commanded by Brant, and the remainder by Sir John Johnson,* the Butlers, and Captain McDonald. A fierce engagement ensued, and it was long doubtful which party would win the laurels of victory. It was finally decided for Sullivan when Proctor's artillery was brought into play and dispersed the terrified barbarians. The invading army rested on the battle-ground that night, and the next morning pushed on in pursuit of the fugitives.

That pursuit was quick and distressing. The army after a perilous

---

* Sir John Johnson, son of Sir William, was born in 1742. His mother was a German girl. He was a stanch and active loyalist; fled to Canada with several hundred followers; in connection with the Indians desolated the Mohawk Valley and its neighborhood, and was defeated by General Van Rensselaer in 1780. He went to England after the war, but soon returned to Canada, where he remained in the capacity of Superintendent of Indian Affairs until his death in 1830.

march encamped before Catharine's Town, near the head of Seneca Lake, on the morning of September 2d, and destroyed the village, the surrounding crops of corn, and the orchards. The flying campaign, charged with the forces of destruction, had now fairly begun. "The Indians shall see," said Sullivan, "that there is malice enough in our hearts to destroy everything that contributes to their support." His men, burning with indignation, eagerly sought to avenge the cruelties of the barbarians and Tories who had made the region of the Mohawk a "dark and bloody ground." The Indians fled before them like frightened deer to cover, and the wail of desolation was heard throughout their pleasant land, from the Susquehanna to the Genesee.

On September 14th General Sullivan and his army encamped before Genesee, the capital of the Senecas, in the beautiful Genesee Valley— the paradise of the Six Nations. There everything indicated the presence of civilization. There was not a wilderness feature in the scene. The rich intervales presented the appearance of cultivation for many generations, and the farms, gardens, and orchards bespoke a degree of comfort and refinement that would be creditable to any civilized community. But a terrible doom hung over the smiling country. The Genesee "Castle" was destroyed and the capital was laid in ashes. "The town," wrote Sullivan, "contained one hundred and twenty-eight houses, mostly large and very elegant. It was beautifully situated, almost encircled with a clear flat extending a number of miles, over which extensive fields of corn were waving, together with every kind of vegetable that could be conceived."

The work of destruction now spread over the whole valley and the surrounding country. Forty Indian villages were burned; one hundred and sixty thousand bushels of corn in the fields and in granaries were destroyed; a vast number of the finest fruit-trees, the product of years of tardy growth, were cut down; hundreds of gardens were desolated; the inhabitants were driven into the forests to starve, and were hunted like wild beasts; their altars were overturned; their graves were trampled upon by strangers, and a beautiful, well-watered country, teeming with a prosperous people and just rising to the level with the productive regions of civilization, was desolated and thrown back a century within the space of a fortnight.

This chastisement awed the barbarians for the moment, but it did not crush them. In the reaction they had greater strength. It kindled the fires of deep hatred, which spread like a conflagration far among the tribes upon the borders of the great lakes and in the valley of the Ohio.

After Sullivan's campaign very few military operations occurred at the North during the remainder of the year. Lafayette had been in France during the summer, and had induced the French Government to promise to send a more powerful fleet and several thousand troops to aid the Americans. Whispers of this intention reached the ears of the British Cabinet, when the evacuation of Rhode Island and the concentration of British troops at New York were ordered.

A land force under General Lincoln and troops sent ashore from the French fleet of D'Estaing made an attack upon Savannah, Ga., in September, and carried on a siege until the second week in October, when it was abandoned in consequence of the sudden withdrawal of the French troops. Lincoln was compelled to cross the Savannah River into South Carolina and retreat to Charleston. Toward that city Sir Henry Clinton sailed from New York at the close of the year with five thousand troops, to open a vigorous campaign in the Carolinas.

In September the intrepid John Paul Jones, in command of the frigate *Bonhomme Richard*, fitted out in a French port, gained a decisive victory in one battle over two British frigates, the *Serapis* and the *Countess of Scarborough*. They fought in the waters of the North Sea, off the north-eastern coast of England.

Sir John Johnson took advantage of the hot indignation of the Iroquois, kindled by Sullivan's chastisement, to make a raid into the Mohawk Valley with five hundred Tories and Indians, in May, 1780. He penetrated the country from Crown Point to the Sacandaga River, and on Sunday night, May 17th, he arrived at Johnstown. Between midnight and dawn his force, divided, began to devastate that region, burning every house excepting those which belonged to Tories. In the course of this raid many persons were slain and homes desolated. Such wild terror was spread all over that region that Sir John was enabled to accomplish the chief object of his visit—namely, the recovery of his family plate, which was buried near Johnson Hall when he fled to Canada in 1776. He recovered twenty of his negro slaves, one of whom was the man who buried the treasure. It filled two barrels, and when it was exhumed it was carried away in the knapsacks of forty soldiers. With this property, his slaves, some prisoners, and much booty, Sir John was allowed by the panic-stricken people to leave for Canada without molestation.

On hearing of this invasion, Governor Clinton, then at Poughkeepsie, ordered a pursuit. He led a division in person to Ticonderoga, where he was joined by some militia from Vermont. Eight hundred militia, under Colonel Van Schaick, pursued the fugitives from Johnstown; but Sir John had such a start that he escaped. He had wisely avoided the lakes on his retreat, and passed through the interior of the country.

In August the Canajoharie and Fort Plain * settlements were desolated by Brant and five hundred Indians and Tories. Fifty-three dwellings and many barns were burned; sixteen inhabitants were killed; between fifty and sixty persons, chiefly women and children, were made captive; implements of husbandry were destroyed, and over three hundred cattle and horses were driven away.

In the autumn of 1780 an extensive expedition against the settlements in Tryon County was planned. The Indians were thirsting for revenge for the wrongs and misery inflicted upon them by Sullivan. The leaders in the expedition were Sir John Johnson, Joseph Brant, and a famous half-breed Seneca chief named Corn Planter. The Indians rendezvoused at Tioga Point, and at Unadilla they formed a junction with Sir John and his forces—regulars, Tories, and Indians—who came from Niagara and Canada by way of Oswego, bringing with them some light artillery. Their plan was to desolate the Schoharie Valley to the Mohawk, and then devastate that beautiful and bountiful region down to Schenectady.

FORT PLAIN BLOCK-HOUSE.

The invaders reached the Schoharie Valley at the middle of October. The inhabitants were taken by surprise. Their barns were filled with the products of a bountiful harvest, and stacks of hay and grain were abundant. The invaders besieged the forts, but failed to capture them. Believing them to be stronger than he had supposed, and fearing re-enforcements were coming, Sir John ordered his forces to sweep the valley with the besom of destruction to the Mohawk. Everywhere they applied the torch. Every house, barn, and stack belonging to a Whig was laid in ashes. Fully one hundred thousand bushels of grain were destroyed during that one day's march. So soon as the invaders had departed the exasperated Whigs burned the spared

---

* After the desolation of the Mohawk and Schoharie valleys in 1778, Fort Plain was erected near the mouth of the Osquaga Creek, and became an important fortress. It stood upon a hill at the (present) village of Fort Plain. It was an irregular quadrangle in form, with earth and log bastions. It finally had a block-house (built in 1780) three stories in height pierced for musketry, the lower story for cannon. It was built of hewn logs. Each story projected about five feet beyond the one below it. The powder magazine was under it.

houses and other property of the Tories. The Schoharie Valley was made a smoking ruin. Several persons were slain during the raid. Sir John remained two days at Fort Hunter, at the mouth of the Schoharie Creek, and destroyed everything belonging to the Whigs in the neighborhood; and on October 18th he began a destructive march up the Mohawk Valley. He burned Caughnawaga and every dwelling on both sides of the river as far as Fort Plain. On the morning of the 19th he sent a detachment to attack a small stockade called Fort Paris, in Stone Arabia, about three miles north of the river.

When Governor Clinton (then at Albany) heard of the invasion of the Schoharie Valley he hastened with a strong body of militia, accompanied by General Robert van Rensselaer, to the aid of the people of the smitten region. They arrived at Caughnawaga while it was in flames. There Clinton gave the chief command of the troops to Van Rensselaer. The latter, apprised of the intended attack upon Fort Paris, ordered its commander, Colonel Brown (distinguished in former campaigns), to march out and meet the invaders. He did so about a mile from (present) Palatine Bridge, was overpowered by superior numbers, and with forty of his soldiers was slain. The remainder of his troops fled to Fort Plain.*

COLONEL BROWN'S MONUMENT.

---

* Colonel John Brown was a citizen of Massachusetts, a graduate of Yale College, and a lawyer by profession. He accompanied the expedition to Canada in 1776, and was specially distinguished in the capture of Fort Chambly. He hung on the rear of Burgoyne's army in 1777, destroying his stores, and so efficiently assisting in the work of his capture. No mention was made of these services in official reports, as Arnold, who had at that time the ear of Gates, prejudiced that officer against him. Colonel Brown and his slain companions were buried in the grounds adjoining the church in Stone Arabia, and fifty-six years afterward (1836), on the anniversary of the battle, a small monument erected on the spot by Mr. Henry Brown, a son of Colonel Brown, of Berkshire, Mass., was dedicated. There was a large concourse of citizens assembled in the church on the occasion, when an address was pronounced by Mr. Gerrit L. Roof, then a young lawyer of Canajoharie, and afterward a clergyman. The above engraving is from a drawing made for the late Dr. Franklin B. Hough, who wrote an interesting and valuable narrative of "The Northern Invasion," of which only eighty copies were printed by the "Bradford Club," of New York.

Sir John desolated Stone Arabia. He halted to rest at a place called "Klock's Field." General Van Rensselaer was in pursuit of him with fifteen hundred men, including a body of Oneidas, led by Chief Louis, whom Congress had commissioned a colonel. Van Rensselaer's movements were so tardy that the invaders were rested before he was ready to attack them. Toward evening a general battle began, when a furious charge made by the patriots caused the invaders to give way and fly It was now twilight, and Van Rensselaer would not allow his impatient troops to pursue until the next morning, when the fugitives were followed by the whole body of the victors as far as the German Flats, where they halted.

Van Rensselaer ordered the Oneidas and Captain McKean, with some volunteers to press on in advance, promising to follow immediately in their support. They had nearly overtaken the fugitives when the pursuers learned that Van Rensselaer had abandoned the pursuit. They retraced their steps as an act of safety, and Sir John and his invading party, who had inflicted such unutterable miseries upon the inhabitants of Tryon County, were allowed to escape to Canada by way of Oswego.

Meanwhile Major Carleton of the British army, with one thousand regulars, Tories, and Indians, went up Lake Champlain, captured and burned Fort Anne, between the head of the lake and the Hudson, and sent forward marauding and incendiary parties toward Fort Edward. At the same time Carleton himself pushed on to the head of Lake George, and captured and destroyed Fort George there. A part of the expedition had landed at Crown Point and made its way through the forest to attack Schenectady, but proceeded no farther than the settlement at Ballston, which they desolated. At about the same time another expedition sent out from Canada fell upon the upper settlements of the Connecticut Valley. These expeditions avoided doing injury to the inhabitants on the New Hampshire Grants (Vermont), because the leaders of those people were then coquetting with the British authorities in Canada. For what purpose will appear hereafter.

When Sir Henry Clinton sailed for the South at the close of 1779 he left the German General Knyphausen in command at New York. The fleet of Admiral Arbuthnot, carrying two thousand marines, bore Clinton's troops. They went first to the coast of Georgia, but soon proceeded to Charleston Harbor and prepared to besiege that city, where General Lincoln was in command of a considerable body of troops. The city, the army, citizens, four hundred cannons, and a large quantity of stores were surrendered on May 12th. The Baron de Kalb had been sent with troops to assist Lincoln, but did not arrive in time.

The fall of Charleston paralyzed the people of South Carolina. Three British detachments proceeded to take possession of the State. Lord Cornwallis was appointed to the chief command in that region. Clinton proclaimed a general truce, and pardon and protection for all who should accept it. The silence of fear overspread the country for a while. Mistaking this lull in the storm of resistance for absolute submission and permanent tranquillity, Clinton, with a large part of his army, sailed in the fleet of Arbuthnot for New York early in June.

Cornwallis unwisely began a reign of terror to overawe the panic-stricken patriots. His course aroused their fiercest indignation, and so soon as an army, first under De Kalb and then commanded by Gates, approached the borders of their State they flew to arms. Energetic partisan leaders like Marion, Sumter, Pickens, and others now appeared, and South Carolina and Upper Georgia became a theatre of active warfare, until Gates was beaten and his army was dispersed in a battle with Cornwallis, near Camden. This disaster seemed again to paralyze the people, and the State lay prone for a while at the feet of the invader.

Cornwallis, now confident of his power, proceeded to invade North Carolina. It was begun, but was soon checked by the defeat of a body of Tory militia, led by Major Patrick Ferguson, in a battle on King's Mountain (October 7th), by the mountaineers of the Carolinas. At the same time Marion and Sumter were keeping British regulars and Tories exceedingly lively in an attitude of defence, until they became thoroughly alarmed. The British called Marion the "Swamp Fox" and Sumter the "South Carolina Game Cock."

While these operations were going on in the South and in the State of New York the American people were inspirited by the presence on their shores of a large land and naval force sent by France to aid them. They arrived at Newport, R. I., on July 10th, 1780. The fleet was commanded by Admiral Ternay. It bore six thousand troops, commanded by Lieutenant-General Count de Rochambeau. This event made Sir Henry Clinton more circumspect and cautious. He had been trying to entice Washington, after he left his winter quarters at Morristown, N. J., to fight; now he changed his course of action, and endeavored to gain, by complotting with a traitor, what he had failed to do by arms.

CHAPTER XXII.

Benedict Arnold was in command of the important post of West Point, in the Hudson Highlands, late in the summer of 1780. He was a brave soldier, and had fought nobly for the independence of his country. But he was never a *true* patriot, or he would never have become a *traitor*. He lacked virtue, and became the slave and the victim of passions unrestrained by conscience.

Arnold was military governor at Philadelphia in the summer of 1778. He there married a beautiful maiden (Miss Shippen), only eighteen years of age. He was forty-eight. He lived in splendor at an expense far beyond his means, became involved in debt, and to meet the demands of his creditors he engaged in practices which caused him to be charged with dishonesty and malfeasance in office. He was tried by a court-

BENEDICT ARNOLD.*

---

* Benedict Arnold, a brave soldier who became a conspicuous traitor, was born at Norwich, Conn., January 3d, 1741; died in London, June 14th, 1804. Apprenticed to an apothecary, he ran away; enlisted as a soldier; deserted; engaged a few years in the business of a bookseller and druggist in New Haven, and a trader with the West Indies. After the affair at Lexington he raised a company of volunteers, and accompanied Allen in the capture of Ticonderoga. He performed gallant service in naval warfare on Lake Champlain the following year. Meanwhile he had made a perilous march through the wilderness from the Kennebec River to Quebec; engaged in the siege of that city; was badly wounded; was chiefly instrumental in winning the battles that resulted in the surrender of Burgoyne, and was again wounded in these conflicts. While in command as military governor at Philadelphia he opened a treasonable correspondence with the British. His attempt to betray West Point failed, and he escaped to the British lines. He served in the British army in predatory warfare upon his countrymen; went to England, where he was despised by all honorable men; became for a while a resident of St. Johns, New Brunswick, where he was hung in effigy. He soon returned to England, where he lived in obscurity. One of his sons became a lieutenant-general in the British army.

martial, and sentenced to be reprimanded by the commander-in-chief of the armies. It was done by Washington in the most delicate manner.

Vengeful feelings took possession of the heart and mind of Arnold, which led him to make an attempt to betray his country. He made treasonable overtures secretly to Sir Henry Clinton, and held treasonable correspondence for several months, under assumed names, with Major André, Clinton's adjutant-general. Before they met face to face Arnold promised to surrender the post of West Point and its dependencies (of which, on his earnest solicitation, he had been made commander in August) into the hands of the enemy. The possession of West Point by the British would secure the control of the Hudson; cut off New England from the rest of the States; facilitate intercourse with Canada, and lead to the speedy accomplishment of all that the expeditions of Burgoyne and St. Leger were expected to effect. Arnold agreed to strike this deadly blow at the liberties of his patriotic countrymen for the consideration of a brigadier's commission in the royal army and $50,000 in gold.

The time chosen for the consummation of this unholy bargain was late in September, 1780, when Washington would be in Hartford, Conn., conferring with the French officers. Arrangements were made for a personal interview between Arnold and André to conclude a final settlement of the details. The place selected by Arnold for the interview was a lonely spot not far below Haverstraw, on the west side of the Hudson, and the time midnight, September 20th.

André ascended the river on the sloop-of-war *Vulture*, and was taken ashore in a boat * sent by Arnold, in charge of his friend, Joshua Hett Smith, who lived between Haverstraw and Stony Point. The complotters met in the dark. André's uniform was concealed by a surtout. He had been instructed to neither carry nor fetch any papers. The conference was protracted. Day dawned and it was not ended. Arnold persuaded André to accompany him to Smith's house to complete the arrangements, without informing him that the dwelling was within the American lines. Meanwhile the *Vulture* had been driven down the river by cannonading from Teller's Point, on the eastern shore.

---

* On the morning at first fixed for his execution (October 1st, 1780) Major André made a pen-and-ink sketch representing his conveyance to the shore from the *Vulture* in a small boat. There are two persons in the boat besides the oarsman. This sketch, with "J. A., fecit, Oct. 1, 1780," written in a corner, was found on his table after his execution, on October 2d; also a pen-and-ink sketch of his own portrait sitting at a table. His servant delivered these sketches to Colonel Crosbie, of the Twenty-second Regiment, on his return to New York.

At Smith's house the final arrangements were made. Clinton was to ascend the river with a powerful force, when Arnold, after making a show of resistance, should surrender the post, pleading as an excuse the weakness of the garrison.

This wicked scheme perfected, André was anxious to return to the *Vulture* that night, but Smith refused to go so far down the river, and it was arranged for the adjutant-general to return to New York by land. Exchanging his uniform for a suit supplied by Smith, and accompanied by that gentleman, he crossed the river at the King's Ferry at twilight, bearing the following passport:

"Permit Mr. John Anderson [an assumed name] to pass the guards to the White Plains, or below, if he chooses, he being on public business. B. Arnold, M. G."

In violation of his instructions, André had received from Arnold some papers explanatory of the condition of West Point and its dependencies, and concealed them in his stockings beneath his feet. He and his attendants passed the night near the Croton River. The next morning he journeyed on alone on horseback, and soon reached the neutral ground in Westchester County.

Near Tarrytown three young militiamen—John Paulding, Isaac van Wart, and David Williams—were playing cards on the edge of a wood when André approached. Paulding, dressed in a British trooper's coat, stepped into the road and hailed him. The young man had been a prisoner a short time, and had been stripped of his better farmer's coat and given the old red one he had on. The traveller, misled by this coat, said:

"Gentlemen, I hope you belong to our party."

"Which party?" asked Paulding.

"The lower party."

"We do."

Thus completely thrown off his guard, André avowed himself to be a British officer, when they said:

"*We* are Americans."

Astonished and alarmed, André now exhibited Arnold's passport. The young men shook their heads. He had avowed himself a British officer. His speech confirmed the truth of that avowal. Their suspicions that he might be a spy were aroused. They invited him to dismount, and then proceeded to search him. Pulling off his boots, the tell-tale papers were discovered.

"My God!" exclaimed Paulding, "he *is* a spy!"

The major offered the young men large bribes if they would let him

TREASONABLE DESIGNS FRUSTRATED. 313

pass on. They refused, and delivered him to Colonel Jameson, then in command of a post at North Castle. Jameson sent the papers found in André's boot by express to Washington, who was returning with his suite from Hartford. André, still maintaining the *rôle* of an American, begged the colonel to inform his (André's) commander at West Point that John Anderson, though bearing his passport, was detained a prisoner. This Jameson thoughtlessly did, and so Arnold was informed of his own peril in time to allow him to escape.

Arnold's headquarters were at the country-house of Beverly Robinson, opposite West Point. Mrs. Arnold had lately arrived there with her

THE ROBINSON HOUSE.

infant son. On the morning of September 25th Washington, with Generals Knox and Lafayette, arrived in the vicinity two days earlier than they were expected. Word was sent to Arnold that they would breakfast with him. Washington and the two generals turned aside to inspect some redoubts, while Colonel Hamilton and others rode on to tell Mrs. Arnold not to detain breakfast for the generals. It was the very day (September 25th) that had been fixed for Clinton to ascend the river and receive the surrender of West Point. Washington's early return frustrated the treasonable designs.

While Arnold and his guests were at breakfast a courier arrived with Jameson's letter, which revealed to Arnold the terrible fact that André was a prisoner ; that all was known—that all was lost. With marvellous self-possession the traitor excused himself to his guests, retired, ordered a horse, and then going to Mrs. Arnold's room, sent for her. In a few words he told her of his peril.

"I must fly instantly," he said. "My life depends upon my reaching the British lines without detection."

He then returned to the breakfast-room, and again excusing himself with the plea that he must hasten to West Point to prepare for the reception of Washington, he leaped into the saddle on his horse at the door and dashed down a path to the river, where his six-oared barge was moored. Quitting his horse, he hurried into his boat, with his pistols in his hands, and ordered the oarsmen to pull to the middle of the stream and then to row with speed to Teller's (now Croton) Point, saying he must hasten and return to meet General Washington. Near that point, sitting in the bow of his barge, Arnold raised a white handkerchief, and ordered his men to row to the *Vulture*, lying within sight. They did so, and the traitor, reaching her deck, was safe from pursuit. The barge was retained and the crew were sent on shore.

Washington took a late breakfast at Arnold's quarters, and then crossed over to West Point, expecting to meet the general there. He had not been there for two days ! Still unsuspicious, the commander-in-chief did not return until about noon. He was met by Colonel Hamilton, who put into his hands evidences of Arnold's treason. Orders had already been issued to attempt to intercept the flight of the guilty fugitive. It was too late.

Arnold had left his wife lying in a swoon. She had not been discovered until some time after her husband's departure. Recovering consciousness, she became frenzied, and for a long time refused to be comforted. Washington went to her room, and succeeded in soothing her. He assured her of the personal safety of her husband, of his own tender regard for her, and also of the personal safety of herself and child. He comprehended the gravity of the situation, but seemed undisturbed. To General Knox he said sadly : "Arnold is a traitor ; who can we trust now ?"

André was conveyed first to West Point, and thence to Tappan, on the west side of the Hudson, then the headquarters of the army, where a board of inquiry was organized (September 30th), composed of fourteen general officers, to consider the prisoner's case. They unanimously reported that "Major André, adjutant-general of the British army, ought to be considered as a spy from the enemy, and that, agreeable to the law and usage of nations, it is their opinion he ought to suffer death."

He was accordingly executed on October 2d, 1780. André was not then twenty-nine years of age.

Great efforts were made to save the life of Major André. It was known that he did not voluntarily become a spy, and almost universal sympathy was then, and has been ever since, evinced for him. Washington would have saved him had the stern rules of war allowed. Sir Henry Clinton might have saved him had honor permitted him to exchange Arnold for André.* His king pensioned his family and knighted his brother; a mural monument to his memory was placed in Westminster Abbey, and in 1882 a granite memorial stone was erected by a citizen of New York (Cyrus W. Field) on the spot where he was hanged as a spy, to commemorate that event. It was destroyed by a miscreant with dynamite on the evening of November 2d, 1885. It bore an inscription written by the late Dean Stanley, of London.

The captors of André were each awarded a silver medal and an annuity of $200 for life. Arnold received his stipulated reward for his treasonable endeavors, and served as a British general in cruel marauding expeditions against his countrymen. None of the British officers would serve with him in the regular army. He was forever afterward shunned and despised by all honorable men on both sides of the ocean.

A few weeks after the execution of André a stirring military event occurred on Long Island. Some refugee Tories from Rhode Island had taken possession of the St. George's Manor-house on Smith's Point and fortified it, and were cutting wood for the supply of the British at New York. Late in November Major Benjamin Tallmadge crossed Long Island Sound in whale-boats from Fairfield, Conn., with eighty dismounted dragoons, and at dawn (November 23d) appeared before the Manor-house, burst through the stockade, rushed across the parade, and assailed the garrison on three sides, shouting, "Washington and glory!" The garrison surrendered without resistance. Having secured three hundred prisoners, they were returning to their boats when they made a detour, and at Coram destroyed three hundred tons of hay gathered there for the use of the British in New York. The expedition returned to

---

* An attempt was made to abduct Arnold from Clinton's headquarters at No. 1 Broadway, New York, and carry him to Washington's headquarters at Tappan. Sergeant Champe, of Lee's Legion, was allowed to play the *rôle* of a deserter. He was met by the traitor with much cordiality. Arrangements were made for a party to seize Arnold while walking in the garden at the British headquarters with Champe, at evening of the day preceding the execution of André. The quasi-deserter was foiled by being sent away with a party of British to Chesapeake Bay on that day.

Connecticut without losing a man. Congress thanked the victors, and Washington warmly commended their valor.*

Civil events in the region known as the New Hampshire Grants created much uneasiness not only in New York, but throughout the Confederacy in 1780. The controversy between New York and the Grants paused, as we have observed, at the beginning of the war for independence ; but the spirit of liberty among the settlers east of Lake Champlain continued conspicuously all through the period of that war. They had assumed a provisional independent political organization, and in 1776 had petitioned the Continental Congress to admit them into the union as such. New York so vehemently opposed their pretensions that their petition was rejected.

At a popular convention held at Westminster in January, 1777, the people of the Grants declared their domain an independent State, forever thereafter to be " known and distinguished by the name of New Connecticut, *alias* VERMONT." This position they maintained until Vermont was admitted into the Union in 1791.

The State of Vermont was much strengthened by the annexation of sixteen towns laying east of the Connecticut River, which were claimed as part of the domain of New Hampshire. The latter State protested ; New York denied the authority of Vermont as independent of her jurisdiction, whilst Congress, appealed to, could do nothing.

In the southern portion of Vermont was the county of Cumberland, one of the fourteen political divisions of New York. Over this county New York exercised authority. Vermont claimed it as her own, and Massachusetts put in a claim for it and a portion of New York, truthfully asserting that the boundary between the Bay State and New York had never been settled. The inhabitants themselves claimed to belong to New York, and in 1779 Governor Clinton gave commissions to persons in that county, whereupon Vermont ordered Colonel Ethan Allen to raise a militia force, march into the disputed district, and assert her authority there. Governor Clinton directed the people to remain firm

---

* A similar gallant feat by soldiers from Connecticut had been performed on Long Island in the spring of 1777. Colonel R. J. Meigs was sent from Guilford with one hundred and seventy men in whale-boats, accompanied by two armed schooners, to destroy British stores at Sag Harbor, on the eastern end of Long Island. At night they crossed over a portion of Long Island to Peconic Bay, carrying their boats with them, and at two o'clock in the morning attacked the British guards. An armed schooner opened fire upon them. The fire was returned with spirit, and the Americans killed or captured the whole British force, destroyed twelve brigs and sloops, one hundred tons of hay, a large quantity of rum and other stores and merchandise, and returned to Guilford with ninety prisoners. Congress thanked Meigs, and gave him an elegant sword.

in their allegiance to New York, and promised them military assistance if required. Congress, having been appealed to, advised the four claimants to authorize that body to determine the respective boundaries; but really independent Vermont paid no attention to the recommendation, and nothing was then done.

At this juncture a question of greater magnitude than these local disputes presented itself. The British authorities in Canada had eagerly watched the progress of the quarrel with Vermont, and now entertained hopes that the latter would be so far alienated from the "rebel" cause, by the opposition of New York and the injustice of Congress, as to be induced to return to its allegiance to the British crown. Accordingly in the spring of 1780 Colonel Beverly Robinson wrote to Ethan Allen from New York, making overtures to that effect. The letter was delivered to Allen in the street at Arlington by a spy disguised as a New England farmer.

Allen laid the letter of Robinson before Governor Chittenden and others, who advised silence. In February, 1781, Robinson wrote another letter to Allen, enclosing a copy of the former. Allen made no reply, but early in March he sent Robinson's letter to Congress, with one from himself, which closed with the words:

"I am as resolutely determined to defend the independence of Vermont as Congress is that of the United States; and, rather than fail, I will retire with the hardy Green Mountain Boys into the desolate caverns of the mountains and wage war with human nature at large."

Meanwhile information of the first letter written by Robinson, and the sending of a delegation from Congress to Vermont, had alarmed the authorities of New York. Governor Clinton, suspecting a combination against his State, wrote to James Duane (October 29th, 1780) that in the event of a certain contingency the New York delegates would be withdrawn from Congress, "and the resources of the State, which have hitherto been so lavishly afforded the Continent, be withheld for the defence of New York." Clinton called the attention of Washington to the apparent danger, when the latter issued orders to General Schuyler to arrest Allen. Schuyler shared in Clinton's apprehensions and wrote from Albany to the governor at Poughkeepsie (October 31st) saying:

"The conduct of some people to the eastward is alarmingly mysterious. A flag, under pretence of settling a contest with Vermont, has been on the Grants. Allen has disbanded his militia, and the enemy, in number upward of six hundred, are rapidly advancing toward us. The night before last they were at Putnam's Point. Entreat General Wash ington for more Continental troops, and let me beg of your Excellency to hasten up here."

This was in allusion to a conference between Allen and Colonel Dundas at Isle aux Noix concerning an exchange of prisoners. At that conference Dundas, under the direction of Governor Haldimand, made verbal proposals to Allen similar to those made by Robinson.* Allen now saw the opportunity for Vermont. He received the overtures with apparent favor. Haldimand and Dundas were delighted with their apparent skill in diplomacy, and readily agreed to a proposition from Allen not to allow hostilities on the Vermont frontier until after the meeting of the Legislature. Hence the dismissal of Allen's militia.

The coquetry of the brothers Allen (Ethan and Ira) and six or eight other leaders in Vermont with the British authorities in Canada continued until the peace in 1783, when dissimulation was no longer necessary. The conclusion of the whole matter may be stated in a few words. The shrewd diplomatists of Vermont had been working for a twofold object— namely, to keep the British troops from their territory and to induce Congress to admit the independence of their domain as a State of the Union. They outwitted the Britons, hoodwinked Congress, and finally gained their point.†

BEVERLY ROBINSON.

* Beverly Robinson, a staunch royalist, was born in Virginia in 1734; died an exile at Thornbury, England, in 1792. He was a major under Wolfe at Quebec. He married a daughter of Frederick Philipse. Up to the Declaration of Independence he opposed the measures of the British Government; then he espoused the cause of the crown. He took an active though generally a secret part in the plot of Arnold and André. He accompanied the latter on his voyage up the Hudson in the *Vulture* to have an interview with Arnold, who occupied Robinson's house as headquarters at that time. He fled to England, and his property was confiscated. The British Government allowed him $80,000 as an indemnity for his losses. His wife died in England in 1822, at the age of ninety-four years.

† Ethan and Ira Allen were remarkable men. They were both born in Connecticut, Ethan in 1737, and Ira in 1751. The latter was Ethan's younger brother. Ethan was one of the proprietors of the iron works at Salisbury, Conn., in 1762. In 1766 he went

Yet the difficulties between New York and Vermont were not settled. Violent measures had ceased forever. Both parties, however, were unwilling to yield. Finally the Legislatures of the two States appointed commissioners late in 1789 to settle all matters of controversy. The only serious difficulty that remained related to compensation for the lands claimed by citizens of New York which had been granted to them by Vermont. It was finally agreed that the State of Vermont should pay to the State of New York $30,000 in settlement of their claims. All other matters in dispute were adjusted, and so, amicably, was ended a bitter controversy which had been carried on for more than twenty-six years, at times threatening immediate civil war. In the spring of 1791 Vermont was admitted into the Union as an independent but not a sovereign State.

The Americans were not subdued at the close of 1780, but their cause was in great peril because of the extreme weakness of material props and the absence of an efficient civil government. The Continental paper money, which had hitherto greatly assisted in sustaining the cause, had become almost worthless. "A wagon-load of money," said a contemporary, "would not buy a wagon-load of provisions." The several States were urged to supply quotas of funds for the common use. Their responses were slow and feeble, for there was no central power competent to levy taxes or demand forced loans. The idea of State sovereignty was all-controlling. Finally a plan of government which had been discussed in Congress since 1775 was adopted late in 1777, and submitted to the State Legislatures for ratification. It was yet unratified, and the Continental Congress had but a shadow of power independent of the States, whose supremacy was made potential by the new constitution of government, which was entitled "Articles of Confederation."

---

to the New Hampshire Grants, then almost a wilderness, and, as we have observed, was a bold leader in the controversy with the settlers and the authorities of New York. He wrote several pamphlets during that controversy. He was outlawed by the authorities of New York; took a conspicuous place in the opening scenes of the Revolution; was carried a prisoner to England; was exchanged in 1778, and invested with the chief command of the Vermont militia. He was a leading coquette with the Canadian authorities; served as a member of the Legislature of Vermont and a delegate in Congress after the war, and died at Burlington, Vt., and was buried there in February, 1789.

Ira Allen was also an active patriot during the old war for independence in military and civil affairs. He was Secretary of State and member of the Council of Vermont. As senior major-general of Vermont, in 1795 he was sent to Europe to purchase arms for his commonwealth. On his way homeward, with muskets and cannons, he was captured and taken to England as a French emissary intending to supply the Irish with arms. He was soon released. He died in Philadelphia in 1814. Allen wrote a *National and Political History of Vermont*.

Thoughtful men were alarmed and perplexed. The young Alexander Hamilton (then in Washington's military family), in a letter to James Duane, one of the four New York members of Congress, denounced this scheme of government as "neither fit for war nor peace. The uncontrollable sovereignty in each State," he wrote, "will defeat the powers of Congress and make our union feeble and precarious." In his letter to Duane he proposed a convention of all the States, for the purpose of constructing a national government under the superintendence of one supreme head, and he proposed a plan, in the form of suggestions, which was substantially adopted several years afterward.

There were no military operations of great importance in the State of New York in 1781 before the arrival of the French troops, under Rochambeau,* from Rhode Island, in the vicinity of the Hudson River, early in July. Sir Henry Clinton had sent the traitor Arnold, at the head of about sixteen hundred British and Tory marauders, into Virginia. Anxious to serve his royal master, Arnold was exceedingly active. He ascended the James River to Richmond, burned it, with a very large quantity of public and private property, and then made a plundering raid down the river. Alarmed by information that the French fleet from Rhode Island had sailed for Chesapeake Bay, he fled up the Elizabeth River and took post at Portsmouth, opposite Norfolk. Great efforts were made to seize him. Lafayette was sent to Virginia with troops to assist the Baron von Steuben,† then in command there. The Virginia militia turned out in large numbers to oppose the traitor.

COUNT DE ROCHAMBEAU.

* Count de Rochambeau was born at Vendome, France, in 1725; died in May, 1807. He entered the army in his youth, and rose rapidly to distinction. With the commission of lieutenant-general he came to America with troops to assist the patriots in their struggle with British power. After the capture of Cornwallis at Yorktown, in 1781, he remained some time in America, returning to France late in 1782. In 1791 he was made a marshal of France and placed in command of the Army of the North. He narrowly escaped the guillotine. Bonaparte pensioned him in 1804, and gave him the decoration of the Cross of Grand Officer of the Legion of Honor.

† Frederick W. A. (Baron) von Steuben was a native of Prussia, born at Magdeburg,

Governor Jefferson offered a reward of $25,000 for his capture, and a portion of the French fleet shut him up in the Elizabeth River. The fleet was soon compelled to retreat, after a conflict with Admiral Arbuthnot.

General Phillips soon afterward joined Arnold with two thousand men, and took the chief command. Finally Lord Cornwallis entered Virginia from North Carolina, joined the forces of Phillips and Arnold, and attempted the subjugation of that State. He was driven back to the coast early in the summer by the forces of Steuben and Lafayette, and took post at and fortified Yorktown, on the York River. Clinton had ordered him to be near the sea, in order to re-enforce the garrison at New York, if necessary. It was then seriously menaced by the combined American and French forces.

STEUBEN'S MONUMENT.

The Count de Grasse, a distinguished admiral, was then in command of a French fleet in the West Indies, and Washington was assured that he was ready to co-operate with the allied armies in any undertaking that promised success. Meanwhile Rochambeau had led the French troops from New England to the Hudson River, and the junction of the Americans and their allies took place near Dobb's Ferry on July 6th. Washington was then contemplating an attack upon the British in the city of New York, but before De Grasse was ready to co-operate with him Sir Henry received

---

in 1730. He held a distinguished place in the Prussian army, and rose to the office of grand marshal in 1764. He joined the Continental army in America in 1777, and was appointed inspector-general, doing excellent service until the close of the war. For his services the State of New York gave him sixteen thousand acres of wild land in Oneida County, where he built a log-house for himself. The National Government gave him an annuity of $2500. He withdrew from society, and dwelt on his domain until his death, in November, 1794. By his will he parcelled his estates among his aides (Colonels North, Popham, and Walker) and twenty or thirty tenants. The State of New Jersey also gave him a small farm. He was kind, generous, and witty, and possessed polished manners. Over his grave in the town of Steuben, about seven miles north-west of Trenton Falls, a plain monument was erected, by private subscription, in 1826—simply a recumbent slab with his name upon it.

re-enforcements (August 11th) of three thousand troops from England. At about the same time Washington was informed that De Grasse could not leave the West Indies just then.

Lafayette had written to Washington that Cornwallis had made a great mistake in intrenching himself at Yorktown, and urged the commander-in-chief to march into Virginia. "Should a French fleet enter Hampton Roads," he wrote, "the British army would be compelled to surrender." For six weeks the allied armies lay in Westchester County, waiting for the arrival of De Grasse to attack New York. When, a few days after the arrival of Clinton's re-enforcements, Washington was informed that De Grasse was about to sail for the Chesapeake, he resolved to march to Virginia and assist Steuben and Lafayette in opposing Cornwallis. He wrote misleading letters to General Greene in New Jersey, and sent them so as to be intercepted by Sir Henry. General Schuyler also wrote a letter to Washington for the same purpose. These letters so adroitly concealed Washington's real intentions that it was ten days after the allies had crossed the Hudson and were marching for the Delaware and beyond before Clinton was convinced the movement was not a feint to cover a sudden descent upon New York. It was then too late to intercept or successfully to pursue the allies, and he sent Arnold with a band of marauders to desolate the New England coast, hoping to recall the Americans.

BARON VON STEUBEN.

Washington was in chief command of the allied armies, and bearing the commission of lieutenant-general from the King of France. He arrived before Yorktown with twelve thousand troops on September 28th, and soon began a siege. De Grasse had already arrived, and was guarding the entrance to Chesapeake Bay. The siege was carried on vigorously, and on October 19th Cornwallis was compelled to surrender to Washington and De Grasse, himself and about seven thousand troops, the post with all its ordnance and supplies, his shipping and seamen. A vast concourse of people, equal in number, it was said, to the military, was assembled from the surrounding country to participate in the event so joyful to the Americans. Clinton appeared at the entrance of Chesapeake Bay a few days afterward with seven thousand troops to reenforce Cornwallis. It was too late, and he sailed back to New York amazed and disheartened.

The surrender of Cornwallis filled the hearts of patriotic Americans with joy, for it was a prophecy of peace and independence. That prophecy was soon fulfilled. The desire for peace, which had long burned in the hearts of the British people, now found such potential expression that it was heeded by the British Ministry.

The news from Yorktown fell like a lighted bombshell in the midst of the war party in Parliament, and public opinion found immediate and vehement expression in both Houses. Lord North, the premier, who had misled the nation for twelve years, retired from office (March 20th, 1782), the advocates for peace came into power, and early in May ensuing Sir Guy Carleton, who had succeeded Clinton as commander-in-chief of the British forces in America, arrived at New York with propositions for a reconciliation.

Measures were immediately taken by Congress and the British Government to arrange a treaty of peace. Commissioners were appointed by the high contracting powers, in which France, an ally of the Americans, was included, and on November 30th a preliminary treaty was signed at Paris. A definitive treaty was signed at the same place on September 3d, 1783, by which the independence of the United States was acknowledged by the King of Great Britain.

War had raged in the South during 1781. General Nathaniel Greene had succeeded General Gates in command of the Southern army, and with the main body took post at Cheraw, east of the Pedee River. Among his most active lieutenants was General Daniel Morgan, who with a thousand men occupied the region near the confluence of the Pacolet and Broad rivers.

Cornwallis was about to march into North Carolina, when he found himself between two fires. He sent the energetic Colonel Tarleton to capture or disperse Morgan's men. The belligerents met in battle at the Cowpens, in Western South Carolina (January 17th, 1781), where Tarleton was defeated with much loss. Congress rewarded Morgan with a gold medal, and his two lieutenants, Colonels Howard and Washington, with a silver medal each.

Morgan started for Virginia with his five hundred prisoners and much spoil. Cornwallis attempted to intercept or overtake him, but failed. Morgan crossed the Catawba before him, and on the banks of the Yadkin he was joined by Greene and his escort.

Now began the famous retreat of the American army, under General Greene, from the Catawba through North Carolina into Virginia. Cornwallis had been detained by the sudden swelling of the Catawba by a heavy rain. He reached the Yadkin (February 3d) just as the Americans were safely landed on the opposite shore. Swelling floods again arrested him. The patriots pressed onward, and Cornwallis was soon again in full pursuit. At Guilford Court-House Greene was joined by his main army from Cheraw, but he was not strong enough to fight. They all continued the flight, and after many escapes the Americans reached the Dan (February 13th), and crossed the rising waters into the friendly bosom of Halifax, in Virginia. Cornwallis, again foiled by a flood, abandoned the chase, and moved sullenly southward through North Carolina.

Greene soon recrossed the Dan, to prevent Cornwallis organizing the Tories in North Carolina. Recruits had swelled his ranks, and at the beginning of March he found himself in command of about five thousand troops. He sought an engagement with Cornwallis, and on March 15th they fought a very severe battle near Guilford Court-House. Although the British remained masters of the field, the victory was almost as destructive for Cornwallis as a defeat. "Another such a victory," said Charles J. Fox, in the House of Commons, "will ruin the British army." The battalions of Cornwallis were so shattered that he could not maintain the advantage he had gained. Thoroughly dispirited, he abandoned Western North Carolina, and moved with his whole army to Wilmington, leaving Lord Rawdon in command of a British force at Camden. Cornwallis soon afterward marched into Virginia.

Greene with all his force pursued Cornwallis some distance, and then marched for Camden. He encamped upon Hobkirk's Hill, within a mile of Rawdon's encampment, where he was surprised by the British forces on the morning of April 25th. After a sharp battle of several hours Greene was defeated, but on his retreat he carried away all his artillery and baggage and fifty British prisoners.

Greene's army began to increase, when Rawdon, alarmed for the safety of his posts in the lower country, abandoned Camden and took position at Nelson's Ferry, on the Santee. Within the space of a week the Americans seized four important posts, and Greene was making rapid marches toward Fort Ninety-Six, on the site of the (present) village of Cambridge, in Abbeville District. In all these operations Greene was greatly aided by Colonel Henry Lee ("Light Horse Harry") and his famous Legion. At the beginning of June the British possessed only three posts in South Carolina—namely, Charleston, Nelson's Ferry, and Ninety-Six.

General Greene began the siege of Ninety-Six on May 22d, but on the approach of Rawdon with a strong force he was compelled to abandon it on June 19th. Meanwhile Lee, Pickens, and others had gained victories on the Savannah River. They captured Fort Galphin, below Augusta, on May 21st, and after a siege of eleven days and a final assault Augusta was surrendered to Lee and Pickens. Then the victors hastened to join Greene before Ninety-Six, and with him they retreated beyond the Saluda River. The Americans finally crossed the Congaree, and the main body encamped during the hot and sickly season on the High Hills of Santee, in Santee District.

Rawdon left his army at Orangeburg with Colonel Stewart and returned to England. Re-enforced by North Carolina troops, Greene crossed the Wateree at the close of August, and marched upon Orangeburg, when Stewart retreated to Eutaw Springs, near the Santee. Greene pursued and overtook him there, and on the morning of September 8th they fought a sanguinary battle. The Americans were victorious at first, but lost the prize for which they contended, by imprudence. Unexpectedly the British renewed the conflict, and after a severe struggle for several hours the Americans were defeated. Stewart, however, thought it prudent to retreat toward Charleston during the night, and on the 9th Greene took possession of the battle-field. Congress rewarded him with a gold medal and other honors.

Annoyed by the active partisan corps in South Carolina, the British soon afterward evacuated their interior posts and retired to Charleston. At the close of 1781 they were confined to the cities of Charleston and Savannah.

CHAPTER XXIII.

The Americans did not relax their vigilance while negotiations for peace were in progress. The army was kept intact, for British troops seemed still disposed to be aggressive. The last blood shed in the Revolution was spilled in a skirmish with a British foraging party not far from Charleston in August, 1782. Already the British troops had evacuated Savannah (July 11th), but they held Charleston until December 14th,

ROOM IN WASHINGTON'S HEADQUARTERS.

when they left it forever, and the city of New York alone was then in possession of the Britons. They remained there almost a year longer.

Meanwhile the State of New York became the theatre of most important events in the career of the Continental army, encamped between Newburgh and New Windsor, above the Hudson Highlands. The headquarters of the army was at Newburgh.* In the autumn of 1782 it was

---

* The quaint old stone house at Newburgh used by Washington as headquarters is yet standing, and is preserved in its original form outside and in. It is the property of the

temporarily transferred to Verplanck's Point, below the Highlands, to meet the French troops on their return from Virginia, preparatory to their marching into New England to embark for France. At that time the Continental army numbered about ten thousand men.

The joy inspired by the prospects of peace was mingled by gloomy forebodings concerning the future. The army, which through the most terrible sufferings had been faithful and become a conqueror, was soon to be disbanded, and thousands of soldiers, many of them made invalids by their hard service in the field, would be compelled to seek a livelihood in the midst of the desolation which war had produced.

For a long time the public treasury had been empty, and neither officers nor private soldiers had received any pay for several months. Murmurings of discontent were heard throughout the army. The weakness of the Confederation was ascribed to its republican form, and many men sighed for a stronger government. A change, to be wrought by the army, was actually proposed by Colonel Nicola, a meritorious foreign officer of the Pennsylvania line. In a well written letter addressed (May, 1782) to the commander-in-chief at his headquarters at Newburgh, he not only urged the necessity of a monarchy, but endeavored to persuade Washington to become *King*, by the voice of the army, in imitation of the actions of the Roman legions. The sharp rebuke administered by the commander-in-chief in his reply checked all further movements in that direction.

Toward the close of the winter of 1783 the discontent in the army assumed a more formidable shape. The officers had asked Congress to make a full settlement of all accounts, past and present. That body, feeble in resources, would not make any definite promises of present relief or future justice. This increased the discontent, and early in the spring (March 11th) a well-written anonymous address, purporting to be from a suffering veteran, was circulated through the American camp. It advised the army to take matters into its own hands, and make a demonstration that should alarm the people and Congress, and thus obtain justice. It declared that to be tame in their present situation would be worse than weakness on the part of the soldiers, and it exhorted them to " suspect the man who could advise to more moderation and longer forbearance." The tenor of the whole address was inflammatory. With it was privately circulated a notification of a meet-

---

State of New York, and in the custody of the corporation of Newburgh. It presents the remarkable feature in one room (which Washington used as a dining-room) of seven doors and only one window, with a huge fireplace, which is large enough to admit of roasting a small bullock whole. The house is filled with relics of the Revolution.

ing of officers at a large building called the Temple, which had been erected for the use of public gatherings and the Free Masons of the army.

These papers were brought to the notice of Washington on the day they were issued. He referred to them in general orders the next morning; expressed his disapproval; invited the general and field-officers of the army to assemble at the Temple at noon on the 19th (March, 1783), and requested General Gates to preside at the meeting. There was a full attendance. Washington stepped upon the platform to read an address which he had prepared for the occasion. As he put on his spectacles he remarked: "You see, gentlemen, I have not only grown *gray* but *blind* in your service." These words touched a tender chord of sympathy in all hearts.

The address was a model—compact in construction, dignified and patriotic in sentiment, mild yet severe in its strictures, and abounding with the most important suggestions concerning the best interests of the army, represented by the men before him, the citizens, the Republic, and human freedom. On closing his address Washington immediately retired, leaving the officers to discuss the subject unrestrained by his presence.

LEMUEL COOK.

The deliberations of the officers were brief. They unanimously condemned the addresses; voted thanks to their chief for the course he had pursued; expressed their unabated attachment to his person; declared their unshaken confidence in the good faith of Congress, and their determination to bear with patience their grievances until they should be redressed.

The author of the seditious addresses was Major John Armstrong, a member of Gates's military family and a young man then twenty-five years of age. He was Secretary of War in Madison's Cabinet in 1814.

A few weeks later the disbanding of the Continental army began at New Windsor and its vicinity. Congress proclaimed a cessation of hostilities on April 19th. The soldiers who had enlisted "for the war" claimed the right to go home. Congress insisted that their terms of enlistment would not expire before a definitive treaty of peace should be effected. Washington exercised the office of mediator and pacificator. He issued long and really indefinite furloughs to all the soldiers excepting those who re-enlisted until a peace establishment should be organized. The furloughed soldiers went home and never returned. A definitive treaty of peace was signed at Paris on September 3d (1783), and on October 18th Congress, by proclamation, discharged the soldiers of the Continental army.*

Before the beginning of the disbandment of the army in June (1783) the officers, at the suggestion of General Knox, formed an association at their cantonment, near Newburgh, having for its chief objects the promotion of cordial friendship and indissoluble union among themselves, and to extend benevolent aid to such of its members as might need assistance. They named the organization the Society of the Cincinnati. Wash-

---

* The number of the soldiers of the Continental army at its disbandment, and its condition, was much the same as it was at the time of the Declaration of Independence, seven years before. On July 4th it consisted of 7754 men present and fit for duty, including one regiment of artillery. Their arms were in a wretched condition. Nearly one half the muskets of the infantry were without bayonets. During the war 231,771 soldiers were enrolled in the Continental army. These were furnished by the respective States, each in number, as follows:

New Hampshire	12,497	Delaware	2,386
Massachusetts	67,907	Maryland	13,912
Rhode Island	5,908	Virginia	26,678
Connecticut	31,939	North Carolina	7,263
New York	17,781	South Carolina	6,417
New Jersey	10,726	Georgia	2,679
Pennsylvania	25,678	Total	231,771

The last two survivors of the Continental army were Lemuel Cook, of New York, and William Hutchings, of Maine. Cook was born at Plymouth, Lichfield County, Conn., in 1764, and died at Clarendon, Orleans County, N. Y., May 20th, 1866, at the age of one hundred and two years. Hutchings was born at York, Maine, October 6th, 1764, and died May 2d, 1866, also nearly one hundred and two years of age. Lemuel Cook entered the military service of his country in the spring of 1781, at the age of seventeen years, and was with the allied armies in the campaign against Cornwallis in Virginia. He was one of the regulars, and was a member of the Second Regiment of Light Dragoons, commanded by Colonel Sheldon, but was soon mustered into the infantry. At the end of the war he was discharged at Danbury, Conn. He soon afterward married Hannah Curtis, of Cheshire, Conn., by whom he had seven sons and four daughters. He married a second wife when he was seventy years of age. In his earlier years he lived in the then almost wilderness region of Utica, N. Y. Most of his children were born in Connecticut. He moved into Central New York with his young family, and lived at Clarendon about thirty years previous to his death. He was a farmer all his life. In 1863 his annual pension was increased from $100 to $200, and the last year of his life to $300. New York has the distinction of having as a citizen the *last surviving soldier of the Continental army.*

ington was chosen its president and General Henry Knox its secretary. This was called the General Society. State societies were formed auxiliary to the general society. To perpetuate the association, its constitution entitled the eldest masculine descendant of an original member to wear the order, or badge, and enjoy the privileges of the society.*

The last act in the drama of the old war for independence was performed at the city of New York late in 1783. The opening scene was the flight of the Loyalists, or Tories. These supporters of the crown were numerous and active, especially in New York City and State. They had aroused the most intense indignation—nay, hatred, of the Whigs against them by their oppressive conduct, civil and military, and when it was known that the British troops were soon to leave the city of New York they hastened, with the utmost consternation, to fly to some place of refuge from the impending wrath of the patriots.

In October a fleet of transports conveyed hundreds of Loyalists, or Tories, to Nova Scotia, and at the evacuation (which was delayed for want of vessels to transport them) other hundreds fled to the same British province.

The property of many Loyalists in the State of New York was confiscated by laws passed for the purpose during the war, but after peace and independence were established justice and policy required a general amnesty. The harsh laws were repealed, and much of the confiscated property was restored. Many of the refugees in Nova Scotia who could procure the means to do so came back, and in the course of a score of years the

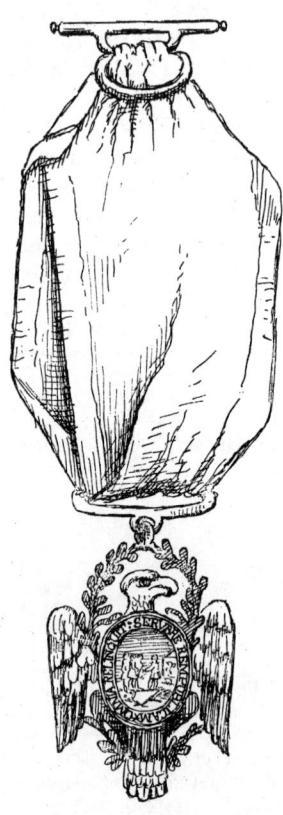

ORDER OF THE SOCIETY OF THE CINCINNATI.

---

* The order or badge of the society consisted of a golden spread eagle, with enamelling, suspended on a ribbon. On the breast of the eagle is a medallion with a device representing Cincinnatus at his plough receiving the Roman senators who came to offer him the chief magistracy of Rome.

social animosities engendered by the war were healed or greatly modified.

The time fixed for the evacuation of New York was November 25th. On the morning of that day General Washington and his staff and Governor Clinton and staff, escorted by General Knox and some troops who came down from West Point, appeared at the (present) junction of Third and Fourth avenues—the "head of the Bowery Lane"—and halted there until noon. At one o'clock, when the British had withdrawn to the water's edge for embarkation, the Americans marched into the city, the general and governor at their head, and before three o'clock General Knox had taken possession of Fort George, at the foot of Broadway, amid the acclamations of thousands of citizens and the roar of artillery. Then Washington and his officers retired to Fraunce's Tavern.* Governor Clinton and the civil officers went to the City Hall and re-established civil government, and at evening the chief magistrate gave a public dinner at Fraunce's Tavern. The last sail of the British fleet that bore away the army and the Loyalists did not disappear beyond the Narrows before twilight.

The final scene in the last act was now performed. Washington assembled his officers in a large room in Fraunce's Tavern on December 4th, and there bade them farewell. He entered the room, and taking a glass of wine in his hand, said:

"With a heart full of love and gratitude I now take leave of you. I most devoutly wish that your latter days may be as prosperous and happy as your former ones have been glorious and honorable." Having tasted the wine, he continued: "I cannot come to each of you to take my leave, but shall be obliged to you if each will come and take me by the hand."

A tender scene ensued. Tears moistened the war-worn cheeks of the veterans before him as each pressed the hand of their beloved commander and received from his lips a kiss upon their foreheads. Then Washington left the room in silence, passed through a corps of light infantry, walked to Whitehall (now the Staten Island Ferry), followed by a large multitude of grateful citizens, and at two o'clock P.M. entered a barge that

---

* This building, yet standing, is on the corner of Broad and Pearl streets. It was partially destroyed by fire in June, 1852. Samuel Fraunce, the proprietor, had a dark complexion, and was called "Black Sam." When President Washington resided in New York Fraunce became the caterer for the Presidential mansion. Freneau, in his "Hugh Gaine's Petition," makes that time-server allude to the cannonade of the *Asia*, man-of-war, and say:

"At first we supposed it was only a sham
Till he drove a round ball through the roof of Black Sam."

conveyed him to Paulus' Hook (now Jersey City), whence he journeyed first to Philadelphia and thence to Annapolis, where the Continental Congress was in session. To that body, assembled in the Senate Chamber of the old State House, at noon on December 23d (1783), he resigned his commission of commander-in-chief of the armies, which he received from them more than eight years before.

From Annapolis Washington journeyed to Mount Vernon in his own carriage, accompanied by his wife, where he arrived on Christmas eve. Then he laid aside his sword and military garments, and, joyfully resign-

FIRST GREAT SEAL OF THE STATE OF NEW YORK.

ing the cares of public life, like Cincinnatus, returned to his plough—a farmer on the banks of the Potomac.

During all the stormy period, from the foundation of the State Government, in the summer of 1777, until the departure of the last hostile foot from its shores, in 1783, New York had been laying the foundations of its future greatness strong and deep, and at the same time it had been just and generous in its fraternal relations with its sister States. It grappled the great task before it with energy and wisdom. It held a commanding position. The prominent part it had taken in the mighty struggle just ended; the fact that it alone of all the States had promptly met every requirement of the Provisional General Government, and even made advances on its own credit to supply the deficiencies of other States; its extensive commerce and large territory, and the ability and patriotism of its leading statesmen, entitled it to special consideration, and gave it great weight in the councils of the nation.

The sessions of the State Legislature were held alternately at Poughkeepsie, New York, and Albany, after the flight from Kingston in the fall of 1777, until the beginning of 1798—a period of about twenty years. At that time Albany became the permanent political capital of the State, and a new great seal was adopted.*

The first care of the Legislature after the war was the adjustment of boundaries, land claims, etc. In this particular New York found itself in a peculiar situation, because of rival claims to its soil. Of the territory which, by the treaty of peace, was ceded by Great Britain to the United States in their collective capacity, each of the individual States claimed such portions as were compre-

SECOND GREAT SEAL OF THE STATE OF NEW YORK.

---

* Three great seals of the State of New York have been made. The first two were pendant, and the third is incumbent. The first great seal, adopted in 1777 by the convention that framed the State Constitution, was rudely engraved on brass. It bore on one side a rising sun; motto, EXCELSIOR; legend, THE GREAT SEAL OF THE STATE OF NEW YORK. On the other side a rock in the midst of the ocean, and the word FRUSTRA. The above engraving is from a drawing of an impression made on beeswax and attached to a commission signed by Governor Clinton. It shows the method of attaching pendant seals to the parchment. It is three and a quarter inches in diameter and about three eighths of an inch in thickness. A second seal was authorized in 1798, and the description was recorded, January 22d, 1799, as follows: "The arms of the State complete, with supporters, crest, and motto; round the same, THE GREAT SEAL OF THE STATE OF NEW YORK. On the reverse a rock and waves beating against it; motto, 'Frustra above; 1798 below.'" The obverse of the seal is delineated above.

In 1809 the great seal (incumbent) now in use was ordered, and was first attached to a document in November of that year. It bears the arms of the State of New York, a little modified in the design. In the second seal the supporters are standing; in the third they are sitting. In both the crest is the same—an eagle preparing to soar from a demi-globe.

hended within their original grants or charters. Massachusetts consequently laid claim to a strip of land equal to its own extent north and south, and extending westward to "the South Sea," or the Pacific Ocean. This included all the territory of New York between the latitude of Troy on the north and the northern part of Duchess County on the south. Connecticut made a similar claim on the same pretext. This would have included nearly all southern New York. Before considering these claims, let us take a brief notice of the rights of older and more legitimate possessors and actual occupants of the soil of New York—the Six Nations.

The conditions of peace with the Six Nations were settled between them and the United States at a treaty held at Fort Stanwix (Schuyler, now Rome) in October, 1784, at which Oliver Wolcott, Richard Butler, and Arthur Lee represented the United States. By that treaty the western boundary of the Six Nations was fixed at the longitudinal parallel of Buffalo. Red Jacket, afterward the great Seneca chief, then first appeared as an orator in opposition to the treaty, which deprived the Confederacy of their hunting-grounds north of the Ohio. The Six Nations were guaranteed the peaceable possession of their lands eastward of the boundary named, excepting a reservation of six miles square around Fort Oswego.

From time to time after 1785 the State and individuals procured lands from the Indians by cession or by purchase. The Tuscaroras and Oneidas first parted with some of their territories in 1785. In 1788 both the Oneidas and the Onondagas disposed of all their lands, excepting some reservations, and in 1789 the Cayugas ceded all their lands to the State, excepting a reservation of one hundred square miles exclusive of Cayuga Lake. In each case the right of free hunting and fishing in all the counties was reserved.

The Senecas parted with most of their territory in 1797. The same year the Mohawks, most of whom fled to Canada at the close of the war, relinquished all their lands to the State for a consideration. So late as 1819 there were about five thousand of the Six Nations in the State, in possession, in eleven reservations, of two hundred and seventy-one thousand acres of land. In 1838 these lands had been disposed of, nearly all the titles extinguished, and the Indian population had removed westward, some of them beyond the Mississippi River. Such was the final act in the drama of the once powerful barbarian republic in the State of New York—the great Iroquois League. It now disappeared from the face of the earth and entered the realm of past history.

The claim of Massachusetts to a part of the territory of New York was amicably adjusted by a convention held at Hartford in December, 1786, when it was agreed that the Bay State should cede to New York all claims to "government, sovereignty, and jurisdiction" over about six million acres of the soil, including what is known as "Western New York." The domain extended from a line drawn north and south between Pennsylvania and Canada on the meridian of Seneca Lake to the western boundary of the territory of the Six Nations, already defined. At the same time New York ceded to Massachusetts and to her grantees and their heirs the right of pre-emption of the soil from the native Indians, and "all other estate, right, title, and property," excepting government, sovereignty, etc. The claim of Connecticut was summarily rejected.*

Massachusetts proceeded to sell the right of pre-emption of this tract. In 1788 Oliver Phelps and Nathaniel Gorham bargained for the whole tract, agreeing to pay $1,000,000. Unable to fulfil the conditions, they took two million six hundred thousand acres. Between that time and 1793 the remainder of the domain was disposed of to several purchasers,† and settlements were soon afterward begun.

After the peace (1783) Congress, considering measures for meeting the claims of public creditors, invited the several States to vest in that body power to levy duties on imports within their respective jurisdictions. All the States had acceded to this request in 1786 excepting New York. This State reserved that right to itself, and refused to make the collectors amenable to and removable by Congress. It also made the duties payable in the bills of credit issued by the State. At this juncture Congress asked Governor Clinton to call a special session of the Legislature, for the purpose of passing a law conformable to those of other States concerning the public revenue. The governor refused compliance.

---

* Under this claim Connecticut made some grants to settlers within the State of New York, also in Pennsylvania and in Ohio. The Wyoming Valley was settled by Connecticut people, so also was the region in Ohio known as the Western Reserve.

† The following is a list of the titles of the subdivisions of the Massachusetts domain in Western New York purchased of the Indians, with the number of acres in each:

Phelps and *Gorham* tract, 2,600,000; *Morris Reserve*, 500,000; *Triangular*, 87,000; *Connecticut*, 100,000; *Cragie*, 50,000; *Ogden*, 50,000; *Cottinger*, 50,000; *Forty Thousand Acre*, 40,000; *Sterritt*, 150,000; *Church*, 100,000; *Morris's Honorary Creditors*, 58,570; *Holland Company's Purchase*, 3,600,000; *Boston Ten Towns*, 230,400. Before the close of the last century a larger portion of the soil of Northern New York was in the possession of land speculators. Among them Alexander Macomb, father of General Macomb, was the most extensive holder, in Franklin, St. Lawrence, Jefferson, Lewis, Oswego, and Herkimer counties. He purchased over two million five hundred thousand acres for eighteen cents an acre, on a long credit, without interest. This reckless squandering of the public domains by the commissioners of the Land Office was severely condemned.

This independent action of New York made the inherent weakness of the Articles of Confederation, as a form of national government, very conspicuous. New York had already taken official action, for the purpose of giving to Congress more power for the collecting of revenue than had yet been proposed.*

Washington had observed with great anxiety the tendency toward ruin of the new government, and he now proposed a convention of representatives of the States to consider amendments of the Articles. A convention was called at Annapolis in September, 1786. Only five States responded. New York was one of them, and was represented by Alexander Hamilton. Nothing was done except to recommend the assembling of another convention at Philadelphia in May the next year. It was done. All the States but New Hampshire and Rhode Island were represented. Robert Yates, John Lansing, Jr., and Alexander Hamilton represented New York. Washington, a delegate from Virginia, was chosen president of the convention. He was ably supported by eminent statesmen from the several commonwealths. The convention was in session from May until September, 1787. It framed a new Constitution—the one (with some amendments) under which the Republic has ever since been governed. Copies of the instrument were sent to the Legislatures of the several States, to be submitted by them to conventions of delegates chosen by the people for approval or disapproval.

Now came the tug of war. Differences of opinion concerning the new

---

* "It is the glory of New York," says Bancroft, "that its Legislature was the first to impart the sanction of a State to the great conception of a Federal Convention to frame a constitution for the United States." The chief instrument in bringing about such action by the Legislature of New York was the then foremost character in the State, General Philip Schuyler, assisted by his son-in-law, Colonel Alexander Hamilton. From the very beginning of the discussion of plans for a national government Schuyler had deprecated the essential weakness of the proposed Articles of Confederation, and urged, on all occasions, the absolute necessity of a strong general government. At length the Continental Congress, in May, 1782, considering the desperate condition of the finances of the country, appointed delegates to explain the common danger to the authorities of all the States. Governor Clinton called an extra session of the State of New York to receive the delegation which had been sent North. They met at Poughkeepsie in July. Hamilton repaired thither and held consultations with the members of the Legislature, especially with his father-in-law. On motion of Schuyler the Legislature resolved itself into a Committee of the Whole on the State of the Nation. They adopted a series of resolutions, drafted, it is believed, by Hamilton, declaring the necessity for a stronger national government, that should have power to provide itself with a sufficient revenue for the public use. The Legislature incited Congress, for the common welfare, "to recommend and each State to adopt the measure of assembling a general convention of the States specially authorized to revise and amend the Confederation, reserving the right of the respective Legislatures to ratify their determinations."

Constitution everywhere prevailed. Radical differences in sentiment had been conspicuous in the convention that framed it. The adherents, respectively, of the idea of a strong central government and of State supremacy were apparently irreconcilably antagonistic.

Two of the New York delegates—Yates and Lansing—were decidedly favorable to the doctrine of State supremacy, while Hamilton* as strongly advocated the plan of a powerful Federal Government wielding supreme authority. Hamilton's opinions prevailed in the convention. Yates and Lansing were so dissatisfied with the evident sentiment of the convention that they withdrew, leaving Hamilton the sole representative of New York in the convention.

This was the birth-time of the stalwart twins—the first two opposing political parties in the United States—the *Federalists* and the *Anti-Federalists*. These parties were of a more pronounced and violent type in New York than elsewhere. Hamilton was the acknowledged leader of the Federalists, and Governor George Clinton of the Anti-Federalists.

ALEXANDER HAMILTON. AFTER CARRACI.

On January 17th, 1788, Egbert Benson † offered in the Legislature of

---

* Alexander Hamilton was born at Nevis, West Indies, January 11th, 1757. He was of Scotch descent. Educated at King's (now Columbia) College, New York, he engaged in the political controversy preceding the Revolution ; became a captain of artillery in March, 1776 ; a member of Washington's military family in the spring of 1777, and served as his secretary and trusted confidant until 1781. He was of essential service to Washington. Hamilton married a daughter of General Philip Schuyler late in 1780. He was colonel of a regiment of New York troops at the siege of Yorktown, soon after which he left the army, studied law, and soon became eminent in his profession. He served as a member of Congress and of the New York Legislature ; was a member of the convention that framed the National Constitution, and was one of its chief advocates through the press. Washington appointed him Secretary of the Treasury in 1789, which post he resigned in 1795. When in 1798 war with France seemed probable, he was made second to Washington in command of the armies of the United States. On July 12th, 1804, Hamilton died of wounds received in a duel with Aaron Burr.

† Egbert Benson was one of the most active and useful men in New York at this time.

New York a resolution providing for a State convention of representatives chosen by the people to consider the new National Constitution. This resolution elicited much and warm debate, but was finally adopted by both branches of the Legislature.

From the moment when the new Constitution was published in New York spirited and sometimes violent contests between the advocates and opposers of the instrument occurred at public gatherings and in the public prints. Acrimonious publications appeared in newspapers and in pamphlets during the canvass and the sittings of the convention. On the one hand it was urged by the opponents of the proposed Constitution that by its adoption a fatal blow would be struck at the so-called " independent sovereignty" of the States, by the gradual absorption of the principal functions of government by the central power ; that the wealth and immense resources of New York especially, instead of being devoted to the development of its vast territory and possibilities, would be largely given to the accumulation of the wealth and power of the National Government, and that its political influence would be greatly diminished. It was argued that the inevitable tendency of such a state of things would be the establishment of a virtually monarchical government.

To these arguments the advocates of the Constitution replied, pointing to the provisions of the instrument itself, that the distribution of the powers of the proposed new government was so carefully arranged that, so far from enabling it to trench upon the jurisdiction of the States, it was itself liable to constant and serious encroachments on their part, and that the existing Confederacy—a mere league of independent States, held together only by the common interests of all its members and subject to disintegration at the pleasure of any—was wholly inadequate to the purpose of a national government. It was at this period that the able essays in favor of the Constitution, written by Hamilton, Jay, and Madison, known collectively as *The Federalist*, were published and scattered widely over the Union with powerful effect.

The sole question which seemed to govern the electors of New York in their choice of delegates to their convention seems to have been whether the candidates were for or against the adoption of the Constitution.

He was born in New York City in 1746 ; died at Jamaica, L. I., in 1833. He was a most efficient member of the Revolutionary Committee of Safety, and was a distinguished jurist, holding a high rank in jurisprudence. He was the first attorney-general of the State of New York, and -member of the first State Legislature ; a delegate to the old Congress in 1784–88 ; a member of Congress, 1789–83 and 1813–15 ; and judge of the Supreme Court of New York 1794–1801. He received the degree of LL.D. from Harvard and Dartmouth colleges, and was the first president of the New York Historical Society. He wrote a " Vindication of Major André."

The members of the convention chosen in the several counties assembled at the court-house in Poughkeepsie on June 17th, 1788, and was organized by the choice of Governor Clinton for its president, John McKesson and Abraham B. Bancker, secretaries, and Nicholas Power, printer to the convention. The convention was composed of sixty-one delegates,* a clear majority of whom were opposed to the new Constitution.

The discussion of the several articles of the Constitution began on June 19th and continued three weeks, during which time several amendments were proposed and adopted.

SIGNATURE OF NICHOLAS POWER.

On July 11th John Jay moved that " the Constitution be ratified, and that whatever amendments might be deemed expedient should be *recommended*."

This motion called out the most vigorous opposition from the Anti-Federalists, and the majority of the convention urged the calling of a new national convention, for the purpose of making additional amendments specified by them. They proposed to amend Jay's motion so that it should read, " that the Constitution be ratified *on the condition* that certain specified amendments should be made." An able and prolonged discus-

---

* The following are the names of the delegates chosen by the people of the several counties :

City and County of New York.—John Jay, Richard Morris, John Sloss Hobart, Alexander Hamilton, Robert R. Livingston, Isaac Roosevelt, James Duane, Richard Harrison, Nicholas Low.

City and County of Albany.—Robert Yates, John Lansing, Jr., Henry Oothout, Peter Vroman, Israel Thompson, Anthony Ten Eyck, Dirck Swart.

County of Suffolk.—Henry Scudder, Jonathan N. Havens, John Smith, Thomas Treadwell, David Hedges.

County of Ulster.—George Clinton, John Cantine, Cornelius C. Schoonmaker, Ebenezer Clark, James Clinton, Dirck Wynkoop.

County of Queens.—Samuel Jones, John Schenck, Nathaniel Lawrence, Stephen Carman.

County of Kings.—Peter Lefferts, Peter Vandervoort.

County of Richmond.—Abraham Bancker, Gosen Ryerss.

County of Westchester.—Lewis Morris, Philip Livingston, Richard Hatfield, Philip van Cortlandt, Thaddeus Crane, Lott W. Sarles.

County of Orange.—John Haring, Jesse Woodhull, Henry Wisner, John Wood.

County of Duchess.—Zephaniah Platt, Melancthon Smith, Jacobus Swartwout, Jonathan Akin, Ezra Thompson, Gilbert Livingston, John De Witt.

County of Montgomery.—William Harper, Christopher P. Yates, John Frey, John Winn, Volkert Veeder, Henry Staring.

Counties of Washington and Clinton.—Ichabod Parker, John Williams, Albert Baker.

I copied the above names from the original printed Journal of the Convention, in my possession. It was printed by Nicholas Power, in quarto form.

340 THE EMPIRE STATE.

Wednesday 10 oClock A.M. July 16th 1776

The Convention met pursuant to Adjournment—

Mr Hobart made a Motion for the Convention to adopt the following Resolution viz.

"Whereas since the time of electing the Delegates &c..☞

The said resolution being read Debates arose thereon

And after some time spent thereon

Ordered that the further Consideration thereof be postponed until tomorrow

FAC SIMILE OF A PART OF THE MS. JOURNAL OF THE CONVENTION.

sion ensued, but before any vote was taken news reached Poughkeepsie that the convention of New Hampshire had ratified the Constitution.

This settled the question. The people of the requisite number of States had now spoken in the affirmative. The question for the people of New York now to decide was not whether they preferred the new Constitution to the Articles of Confederation, but whether they would secede from the Union. The Anti-Federalists decided wisely and patriotically. The Federalists proposed a compromise between Jay's proposition and that of their opponents. The latter, not without hesitation and reluctance, yielded their assent to the following resolution :

"*Resolved*, That the Constitution be ratified, *in full confidence* that the amendments proposed by this convention will be adopted."

A most remarkable speech of three hours by Alexander Hamilton and a patriotic one by Gilbert Livingston, of Duchess, effected the happy result. There were fifty-seven members present and voted, thirty of them for the ratification of the Constitution and twenty-seven against it —a majority of three. This decision was taken on July 28th, and on that day the convention finally adjourned. On September 13th Governor Clinton officially proclaimed the National Constitution as the fundamental law of the Republic.

At a special session of the Legislature of New York, begun in the city of New York on December 8th (1788), they chose delegates to represent the State in the concluding session of the Continental Congress. They also appointed presidential electors and provided for the election, by the people, of six members of Congress. Under this provision Egbert Benson, William Floyd, John Hathorn, Jeremiah van Rensselaer, and Peter Sylvester were elected the first representatives of New York to seats in the National Congress under the new Constitution. The two Houses of the Legislature could not agree upon a method of choosing United States Senators, and none were appointed at that session. The State remained unrepresented in the National Senate during the first session of the first Congress. Finally the Legislature, convened in special session, by joint resolution passed on July 19th, appointed General Philip Schuyler and Rufus King* Senators. The latter gentleman had only recently become a citizen of the State of New York.

---

* Rufus King was born at Scarborough, Me., in March, 1755, and died at Jamaica, L. I., in April, 1827. He was a graduate of Harvard ; became a lawyer ; married the daughter of John Alsop, a rich merchant of New York, and ever afterward made that city his home. Mr. King, like Schuyler, was a leading Federalist. From 1798 to 1804 he was United States minister at the court of Great Britain. He was again in the Senate, for the third time, in 1818. Always an anti-slavery man, he was one of the leaders of the opposition to the admission of Missouri as a slave-labor State. He again went to England as American minister in 1825, but soon returned in feeble health.

CHAPTER XXIV.

So soon as the questions concerning territory, boundaries, ownership, and government, which had occupied the minds of the people of New York, were settled and adjusted, the virgin soil and topography of the State attracted the attention of enterprising people, and settlements began to carry light and civilization into the dark wilderness.

New political divisions were rapidly organized. In 1770 Albany County embraced all of New York northward of Ulster County and west of the Hudson River, also all north of Duchess County and eastward of that river. In 1772 Charlotte and Tryon counties were taken from Albany. The name of the former was changed in 1784 to Washington, and that of the latter to Montgomery. A part of Charlotte was included in the counties of Cumberland and Gloucester in forming the State of Vermont.

Tryon County included all the province west of a longitudinal line running nearly through the middle of Schoharie County. In 1789 Ontario County was taken from Montgomery County, and included all the land of which pre-emptive right had been ceded to the State of Massachusetts.

No State in the Union presented so wide a range for enterprise and exertion as New York after the war, especially in the industries of agriculture and commerce. The borders of its great river were then settled with wealthy, industrious, and thriving people. Campaigns against the Indians, especially that of Sullivan in 1779, had revealed to soldiers of the latter, who were largely New Englanders, the richness of the soil of the interior, and they gave glowing accounts to their friends of the beauty and fertility of the land they had traversed. The purchase of great tracts of land for speculative purposes, already mentioned, followed, and set in motion emigration from the east into that region.

The first emigrant from New England was Hugh White, of Middletown, Conn., with his own family and those of four of his neighbors. They seated themselves, at the beginning of 1784, about four miles west of (present) Utica. This settlement was the first rose that blossomed in the wilderness of Central and Western New York. The now beautiful and thriving borough of Whitestown is of itself a grand monument to the memory of its founder, who died there, in 1812, at the age of eighty years. Before 1790 scores of families flocked into that region, largely from New England, and thenceforth emigrant wagons with families, implements of labor on farms and for domestic purposes were continually carrying forward population farther and farther into the wilderness of Western New York.

In 1788 Mr. Phelps, one of the purchasers of the six million acres tract, penetrated to the country of the Genesee. He and some friends went up the Mohawk in boats from Schenectady as far as possible, and made their way to the outlet of Canandaigua Lake, where they planted the seed of a flourishing settlement by constructing some log-huts and making it the business capital of the domain. The Rev. Samuel Kirkland, an earnest missionary laborer among the Oneidas, was their interpreter. Gorham procured cessions of lands from the Senecas.

In 1791 a party of emigrants constructed a wagon-road from Whitestown to Canandaigua, the first ever opened from the Mohawk River to the Genesee country. These pioneers suffered great hardships in the performance of their task, for the route lay over lofty hills and deep ravines, broad marshes and swift-running streams; yet they persevered, and made a highway for swarms of emigrants from New England, who soon made it a beaten path. It was soon afterward continued to the foot of Lake Erie, at the site of Buffalo. In this work the Government did nothing; private individuals did everything. This highway was the first work of internal improvement in the State of New York. Others of greater importance will be noticed presently.

When the National Constitution was adopted by the requisite number of States the patriotic opponents of the instrument generally acquiesced in the decision. Judge Yates, who in the National and State conventions had strongly opposed it, now, in his first charge to the Grand Jury at Albany after the ratification, said:

"Before the Constitution was ratified I had been opposed to it; it is now mine and every other man's duty to support it."

But it was not long before party strife became more violent than ever throughout the country, especially in the State of New York, where party lines were sharply drawn between the *Federalists* and *Anti-Federalists*. Washington identified himself with the former. The Constitution was not all that he could have wished, yet he regarded its adoption as a real blessing to the country. In a letter to General Schuyler on the subject he wrote:

"That invisible Hand which has so often interposed to save our country from impending destruction seems in no instance to have been more remarkably exerted than in that of disposing the people of this continent to adopt, in a peaceable manner, a constitution which, if well administered, bids fair to make America a happy nation."

The choice of the first President of the United States under the National Constitution was done very quietly, for there was no partisanship displayed. The eyes and the hearts of the whole people were instinctively turned toward Washington, the "Saviour of his Country," as the fittest man to guide the vessel of State, with its precious freight, on

THE CITY HALL IN WALL STREET, 1789.

its first necessarily perilous voyage. He received every vote in the Electoral College. John Adams was chosen Vice-President.

The Continental Congress had decreed that the city of New York should be the residence of the National Government. The City Hall, in Wall Street, fronting the head of Broad Street, was fitted up for the use of the National Legislature. March 4th (1790) was the day designated for the organization of the new government. That auspicious day was ushered in by the ringing of bells and the booming of cannons; but the members of Congress were tardy in their journeys to the capital, owing to the wretched state of the roads. On the appointed day only a few of them were present. It was April 6th before a quorum was assembled, when the two Houses proceeded to count the votes for President and Vice-President and declare the result.

The Vice-President reached New York on April 21st. The President arrived two days later. His journey from Mount Vernon had been an almost continuous ovation. A committee of Congress met him at Elizabethtown, N. J., and from its port he was conveyed in a barge to the foot of Wall Street, at the East River, where he was met by the governor, the municipal authorities, and a vast concourse of citizens, who formed a procession and conducted him to the mansion in Cherry Street, near Franklin Square, prepared for his residence. That was then the most fashionable part of the city. That evening the whole town was illuminated.

At noon on April 30th, after religious services had been held in all the churches in the city, Washington left the presidential mansion, escorted by a procession formed of members of Congress

ROBERT R. LIVINGSTON.

and heads of departments in carriages, led by the City Cavalry, and proceeded to the City Hall, where, in its street gallery, in the presence of a vast multitude of people, the inaugural ceremonies were performed. The oath of office was administered by Robert R. Livingston,* the first Chancellor of the State of New York. Returning to the Senate Chamber, the President read his inaugural address, after which the whole assembly went on foot to St. Paul's Chapel, on Broadway, where prayers

---

* Robert R. Livingston was born in New York City November 27th, 1747; died at the Livingston Manor-House February 26th, 1813. He was graduated at King's (now Columbia) College, became a successful lawyer, and was recorder of the city of New York in 1773. He was elected a member of the Continental Congress in 1775; was one of the committee to draft the Declaration of Independence, but necessary absence from Philadelphia prevented his voting for and signing it. He was appointed the first chancellor of the State of New York, which position he held until 1801. He was secretary for foreign affairs of the General Government from 1781 to 1783; a member of the committee that framed the National Constitution; minister of the United States to France in 1801–1804, and negotiated for the purchase of Louisiana, and was the efficient coadjutor of Robert Fulton in perfecting navigation on the Hudson River by steam.

were read by the chaplain of the Senate. Then the President was escorted to his residence. The ceremonies of the day were concluded by a display of fireworks in the evening.

General Schuyler, John Jay, and Colonel Alexander Hamilton were the chief leaders of the Federal Party in New York, and had great influence with President Washington. Schuyler and Hamilton were uncompromising partisans, as all men of strong moral convictions are apt to be, and they induced the President to bestow Government patronage upon men who were, either personally or politically, opposed to Governor Clinton. Jay was appointed Chief Justice of the United States; James Duane, Judge of the District of New York; Richard Harrison, United States Attorney; and William S. Smith, Marshal. Hamilton, who was the soul of the Federal Party, was called to the Cabinet as Secretary of the Treasury.

The spirit of the Constitution of New York was less democratic than that of any other State. It placed an enormous amount of power and patronage in the hands of the governor. With this advantage Clinton and his friends were enabled to carry on a political warfare with great vigor and success for a very long time; but the Constitution afforded a check upon an undue exercise of that power when bearing upon the control of offices by the provision of a Council of Appointment. That Council, as we have observed, was created by the choice of the Assembly, of one Senator each year out of each Senatorial district, and these, with the governor, formed the Council. The governor had a right to give a casting vote, but had no vote for any other purpose. He was *ex-officio* president of the Council, and was required, "by the advice and consent of the Council, to appoint all officers" whose appointment was not otherwise provided for.

After the inauguration of Washington political parties in New York became mixed. The Federalists determined to form a coalition for the purpose of breaking the Anti-Federalist ascendency. They induced the Anti-Federalist Judge Yates to accept from them the nomination for governor in opposition to Clinton. The coalition was unsuccessful, and Clinton was re-elected by a strong majority. The election was warmly contested. The whole number of votes cast in the State was 12,343. The census of 1790 certified the number of the population then in the State to be 340,120, an increase of more than 85,000 in five years. This increase had been caused largely by emigration into the northern and western parts of the State. The city of New York then contained a population of 33,131.

The subject of improving the internal navigation of the State now engaged the earnest attention of thoughtful men. General Schuyler saw, when in England in 1761, the canal constructed by the Duke of Bridgewater. He was deeply impressed with what he saw and heard, and as opportunities offered he urged the importance of improving the navigation of the Mohawk River by short canals around rifts and shallows. He suggested that by a short canal between the Mohawk and Wood Creek, which flows into Oneida Lake, and the improvement of the navigation of that stream and the outlet of Oneida Lake into the Oswego River, continuous navigation between the Hudson and Lake Ontario might be effected. At Schuyler's suggestion, Governor Sir Henry Moore presented the subject to the Colonial Legislature in 1768.

So early as 1772 Christopher Colles * lectured in New York and Albany on Inland Lock Navigation, and warmly advocated Schuyler's project. Schuyler also urged the construction of a canal between the Hudson and Lake Champlain so early as 1776. In 1784 Colles presented a memorial to the Legislature proposing the improvement of the navigation of the Mohawk, and that year he penetrated the country to Wood Creek, published an account of his observations in a pamphlet, and in the winter of 1786 the Legislature made a report favorable to his project. Nothing more seems to have been done.

At about that time Washington made a tour in the interior of the State of New York. He was then much interested in the subject of internal navigation in his own State. He passed over Lake George and down Lake Champlain as far as Crown Point. Returning to Schenectady, he went up the Mohawk to Fort Schuyler (now Rome), and visited Otsego Lake and its vicinity. He observed the feasibility and commended the importance of inland navigation in the State of New York.

Soon after this Elkanah Watson appears upon the scene as a most earnest advocate of a continuous water communication between the

---

* Christopher Colles was born in Ireland about the year 1737, and was educated by Richard Pococke, the Oriental traveller. After the death of his patron, in 1765, he came to America, and, as we have observed, became an earnest advocate of canal navigation. He was a skilful engineer. He proposed plans for supplying the city of New York with pure water so early as 1774. In 1797 he proposed to bring the waters of the Bronx River, in Westchester County, into the city. He constructed a series of sectional road maps for the use of travellers. His active mind kept his hands busy in a variety of employments. At one time he was the actuary of the Academy of Fine Arts. He was also a notable inventor, and enjoyed the friendship and esteem of De Witt Clinton, Dr. Samuel L. Mitchell, Dr. Hosack, Jarvis, the painter, and other distinguished men of New York. The effigy of Colles was borne in the grand procession in New York which celebrated the completion of the Erie Canal. He had then been in his grave about four years, having died in the autumn of 1821. His remains lie unhonored in the burying-ground of the Episcopal Church in Hudson Street.

Hudson River and Lake Ontario. In this project he spent much time for years, and was a most efficient supporter of General Schuyler's canal projects. He made journeys westward from Albany to gather up facts, and he penetrated the country to Seneca Lake.*

The final result of the endeavors of these public-spirited men was the passage of an act by the Legislature of New York, in January, 1792, for chartering two inland lock navigation companies. One was called the Western Inland Lock Navigation Company, and the other the Northern Inland Lock Navigation Company. These companies were formed, and General Schuyler was unanimously chosen president of each company. Thomas Eddy, an enterprising Quaker, was appointed treasurer of the Western Company.

Accompanied by Goldsbrow Banyer and Elkanah Watson and surveyors and engineers, Schuyler made a thorough exploration of the whole route for the western enterprise, from Schenectady to the waters of Lakes Seneca and Ontario, in August and September, 1792. They also explored the route for the northern canal, from the head of tide-water of the Hudson, just above Albany, to the head of Lake Champlain, at (present) Whitehall. These explorations were satisfactory to both companies, and in the spring of 1793 the Western Company began work at the Little Falls, in Herkimer County, with artificers and about three hundred laborers.

ELKANAH WATSON.

---

* Elkanah Watson was born at Plymouth, Mass., in January, 1758, and died at Port Kent, Essex County, N. Y., in December, 1842. He was a clerk in the employ of John Brown, of Providence, R. I., who sent him to Boston with a large amount of powder for the patriot army besieging it in 1775. Before he was nineteen years of age Brown sent him to Charleston and other Southern ports with $50,000, to buy cargoes for the European markets. At the age of twenty-one Congress sent despatches by him to Dr. Franklin, in Paris. He remained in France until 1784, engaged in a commission business at Nantes in connection with Mr. Brown. He went to Albany in 1789, and became greatly interested in General Schuyler's canal projects. He afterward travelled in Europe, and in 1807 settled at Pittsfield, Mass., as a farmer, and made many improvements in agriculture. After a visit to the lake region in the North-west he settled at Port Kent, on the west side of Lake Champlain, where he resided until his death. His autobiography was completed and published by his son, Winslow C. Watson, in 1856.

The Northern Company began work at Stillwater the same year. Delays followed, chiefly on account of a want of funds, and yet so vigorously did the president and his associates, especially Mr. Watson, push on the work when means were at command, that boats of sixteen tons burden passed over the whole route, from Schenectady to Oneida Lake, in 1796, without interruption. There were only about six miles of canalling altogether.

Unfortunately, the locks in the canals had been constructed of wood, and were too perishable. William Weston, a distinguished canal engineer, came to this country from England early in 1795. He was employed to examine the whole work of the companies with General Schuyler, and the result was an order for him to reconstruct the locks of stone. This operation exhausted the funds of the company.

In 1793 Isambert Brunel, a distinguished French engineer, arrived with a letter of introduction to General Schuyler. He was employed in 1794 in a survey of the Northern or Champlain Canal. That was almost fifty years before he completed the famous tunnel under the Thames, at London, and received the honors of knighthood from the then young Queen of England.

In 1796 Mr. Weston, under the direction of the Western Company, made an exploration of a route for a canal between the Mohawk and Seneca rivers. A canal was speedily constructed, and became the living germ of the grand Erie Canal which was afterward built by the State. It led Gouverneur Morris, in 1801, to conceive the greatest of canal projects—namely, the connection of Lake Erie with the Hudson by an artificial river, a work that was completed a little more than twenty years afterward. This great work will receive special notice presently.

The interest of General Schuyler in canal navigation never flagged during his life. So late as the summer of 1802, when he was almost sixty-nine years of age, he endured the hardships incident to an exploration of the whole line of the Western Canal route, and gave his personal attention to the construction of new locks, repairing old ones, and removing obstructions. His manuscript journal kept during that exploration is before me, and is filled with vivid pictures of the labors and privations which he then endured. To General Schuyler is undoubtedly due the honor of the paternity of the canal system of New York, which contributed so much to its prosperity.

Immediately after the war for independence the city of New York—the commercial metropolis of the State—began the task of recuperation. Fire had consumed a vast number of its dwellings; its churches had been desecrated and laid waste; its commerce had been destroyed by the war, and its people had been estranged from each other by differences in political opinions. New York was compelled to begin life anew, as it were. The tribute which it paid to the cause of human freedom was large, but had been most freely and cheerfully given.

The Whig refugees returned to the city, many of them to find their dwellings in ruins. The old charter was resumed, and municipal government was soon re-established. In February, 1784, James Duane,* an ardent Whig, was chosen mayor. He had found his dwelling on his farm, near (present) Gramercy Park, in ashes and his fortune wrecked. Although the vitality of the city had been paralyzed, yet men—" high-minded men" who " constitute a State," were left, and their influence was soon manifested in the visible aspects of public spirit and the revival of commerce. But not much was done in the way of public improvements before the close of the century.

One hundred years ago there was only here and there a house above Murray Street on the west side of the city of New York, and above Chatham Square on the east side. Not a bank or insurance company existed in the city. Wall Street was the seat of wealth, elegance, and fashion. Its dwellings were chiefly of wood and roofed with shingles, and the sides of many of them were of the same materials. Between Broadway and the Hudson River above Reade Street might be seen scores of cows belonging to the citizens grazing in the fields. In 1790 the first sidewalks in the city were laid on each side of Broadway,

JAMES DUANE.

---

* James Duane was born in New York City in February, 1733. He inherited a large estate in the lower Mohawk region, and began a settlement there in 1765. Duanesburg was the product. He married a daughter of Colonel Robert Livingston. A member of the first Continental Congress, he was an active patriot all through the war that ensued. He was residing in New York City at the breaking out of the war; left it when the British took possession of it, but returned immediately after the British evacuated it. He was made the first mayor under the new order of things. He was a member of the State Council of Appointment and of the Senate, also of the convention that ratified the National Constitution. He was United States District Judge from 1789 to 1794. Judge Duane died at Duanesburg in February, 1797.

between Vesey and Murray streets. They were of stone and brick, and so narrow that only two persons might walk abreast.

The city was the seat of the National Government from 1785 until 1790, when it was transferred to Philadelphia. During the session of the State Convention at Poughkeepsie in the summer of 1788 the city was much excited by the discussions of opposing factions. Congress was then in session at New York. On July 8th, eighteen days before the Constitution was ratified, its ardent friends in New York, feeling confident of success, fitted up a little frigate on wheels, and called it

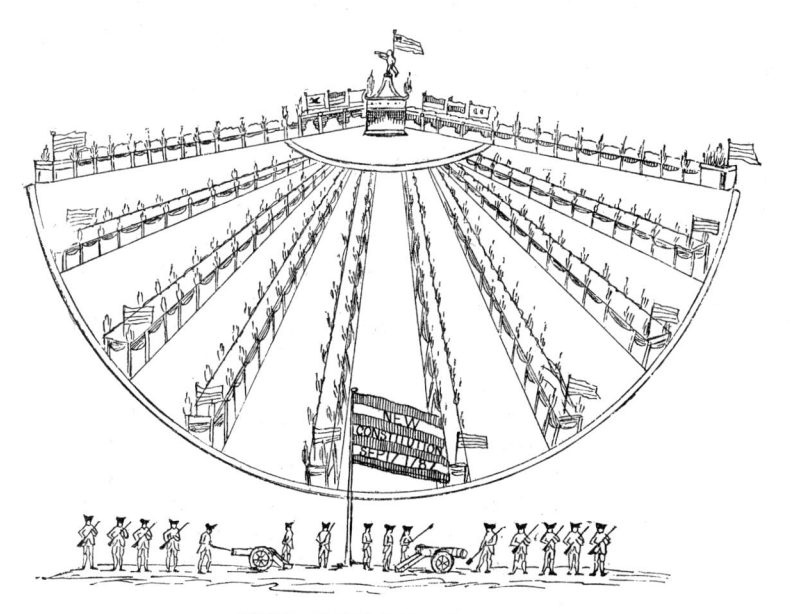

TABLES AT THE FEDERAL DINNER.

the Federal Ship *Hamilton*. It was commanded by Commodore Nicholson and manned by thirty seamen and mariners. Accompanied by a great procession, it was drawn by ten horses from the Bowling Green to Bayard's Farm, near Grand Street and the Bowery, where tables were spread and dinner was provided for four or five thousand people. At a circular table, which was a little elevated, were seated members of Congress, heads of departments, foreign representatives, and other distinguished persons. From this table thirteen other tables diverged, at which sat the multitude.

An Anti-Federal newspaper (Greenleaf's *Patriotic Register*) lampooned the procession and its promoters. The Federalists were greatly irritated, and when the Constitution was ratified a mob broke into the office of the offending newspaper and destroyed the press and types. They then attacked the house of General Lamb, the Collector of the Port,* in Wall Street. He had been forewarned, and was forearmed. He had barricaded the lower story of his house, and with two or three friends with muskets, in the second story, and his daughter, a young lady from Connecticut, and a colored servant in the attic well supplied with tiles and glass bottles to shower on the heads of the rioters, they so well defended the castle that the assailants were compelled to raise the siege and retire discomfited.

The city of New York was several times scourged by yellow-fever. It appeared there in 1742, but its most frightful ravages occurred during the closing decade of the last century. It broke out in 1791, but it was so late in the season that frosts soon checked it. In 1795 it slew 772 persons. Its most fearful visit was in 1798, when it raged from July until November, and killed 2100 persons in the city and 300 residents who had fled from it. In 1799 and 1800 this plague prevailed, but in a mild form; but in 1803 the disease slew about 600 persons. When it again broke out in 1805 with much violence, so great was the panic that one third of the population, then numbering 75,000, fled to the country.

The city was almost entirely exempted from this dreadful scourge from 1803 until 1819, when yellow-fever raged there to a considerable extent. It again appeared in 1822 and 1823, but in a comparatively mild form. Since the latter year only sporadic cases have been known. It has never appeared in the form of an epidemic. This disease never originates or scarcely ever exists north of the latitude of the city of New York, unless the seeds of the malady shall be carried by fugitives from the plague in lower latitudes.

---

* A part of Lamb's residence was used for the Custom House, the business of the port of New York not then being extensive enough to need the space or warrant the expense of a separate building.

CHAPTER XXV.

George Clinton, the Republican governor, was re-elected in the spring of 1792, with Pierre van Cortland as lieutenant-governor. The opposing candidates were John Jay and Stephen van Rensselaer, the latter a son-in-law of General Schuyler and the last of the patroons. In the autumn of the same year presidential electors were chosen, and Washington was re-elected by the unanimous vote of the Electoral College.

The dividing line between the two great political parties—Federalists and Republicans—was now more distinctly drawn than ever, owing to the influence of the French Revolution. When that great movement began, and until it had progressed some time, there was only one feeling among Americans in regard to it, and that was earnest sympathy for their old ally. But when the movement fell under the control of violent demagogues, and conservative men like Lafayette were driven from their country; when the civilized world was shocked by the terrible excesses of the Jacobins, many of the leaders of opinion in America paused. Apprehending that the intrigues of the French and the generous sympathy of the Americans might involve the young Republic in a European war, they not only withdrew their sympathies, but soon went so far as to denounce the original revolution. These were chiefly Federalists.

The Republicans, on the other hand, advocated the French Revolution with great warmth, hailing its authors and promoters as friends and brothers. They wrongly charged the Federalists with hostility to the principles of the French Revolution, with friendship for their late enemy, Great Britain, and even with anti-republican and monarchical tendencies. This antagonism of opinion grew more and more intense when, in the spring of 1793, E. C. Genet—"Citizen" Genet, as he was styled—arrived in this country as the representative of the French Republic.

Mr. Jefferson, a member of Washington's Cabinet as Secretary of State, was in France when the revolution there broke out, and he had come home filled with admiration and love for the cause, which had not then been stained by the outrages of the Jacobins. He expected to find equal enthusiasm among his countrymen; but when he reached New York he was chilled by the frigidity which he encountered. He was cordially received by the wealthier and more refined classes of society at New York, but these were composed largely of members of the old Tory families, whose opinions, frankly spoken, often shocked him. He became painfully sensitive, and he soon regarded the conservatism of Washington, Adams, Hamilton, and other conspicuous Federalists as evidence of their unfaithfulness to the cause for which they had so zealously contended. Toward Hamilton he indulged positive dislike, and considered him a dangerous citizen.

By common consent Mr. Jefferson became the leader of the rapidly growing Republican Party, which hailed with enthusiasm the tidings of the death of the French King, the proclamation of the Republic with all its horrors, the virtual declaration of war by France against all monarchical Europe, and its actual conquest of a part of the Netherlands, a friend of the United States. Perceiving the danger with which such blind enthusiasm menaced the Republic, Washington issued a proclamation of neutrality in the spring of 1793. It was bitterly denounced by the French Party, as the Republicans were now called.

EDMUND C. GENET.

It was in the midst of this excitement in the public mind that Citizen Genet arrived * at Charleston, S. C., and in defiance of the proclamation, proceeded to fit out privateers (which were manned chiefly by American citizens) to prey upon British commerce in our waters. One

---

* Edmund Charles Genet was born at Versailles, France, in January, 1763, and died at Greenbush, opposite Albany, N. Y., in July, 1834. He was a precocious lad, who early developed a taste and talent for literature, like his notable sister, Madame Campan. He was attached to foreign embassies in his youth, and had been trained in the arts of diplomacy before he came to America. As will be observed in the text, his conduct as representative of the French revolutionists became very obnoxious to our Government. Such changes took place in France that Genet dared not return. He remained in New York, and married the daughter of Governor George Clinton, and became one of the best citizens of the commonwealth. He was twice married, his second wife being the daughter of Mr. Osgood, the first Postmaster-General under the National Constitution. Fond of agriculture, he took great interest in its pursuit. His last illness was occasioned by attendance at a meeting of an agricultural society of which he was president.

of these—*L'Ambuscade*—the frigate that brought the minister to our shores, went prowling up the coast, seizing English vessels, and proceeded to Philadelphia, bearing at her masthead and elsewhere liberty-caps. She was greeted by a multitude of citizens with " peals of exultation," Jefferson wrote to Madison. Genet soon followed. He had received everywhere on his land journey demonstrations of delight. He was met at the Schuylkill by a crowd of citizens and escorted into Philadelphia, where he was entertained at a public banquet by his Republican friends before he had presented his credentials to the President of the United States ! He had changed the name of *L'Ambuscade* to *Little Democrat*, in French, and from that time the Republicans were called " Democrats" in derision.*

Genet bore secret instructions from his Government to foment discord between Great Britain and the United States, and to set the American Government at defiance, if necessary, to accomplish his purpose ; and yet when he presented his credentials to the President he uttered the most vehement protestations of the peaceful and friendly intentions of the French Republic. " Nothing," wrote Jefferson, " could be more affectionate, more magnanimous than the purport of Genet's mission. . . . He offers everything and asks nothing." But when Genet left the presence of Washington the minister's pride was touched and his hopeful ardor was chilled. He had found himself in an atmosphere of the most profound dignity in that presence, and he was made to realize

---

* Madness appears to have seized some of the staid citizens of Philadelphia at that moment. The sympathizers with the French revolutionists at that banquet (May 23d, 1793) presented some strange scenes. Governor Mifflin was among the guests. The chief music was the air of the " Marseillaise." A Liberty Tree crowned the table. The flags of the two nations were fraternally enfolded. A red cap of liberty was first placed on the head of Genet and then upon the head of each guest, who, while it rested there, uttered some patriotic sentiment. A roasted pig on the table received the name of the murdered King of the French. The head of the pig was severed from the body and carried round to each guest, who, after placing the liberty-cap on his head, pronounced the word " tyrant," and proceeded to mangle with his knife the head of the luckless porker ! Earlier than this, at a public dinner in Philadelphia to celebrate the alliance with France (February 6th, 1778), a pike at the head of the table bore upon its point a *bonnet rouge* entwined with the flags of the two nations.

There was a strange political demonstration at Boston a few days earlier. An ox was roasted whole, decorated with ribbons, and borne in a procession through the streets on a car drawn by sixteen horses, followed by carts carrying sixteen hundred loaves of bread and two hogsheads of punch, which were distributed among the people. Three hundred citizens, with Samuel Adams at their head, sat down to a banquet. The children of all the schools were paraded in the streets, to whom cakes were presented bearing the stamped words, *Liberty and Equality*.

The citizens of New York did not indulge in such extravagances at that time.

his own littleness while standing before that noble representative of the best men and soundest principles of the American Republic. He withdrew from the audience abashed and subdued. He had heard sentiments of sincere regard for the French nation that touched the sensibilities of his heart, and he had felt in the genuine courtesy and severe simplicity and frankness of the President's manner, wholly free from effervescent enthusiasm, a withering rebuke, not only of the adulation in public places, but also of his own pretentious aspirations and ungenerous duplicity. He had already been rebuked by the action of more than three hundred merchants and other substantial men in Philadelphia, who on the day of his arrival had signed and presented to President Washington an address expressing their unswerving loyalty to the letter and spirit of his proclamation of neutrality.

The Republicans were irrepressible. In their infatuation they formed Democratic societies in various cities, in imitation of the Jacobin clubs of Paris. Their operations were in secret, and their proceedings were often extremely disloyal. In servile imitation of their prototypes, they adopted the peculiar phrases of the populace of Paris, and a powerful faction was soon visible in the United States more French than American in their habits of thought and political principles.

The Government went straight forward in the performance of its duty, satisfied that it would be sustained by the great mass of the American people. British vessels captured by privateers were restored to their owners; American citizens acting as privateers were prosecuted; collectors at ports of the United States were ordered to seize all privateers that entered them; Chief Justice Jay declared it to be the duty of all Grand Juries to present for trial persons engaged in such violation of the laws of nations; and the privateers were ordered to leave American waters forthwith.

Genet and his American partisans were greatly irritated. Encouraged by the disloyal faction, Genet vehemently protested against the acts of the Government, and even threatened to "appeal from the President to the people"—in other words, to incite an insurrection. He actually began to fit out a privateer at Philadelphia, when Governor Mifflin, though a Republican, threatened to seize the vessel if he persisted. Jefferson soon found his French friend exceedingly troublesome. He begged him to pause in his outrageous career. The minister refused to listen, and raved like a madman. Jefferson, disgusted with his conduct, joined Washington in requesting the French Government to recall their obnoxious representative. Genet went to New York, where he was received with more enthusiasm, if possible, than at Philadelphia.

He was welcomed by ringing of bells and salvos of cannon fired in honor of the success of the Republicans of France. A great meeting had been held in the Fields (now City Hall Park), at which a committee of forty had been appointed to meet him at Paulus Hook (Jersey City) and escort him into the town. The Federalists, supported by the Chamber of Commerce, held counter meetings, denounced Genet's conduct, and warmly endorsed the Proclamation of Neutrality.

The Republican newspapers in New York had zealously espoused the French cause, and the minister was *fêted* and caressed to his heart's content. The liberty-cap was raised upon the flag-staff at the Tontine Coffee-House; tri-colored cockades were worn by many citizens; the Marseillaise Hymn was chanted and the *carmagnole* * was performed in the streets. For a time New York seemed transformed into a French city.†

Genet was recalled. A political change had taken place in France. He was of the Girondist or more moderate faction, who ruled when he came here. They had fallen, and the Jacobins were conducting the dreadful Reign of Terror. He dared not return, so he married a daughter of Governor Clinton, and remained in the State of New York.

During the Reign of Terror in France an immense number of its wealthier and more refined population fled to other countries. America became the favorite refuge for these *emigrès*, and the city of New York

---

* A dance, with singing, performed in the streets of Paris during the Revolution.

† At a meeting of the Democratic Society in New York the following song, composed by Thelwall, an English Radical, was sung to the air of "God Save the King:"

"God save the Guillotine!
Till England's King and Queen
  His power shall prove;
Till each anointed knob
Affords a clipping job,
Let no rude halter rob
  The Guillotine.

"France, let thy trumpet sound—
Tell all the world around
  How Capet fell;
And when Great George's poll
Shall in the basket roll,
Let mercy then control
  The Guillotine.

"When all the sceptred crew
Have paid their homage due
  The Gullotine,
Let Freedom's flag advance
Till all the world, like France,
O'er tyrants' graves shall dance
  And peace begin!"

was their principal resort. They produced a sensible effect upon society there. French fashions, French furniture, French manners and customs, and the French language became prevalent. Even when the emigrants were permitted to return home after the downfall of Robespierre and they had left this country, their influence continued to be felt in social life in New York for many years.

The disloyalty and insubordination of the Republican faction, inaugurated by the official acts of Genet, were conspicuously manifested the following year in the event known in our history as "The Whiskey Insurrection;" and the violence of political antagonisms was as conspicuously displayed in 1795, when the provisions of a treaty with Great Britain, which Mr. Jay had negotiated, were made known. That treaty was the result of an attempt on the part of the President to avert the calamities of war with Great Britain, which circumstances seemed to be engendering. The British Government had failed in complying with the treaty of peace of 1783, in giving up forts in the western country and in other matters. This event, on one side, and the hostile attitude toward Great Britain and partiality for France of the Republicans, on the other side, so menaced the peace between the two nations that Washington sent Jay on the righteous errand to secure tranquillity and justice. The Republicans opposed the mission as a cringing to Great Britain and an affront to France, and when it was known that the treaty had not secured all that the United States demanded, and especially that it bound our Government to a strict neutrality in all wars between Great Britain and other nations (the spirit of the proclamation of neutrality), there was a burst of indignation from the opposition which knew no bounds for a while. They used the most strenuous efforts to induce the President and Senate to refuse their ratification of the treaty.

The first public demonstration in that direction was made in Boston. An anonymous handbill was distributed throughout New York, calling on the citizens to meet in front of the City Hall, in Wall Street, on July 18th (1795), to join the Bostonians in expressing their opposition to the treaty. The meeting assembled. Aaron Burr, Chancellor Livingston, and Brockholst Livingston (the latter a brother-in-law of Jay, who had joined the Republican Party) were leaders of the opposition. The Federalists had gathered there in full force, and were led by Alexander Hamilton and Richard Varick.* They succeeded in electing a chairman

---

* Richard Varick was a descendant of one of the earlier Dutch settlers of New York. He was born in Hackensack, N. J., in 1753, and died in New York City in July, 1831. When the war for independence broke out he was a young lawyer in New York. He entered the military service, and was General Schuyler's military secretary until after the

from among their number, and then proposed to adjourn. The Republicans objected. Then it was moved that the disposition of the treaty be left to the President and Senate. The question being taken, both sides claimed the majority, when a scene of violence ensued. Hamilton, standing upon the elevated "stoop" of a Dutch house on the corner of Wall and Broad streets, attempted to speak in defence of the treaty, when he was stoned, dragged to the ground by the Republicans, and roughly handled in the street. A motion was made to appoint a committee of fifteen to report three days later. It was pronounced carried. Then the tumult increased. Some person in the crowd shouted:

"All you who agree to adjourn to Bowling Green and burn the British treaty will say Aye."

There was a tremendous affirmative response, and the excited opposition ran, shouting, to the Bowling Green, where a copy of the treaty was burned beneath the entwined folds of the American and French flags, while the *carmagnole* was performed. At the adjourned meeting, on the 21st, attended mostly by Republicans, a series of resolutions was adopted condemnatory of the treaty. The next day the Chamber of Commerce adopted counter resolutions.

RICHARD VARICK.

Mr. Jay was violently abused. He was denounced as a "traitor who had sold his country for British gold." In Charleston the populace trailed the British flag in the dust and burned it at the door of the British consul. Some of the more violent Republicans longed for the guillotine, while leaders in Virginia, ever ready with the panacea of *dis-*

---

surrender of Burgoyne. He was inspector-general at West Point until after the treason of Arnold, when he became a member of Washington's military family, and was his recording secretary until the close of the war. After the British evacuated the city of New York, in November, 1783, he was appointed recorder of that municipality, and held the office until 1789, when he became attorney-general of the State, and subsequently mayor of the city, which position he held until 1801. He had been associated with Samuel Jones in making a revision of the laws of the State (1786-88). In 1787 he was speaker of the Assembly. Colonel Varick was one of the founders of the American Bible Society and one of its most efficient members.

union, offered their prescription in vehement language. The treaty was ratified in August, and the effervescence of passion soon ceased.

These turbulent events in New York and elsewhere, and the support given them by the secret Democratic societies, caused Washington to denounce secret associations as dangerous to the public welfare. The Tammany Society, or Columbian Order, which had been formed at the beginning of his administration as a patriotic and benevolent institution, regarding itself as pointed at, and being largely composed of Republicans, or Democrats, was transformed into a political organization in opposition to the Federalists. It still exists, and plays an important part in the politics of the State of New York.*

In his message to the Legislature, which convened at Poughkeepsie on January 6th, 1795, Governor Clinton reminded that body that while liberal provisions had been made for the endowment of colleges and other higher seminaries of learning, no legislative aid had yet been given to *common schools*. He recommended that provisions be made for their encouragement and improvement. This was the first official movement in the State of New York for extending the fostering care of the

---

* The Tammany Society, or Columbian Order, was formed chiefly through the exertions of William Mooney, an upholsterer in the city of New York, in May, 1789. Its first meeting was held on the 13th of that month, a fortnight after the inauguration of Washington. It took its name from a great and good Delaware chief, who was supposed to have been one of those who made the famous treaty with William Penn. He was revered by the Delawares, and the early settlers called him " Saint Tammany," or Tamenand. He " loved liberty better than life," it was asserted, and the new society professed the same. The officers consisted of a grand sachem and thirteen inferior sachems, representing the President and the governors of the thirteen States in the Union. There was also a grand council, of which the sachems were members. It was patriotic in its influence and very popular, and its membership comprised many of the best men of New York. For reasons given in the text, Mooney and others adhered to the organization, but took part with Jefferson and the Democratic Party. They first met as a political organization at Martling's Long Room, at the south-east corner of Nassau and Spruce streets. They built a wigwam on the spot. The corner-stone of the hall was laid in May, 1811, and the building was completed the following year. The venerable Jacob Barker, who died in Philadelphia in 1871, at the age of ninety-two years, was the last survivor of the building committee. The certificate of membership of the reorganized Tammany Society bore a device of an arch composed of two cornucopias ; the supports, resting upon a solid stone arch composed of eighteen blocks, represented the seventeen States and one Territory then in the Union, that of Pennsylvania forming the keystone. Under the cornucopia arch are the words :

" Civil Liberty the Glory of Man. This Sheweth a Link of that Bright and Lasting CHAIN of Patriotic Friendship which binds together

THE SONS OF TAMMANY."

Then follows the certificate, with the seal and signatures of the grand sachem, sagamore, and sentry.

commonwealth to these most important institutions—far more important to the welfare of the commonwealth than colleges and universities. The Legislature heeded the recommendation of the governor, and at that session passed a law appropriating annually for five years $50,000, and directed the specific sums to be paid by the State treasurer to each county. The act provided that the supervisors of the several counties should apportion the money among the respective towns, and a sum equal to one half the sum received from the State by the several towns was required to be raised by a tax in such towns and added to the bounty of the State. The sum thus made up was to be distributed in each school district, under the direction of the town commissioners.

A Literature Fund was created by the operation of an act passed in April, 1801, which authorized four lotteries, for the purpose of raising $100,000 for the joint benefit of colleges, academies, and common schools, but chiefly for the latter. This fund has been increased from various sources from time to time. It was managed by the regents of the University until 1832, when it was transferred to the comptroller for investment, the Legislature appropriating the proceeds annually.

The State of New York has been and continues to be very liberal in its provisions for popular education. During the closing year of the first century of the Republic (1875) the expenditure from the public treasury of the State for educational purposes amounted to about $11,364,000, of which amount about $2,960,000 were the proceeds of a direct tax of $1\frac{1}{4}$ mills for common schools.*

---

* There was no general system of primary education in the State of New York before the Revolutionary War. The schools were chiefly of a private character, and education was confined largely to the wealthier classes. In 1789 an act was passed appropriating certain portions of the public lands for gospel and school purposes. The regents of the University in 1793 recommended the establishment of a general system of common schools, and this led to the recommendation of Governor Clinton in his message mentioned in the text. In the spring of 1801 Judge Peck, of Otsego County, then a member of the Legislature, introduced a bill which by its provisions created the Literature Fund mentioned in the text.

The great benefits of the common-school system were immediately apparent, and successive governors recommended the passage of new laws for the encouragement and support of common schools. Nothing definite was accomplished until 1811, when five commissioners were appointed to report a complete system for the organization and establishment of common schools. In 1812 the Legislature passed a bill in accordance with their report, under which Gideon Hawley was appointed State Superintendent of Common Schools. The office was abolished in 1821, and his duties were assigned to the department of the Secretary of State. In 1835 teachers' departments in academies, one in each senatorial district—a sort of normal school—were authorized. In 1838 the school district library system was established, and in 1841 the office of deputy superintendent was created—in other words, county superintendent; and in 1843 the Board of Town

The Board of Regents of the State of New York alluded to was established in 1784, when the name of King's College was changed to Columbia College, and that institution was to be made the centre of a devised extensive system of education. Subordinate branches were to be established in different parts of the State, the whole to be under the control of the regents. The board was to be composed of the principal State officers—two persons from each county, and one chosen by each religious denomination. The number of the regents was afterward increased by adding thirty-three others, twenty of whom were to reside in the city of New York. The authorship of this scheme is attributed to Alexander Hamilton, then in the Assembly, assisted by Ezra L'Hommedieu,* then in the Senate. It was found to be impracticable, and by an act passed in April, 1787, it was superseded by a system which has continued, with slight modifications, until the present time. The officers of the board are a chancellor, vice-chancellor, and secretary. They have the general supervision of all the educational institutions of the State and the distribution of a portion of the Literature Fund. They appoint the librarian and assistants of the State Library and a curator of the State Cabinet. Six members form a quorum for the transaction of business.

Both Governor Clinton and Lieutenant-Governor Van Cortlandt declined to be a candidate for re-election in the spring of 1795. It was

---

Inspectors and School Commissioners was abolished and the office of town superintendent was substituted. In 1847 a State normal school was established at Albany for the instruction of teachers. In the same year the office of county superintendent was abolished, and teachers' institutes were legally established.

By act of the Legislature in the spring of 1849 free schools were established throughout the State, and the condition of the rate-bill system was abolished. It was soon found not to work well in practice. The law was repealed in 1851, and the rate-bill system was restored. In 1853 Union free schools were permitted under certain conditions.

In the spring of 1854 the office of superintendent of public instruction was created—a virtual restoration of the office filled by Gideon Hawley from 1813 to 1821. In 1855 the regents of the University were authorized to designate certain academies in the several counties in which teachers' classes might be taught free, allowing $10 for each pupil so taught, to a number not exceeding twenty in each academy. The office of school commissioner was created in 1856—really a reinstatement of the office of county superintendent.

* Ezra L'Hommedieu was born at Southold, Long Island, N. Y., in August, 1734, and died there in September, 1811. He was of a Huguenot family from Rochelle, France. Ezra was a lawyer, an active patriot, and a member of the New York Provincial Congress, 1775–78. He assisted in framing the first State Constitution, and was for many years a member of the Continental Congress. He was also a State senator from 1784 until 1809. He had been a member of the State Assembly from 1777 to 1783. Once he was a member of the Council of Appointment, and he was a regent of the University from 1787 until his death. In politics he was a Federalist.

evident that the horrors of the French Revolution had largely diminished the number of American sympathizers with the cause of the French Republicans, and there seemed little doubt that the Federalists were about to assume political control of the State. Clinton had been governor, by successive re-elections, since 1777, and had served the public with ability and faithfulness. The Federalists nominated John Jay for the exalted station. He was then in England, but was elected by a large majority, with Stephen van Rensselaer (the patroon) as lieutenant-governor. The Federalists also secured a majority in both branches of the Legislature.

None but freeholders—men in possession of property of a prescribed character and value—were then allowed to vote. There were about 36,000 freeholders in the State. Of these, 25,373 cast their votes at that election. The western portion of the State had rapidly increased in population. New counties had been organized. Forty-four senators had to be chosen—a score more than in 1777. Seventeen of the new senators were chosen from the western district.

At the first session in Governor Jay's administration a bill was introduced for the gradual abolition of slavery in the State of New York, a measure in which the governor felt deeply interested. After a long debate the bill was rejected in the Assembly by the casting vote of the chairman of the Committee of the Whole. The vote stood 32 to 31.

The Federalists continued to increase in numerical strength, but in the presidential canvass in 1796 (Washington having declined to be a candidate) there was a division in the Federal Party as to their candidate. John Adams and Thomas Pinckney were nominated by the Federalists, and Thomas Jefferson by the Republicans. The State of New York gave Adams its twelve votes in the Electoral College. He was elected President, with Mr. Jefferson as Vice-President.*

The twentieth session of the Legislature convened at New York on November 1st, and sat till November 11th. A second meeting began at Albany on January 2d, 1797, and from that time until now that city has been the political capital of the State. During this session the office of comptroller was first created. The law made him the highest financial

---

* Under the Constitution as originally adopted the candidates for President and Vice-President were voted for in the Electoral College of each State, without designating which the elector intended for the first and which for the second office. Lists of these were transmitted to the seat of Government, and the candidate having the greatest number of votes (of a majority of the whole) became President, and the one having the next greatest number Vice-President. The Twelfth Amendment of the Constitution changed the mode of voting for the two officers, the electors being required to vote by separate ballots for President and Vice-President.

officer of the State, and the treasurer merely a clerk to him. Samuel Jones, a member of the Senate, was appointed by the Council of Appointment the first comptroller of the State of New York.

On February 6th, 1796, there was a notable celebration at New York by the Republicans and the many French temporary residents of that city, of the nineteenth anniversary of the treaty of alliance between France and the United States. There were a banquet, speeches, and toasts. Chancellor Livingston offered the sentiment:

"May the present coolness between France and America produce, like the quarrels of lovers, a renewal of love."

The chancellor had been an ardent Federalist, but, with others of the Livingston family, had become an Anti-Federalist in 1790, because, it was said, of his opposition to the views of Colonel Hamilton contained in the famous report of the latter as Secretary of the Treasury, and especially those in relation to the funding of the national debt. The change was attributed also by his political antagonists to his disappointment in not having been made Chief Justice of the United States.

The coolness between France and the United States alluded to by Livingston continued to increase until, during the administration of John Adams, both nations prepared for war, and hostilities upon the ocean actually occurred; yet neither party made a declaration of war. Bonaparte overturned the republican government of France in 1799, and in the earlier portion of the opening year of the nineteenth century there was peace and friendship between France and the United States.

The Republican Party had been making desperate efforts to maintain its ascendency. A wide breach in the Federal Party promised it success in the spring of 1799, but a dishonorable transaction of Colonel Aaron Burr, who was at the head of the Republican ticket in New York City, caused its defeat. The stock of the Bank of New York, chartered in 1791—the first bank established in the State—happened to be chiefly owned by Federalists. After the election of Adams to the presidency, in 1797, party spirit was nowhere so violent as in the State of New York. Suspicion was on the alert. The Republicans suspected the Federalists of using the funds of the bank for partisan purposes, and they determined to procure a charter for another bank that should be under Republican control. As the majority of the members of the Legislature were Federalists, they saw the necessity of adroit management to obtain a charter. This was left to Colonel Burr, who was equal to the occasion.*

---

* Aaron Burr was born at Newark, N. J., February 6th, 1756; died on Staten Island, N. Y., September 14th, 1836. At the age of nineteen years he entered the Continental army at Cambridge as a private soldier, and accompanied Arnold in his expedition

The yellow-fever had devastated the city of New York in 1798. Its general prevalence was attributed to the use of unwholesome water. Colonel Burr originated a scheme ostensibly for the cure of the evil. He drew up and presented to the Legislature a bill for the chartering of a company for "supplying the city of New York with pure and wholesome water." As the amount of the capital which might be needed was uncertain, he asked for authority to raise $2,000,000. As that sum would probably not be absorbed in the construction of the water-works, he asked for a provision that the "surplus capital might be employed in any way not inconsistent with the laws and Constitution of the United States or of the State of New York." This request appeared reasonable. Under the authority of these few words the Manhattan Company, as the corporation was called, was given banking privileges—really the chief object to be attained by the charter. The bill was rushed through the Legislature at near the close of the session, the greater number of the members having no suspicion that they were chartering a powerful banking institution under the control of Burr and other Republican leaders. Such was the origin of the Manhattan Bank in the city of New York, which still exists. Water-works were established by the corporation, but were inadequate for the promised service. This trick

AARON BURR.

---

through the Wilderness to Quebec. On the way he was sent with despatches to General Montgomery, and joined Arnold at the siege of Quebec. In the spring of 1776 Burr joined Washington's military family, but soon left it, and in 1779 retired from military life and became a lawyer and an active politician. He was twice a member of the New York Legislature (1784, 1798). He was adjutant-general of the State in 1789, and United States senator from 1791 to 1797. In 1801 he was chosen Vice-President of the United States. In 1804 he was ruined politically and socially by his slaying of Alexander Hamilton in a duel. In 1805-1806 Burr was engaged in a supposed treasonable scheme in the Mississippi Valley, and was tried and acquitted—"not proven." He lived abroad several years, returning to New York in 1812, where he resumed the practice of the law, living in obscurity and comparative poverty. In 1834 he married a wealthy widow of a Frenchman, but they soon parted.

produced widespread indignation, and, as we have observed, caused the defeat of the Republicans in the city and throughout the States..

A young man, notable for the dignity of his personal presence, appeared on the stage of political action as a member of the Assembly in 1797, who afterward became a leading figure in the history of New York. He was De Witt Clinton, son of General James Clinton, a graduate of Columbia College, and having the reputation of high scholastic attainments, and then twenty-eight years of age. He had been the private secretary of his uncle, the governor, and had already engaged, with his pen, in political discussions. It was hoped that he would join the Federal Party; but he did not. He was a conspicuous Republican leader until the "era of good feeling"—the period of the dissolution of the two great parties—during Monroe's administration. We shall meet him very frequently hereafter. He took an active part in New York in the presidential canvass of 1800, which resulted in the triumph of the Republicans in the State and nation. Jefferson and Burr were rival candidates nominated by the Republicans, and John Adams was the Federalist candidate for re-election. Jefferson and Burr having an equal number of votes, the choice was made by the House of Representatives. It was given to Jefferson, and Burr became Vice-President. A jubilant Democratic rhymer of the day wrote:

> "The *Federalists* are down at last!
> The *Monarchists* completely cast!
> The *Autocrats* are stripped of power—
> Storms o'er the *British factions* lower.
> Soon we *Republicans* shall see
> Columbia's sons from bondage free.
> Lord! how the *Federalists* will stare
> At JEFFERSON in ADAMS' chair!"

From that time the Republicans were generally called "Democrats," and so we will designate them hereafter.

Washington had died at near the close of the previous year (December 14th, 1799). The event cast a gloom over the whole country, for he was beloved by the nation. The asperity with which he had been assailed by political antagonists had already been transformed into profound respect and reverence. His death was felt as a national calamity—an irreparable loss. It was especially so to the Federalists, with whom he was identified, for his name was a tower of strength. After his death the party was weakened by factions. The most imposing funeral honors were paid to the memory of Washington everywhere. In the city of New York particularly all parties joined in expressions of profound and tender regard.

CHAPTER XXVI.

At the beginning of this century the population of the State of New York was 589,000, and of the city of New York, its commercial metropolis, it was 60,000. The decidedly Dutch aspect of the city in architecture and social manners had almost disappeared. The houses, the furniture, the amusements, and the dress of the people were imitations of English life. To London the ladies and gentlemen looked for fashions, and even in the Dutch Reformed churches the language of Holland was now seldom heard in the pulpit. New York was a complete transformation of New Amsterdam.

That metropolis, now (1887) numbering, with its suburban municipalities, fully 2,500,000 inhabitants, was then only a large village in comparison. Its northern boundary on the west was Harrison Street, some distance below Canal Street; on the east, Rutgers Street, and at the centre by Anthony (now Worth) Street. North of there, and extending from river to river over a hilly country, were fields and orchards, farmhouses and pretty country-seats. Broadway, which crossed by a stone arched bridge the little sluggish stream that passed between the Fresh Water Pond (where the Tombs, or Halls of Justice, now stands) and the Hudson River, through Lispenard's oozy meadows on the line of Canal Street, was terminated by a picket-fence across the road at Astor Place. That was the southern boundary of the farm of Captain Randall, the founder of the Sailors' Snug Harbor, who gave it for an endowment for that institution. From near this point the Boston Road led, by a crooked way, to Harlem, which had been founded by the early Dutch settlers. There Dutch farmers were seated, and on Harlem Plains they raised vegetables for the traders at New Amsterdam. The Middle Road, beginning at the Randall farm, also extended to Harlem by a devious way, to avoid rocks and morasses, and the King's Bridge, or Bloomingdale Road, extended by present Central Park and Manhattanville to the famous bridge which spanned Spuyten Duyvil Creek. It was the beginning of the post road to Albany.

On the site of Washington Square, a portion of which was a swamp, was the new Potter's Field, a burial-place for paupers and strangers. The Jews' burial-ground was near Chatham Square, and the negro burial-ground was at the north-east corner of Broadway and Chambers Street.

Burial-grounds were also attached to the several churches. Burials below Canal Street were prohibited in 1813.

There were two little villages on the Hudson River (Greenwich and

NEW YORK COSTUMES AT THE BEGINNING OF THE NINETEENTH CENTURY.

Chelsea), not far north of the city proper. At Greenwich was the States Prison, a strong stone building. It was the second States prison built in the United States. At the foot of Park Place was Columbia

College; and on Broadway, between Pearl and Duane streets, was the New York Hospital, chartered in 1771. The only medical school in the city was the Medical Faculty of Columbia College.

The benevolent institutions were the Chamber of Commerce;* the Marine Society, for the benefit of the families of seamen; the Humane Society, for the relief of distressed debtors and of the poor in general; the Manumission Society, composed chiefly of Friends, or Quakers, designed for the amelioration of the condition of the slaves and the accomplishment of their freedom ultimately; the Sailors' Snug Harbor, for the comfort of decrepit and worn-out seamen; the General Society of Mechanics and Tradesmen, for the

JOHN CRUGER.†

benefit and relief of the families of necessitous members; the Society of the Cincinnati; the Tammany Society, already mentioned; a Dispensary,

---

* This most useful organization was formed in 1768 at the Queen's Head Tavern, afterward Fraunce's Tavern, where Washington parted with his officers, and yet standing, at the corner of Pearl and Broad streets. It was founded by twenty leading merchants, some of whom afterward appeared conspicuous in public affairs. They avowed the purpose of the association to be "promoting and extending all just and lawful commerce, and for affording relief to decayed members, their widows and children." It was incorporated in March, 1770. The following are the names of the original members: John Cruger, Elias Desbrosses, James Jauncey, Jacob Walton, Robert Murray, Hugh Wallace, George Folliot, William Walton, Samuel Verplanck, Theophylact Bache, Thomas White, Miles Sherbrook, Walter Franklin, Robert Ross Waddel, Acheron Thompson, Laurence Kortright, Thomas Randell, William McAdam, Isaac Low, and Anthony van Dam. John Cruger was the first president. Robert Murray and Walter Franklin represented the Quaker element in the commercial features of New York. Its sittings were interrupted when the British took possession of the city in 1776, but in 1779 the Tory members who remained in the city met at the Merchants' Coffee-House, corner of Wall and Water streets, and renewed the sessions. It was rechartered by the State Legislature in 1784, and its first president was John Alsop. The Waltons were among the most eminent and opulent merchants of the city. The Walton House, on Franklin Square, was long the most magnificent dwelling in the city of New York. It is now devoted to the uses of various kinds of business. It is opposite the publishing house of Harper & Brothers.

† John Cruger was mayor of the city of New York when the Chamber of Commerce was founded, and the next year (1765) was speaker of the Assembly from 1769 to 1775. During the perilous time just preceding the outbreak of the Revolution his influence was

on Tryon Row, not far from the site of the (present) City Hall; the St. Andrew's Society, and several Masonic Lodges.

There were twenty-six churches in the city—namely, 3 Dutch Reformed, 1 German Reformed, 7 Protestant Episcopal, 1 Lutheran, 5 Presbyterian, 2 Baptist, 3 Methodist, 1 Moravian, 1 Friends' Meeting-House, 1 Roman Catholic, and 1 Jews' Synagogue. The only public library in the city was the Society Library, founded in 1754. The Post-Office was kept in a room of the dwelling of the postmaster (General Bailey), on the corner of William and Garden streets, and contained one hundred boxes. There was only one theatre in the city. The Manhattan Water Company had a distributing reservoir on Chambers Street, then quite "out of town."

The most noted of the country-seats on Manhattan Island were those of Roger Morris, on Harlem Heights; of Robert Murray, on the Inchberg (now Murray Hill); the Apthorp Mansion, on the Bloomingdale Road; "The Grange," Hamilton's residence near Carmansville, yet (1887) standing, and of Richmond Hill, at the junction of Charlton and Varick streets, then the residence of Colonel Aaron Burr.

Such is an outline picture of the city of New York less than one hundred years ago.

The State Constitution made no provisions for its own alteration or amendment. A necessity for an amendment appeared at the beginning of this century. In accordance with its provisions, the members of the Legislature, and particularly of the Senate, were increasing in numbers to a degree that was already inconvenient. Governor Jay, in his speech at the opening of the session of the Legislature, in January, 1801, called the attention of that body to the subject. Having no legal power under the Constitution to *order* a convention, to consider amendments, they *recommended* such a convention, to consist of delegates from the several counties, equal in number to the members of the Assembly. It was done. The delegates were chosen in August, and assembled at Albany on October 13th. Aaron Burr was chosen President of the convention. It remained in session until the 27th, and adopted, by unanimous vote, an amendment proposed by De Witt Clinton, which provided that the number of the members of the Assembly should never exceed one hundred and fifty, and of the Senate, thirty-two. At that time

---

powerful in maintaining public order among the citizens of New York. He was an active member of the Stamp Act Congress in 1765, and prepared its famous Declaration of Rights. He was also a prominent member of the New York Provincial Congress, 1775. Mr. Cruger left the city before the British took possession of it in 1776. He died in New York City in 1791–92, at the age of eighty years.

there were one hundred assemblymen. An amendment was adopted requiring an increase of assemblymen, at the rate of two each year—after the return of every census—until the whole number should amount to one hundred and fifty. The people ratified the amendments.

The Democrats now held the political ascendancy in the State and the nation. Ex-Governor George Clinton was elected Governor of New York, and in February, 1802, his nephew, De Witt Clinton, was chosen to fill the place of General Armstrong (who had resigned) in the Senate of the United States. Clinton was then about thirty-three years of age. He was also a member of the Council of Appointment, and was regarded as one of the ablest of the younger public men of the State.

Colonel Burr, the Clintons, and the Livingstons were then the acknowledged leaders of the Democratic Party in the State; but Burr's popularity had already begun to wane. His ambition had impelled him to acts which rendered him an object of suspicion and the animadversions of leading members of his party. The Clintons and the Livingstons disowned him as a Democrat, and on the distribution of the great offices of the State by the Council of Appointment not one of Burr's friends received a place.

The Democratic Council of Appointment divided the offices among the two leading families in the State—the Clintons and the Livingstons—and their immediate friends. Edward Livingston was created Mayor of New York City. The Secretary of State was removed in order to make a place for Dr. Tillottson, a brother-in-law of Chancellor Livingston. Morgan Lewis, another brother-in-law, was made Chief-Justice of the State Supreme Court; General Armstrong, another brother-in-law of the chancellor, was appointed United States Senator. Brockholst Livingston and Smith Thompson (the latter married a Livingston) were created Judges of the Supreme Court. These persons, connected with the Livingston family by marriage or otherwise, were all able men. Governor Clinton had declared, on taking office again, that the heads of State Departments especially and the incumbents of minor offices should be men in political accord with the majority of the voters who appeared at the poles. This was a mild expression of the political maxim enunciated long years afterward—"To the victors belong the spoils."

Chancellor Livingston having been disqualified by age to hold the office of chancellor longer, Judge John Lansing succeeded him, and Mr. Livingston was appointed by President Jefferson Minister at the Court of the First Consul of France, where he negotiated the purchase from that power of the immense territory known as Louisiana, for $3,000,000.

In the summer of 1802 a most bitter political and personal warfare was waged between Colonel Burr and his partisans, and the Clintons and Livingstons and their adherents. The latter established a newspaper, called the *American Citizen*, as the organ of the Democratic Party, which was under the control of De Witt Clinton. It bitterly charged Burr with treason to the Democratic cause, and also with intriguing with the Federalists to prevent the election of Jefferson, in order to secure for himself the presidential chair. An Englishman named Cheatham was the editor-in-chief. To meet this formidable opponent in battle, Colonel Burr and his friends established the *Morning Chronicle*, edited by Peter Irving, an elder brother of Washington Irving.

The *Chronicle* carried the war into the camp of the Clintons and Livingstons with great vigor. It charged them with inordinate personal ambition; with endeavoring to exercise dictatorial power over the Democratic Party, and appropriating to themselves the spoils of the political victories. It affirmed that they were jealous of Burr, and wished to get rid of him, because he was an obstacle in the way of their efforts to place a member of one of their families in the exalted position (Vice-President of the United States) then filled by the colonel, and ultimately in the principal chair. So heated did the controversy become, that the two sections of the Democratic Party became personally hostile.

Burr's opponents managed to gain control of the Manhattan Bank (already mentioned), and wielded its power against him and his friends. Colonel John Swartwout, one of Burr's most devoted partisans, was turned out of the direction of the bank. Though his private character was unimpeachable, De Witt Clinton—who was too apt to speak of every man who opposed him as a knave or a fool—spoke of Swartwout as a "liar, a swindler, and a villain." Swartwout challenged Clinton. A duel ensued. Five shots were exchanged. Nobody was hurt. Richard Riker, afterward the famous Recorder of the city of New York, was Clinton's second and warm personal friend. He so vigorously defended Clinton, through the press, that a brother of Swartwout challenged Riker.

In a duel that ensued, Riker was so severely wounded that he was lamed for life.[*]

---

[*] Richard Riker was long a conspicuous figure in official life in New York. He was born on Long Island in September, 1773, upon land ceded to his ancestor, Geysbert Riker, in 1630. His father was an active patriot of the Revolution of 1775–83. When quite a young man Richard was made Attorney-General of the State of New York. He was first chosen Recorder of the city in 1815. He was again chosen in 1821 and 1824, serving fourteen years successively in his last term. He died in October, 1842. Mr.

Cheatham published a pamphlet against Burr, and William P. Van Ness (Burr's second in his duel with Hamilton) published in the same form, over the signature of "Aristides," a most violent attack upon the character of the whole Livingston family. He also attacked De Witt Clinton and Ambrose Spencer with special severity.

In forming a judgment concerning this virulent controversy, it may be well to remember the words of Lady Betty Germain—"I have lived long enough never wholly to believe any side or party against the other."

This schism in the Democratic Party in the State vexed the leaders a long time. Colonel Burr lost the confidence of his party not only at home, but at the national capital; but the continually increasing majorities of the party at every election inspired his friends with hope. They resolved to bring out Burr as a Democratic candidate for Governor of New York against any regular nominee of the party. In February, 1804, his friends in the Legislature held a meeting at Albany, and formally nominated him. A meeting in New York City ratified it. There being no chance for the election of a Federalist, leaders of that party proposed to take up Burr as their candidate, so as to defeat the Democrats by the coalition.

At a private meeting of Federalists for consultation, held at Albany a few evenings after Burr's nomination, General Alexander Hamilton, then on legal business at Albany, took a conspicuous part. He advocated voting for Chancellor Lansing, in case they had no candidate of their own, declaring that no reliance ought to be placed on Colonel Burr. He repeated his declaration in substance at a private dinner-table. One of the guests on that occasion (Dr. Cooper), in a letter to a friend, repeated the substance of Hamilton's remarks in such a careless use of words that they conveyed the erroneous impression that they impeached the *private* character of Burr. He wrote that both Hamilton and Judge Kent[*] looked upon Burr as a dangerous man, and one who ought not to

---

Riker was one of the most notable of the recorders of the city—efficient, amiable, just, and beloved by everybody. Fitz-Greene Halleck wrote:

> "My Dear Recorder, you and I
> Have floated down life's stream together,
> And kept unharmed our friendship's tie
> Through every change in Fortune's sky,
> Her pleasant and her rainy weather."

[*] James Kent was born in Putnam (then a part of Duchess) County in July, 1763. He was graduated at Yale College; became a lawyer and a profound jurist; in politics he was a Federalist, and in 1791 made New York City his residence, where he formed an intimate friendship with Colonel Hamilton. He became a judge of the Supreme Court of New York in 1798 and chief justice in 1804. In 1814 he became chancellor, retired

be trusted with the reins of government, and added : " I could detail to you a still more despicable opinion which General Hamilton has expressed of Burr." This letter was shown to many politicians before the election, which took place in April, and soon after that event it found its way into the newspapers. Many Federalists voted for Burr, but he was defeated by a large majority of votes given to Morgan Lewis,* the regular nominee of the party. He attributed his failure to gain the prize to the adverse influence of Hamilton. When he saw Cooper's letter in the newspapers his indignation knew no bounds. He at once wrote a note to Hamilton (June 18th, 1804), demanding a " prompt and unqualified acknowledgment or denial of the use of any expression which would warrant the assertions of Mr. Cooper." An unsatisfactory correspondence ensued. Burr finally challenged Hamilton to fight a duel. The latter did all in the power of an honorable man to avoid a personal *rencontre*. Burr was persistent. Yielding to the then prevailing public opinion about the miscalled code of honor, Hamilton, in violation of his moral and religious convictions, felt compelled to accept the challenge. His son Philip was killed in a duel not long before.

MORGAN LEWIS.

On the morning of July 11th, 1804, the belligerents crossed the Hudson in boats to the duelling-ground at Weehawken, with their

---

from the office in 1823, and became law professor in Columbia College the second time. His *Commentaries on American Law*, four volumes, is a standard work. He died in New York in December, 1847.

* Morgan Lewis was born in New York City in October, 1754, and died there in April, 1844. He was a son of Francis Lewis, a signer of the Declaration of Independence. He was educated at Princeton ; studied law with John Jay ; entered the Continental army at Cambridge in June, 1775, and was a gallant soldier, serving faithfully until 1780, when he left the army, having been promoted to colonel on the staff of General Gates. He began the practice of law in Duchess County, N. Y. ; married a sister of Chancellor Livingston ; became a judge ; attorney-general of the State in 1791 ; justice of the State Supreme Court and chief justice in 1801. He was Governor of the State in 1804 ; was made quartermaster-general with the rank of brigadier in 1812, and major-general in 1813. He served well during the war. Late in life he devoted himself to literature and agriculture. In 1835 he was president of the New York Historical Society.

respective seconds—Mr. Van Ness with Burr, Mr. Pendleton with Hamilton. The chosen weapons were pistols. At the given word, Burr took deliberate aim and gave his antagonist a fatal wound. The latter did not fire at Burr. The wounded statesman was taken across the river to the home of his friend, Colonel Bayard, at Greenwich, where he died in the afternoon of the following day. The Federal Party in New York thus lost its most efficient leader, and the nation was deprived of a mighty pillar of support. The remains of Hamilton rest in Trinity Churchyard, near Broadway.

The death of Hamilton at the hand of Burr created the most intense excitement among all classes of society, first in the city of New York and then throughout the Republic. It was regarded as a deliberate murder. The recollection of Hamilton's past services, his transcendent abilities, his marvellous powers for usefulness as a citizen, caused universal mourning among his countrymen. Even his political enemies dropped a tear of sensibility.

At the moment when Hamilton fell Burr became politically dead. He fled from righteous wrath, and became a fugitive. At length he ventured to engage in some mysterious scheme—treasonable it was believed—for his own aggrandizement. He was arrested, and tried on a charge of treason, but escaped conviction. It was virtually a Scotch verdict—"Not proven." He lived thirty years afterward in obscurity.

At near the close of the last century a National Military Academy was founded at West Point, among the Hudson Highlands, with pupils composed of cadets attached to corps of artillerists and engineers then stationed there for the purpose. Its first commander, or superintendent, was Major Jonathan Williams. The institution rapidly grew in the number of the pupils and in tangible usefulness. The Academy was reorganized in 1812, when the number of cadets was limited to two hundred and sixty. Then the broad foundation upon which the institution now rests was laid. The first graduate of this military academy was the late General Joseph G. Swift, under whose directions the fortifications on and around New York or Manhattan Island were constructed during the War of 1812–15.

The election of Judge Lewis Governor of the State of New York left the office of Chief-Justice of the Supreme Court vacant. James Kent was soon afterward appointed to fill the seat, and Daniel D. Tompkins was created Associate Justice. Mr. Jefferson was re-elected in the autumn of 1804, with George Clinton as Vice-President.

In a special message in January, 1805, Governor Lewis urged the application of the proceeds of the sales of the public lands of the State (one million five hundred thousand acres) to the improvement and elevation of the common schools. The Legislature made an appropriation of five hundred thousand acres for that purpose, and thus was laid the foundation for a permanent school fund. At the same session the Society for Establishing a Free School in the city of New York, for the education of destitute children, was incorporated. De Witt Clinton, the first signer to the petition for the incorporation, was made its first president. It was the legitimate offspring of the Female Association for the Relief of the Poor, founded in 1802 by benevolent women of the Society of Friends. They opened a school for the free education of white girls. Its influence rapidly extended, and at one time it had several large elementary schools.

The first school of the Society for Establishing a Free School was opened on Madison Street, in May, 1806. Colonel Henry Rutgers soon afterward gave land on Henry Street as a site for a school-house. The pupils increased so rapidly that other buildings were provided. The Legislature, Trinity Church, and the Municipal Corporation gave the society pecuniary aid. In 1808 the name of the society was changed to Free School Society of the City of New York; and late in 1809 a school was opened in the old arsenal building,* on Chambers Street, as "Public School No. 1." It was held in a room large enough to accommodate fully five hundred children. It was agreed that the children in the Almshouse should be taught there. At the opening of the school, De Witt Clinton pronounced a memorable address, which was spoken of nearly fifty years afterward in a Public School Report, as "sowing the seed-wheat of all the harvests of education which subsequent years have gathered into our garners."

In the State of New York one of the most important achievements in

---

* This was a brick building on Chambers Street and Tryon Row. The city corporation appropriated $1500 for the remodelling of the building inside and out, for the purpose of a school. Among the most conspicuous working members of the society at that time was De Witt Clinton, Thomas Eddy, Samuel Wood, Thomas Brown, John Griscom, Joseph Curtis, Charles Wilkes, Cadwallader D. Colden, and Dr. John W. Francis.

the history of human progress was accomplished in 1807, in the permanent establishment of steam-navigation. Some feeble attempts to accomplish this end had been made before in Europe. Robert Fulton,* an American citizen, a professional portrait-painter, had lived some years in Paris, had travelled in Great Britain, and had studied the subject and made some experiments.

In Paris he had interested Chancellor Livingston in steam-navigation projects, and on his return home, in 1806, Fulton, in conjunction with Livingston, built a steamboat far up the Hudson River, and named it the *Clermont*. She was one hundred and thirty feet long, sixteen feet wide, and was one hundred and sixty tons burden. She was furnished with a Watts & Boulton steam-engine.

THE CLERMONT.

On the morning of August 7th, 1807, the *Clermont* started from New York City on a trial-trip to Albany, one hundred and fifty miles. It was successful, and was accomplished in thirty-six hours, against wind and tide. Steam-navigation was now no longer an experiment; it was a demonstration. On September 1st the *Clermont* began regular trips over that route. Livingston had obtained from the Legislature the exclusive right of steam-navigation on the Hudson for twenty years. In

---

* Robert Fulton was born in Lancaster County, Penn., in 1765. He was of Irish descent; died in New York City February 21st, 1815. He became a skilful painter of miniature portraits in Philadelphia, and went to England to study under Benjamin West. He there made himself familiar with the steam-engine, then just improved by Watt, and turned his attention to invention. He was seven years an inmate of Joel Barlow's house in Paris, studying languages and science and considering inventions. One of these was a torpedo for use in naval warfare. He unsuccessfully offered his invention to the French and English governments. He became acquainted in Paris with Robert R. Livingston, and was aided by him pecuniarily in perfecting his invention for navigation by steam. Fulton returned to New York in 1806, and with Livingston built a boat, which was successfully propelled by steam between New York and Albany in 1807. He could not induce his Government to adopt his torpedo. He built steam ferry-boats, and in 1814 the Government appointed him to superintend one or more floating batteries. He built a war steamer (the first ever constructed), which after his death was named *Fulton the First*.

less than six years from the exploit of the *Clermont* there were six steamboats navigating the Hudson, or North River, as it was then usually called.

From the port of New York went out the *Savannah*, in 1819, the first steam-vessel that crossed the Atlantic Ocean to Europe; but the regular navigation of the sea was postponed until the summer of 1838, when the *Great Western* steamship crossed from Bristol and entered the harbor of New York.

New York was the most famous commercial mart in the United States early in the century, and has remained so. Her merchants suffered severely from the reckless football-playing with the world's commerce, by Great Britain and France, for several years. By the operation of British Orders in Council, and Decrees issued by the Emperor Napoleon, all American commerce in neutral ships with either of the belligerent nations was suspended.

FULTON THE FIRST.*

Late in October, 1807, Congress, as a countervailing measure, laid an embargo on all vessels in the harbors of the United States. These measures were disastrous to the mercantile and shipping interests of the whole country, and to that of the city of New York especially. The Federalists and many Democrats strenuously opposed the Embargo Act, but it was supported by most of the Democratic Party. The Federalists justified the British Orders in Council, and the Democrats justified the French Decrees. The Embargo Act was repealed early in 1809. Another embargo was laid in the spring of 1812. American commerce was now prostrated; it was annihilated in the ensuing summer by the declaration of war against Great Britain. For several years the trading interests of New York City were subjected to many vicissitudes

---

* Early in 1814 the first steamship of war was constructed at New York, at Noah Brown's ship-yard, and named *Fulton the First*. It was a sort of catamaran. The hull consisted of two boats, separated by a channel fifty feet wide. One boat contained the copper boiler for generating steam, the other contained the machinery. The propelling wheel revolved in the space between them. A deck extended over the whole. The vessel was arranged for sails. It was designed for harbor defence. The *Fulton the First* made a trial-trip a short distance at sea. She made six miles an hour with steam alone. She was only a floating battery.

Meanwhile the political quarrels in the State of New York had raged with great violence. The schism in the Democratic Party continued, and yet that party was so powerful in numbers that it continued its domination in the State with continually increasing strength. One faction was led chiefly by the Livingstons, and the other faction was led by De Witt Clinton and his friends. The Federal Party had fallen to rise no more into permanent existence.

The chief cause of the overthrow of the Federal Party was the mistakes made by earnest but injudicious leaders in taking occasions to show their partiality to the British nation.* This was natural in the fever of excitement, because the Democrats were more demonstrative in tokens of their partiality for the cause of Napoleon, then scourging Europe with his armies. Besides, many Tories of the Revolution and their friends had become attached to the Federal Party, and so increased the animosity and the suspicions of the Democrats.

Although Colonel Burr himself was politically dead and buried, his friends, who formed a considerable faction, were very much alive and aggressive. There appears to be evidence that De Witt Clinton and his friends coquetted with the "Burrites," in order to gain their support in the warfare with Governor Lewis; and that as Clinton had not the power at that time to give offices to Burr or his friends, it was proper that he should give "pecuniary" aid, through the medium of the Manhattan Bank, of which Clinton was a prominent director.† The revela-

---

* One instance will suffice to illustrate this point. Previous to celebrating the anniversary of independence at Albany, in 1805, the Common Council of that city, composed of a majority of Federalists, passed a resolution that the Declaration of Independence should not be read on that occasion, because the reading of that instrument, it was alleged, tended to perpetuate prejudices against the British nation, when the causes of hostility had long since ceased to exist.

† Matthew L. Davis, the bosom friend and biographer of Colonel Burr, states in a pamphlet, composed of a series of letters published in a newspaper, over the signatures of "Marcus" and "Philo Cato," that in December, 1805, Levi McKean, a Burrite from Poughkeepsie, a neighbor and friend of General James Tallmadge, a zealous "Clintonian," arrived in New York, and stated to his political friends there that overtures had been made "by the Clintonians to form a union with the Burrites," and that he had conversed with General Bailey, the postmaster, on the subject. Mr. Davis states that early in January, 1806, Colonel Swartwout, Burr's warm friend, accepted an invitation from General Bailey to a personal interview, the latter avowing himself as the agent of De Witt Clinton ; also that an agreement was made that :

1. Colonel Burr should be recognized by the coalition as a Democrat.

2. That attacks upon him should cease, and that the Burrites should not be regarded as *returning* to the Democratic Party ; and

3. That the friends of Burr should be placed on the same footing as the most favored Clintonians as respected appointments to offices of honor and profit throughout the State.

tions of this coalition and its conditions produced intense indignation in the Democratic Party. At a meeting at Martling's Long Room (Tammany Hall) it was denounced. Mr. Clinton was then in Albany. He wrote a letter to General Bailey, approving in general of the proceedings of the meeting, and declaring that the support of the Democratic Party by the Burrites would be universally agreeable, but it ought not to be purchased by a promise of offices.

There being menaces of war between the United States and Great Britain, the governor, in his speech at the opening of the Legislature in 1806, urged the necessity of placing the State in a position of defence, for it would be exposed to attacks by land on the north and from the sea on the south. Very little was then done to this end. The National Government built Fort Jay and Castle William on Governor's Island, in New York Harbor.

DANIEL D. TOMPKINS.

In 1806 the Democrats elected Daniel D. Tompkins * Governor of the State of New York, which position he held from 1807 until 1817. He filled the office with great distinction and efficiency during the trying times of the War of 1812-15. In 1808 the Democrats elected James

---

Davis further stated that Clinton, with some friends, among them a zealous partisan of Burr, afterward met Colonel Swartwout at the house of General Bailey, when congratulations on the coalition were exchanged; and that in February, at a supper at a hotel near New York, the Clintonians and Burrites exchanged toasts and congratulations.

When these letters appeared Mr. Clinton denied the truth of their allegations, and publicly threatened to prosecute their author for libel. Mr. Davis gave notice that he could prove all his assertions. The case was never brought to trial.

* Daniel D. Tompkins was born in Westchester County, N. Y., in June, 1774, and died on Staten Island in June, 1825. He was educated at Columbia College; became a lawyer, and in 1801 was a member of the convention that revised the State Constitution. He served in the State Legislature, and was a member of Congress in 1804-1805. He was made a judge of the State Supreme Court in 1804; was chosen governor in 1806, and served ten consecutive years, and was elected Vice-President of the United States in 1816. He was chancellor of the University of the State of New York, and president of the convention, in 1821, which revised the State Constitution. He had recommended, by a special message to the Legislature, the abolition of slavery in the State of New York. Owing to reports of crookedness in his public financial affairs, he failed to secure a nomination for the Presidency of the United States, for which he was an aspirant.

Madison President of the United States, with George Clinton Vice-President. These gentlemen took their official seats in the spring of 1809.

The great business depression, in consequence of the embargo and the quarrels of the Democratic factions, caused a temporary revival of the strength of the Federal Party, and at the spring election in 1809 they gained ascendency in the State of New York—the first time in ten years.

The act repealing the Embargo Law went into effect on June 10th, 1809. On that day there were public rejoicings throughout the State, and particularly in the city of New York. But the jubilant feelings of the people were soon repressed by the peremptory refusal of the British Government to repeal the Orders in Council, in accordance with a treaty made with its accredited agent. This refusal caused intense indignation against the British authorities, which the Federalists were powerless to assuage.

CHAPTER XXVII.

The great canal which bisects the State of New York, from the Hudson River to Lake Erie, a distance of three hundred and sixty-three miles, is a monument of unsurpassed magnificence, commemorative of the profound statesmanship, the prophetic wisdom, the far-reaching sagacity, and the exalted public spirit of the leaders of opinion in the State during the earlier years of this century.

Who first conceived the grand idea of so wedding the great lakes and the beautiful river is an unsolved question. Undoubtedly it was nebulous in the minds of many thoughtful persons before it found symmetrical expression. Perhaps it was a dream of Joel Barlow the poet (who so early as the year 1787 gave to the world his "Vision of Columbus") when he wrote:

> "He saw, as widely spreads th' inchannell'd plain,
> Where inland realms for ages bloom'd in vain,
> Canals, long winding, ope a watery flight,
> And distant streams, and seas, and lakes unite.
>
> "From fair Albania, toward the setting sun,
> Back through the midland length'ning channels run;
> And the fair lakes, their beauteous towns that lave,
> And *Hudson's* joined to fair *Ohio's* wave."

A dozen years later Gouverneur Morris,* while he was on a tour to the

---

* Gouverneur Morris was born at Morrisania, N. Y., in 1752, and died there in November, 1816. He was a son of Chief-Justice Lewis Morris; was a graduate of King's College, and became a practising lawyer in 1771. In 1775 he was a delegate to the New York Provincial Congress, and one of the committee that drafted the State Constitution. From 1777 to 1780 he was a member of the Continental Congress, and was an efficient member of several committees. In 1780 he removed to Philadelphia, where, thrown from his carriage, his leg was fractured, and amputation was necessary. In 1786 he

Falls of the Niagara, uttered a few prophetic words in a letter to a friend in London. After alluding to the budding commerce on the lakes, and the probability that swarms of ships would appear there in the near future, he wrote:

"Shall I lead your astonishment up to the verge of credulity? I will. Know, then, that one-tenth part of the expense borne by Britain in the last campaign [against Bonaparte] would enable ships to *sail from London through the Hudson River into Lake Erie.*"

To friends at home Morris suggested a direct canal from Lake Erie through the centre of the State to the Hudson. In 1803 he submitted an outline of a plan of such a work to Simeon De Witt, the Surveyor-General of the State, who regarded it as visionary. In conversation with James Geddes, a land surveyor of Onondaga County, the next year, De Witt told him of the impracticable plan of Morris. Geddes viewed the matter in a different light. He regarded it as the best that had been suggested. He conferred with Jesse Hawley, a sagacious and public-spirited citizen of Central New York. The latter, satisfied of the feasibility of the project, wrote a series of essays on the subject, over the signature of "Hercules." They were published in a Pittsburgh paper and in the *Genesee Messenger*, at Canandaigua, during the years 1807 and 1808, and commanded wide and earnest attention. They were the first writings ever put forth in favor of the Erie Canal.

In 1808 Joshua Forman, an intimate associate of Mr. Geddes, was a member of the New York Assembly, and on February 4th introduced a resolution, with a preamble, for the appointment of a joint committee to "take into consideration the propriety of exploring and causing an accurate survey to be made of the most eligible and direct route for a canal to open communication between the waters of the Hudson River and Lake Erie, to the end that Congress may be enabled to appropriate such sums as may be necessary to the accomplishment of that great national object." *

---

retired to the estate at Morrisania as sole owner. He was the colleague of Robert Morris, Superintendent of Finance in 1781. The literary construction of the National Constitution is the work of his hands. He was sent minister to France in 1792, returned home in 1798, and was chosen senator in 1800. He was a canal commissioner from their first appointment until his death. In politics he was a Federalist.

* President Jefferson in his message to Congress, in December, 1807, proposed the application of the surplus funds in the National Treasury to the great national objects of opening canals and making turnpike roads. In his preamble Mr. Forman pointed out the fact that the State of New York possessed the best route of communication between the Atlantic and Western waters, "by means of a canal between the tide-water of the Hudson and Lake Erie."

The resolution was adopted, and the sum of $600 was appropriated for surveys to be made under the direction of the surveyor-general. This was the first legislative movement in reference to the Erie Canal.

Surveyor-General De Witt employed Mr. Geddes to survey a route from Lake Erie to the Genesee River, and thence to the waters flowing into Seneca Lake. His favorable report attracted great attention. De Witt Clinton was then a member of the State Senate, and became deeply interested in the matter. He warmly espoused the project. So also did Stephen van Rensselaer in the Assembly. The matter rested until the next year, when, on motion of Senator Jonas Platt, commissioners were appointed to explore the whole route for a canal through the centre of the State from Lake Erie to the Hudson River.* It was accomplished.

In April, 1811, an act was passed to provide for the "improvement of the internal navigation of the State." Efforts were made to obtain aid from the National Government and otherwise. The commissioners were authorized to make application to Congress or to any State or Territory, and request them to co-operate with New York in the project. Robert R. Livingston and Robert Fulton were added to the commission.

Early in December Messrs. Clinton and Morris appeared before Congress and endeavored to obtain an appropriation for the work, but were unsuccessful. This failure was a fortunate circumstance, for it allowed the State of New York to construct the canal alone and unaided, and so to secure to itself the undivided honor of the achievement and the undisputed possession and control of the great work for all time. The pride and patriotism of the people of the State were effectually appealed to, and in June, 1812, the Legislature passed an act authorizing the commissioners to borrow $5,000,000 on the credit of the State. But the war with Great Britain, which broke out at that time, caused a suspension of the work, and the law was repealed in 1814.

A few months after the restoration of peace the subject was revived. By the exertions of Thomas Eddy † a public meeting was held at New

---

* The commissioners were Gouverneur Morris, Stephen van Rensselaer, De Witt Clinton, Simeon De Witt, William North, Thomas Eddy, and Peter B. Porter.

† Thomas Eddy was a philanthropist and an eminently public-spirited man. He was born in Philadelphia in September, 1758, and died in New York City in 1827. His parents were Quakers, and he, a birthright member, remained so until his death. He made New York his residence in early life, and was a successful insurance broker there Mr. Eddy was active in originating the "Penitentiary System" of New York, and in 1801 he published an admirable work on the State prisons of New York. He was long a governor of the New York Hospital, and a director of the Bloomingdale Asylum for the Insane. Mr. Eddy was one of the chief promoters of the canal system in the State of

York in the autumn of 1815, which was addressed by Mr. Platt, Mr. Clinton, and others. The latter more vigorously than ever pressed upon the public attention the importance of constructing the projected canal. He devoted his wonderful energies to the subject. In a memorial of the citizens of New York, prepared by Mr. Clinton, such a powerful argument in its favor was produced that not only the majority of the people of his State approved it, but of other States. Favorable action was taken by the Legislature of New York in the spring of 1816, and a Board of Canal Commissioners was created.

In the spring of 1817 the Legislature authorized the beginning of the construction of the canal. The first contract was made in June, and the first spadeful of earth in the process of excavation was thrown up at Rome, Oneida County, on July 4th. The middle section, extending from the Seneca River to Utica, including a branch from Syracuse to Onondaga Lake, was rendered navigable in October, 1819. The great work was completed in 1825, and the first boat—the *Seneca Chief*—with Mr. Clinton, then Governor of the State, on board, passed from Lake Erie to the Hudson late in the autumn of that year. The entire cost of the canal was over $9,000,000. It was a little over eight years a-building.

DE WITT CLINTON.

De Witt Clinton* had taken his seat as Governor of the State in the summer of 1817. He used all his official and private influence in favor

---

New York, beginning with the Inland Lock Navigation system. The Bible Society found in him an efficient friend, and he was an originator and promoter of banks for savings. His benevolent works won for him the title of the "American Howard." He lived to see the great Erie Canal in successful operation.

* De Witt Clinton, son of General James Clinton, was born at Little Britain, Orange County, N. Y., March 2d, 1769; died at Albany, February 11th, 1828. Was graduated at Columbia College, and became a lawyer, but practised his profession very little. He was for a long time private secretary to his uncle, Governor George Clinton; served in both branches of the New York Legislature, and from 1798 to 1802 was the Democratic leader in the State Senate. Between 1803 and 1814 he served as Mayor of New York City eight years. He took a very active part in promoting public education; was one of the founders of the New York Historical Society and of the Academy of Fine Arts, and, being opposed to the War of 1812-15, he was the peace candidate for President of the

of the canal. There was continual and powerful opposition to the project almost to the hour of its completion; but his faith in its vast importance to his native State and the whole country never wavered. He lived not only to see it completed and to be a participant in the triumph, but to enjoy most abundant demonstration of the wisdom and sagacity which had conceived and carried out to completion that mighty work. To De Witt Clinton more than to any other man our country is indebted for the Erie Canal; and the city of New York owes him a debt of gratitude it can never repay for its wonderful growth in wealth and population to which that great work so powerfully contributed. It is not creditable to the citizens of the metropolis that among the many statues of eminent Americans and foreigners which appear in their public places no memorial of stone or bronze has ever been erected in their city in commemoration of their great benefactor, DE WITT CLINTON.

At the beginning of 1810 the two great political parties in the State of New York were nearly equal in numerical strength. The Democrats renominated Tompkins for governor, and the Federalists nominated Jonas Platt, of Oneida, for the same office. The canvass was very active, and the election was hotly contested. The Federalists felt that if Tompkins should be re-elected their recently gained political ascendancy in the State might be lost, perhaps forever. Yet they had strong hopes of their success. Their opponents were doubtful of the result, and both parties struggled mightily for victory. Contrary to the expectation of both, the Democrats completely overthrew the Federalists. Tompkins was re-elected by ten thousand majority. The Legislature was made strongly Democratic. A new Council of Appointment was chosen, and very soon there was an entire change in the incumbency of offices throughout the State. Political proscription was sweeping and severe.

Three causes combined to effect this second overthrow of the Federal Party in the State at this time—namely, 1. The adoption by the National Government of the more acceptable policy of non-intercourse instead of embargoes; 2. The rapidly growing feeling of hostility to Great Britain because of recent events, the germ of a war party having already appeared; and, 3. The influence of the patronage wielded by the National Government.

The quarrel between De Witt Clinton and a portion of the Democratic

---

United States in 1812, but was defeated by Madison. Mr. Clinton was one of the founders of the Literary and Philosophical Society of New York, and the most efficient promoter of the construction of the Erie Canal. He was Governor of the State in 1817-22 and 1824-28.

Party in the city of New York, who made Martling's Long Room (then beginning to be known as "Tammany Hall") their rallying-place, was then as bitter as ever. Early in 1811 Clinton was nominated for lieutenant-governor. The "Martling Men," or "Tammanyites," nominated Colonel Marinus Willett, and the Federalists nominated Colonel Nicholas Fish. A majority of the Martling men evidently voted for Fish in order to defeat Clinton. The latter received in the city only 590 votes, and Willett 678, while Fish received 2044. The Federalists carried the Assembly ticket by a majority of 1400. The vote in the State was generally favorable to the Democrats. Clinton was elected by the country votes.

The year 1812 was made memorable in our history by the beginning of a two years' war between the United States and Great Britain. For several years incitements to this result had abounded. The British maintained the doctrine that a British subject can never become an alien, and they claimed the right to search neutral vessels for deserters from the royal navy, and to carry them away and impress them into the naval service of Great Britain without hindrance. The commanders of British cruisers had practically asserted this right for many years, and thousands of American seamen had been taken from American vessels on the pretence that they were suspected deserters, and compelled to serve under a flag which they detested. To every earnest remonstrance through the voice of diplomacy the invariable answer had been : "It is our ancient custom, and we cannot consent to suspend a right upon which the naval strength of the empire mainly depends;" and, governed by the ethics of the mailed hand—"might makes right"—they persisted.

The affair of the *Chesapeake* and *Leopard*, in 1807, in which the officers of the latter (a British frigate) forcibly boarded the former (an American frigate) and carried off some seamen, one an American, under pretence that they were deserters, aroused a war spirit in the United States. It was again awakened in 1809 by the disavowal by the British Government of an arrangement made in good faith with the British Minister at Washington concerning a repeal of an Order in Council, already alluded to ; and again in 1811, when British cruisers were sent to prowl along the American coast with authority to seize American merchant vessels and send them to England as lawful prizes.

These recent outrages, coupled with those of the past, and that of inciting the Indians in the North-west to make war on the frontier settlements of the United States beyond the Ohio River, became unendurable. On June 20th, 1812, President Madison, by the authority of Congress, issued a declaration of war against Great Britain, and Congress made provision accordingly. A large majority of that body and the people of the republic favored the measure, yet there was general anxiety to avoid the calamity of war if possible. There was also a large and powerful party, composed chiefly of Federalists, who were decidedly opposed to hostilities, and considered the declaration of war as premature. There was also an active faction known as the "Peace Party," pledged to cast obstacles in the way of the Government so long as hostilities should last. This disloyal faction was exceedingly mischievous during the whole war.

The authorities of several States took positive action against affording aid to the Government in carrying on the war. The governors of Massachusetts, New Hampshire, and Connecticut refused to comply with the requisition of the National Government for militia, and set the President at defiance. The governors of two or three other States approved their course, and others were lukewarm, while others took their places promptly on the side of the National Government. The Legislature of Pennsylvania rebuked the governors of the three New England States; that of Ohio did the same, and said: "The man who would desert a just cause is unworthy to defend it." The governor of the then new State of Louisiana, just admitted into the Union, said: "If ever war was justifiable, the one which our country has declared is that war. If ever a people had cause to repose in the confidence of their Government, we are the people." Vermont was also loyal, and the Governor of the State of New York (Mr. Tompkins), which then contained a population of fully one million, exhorted the people to give a hearty support to the National Government. The New York delegates in Congress did not vote for a declaration of war.

During the war that ensued the inhabitants of New York bore their full share of the burdens imposed, as active participants in the stirring events or as passive sufferers of calamities incident to a state of war. In that contest, as in former times, the northern frontiers of the State were peculiarly exposed to invasion by land and water.

At the time of the declaration of war the troops and military defences on the northern frontier of New York possessed very little aggregate strength. So on the other side. There were only about fifteen hundred regular troops in Upper Canada, but in Lower Canada there were about six thousand. At the foot of Lake Erie, opposite Buffalo, was Fort Erie, with a small garrison. At near the mouth of the Niagara River was Fort George, a small earthwork with wooden palisades, mounting a few guns not heavier than nine-pounders; and a little above Niagara Falls was Fort Chippewa, a small stockade. At York (now Toronto), on the north shore of Lake Ontario, was an old fort and a block-house, and at the eastern extremity of the lake, near Kingston, was a small battery of nine-pounders.

There was very little hostile movement on the soil of New York, excepting that of preparation, until mid-autumn in the year 1812. War had actually begun in the West and on the ocean. Colonel William Hull, then Governor of Michigan, was commissioned a brigadier-general and authorized to invade Canada on its western frontier in the summer of 1812. He crossed the Detroit River with a small force and encamped at Sandwich, but was soon compelled to return to Detroit, where he was menaced by a British force under General Sir Isaac Brock early in August. Alarmed by intelligence from the north, he surrendered his whole army and the territory to the British on August 16th. Meanwhile Fort Mackinaw, one of the strongest posts of the United States in the Northwest, had been surprised and captured (July 17th) by an allied force of British and Indians. An escort of supplies for Hull, under Major Van Horne, had been defeated below Detroit, and Fort Dearborn, on the site of the (present) great city of Chicago, had been taken by Indians, and most of the garrison, with women and children, had been slaughtered.

These events aroused the most intense indignation throughout the country. Volunteers from Kentucky and Ohio pressed toward the North-west to retrieve the disaster at Detroit, and the most active preparations were made for an invasion of Canada on the Niagara frontier.

The authorities of the State of New York had been vigilant ever since light war-clouds had been seen in the political firmament, so early as 1807. In order to enforce the revenue laws on the Canadian frontier, the Governor of New York, in February, 1808, ordered five hundred stand of arms to be deposited at Champion, in (present) Jefferson County, and the following year he caused an arsenal to be built at Watertown, on the Black River, twelve miles from Sackett's Harbor.

By a general order issued from the War Department on April 21st, 1812, the detached militia of the State of New York were arranged in two divisions and eight brigades. Stephen van Rensselaer (the patroon), of Albany, was commissioned major-general and assigned to the command of the First Division, and Benjamin Mooers, of Plattsburg, was appointed to the same office and assigned to the command of the Second Division. The commanders of the eight brigades were: Gerard Steddiford, of the city of New York; Reuben Hopkins, of Orange County; Micajah Pettis, of Washington County; Richard Dodge, of Montgomery

County; Jacob Brown,* of Jefferson County; Daniel Miller, of Cortland County; William Wadsworth, of Ontario County, and George McClure, of Steuben County.

In May a regiment, commanded by Colonel C. P. Bellinger, was stationed at Sackett's Harbor, and in June the first detachment of New York's quota of militia called for by the President was placed under the command of General Brown, who was charged with the defence of the northern frontier from Oswego to Lake St. Francis, a distance of about two hundred miles.

An armed brig named *Oneida* had been built at Oswego, on Lake Ontario, in 1809, by Christian Bergh and Henry Eckford, to enforce the revenue laws. In the spring of 1812 she captured several British vessels—violators of these laws. Retaliation followed. When news of the declaration of war reached Ogdensburg, on the St. Lawrence, eight American trading vessels were lying there. They tried to escape to Lake Ontario, bearing away some frightened families. Two of them were captured by armed men in boats led by a Canadian partisan, and were plundered and burnt. The other six returned to Ogdensburg. This was the beginning of war on the northern frontier of New York.

Lieutenant Melancthon Woolsey was in command of the *Oneida*, and he and General Brown were vested with full authority to repel invasion from Canada and to protect the inhabitants on the frontier. Re-enforcements of militia were called out from the northern counties, and measures were taken to concentrate a considerable force at Ogdensburg and Cape Vincent, for the twofold purpose of guarding the frontier and keeping Kingston, the chief military station of the British on the lake, in a state of continual alarm.

Late in July a squadron of five small British armed vessels entered Sackett's Harbor. They carried an aggregate of eighty-two guns. The *Oneida* was in the harbor, and seemed to be in great peril. Woolsey attempted to gain the lake, but failed. He moored his vessel to a position where her broadside of nine guns might be brought to bear on

---

* Jacob Brown was born in Pennsylvania in May, 1775, of Quaker parentage. He died in Washington City in February, 1828. He was first a school-teacher, then a land surveyor, and finally became a lawyer. While General Hamilton was acting chief commander of the army intended to fight the French in 1798, Brown was his secretary. He settled upon lands he had purchased on the Black River, not far from Sackett's Harbor, and was the founder of Brownsville. He became a county judge, a militia general, and was placed in command of the northern frontier of New York in 1812. He performed eminent service during the war, and received the thanks of Congress and a gold medal. He was made general-in-chief of the army in 1821. At his death his remains were interred in the Congressional burying-ground.

the enemy. The remainder of her guns were taken out and placed in battery on land. An iron thirty-two-pounder had already been placed in a battery, with three nine-pounders, on a rocky bluff at the foot of the main street of the village. It had long been lying in the mud near by, and was named the *Old Sow*. These guns, with two nine-pounders and two six-pounders, constituted the artillery for the defence of the harbor. The soldiers consisted of a few regulars, three hundred militia, and a portion of the crew of the *Oneida*, with Woolsey at their head.

The flag-ship of the attacking squadron was the *Royal George*. When the vessels were near enough for action the battle was begun by a shot from the big iron cannon on shore. It was harmless, and drew peals of derisive laughter from the crew of the flag-ship, followed by two shots. Firing was kept up for about two hours, the squadron standing, off and on, out of range of the smaller guns. Most of the enemy's shot had fallen against the rocks below the battery. At length a thirty-two-pound ball came over the bluff, struck the earth, and ploughed a deep furrow. It was picked up by a sergeant, who ran with it to Captain Vaughan, who was in command of the *Old Sow*, exclaiming:

"I've been playing ball with the redcoats, and have caught 'em out. See if the British can catch back again."

The ball exactly fitted the old cannon, while those which had been sent did not. At that moment the *Royal George* was nearing, to give a broadside, when the big gun sent back the captive ball with such force and precision that it struck her stern, raked her completely, sent splinters as high as her mizzen-topsail, and killed fourteen men and wounded eighteen.

The flag-ship had already received a shot that went through her sides, and another between wind and water. Two other vessels had been severely crippled, and a signal for retreat was speedily given. The squadron sailed out on the lake while the band on shore played "Yankee Doodle" in the liveliest manner, and the soldiers and citizens cheered the retreating enemy in their departure. It was a serene Sabbath morning, and at evening the village was as quiet as ever.

The command of Lake Ontario was now an object of great importance to both parties, and each put forth extraordinary exertions to that end. To obtain this advantage required the speediest preparation. The six American trading vessels were yet at Ogdensburg. To save and arm them was an important object to the Americans; to destroy them was an equally important object to the British. The latter sent two armed vessels down the St. Lawrence to destroy them; the Americans sent a small force to protect them. The belligerents met eleven miles above

Ogdensburg and fought three hours, when the British vessels withdrew to the Canada shore. The armistice that soon followed allowed the six vessels to be taken to the lake and converted into warriors.

Captain Isaac Chauncey was appointed commander-in-chief of the navy to be created on Lake Ontario. In September (1812) he sent forty ship-carpenters to Sackett's Harbor, with Henry Eckford * at their head. Others soon followed. Commander Woolsey was directed to purchase merchant vessels for the service. Later, in September, one hundred officers and men, with guns and other munitions of war, left New York for Sackett's Harbor, and very soon a respectable little American fleet was afloat on the lake. At the same time the British had been busy at Kingston in creating a navy having a weight of metal double that of the Americans.

HENRY DEARBORN.

During the summer of 1812 the National Government matured a plan for the invasion of Canada on the Niagara frontier. The militia of the State of New York under General Van Rensselaer were ordered to concentrate near the Niagara River, chiefly at Lewiston; and from that point the first demonstration against the neighboring province from New York was made. In contemplation of such a movement, the British posted troops in a strong position at Queenstown, opposite Lewiston.

General Dearborn,† the commander-in-chief of the Northern Depart-

---

* Henry Eckford was a famous naval constructor. He was born in Scotland in March, 1775, and died in Constantinople in November, 1832. He learned the art of ship-building at Quebec, and began the business on his own account at New York in 1796, where he soon took the lead in his profession. He constructed many vessels for the Government during the War of 1812–15, and soon afterward built the steamship *Robert Fulton*, in which, in 1822, he made the first successful trip in a craft of that kind, to New Orleans and Havana. He was naval constructor at the Brooklyn Navy-Yard several years, and afterward made ships of war for European powers. In 1831 he built a war vessel for the Sultan of Turkey, and, going to Constantinople, organized a navy-yard there.

† Henry Dearborn was born in New Hampshire in February, 1751, and died at Roxbury, Mass., in June, 1829. He became a physician, studied military science, and joined the little patriot army at Cambridge with sixty volunteers on the day after the skirmish at Lexington. As a captain in Stark's regiment he fought at Bunker (Breed's) Hill, accompanied Arnold in his expedition against Quebec, and was made prisoner

BATTLE OF QUEENSTOWN.

ment, had concluded an armistice in the summer with the chief British commander in Canada, and this caused delay in the gathering of troops on the Niagara. But at length Van Rensselaer found himself in command of about six thousand troops scattered along the river from Lewiston to Buffalo, and he resolved to invade the neighboring province, from Lewiston, on the night of October 12th, and take the British by surprise.

Intense darkness brooded over the waters and the land, for a heavy storm was just ending. It was three hours past midnight when Colonel Solomon van Rensselaer, in command of six hundred men, was ready to cross the swift-running stream in boats to storm the British works on Queenstown Heights. There were only boats enough to convey less than one half his force. With the brave three hundred he pushed across in the gloom. The British were on the alert, for they had discovered the movement of the New Yorkers; and when Van Rensselaer landed, his little force was fiercely assailed with musketry and a small field-piece. A battery on Lewiston Heights responded to this firing, when the British fled toward Queenstown, followed by some regulars under Captains Wool and Oglevie, who, pushing gallantly up the hill, pressed the British back to the plateau on which the village stands, fought them there, and finally gained possession of Queenstown Heights.

Colonel Van Rensselaer, who had followed with the militia, was so severely wounded that he was compelled to relinquish the command and recross the river. Wool, who was now in chief command, was also badly wounded, a bullet having passed through the fleshy part of both his thighs; but, unmindful of his wounds, he would neither leave the field nor give up the command until the arrival of his senior officer, Lieutenant-Colonel Christie, who had been in a boat which lost its way in the darkness in crossing the river.

General Sir Isaac Brock, the Governor of Upper Canada, to whom General Hull had surrendered in August, was at Fort George, several miles below Queenstown, when the firing began. He hastened to the scene of action, and with his staff pressed up the heights to a redan battery, where they dismounted. They were suddenly startled by the

---

there. He served faithfully during the whole war, and in 1781 was one of Washington's military family, with the rank of colonel, at the siege of Yorktown. He filled several civil offices after the war, and was a member of Congress from 1793 to 1797. Jefferson appointed him Secretary of War in 1801. From 1809 until called to the head of the Army of the Northern Department by Madison, in 1812, he was collector of the port of Boston. In 1822 he was sent to Portugal as American Minister, where he remained two years, when he returned to Roxbury.

crack of musketry. Wool and his followers were close upon them. Brock and his aides had not time to remount, but fled down the hill, leading their horses at full gallop. They were followed by the dozen men who manned the battery, and in a few moments afterward the American flag was unfurled over that little work.

AN INCIDENT AT THE BATTLE OF QUEENSTOWN.

Brock placed himself at the head of some troops to retake the battery and drive Wool from the heights. The Americans were pressed back to the verge of the precipice two hundred feet above the rushing Niagara. Seeing the peril of the little band, who were in danger of being hurled into the flood below, Captain Oglevie raised a white handkerchief on the point of a bayonet in token of surrender. Wool sprang forward, snatched the token of submission, addressed a few stirring words to his men, begging them to fight as long as they held a weapon, and then, waving his sword, so inspirited his comrades to a renewal of the fight, that they soon made the British veterans break and fly down the hill in confusion. Brock rallied them, and they were about to reascend the heights when their commander was mortally wounded at the foot of the declivity. At the end of a brief struggle the British fled a mile below Queenstown. After three distinct battles young Wool (then only twenty-four years of age) was left master of the heights, with two hundred and forty men. Soon afterward Brigadier-General Wadsworth, of the New York militia, took the chief command.

General Sheaffe succeeded Brock in command, and rallied the troops. Lieutenant-Colonel Winfield Scott, who had arrived at Lewiston, crossed the river and joined the troops as a volunteer, when he was requested to take active command. Early in the afternoon quite a large number of Indians, painted and plumed and led by John Brant, a son of the famous chief, fell with great fury upon the American pickets, uttering the horrid war-whoop. The militia were about to flee, when Scott, by his voice and commanding presence, inspired the troops to fall upon the barbarians. The Indians fled to the woods in terror.

STEPHEN VAN RENSSELAER.

General Van Rensselaer,* who stood by the side of Scott, seeing the troops under General Sheaffe pressing forward, hastened across the river

---

* Stephen van Rensselaer, the last of the patroons, was born in New York City, November 1st, 1764; died at the Manor House at Albany, January 26th, 1839. He was the fifth in lineal descent from Killian van Rensselaer, the first patroon. His mother was a daughter of Philip Livingston. He married a daughter of General P. Schuyler. Mr. Van Rensselaer served in both branches of the Legislature, and from 1795 to 1801 he was Lieutenant-Governor of the State. He presided over the Constitutional Convention of the State in 1801, and was made one of the first Canal Commissioners in 1810. He was

to send over re-enforcements of militia. They refused to go, pleading that they were not compelled to leave the soil of their country and invade that of another. Very soon overwhelming numbers compelled the Americans to surrender, and they were made prisoners. They lost on that memorable day (October 13th, 1812), in killed, wounded, and prisoners, about eleven hundred men. Van Rensselaer left the service, and was succeeded by General Alexander Smythe, of Virginia, who accomplished nothing of importance during the remainder of the season.

---

president of the Canal Board fifteen years. He was made commander of the State cavalry in 1801, with the rank of major-general; and when war began in 1812 he was the chief of the militia of the State. He became a Regent and Chancellor of the State University; was a member of the State Constitutional Convention in 1821, and of Congress from 1823 to 1829. At his own expense and under his direction a geological survey of the State was made in 1821-23, and in 1824 he established at Troy, N. Y., a scientific school for the instruction of teachers.

CHAPTER XXVIII.

WHILE the American armies were suffering defeat and humiliation, and the disasters became a staple topic for rebuke of the Democratic administration in the mouths of its opponents, the little American navy was winning honors and renown for its skill and prowess on the ocean. At that time the British navy comprised one thousand and sixty vessels, while that of the United States, exclusive of small gun-boats, numbered only twenty. Two of these were unseaworthy, and one was on Lake Ontario. Nine of the American vessels were of a class less than frigates, and none of them could well compare in appointments with those of the enemy. Yet the Americans went boldly out upon the ocean in their ships to meet the war-vessels of the proudest maritime nation on the earth, and won victory after victory.

Commodore Rodgers[*] was at Sandy Hook, N. Y., with the frigates *President*, *Congress*, and *United States*, and the sloop-of-war *Hornet*, in June, 1812; and on the day after the declaration of war was proclaimed he put to sea in pursuit of a British squadron which had sailed as a convoy of the West India merchant fleet. He abandoned the chase at midnight, and returned to his anchorage. He had a slight skirmish with the enemy.

On August 19th the American frigate *Constitution*, Commodore Isaac Hull, fought the British frigate *Guerriere*, Captain Dacres, some distance off the American coast, in the present track of ships plying between New York and Great Britain. The contest lasted about forty minutes. Hull was victorious. The *Guerriere* had become such a complete wreck that he burned her. This victory had a powerful effect on the public mind in both countries.

On October 18th the American sloop-of-war *Wasp*, Captain Jones, captured the British brig *Frolic* off the coast of North Carolina, after a

---

[*] John Rodgers was born in Maryland in 1771, and died in Philadelphia in August, 1838. He entered the navy as lieutenant in 1798, and was executive officer of the frigate *Constitution* under Truxton. From 1802 to 1806 he did good service in the Mediterranean. In the spring of 1811, in command of the *President*, he had an encounter with the *Little Belt*. His services were conspicuous during the War of 1812–15. He was acting Secretary of the Navy in 1823. For a long time he was a member of the Board of Naval Commissioners, which he left the year before his death.

severe conflict of forty-five minutes. Out of the *Frolic's* company of eighty-four men and boys only three officers and one seaman remained unhurt at the close of the battle. They had been either slain or badly wounded. The *Wasp* lost only ten men. In the afternoon of the same day the British ship *Poictiers*, seventy-four, recaptured the prize and seized the victor. A week later (October 25th) the American frigate *United States*, Captain Decatur, fought the British frigate *Macedonia*, westward of the Canary Islands, for almost two hours, and captured her. She had been greatly damaged in the conflict, and lost more than one hundred men, killed and wounded, while Decatur lost only five men killed and seven wounded. A few weeks later (December 29th) the *Constitution*, Commodore Bainbridge, captured the British frigate *Java*, after a fierce battle for almost three hours, off San Salvador, on the coast of Brazil. The *Java* had four hundred men on board, of whom more than one half were killed or wounded. The *Java* was so much injured that she could not be kept afloat, and was burned.

These victories greatly elated and inspired the Americans. They had also sent out numerous privateers that struck British commerce heavy blows in every direction. During the latter half of the year 1812 upward of fifty British armed vessels of various sizes, and two hundred and fifty merchantmen, with an aggregate of over three thousand prisoners and a vast amount of booty, were captured by the Americans. British pride was fearfully wounded in a tender part, and the favorite national song,

"Britannia, Britannia rules the waves,"

was sung in a minor key by the boasted "Mistress of the Seas."

These events strengthened the national administration, and Mr. Madison was re-elected President of the United States in the autumn of 1812 by an increased majority, with Elbridge Gerry, of Massachusetts, Vice-President. Gerry's venerable predecessor, George Clinton, had died in the spring of the same year.*

---

* George Clinton was born in Ulster County, N. Y., in July, 1739, and died in Washington, D. C., in April, 1812. In early youth he made a successful cruise in a privateer during the French and Indian War, and was in the expedition against Fort Frontenac in 1758. He studied law under William Smith, became a member of the Provincial Assembly of New York in 1768, and was a leading Whig. In 1775 he became a member of the Continental Congress, and voted for the resolution for independence in June, 1776, but was in the military service when the Declaration of Independence was adopted. As brigadier he performed important services. He was elected the first Governor of the State of New York in 1777, and retained the office, by re-election, eighteen years. In 1788 he presided over the convention at Poughkeepsie which ratified the National Consti-

A BANK CHARTER IN POLITICS.

The political situation in New York was still in a state of effervescence owing to the continued bitterness of the quarrel between the "Clintonians" and the "Martling men," or the "Regular Democracy." The latter had "read" De Witt Clinton "out of the party;" but he was a power too strong to be repressed by such "paper blockades." At the same time another important and disturbing question arose for discussion—namely, a proposition for an increase of the paper currency of the States, by chartering a bank to be located in the city of New York, with a capital of $6,000,000, to be called the "Bank of America."

The petitioners for the charter of the bank offered the extravagant bonus of $600,000, to be paid in the following manner and for the following purposes: $400,000 to the common-school fund; $100,000 to the literature fund; and $100,000 to be paid into the Treasury at the end of twenty years, provided no other bank should in that time be chartered by the State. The sum of $1,000,000 was also to be loaned to the State at five per cent interest, to be laid out in constructing canals, and $1,000,000 to be loaned to farmers. Solomon Southwick, then a brilliant young man and editor of the Albany *Register*, the accredited organ of the Democratic Party in the State, and a devoted and confidential friend of De Witt Clinton, was one of the most persistent and efficient agents in efforts to procure the proposed bank charter.

GEORGE CLINTON.

It was suspected that the bank would be used as a political machine, like the Manhattan Bank, and there was much opposition to it. Mr. Clinton avowed that he was opposed to it on other grounds, and protested against making support of or opposition to it a test of political merit. Mr. Southwick echoed Mr. Clinton's sentiments in the *Register* by saying: "He who supports or opposes a bank upon the grounds of Federal-

---

tution, to which he was opposed. He was again elected governor in 1801, and in 1804 was chosen Vice-President of the United States, which office he filled until his death. His remains rest in the Congressional burying-ground at Washington.

ism or Republicanism is either a deceiver or deceived, and will not be listened to by any man of experience."

The friends of the bank in the Legislature determined that nothing of importance should be done in that body until their favorite measure should be adopted. They resorted to another measure to force Mr. Clinton and his friends to favor the bill for the charter of the bank. They all professed to favor his nomination for the presidency of the United States, to which he aspired, by a legislative Democratic caucus; but by one pretence and another they refused to go into caucus on that subject until after the question of chartering the bank should be disposed of. This course exceedingly annoyed Mr. Clinton, for he desired that the nomination, if made by the Legislature of New York, should be announced before a Congressional nomination of Mr. Madison should be declared.

A crisis was suddenly reached. Late in March the enacting clause of the bank charter bill was passed by a vote of 52 to 46, when some startling disclosures were made of attempts to bribe members of both houses by friends of the measure. Notwithstanding these damaging disclosures, the bill was passed by a vote of 58 to 39. It was sent to the Senate, where it was evident it would be almost immediately adopted. Governor Tompkins, who had watched the measure with keen vigilance, satisfied that it would be forced through by corrupt means, prorogued the Legislature on March 27th until May 21st. His message announcing his act fell like a thunderbolt on both houses, and a scene of wildest confusion and uproar ensued; but the legislators were compelled to submit to the inevitable.

When the Legislature reassembled the bill for the charter of the Bank of America, which had produced so much social and political commotion, was promptly passed, all the Federalists in both houses voting for it. Immediately afterward a meeting of the Democratic members of the Legislature was held (May 28th, 1812), by which Mr. Clinton was nominated as the candidate of the State of New York for the presidency of the United States. They recommended his support to the Democratic Party throughout the republic.

Mr. Clinton and his friends having been rather lukewarm on the subject of war, the Federalists felt kindly toward him. The Clintonian members of Congress from New York voted against the declaration of war. At the election most of the Federalists voted for Mr. Clinton. In the Electoral College he received eighty-nine votes, and Mr. Madison received one hundred and twenty-eight votes. Clinton's course, regarded as coquetry with the Federalists, lost him the friendship of many of his party at home. An immense majority of the Democrats of New York City, where the "Tammanyites" were influential, became opposed to him politically, and these influenced the party in the State.

There were some hostile movements on the Canada frontier of New York near the St. Lawrence in the autumn of 1812 and in the winter of 1813. Late in September Major Benjamin Forsythe, with a company of riflemen, appeared on the southern bank of the St. Lawrence, and after some exploits among the Thousand Islands, he took post at Ogdensburg. General Brown arrived there on October 1st, and on the same day a large flotilla of British bateaux, escorted by a gun-boat, appeared at Prescott, on the opposite side of the river. On October 4th this flotilla bore armed men across the stream to attack Ogdensburg, when about fifteen hundred American regulars and militia at that place repulsed the invaders.

Nearly three weeks later a detachment of about two hundred militia, chiefly from Troy, N. Y., led from French Mills by Major G. D. Dudley, captured a larger portion of a British detachment stationed at the Indian village of St. Regis, which lies on the boundary-line between the United States and Canada. The late Governor Marcy, of New York, then a lieutenant, captured a British flag with his own hands. It was the first trophy of the war taken on the land.

Early in November Commodore Chauncey[*] appeared on Lake Ontario with a little squadron of armed schooners. With these he made a cruise toward Kingston, and after a slight skirmish he blockaded a British squadron in Kingston Harbor. In this cruise of a few days he disabled the *Royal George*, destroyed one armed schooner, captured three merchant vessels, and took several prisoners. Leaving vessels to blockade the harbor until ice should seal it, he cruised toward the western end of the lake, and soon returned to Sackett's Harbor. The aggregate amount of metal carried by his squadron was less than fifty guns, and the aggregate number of his men was only four hundred and thirty, including marines.

Meanwhile some stirring events had occurred at the head of the

---

[*] Isaac Chauncey was born in Connecticut in February, 1772, and died at Washington, D. C., in January, 1840. At the age of nineteen he commanded a merchant ship, and he made voyages to the East Indies in ships belonging to J. J. Astor. He entered the navy as lieutenant in 1802, and had become captain in 1806. During the War of 1812-15 he was commander-in-chief of the United States naval force on Lake Ontario. After the war he commanded the Mediterranean squadron, and assisted in negotiating a treaty with Algiers. He was Naval Commissioner at Washington in 1820, and held the same position from 1833 until his death. His remains lie in the Congressional burying-ground.

Niagara River. Black Rock, near Buffalo, had been chosen as a place for the construction of war-vessels for service on Lake Erie. Lieutenant J. D. Elliott had been sent thither by Chauncey as superintendent. A few days before the affair at Queenstown two British merchant vessels—*Caledonia* and *Detroit*—had come down the lake and anchored under the protection of the guns of Fort Erie, opposite Buffalo. Elliott determined to seize them. At midnight (October 8th) he crossed the river in boats with one hundred and twenty men, and surprised and captured both vessels with all their people. The shouts of men at Buffalo and Black Rock who witnessed the exploit aroused the garrison at Fort Erie, who brought great guns to bear upon the assailants. A fierce struggle for the possession of the captured vessels ensued. The *Caledonia* was

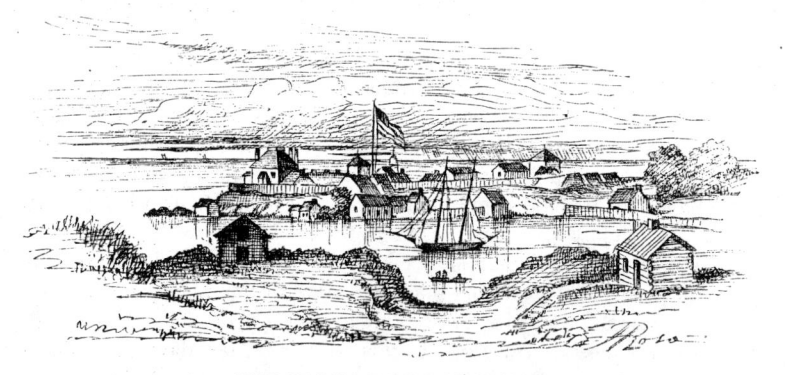

FORT NIAGARA FROM FORT GEORGE.

secured by the Americans, and was afterward converted into a war-vessel. The *Detroit* was burned.

Near the mouth of the Niagara River stood old Fort Niagara, lightly garrisoned by the Americans. On November 21st (1812) a heavy artillery attack upon this post was carried on from the morning until the evening twilight by five detached batteries on the Canada shore. Two thousand red-hot balls and a tempest of bomb-shells were projected upon the American works during the day. The cannonading and bombardment was returned with spirit. The village of Newark, on the Canada side, was set on fire several times by bombs, and little Fort George was severely pounded by round-shot. Night ended this artillery duel.

This cannonade and bombardment aroused General Smythe, Van Rensselaer's successor in command at Buffalo, to spasmodic action. He made preparations for invading Canada at once. In a flaming proclamation he said to his soldiers : " Hearts of war ! to-morrow will be memorable in the annals of the United States. Neither rain, snow, nor frost will prevent the embarkation. . . . The landing will be effected in despite of cannon."

"To-morrow" was "memorable" for the failure of the boaster to cross the Niagara. He was afraid of Lieutenant-Colonel Bisshopp, who commanded a small British force on the Canada side. Smythe was dismissed from the service. He petitioned Congress to be reinstated, asking to be allowed to "die for his country." A wag wrote with a pencil on the panel of a door of the House of Representatives :

> "All hail, great chief, who quailed before
> A Bisshopp on Niagara's shore,
> But looks on Death with dauntless eye,
> And begs for leave to bleed and die.
>   Oh my !"

It is not our province to give more than the briefest notices of events not specially connected with the history of the State of New York ; therefore we present only an outline of stirring scenes elsewhere.

We have observed that the surrender of Hull and the atrocities of the barbarians on the north-western frontier aroused the hottest indignation and intense patriotism of the people west of the Alleghany Mountains. In the valleys of the Ohio and the Mississippi the spirit of the old crusaders seemed to have been awakened. Volunteers gathered in every settlement, and for weeks they found employment in driving the hostile Indians from post to post in Ohio, Indiana, and Illinois, desolating their villages and plantations, and exciting the terrible wrath of the barbarians. The people were so eager to smite the British and their dusky allies that the campaign of 1813 opened at midwinter, and volunteers were more plentiful than were needed.

General Hull had been succeeded in the command of the Army of the North-west by General William H. Harrison (afterward President of the United States), and General Sir George Prevost became the successor of Brock in Canada. Harrison marched a crude and undisciplined army through a savage wilderness toward Detroit. They built roads and block-houses by the way, created magazines of provisions and defended them, and protected in a measure a frontier of several hundred miles in extent against the tomahawk and the scalping-knife of murderous savages. Harrison made the vicinity of the Maumee Rapids, toward the western end of Lake Erie, the place of general rendezvous.

General James Winchester, with eight hundred young Kentuckians, arrived at the Maumee Rapids in January, 1813. Informed that British and Indians were occupying the little settlement of Frenchtown (now Munroe, Mich.), on the river Raisin, he hastened thither to dislodge the intruders. His advanced detachment had driven them out of the hamlet on his arrival on the 20th. General Proctor, with a force of British and Indians (the latter commanded by Tecumtha), then occupied Malden, on the Detroit River. With fifteen hundred men of this motley army he surprised Winchester at dawn on the 22d, made him a prisoner, and slew many of his men. Winchester surrendered his troops to Proctor on the condition that they and the settlement should be protected against the fury of the barbarians. This promise was quickly violated. The sick and wounded Americans were left behind when the prisoners were marched away. The Indians soon turned back, murdered and scalped those who were unable to travel, and took the remainder to Detroit, twenty-five miles to the north, in order to procure exorbitant sums for their ransom. This perfidy and massacre created intense excitement in Kentucky, for the victims were of the flower of society in that State. After that the war-cry of the Kentuckians was, "Remember the river Raisin!"

Harrison advanced immediately to the Maumee Rapids, where, opposite the site of present Perrysburg, he built a strong earthwork, with bastions, and named it Fort Meigs. There he was besieged many weeks afterward by Proctor and Tecumtha and their respective followers. The assailants appeared before the fort at the close of April, and though the post was strong and the garrison had many great guns mounted, they were in imminent peril for a while. The fort was relieved by the arrival of forces under General Green Clay, of Kentucky, early in May, and the siege was abandoned. Active military operations in the West then ceased for a while.

At Lower Sandusky (now Fremont, Ohio) was a regular earth and stockaded military work named Fort Stephenson, garrisoned by one hundred and sixty men under the command of young Major George Croghan, then only twenty-one years of age. In July Proctor and Tecumtha, with four thousand followers, again appeared before Fort Meigs, but soon left it and pushed across the country to fall upon Fort Stephenson. They made a furious attack upon it, but Croghan and his men so skilfully and gallantly defended the post and made such havoc among the assailants that the latter fled in haste and great confusion to Detroit.

The control of Lake Erie was as important to both parties as was that of Lake Ontario, and to secure it the Americans and the British each hastened to create a fleet of war-vessels thereon. The British built at Malden, the Americans built at Presque Isle, now Erie, Pa.

Captain Oliver Hazard Perry,* a zealous young naval officer of Rhode Island, offered his services on the lakes. At the middle of January, 1813, he was ordered to report to Commodore Chauncey, and to take with him all the best men from a flotilla of gun-boats which he had commanded on Narraganset Bay. He sent them forward in three companies, fifty in each. Meeting Chauncey at Albany, they journeyed together through the dark wilderness to Sackett's Harbor in a sleigh. Perry soon proceeded to Presque Isle to superintend the construction and equipment of a navy in that sheltered harbor to co-operate with Harrison in an attempt to recover Michigan.

At Black Rock Henry Eckford had fashioned five merchant vessels into war-craft. These were sent to Presque Isle, where Perry had four vessels built. Early in July he had a squadron of nine vessels ready for men and supplies. These were delayed several weeks, while a British squadron under Commodore Barclay was proudly and defiantly patrolling the lake. Late in July Perry wrote to Chauncey: "Send me men and I will have them all [the British vessels] in a day or two. . . . Barclay has been bearding me for several days; I long to be at him."

OLIVER HAZARD PERRY.

At length Perry left the harbor, his vessels fully manned, and on September 10th the two squadrons met toward the western end of the lake and engaged in a fierce and sanguinary battle. The flag-ship *Lawrence*, bearing on a blue burgee the words of the dying hero in whose honor she had been named—"Don't give up the ship"—bore the brunt of conflict about two hours, when she lay upon the water an

---

* Oliver Hazard Perry was born at South Kingston, R. I., August 23d, 1785; died in Trinidad, W. I., of yellow fever, August 23d, 1819. He entered the navy as a midshipman in 1799, served in the Tripolitan War, and was called to the command of a fleet on Lake Erie in the summer of 1813, having first served with Chauncey on Lake Ontario. In a battle on Lake Erie on September 10th, 1813, with a British squadron he gained a signal victory. Perry assisted Harrison in retaking Detroit, late in 1813. In 1815 he commanded the *Java* in Decatur's squadron on the Mediterranean.

almost total wreck. The slaughter had been dreadful. The *Niagara*, a stanch vessel, was near and unhurt. To her Perry went in a boat, through a tempest of bullets and grape-shot. He hoisted his pennant over her, dashed through the British line, and in eight minutes afterward the colors of Barclay's flag-ship, the *Detroit*, were struck, and all but two vessels of his squadron were surrendered. Resting his naval cap on his knee, Perry wrote to Harrison, with a pencil on the back of a letter, his famous despatch :

"We have met the enemy and they are ours ; two ships, two brigs, one schooner, and one sloop."

The control of Lake Erie by the Americans was now secured. Harrison pushed forward toward Detroit. A part of his troops were taken across the lake on Perry's vessels. Proctor set fire to Malden, and fled into the interior of Canada with Tecumtha and his Indians.

Harrison crossed the river and pursued the fugitives. He overtook them at the Moravian Towns on the little river Thames, where a sharp battle was fought on October 5th, 1813. Tecumtha was killed, the British were defeated, and Proctor, with a few followers, escaped to the head of Lake Ontario. At this battle the Americans recaptured six brass field-pieces which had been surrendered by Hull, on two of which were engraved the words : "SURRENDERED BY BURGOYNE AT SARATOGA." These precious relics of the old war for independence are now at West Point, on the Hudson.

All the territory which Hull had lost was now recovered. The Indian Confederacy on the north-western border of the republic was broken up, and war in that region was ended.

During the summer of 1813 the United States were involved in war with the Indians in the region of the Gulf of Mexico. In the spring Tecumtha went among them to arouse them to wage war on the white people. The powerful Creeks yielded to his persuasions. Late in August a large party of them surprised and captured Fort Menis, on the Alabama River, and massacred about four hundred men, women, and children. This event aroused the whole South to vigorous retaliation, and General Andrew Jackson, afterward President of the United States, led twenty-five hundred Tennesseeans into the Creek country, where he waged a destructive subjugating war against them.

Early in November General Coffee, Jackson's second in command, with nine hundred men, surrounded an Indian force at Tallashatchee, and slew two hundred of them. Not a warrior escaped. Within ten weeks afterward bloody battles had been fought at Talladega (November 8th), Autosee (November 29th), and Emuckfaw (January 22d, 1814), and several skirmishes had taken place. The Tennesseeans were always victorious, yet they lost many brave soldiers. The Creeks finally established a fortified camp at the Great Horseshoe Bend of the Tallapoosa River, and there a thousand warriors, with their women and children, determined to make a last decisive stand. On March 27th, 1814, they were surrounded by Jackson's troops and attacked. The dusky warriors fought desperately, for they knew that there would be no future for their nation in case of a defeat. They disdained to surrender, and almost six hundred of them were slain. Only two or three were made prisoners, with about three hundred women and children. The result of the battle crushed the spirit and the power of the Creek nation. It was a sad picture for the eyes of good men to see one of the ancient tribes of our land, who were then making rapid strides in the progress of civilization, so ruthlessly and utterly ruined by the destructive hand of war.

CHAPTER XXIX.

EARLY in 1813 important military movements occurred at Ogdensburg and its vicinity. There were hostile incursions by both parties across the St. Lawrence. Major Forsythe, in command at Ogdensburg, had crossed over to Brockville early in February, released all the prisoners in jail there, and seized some troops and citizens, who were carried to his camp in triumph.

Retaliation soon ensued. Sir George Prevost, Governor-General of Canada, arrived at Prescott, opposite Ogdensburg, on his way to York, the capital of Upper Canada, and assented to a proposal for troops to cross the river on the ice and assail the American village. Considering his own person in danger of capture, Sir George hastened forward toward York, directing Lieutenant-Colonel McDonnell to conduct the attack.

At dawn on the morning of February 22d McDonnell appeared on the frozen river with about eight hundred soldiers, in two columns, and pushed on to the village at separate points. Forsythe, informed by spies of this intended assault, had prepared to receive the invaders; but he could not withstand them. It was a sort of surprise. Some of the inhabitants were in bed, others were at breakfast. They nearly all fled in consternation, and after a conflict of an hour in the streets, Forsythe and his troops retreated to Black Lake, eight or nine miles distant. The British became masters of the village. They plundered every house in the town excepting three, burned the barracks near the river and two gun-boats and two armed schooners frozen in the ice, and returned to Canada with a great amount of plunder. These events accelerated the gathering of militia on the northern frontier, especially at Sackett's Harbor.

General Dearborn, the commander-in-chief of the Northern Department, unable to afford assistance to the exposed points of the frontier of New York, resolved to invade Canada. He was then in direct command of the Army of the North, which was about six thousand strong, and were all within the State of New York. These were to defend the frontier from Buffalo to St. Regis. Dearborn determined to attempt the capture of Montreal, in Lower Canada, and York (now Toronto), the capital of the upper province. Chauncey, as we have seen, had

EXPEDITION AGAINST YORK (TORONTO).

gained the control of Lake Ontario, and believed he could keep the ice-bound British navy in the harbor of Kingston until the reduction of York.

Dearborn concentrated troops at Sackett's Harbor and Buffalo; but in March (1813) he found only three thousand troops at the former place. He directed General Brown to summon several hundred militia to the field, and called Brigadier-General Z. M. Pike to the harbor with four hundred of his best men, then at Plattsburg, on Lake Champlain. Henry Eckford was charged with the building of six war schooners at the harbor, and Chauncey was authorized to purchase as many vessels as the exigencies of the service might require.

At the middle of April a plan was matured for a land and naval force to cross the lake, capture York, and assail Fort George, near the mouth of the Niagara River. At the same time troops were to cross the river at Buffalo, capture Fort Erie and the redoubt at Chippewa, and meeting the force from York at Fort George, reduce that work, and then all press on to the capture of Kingston.

ZEBULON MONTGOMERY PIKE.

On April 25th (1813) seventeen hundred troops, under the immediate command of General Pike, sailed from Sackett's Harbor in Chauncey's fleet, and on the morning of the 27th appeared before York, then pretty strongly fortified. The land forces were disembarked about two miles west of the British outworks in the face of a destructive fire from regulars and Indians under General Sheaffe. The former were soon driven to their fortifications, and the Americans, led by Pike,* pressed forward and captured two redoubts. At the same time Chauncey was smiting the foe with a tempest of grapeshot from his naval cannons. The Indians, terrified by the roar of artil-

---

* Zebulon M. Pike was born at Lamberton, N. J., in January, 1779. He entered the army in his youth, and was made captain in 1806. In 1805 and 1806 he was engaged in searching for the sources of the Mississippi River, and exploring a portion of the vast territory of Louisiana. He was commissioned a major in 1808, and rose to brigadier-general in 1813. Early in that year he was appointed adjutant and inspector-general in the Northern Department. He lost his life in an attack upon York, April 27th, 1813.

lery, had deserted the British at the beginning, and fled as fast as their legs could carry them.

Sheaffe now took post with the garrison near the governor's house, and opened a heavy fire of round and grape-shot from a battery. This battery was soon silenced by Pike's heavy guns, and he was expecting a white-flag token of submission, when an awful catastrophe occurred. The British, unable to hold the fort, fired a magazine of gunpowder on the edge of the lake. The explosion which followed was terrible in its effects. Timbers and stones, of which the magazine was built, were scattered many hundred feet in every direction, carrying death and destruction. Fifty-two Americans and forty British soldiers were slain, and a much larger number were wounded.

General Pike at the time of the explosion was sitting on the stump of a tree talking with a captive British officer. The general, two of his aides, and the captive officer were mortally hurt by the flying missiles. The dying leader was taken on board Chauncey's flag-ship. His dulled ears heard the shouts of victory, and just before he died the captured British flag was brought to him. He smiled, and made a sign to have it placed under his head. It was done, and a moment afterward he expired.

Early in May the victorious Americans sailed from Sackett's Harbor to attack Fort George. The British had at that post and smaller works along the Niagara River about eighteen hundred men, commanded by General Vincent. The American troops landed and encamped five miles east of Fort Niagara, where they prepared for the task before them. On the morning of May 27th they were conveyed by Chauncey's squadron to the mouth of the Niagara on the Canada side.

Led by Colonel Winfield Scott and Commodore Perry, the latter in command of the boats, the invaders ascended the bank in the face of a shower of bullets and of glittering bayonets, and after a sharp conflict they pushed back the British. Vincent, discouraged, ordered the guns of Fort George to be spiked, the ammunition to be destroyed, and the garrison to join him in a retreat toward Burlington Bay, at the west end of Lake Ontario. The whole British force retreated first to a strong position in the hilly region of the Beaver Dams, where Vincent had a magazine of stores and provisions. Forts Erie and Chippewa were abandoned, and the Niagara frontier in Canada passed into the possession of the Americans.

Generals Chandler and Winder were sent in pursuit of Vincent. They encamped at Stony Creek on the night of June 6th, seven miles east of the British forces, where they were attacked by the latter at midnight. The darkness was intense ; surprised and confused in the gloom, the two American generals were made prisoners. Expecting a renewal of the attack, the Americans made a hasty retreat toward the Niagara, menaced on the way by a British squadron on the lake at their left, and by barbarians and local militia on the heights at their right. They reached Fort George in safety.

Sackett's Harbor was now the chief depot of the military and naval supplies of the Americans on Lake Ontario, and offered a tempting object to the enemy. When the British at Kingston heard of the departure of a large portion of Chauncey's squadron with the land troops from the harbor, they resolved to attempt the capture of that post.

On the evening of May 27th Sir James Lucas Yeo,* the commander of the British squadron, sailed from Kingston, and at about noon the next day appeared off Sackett's Harbor with six armed vessels and forty bateaux, bearing over a thousand land troops, the whole armament under the command of Sir George Prevost, the governor-general.

There were only a few regular troops at the harbor, commanded by Colonel Backus. General Brown, who was at his home a few miles distant, hastened to the threatened post. He sent expresses in all directions to summon the militia to the field, and fired alarm-guns to rouse the inhabitants. The militia on their arrival were sent to Horse Island, close by, where it was supposed the invaders would first attempt to land.

The British troops were embarked from the war-vessels in bateaux, but were soon ordered back, when the whole squadron put to sea. Sir George, who was a timid man, had been alarmed by the appearance of some American gun-boats bearing a regiment from Oswego to re-enforce the little garrison at the harbor. As soon as he perceived the real weakness of the approaching foe he returned, and on the morning of the 29th landed a considerable force, with artillery, upon Horse Island. The American militia were called from the island and placed behind a gravel-

---

* Sir James Lucas Yeo was born in Southampton, England, in 1782, and died in his native country in 1819. He was an active but very cautious officer. He was given to boasting and promising more than he could perform. Offended with Captain Porter, of the American ship *Essex*, because of the latter's disparaging remarks concerning the baronet, he sent, by a paroled prisoner, a message to Porter inviting him to a combat between their two ships, saying he " would be glad to have a *tête-à-tête* anywhere between the Capes of the Delaware and the Havana, when he would have pleasure to break his own [Captain Porter's] sword over his d—d head, and put him down forward in irons." Porter accepted the challenge in more decorous terms, but owing to the *extreme caution* of Sir James, the meeting never occurred. His conduct on Lake Ontario on two or three occasions was such that the wits of the day interpreted his cautious movements as specimens of " heart disease" known to cowards. He had been instructed to " risk nothing."

ridge on the main, from which they scampered at the first fire of the invaders. The indignant General Brown attempted to rally them while the regulars and a few Albany volunteers disputed the advance of the foe inch by inch. At that moment a dense smoke arose in the rear of the American forces. Brown was alarmed, but was soon relieved of anxiety when he learned that a friend and not a foe was the incendiary. When the militia fled the officer in charge of the public property at the harbor, believing the post would be taken, set fire to the store-houses and their contents, and a ship on the stocks.

General Brown sent some regulars to intercept the fugitive militia. These, with the gathering of others, deceived and alarmed Sir George. He had mounted a high stump and swept the horizon with his field-glass. Seeing numerous men, he supposed them to be re-enforcements of regulars in large numbers, and immediately ordered a retreat. That movement became a disorderly flight. The fugitives left their dead and wounded behind, fled pell-mell to their vessels, and the whole squadron hastily withdrew from the harbor. The post and the ship on the stocks were saved, but stores worth half a million dollars were lost. Sackett's Harbor was never again attacked, and it remained a chief place of deposit of supplies for the Northern Army during the remainder of the war.

General Vincent established an advanced post at the Beaver Dams under the command of Lieutenant Fitzgibbon. Late in June Colonel Bœrstler was sent from Fort George, with six hundred men, to capture the garrison and stores at the Beaver Dams. Informed of their approach, Fitzgibbon was prepared to receive them. Furiously assailed by Indians under John Brant, and alarmed by an exaggerated account of the number of the foe, Bœrstler surrendered his whole force, when the British pressed forward and menaced Queenstown and Fort George. The infirmities of General Dearborn now caused him to resign his command, and he was succeeded by General James Wilkinson, another officer of the old war for independence.

The attempts to seize Canada had been decided failures, and yet the Government seemed not to have learned wisdom by dear-bought experience. The Secretary of War was John Armstrong,[*] who had been a

---

[*] John Armstrong was born at Carlisle, Pa., in November, 1758, and died at Red Hook, N. Y., in April, 1843. He was a student at Princeton when the Revolutionary War broke out, joined a Pennsylvania regiment as a volunteer, and was on the staff of General Mercer. He was afterward on the staff of General Gates with the rank of major, and remained so until the end of the war. He wrote the famous "Newburg Addresses." He held important civil offices in Pennsylvania; conducted military operations

subaltern in the war for independence. He was possessed of a fiery and obstinate spirit. He and Wilkinson could not agree. There was another fiery spirit in the field in New York at that time—Wade Hampton, of South Carolina—the largest slaveholder in the republic, who had been a partisan officer with Marion. He was haughty and imperious, and could not brook official control. These old Revolutionary officers, jealous of each other, could not bear with complacency commands from one of their number who might be superior in official station. They were a decided disadvantage to the service from the beginning, and until they were succeeded by younger men the American armies were generally unsuccessful.

Made bold by their success at the Beaver Dams, the British became aggressive on the Niagara frontier. They closely invested Fort George. On the night of July 4th, 1813, a few Canadian militia and Indians crossed the river to Schlosser, and captured a guard, arms, ammunition, and stores. On the 11th Lieutenant-Colonel Bisshopp, with a motley force of four hundred regulars, Canadians, and Indians, crossed the river from Fort Erie and surprised the post at Black Rock, a little before dawn. His object was to seize the stores collected there and the shipyard. They were defended by a few militia. These, with others at Buffalo, two miles distant, were under the command of General Peter B. Porter. The militia at Black Rock fled. Porter rallied a portion of them, and with fifty volunteer citizens drove the invaders across the river. Bisshopp was mortally wounded in the flight, and died five days afterward.

JOHN ARMSTRONG.

Wilkinson prepared for another invasion of Canada, or to "strike a deadly blow somewhere." He left eight hundred troops at Fort George,

---

against settlers in the Wyoming Valley, in 1784; and declined the office of judge for the North-western Territory, in 1787. Two years later he married a sister of Chancellor Livingston, and purchasing a farm within the bounds of the Livingston Manor, devoted himself to agriculture. He was United States senator in 1800–1804, and succeeded his brother-in-law, Livingston, as minister at the French Court. In 1812 he was commissioned a brigadier-general, and entered Madison's cabinet the next year as Secretary of War, resigning in 1814. He never entered public life afterward.

under Colonel Winfield Scott, and with the remainder of the forces on the Niagara frontier he sailed eastward to undertake an expedition against Montreal. He instructed Scott, in case the British should leave that frontier, to join his expedition on the St. Lawrence. This contingency soon occurred. When Vincent heard of the defeat of Proctor on the Thames, he called his troops from the Niagara to Burlington Heights. Meanwhile the Secretary of War (Armstrong) had come on to reconcile differences between Wilkinson and Hampton, and to assume the conduct of the invading expedition. Armstrong established the seat of the War Department at Sackett's Harbor.

JAMES WILKINSON.

When Wilkinson * took command of the Army of the North in the summer of 1813, military affairs on Lake Champlain and in its vicinity were in a peculiar position. Captain Thomas Macdonough had been charged with the construction of a fleet on the lake in the spring. At the beginning of June he had two stanch armed vessels—*Eagle* and *Growler*—ready for service. They were sent to the foot of the lake to look after some British gun-boats that were depredating there. They ran far into the Sorel, when, turning southward, they were chased by British armed vessels and assailed by land troops on each side of the narrow river. The *Eagle* was sunk by a heavy round-shot, and the *Growler* was captured.

---

* James Wilkinson was born in Maryland in 1757, and died near the city of Mexico in December, 1825. He joined the Continental Army at Cambridge in 1775, and was an active subaltern officer during the whole war. At its close he engaged in mercantile business in Lexington, Ky. He was lieutenant-colonel in an expedition against the Indians in 1791, and was made brigadier-general the next year. He commanded the right wing of Wayne's army on the Maumee in 1794, and was general-in-chief of the United States Army from 1796 to 1798 and from 1800 to 1812. He was one of the commissioners to receive Louisiana from the French late in 1803, and was governor of that territory from 1805 to 1807. Wilkinson became entangled with Burr. Made major-general in 1813, he was ordered to the command on the northern frontier. His campaign against Montreal was a failure, chiefly because of the conduct of Wade Hampton. He left the army at the close of the war. Having become possessed of large estates in Mexico, he removed to that country, and died there.

Early in August Macdonough had three armed schooners and six gun-boats ready for service, fitted and manned. At about the same time Plattsburg, on the west side of the lake, left uncovered by any military force, had been seized, plundered, and scorched by a British land and naval force, fourteen hundred strong, under Colonel Murray, while General Hampton, the commander of that region, lying at Burlington, twenty miles distant, with four thousand troops, had made no attempt to oppose the invaders.

In the mean time Chauncey had been busy on Lake Ontario. He sought a conflict with Sir James Yeo, but the latter evaded him for weeks, for he had been instructed to "risk nothing." The saved ship at the harbor had been completed and named the *General Pike*. Chauncey made her his flag-ship. He had twelve other vessels, mostly merchantmen altered into war-craft. Sir James had six vessels built at Kingston expressly for war.

One night in July the belligerents were about to engage in an encounter when a sudden tornado capsized two of Chauncey's vessels, and all on board perished excepting sixteen men. Finally, at the middle of September, Chauncey compelled the baronet to fight. The *Pike* fought the heavier vessels of the foe. The conflict was quick, sharp, and decisive. The *Wolfe*, Yeo's flag-ship, too much bruised to fight any longer, hurried away before the wind, covered by the *Royal George*. Chauncey pursued to Burlington Bay, but the equinoctial gale made it prudent for him to return to Niagara. He did little more during the season than to watch the enemy and assist the expedition on the St. Lawrence.

Armstrong directed Wilkinson to command the expedition against Montreal, and ordered Hampton, who was in command of the right wing of the army, to co-operate with the forces on the St. Lawrence. Hampton moved forward from Plattsburgh at about the middle of September with four thousand effective infantry, a squadron of cavalry, and a train of artillery, and on the 24th encamped on the Chateaugay River near the site of the present village of Chateaugay, where he awaited orders.

At the middle of October the troops destined for Montreal sailed from Sackett's Harbor in a flotilla of open boats, and at the same time Hampton was ordered to push on to the St. Lawrence, at the mouth of the Chateaugay. The flotilla was dreadfully smitten by a gale on the lake, and was dispersed. Much property was lost. The scattered troops rendezvoused at Grenadier Island, excepting a detachment under General Brown, which pushed on to French Creek, now Clayton, on the St.

Lawrence, where, on November 1st, they had a sharp but successful encounter with British infantry on gun-boats and schooners.

The whole expedition was concentrated at French Creek in the first week in November. On the 5th the whole armament moved down the river in three hundred open boats. A Canadian winter was just at hand. Snow had already fallen, and the cold was becoming severe. Their flags were furled and their music was silent, for they wished to elude the vigilance of the British; but they were discovered and pursued by troops in a heavy-armed galley and some gun-boats through the sinuous channels of the Thousand Islands. They had a battle by moonlight in Alexandria Bay.

Land troops from Kingston arrived at Prescott before Wilkinson could reach Ogdensburg, on the opposite shore. He disembarked above that village, marched around it to avoid the artillery on the Canada shore, and at a point a few miles below re-entered the boats, which had been safely taken past the batteries by General Brown. On November 10th the flotilla lay anchored a short distance above the head of the Long Rapids.

Meanwhile British troops under Lieutenant-Colonel Morrison, in boats and on shore, had pursued the flotilla, and some of them were posted at the foot of the rapids to intercept the Americans when they should come down. Many of the latter, under Generals Brown and Boyd,* were on the Canada shore. Brown pushed forward with a detachment to dislodge the British at the foot of the rapids, and on the 11th Boyd met the enemy face to face, who were in battle array on the farm of John Chrysler, a few miles below Williamsburg, in Canada. A severe battle was fought in sleet and snow. Boyd was ably supported by Generals Swartwout and Covington, and Colonels Coles, Ripley, and Swift. The Americans were driven from the field with considerable loss. General Covington was mortally wounded. Under cover of night the little American force withdrew to the flotilla, which descended the Long Rapids with safety the next morning.

General Wilkinson was then very ill. Word came that General

---

* John Parker Boyd was born at Newburyport, Mass., in December, 1768, and died in Boston in October, 1830. He entered the military service and soon afterward went to the East Indies, where he entered the Mahratta service and soon rose to the rank of commander, leading, at one time, 10,000 men. He served for some time, when, his presence being no longer needed, he sold out and went to Paris. He returned home in 1808 and re-entered the United States Army as colonel. He was distinguished in the battle of Tippecanoe. In 1812 he was commissioned a brigadier-general, and commanded an important part of Wilkinson's expedition down the St. Lawrence in 1813. General Boyd was made naval officer at Boston in 1830, but died soon afterward.

Hampton could not form the ordered junction with the expedition, but would return to Lake Champlain. He would not serve under Wilkinson. The expedition did not proceed farther, but went into winter quarters at French Mills, on the Salmon River. So ended in disaster another attempt to invade and conquer Canada.

Distressing events closed the campaign of the Northern Army on the Niagara frontier. Early in December General McClure, regarding Fort George as untenable with his little garrison of forty men, abandoned it and crossed over to Fort Niagara. Before leaving Canada he set fire to the beautiful village of Newark. One hundred and fifty houses were destroyed (December 10th), and scores of men, women, and children were turned into the keen wintry air, homeless wanderers. This savage act created the most fiery indignation, and fierce retaliation followed The British captured Fort Niagara and massacred a part of the garrison. The Indians were given full liberty to plunder and destroy. Every village and hamlet on the New York side of the river was sacked and burnt. Black Rock and Buffalo, though defended by some troops, did not escape. The latter village contained about eighteen hundred inhabitants. All but four of its buildings were laid in ashes. An immense amount of public and private property was destroyed. With these events the campaign of 1813 in the north was closed. We have already considered the war with the Indians in the region of the Gulf of Mexico.

The naval operations on the ocean during 1813 were very important. As these were not specially connected with the history of the State of New York, it is our province only to notice them very briefly.

The United States sloop-of-war *Hornet*, Captain Lawrence, fought the British brig *Peacock* (February 24th, 1813) off the mouth of the Demarara River, South America. The *Peacock* surrendered after a sharp contest of fifteen minutes, and immediately sunk, carrying down with her nine British seamen and three Americans. The generous conduct of Lawrence on that occasion drew from the survivors of the *Peacock* a letter of thanks after their arrival, as prisoners, at New York.

Lawrence was promoted to the command of the American frigate *Chesapeake*. On June 1st he sailed from Boston to respond to a challenge by the commander of the frigate *Shannon*, Captain Broke. He found the boaster on the same day thirty miles from Boston Light. At five o'clock in the afternoon a furious struggle began. The vessels became entangled. The Britons boarded the *Chesapeake*, and after a desperate hand-to-hand combat the Americans were overpowered and the British flag was hoisted over the dreadfully injured vessel. Early in the conflict a musket-ball mortally wounded the gallant young Lawrence. As he was being taken to the cockpit he said: "Tell the men to fire faster and *not to give up the ship.* Fight her till she sinks!" These dying words of Lawrence—" Don't give up the ship!' "—became a battle cry of the Americans. The loss of men on the *Chesapeake* was fearful. She was taken to Halifax. Lawrence died on the way. Public honors were awarded him. His monument stands in Trinity church-yard, New York City.

In the spring of 1813 the American brig *Argus*, Captain Allen, carried Mr. Crawford to France as the accredited American Minister at the French court. For two months after her arrival in Europe she greatly annoyed the British shipping in the English Channel. Several vessels were sent out to capture her. At the middle of August she surrendered to the *Pelican*, sloop-of-war. Perry gained his great victory on Lake Erie less than a month afterward, and on September 5th the British brig *Boxer*, Captain Blythe, surrendered to the American brig *Enterprise*, Lieutenant Burrows, after a contest of forty minutes, off the coast of Maine. Both commanders were slain, and their bodies were buried in one grave at Portland. During the year 1813 the American frigate *Essex*, Captain Porter, made a long and successful cruise in the Atlantic and Pacific oceans. She carried at her masthead the popular motto: "Free Trade and Sailors' Rights." In the spring of 1814 she was captured in the harbor of Valparaiso by the British frigate *Phœbe* and the sloop-of-war *Cherub*, after a most desperate struggle. Porter wrote to the Secretary of War: "We have been unfortunate, but not disgraced."

While Porter was performing great exploits on the calm Pacific Sea, Commodore Rodgers was out on a long cruise on the stormy Atlantic in the American frigate *President*. He sailed from Boston at the close of April, 1813, and returned to Newport, R. I., after a cruise of one hundred and forty-eight days. He had captured eleven British merchant vessels and the armed British schooner *Highflyer*.

During the spring and summer of 1813 a most distressing amphibious warfare was carried on along the coast of the United States from Delaware Bay to the harbor of Charleston by a British squadron commanded by Admiral Cockburn, which bore some land troops. This force destroyed American shipping in Delaware River, cannonaded the town of Lewiston on the shores of Delaware Bay, and plundered and burnt the villages of Frenchtown, Havre de Grace, Georgetown, and Frederickton, on the shores of Chesapeake Bay. It sailed into Hampton Roads and menaced Norfolk. Driven off by troops on Craney Island, in the Elizabeth River, under Major Faulkner (June 22d), the squadron made a marauding voyage down the coast of North Carolina, and carried away a great many negroes, whom Cockburn sold as booty in the West Indies. In pleasant contrast with the conduct of Cockburn was the deportment of Commodore Hardy, who commanded a blockading squadron on the New England coasts during the same season. He was a high-minded gentleman and a generous enemy.

During most of the year 1813 the Americans had only three frigates afloat on the sea—namely, the *President*, the *Congress*, and the *Essex*. The *Constitution* was undergoing repairs, the *Constellation* was blockaded during the summer at Norfolk, and the *Macedonia* and *United States* were blockaded in the harbor of New London. The *Adams* was undergoing repairs, the *John Adams* was unfit for service, and the *New York* and *Boston* were virtually condemned. All the brigs had been captured excepting the *Enterprise;* and yet the Americans, with indomitable courage, determined to continue the war on the ocean, with vigor.

CHAPTER XXX.

EARLY in the year 1814 the British Government seemed disposed to prosecute the war against the United States with increased vigor. The allied forces of Europe had checked the victorious career of Napoleon. They had united to crush him and to sustain the sinking Bourbon dynasty in France. Their armies, approaching from different directions, reached the suburbs of Paris at the close of March, when the emperors of Russia and Prussia entered the city. Nearly half a million disciplined troops were back of them. Napoleon, hoping to secure his crown for his son, abdicated in his favor (April 4th, 1814), and retired to the island of Elba. Peace for Europe appeared to be secured. British troops were withdrawn from the Continent, and early in the summer of 1814 fourteen or fifteen thousand of Wellington's veterans were sent to Canada to defend that province or to invade the State of New York.

At the beginning of 1814 British war vessels swarmed in American waters, and kept the seaport towns in such a state of continual alarm that all projects for the conquest of Canada were kept in abeyance for a while. They were not abandoned, however.

At this time the people of the United States were more united in support of the war than ever before. The best men of the Federal Party patriotically aided the Government in its struggle. There were but few opponents of the Government outside of the unpatriotic Peace Faction and the sphere of its influence. The bulk of that faction was in New England. They did everything in their power to embarrass the Government, especially in its financial operations. They upheld violators of the revenue laws; encouraged smuggling; secretly furnished the British blockading squadron off the New England coasts with supplies, and rejoiced when disasters befell the arms of the United States. At length their mischievous disloyalty and treason became so conspicuous and obnoxious that the great bulk of the inhabitants of New England vehemently condemned their course, and they gradually disappeared from public view. To the credit of the State of New York, very few members of the Peace Faction resided within its borders.

In February (1814) General Wilkinson with a part of his force removed from the vicinity of the St. Lawrence to Plattsburgh, on Lake Champlain, and General Brown, with two thousand men, marched to

Sackett's Harbor, preparatory to his departure for the Niagara frontier. Late in March Wilkinson erected a battery at Rouse's Point, at the foot of Lake Champlain, on the Canada border. He had resolved to march on Montreal, with or without orders from Washington. Informed that a considerable British force was about to be gathered at La Colle Mills, three or four miles within the Canada line, he pressed forward with about four thousand men to preoccupy the place. The British arrived there first, and were garrisoned in a very strong stone mill. They were regulars under Major Hancock. Although Wilkinson was informed that re-enforcements for Hancock were approaching and were near, he persisted in making an effort to dislodge the troops in the mill and in a strong position near it. After a sharp engagement for two hours the Americans were repulsed, with a loss of sixty-three men. With this event the military career of Wilkinson was ended. He was tried by a court-martial, but was acquitted. Suspended from command at the time, he left the army and his troops were assigned to General Izard.

Both parties had been preparing during the winter and spring to make a struggle for the mastery of Lake Ontario. As soon as the ice in Kingston Harbor gave way, Sir James Yeo, in command of a British squadron there, went out upon the lake with about three thousand fighting men. On May 5th he appeared off Oswego with the design to attempt the seizure of a large quantity of provisions and naval stores which the Americans had gathered at the falls of the Oswego River, at the (present) village of Fulton. The post was defended by a fort on the bluff at the east side of the harbor and garrisoned by three hundred men commanded by Colonel Mitchell, and a small flotilla under Captain Woolsey. Commodore Chauncey was not quite ready to leave Sackett's Harbor. The British effected a landing at Oswego, and after a sharp skirmish with the little garrison, in the open field, the latter retired, and the invaders took possession of the fort. But they dared not attempt to penetrate the country in quest of the coveted prize, but hastily withdrew early on the morning of the 7th, carrying away as prisoners several prominent citizens. The British lost in the contest two hundred and thirty-five men.

The principal military force of the British in Upper Canada was now placed under the command of Lieutenant-General Drummond, and were stationed chiefly on the peninsula west of the Niagara River. Toward that frontier General Brown marched from Sackett's Harbor at the close of June, and on July 1st he was on the eastern bank of the Niagara near the desolated town of Buffalo.

Brown had orders from Washington to invade Canada. He regarded his force sufficient for that achievement. It consisted of two brigades of infantry, commanded respectively by Generals Scott * and Ripley; some artillery under Captains Towson and Hindman, and a small squadron of cavalry led by Captain S. D. Harris. These were all regulars. He also had a brigade of New York and Pennsylvania volunteers, and nearly six hundred Indians. The latter comprised almost all of the military force of the Six Nations remaining within the State of New York, of whom Red Jacket † was the chief. This combined force was commanded by General Peter B. Porter.

WINFIELD SCOTT, 1820.

The Americans made the first aggressive movement on July 3d, when Generals Scott and Ripley crossed the Niagara River to attack Fort Erie, nearly opposite Buffalo, which was then the chief impediment in the way of an invasion of Canada. Scott led several regiments and a corps of artillery to the Canada shore, in boats, before the dawn on the 3d. He was followed by General Brown and his staff. It was a late hour before the more tardy Ripley joined them with several regiments,

---

* Winfield Scott was born in Petersburg, Va., in June, 1786, and died at West Point, N. Y., in May, 1866. He was admitted to the bar in 1806, but entered the army as captain of artillery two years later. He became lieutenant-colonel in 1812, and adjutant-general, with the rank of colonel, early in 1813. He was made prisoner at the battle of Queenstown. In the spring of 1814 he was commissioned a brigadier-general, and fought battles on the Niagara frontier for which he received the thanks of Congress and a gold medal. After the war he was sent to Europe in a military and diplomatic capacity. He remained in the army. His services in the South—in Charleston during the nullification movements, in the war with the Seminoles and Creeks, and in the partial removal of the Cherokees from Georgia in 1838—were very salutary. He was a discreet pacifier of trouble on the northern frontier in 1839, and on the borders of New Brunswick. He performed admirable service in the war with Mexico. When the Civil War broke out, in 1861, he was general-in-chief of the armies of the United States, but being infirm he soon resigned his trust. In 1852 he was an unsuccessful candidate for the Presidency of the United States.

† Red Jacket (*Sa-go-ye-wat-ha*) was a celebrated Seneca orator. He was born near Buffalo, N. Y., in 1751. His nation was on the side of the British during the old war for independence. He was conspicuous for his oratory at a council held at Fort Stanwix (Schuyler) in 1784, in a speech against ceding lands to the white people. In an interview with President Washington he received from the latter a silver medal, which he ever

when the combined troops invested the fort. Brown demanded its surrender. There was a parley, but little fighting, and in the afternoon the fort was given up. At six o'clock the little garrison, commanded by Major Buck, marched out and laid down their arms. They were sent across the river and marched to the Hudson, prisoners of war. During the forenoon cannons had been fired from the fort, which killed four Americans and wounded two or three. The Americans had driven in the British pickets and killed one man. This was all the blood shed in the capture of Fort Erie.

Measures were promptly take to secure the advantages of th victory to the Americans. General Riall, an able soldier and chief commander of the British under Drummond on that frontier, was marching toward Fort Erie when he heard of the investment of that post. He at once sent forward some veterans to re-enforce the garrison. At Chippewa they heard of the capture of the fort, when Riall resolved to press forward and attack the invaders at once. Informed that re-enforcements were coming to him from York, he postponed the attack until the next morning. General Brown sent General Scott with his brigade, accompanied by Towson's artillery, to meet this force. Scott moved early on the morning of the 4th (July, 1814). General Ripley was ordered in the same direction, but always tardy and slow to obey, it was late in the afternoon before he was prepared to move. Scott pushed on toward Chippewa, and drove in a British ad-

RED JACKET.

afterward wore with pride. It is in possession of Colonel Parker, now (1887) chief of the remnant of the nation. In 1810 he informed the United States Government of the attempt of Tecumtha to draw the Senecas into the North-western Confederacy. He fought for the United States in the War of 1812-15. Red Jacket was a persistent opposer of Christian missionaries. His influence over the remnant of his nation was supreme. He remained a thorough Indian, and held in contempt the language, dress, and customs of the English-speaking people. Late in life he became an intemperate man. In 1884 a beautiful monument to his memory was erected in a cemetery at Buffalo (where he died in January, 1830), under the auspices of the Buffalo Historical Society. Colonel William L. Stone wrote and published a life of Red Jacket.

vanced detachment about a mile from that post. There he was joined at evening by Brown's entire force, and on the morning of the 5th the hostile armies were only two miles apart.

Scott was joined by General Porter, with his volunteers and Indians, at noon on the 5th. Riall had been re-enforced. There was skirmishing during the afternoon. Toward evening Riall advanced with his whole force. A desperate battle ensued between Street's Creek and Chippewa. It was very sanguinary. At length the British line gave way under the pressure of a flank movement by Major McNeil and a terrific fire from a corps under Major Jesup. The foe broke and fled to the intrenchments at Chippewa, tearing up the bridge over Chippewa Creek behind them, and so leaving an impassable barrier between themselves and the victorious Americans. The battle-field was strewn with the dead and wounded—six hundred and four of the British, and three hundred and fifty-five of the Americans. A shower of rain descended like an angel of mercy that night, and gave comfort to the maimed and dying of both armies, who were tenderly cared for. Much of the next and following day were spent by the Americans caring for the wounded and in burying the dead.

Drummond was mortified by this discomfiture of his veteran troops by what he deemed to be raw Americans, and he resolved to wipe out the stain. He gathered troops from every available point, in number about one third larger than that under Brown, and soon advanced to meet the invader.

Brown was anxious to push on toward the mouth of the Niagara, where he expected Chauncey would co-operate with him. He crossed the Chippewa Creek in boats with a part of his army before daylight on the morning of the 8th, when Riall fled to Queenstown, put some of his troops into Forts George and Mississaugua, and established his headquarters near the lake, twenty miles westward. Brown pushed on to Queenstown and menaced Fort George. After waiting many days he learned that Chauncey was sick and his squadron was blockaded at Sackett's Harbor. Hopeless of aid from the navy, he ordered the army to fall back to the battle-ground of Chippewa and await developments. They did not rest long, for on the morning of the 24th Brown was startled by the intelligence that Drummond had landed with a thousand troops at Lewiston, many of them Wellington's veterans; that a British force occupied Queenstown, and that Riall had joined the lieutenant-general with his own troops and a body of loyal Canadians.

Brown now ordered Scott to march rapidly with a part of the army and menace the forts at the mouth of the Niagara. He pushed forward toward evening with his brigade, Towson's artillery, and some mounted men, and near the verge of the great cataract he saw some British officers come out of a house, leap into their saddles, and ride swiftly away. He dashed into the woods, expecting to find a small detachment of the British army, but soon discovered that Riall was there with a force larger than he led at Chippewa. Scott measured the peril of his situation instantly. To stand still would be fatal, and to retreat might demoralize the army he had just left; so he resolved to fight with great odds against him.

A desperate battle began at sunset, and did not cease until almost midnight. The British line encountered by Scott, eighteen hundred strong, was on a hill over which passed a high ay known as Lundy's Lane. Near its crest the British had a fine battery of brass cannon, which inflicted fearful havoc in the ranks of the Americans. While Scott was hotly engaged with Riall, Major Jesup secretly led a small force in the gloom to the rear of the British and kept back re-enforcements sent by Drummond. Meanwhile General Brown, apprised of the situation by the booming of cannons and from messengers, pushed forward with his whole army. Perceiving the battery on the hill to be the key to the enemy's position, he turned to Colonel James Miller and asked:

"Can you storm that work and take it?"

"I'll try!" said Miller.

The battery was soon taken, and the exploit led to victory. Miller was promoted to brigadier-general.

Scott, fighting gallantly, was severely wounded in his shoulder by a musket-ball. Brown, too, was badly wounded, and the command devolved upon the inefficient Ripley. The British had already been driven from the field, notwithstanding Drummond had brought them a re-enforcement of fifteen hundred men. The Americans retired to Chippewa, a short distance off, but could not take the captured battery with them. Brown ordered Ripley to return after a brief rest and take possession of the battle-field and the battery before daylight. That always tardy and disobedient officer hesitated to obey. The British returned, retook the battery, and held the field, while Ripley led the little American army back to Fort Erie, and deprived them of all the advantages they had gained at this battle of Lundy's Lane. He was immediately superseded by General E. P. Gaines. Both parties claimed the victory.*

Drummond was wounded in the battle. As soon as he was able he

---

* The British had about four thousand five hundred troops in this battle, and the Americans two thousand six hundred. The latter lost about one third of their number, and the British lost a few more. The conflict is sometimes called the battle of Bridgewater, from a hamlet near by, and also the battle of Niagara, it having been fought in sight of the great cataract.

pushed forward and besieged Fort Erie with about five thousand men. From the 7th to the 14th of August (1814) almost continuous cannonading between the besiegers and the besieged was kept up. At evening twilight on the 14th a shell hurled from a British mortar came screaming into the fort, lodged in an almost empty magazine, and blew it up. Drummond, supposing he had fired one of the principal magazines of the fort, proceeded to assail the works in strong force. Before dawn on the 15th fifteen hundred of his men furiously attacked the fort. They gained a bastion, but were repulsed at all other points. They held the bastion with tenacity. The Americans mined it and blew it up. The explosion was terrific. Mingled earth, timbers, stones, and human bodies rose one hundred feet in the air and spread a shower of ruins to a great distance. The British, amazed, soon afterward broke and fled, and victory remained with the Americans.

Both parties prepared to renew the struggle. General Brown had recovered, and was again in command of his army. Drummond's force again invested Fort Erie, but, occupying low ground, many died of typhoid fever.

On September 17th a sortie was made from the fort, and after a severe contest the Americans captured the advanced works of the enemy. The British were driven back to Chippewa, with a loss of almost a thousand men, killed, wounded, and prisoners. "Thus," wrote General Brown to the Secretary of War, "one thousand regulars and an equal proportion of militia destroyed the fruits of fifty days' labor, and diminished his [Drummond's] effective force one thousand men."

GENERAL IZARD.

This victory, won by the Americans so soon after those achieved at Chippewa and Lundy's Lane, and occurring a few days after a triumph of their arms at Plattsburgh, on Lake Champlain, and the expulsion of the British from Baltimore, diffused great joy throughout the country, and dispelled the gloom which the recent capture of the national capital by the enemy had spread over the land.

General Izard,* the successor of General Wilkinson, led about five

---

* George Izard was a native of South Carolina, where he was born in 1777, and died at Little Rock, Ark., in November, 1828. He was educated in England, and soon after

thousand troops to the Niagara frontier in October, and, ranking Brown, took the chief command. The combined forces, numbering about eight thousand men, were preparing to attack Drummond, when he withdrew to Fort George and Burlington Heights. Perceiving that further offensive operations on the Canadian peninsula would be perhaps perilous, Izard caused Fort Erie to be abandoned and blown up early in November, and, leaving Canada, he crossed the Niagara and put the troops into winter quarters at Buffalo, Black Rock, and Batavia.

There were stirring scenes on Lake Champlain early in September, 1814. When, in August, Izard marched westward he left about fifteen hundred regulars near Plattsburgh under the command of General Alexander Macomb. General Benjamin Mooers * was at the head of the militia force in that region.

During the summer the Americans and the British had been busy in the preparation of vessels of war on Lake Champlain. The American squadron was placed in charge of Captain Thomas Macdonough

BENJAMIN MOOERS.

and was ready for service at the middle of August. At the beginning of September Macomb was in command of about three thousand four hundred armed men all told. With great exertions he had completed redoubts and block-houses there and other preparations for defence. He also took measures to prevent expected invaders from Canada crossing the Saranac River. He had learned that fifteen thousand of Wellington's

---

his return he entered the army (1794) as a lieutenant of artillery. In 1799 he was appointed aide to General Hamilton, and resigned his office in 1803. He was appointed colonel of artillery in the spring of 1812, and brigadier-general a year later. On Lake Champlain and on the Niagara frontier, he commanded with skill and prudence, with the rank of major-general. In 1825 he was appointed governor of the Arkansas Territory, and so remained until his death.

* Benjamin Mooers, born in Massachusetts in 1761, was a young soldier in the old war for independence. He was chosen commander of one of the two great divisions of the militia of the State of New York in 1812, but did not appear active on the field until the invasion of the Champlain region by the British in 1814, when he was in command of the militia who defended Plattsburgh. In that position he did his duty nobly. He died at his residence on Cumberland Head, in February, 1838.

veterans were at Montreal, under the command of Sir George Prevost, the Governor-General of Canada, who was preparing to invade the State of New York.

At the beginning of September Prevost,* with fourteen thousand men, chiefly Wellington's soldiers, penetrated the country from the St. Lawrence to a point a few miles from Plattsburgh. He avowed his intention to seize and hold Northern New York as far south as Ticonderoga, and by proclamation called on the inhabitants to cast off their allegiance to their government and to furnish him with supplies. At the same time the British squadron, built on the Sorel, moved into Lake Champlain, under the general command of Commodore Downie.

On the morning of September 6th Prevost advanced upon Plattsburgh in two columns. One of these encountered and had a severe skirmish with a small force of regulars and militia under Captain Wool, the hero of Queenstown.

STONE MILL AT PLATTSBURGH.

The Americans were pressed back by overwhelming numbers, and retired to the south side of the Saranac, tearing up the bridges behind them and using the timbers for breastworks. In trying to force their way across the Saranac the British were repulsed by a company of musketeers in a strong stone mill. Prevost soon learned that his invasion was not to be a pleasant holiday excursion, and he paused for the coming up of batteries and supplies, and for the construction of works to command those of the Americans on the south side of the river.

Meanwhile the British naval force had appeared off Cumberland Head, at the entrance to Plattsburgh Bay, in which lay the squadron of Mac-

---

* Sir George Prevost was born in New York in 1767, and died in England in 1816. He entered the British Army in his youth, and served with distinction in the West Indies late in the last century. In 1805 he was commissioned a major-general, and the same year was created a baronet. He was second in command at the capture of Martinique in 1808, and became Governor of Nova Scotia the same year. He was made lieutenant-general in 1811, and the same year was appointed Governor-General of Canada. He retained that office until his return to England, in 1814.

donough.* His flag-ship was the *Saratoga*, which was assisted by one brig, two schooners, and ten gun-boats, or galleys. Downie's flag-ship was the *Confiance*, which was assisted by one brig, two sloops, and twelve gun-boats. The British land and naval forces began an attack at about the same time on the morning of the 11th. The battle was opened by the navy. Macdonough was only thirty-one years of age, pious, and trustful in Providence. When his ship was cleared for action he knelt on her deck, with his chief officers around him, and implored the aid of the Almighty. Very soon the thunders of great guns boomed over the lake, and a sharp naval battle, which lasted nearly two hours and a half, began.† The sublime spectacle was seen by hundreds of spectators on the headlands of the Vermont shore of the narrow lake. The battle ended in a complete victory for the Americans. Both squadrons were dreadfully shattered. "There was not a mast in either squadron," Macdonough wrote, "that could stand to make a sail

THOMAS MACDONOUGH.

* Thomas Macdonough was born in Delaware in December, 1783, and died at sea, November 14th, 1825. He was of Scotch-Irish descent. He became a midshipman in the United States Navy in 1800, lieutenant in 1807, and commander in 1813. He had served with Decatur and Bainbridge in the Mediterranean, and won a signal victory in a naval battle off Plattsburgh on September 11th, 1814, for which service he received the thanks of Congress and a gold medal, and other rewards. Civil honors were bestowed upon him in several places. His health declined from the close of the war, and he lived but ten years afterward.

† At the beginning of the battle a shot from a British vessel demolished a hen-coop on the *Saratoga*, where a young game-cock which the sailors had brought from the shore, released from confinement and startled by the sound of cannons, flew up on a gun-slide, and flapping his wings, crowed lustily and defiantly. The sailors regarded the incident as an omen of victory, and felt their courage strengthened. In a rhyming *Epistle of Brother Jonathan to Johnny Bull*, written at the close of the war, is the following allusion to this event:

> "O, Johnny Bull, my Joe, John,
> Behold on Lake Champlain,
> With more than equal force, John,
> You tried your fist again;
> But the cock saw how 'twas going, John,
> And cried 'cock-a-doodle-doo,'
> And Macdonough was victorious, John
> O, Johnny Bull, my Joe."

on." "Our masts, yards, and sails," wrote an officer of the *Confiance*, "were so shattered that one looked like so many bundles of matches, and the other like so many bundles of rags." The Americans lost one hundred and ten men, the British over two hundred. Among the latter was Commodore Downie, who was slain, and was buried at Plattsburgh.

There was a sharp and decisive conflict on the land at Plattsburgh while the battle was raging on the water. At the discharge of the first gun on the lake the British troops moved forward in three columns to force their way across the Saranac at the sites of the two destroyed bridges and at a ford three miles from the mouth of the river, to carry the American works by storm. After a desperate battle for about two hours, with varying fortunes for both sides, the British were repulsed by the brave men under Macomb* and Mooers. The Americans were driving back some of the enemy who had forced their way across the river, when Hiram Walworth (afterward Chancellor of the State of New York) dashed up, his horse flecked with foam, and announced that the British squadron on the lake had surrendered ! The Americans gave hearty cheers. The enemy wavered. The timid Prevost, seeing the militia, who had come streaming over from Vermont and from the surrounding country, gathering on his flanks and rear, sounded a retreat. At midnight he fled Canadaward with such precipitation that he left his sick

ALEXANDER MACOMB.

* Alexander Macomb was son of a fur merchant, and was born in Detroit in April, 1782. Died in Washington, D. C., in June, 1841. He entered the army as cornet of cavalry in 1799. At the beginning of the second war for independence (1812-15), he was a lieutenant of engineers and adjutant-general of the army. In the artillery service, he distinguished himself on the Niagara frontier. He was promoted to brigadier-general early in 1814, and was left in chief command in the Lake Champlain region in the summer of that year. His victory over the British at Plattsburgh in September won for him great honors—the thanks of Congress and a gold medal, and awards from others. On the death of General Brown, in 1835, he was made general-in-chief of the armies of the United States, which position he held at the time of his death. His remains repose beneath a handsome monument in the Congressional burying ground at Washington.

and wounded and a vast amount of stores behind. A pursuit was begun, but heavy rains compelled the pursuers to give up the chase. The British had lost in killed, wounded, and deserted, from the 6th to the 11th of September, about twenty-five hundred men. Macomb and Macdonough became the recipients of high honors and of solid rewards.

The flight of Prevost to Canada ended military operations of importance on the northern frontier of New York.* The active and efficient Chauncey had been compelled to remain inactive during a large portion of the season. He was blockaded at Sackett's Harbor by a British squadron, and when he was ready to go o. and fight the blockaders he was prostrated by severe sickness. While convalescing he went out on a cruise and blockaded the British squadron in Kingston Harbor. A

---

* The victory at Plattsburgh and the flight of Prevost formed the burden of one of the most popular of the many songs composed during the war. It was written by Micajah Hawkins, and was first sung at a theatre in Albany by him, in the character of a negro sailor. It was entitled

THE SIEGE OF PLATTSBURGH.

Tune, "*Boyne Water.*"

Backside Albany stan' Lake Champlain,
   Little pond half full o' water ;
Plat-te-burgh dar too, close 'pon de main :
   Town small, he grow bigger, do, herearter.
On Lake Champlain Uncle Sam set he boat,
   An' Massa Macdonough sail 'em ;
While Gineral Macomb make Plat-te-burgh he home
   Wid de army whose courage nebber fail 'em.

On 'lebenth day Sep-tem-ber,
   In eighteen hun'red and fourteen,
Gubbernor Probose an' he British so-jer
   Come to Plat-te-burgh a tea-party courtin'.
An' he boat come, too, arter Uncle Sam's boat.
   Massa 'Donough look sharp out de winder ;
Den Gineral Macomb (ah ! he always at home)
   Cotch fire too, Sirs, like tinder.

Bang ! bang ! bang ! den de cannons 'gin to roar
   In Plat-te-burgh an' al! 'bout dat quarter ;
Gubbernor Probose try he han' 'pon de shore,
   While he boat take he luck 'pon de water.
But Massa Macdonough knock he boat in he head,
   Break he heart, break he shin, 'tove he caff'n in ;
An' Gineral Macomb start ole Probose home,
   'Tot me soul den I muss die a laffin.

Probose scare so he lef' all behine,
   Powder, ball, cannon, tea-pot an' kittle ;
Some say he cotch a cole—trouble in he mine,
   'Cause he eat so much raw an' cole vittle.
Uncle Sam berry sorry, to be sure, for he pain ;
   Wish he nuss hisself up well an' hearty,
For Gineral Macomb and Massa 'Donough home
   When he notion for anudder tea-party.

vessel named *St. Lawrence*, pierced for one hundred and twelve guns, was completed at Kingston on September 1st, when Chauncey prudently raised the blockade and returned to the harbor. That ship, carrying over one thousand men, with other vessels of war, made Sir James Yeo lord of the lake during the remainder of the season. The Americans determined to match the *St. Lawrence*, and laid the keels of two first-class frigates at Sackett's Harbor. The *New Orleans*, nearing completion when peace came early in 1815, is still on the stocks at the Harbor.

A land and naval force was prepared in the spring of 1814 for the purpose of recapturing Fort Mackinaw in the far North-west. It left Detroit early in July. It destroyed the post of the North-west Fur Company at the Falls of St. Mary. The agents of this company had been persistent in inducing the Indians to make war on the frontier settlements of the United States beyond the Ohio. The garrison of the fort to be taken was too strong for the small American force, and the enterprise was abandoned.

CHAPTER XXXI.

WHILE the military events we have considered in the preceding chapter were occurring on the borders of the State of New York during 1814, others of equal importance were taking place at various points in the republic.

Late in August (1814) General Duncan McArthur, with seven hundred mounted men of Kentucky and Ohio, left Detroit, crossed into Canada, and made a terrifying raid through the western portion of the province from Lake St. Clair eastward to the Grand River, and back to Sandwich. He spread alarm everywhere. Fear magnified the number of his men to thousands. The object of the raid was to create a diversion in favor of the Americans on the Niagara frontier. It was effectual. For four weeks McArthur skurried hundreds of miles through the enemy's country, disarming and paroling the militia, and destroying public property; but he was generous to inoffensive citizens.

New England had experienced very little actual war before the year 1814. From the end of 1813 until the close of the contest, British blockading squadrons and single cruisers hovered along its coasts, barred its sea-ports against commerce, and kept its maritime cities and villages in a state of continual alarm and dread.

Pursuant to an order of the British Admiral Cochran given to the commanders of war-vessels to "destroy the sea-port towns and desolate the country," much property was wasted on the coasts of Maine and Massachusetts; and Stonington, in Connecticut, a little east of New London, suffered a severe bombardment. Formidable squadrons blockaded the Delaware River, New York Harbor, New London, and Boston. The largest of these squadrons on the New England coast was commanded by Commodore Sir T. M. Hardy.

After seizing a portion of Eastern Maine, Hardy menaced Portsmouth and Boston. The last-named city was almost defenceless. Stimulated by alarm and the instinct of self-preservation, citizens of Boston of every class turned out daily with implements of labor, and worked energetically in the construction of defences for the town. Informed of these preparations, and having a wholesome fear of Fulton's torpedoes, with which common report said some of the American sea-port harbors were strewn, Hardy did not venture within the roads, and Boston was saved.

New York was equally excited by patriotism and alarm. In daily expectation of an attack by a British land and naval force which had been operating in Chesapeake Bay, men of all classes and occupations worked daily in building fortifications at Brooklyn and Harlem. De Witt Clinton was then mayor of the city of New York. He issued a stirring appeal (August 2d, 1814) to the patriotism and the interests of the citizens, calling upon them to offer their personal services and pecuniary means to aid in the completion of the unfinished fortifications around the town. The response to this appeal was prompt and generous.* Members of various churches and of social and benevolent organizations went out in groups, as such, to the patriotic task. So also did different craftsmen under their respective banners :

> "Plumbers, founders, dyers, tinners, tanners, shavers,
> Sweeps, clerks, and criers, jewellers, engravers,
> Clothiers, drapers, players, cartmen, hatters, nailers,
> Gaugers, scalers, weighers, carpenters, and sailors."

Within four days after Clinton's address three thousand persons were at work on the fortifications under the direction of a Defence Committee and engineers guided by lines drawn by General Joseph G. Swift. The enthusiasm of the people was intense. School-teachers and their pupils went together to the patriotic task, and little boys, too small to handle a spade or pickaxe, carried earth on shingles, and so added their mites in rearing the breastworks. New York City was soon well defended by fortifications and numerous militia, and no blockader ventured within the harbor. Samuel Woodworth concluded a stirring poem published at that time with the following lines, addressed to the British :†

> "Better not invade ; recollect the spirit
> Which our dads displayed and their sons inherit.

---

* Money to erect fortifications must be had at once. The Legislature was not in session. The credit of the National Government was so low at that, the most critical period of the war, that the banks would not loan money on its stock or its Treasury notes without other security. It was understood, however, that if Treasury notes were deposited, endorsed by Governor Tompkins, the banks would advance four or five hundred thousand dollars. Rufus King went to the governor and said, "The time is arrived when it is the duty of every man to put his all at the requisition of the Government," and that he himself (though a leader of the opponents of Mr. Madison) was ready to do so. The governor said he should be obliged to take the responsibility, and should be ruined. "Ruin yourself if it becomes necessary to save your country," said the patriotic Mr. King, "and I pledge you my honor that I will support you in whatever you do." The governor endorsed the notes and the banks loaned the money.

† The whole poem, in eight stanzas, may be found in Lossing's *Pictorial Field Book of the War of* 1812, page 970.

THE NATIONAL CAPITAL THREATENED.

> If you still advance, friendly caution slighting,
> You may get, by chance, a bellyful of fighting.
>   Pick-axe, shovel, spade, crowbar, hoe and barrow ;
>   Better not invade ; Yankees have the marrow."

Philadelphia exhibited a similar spirit on a like occasion at that time, and the amphibious marauders met with such resistance at every point that the terrible order of Cochran could not be executed. Hardy was kept out of the Thames and from New London by Commodore Lewis with some gun-boats on Long Island Sound, and he was discomfited at Stonington and driven away by a few determined men.

Early in January, 1814, the National Government was informed that four thousand British troops destined for the United States had landed at Bermuda. At the close of April intelligence was received of the temporary downfall of Napoleon, as we have observed, which would release many British troops from service on the Continent and allow them to come to America ; and on July 1st official intelligence reached the President that a fleet of transports with a large land force bound to some port in the United States, " probably in the Potomac," was about to sail from Bermuda.

The Government gave little heed to these warnings, and when, at the middle of August, a British squadron of about sixty sail appeared in Chesapeake Bay, with six thousand land troops under General Ross, one of Wellington's best officers, destined for the capture of the national capital, there was no force to oppose the invaders excepting a small flotilla of armed barges and a schooner under Commodore Joshua Barney, and a few scattered militia. The British fleet drove Barney's flotilla into the Patuxent River, and blockaded it there. The flotilla went far up the river to a point not to be reached by the British ships.

Meanwhile the invaders in armed barges pursued the flotilla, when Barney blew it up, and with his marines joined the forces which General Winder,[*] the commander of the district, was hastily gathering. Five thousand of the British force landed at Benedict, thirty miles from the mouth of the Patuxent. Finding the American flotilla a smoking ruin,

---

[*] William H. Winder was a native of Somerset County, Md., and was born in February, 1775. He died in Baltimore in May, 1824. He was a successful lawyer in Baltimore from 1798 until 1812, when he was appointed colonel of infantry in July, and served on the Niagara frontier. In the spring of 1813 he was commissioned brigadier-general ; made prisoner at Stony Creek, Canada ; was exchanged, and made inspector-general in May, 1814. He commanded the Tenth District, and was engaged in the defence of Washington City and the city of Baltimore in the summer of 1814. After the war he resumed the practice of his profession, and served with credit in important civil stations. He was a State senator of Maryland at one time.

they pressed forward toward Washington. Winder, who had only about three thousand men, most of them undisciplined, retreated in the direction of the capital, and that night (August 23d) the invaders, who had been joined by Cockburn and his amphibious marauders, encamped within ten miles of Washington.

Winder left some troops at Bladensburg, four miles from the capital, and with others watched the highways leading from it, uncertain what point might be first attacked. On the morning of the 24th, while Winder and the Cabinet were in consultation, word came to the general that the British were pressing toward Bladensburg. He hurried to that village with re-enforcements. His little army was in great peril, for the invaders were overwhelming in number. To retreat would be perilous. He must either fight or surrender. He chose to fight, and at a little past noon a sharp battle was begun. Many of the militia soon fled. Barney and his men sustained the brunt of the conflict until that leader was badly wounded, when Winder, seeing no ground for hope of a victory, ordered a retreat. The invaders had lost fully five hundred men in killed and wounded during a struggle of four hours. Among their lost were several officers of distinction.

The President (Madison) and some of his Cabinet, who had watched the battle, hastened back to the city as fast as fleet horses could carry them, conveying the first news of impending danger. The victors followed, and entered the city at evening twilight. They at once began to plunder and destroy. The President's house, the Capitol, the Treasury buildings, the arsenal and the barracks were burned. Of the public buildings only the Patent Office was saved. Some private houses were sacked and some were burnt. Meanwhile the commandant of the Navy-Yard fired the public property there—buildings, vessels, and stores—in obedience of an order to prevent their falling into the hands of the enemy. Altogether property of the estimated value of $2,000,000 was laid waste.

While the people of England loudly condemned and deplored this barbarous act, the British Government caused the Tower guns to be fired in honor of Ross's victory, and at his death, a few weeks later, it decreed him a monument in Westminster Abbey. This was well, for he was a brave and humane soldier.

The British now menaced Baltimore. They started from Washington on the night of the 25th, and after resting and recruiting at the mouth of the Patuxent, they appeared in force on Patapsco Bay, at the head of which Baltimore stands, then a city of forty thousand inhabitants. The people of that city had wisely prepared for the reception of the invaders.

Fort McHenry, which defended the harbor, was garrisoned by a thousand men under Major Armistead; redoubts were erected, and a large number of troops were gathered around the city.

On the morning of September 12th General Ross, with nine thousand troops, landed at North Point, twelve miles from Baltimore. The Americans had about the same number within call. Three thousand of these, under General Stricker, were sent out to watch the invaders. Confident of success, Ross and Cockburn were riding gayly at the head of the advancing British troops, when a rifle-ball from a company of concealed sharpshooters mortally wounded the British commanding general. The troops were then led by Colonel Brooke. They pressed on toward Baltimore, encountering General Stricker's advanced troops in a sharp engagement. The British bivouacked on the battle-field that night.

In the mean time a heavy British naval force was anchored before Fort McHenry out of range of its moderate-sized guns, and prepared to bombard it and its supporting redoubts the next morning (September 13th), when the British land force should move upon Baltimore. This was done at the appointed time. Armistead gallantly defended the fort through all the bombardment, and kept the assailants at bay. The contest continued twenty-five hours, during which time fully twenty-five hundred shells were thrown.* The land forces of the enemy were confronted by determined troops under Generals Stricker and Winder. Very soon the British commanders became convinced that they could not take Baltimore, and the bombardment of Fort McHenry suddenly ceased on the morning of the 14th. The British troops hastily withdrew to their ships in darkness and rain at three o'clock in the morning, and the entire armament went down the bay, greatly crestfallen. Sir George Prevost, who had returned to Montreal from Plattsburgh, postponed rejoicings there because of the capture of Washington until he should hear of the

---

* The bombardment of Fort McHenry was the occasion which inspired Francis S. Key to write the popular song, "The Star-spangled Banner." Dr. Beans, a distinguished and much-loved physician of Maryland, had been carried by the British, when retreating from Washington, on board their ship. Mr. Key and Mr. Skinner, of Baltimore, went to the fleet with a flag, to procure Dr. Beans's release. They also were detained on board as the fleet was about to sail for Baltimore. They were compelled to witness the bombardment from one of the British ships. Their anxiety was very great when, before the dawn of the 14th, the fort was silent. They did not know whether it had surrendered or not. They were rejoiced when, "at the dawn's early light," they saw that "our flag was still there," waving over the fort. It was while pacing the deck at that early hour in the morning, filled with doubt, that Key composed that stirring song. The prisoners were sent on shore when the fleet departed.

seizure of Baltimore, that both events might be celebrated at the same time. He was denied that gratification.

Let us turn for a moment to the consideration of operations on the ocean during the remainder of the war.

In May, 1814, Captain Johnston Blakely crossed the sea with the sloop-of-war *Wasp*, of eighteen guns, and spread terror among the British shipping in the English Channel. She captured one sloop-of-war and fought others. During the autumn she was lost somewhere with all her company. She was never heard of afterward.

Captain Warrington had sailed on a cruise from New York in the sloop-of-war *Peacock*, and in April captured the British sloop-of-war *Epervier*, a valuable prize having $118,000 in specie on board of her. In a later cruise to the shores of Portugal the *Peacock* captured fourteen vessels, and returned to New York in October.

The frigate *Constitution* was thoroughly repaired after Bainbridge relinquished the command of her, and she went to sea under the command of Captain Charles Stewart * late in 1813. She sailed to the coast of Surinam, South America, captured the sloop-of-war *Pictou*, and, returning to the New England coast, was chased into the harbor of Marblehead by two powerful British frigates. She did not go to sea again until near the close of December, 1814, when she started on a cruise, crossed the Atlantic, and late in February, 1815, she fought at the same time and captured two British vessels (the frigate *Cyane* and sloop-of-war *Levant*) off the coast of Portugal. Peace had then been declared.

This exploit gained for Stewart great renown. Congress gave him thanks and a gold medal, and the city of New York awarded him the honor of the freedom of the city in a gold box. After that the *Consti-*

---

* Charles Stewart was born in Philadelphia in July, 1778; died at Bordentown, N. J., in November, 1869, in the ninety-second year of his age. He was the youngest of eight children, and lost his father when he was two years old. He went to sea as a cabin boy, and became captain of an East Indiaman when he was eighteen years of age. In 1798 he was commissioned a lieutenant in the navy, and was in command of the schooner *Experiment*, in 1800, in a fight with the French schooner *The Two Friends*, which he captured. He soon made other conquests. He served gallantly against the Barbary powers, and in May, 1804, became a master commandant, and was placed in charge of the frigate *Essex*. He became captain in 1806. In 1812 he was placed in command of the *Constellation*. His chief exploit was the capture of two vessels at the same time with the *Constitution*. After the War of 1812–15 he was in command of the Mediterranean squadron, and was almost continually in the naval service until the breaking out of the Civil War in 1861. In 1857 he was placed on the retired list, but in 1859 he was replaced on the active list (then eighty-one years of age) by special legislation. In 1862 he was promoted to rear-admiral on the retired list.

tution was called *Old Ironsides*, and Stewart bore the same title until his death in 1869, when he was in the ninety-second year of his age, and held the rank of rear-admiral. The *Constitution* still (1887) survives.

In the summer of 1814 Commodore Decatur, whose vessels had been blockaded at New London a long time, was placed in command of the frigate *President* and three other vessels—*Peacock*, Captain Warrington; *Hornet*, Captain Biddle, and a store-ship—destined for a raid on the British shipping in the East Indies. The *President* left the harbor of New York at the middle of January, 1815, eluded the blockades at Sandy Hook, and put to sea. She was chased by four British ships-of-war. Heavily laden for a long cruise, the *President* could not sail fast,

A CLIPPER-BUILT SCHOONER.

and after a protracted chase and running fight she was compelled to surrender.

Late in January the commanders of the other vessels of Decatur's squadron, ignorant of the fate of the *President*, put to sea and sailed for an appointed place of rendezvous at one of a group of islands in the South Atlantic Ocean. There the *Hornet* met the British sloop *Penguin*. They had a desperate fight, and the *Hornet* gained the victory in twenty minutes. This brilliant exploit won for Biddle honors and rewards. Captain Warrington proceeded to the East Indies, and in June, 1815, the *Peacock* captured the *Nautilus* in the Straits of Sunda. Informed the next day of the ratification of the treaty of peace some months before, Warrington gave up the prize. On his return home he also received honors. The war was over, and every American cruiser, public and private, had returned to port.

The achievements of American privateers upon the ocean during the war were wonderful. The romantic story of their exploits has filled a large volume (Coggeshall's *History of American Privateers*), and yet the half has not been told. These exploits were but a repetition of the doings in the regular service. After the first six months of the war the bulk of the naval conflicts upon the sea on the part of the Americans was carried on by private armed vessels, which "took, burned, and destroyed" *sixteen hundred* British merchantmen, of all classes, in the space of three years. The most famous of these privateers for speed and efficiency were the Baltimore clippers.

A large number of privateers were sent out from the port of New York, and many merchants reaped more bountiful pecuniary harvests by this means than they could have done by the slower processes of commerce. The most noted of these New York privateers was the *General Armstrong*, Captain Samuel C. Reid.* In September, 1814, while she was lying in the harbor of Fayal, at one of the islands of the Azores, of the same name, belonging to Portugal, she was suddenly attacked by a part of a large British squadron. The attacking vessels carried one hundred and thirty-three guns in the aggregate, while the *General Armstrong* carried only seven. There were three attacks between the evening and the morning twilight. A terrific conflict lasting forty minutes occurred at midnight. At each attack the plucky *Armstrong* repulsed her assailants, who lost in the struggle of ten hours over three hundred men, while the Americans lost only two killed and seven wounded.

CAPTAIN SAMUEL C. REID.

---

* Samuel Chester Reid was born at Norwich, Conn., in August, 1783; died in New York in January, 1861. He went to sea when only eleven years of age. He was an acting midshipman under Commodore Truxton; became enamored with the naval service, and began the adventurous business of a privateersman at the beginning of the War of 1812-15. After the war he was appointed sailing-master in the navy, and held that position until his death. He was for a time warden of the Port of New York, and the inventor of the semaphore or telegraph used at the Narrows before the electro-magnetic telegraph was perfected. Captain Reid has the honor of being the designer of the present form of our national flag—that is, retaining only thirteen stripes, and adding a star for each State admitted to the Union.

War at the North was now ended, but there was trouble in the Southwest late in 1814. We have considered Jackson's campaign against the Creek Indians. The British, favored by the Spanish governor of Florida, had given the Creeks hope, and induced them to join the forces from Great Britain against the Americans. A British squadron, by permission of the Spanish authorities, took possession of Pensacola, and there fitted out an expedition against the fort at the entrance to Mobile Bay. British land troops and Creek Indians attacked it at the middle of September. They were repulsed.

General Jackson, then at Mobile, holding the Spanish governor responsible for the attack on the fort, marched from that town with two thousand Tennessee militia, seized Pensacola, drove the British from the harbor, and compelled the Spanish governor to beg for mercy and to surrender the town and the military works unconditionally. On returning at once to Mobile, the victorious general found messengers with urgent calls for him to hasten to New Orleans to assist in defending that city and Louisiana from a threatened formidable invasion. The British cruising in the Gulf of Mexico had been re-enforced by thousands of troops from Great Britain.

Jackson instantly obeyed the call. He arrived at New Orleans on December 2d (1814), and found the people in a state of fearful alarm and confusion. He assumed heavy responsibilities. He declared martial law, and by vigorous measures under that rule he soon placed the city in an attitude of comparative security. When an efficient officer fresh from the Spanish peninsula, General Pakenham, with about twelve thousand troops, most of them Wellington's veterans, entered Lake Borgne, Jackson felt confident of success even against such fearful odds.

After a naval struggle on Lake Borgne, in which a flotilla of American gun-boats was destroyed, twenty-four hundred British troops under the Irish General Keane pushed on to the Mississippi River, nine miles below New Orleans, with the expectation of taking that city by surprise. Keane was betrayed by an escaped prisoner, and in the gloom on the night of December 23d he was attacked and defeated by Americans led by General Jackson in person. In this affray the Americans lost in killed and wounded about two hundred men; the British lost about four hundred. The Americans were assisted by an armed vessel on the river, which produced a panic.

New Orleans was saved from surprise; now it had to be saved from open invasion. General Pakenham took the chief command of the troops, and pushed on toward New Orleans. Across his path from the Mississippi to a deep cypress swamp Jackson cast up a line of breastworks with great celerity. When the invader approached to the plain of Chalmette (January 8th, 1815) with his whole land force, and stood in battle array before the improvised fortifications, hope for the Americans seemed very dim.

Behind those breastworks there was an ominous silence as the British veterans approached to the attack. When they had reached within cannon-shot range of Jackson's batteries the latter opened upon them with terrible effect, cutting fearful lanes through the ranks of the British. Yet the latter pressed forward until they were within range of the American rifles, when a host suddenly arose and with a deadly tempest of bullets swept the British line. Whole platoons were mown down like grass before a scythe. Officer after officer was slain. Pakenham fell, bleeding and dying, into the arms of McDougall, his favorite aide. Very soon the assailants broke and fled, their retreat covered by General Lambert at the head of reserves. The slaughter and maiming had been dreadful. The vanquished left seven hundred of their dead and fourteen hundred of their wounded on the field, and five hundred were made prisoners. The Americans lost only eight killed and thirteen wounded. They had been protected by breastworks, while the invaders were exposed on an open plain.

The vanquished Britons, led by General Lambert, stole away under cover of darkness on the night after the battle, and escaped to their ships. General Jackson and his men entered New Orleans as victors. There special honors were bestowed upon the conqueror as a deliverer. He had saved the city and the State. Thirteen years afterward the people of the United States chose him to be the Chief Magistrate of the republic.

Before this conflict on the plain of Chalmette peace between the United States and Great Britain had been secured by a treaty negotiated and signed at Ghent, in Belgium. Commissioners of the two governments,* chosen for the purpose, met in August, 1814, and concluded their labors on December 24th following. The treaty was ratified by the British Government on the 28th, and by that of the United States on February 17th, 1815. As the news of peace went slowly over the land intense joy and satisfaction were everywhere felt.

Nowhere was the intelligence more welcome than in the commercial city of New York. The news was brought to that port on the evening of February 11th by the sloop-of-war *Favorite*, forty-two days from

---

* The United States Commissioners were John Quincy Adams, James A. Bayard, Henry Clay, Jonathan Russell, and Albert Gallatin. The British Commissioners were Lord Gambier, Henry Goulbourn, and William Adams.

Portsmouth. Now it might come in forty-two seconds! The streets were speedily thronged with an excited multitude. Placards were printed by the *Mercantile Advertiser*, announcing the happy event, and thrown out of the window. They were caught up and read with the greatest avidity by the people. The air was soon resonant with huzzas. Cannons thundered, bells were rung, and bonfires blazed. In cities and large villages all over the land the abounding joy was manifested by banquets, orations, and illuminations. There were rejoicings in Great Britain; and there were rejoicings in Canada because of the deliverance of the people from the fear of invasion.

This sudden outbreak of joy was soon tempered by the unpleasant reflection that much advantage expected to be gained by the war and the treaty had not been acquired. Indeed, the subjects of impressments, the right of search, the orders in council and paper blockades, had all been passed over without specific notice in the treaty. These omissions were made powerful weapons in the hands of the opponents of the war. The New York *Evening Post*, anticipating this failure, printed in the "New Year's Address" of its carriers, several weeks before the arrival of the treaty, the following stanza:

> "Your commerce is wantonly lost,
> Your treasures are wasted and gone;
> You've fought to no end, but with millions of cost;
> And for rivers of blood, you've nothing to boast,
> But credit and nation undone."

But the war did secure the positive and permanent independence of the United States, and gave our republic a position among the most conspicuous of the nations of the earth.

The haughty spirit manifested by the British Government during the negotiations at Ghent in demanding terms which were humiliating to the Americans had excited anew the war spirit here, and the Government determined to prosecute the struggle with more vigor than ever. Conscription was resorted to in the early fall of 1813. This measure, which offended State pride, brought matters to a crisis in New England, where the Peace Faction was yet quite powerful. The people of that section had been suspected of disloyalty to the National Government, while the latter adopted some injudicious measures calculated to promote such a feeling. Suspicions and discontents culminated in a conference of sympathizing New England States to consult upon public matters and to consider a radical reform in the National Constitution. A convention composed of twenty-six delegates assembled at Hartford, Conn., on December 15th, 1814, and held their sessions in secret.

The sittings of the Hartford Convention continued about three weeks. At the time of its adjournment it was believed a necessity might require the members to assemble again, and the seal of secrecy was not removed from their proceedings. This gave rise to wild rumors, conjectures, and suspicions. The convention had been suspected of treasonable designs, and had been closely watched; now the members were regarded as disloyal to the Government, and dared not avow it. When, in after years, the proceedings were made public, it was perceived that the Hartford Convention was composed of as loyal and patriotic men as any in the land. Their political opponents, however, made the most of the public prejudice which had been created, and for more than a score of years afterward the partisan cry, "a Hartford Convention Federalist!" cast in some degree a sort of undefined odium on the man to whom the epithet was applied.

CHAPTER XXXII.

During the war we have just been considering, and which made the northern and western frontiers of the State of New York the theatre of almost continually stirring military events, the civil affairs of the commonwealth were conducted in an admirable manner under the guiding hand of Daniel D. Tompkins, who was Governor of the State from 1807 until 1817. He was energetic, judicious, courageous, and patriotic. In politics he was of the " Jefferson School." He had served his country in the State Constitutional Convention ; in the State Legislature ; in Congress ; as Judge of the Supreme Court of the State, and as Chancellor of the University. He was commander of the Third Military District during the war, and he contributed greatly to the success of the national arms by his energy in calling out and equipping troops for the service. Governor Tompkins was Vice-President of the United States during the eight years of Monroe's administration, and early in the last year of his governorship he won immortal honor by recommending to the Legislature in a special message the total abolition of slavery in the State of New York after July 4th, 1827.

During the first quarter of this century De Witt Clinton was undoubtedly the foremost public man of the State in point of mental force, wisdom, sagacity, energy, and statesmanship ; and he was more active and effective in the promotion of measures for the general benefit of society than any other citizen of his time. We have noticed his career up to the breaking out of the War of 1812–15. He was appointed Mayor of the city of New York in 1803, and held that important position continuously until 1815 (excepting two years when he was lieutenant-governor) with great acceptance to the people. He divided the nation with Mr. Madison as a candidate for the presidency, but did not win the prize. In 1817 he was chosen Governor of the State almost without a contest, and was re-elected in 1820, and again in 1824. His was the chief moral and intellectual force which carried forward from conception to completion the great Erie Canal.

It was in the year 1812 that Martin Van Buren,[*] who so long held a

---

[*] Martin Van Buren, the eighth President of the United States, was born in Kinderhook, N. Y., December 5th, 1782 ; died there July 24th, 1862. He was admitted to the bar in 1803. Fond of politics, he took an active part in elections while yet a youth. At the age of twenty-four he was appointed Surrogate of Columbia County, and in 1812 was

conspicuous position in the politics of the State and nation, made his first appearance in a legislative capacity as a senator from the Middle District of New York. His mental abilities, tact, and capacity for adroit management of men speedily gave him the position of leader of the Democratic members of the Legislature. He was a zealous " Clintonian" then, and an earnest advocate of the war.

It was at this period that the Legislature took a step which was of vast benefit to the cause of popular education. At the middle of January, 1812, they appointed Gideon Hawley, an energetic, hard-working, benevolent-minded and modest young lawyer of Albany, Superintendent of Public Schools, under the provisions of an act passed at the previous session. He perfected a system for the management of the school fund and for its equitable distribution into every school district in the State, which he had organized in every neighborhood. He devised a plan of operations by which this vast machinery might be moved and managed by a single individual. For these important services, with others, the State paid Mr. Hawley $300 a year ! Posterity has rewarded this fine scholar and public benefactor with full appreciation and unstinted praise when contemplating the result of his benevolent labors. Mr. Hawley died in 1870 at the age of eighty-five years, having served as a Regent of the University twenty-seven years, and a Regent of the Smithsonian Institution twenty-four years.*

MARTIN VAN BUREN.

---

sent to the State Senate. From 1815 to 1819 he was Attorney-General of the State. In 1819 he began a reorganization of the Democratic Party, and became the leader of the politicians known as the "Albany Regency." In 1821 he became a member of the United States Senate, and again in 1827 ; was chosen Governor of New York in 1828 ; entered President Jackson's Cabinet as Secretary of State in 1829, and was sent Minister to England in 1831. The Senate refused to ratify his appointment, and he was chosen Vice-President of the United States. He was elected President in 1836. His administration was marked by great commercial troubles. In 1848 he was an unsuccessful candidate of the "Free Soil" Party for President. He visited Europe in 1853-55. When the Civil War broke out Mr. Van Buren took decided grounds against the enemies of the Republic.

* Gideon Hawley was born in Huntington, Conn., in 1785 ; died at Albany, N. Y., in August, 1870. He was a graduate of Union College. In 1794 he took up his abode at

CIVIL AFFAIRS IN THE STATE. 447

In the session of the Legislature early in 1813 sharp collisions began to occur between the two houses on all questions which related to the prosecution of the war. The militia which had been called out the previous autumn by the governor had returned dissatisfied with the service. The Federal politicians took advantage of this dissatisfaction, and promoted it so as to increase their own power and influence.

The National Government had already become embarrassed by lack of money to carry on the war ; and this, too, was used as a weapon of attack by the Federalists. A resolution which was adopted by the State Senate to loan to the National Government $500,000 was defeated by the Federalists in the Assembly. During the same year Solomon Southwick,* the able editor of the *Albany Register*, the organ of the Democratic Party, showed lukewarmness in support of the war, and lost the confidence of the party leaders. They made the *Argus*, just established by Jesse Buel,† their organ.

The next session of the Legislature (1814) was marked by liberal appropriations of money to be raised by lottery for the benefit of Union,

---

Saratoga. In 1813 he was admitted to the bar in Albany, and the next year became secretary to the Regents of the University. He was a regent of the University from 1814 to 1841, and of the Smithsonian Institution from 1846 until his death. Mr. Hawley wrote and printed for private distribution *Essays on Truth and Knowledge*.

* Solomon Southwick was for some years a brilliant journalist in Albany. He was a son of Solomon Southwick, a journalist of Newport, R. I., where this son was born in 1774. He learned the trade of a baker, but became a practical printer in Albany. About the year 1800 he was the assistant editor of the *Albany Register*, which finally became the accredited organ of the Democratic Party. Southwick became sole editor in 1807, and conducted it with great ability. He was personally popular, with a handsome face and pleasing deportment. He was a firm supporter of De Witt Clinton and his friends. In 1809 he was appointed Sheriff of Albany, and in 1811 was a bank president there. He was printer to the State ; also a regent of the University. He quarrelled with his party leaders, when the *Register* was abandoned by them, and in 1818 it died. He had been superseded as State printer, and he lost the office of postmaster at Albany in 1822. Various speculations of his were unsuccessful. In 1821 he established *The Ploughboy*, and then the *National Democrat*. Both were short-lived. He became a candidate for governor of the State in 1822, when he was defeated by an overwhelming vote. He was again a candidate for the same office in 1828, representing the Anti-Masonic Party, and at the same time became the editor of the *National Observer*, an Anti-Masonic journal. Mr. Southwick died in 1839.

† Jesse Buel was born in Coventry, Conn., in 1778, and died in Danbury, 1839. He was educated a printer. He published the *Ulster Republican*, and in 1813 went to Albany, where he established the *Argus*, which, on the party defection of Solomon Southwick, became the organ of the Democratic Party. He was soon chosen State printer. He left the *Argus* in 1821, having acquired a competency. Buel was Whig candidate for governor in 1836. Two years before, he established *The Cultivator*, a periodical devoted to agriculture, which for years exerted a wide and salutary influence among farmers. At the time of his death Mr. Buel was a regent of the University.

Columbia, and Hamilton colleges; an African church; the New York Historical Society, and various medical colleges. At the same session James Kent was appointed Chancellor of the State of New York, and Smith Thompson Chief-Justice of its Supreme Court. They were both natives of Duchess County.

The Legislature put forth the most vigorous exertions to place and maintain the State in an attitude of secure defence against invasion, and to aid the general Government against the enemy. They increased the pay of the militia, and passed an act to encourage privateering by authorizing associations for that purpose. This was done in spite of a very learned protest from Chancellor Kent[*] and others. The chancellor was answered, and a controversy in the newspapers occurred, in which Judge Kent, Colonel Samuel Young, and Martin Van Buren participated. A law was passed for enlisting twelve thousand men for two years; and another was adopted for raising a corps of "sea fencibles," a sort of minute-men; and still another for raising a regiment of colored men, among whom slaves might be enlisted by consent of their masters, and who were to be manumitted when honorably discharged.

JAMES KENT.

Intelligence of the prompt passage of these several laws by the Legislature of New York at the short session in the fall of 1814 was received by President Madison with great joy and satisfaction, for the event

---

[*] James Kent, an eminent jurist, was born at Phillipstown, Putnam (then Duchess) County, N. Y., in July, 1763; died in New York City in December, 1847. He studied law with Egbert Benson, and began its practice at Poughkeepsie in 1787. From 1790 to 1793 he was a member of the New York Assembly. In the latter year he became professor of law in Columbia College; in 1796 he was made Master in Chancery; Recorder of New York City in 1797; Judge of the Supreme Court of New York in 1798; Chief Justice in 1804, and was Chancellor of the State from 1814 to 1823. He took an active part in the State Constitutional Convention in 1821, and soon afterward again became law professor in Columbia College. The lectures he delivered there form the basis of his famous *Commentaries on the United States Constitution*, published in four volumes. Judge Kent was one of the clearest legal writers of his time. In 1828 he was chosen President of the New York Historical Society. In his later years he revised his *Commentaries*.

added much strength to the then exceedingly weak Government. Oppressed by painful apprehensions, the President gratefully tendered to Governor Tompkins the important position in his Cabinet of Secretary of War, which General John Armstrong, of New York, had lately resigned. The governor declined.

The Federalists gained political ascendancy in New York in 1815, and the Council of Appointment, influenced by the many political enemies of De Witt Clinton, proceeded to deprive him of the lucrative office of Mayor of New York. This left him in straitened pecuniary circumstances with a large family, but he maintained his dignity of deportment and his cheerfulness of spirits. He engaged in literary pursuits, and increased his efforts to induce the State to construct the great Erie Canal. He was successful, as we have observed.

Governor Tompkins was now one of the most popular men in the State, and was an aspirant for the office of President of the United States. At the close of the war Mr. Madison began to give tokens that he expected Mr. Monroe to be his successor. Already the President of the republic had been taken from Virginia twenty-four out of twenty-eight years of the existence of the National Government. This continuation of the "Virginia dynasty," as it was called, had become distasteful, especially to New Yorkers. At the same time the Virginians were evidently jealous of New York because of her rapid growth in population, commerce, wealth, and political influence.

When the congressional caucus assembled to nominate a candidate for the presidency, it was found that nearly the whole delegation from New York were for Governor Tompkins. The majority of other Democratic members were from the South, and were opposed to him; while the New England delegates were all Federalists. Monroe was nominated and elected in 1816, and Tompkins was chosen Vice-President.

Great was the rejoicing in the legislative halls and among the people all over the State when the news of peace and of the victory at New Orleans was spread over the commonwealth. Then the thoughts of all were directed to the pursuits of peace, the readjustment of business relations, and the development of the resources of the State, especially to the importance of a speedy construction of the projected great canal. The friends of that project moved with vigor. A most important meeting held in New York City in the autumn adopted strong resolutions in its favor, and a powerful memorial to the Legislature was drawn up by De Witt Clinton, and widely circulated and signed, commending the project.

This movement in New York City was followed by a large gathering at Canandaigua, Ontario County, of leading gentlemen in Western New York. At that meeting Myron Holley, one of the canal commissioners and one of the brightest and wisest men in the State, was the chief actor.* Governor Tompkins, in his message at the opening of the session of the Legislature in 1816, expatiated upon the vast importance of such a work not only to the State of New York, but to the nation; and at a large meeting of citizens at Albany earnest resolutions in favor of the project were adopted.

Notwithstanding the treasury of the commonwealth had been nearly exhausted by the efforts to sustain the National Government in its prosecution of the war, and all aid from that Government in carrying out the project had been withheld; notwithstanding the resources of private enterprise had been crippled by the financial embarrassments of the crisis and the prevalence of an impression that the scheme was altogether visionary, the leaders of sober thought and opinion in the State were strong enough to induce the Legislature to authorize the prosecution of all necessary surveys for the great work; to appropriate $20,000 for the purpose, and to appoint a new Board of Canal Commissioners.†

The most powerful advocates of the measure at that time were De Witt Clinton, Martin Van Buren, and Samuel Young. It was observed that most of the leaders of the opposition to the canal project were political enemies of Mr. Clinton; and so strong was this partisan enmity that it formed the chief constituent of their motives in opposing the scheme.

At the opening of the session of 1817 Governor Tompkins, as we have

---

* The meeting in New York City was assembled through the instrumentality of Thomas Eddy, Judge Jonas Platt, De Witt Clinton, John Pintard, and a few others, the zealous, persistent, and earlier friends of the project. They sent cards of invitation to about one hundred gentlemen of that city, to meet at the City Hotel, to consult concerning the Canal. William Bayard presided at the meeting, and John Pintard was the secretary. Judge Platt made a convincing address to the meeting. A resolution was passed approving the scheme, and a committee, composed of De Witt Clinton, Thomas Eddy, Cadwallader D. Colden, and John Swartwout, was appointed to prepare and circulate a memorial to the Legislature in favor of the canal. That memorial—a masterpiece—was drawn by Mr. Clinton.

The meeting at Canandaigua was held on January 8th, 1817. Gideon Granger, afterward Postmaster-General, was the chief speaker on that occasion. Important resolutions, drawn by Myron Holley, were adopted. These resolutions, it was observed, "both in matter and style may be justly denominated a *near relation* of Mr. Clinton's memorial." The proceedings of this meeting made a deep impression on the public mind, and powerfully contributed to the enlightened policy which the Legislature subsequently pursued.

† Stephen van Rensselaer, De Witt Clinton, Samuel Young, Joseph Ellicott, and Myron Holley.

observed, recommended the unconditional and entire abolition of the slave system in the State of New York after July 4th, 1827. The recommendation was concurred in by the unanimous voice of the Legislature. Thus were the persistent benevolent efforts of the Society of Friends, or Quakers, to erase from the escutcheon of the State of New York the dark stain of human slavery given encouragement and final success. In bringing about this act of the Legislature in 1817 they were powerfully aided by Cadwallader D. Colden (grandson of Governor Colden), Peter A. Jay, William Jay,* Governor Tompkins, and other earnest laborers in the cause.

On March 10th, 1817, the canal commissioners presented to the Legislature an elaborate report. Most strenuous opposition to the canal scheme was then manifested in and out of the Legislature. It was ridiculed as the conception of lunatics; condemned as a project which, if attempted, would ruin the State financially; and its advocates were declared to be enemies of the commonwealth. The excitement throughout the State was intense. But common-sense and sagacity prevailed in the Legislature, and on April

WILLIAM JAY.

---

* William Jay, LL.D., was an eminent jurist and earnest philanthropist, son of Governor John Jay. He was born in New York City in 1789, and died at Bedford, Westchester County, N. Y., in October, 1858. He was a graduate of Yale College. On account of weak eyes he was compelled to abandon the practice of law, for which he was prepared. He was one of the founders of the American Bible Society, in 1815, and was ever an active member of it. He was one of the earliest advocates of the temperance reform, and founded a temperance society in 1815. He was active in founding and promoting the work of tract, missionary, and educational societies. In 1818 he was appointed Judge of the Court of Common Pleas of Westchester County, and was first judge from 1820 to 1842, when he was superseded on account of his radical anti-slavery sentiments. He was one of the founders and most efficient supporters of the American Anti-Slavery Society. In 1843 Judge Jay visited Europe, and with the eminent Egyptologist, Sir Gardiner Wilkinson, investigated the subject of slavery in Egypt. Judge Jay held a vigorous pen, and wrote much on the subject of temperance, slavery, and peace. He was for several years President of the American Peace Society. His numerous publications were widely circulated, and exercised great and good influence. Judge Jay prepared a biography of his father, John Jay, and a collection of his writings, in two volumes, which was published in 1833.

17th it passed an act authorizing the construction of the great work of internal improvement. The work upon it was begun less than three months afterward.

With kaleidoscope rapidity and variety were the changes in the position of the leaders of political parties and factions in New York at that time. They were then in a sort of transition state. Each faction was controlled by a few men. Personal politics was the rule. It was at this time that a small clique of shrewd politicians known as the "Albany Regency" came into power and ruled the State, in a degree, for almost twenty years. The leader of the "Regency" was Martin Van Buren, and his chief associates were Benjamin F. Butler, Edwin Croswell, and William L. Marcy.

We have seen De Witt Clinton, in 1815, "shelved" by the Council of Appointment, which was composed chiefly of men of his own party, and he was relegated to the class of political fossils. Judge Spencer,[*] between whom and Clinton there had long been maintained bitter political and personal animosity, and who had been a power in the politics of the State and puissant in the annual creation of the Council of Appointment, had been the chief instrument in destroying the confidence of the Democratic Party in Mr. Clinton. Now Spencer was menaced with a similar fate, and sought to avert it. The popularity of Tompkins and the talents and fascination of Van Buren made them exceedingly influential among the members of the Legislature, with whom they were in constant intercourse. They were now the political antagonists of Clinton, and disposed to give the cold shoulder to Spencer. The latter well knew that there was no man who could neutralize the influence of these rivals more effectually than Mr. Clinton, and Spencer sought and obtained a reconciliation with his old friend and kinsman. Mrs. Spencer was a sister of Clinton.

In February, 1817, Governor Tompkins resigned his seat to occupy

---

[*] Ambrose Spencer, LL.D., was the son of a farmer and mechanic, and was born in Salisbury, Conn., in 1765. He died at Lyons, N. Y., in March, 1848. He was graduated at Harvard, and studied law with John Canfield, of Sharon, Conn., whose daughter he married before he was nineteen years of age. After her death he married a sister of De Witt Clinton. They settled in Hudson, N. Y. In 1793 he was elected to the Assembly, and was State senator from 1795 to 1802. He was the author of a bill which abolished the penalty of death excepting for the crimes of treason and murder ; also for the erection of a State prison near New York, and for the amelioration of the condition of prisoners. In 1802 he was appointed attorney-general, and in 1804 was made Chief-Justice of the State Supreme Court. Judge Spencer was always an active politician. He was a member of the State Constitutional Convention in 1821 ; was Mayor of Albany, and from 1829 to 1831 a member of Congress. In 1839 he removed to the village of Lyons, where he died.

that of Vice-President of the United States. There appeared a strong disposition in the Legislature to nominate Mr. Clinton for governor. Mr. Van Buren and his friends opposed it. Spencer worked valiantly for it. Clinton was nominated, and in April was elected by an almost unanimous vote. The Federalists did not make any nomination, and they generally voted for Clinton.

How "the whirligig of time brings about its revenges"! Only two years before, Mr. Clinton had been expelled by his party from the office of Mayor of New York, denounced by the leading Democrats in his native State and the nation as utterly unworthy of their confidence, and consigned to political perdition ; now we see him elevated to the highest official position in his State by a majority of the Democratic Party and of the opposing party as their best man !

A formidable political faction opposed to Governor Clinton soon appeared, and gave origin to two distinctly marked parties known as "Bucktails," or Democrats, and "Clintonians." *

Little of special importance outside of the political arena occurred in the State of New York during the remainder of Governor Clinton's administration. The construction of the great water highway across the State was pushed on with vigor, and on October 22d, 1819, the first boat on the Erie Canal floated between Rome and Utica, with the governor and other distinguished citizens on board.

In the spring of 1820 a hot contest for the governorship of the State occurred. The Bucktails nominated Vice-President Tompkins for that position, and the Clintonians renominated Mr. Clinton. The canvass was very spirited, and resulted in the re-election of Mr. Clinton by about fourteen hundred majority.

Just before the election a most singular movement took place among the politicians of the State, designed to "put down Mr. Clinton at all hazards." On April 14th fifty professed Federalists, representing the intelligence and wealth of the State (among them sons of the late General Hamilton and also of Rufus King), issued an address to the people, in which they affirmed that the Federal Party no longer existed, and avowed their intention to support Mr. Tompkins for governor and to attach themselves to the great Democratic Party of the nation—the

---

* There was an order in the Tammany Society who, on certain occasions, wore a portion of the tail of a deer in their hats. The Tammanyites were all opposed to Clinton, and had a controlling influence in the Democratic Party in the State. The friends of Clinton gave to them the name of "Bucktails," as the order that wore that insignia was a leading one in the society. Hence the party opposed to Mr. Clinton was called, for a long time, the Bucktail Party.

Bucktails in New York. They did not object to Mr. Clinton's capacity, his morals, or his public measures, but opposed him solely because, they alleged, he was attempting to form a "personal party." At the same time Mr. Van Buren and his friends were as strenuously opposing Mr. Clinton, solely on the professed ground that the Federal Party *did exist* in the State, and that he was secretly inclined to favor it. They, too, admitted the talents and virtues of Mr. Clinton, and did not object to his public measures, but they suspected him of political coquetry! The common-sense of the better people of the State perceived the absurdity of the actions of the intriguing politicians, and gave Mr. Clinton a triumphant majority vote. Governor Clinton's success at this time was largely due to his popularity as the leading champion of the canal interest.

At a session of the Legislature held in November (1820) Governor Clinton recommended the passage of a law for the choice of presidential electors directly by the people; also another for the calling of a convention for the consideration of amendments to the State Constitution. A bill for the latter purpose was passed by both houses in January following, but was rejected by the Council of Revision * by the casting vote of the governor, who did not approve of some of its provisions.

Early in the session of 1821 another bill providing for a convention was passed, and became a law. The Legislature and the Council of Appointment were politically opposed to the governor, and the latter body soon set the work of official decapitation in motion. One of the victims was Gideon Hawley, the wise and able Superintendent of Common Schools, whose removal was without excuse. They proceeded to fill his place by appointing to the position a young lawyer who was utterly incompetent to perform the duties. The removal of Hawley was regarded as so gross an outrage against the best interests of society that the political friends of the Council in the Legislature would not submit to it. By an almost unanimous vote the Legislature abolished the office

---

* The Council of Revision, as we have observed on page 259, like the Council of Appointment, was a part of the machinery of the Executive Department of the State Government. It possessed and exercised the veto power. All bills passed by the Legislature were submitted to its inspection and revision before becoming laws. But if, after bills had been rejected and returned to the Legislature with objections stated, by the Council of Revision, they should again be passed, by a vote of two thirds, they became laws. This council, after an existence of about forty years, was abolished by the Convention of 1821, and its power lodged in the hands of the governor by the Constitution framed that year. During its existence the Council returned one hundred and sixty-nine bills, with their objections, to the Legislature. Fifty-one of the bills so returned were passed into laws by the Legislature by a two-thirds vote.

of Superintendent of Common Schools, and assigned the duties of that official to the Secretary of State.

So eager were the people for a revision of the State Constitution that at the April election (1821), when the subject was submitted to them, there was a majority of nearly seventy-five thousand votes in favor of a convention. On the third Tuesday in June elections of delegates to a constitutional convention were held throughout the State. Some of the most distinguished men in the commonwealth were chosen delegates, some of them having been selected on account of their superior ability rather than for any partisan consideration; yet a larger portion of the representatives were Democrats.

The convention assembled at the Capitol * in the city of Albany on August 28th, when one hundred and ten delegates were present. They presented an array of talent, experience, and weight of personal character unsurpassed by any similar body of men ever before assembled in the republic.† They chose Vice-President Tompkins to preside over their deliberations, and John F. Bacon and Samuel L. Gardiner to record the proceedings. William L. Stone, editor of the *New York Commercial Advertiser*; N. H. Carter, of the *Statesman*; and M. I. Cantine were the official reporters.

The convention remained in session nearly two months and a half, and made many important changes in the fundamental law of the State. The debates, especially those concerning the right of suffrage, were marked by signal ability, and were exceedingly interesting. The labors

---

* The State Capitol at that time stood on the site of the new one not yet (1887) completed, at the head of State Street, one hundred and thirty feet above tide-water. Its corner-stone was laid in 1806. It was a substantial stone building, veneered with brown sandstone from quarries below the Hudson Highlands. The columns, pilasters, and decorations of the doors and windows were of white or gray marble from Berkshire, Mass. As it was in part designed for city offices, it was erected in part at the expense of the city of Albany. The whole expense was a trifle over $120,000, of which amount the city paid $34,000. It was begun in 1803 and finished in 1807.

† The following gentlemen were among the most distinguished delegates elected by the Democrats: Nathan Sandford, Jacob Radcliff, William Paulding, Henry Wheaton, Ogden Edwards, John Oliver, Samuel Nelson (afterward chief-justice of the State), Martin Van Buren, Daniel D. Tompkins, Samuel Young, Jacob Sutherland, Erastus Root, Rufus King (the latter had been a very prominent leader among the Federalists), General James Tallmadge, and Peter R. Livingston. Those most distinguished who were elected by the other party were Stephen van Rensselaer, Chancellor Kent, Ambrose Spencer, Abraham van Vechten, William W. Van Ness, Elisha Williams, J. Rutsen van Rensselaer, Peter A. Jay, Judge Jonas Platt, and Ezekiel Baum. The labor of reporting and preparing for the press the proceedings of the convention was performed almost wholly by Colonel W. L. Stone. It was done with remarkable accuracy.

of the convention were ended on November 10th (1821), when it adjourned *sine die*.*

Allotted space will allow only brief allusion to the most important labors of the convention and the chief new features given to the instrument then adopted. The subjects of (1) the Legislative Department; (2) the Executive Department; (3) the Judiciary Department; (4) the Council of Revision; (5) the Council of Appointment; (6) the Right of Suffrage; (7) the Rights and Privileges of Citizens; (8) Miscellaneous Matters; (9) the Legislative Year and Terms of Elective Officers; (10) the Mode of Making Future Amendments, were referred to standing committees.

The Legislative Department was declared to consist of a Senate composed of thirty-two members, distributed equally over eight Senate districts, elected for four years, one fourth of this number going out each year and presided over by the lieutenant-governor, with a casting vote; and an Assembly consisting of one hundred and twenty-eight members, apportioned among the several counties according to population, and annually elected.

The Executive Department to consist of a governor and lieutenant-governor to be elected biennially, and the several State officers, with the exception of the adjutant-general, chosen by joint ballot of the Senate and Assembly once in every three years. Sheriffs, county clerks, and coroners to be elected by the people of the several counties for a term of three years.

The judiciary system was remodelled by the substitution of circuit courts in eight judicial districts into which the State was divided, in place of the previous system of trials of important issues before one of the judges of the Supreme Court; the reduction of the Supreme Court to a chief-justice and two assistant justices, with the right of appeal to the Senate, chancellor, and judges of the Supreme Court, sitting as a court for the correction of errors, the several judges to hold office until the age of sixty years, unless previously removed for cause; and the appointment of a chancellor, for the determination of all cases of equity jurisdiction, subject to the same right of appeal. Judges of the county courts of Common Pleas and justices of the peace to be appointed by the governor and Senate.

---

* It was during this year that Martin Van Buren was chosen to represent the State of New York in the Senate of the United States, a field commensurate with his ambitious aspirations and his eminent intellectual ability. He now entered the arena of national politics, and rose to the highest station in the republic.

IMPORTANT FEATURES OF THE NEW CONSTITUTION.

The Councils of Revision and Appointment * were abolished. The functions of the latter were devolved upon the governor and the Senate, and of the former upon the governor, who was vested with the veto power.

The right of suffrage was extended to every male citizen of the age of twenty-one years and upward, with no other restrictions than that of residence and exemption from criminal conviction, and the requisition of a freehold qualification of $250, in the case of colored voters.

A section requiring the call of future conventions for the amendment of the Constitution on the expiration of each period of twenty years thereafter was adopted. Also another, authorizing the Legislature, in the mean time, by a two-thirds vote, to submit any amendment deemed requisite to a popular vote for its ratification. At a special election held in February, 1822, the new Constitution was ratified and adopted by a majority of thirty-four thousand votes.

---

* The Council of Appointment was one of the most gigantic political machines subject to partisan purposes ever put in motion. That it did not work more political mischief than it did must be credited to the prevalence of great public virtue. At the time of its abolition the Council had at its disposal six thousand six hundred and sixty-three civil offices and eight thousand two hundred and eighty-seven military offices. The patronage dispensed by the civil officers was enormous in amount. The Council could appoint and dismiss at pleasure, and as its political complexion was subject to frequent and sudden changes, the tenure of office was as weak as a rope of sand. Such a condition was most demoralizing to the civil service.

CHAPTER XXXIII.

The population of the State of New York at the time of the adoption of the new Constitution was about one million four hundred thousand, of whom forty thousand were colored, including a little more than ten thousand slaves. Albany, the political capital of the State, contained between twelve and thirteen thousand inhabitants, and New York City, its commercial metropolis, had a population of one hundred and twenty-five thousand. Its agricultural products; its mineral resources; its manufactures, commerce, and trade; its accumulated wealth and its political influence in the nation gave New York even then a fair claim to the title of *The Empire State.*

The Algerine corsairs in the Mediterranean Sea had been suppressed and the piratical Barbary Powers had been humbled by a squadron of the United States Navy, commanded by Commodore Decatur.* American commerce, thus untrammelled, was making its way even to the Levant and the Golden Horn, and her white-winged ships flecked the seas of far-off India. New York had begun to send its argosies everywhere, and held a proud position among its sister commonwealths. Sagacious men saw clearly that it was at the entrance upon a far more wonderful career of commercial activity and general prosperity than ever before, for the Erie Canal, with all its possibilities foreshadowed, was well advanced toward completion.

But little of importance was done by the Legislature which convened early in January, 1822, excepting to provide for setting in motion the machinery of civil government under the amended Constitution. Governor Clinton congratulated the Legislature upon the great progress made in the construction of the canals—the Erie and the Champlain—and recommended various modifications of the civil and criminal laws.

---

* Commodore Stephen Decatur was sent to the Mediterranean with a squadron to humble the Barbary Powers and to break up the nests of pirates that infested those waters. He captured two pirate vessels and then sailed for Algiers, when he demanded the instant surrender of all American prisoners, full indemnity for all property destroyed by English vessels which were not allowed to enter his harbor, and absolute relinquishment of all claim to tribute from the United States. The Dey of Algiers yielded. Decatur then visited Tunis and Tripoli with a similar result. He received from the two latter powers $71,000. This cruise gave full security to American commerce in the Mediterranean Sea.

The new Constitution having provided that no lottery should thereafter be authorized in the State, and the sale of tickets prohibited excepting in lotteries already established, two persons (Messrs. Yates and McIntyre) were appointed managers of the State Lottery for the provision of funds for colleges, etc. At the termination of this lottery soon afterward this vicious system of supporting institutions of learning in the State was abandoned forever.

The new Constitution changed the time for holding the general State elections from April to November. Mr. Clinton was not renominated for governor. Indeed, in the gradual disintegration of parties then in progress, the Clintonian party had nearly disappeared. So, also, had the Federal Party in the State. There was unusual quiet in the political arena throughout the republic. This state of things gave to the second term of Mr. Monroe's administration the title of "The Era of Good Feeling." Joseph C. Yates,* of Schenectady, was elected Governor of New York with no other opposition than a few scattering votes in different parts of the State given for Solomon Southwick, a self-nominated candidate for governor. Both branches of the Legislature were overwhelmingly Democratic.

JOSEPH C. YATES.

At the first meeting of the Legislature under the amended Constitution (January, 1823) measures were taken for adjusting the government machinery in accordance with its requirements. John Savage was made Chief-Justice of the Supreme Court, and Jacob Sutherland and John Woodworth were created associate justices. Nathan Sandford was appointed Chancellor; J. Van Ness Yates, Secretary of State; W. L.

---

* Judge Yates was born in Schenectady, N. Y., in November, 1768, and died there in March, 1837. He was a son of Colonel Christopher Yates of the Revolution; gained eminence as a lawyer, and from 1803 till 1822 was a judge of the State Supreme Court. He was one of the founders of Union College, in 1795; was Mayor of Schenectady in 1798, and State senator in 1806–1807. He was governor of the State in 1823–24, and afterward remained in private life.

Marcy, Comptroller; S. A. Talcott, Attorney-General, and Simeon De Witt, Surveyor-General, an office he had then held about fifty years. To the classical taste of Mr. De Witt the interior of the State of New York is indebted for its burden of ancient names given to townships and villages. One might easily suppose that region had been settled by Greek and Roman colonies.*

The puissant Democratic Party in the State was split asunder at the fall elections in 1823 largely by the question of submitting the choice of presidential electors to the people. A new organization sprang up known as "The People's Party," and carried several of the largest Democratic counties of the State. Its strength was increased by the unwise action of the Legislature early in 1824 in refusing to give the people the power to choose presidential electors, and by an extraordinary exhibition of personal enmity toward Mr. Clinton. The Senate passed a resolution for the removal of Mr. Clinton from the office of canal commissioner. The Assembly immediately concurred by a large majority.†

This unwarrantable and purely partisan conduct produced intense indignation throughout the State. Large public meetings were held in many places, at which the conduct of the Legislature was denounced and the high character and valuable public services of Mr. Clinton were recounted and approved. A State Convention held at Utica nominated him for governor, and at the November election he was chosen for that office over Samuel Young by a majority of nearly seventeen thousand votes. General James Tallmadge, of Duchess, was elected lieutenant-governor over General Root by thirty-four thousand four hundred and nine majority, having received the combined votes of the Democratic and the People's parties.

---

* Simeon De Witt was born in Ulster County, N. Y., in December, 1756; died in Albany in 1834. He was a graduate of Queens (Rutgers) College, N. J.; entered the Continental Army, where he held the position of "geographer," and was with Gates at the surrender of Burgoyne. He was also at the surrender of Cornwallis. He was Surveyor-General of the State of New York from 1784 until his death. In 1796 he declined the office of Surveyor-General of the United States. In 1798 he was appointed a regent of the University; 1817, Vice-Chancellor, and in 1829, Chancellor of the State. He made a map of the State of New York in 1804. Mr. De Witt was a member of many literary and scientific societies.

† This movement was probably preconcerted. Only a short time before the hour fixed for the adjournment of the Legislature—"perhaps I may say minutes," wrote Mr. Hammond—Mr. Bowman, a senator from Monroe County, submitted a resolution for the removal of Mr. Clinton from the office of canal commissioner. It was acted upon immediately, all but three senators voting in the affirmative. The resolution was forthwith sent to the Assembly, where it was immediately passed by a vote of sixty-four against thirty-four. This action caused the political death of Mr. Bowman.

At the middle of August, 1824, Lafayette arrived in the United States as the guest of the nation, after an absence of forty years. He landed at Staten Island, and remained there, the guest of Vice-President Tompkins, until the next day, when he was escorted to the city of New York by a large fleet of vessels of every kind. There he was received with great honors—booming of cannons, pealing of bells, and shouts of a multitude—and was welcomed by the municipal authorities. He was conducted to the City Hall, and was the guest of the corporation for several days. He visited the principal institutions, and held crowded receptions of the citizens. He made an extensive tour through the

CASTLE GARDEN IN 1852.

United States. It was a continued ovation. In September the following year, after a brilliant reception at Castle Garden by the citizens of New York, he departed for his home in France. He was conveyed to his country in the frigate *Brandywine*, so named in compliment to him. He was wounded at the battle on Brandywine Creek.

While Lafayette was in the United States a presidential election occurred, and resulted in the choice of John Quincy Adams, son of ex-President John Adams, as Chief Magistrate of the republic. There were five candidates in the field—namely, John Quincy Adams, Henry Clay, William H. Crawford, Andrew Jackson, and John C. Calhoun. The Electoral College failed to make a choice, and that duty devolved upon the House of Representatives for the second time in the history of the Government. One of the earliest acts of President Adams after his inauguration on March 4th, 1825, was to offer Governor Clinton the position of Minister of the United States to Great Britain. It was respectfully declined, when it was conferred upon Rufus King, of New York.

In his message to the Legislature at the beginning of 1825, Governor Clinton recommended the passage of a law giving the choice of presidential electors to the people; the creation of a Board of Internal Improvements for the completion and extension of the canal system of the State, and the construction of a great highway through the southern tier of counties, then rather sparsely settled. The Legislature passed an act for the appointment of these commissions to explore and cause to be surveyed a route for such road. It was never built by the State, but canals were rapidly multiplied soon afterward.*

The year 1825 was a memorable one in the history of the State of New York. It was the beginning of a new era in its wonderful career of prosperity. The great Erie Canal, which traversed the State from west to east—the most gigantic work of the kind in the world—was completed in the autumn of that year—an artificial navigable river more than three hundred and sixty miles in length. Governor Clinton, its mightiest champion, had made a tour the previous summer, first to Philadelphia, and then to Ohio and Kentucky, for the purpose of inspecting public improvements in progress in those States. He was everywhere received with earnest demonstrations of respect, for his fame was now national—nay, even international.

The half decade of years previous to 1830 presented in the State and city of New York a most exciting drama to the eye of the social observer. It was the great transition period from the stagnation of business and enterprise caused by the late war to the awakening to new and prosperous life throughout the whole country. Nowhere in our broad land was that awakening more pronounced and the results more marvellous than in the State of New York and its great seaport. The grandest and most puissant of the forces which produced this awakening in New York and

---

* The Champlain Canal was completed in the summer of 1822. A gentleman engaged in the lumber trade in Northern New York wrote to his brother from Fort Edward on August 29th, 1822: "This morning, at eight o'clock, I had the satisfaction of seeing the water pour over the big dam [a feeder for the canal]. It filled in about sixty-two hours after the planks were laid down, which was much quicker than was anticipated, in consequence of the river being so very low. The canal will be in full operation by Saturday." This canal connects Lake Champlain with the Hudson River at Fort Edward.

the region west of it was the putting into operation the great Erie Canal. It had occupied in its construction the time of eight years and four months from its commencement at Rome on July 4th, 1817, until the celebration of its completion on November 4th, 1825. That celebration presented one of the most remarkable pageants ever before seen in the State or nation.

The first flotilla of canal-boats left Buffalo, on Lake Erie, for the city of New York on the morning of October 26th. On that morning the waters of Lake Erie first flowed into the "Great Ditch," as doubters and opposers of the canal contemptuously called it. Tidings of this event were sent from Buffalo to New York, in the space of one hour and twenty minutes, on the wings of sound produced by discharges of cannons placed at intervals along the line of the canal and the Hudson River.

The flotilla, beautifully decorated, was led by the barge *Seneca Chief*, drawn by four powerful gray horses. It bore as passengers Governor Clinton, Lieutenant-Governor Tallmadge, General Stephen van Rensselaer (the *patroon*), General Solomon van Rensselaer, Colonel W. L. Stone,* a delegation from New York City, and gentlemen and ladies who were invited guests. One large boat called *Noah's Ark* contained a bear, two fawns, two live eagles, and a variety of birds and "four-footed beasts," with two Seneca Indian youths in the costume of their dusky nation.

WILLIAM L. STONE.

---

* William Leet Stone was born at Esopus, N. Y., in April, 1792; died at Saratoga Springs in August, 1844. He made his residence at Cooperstown in 1809, and there learned the art of printing. In 1813 he became editor of the *Herkimer American*. Afterward he was an editor at Hudson, and at Albany, N. Y., and at Hartford, Conn. From 1821 until his death he was the able editor of the *New York Commercial Advertiser*. For some years he was Superintendent of Common Schools in the city of New York, and did efficient service in the cause of education. Colonel Stone held a ready pen, and wrote and published several volumes of much value. The most conspicuous of these are *The Life of Joseph Brant*, *The Life of Red Jacket*, and *Border Wars of the American Revolution*. At the time of his death he had completed the collection and arrangement of materials for a life of Sir William Johnson, which was finished and published by his son, William L. Stone, himself an accomplished writer.

Crowds gathered at villages and hamlets along the route at all hours of the day and night to see and greet the novel procession. At Rochester, where the canal crosses the Genesee River, a man was stationed as a sentinel in a boat on the Genesee, and when the *Seneca Chief* entered the aqueduct he called out:

"Who comes there?"

"Your brothers from the West, on the waters of the Great Lakes," answered a voice from the *Chief*.

"By what means have they been diverted so far from their natural course?" the sentinel inquired.

"Through the channel of the grand Erie Canal," responded the same voice.

"By whose authority and by whom was a work of such magnitude accomplished?" asked the sentinel.

"By the authority and by the enterprise of the people of New York," cried many voices as one from the deck of the *Chief*.

A canal-boat called *The Young Lion of the West*, having on board several distinguished gentlemen, two living wolves, a fawn, a fox, four raccoons, and two eagles, here joined the flotilla, which was everywhere greeted with demonstrations of joy as it glided down the beautiful Mohawk Valley. At Albany, the eastern terminus of the canal, where it is connected with the Champlain Canal, the voyagers were received by a grand civic and military procession, who escorted the governor and his travelling companions to the Capitol, where interesting services were held while bells rang and cannons thundered. People had gathered at the State capital from all parts of Northern New York, Vermont, and even Canada to witness the imposing spectacle. Philip Hone,[*] the Mayor of New York, made a congratulatory speech, and in the name of his constituents invited the Corporation of Albany to accompany the voyagers down the river and partake of the hospitality of the commercial metropolis. There was a grand illumination in Albany that evening.

---

[*] Philip Hone was a prosperous and public-spirited merchant of New York City, where he was born in 1781 and died in 1851. He was a very popular man of business, and in social life a fluent public speaker, and active in all important movements in the city of his birth. Mr. Hone was the chief founder of the Mercantile Library Association of New York. In 1825-26 he was Mayor of New York. He was the life of the Hone Club, composed of the literary and other celebrities of the city. President Taylor appointed him naval officer at New York, which post he held at the time of his death. Dr. J. W. Francis wrote of Mr. Hone as a public-spirited citizen: "From the laying of a Russ pavement to the elaboration of a church portico, from the widening of a street or avenue to the magnificent enterprise which resulted in the Croton Aqueduct, he was the efficient coadjutor of his fellow-citizens."

A flotilla of canal-boats was towed from Albany to New York by Hudson River steamboats. The *Chancellor Livingston* was the flagship of the squadron, having in tow the *Seneca Chief*, whose passengers were now transferred to her escort, and were joined by many others.

The aquatic procession moved at an early hour in the morning. It was greeted by groups or crowds of men, women, and children, the firing of great guns, and the waving of flags all along the banks of the Hudson. The flotilla was fully twenty-four hours descending the noble stream; and when it anchored off Greenwich Village, a suburb of the great city, before the dawn of November 4th, the people of the metropolis were astir, for ample preparations had been made for celebrating the event.

The day was welcomed by the ringing of bells and the roar of cannons. At a signal given from the *Chancellor Livingston* flags were unfurled all over the city, and the new steamboat *Washington*, handsomely decorated and bearing the banner of the corporation, proceeded to the fleet, conveying a committee of the municipal authorities and the officers of the governor's guard. When within hailing distance of the *Seneca Chief*, one of the officers of the *Washington* inquired of the strange craft, "Where are you from and what is your destination?"

PHILIP HONE.

The response was, "From Lake Erie and bound for Sandy Hook." At an early hour the waters at the mouth of the Hudson and the harbor of New York were dotted with floating craft of every kind. The fleet from Albany took a position between the Battery and Governor's Island, where it was joined by several steamboats conveying naval, military, and civil officers and invited guests. After receiving salutes from the Battery, Castle Williams on Governor's Island, and two British ships-of-war lying in the harbor, a grand procession was formed, composed of twenty-nine steamboats and sailing ships, schooners, barks, canal-boats, and sail-boats in large numbers, led by the *Chancellor Livingston*, and moved toward the sea. After passing the Narrows and receiving salutes from the forts there, the United States schooner *Dolphin* approached, as a "messenger from Neptune," to inquire who the visitors were and what was the object of their coming. This query answered, the motley fleet formed a circle around the *Dolphin* about three miles in circumference, preparatory to the performance of the grand nuptial ceremonies of wedding the gentle lakes and the sturdy Atlantic Ocean.

The *Seneca Chief* had brought from Buffalo two handsomely painted kegs filled with water from Lake Erie. One of these kegs was received by Governor Clinton on the deck of the *Chancellor Livingston*. Then there was silence and eager watching among the vast multitude floating on the unruffled bosom of the Atlantic under a serene and cloudless sky. Then Governor Clinton, lifting the keg of Erie water in full view of the spectators, stepped to the side of the *Chancellor Livingston* and poured its contents into the sea, saying:

"This solemnity, at this place, on the first arrival of vessels from Lake Erie, is intended to indicate and commemorate the navigable communication which has been accomplished between our Mediterranean seas and the Atlantic Ocean, in about eight years, to the extent of more than four hundred and twenty-five miles, by the wisdom, public spirit, and energy of the people of the State of New York; and may the God of the heavens and of the earth smile most propitiously on this work, and render it subservient to the best interests of the human race."

After a long address by Dr. Samuel L. Mitchell,* personal congratulations between men of the seaboard and Western New York, and the firing of a salute, the fleet, enlivened by the music of several bands, moved back to the city in a grand triumphal procession, the passengers on the steamboats partaking of a collation on the way.

Meanwhile a vast civic procession such as had never before been seen

---

* Samuel Latham Mitchell, M.D., was an eminent scientist, born at Hempstead, L. I., in August, 1764, and died in New York City in September, 1831. He studied both law and medicine. He was a member of the New York Legislature in 1790; made Professor of Chemistry, Natural History, and Philosophy in Columbia College in 1792, and in 1796 published a report of his tour along the Hudson River which gave him fame at home and abroad. He was one of the founders of a Society for the Promotion of Agriculture, Manufactures, and the Useful Arts. He was a member of the lower house of Congress twice between 1801 and 1813, and was United States Senator, 1804–1809. Was active in the College of Physicians and Surgeons and the Rutgers Medical School, in New York. With other eminent men he founded the New York Literary and Philosophical Society. A warm friend of Fulton, he accompanied him on the trial trip of the *Clermont*, in 1807. Dr. Mitchell was endowed with a remarkably retentive memory, and possessed great learning.

in the city of New York had been formed and paraded through the principal streets. It was composed of representatives of every respectable class in the metropolis arranged in organized groups. The benevolent, literary, and scientific institutions were represented, also the Fire Department, the bar, the pulpit, and various occupations. Every society seemed emulous to excel in the richness and beauty and art excellence of its banner and designs. Twenty-two industrial societies had furnished themselves with large platforms, upon which the artisans were employed in their several occupations as the procession moved through the streets. Upon one car was a printing-press, from which were continually issued and scattered among the people copies of a long "Ode for the Canal Celebration," opening with the following stanzas:

KEG WITH LAKE ERIE WATER.

"'Tis done! 'Tis done! The mighty chain
Which joins bright ERIE to the MAIN
For ages shall perpetuate
The glory of our native State.

*   *   *   *   *

"To-day the *Sire* of *Ocean* takes
A sylvan maiden to his arms,
The Goddess of the crystal Lakes
In all her native charms!"

The festivities of the day were closed in the evening by the illumination of the public buildings. On the following day (Saturday) the delegations from the West were entertained at a banquet given in their honor on board the *Chancellor Livingston*. The public institutions were opened to them. Sunday was passed quietly, and on Monday, the 7th, the festivities of the "canal celebration" were closed in the evening by a grand ball in the vast rooms of the Lafayette Amphitheatre in Laurens Street, near Canal Street. It was a brilliant assemblage (estimated) of more than three thousand persons. Among these were Governor Clinton and his wife.

To every guest of the corporation of New York on that occasion, both ladies and gentlemen, a beautiful medal was presented, bearing on one side the image of Pan and Neptune in loving embrace, and also a well-filled cornucopia showing the productions of the land and sea, with the words, "UNION OF ERIE WITH THE ATLANTIC." On the other side were the arms of the State of New York—the State which had borne the whole burden in the construction of the great work—and a representation of a section of the canal, its locks and aqueducts, and a view of the harbor of New York. On this side were the words, "ERIE CANAL, COMMENCED 4TH DAY OF JULY, 1817; COMPLETED 26TH OCTOBER, 1825. PRESENTED BY THE CITY OF NEW YORK."*

Wise and sagacious men had prophesied that this canal, when completed, would give an impetus to business of every description in the city of New York and in the interior of the State, and produce a wonderful increase in the population, commerce, and wealth of both sections. This prophecy was speedily fulfilled.† The canal did more. It presented an ample outlet to the sea for the products of the then rapidly developing region in the vicinity of the great lakes and the valley of the Ohio, which added untold millions to the value of that then almost wilderness region; and thus it became a national benefaction. It changed the whole aspect of commercial affairs in the lake region. The total area of these four great inland seas is about nine thousand square miles, and their inlets drain a region estimated at about three hundred and thirty-six thousand square miles. Upon its bosom have floated products of the North-western States and Territories valued at billions of dollars. In the year 1872 the value of property transported on that canal, notwithstanding a three-track railway lies parallel with it, was about $168,000,000.

The Erie Canal was built by the State of New York at a cost of $9,000,000. A greater portion of the country through which it passes was then an uncultivated wilderness. It was by far the most extensive public work ever attempted in this country up to that time, and excited

---

* The medals were made of white metal. Some were made of silver, and fifty-one gold ones were struck and sent to European monarchs and other distinguished persons. They were presented by a committee composed of Recorder Richard Riker, John Agnew, and William A. Davis.

† In the year 1812, five years before the construction of the canal was begun, the lately appointed canal commissioners—Gouverneur Morris, Stephen van Rensselaer, De Witt Clinton, and Peter B. Porter—gave the following prophetic utterance:

"Viewing the extent and fertility of the country with which this canal is to open communication, it is not extravagant to suppose that, when settled, its product will equal the present export of the United States [$58,000,000]. Will it appear improbable that twenty years hence [1832] the canal should annually bring down 250,000 tons?" Twenty years after the completion of the canal (1845), there came upon it to tide-water 1,107,000 tons of produce, valued at $45,000,000, the tolls upon which amounted to $2,500,000.

universal admiration. It has been twice enlarged, and is now seventy feet wide on the surface east of Rochester (and larger westward of that city), fifty feet wide at the bottom, and seven feet deep.

The canal system of New York rapidly extended after the completion of the Erie Canal, embracing nearly every section of the State. The whole number of the canals is fifteen.* The larger ones after the Erie are the Champlain Canal, 64 miles in length, finished in 1822; the Black River Canal, with its feeder, 87.5 miles in length, finished in 1849; the Genesee Valley Canal, with its Danville branch, 125 miles

BUFFALO IN 1815.

long, begun in 1826 and finished in 1861; and the Chenango Canal, 97 miles in length, completed in 1836.

The marvellous influence of the Erie Canal in promoting the increase of population in Western New York may be approximately estimated by the growth of two of its chief cities—Buffalo and Rochester. The British, as we have observed, literally "wiped out" Buffalo in 1813. In 1825, on the completion of the canal, it contained a population of about sixty-three hundred. Five years later the population had doubled. Now (1887) it is over two hundred thousand. Rochester was a wilderness three fourths of a century ago. The first dwelling—a log-cabin—

---

* Erie Canal, 364 miles in length; Champlain Junction, 64; Waterford Junction, 2; Oswego, 38; Cayuga and Seneca, 21; Crooked Lake, 8; Chemung, 39; Chenango, 97; Genesee Valley, 108.5; Danville Branch, 11; Black River, 77.5; Black River Feeder, 10; Delaware and Hudson, 83; Oneida, 8. Total length of canals in the State, 946.10 miles.

was built there in 1812. The picture shows an actual occurrence at that time. In 1825 it had a population of about eighteen hundred. Five

ROCHESTER IN 1812.

years later it was eleven thousand. Now the population is probably one hundred and fourteen thousand.*

---

* At the beginning of 1813 the Seneca Indians, at a great gathering of the tribe, encamped on the site of Rochester, performed pagan rites there. It was a "great sacrifice and thanksgiving" after the corn harvest was secured and the barbarians returned from their first hunting. The festival occupied several days. Two dogs, as nearly pure white as could be found, were killed by strangulation (for the effusion of blood would spoil the victim for sacrificial purposes) at the door of the council-house. The dogs were then painted with bright colors, decorated with feathers, and suspended about twenty feet above the ground at the centre of the camp. Then the ceremonies, which consisted chiefly of feasting and dancing, began.

Two carefully chosen bands, one of men the other of women, ornamented with trinkets and feathers, each person furnished with an ear of corn in the right hand, danced in a circle around the council-fire, their steps regulated by rude music. Thence they went to every wigwam in the camp, and in like manner danced in a circle around each fire. On another day, several men, clothed in the skins of wild beasts, covering their faces with hideous masks and their hands with the shells of tortoises, went among the wigwams, making frightful noises, taking the fuel from the fire and scattering the embers and the ashes about the floor for the purpose of driving away evil spirits.

These persons were supposed thus to concentrate within themselves all the sins of their tribe. These sins were transferred into one of their own number, who, by magic, worked off from himself into the two suspended dogs the concentrated wickedness of the tribe. The dogs were then placed on a pile of wood which was ignited, while the surrounding multitude cast tobacco and other "incense" upon the flames, the odor of which was supposed to be a "sweet-smelling savor," which would conciliate the favor

In his message at the opening of the session of the Legislature early in January, 1826,* Governor Clinton urgently called attention to needed improvements in the common-school system of the State, and recommended the establishment of normal schools for the education of teachers. In accordance with this recommendation John C. Spencer, a son of Judge Ambrose Spencer, submitted an able report from the Literature Committee of the Senate, early in February, concurring with the governor's recommendation and directing the attention of the Legislature to the propriety of employing the various academies of the State for the purpose; also appropriating a specific portion of the public funds to this important end. The report also suggested the expediency of a plan of county supervision of the common schools; resolutions recommending the election of justices of the peace by the people and an amendment of the State Constitution removing all restrictions to the right of voting, excepting only citizenship and a residence of six months. These resolutions were adopted by the Legislature, and the amendment was made accordingly. So, in the year 1827, the people of the State of New York were forever freed from the control over public opinion by the central power, and universal suffrage has since prevailed.

Early in the autumn of 1826 an event occurred in Western New York which produced a great effect on society in general, and upon the political parties in this State and in several other States in the Union. William Morgan, a native of Virginia, a printer by trade, and a Royal Arch Free Mason, living in Batavia, N. Y., determined, for some reason, to publish a pamphlet in which the secrets of Free Masonry were to be disclosed. Some of his fellow-members discovered this intention, and it was soon made known to Masonic lodges in Western New York. On September 11th Morgan was arrested at his home, on a charge of theft, at the instance of the master of a lodge of Masons at Canandaigua, and by him and other members of the order was hurried into a coach and taken to that town. He was discharged by a justice because he found no cause

---

of the Great Spirit. When the dogs were partially consumed, one was taken from the sacrificial pyre, put into a large kettle with vegetables of various kinds and boiled over a fire, when the whole company devoured the contents of the caldron. After this they performed the dances of war and peace, and smoked the calumet. Thus purified from sin, they returned to their homes and began the occupations of the new year.

* The year 1826 is memorable in our national history because of the almost simultaneous deaths of two of the leading founders of our Republic—Thomas Jefferson and John Adams. They both died on July 4th, within a few hours of the same time. It was the fiftieth anniversary of the signing of the Declaration of Independence. They were both on the committee which was appointed to draw up that Declaration. Jefferson wrote it, and both signed it.

of action. He was immediately rearrested on a civil process for a trifling debt and cast into jail.

On the following night Morgan was taken from the jail by a number of Free Masons, thrust into a carriage in waiting, taken by a relay of horses to Fort Niagara, at the mouth of the Niagara River, and confined in the powder magazine there. He was taken from that prison on the night of September 29th, and was never heard of afterward.

It was known that Morgan's brethren had made violent attempts to suppress his book, and when this outrage was made public the Free Masons were charged with its perpetration. There was widespread excitement. A public meeting held at Batavia appointed a committee to investigate the affair. They found evidence of what they believed to be an extended conspiracy to effect Morgan's death, with many agents moved by powerful motives. Similar meetings were held elsewhere. Public excitement continually deepened and widened, and a strong feeling soon pervaded the public mind that the Masonic institution was responsible for the crime.

The profound mystery in which the affair was involved gave wings to a thousand absurd rumors. Mutual criminations and recriminations became very violent, and entered into all religious, social, and political relations. A very strong Anti-Masonic party was soon created, at first only social in its character, but very soon it assumed a decided political aspect. This feature of the party first appeared at town meetings in the spring of 1827, when it was resolved by considerable majorities that no Free Mason was worthy to receive the votes of free men.

A political party formed for the exclusion of Free Masons from public offices was spread over the State of New York and into several other States, and continued several years. In August, 1830, an Anti-Masonic Convention at Utica nominated Francis Granger for Governor of New York. Enos T. Throop was the opposing candidate. Throop received 128,842 votes and Granger 120,861 votes. This result showed a powerful anti-Masonic sentiment in the State. Mr. Granger was again nominated for governor in 1832. In the same year a National Anti-Masonic Convention was held in Philadelphia, at which several States were represented. William Wirt, of Virginia, was nominated for President of the United States. The party polled a considerable vote, but soon afterward it began to gradually fade, and speedily became extinct as a political organization.

The fate of Morgan will never be known. It is believed that he was taken in a boat from Fort Niagara, cast into the water, and drowned.*

* In a series of letters written by Colonel W. L. Stone and addressed to John Quincy Adams, and published in a volume of over five hundred pages, a full and important history of the events I have alluded to is given.

CHAPTER XXXIV.

In the fall of 1826 Governor Clinton was re-elected, with Nathaniel Pitcher as lieutenant-governor. The chief events in the history of the State during this—the fourth—term of Mr. Clinton as governor were the Morgan episode and a State Convention held at Albany on July 27th, 1827, to appoint delegates to a National Tariff Convention, which was held at Harrisburg, Pa., on the 30th of the same month.

At the close of the war foreign goods, admitted almost free, prevented the revival of American manufactures, especially of woollen goods. A moderate tariff law was passed in 1818, and continued seven years. It was inadequate, and the manufacturers of New England and the Middle States clamored for protective laws. An act imposing heavier duties was passed in 1824. Still the northern manufacturers clamored for more protection, and called a convention at Harrisburg, Pa.

The cotton-growers of the South, meanwhile, perceiving that the tariffs were injurious to their interests, opposed them. Only four of the slave-labor States were represented at Harrisburg. Those of the North were numerous. New York sent about ten delegates to the convention. That body adopted a memorial to Congress on the subject, and Congress passed laws in 1827-28 which established a most stringent tariff. It was denounced by the Southern people as unjust and unconstitutional; and it led to the "nullification movement" in South Carolina in 1832. These tariff laws, of which Henry Clay was the principal champion, formed the foundation of the "American System," so called, for protecting home manufactures.

The State of New York and, indeed, the whole country now experienced a severe loss. Governor Clinton had suffered symptoms of organic disease of the heart for several months. On the evening of February 11th, 1828, while sitting in his study conversing with two of his sons, he suddenly fell forward and expired. His death caused deep and sincere sorrow throughout the State and nation. The voice of partisanship was hushed. Mr. Van Buren, long his most persistent political antagonist, said in a public address: "The triumph of his talents and patriotism cannot fail to become monuments of high and enduring fame." Alluding to their political antagonism and mutual personal respect, Mr. Van

Buren said: "I, who, while living, never, no, never, envied him anything, now that he has fallen, I am greatly tempted to envy him his grave with its honors." Lieutenant-Governor Pitcher performed the duties of governor during the remainder of the term.

An act was passed during the session of 1828 for the organization in the city of New York of a Superior Court of Common Pleas for the trial of civil actions, of which Chancellor Samuel Jones * was appointed chief-justice, and J. Ogden Hoffman and Thomas J. Oakley assistant justices. In the same year a contest for the Presidency of the United States occurred between John Quincy Adams and General Andrew Jackson, which resulted in the election of the latter, with John C. Calhoun as Vice-President. The New York Legislature chose twenty electors favorable to Jackson and sixteen favorable to Adams. In the election for State officers in the fall, Martin Van Buren was chosen Governor of New York.

In his message at the opening of the Legislature in 1829 Governor Van Buren recommended the appropriation of the surplus funds of the State and a judicious use of its credit to an extension of the system of internal improvements; also the establishment of a safety fund for the ultimate redemption of the notes of the several State banks, the choice of presidential electors by the people, and the promotion of the interests of popular education. A safety-fund bill planned by Joshua Forman, of Onondaga, was passed, and thirty-one banks, exclusive of three of the city of New York, were rechartered under the law. This excellent safety-fund system prevailed in New York until the establishment of our present national currency during the late Civil War.

In March, 1829, Governor Van Buren accepted the position of Secretary of State of the United States in the Cabinet of President Jackson, and forthwith he resigned his chair, which was filled by Lieutenant-Governor Throop. The fall election gave a very large majority of the political friends of Jackson (Democrats) to both branches of the Legislature. The Anti-Masons carried fifteen of the western counties and polled sixty-seven thousand votes.

---

* Samuel Jones was born in New York in 1769; was educated at Columbia College; studied law with De Witt Clinton in his father's office, the Chief-Justice of New York and "father of the New York bar," and became an eminent jurist. He was a member of the New York Assembly, 1812–14; Recorder of New York City in 1823; appointed Chancellor of the State in 1826, and accepted the office of Chief-Justice of the Superior Court in New York City in 1828. In 1847–49 he was a justice of the Supreme Court of the State and *ex-officio* a judge of the Court of Appeals. Judge Jones died at Cold Spring, L. I., in August, 1853.

It was at this time that Silas Wright,* who became conspicuous in the State and nation, appeared very prominent in public affairs in New York. He had been State Senator and member of Congress; he was now made comptroller—the manager of the complicated financial operations of the State. He proved himself competent and trustworthy. After conducting that office with signal ability for some years, he was transferred to the Senate of the United States.

Early in 1830 the Anti-Masons established at the seat of the State government the *Albany Evening Journal*, with Thurlow Weed † as editor. It took a conspicuous place in journalism from the start, and for a generation, under the management of Mr. Weed, it exerted marvellous power over the politics and politicians of the State. Mr. Weed, wrote Hammond,‡ was "one of the most shrewd and sagacious political

SILAS WRIGHT.

---

* Silas Wright was born at Amherst, Mass., in May, 1795; died at Canton, N. Y., in August, 1847. He was admitted to the bar in 1819, and began the practice of law at Canton. He was appointed surrogate of the county (St. Lawrence) in 1820. In 1823 he became State Senator, and a member of Congress 1827-29. In 1829 he was made Comptroller of the State of New York; United States Senator in 1833; defended Jackson's course in his warfare on the United States Bank; voted for the annexation of Texas; declined to be made a justice of the Supreme Court, and in 1844 declined the nomination for the vice-presidency. The same year he was elected Governor of New York. The next year he was offered the place of Secretary of the Treasury in President Polk's Cabinet. He retired to private life on leaving the chair of Governor of New York, and died soon afterward.

† Thurlow Weed was born in Cairo, N. Y., in November, 1797. He was a cabin-boy on a North River sloop at ten years of age; learned the printer's trade at Catskill, and in 1812 was a volunteer in the military service on the northern frontier of New York. He unsuccessfully attempted the establishment of a newspaper in Central New York, and in 1826-27 he edited the *Anti-Masonic Enquirer*. He was twice elected to the Assembly. In 1830 he became the editor of the *Albany Evening Journal*, and very soon became a prominent leader of the Whig and then the Republican Party, but he would never accept public office of any kind. In 1861 President Lincoln sent him to Europe in a semi-diplomatic capacity. He returned home in June, 1862. Then for a while he was editor of the *New York Commercial Advertiser*. In 1865 he took up his permanent abode in the city of New York with his family, and died at his home there on November 22d, 1882. He had visited Europe several times, the last in 1871.

‡ *Political History of New York*, by Jabez D. Hammond, LL.D., vol. ii., p. 339.

editors and eagle-eyed politicians the State of New York ever produced."

A "Workingmen's Party" was formed in the State of New York in 1830, but was short-lived. It was complained that workingmen did not receive a fair share of the public offices and emoluments. Others besides workingmen flocked to the new standard. General Erastus Root was nominated by the party for governor. It was professedly opposed to banks and paper money. It was soon controlled by others than workingmen—aspiring politicians—and, like all organizations effected and ruled by demagogues, it flourished awhile and then disappeared.

The rapid influx of population into the city and State of New York, especially from the New England States, after the completion of the Erie Canal, speedily put an end to the reign of the Knickerbocker element on society. Fashions, customs, and the general aspects of social life were modified by this immigration, and New York soon became largely, what it is to-day, a cosmopolitan city.*

It was at this period that William H. Seward, then a very young man, was sent to the State Senate. He took his seat in January, 1831, when only thirty years of age. He had been elected by the Anti-Masonic Party, who at the same time chose thirty members of the Assembly. That party nominated Francis Granger for governor and Samuel Stevens for lieutenant-governor in 1832, with an electoral ticket led by Chancellor Kent and John C. Spencer. The "National Republicans," as the adherents of Henry Clay called themselves, adopted the Anti-Masonic ticket; but the Democratic majority in the State at the election was thirteen thousand. General Jackson was re-elected President and Martin Van Buren Vice-President. With this contest the existence of the political Anti-Masonic Party, State and National, was virtually terminated. The institution of Free Masonry soon recovered from the shock and regained its good reputation and influence.

---

* The older reader will remember the fashions of the ladies about 1832. They were generally rather plain, but rich in material and colors. The walking-dress was lavender gray in color. The sleeves were tight from the elbow to the wrist, and very full above. They were called "mutton-leg sleeves." A *ruche* trimmed the corsage and extended straight down the front of the dress, which was short, showing the whole of the black prunella gaiter-shoes. The bonnet was Leghorn straw, with square brim lined with green satin. The crown was trimmed with three bands of green ribbon and a full cockade in the centre. The neck-knot was a green ribbon. The evening-dress was of Chinese green faced with dark green velvet and "mutton-leg" sleeves with velvet cuffs. The trimming of the skirt was a velvet band from which depended large leaves. The hair was dressed in full curls on the forehead, and in bows of moderate height on the top of the head. A wreath of roses and bluebells surrounded the base of the bows. Delicate morocco or satin slippers covered the feet.

In 1832 the Whig Party was formed in this wise: James Watson Webb, the editor and proprietor of the *New York Courier and Enquirer*, who attended as a spectator the Anti-Masonic Convention at Philadelphia

NEW YORK COSTUMES ABOUT 1832.

which nominated William Wirt for President, wrote a letter to his journal, in which he pointed out the folly of the different parties wasting their energies in separately opposing General Jackson. He proposed a coalition of the general's opponents under one rallying name to "fight the dangerous democracy." He claimed that these parties were contending for the Constitution against executive usurpation, while their opponents were battling to sustain such an usurpation. "We, therefore, are *Whigs*," he said, "while they are *Tories*. Why not, then, take to ourselves the name of *Whig*, which represents our principles, and give to our opponents the name of Tories?"

This letter was read to a very large meeting assembled at Masonic Hall, Broadway near Pearl Street, New York, by Philip Hone, who presided, and who suggested the adoption of the name of "Whig." It was done. The press and the people all over the country acquiesced. Thus it was that the great historic "Whig Party" received its name.

At this period the State of New York took the lead in a most important measure of reform, marked by justice and humanity. Enos T. Throop * took his seat as Governor of the State early in 1831. In his message to the Legislature he recommended the passage of a law for the abolition of imprisonment for debt; also for restricting the death penalty to only one specific crime. A law for the abolition of imprisonment for debt was passed at that session, and so New York acquired the honor of being the pioneer among the States in the work of abolishing from its statutes that absurd and barbarous law.

ENOS T. THROOP.
(From a painting by Charles L. Elliott.)

The embittered opponents of Anti-Masonry had joined in the support of Mr. Throop, and his election by over eight thousand majority gave to

---

* Enos T. Throop was born at Johnstown, N. Y., in August, 1784; died at Auburn, N. Y., November 1st, 1875. He acquired by hard study a classical and legal education, while performing the duties of an attorney's clerk. He settled in Auburn, N. Y., rose to eminence in his profession and as an acute politician, and was appointed circuit judge in 1823. He was a member of Congress, 1815-17, and in 1828 was elected Lieutenant-Governor of the State of New York. In 1830 he was elected governor. In 1838 Governor Throop was appointed *chargé d'affaires* to the two Sicilies.

RENEWAL OF THE U. S. BANK CHARTER OPPOSED. 479

the Jackson party a large and permanent accession of voters in the State of New York. William L. Marcy,* a distinguished jurist, ripe scholar, and expert politician, was elected governor by that strengthened party, and took his seat early in January, 1833. He was a member of the United States Senate at the time of his election, and in that body he had frankly promulgated the maxim that "to the victor belong the spoils." His seat there was filled by Silas Wright, and the vacant seat of another New York Senator was given to Nathaniel P. Tallmadge, of Duchess County.

The State of New York became very early a party to the vehement discussion, which took a national range, concerning the renewal of the charter of the United States Bank, for the destruction of which President Jackson was then waging an uncompromising war. Its charter would expire in 1836. In the winter of 1832 the bank applied to Congress for a renewal of its charter. During the sitting of the Legislature of New York the same winter a joint resolution was passed, after a warm debate, instructing the senators and requesting the members of the House of Representatives to resist such renewal. The resolution received an overwhelming majority of votes.

WILLIAM L. MARCY.

Mr. Van Buren, then designated the "Favorite Son of New York," felt the effects of this vote. He was known also as the "court favorite"

---

* William Learned Marcy was born in Southbridge, Mass., in December, 1786; died at Balston Spa, N. Y., July 4th, 1857. He was graduated at Brown University in 1808; taught school in Newport, R. I., awhile; studied law and began its practice at Troy, N. Y. He joined the army as a volunteer in 1812, and assisted in the capture of Canadian militia at St. Regis, the first prisoners taken on land. In 1816 he was Recorder of Troy. He edited the *Troy Budget* for a time as the leading Democratic organ in Rensselaer County, and was made Adjutant-General of the State in 1821. In 1823 he was State Comptroller, and in 1829 justice of the State Supreme Court. In 1831 he was chosen United States Senator, and was elected Governor of the State in 1833. He held that office by re-election until 1839. He was Secretary of War in Polk's Cabinet from 1845 to 1849, during the war with Mexico. He was United States Secretary of State, 1853–57. Governor Marcy was the author of several important State papers.

—the pet of the President, who desired him to be his successor in the presidential chair. Jackson appointed him Minister to England during the recess of the Senate. He sailed to that country, and was installed as accredited Minister of the United States. Henry Clay was a candidate for the presidency. By his tact and talent he succeeded in forming a party in the Senate opposed to the President. It consisted of a majority of the members of that body. The Senate was induced to refuse to ratify the appointment of Van Buren, and the unconfirmed minister was compelled to return home a private citizen.

The rejection of Mr. Van Buren produced intense indignation, especially in the State of New York. Indignation meetings denounced the act in no measured terms. Van Buren was considered by a large proportion of the American people a victim of persecution, and their love of fair play and their admiration for his ability caused them to elect him President of the United States as the successor of General Jackson.

It was at this period that the country was violently agitated by a movement in South Carolina to carry into practical effect the doctrine of supreme State sovereignty by an attempt to nullify or to defy laws of the United States. President Jackson promptly met this revolutionary movement by issuing a proclamation,* in which he denied the right of any State to nullify a law of the National Government, and commanded immediate obedience to all the laws. The proclamation was followed by prompt action, and very soon the country was relieved from menaces of civil war. The President was sustained by the loyal and patriotic men of both parties.

The most effective blow given to the United States Bank by the President in his warfare upon that institution was the removal from its custody of the deposits of the national funds, amounting to about $10,000,000, and placing the money on deposit in the State banks in the fall of 1833.

The Legislature of New York, then strongly Democratic, passed a resolution early in 1834, by a large majority, approving of the action of the President in ordering the removal of the deposits. It was believed that the deposit of the funds in the State banks would be of great benefit to the business community by affording facilities for acquiring loans from the banks. So it did; but the final result was anything but salutary. It led to the creation of a vast and dangerous credit system and wild speculations, which ultimately caused widespread disaster, as we shall perceive presently.

---

* This proclamation was written by the able Secretary of State, Louis McLane.

The managers of the United States Bank "got even" with the New Yorkers by bringing to bear upon them with peculiar severity, because of that resolution, the system they had adopted at the time of the removal of the deposits, of a great and sudden curtailment of discounts, and making forced collections from debtors. Their loans then amounted to $60,000,000. This severity brought the banks of New York to the verge of suspension of specie payments. To avert this calamity the Legislature, on the recommendation of the governor, tendered a loan to the banks of the credit of the State to the amount of $5,000,000, should relief become necessary. There was widespread commercial distress and a panic for a while. Very soon the great bank afforded relief by a sudden enlargement of discounts and a great expansion of its circulation, allowing the State deposit banks to loan freely. This revelation of the inherent power of the bank for working mischief attested the wisdom of the President in making war upon it.

By an act of the Legislature passed in March, 1834, the people of New York City were empowered for the first time to elect their own mayor. Hitherto that officer had been chosen by the Council of Appointment or by the Governor and Senate of the State. The first mayor elected by a popular vote was Cornelius W. Lawrence.

At that time a feud in the ranks of the Democratic Party in the city was disturbing its harmony, distracting its organization, and weakening its power. There had been formed, under the teachings of Fanny Wright and others of communistic proclivities, a "Radical" or "Equal Rights" faction, which appealed to the sympathies of the workingmen. It occasioned a split in the Democratic Party and the application to it of a nickname that adhered for several years. At a meeting in Tammany Hall just before the election in the fall of 1835, both sections of the party zealously claimed the right to the chair and the management of the proceedings. Violence ensued, and a grand row was the consequence. In the midst of the affray the gas was turned off and the room was left in darkness. One of the Equal Rights Party having some "loco-foco" matches in his pocket, relighted the lamps, and the business of the meeting proceeded. "I was one of the vice-presidents," wrote an actor in the scene, "and the next day I was compelled to buy a suit of new clothes. In a short time the whole Democratic Party were known as '*Loco-focos*.'"

In January, 1836, the Equal Rights Party organized as distinct from the Democratic Party, and adopted a Declaration of Rights, which condemned all monopolies and the issuing of a paper currency by banks. They declared no man eligible for nomination for office by this party unless he had signed the Declaration. One of the active members—John Windt, a printer—issued a journal called *The Democrat* as the organ of the new party. They nominated a candidate for Mayor of New York in the spring; proposed to nominate Colonel Samuel Young for governor, and attempted to form a State Equal Rights Party at a convention held at Utica in September, when they nominated Isaac S. Smith, of Buffalo, for governor, Robert Townsend, of New York, for lieutenant-governor, Frederick A. Tallmadge for State Senator, and a full Assembly ticket. They appointed a State Corresponding Committee. At the municipal election in the spring of 1837 their candidate for mayor received over four thousand votes. At a convention held at Utica in September they devised a State Constitution

The days of the Equal Rights Party were few. In the fall of 1837, finding very few adherents to the party outside of the city of New York, they effected a reunion with the Tammany party, or the old Democrats. Probably no political party in the State ever received more severe attacks and scathing animadversions than this. All the banks and the whole influence of chartered corporations and associated wealth were against them. Also the press of both parties, excepting the *Evening Post*, conducted by William C. Bryant and William Leggett.* The *Post* did not approve of a separate party organization, but warmly advocated its principles.

This was also a period of a radical revolution in journalism, which was inaugurated in the city of New York by James Watson Webb,† Benja-

---

* William Leggett was a powerful writer and a radical reformer in his proclivities. He was born in the city of New York in 1802; died at New Rochelle, N. Y., in May, 1839. He was a graduate of Georgetown (Roman Catholic) College, and was a midshipman in the United States Navy, 1822–26. Then he devoted himself to literary pursuits chiefly. He was a constant contributor to Morris's *New York Mirror* and other publications for years, under the title of "Tales by a Country Schoolmaster." In the autumn of 1828 he established in New York City a weekly literary periodical called *The Critic*. It was soon united with the *Mirror*. In 1829 he became associated with William Cullen Bryant in the management of the *New York Evening Post*, and was its chief editor in 1834–35. He sympathized with the anti-slavery movements of that day, and ably defended the right of free speech and discussion. In 1836 he established *The Plain Dealer*, devoted to politics and literature, but failing health soon compelled him to relinquish literary labor. Appointed diplomatic agent to the republic of Guatemala, he was preparing for a voyage thither when he suddenly died at his home.

† James Watson Webb, son of General Samuel B. Webb, of the Revolution, was born at Claverack, N. Y., in February, 1802. He entered the army as second lieutenant in August, 1819; was first lieutenant in 1823; resigned in 1827, and entered the arena of journalism in the city of New York, in which he wrought with power for thirty-six years —1827–61. He formed a conspicuous part of the social and political history of the city of New York. He was the publisher and chief editor of the *Morning Courier and Enquirer*

min H. Day, and James Gordon Bennett. Colonel Webb initiated the enterprise of collecting news by sending a fast-sailing clipper-built schooner many miles at sea to meet vessels from foreign ports, gather the latest news from abroad, and speedily publish it to the world. His contemporaries soon followed his example.

On September 3d, 1833, Mr. Day issued the first number of the *Sun*, the first one-cent daily newspaper ever published. Imitations soon followed. On May 6th, 1835, Mr. Bennett issued the first number of the permanently established *Herald* on a nominal capital of $500, and introduced a new feature in journalism — the "Money Article." His contemporaries followed his lead. At that time (1835), of the fifteen daily newspapers published in the city of New York, then having a population of two hundred and seventy thousand, only the *Sun* had a circulation of over six thousand daily.

This was also a period of riots in the city of New York. Emigration had recently given to the city a large population of ignorant, excitable, and often vicious foreigners, and these were speedily transformed, by unwise naturalization laws, into citizens and legal voters. This class of voters was out in full force at the first popular election of a mayor of the city in the spring of 1834. They generally affiliated with the Democratic Party, and were always the pliant tools of demagogues.

JAMES WATSON WEBB.

Early in the morning of the first day of the election (the polls were then opened three days in succession) riotous symptoms appeared. The

---

from 1830. In 1842 he was wounded in the leg in a duel with Thomas F. Marshall, of Kentucky—an affair which was the result of gross misrepresentations. In 1846 he was made military engineer-in-chief of the State, and ever after he bore the title of "general." In 1861, after declining a mission to Constantinople, he was appointed by President Lincoln Minister to Brazil, where he performed efficient services, and returned home in 1861, when he retired from public life. General Webb died at his residence in New York on June 7th, 1884.

The above portrait represents him when over eighty years of age. General Webb, through his personal intimacy with the Emperor Napoleon III., was instrumental in procuring the withdrawal of the French troops from Mexico during our Civil War.

Democratic leaders were exasperated by the opprobrious name of *Tories* applied to their party by their opponents, and seemed determined to win the victory at all hazards. The Whigs were numerous and strong; the Democrats had been weakened by discord.

In the Sixth Ward, where there was a large foreign population, a mob was soon gathered, and, led by an ex-alderman, rushed into the Whig committee-room, tore down the political banners, destroyed the ballots, and made a wreck of everything. They had felled to the floor, bruised and bleeding, about twenty of the inmates. The remainder escaped with bruises and torn garments. Clubs and even knives had been used, and one man was carried out in a dying condition. This occurrence gave the ward the title of the "Bloody Sixth."

This outrage aroused the opposite party to vigorous action, and under the lead of Colonel Webb an organized force of Whigs preserved comparative order, especially at the polls, the next day; but at night an enormous mob assembled in the City Hall Park. A cross had been set up near by bearing the words, "DOWN WITH THE COURIER AND ENQUIRER BUILDING," a five-story structure in Wall Street. Colonel Webb, the editor and proprietor of that journal, was the chief object of the wrath of the assembled multitude, who were required to march by and touch the cross. Then speakers in the park urged the excited populace to proceed to Wall Street. They did so with shouts and yells, which sent a thrill of alarm throughout the city. They found Colonel Webb's castle so strongly fortified, with him at the head of a well-armed and determined garrison, that they not only refrained from attack, but, cowards as they were, scampered away as fast as their legs could carry them.

On the following day there was a fierce collision in Broadway in front of Masonic Hall, where Mayor Gideon Lee, who attempted to quell the disturbance, was severely beaten. The rioters prepared to seize the Arsenal, when the mayor called out the (now) Seventh Regiment, National Guards, when order was soon restored by them; but the city was kept in a state of excitement for nearly two days longer. The Democrats had elected their candidate for mayor, Mr. Lawrence.

The election riots of 1834 and the increasing numbers and influence of foreign-born citizens finally alarmed thoughtful men. It was found that these adopted citizens held the balance of power between the Whig and Democratic parties, and that whichever party gained a victory they claimed an unreasonable share of the "spoils." The best citizens of New York, believing it to be their duty to check this influence, so menacing to our free institutions through the instrumentality of the ballot-box, combined, in the winter of 1842-43, in forming a new political organization for the purpose, which was called the Native American Party. They elected James Harper,* of the publishing house of Harper & Brothers, Mayor of New York in the spring of 1844, by a majority of over four thousand. From this auspicious beginning the party spread over the State and the republic, but its policy became so narrow and so really anti-American in character that after the presidential election in 1856, when its candidate for President of the United States was Millard Fillmore, it was dissolved.

The passions of the lower orders in New York City were so excited to do mischief by the election riots, that immediately afterward they were incited by the demagogues who had led them before to engage in a fearful public disturbance known as "The Abolition Riots." New York City was the headquarters of the American Anti-Slavery Society. Their meetings were frequently disturbed by their ignorant or unreasoning opponents. In July, 1834, these disturbances blossomed out into a wild riot, which spread terror over the entire city. Houses of humane citizens were sacked, the property of others was destroyed, and no less than five churches in the city were attacked and partially demolished. Again the (now) Seventh Regiment, National Guards, was called out to suppress the dangerous tumult and to restore order. In this effort it succeeded admirably.

In the years 1834 and 1835 a spirit of wild speculation scourged the land. Trade was brisk; the shipping interest was prosperous; prices ruled high; luxury abounded, and nobody seemed to perceive the undercurrent of disaster that was surely wasting the foundations of the absurd credit system and the real prosperity of the people. The credit system collapsed at the touch of the Ithuriel spear of Necessity. The Bank of England, seeing exchanges running higher and higher against that country, contracted its loans and admonished houses giving long credits to Americans by the use of money borrowed from the bank to curtail that hazardous business. At about the same time the famous "Specie Circular" went out from our Treasury Department (July, 1836) directing

---

* James Harper, the senior member of the original firm of Harper & Brothers, was the son of Joseph Harper, of Newtown, L. I., where he was born in April, 1795. At sixteen years of age he went to New York to learn the art of printing. Industrious and thrifty, he was able, soon after his majority, to begin business on his own account. In the course of time his three brothers, John, Joseph Wesley, and Fletcher, became associated with him in the printing and publishing business under the firm name of Harper & Brothers. This brotherhood remained unbroken forty-three years, when, in March, 1839, James died at St. Luke's Hospital, New York, whither he had been taken, mortally hurt by being thrown from his carriage while his horses were running away. Mr. Harper was ever prominent in good works.

the collectors of the public money to receive nothing but coin. From the parlor of the Bank of England and from the Treasury of the United States went forth the unwelcome fiat, "Pay up!" American houses in London failed for many millions, and every bank in the United States suspended specie payments in 1837. In 1839 the Bank of the United States, which had been rechartered by the State of Pennsylvania, fell into hopeless ruin, and with it went down a large number of the State banks of the country. A general Bankrupt Act, passed in 1841, relieved of debt about forty thousand persons, whose aggregate liabilities amounted to about $441,000,000.

The business men of the city and State of New York suffered intensely from these financial troubles. Already the merchants of the city had been severely smitten by a fearful conflagration on a bitterly cold night—December 16th, 1835—which reduced to ashes and cinders in the space of a few hours property valued at almost $20,000,000. But from this calamity and the financial troubles of 1837 the merchants of New York, by their energy and pluck, presented the spectacle of a speedy and marvellous rebound.

The construction of the Croton Aqueduct for the sanitary and other uses of the inhabitants of the city of New York had been begun a few weeks before the great fire. It was completed in 1842 at a cost of $10,375,000, including $1,800,000 for distributing pipes and amounts paid for the right of way. It extends from the Croton River, in Westchester County, where the waters of that stream are collected in a large reservoir, to the distributing reservoir at Forty-second Street and Fifth Avenue, in New York City, a distance of about forty miles. The aqueduct is tubular in form, and crosses the Harlem River over the magnificent High Bridge. The receiving reservoir within the Central Park covers an area of thirty-five acres.

CHAPTER XXXV.

Governor Marcy's administration extended from 1833 to 1839, during which time wise and important measures were adopted by the Legislature on his recommendation. The most conspicuous of these measures was a provision, at the session of 1835, for the enlargement of the Erie Canal and for the promotion of popular education and enlightenment. The Legislature responded generously. It instructed the canal commissioners to "enlarge and improve the Erie Canal, and construct a double set of lift-locks therein." These improvements were finally made, at an expense far greater than the cost of its original construction. This enlargement had become necessary because of the increasing business of the canal within ten years after it was completed.

This provision for the material prosperity of the State was supplemented in April, 1835, by a provision for the intellectual advancement of the people of the commonwealth. A law was passed for the establishment of a free library in every school district in the State, then numbering over nine thousand six hundred. Governor Marcy took special interest in the matter, and made untiring efforts to accomplish this important object—this grand feature of our common-school system. He desired to afford an opportunity to every child within the border of the commonwealth, of whatever color, race, creed, or condition, to acquire intellectual and moral cultivation and enlightenment. The late General John A. Dix was the Secretary of State and Superintendent of Common Schools when these libraries were established. To his wisdom and sound judgment, aided by his deputy, S. S. Randall, the people of the State were indebted for the excellence of the selection of the books for the libraries.* These were pretty generally established in 1838, when the

---

* In the selection of books the following directions were adhered to :

"1. No works written professedly to uphold or attack any sect or creed in our country claiming to be a religious one shall be tolerated in the school libraries.

"2. Standard works on other topics shall not be excluded because they incidentally and indirectly betray the religious opinions of their authors.

"3. Works avowedly on other subjects which abound in direct and unreserved attacks on or defence of the character of any religious sect, or those which hold up any religious body to contempt or execration by singling out or bringing together only the darker part of its history or character, shall be excluded from the school libraries. In the selection of books for a district library, information and not mere amusement is to be regarded as

pupils attending the district schools of the State numbered about five hundred thousand five hundred. An annual appropriation of $55,000 was made for the purchase of books for the libraries. In 1844 a State Normal School (the first in the commonwealth) was established at Albany, of which David P. Page was the first principal. It occupied a

STATE NORMAL SCHOOL BUILDING AT ALBANY.

building on State Street (117) originally erected by the Mohawk and Hudson Railroad Company for a passenger depot.*

It was at this period that great improvements were made in the system of popular education in the city of New York. The Lancastrian or monitorial form of government and instruction had long prevailed there

---

the primary object. Suitable provision should, however, be made for the intellectual wants of the young by furnishing them with books which, without being merely juvenile in character, may be level to their comprehension and sufficiently entertaining to excite and gratify a taste for reading. It is useless to buy books that are not read."

* A spacious building for the use of the State Normal School was completed late in 1885, and the school was opened therein on September 9th, with representatives from forty-three of the sixty counties of the State. During the first term in the new structure the attendance in the Normal Department was three hundred and sixty.

and in other parts of the State.* The Pestalozzian † system had also been pretty extensively adopted. In 1832 a new organization of the public schools was effected, and these two grafts from foreign systems were pruned away. The schools in the city were placed upon a perfectly free basis, and were graded in 1834. The six schools for colored children were transferred to the Public School Society (the formation of which has already been noticed), and placed on an equality with the other schools.

Toward the close of 1837 a popular outbreak occurred in the neighboring British provinces of Upper and Lower Canada, which caused intense excitement among the people of the northern portions of New York. Their sympathies with the insurgents were aroused, and citizens of the State engaged in an unlawful invasion of the territory of a friendly neighbor.

There had been popular discontent in these provinces for some time. It finally assumed the aggressive form of a concerted attempt in both territories to cast off dependence upon Great Britain. The chief leaders in this movement were William Lyon McKenzie, in Upper Canada, and Joseph Papineau, in Lower Canada. McKenzie was a Scotchman, a journalist of rare ability, and a restless political agitator. Papineau, of French descent, was an extensive land-owner in the Lower Province, of cool judgment, and very influential among the French inhabitants in that region. Both leaders were republicans in sentiment.

This movement was regarded as patriotic by the Americans, and the active sympathy of the New Yorkers along the frontier was evoked. At the middle of December (1837) nearly a thousand New York volunteers, with provisions and twenty pieces of artillery, seized Navy Island, in the Niagara River, two miles above the falls. There they were joined by McKenzie, who was already a fugitive. They employed a small

---

* It was so called after Joseph Lancaster, a member of the Society of Friends, or Quakers, who at the beginning of the century introduced into the schools in England the monitorial system, which consisted of the employment of monitors, so called, composed of some of the brightest boys and girls in school, who each had charge of the discipline and tuition of a section of the school. They enforced discipline by watchfulness and prompt reporting to the teacher. The system was designed to carry on the public teaching of children in the most economical way. By this means a teacher could manage a school of three or four hundred children. But this system of espionage was mischievous.

† The Pestalozzian system originated with John Pestalozzi, a Swiss teacher and reformer, and was designed to educate infant pupils by a combination of industrial, entertaining, intellectual, and moral instruction, without the use of books and by oral and object teaching entirely—the fundamental basis of the kindergarten system of Froebel. It was put in practice first in New York by the Infant School Society, founded by Mrs. Divie Bethune and others, in 1828.

steamboat named the *Caroline* as a ferry-vessel between the New York shore and the island. On a dark night at the close of December, while persons on board of her were asleep, a party of armed Canadian loyalists from Chippewa seized her, killed some of her people, cut her loose from her moorings, set her on fire, and allowed her to go blazing down the fearful rapids and over the crown of the mighty cataract into the seething gulf below. It is believed that some persons were alive on board and perished with the vessel.

McKenzie, whose rashness imperilled the cause at the outset, fled to New York. The Governor of Canada made requisition upon Governor Marcy for the surrender of the arch-agitator. Marcy declined to do so, for McKenzie's offence was *political*, not *criminal*, and he was seeking an asylum on neutral territory.

Meanwhile all along the New York frontier, from Cape Vincent to Rouse's Point at the foot of Lake Champlain, American sympathizers continued to cross into Canada and join the insurgents. At Clayton, on the New York shore of the St. Lawrence, lived William Johnston, a bold British subject, who was appointed commodore of the naval force of the insurgents by their authority.* He kept up an amphibious warfare among the Thousand Islands, and others on the Canada shore kept the frontier in continual excitement for months. At length the President of the United States (Van Buren) issued a proclamation forbidding American citizens engaging in the insurrectionary movement. General Scott was sent to Northern New York to preserve order. Governor

---

* William Johnston was born at Three Rivers, Canada, in February, 1782. His father was an Irishman, and a Dutch girl from New Jersey was his mother. He was living at Clayton (French Creek), on the St. Lawrence, when the insurrection broke out. Cordially hating the British Government and its employés, and fond of adventure, he was easily persuaded to join in the strife. He was bold and courageous. The "Patriots" commissioned him "commodore" and commander-in-chief of the navy on the lake, among the Thousand Islands, and on the St. Lawrence River. After he had burned a British steamboat and committed other excesses, a reward for his apprehension was offered by both governments, and for a long time he was a fugitive, hiding among the islands and supplied with food by his charming daughter, a girl of eighteen years, who was expert in the management of a boat. He finally gave himself up to the American authorities. He was sentenced to one year's imprisonment and a fine, and was confined in jail at Albany, where his daughter joined him to solace him in his solitude. They managed to escape, and Johnston was unmolested. When I visited him in 1860, at Clayton, he was the keeper of a light-house a few miles below. His daughter, the "Heroine of the Thousand Islands," was then a matron with several children, but retaining many traces of her former beauty. Johnston gave me his photograph; also his commission from the Grand Council, the Western Canadian Association, the Grand Eagle Chapter, and the Grand Eagle Chapter of Upper Canada, creating him "Commodore of the Navy, Commander-in-Chief of all the Naval Forces of the Canadian Provinces on Patriot service."

Marcy also issued a proclamation of the tenor of that of the President. The open contest soon ceased, but for some time secret associations called "Hunters' Lodges" on New York soil kept up the excitement. These lodges numbered about twelve hundred. They were suppressed by President Tyler in 1842.

Early in January, 1841, an incident occurred on the Niagara frontier which for a moment threatened to disturb the existing amity between the governments of the United States and Great Britain. Alexander McLeod, a resident of Chippewa, being at Lewiston, on the New York shore of the river, boasted that he was a participant in the destruction of the steamer *Caroline* and in the murder of one of her men. He was arrested and sent to the Lockport jail. He was indicted for murder, and the owner of the vessel instituted a civil suit against him. Mr. Fox, the British Minister at Washington, demanded of our Government the release of McLeod, and avowed and justified the destruction of the *Caroline* as an act of his Government. The Secretary of State (Mr. Webster) informed Mr. Fox that it was a State affair, and the National Government had no right to interfere with the judicial proceedings of a State ; that the matter was before the Supreme Court of New York, and that he believed that tribunal would agree with him that the prisoner ought to be given up, for he was acting in obedience to orders from a superior. That court remanded McLeod for trial before a special circuit court sitting at Utica. After an exciting trial the innocence of the prisoner was proven, he having made the boast in a spirit of bravado while intoxicated. He was acquitted.

Martin Van Buren was nominated for the Presidency of the United States in 1836. Perceiving the necessity of taking ground against the Abolitionists, now organized and aggressive, in order to secure the votes of the Southern States, he did so, and was elected, taking his seat as Chief Magistrate in the spring of 1837. Governor Marcy also took a position antagonistic to the Abolitionists ; and so the Democratic Party of the State and nation became wedded to the upholders of the system of slavery. The nuptials proved disastrous to the party.

Never did any political party seem to stand on a more secure foundation than did the Democratic Party in New York in the winter of 1836-37. Alas ! before the lapse of a year it was utterly overthrown. In the fall the Whigs elected one hundred and one of the one hundred and twenty-eight members of the State Assembly, and carried six of the eight senatorial districts. The country had been swept by a fearful tornado of financial disaster. The banks of New York were compelled to suspend specie payments ; commercial distress was the rule, and the huge, hollow credit system fell into ruins. All this had followed the terrible fiat of the "Specie Circular" and cognate instrumentalities. The Whig leaders adroitly charged the public calamities to the misrule of the Democratic Party. The rank and file accepted the solution, and the overthrow of Democratic domination in New York was the logical consequence. William H. Seward was elected Governor of the State in the fall of 1838, over Governor Marcy, by a majority of about ten thousand.*

WILLIAM H. SEWARD.

The finances of the State at this juncture were admirably managed. The banks conducted their business with so much prudence that they were able to resume specie payments in 1839. A Free Banking Law had been enacted in 1838 on the recommendation of Governor Marcy. Governor Seward in his message in 1839 spoke highly of the measure, and he eulogized the financial position of the State of New York, saying:

"History furnishes no parallel to the financial achievements of this State. It surrendered its share in the national domain, and relinquished

---

* William Henry Seward was born at Florida, Orange County, N. Y., in May, 1801; died at Auburn, N. Y., in October, 1872. He was a graduate of Union College, and began the practice of law at Auburn in 1823. He soon acquired a high reputation in his profession. He first appeared conspicuous in politics as president of a State convention of young men who favored the election of John Quincy Adams to the Presidency of the United States. He was a member of the State Senate, 1830-34, and became a leader of the newly-formed Whig Party. He was elected Governor of New York in 1838, and again in 1840. For several years he quietly pursued his lucrative profession. In 1849 he was chosen United States Senator, which position he held until called to the seat of Prime Minister (Secretary of State) in the Cabinet of President Lincoln in the spring of 1861. He filled the office with great honor to himself and the nation during the trying period of the Civil War. He continued in the same office in the Cabinet of President Johnson. Mr. Seward was regarded for many years as one of the leading and most efficient opposers of the system of slavery. Early in 1865 he was confined to his bed by an accident, and on the night of the murder of President Lincoln an assassin found his way into Mr. Seward's home and attempted to slay him. He never recovered from the shock. In the spring of 1869 he retired from public life. In August, 1871, he started with some friends on a tour around the world. He was everywhere received with marks of great respect. Mr. Seward died at Auburn, October 10, 1872. One of the most notable of his public acts was the purchase of Alaska from Russia for $7,200,000 in gold, in 1867.

for the general welfare all the revenues of its foreign commerce, equal generally to two thirds of the entire expenditure of the Federal Government. It has, nevertheless, sustained the expenses of its own administration, founded and endowed a broad system of education, charitable institutions for every class of the unfortunate, and a penitentiary establishment which is adopted as a model by civilized nations. It has increased fourfold the wealth of its citizens, and relieved them from direct taxation ; and in addition to all this has carried forward a stupendous enterprise of improvement, all the while diminishing its debts, magnifying its credit, and augmenting its resources.'' *

Governor Seward recommended the Legislature (1840) to provide for the speedy completion of the enlargement of the Erie Canal, but told them frankly that the cost, which the State officers had estimated at $12,000,000, would be at least $23,000,000—possibly $25,000,000. He also urged the construction of the Genesee Valley and Black River canals, which would require an expenditure of $6,000,000. In the same message he invited the attention of the Legislature to the fact that he had received from the Governor of Virginia a demand for the return of three colored "fugitives from justice," charged with stealing a negro-slave. Governor Seward refused compliance on the ground that such alleged felony was not recognized as such by the laws of civilized nations or those of the State of New York.† This was Mr. Seward's first official encounter with the slave power.

---

* The State of New York has the honor of having within its borders the first passenger railway built in the United States. The first railway charter granted in America was given by the Legislature of New York, in 1825, to the Mohawk and Hudson Railway Company. Their road extended from Albany to Schenectady, a distance of about fifteen miles, and was completed in the fall of 1831.

† The Governor of Virginia in his next annual message referred the matter to the Legislature of his State, and haughtily declared that if the construction of the Constitution of the United States by the Governor of New York should be allowed to prevail, and no relief could be obtained against a "flagrant violation of the rights of Virginia" to reclaim her fugitive slave, it would be proper for her "to appeal from the cancelled obligations of the national compact to original rights ;" in other words, to secede from the Union.

The matter did not end here. The Virginia governor entered upon the work of retaliation. A citizen of New York charged with the crime of forgery fled to Virginia. Governor Seward forwarded a requisition for him to be surrendered as a fugitive from justice. The Governor of Virginia refused compliance, and kept the prisoner in jail a long time waiting for the Governor of New York to give up the three colored Virginia fugitives. This unjustifiable conduct on the part of the governor was disclaimed by the Virginia Legislature. The Legislature of New York adopted a joint resolution sustaining the claim of the Governor of Virginia for the three fugitives, and directed Governor Seward to transmit the resolution to the executive of Virginia. He declined to do so, and suggested the employment of some other agent than himself to perform that task. Here the matter was dropped.

The Whig Party had now the entire political control of the State of New York, and the result of the presidential election that year (1840) gave them the political control of the nation for a while. In New York Governor Seward was re-elected, and the Whig candidate for the presidency, General William Henry Harrison, of Ohio, was chosen by a very large majority, after an exciting and demoralizing canvass, known in political history as "The Hard-Cider Campaign." *

President Van Buren had made himself very unpopular with the banking and commercial interests of the country because of his successful exertions in the establishment of the independent treasury ; also with a large portion of the people of the non-slaveholding States because of his alleged subserviency to the Southern slave oligarchy. Harrison took his seat on March 4th, 1841, and died just one month afterward. Then Vice-President John Tyler, of Virginia, assumed, by constitutional provision, the exalted position of President of the United States.

At this time the population of New York was about two million five hundred thousand. Of this number, it was estimated that about thirty thousand children were uneducated, of whom fully one third were of foreign parentage. These were destined to become future citizens. In view of these facts thoughtful men pondered the matter with anxiety. Governor Seward was keenly alive to the foreshadowed danger, and in his message to the Legislature in 1841 he strongly urged that body to provide by law for the elementary education of the children of foreigners, of whatever nationality or religious belief. He said :

"I could not enjoy the consciousness of having discharged my duty if any effort had been omitted which was calculated to bring within the schools all who are destined to exercise the rights of citizenship ; nor shall I feel that the system is perfect or liberty safe until that object be accomplished."

The wise and cultivated citizen, John C. Spencer,† was then the

---

* General Harrison lived in the growing West, and his dwelling had once been a log-cabin, at North Bend, Ohio, where he exercised great hospitality. In the campaign referred to his partisans made a log-cabin a symbol of his democracy—a man of the people—and a barrel of cider symbolized his hospitality. In hamlets, villages, and cities log-cabins were built as rallying-places for the members of the party, and there cider was freely given to all. Drinking carousals were the results, and the demoralization of young men was fearful. Horace Greeley edited a campaign paper called *The Log-Cabin*, which became the predecessor of the *New York Tribune*.

† John Canfield Spencer, son of Judge Ambrose Spencer, was born at Hudson, N. Y., in January, 1788 ; died in Albany in May, 1855. He was a graduate of Union College ; studied law and began its practice at Canandaigua, N. Y., in 1809. At the age of nineteen he had been private secretary of Governor Tompkins, and was ever afterward prom-

Secretary of State and State Superintendent of Common Schools. He was in full accord with the views of Governor Seward. In response to petitions from the city of New York upon this subject, which were referred to him, he made an able report, in which he recommended the election of a Board of Commissioners of Common Schools in that city, authorized to establish and organize a system of ward schools, which should co-operate with those of the Public School Society in furnishing the requisite facilities for the education of all classes of children. On Mr. Spencer's recommendation provision was made for a State Deputy Superintendent of Common Schools, to which important office S. S. Randall, who had been Secretary Dix's deputy, was appointed. Provision was also made for the election of county superintendents throughout the State. A liberal appropriation was made for the support of the *Common School Journal*, which was devoted to the interests of popular education.*

Out of these and cognate proceedings grew a violent controversy which had been begun mildly many years before. Its essence was the

---

inent in the public affairs of the State. In 1811 he was appointed master in chancery, and in 1813 judge-advocate in active military service on the frontier. In 1814 he was postmaster at Canandaigua, and was assistant attorney-general in 1815. He was a member of Congress, 1817–19, and a member of the Assembly and its Speaker in 1820. He was State Senator, 1824–28, and in 1827 was one of the commissioners to revise the statutes of New York. He became an anti-Mason, and was a special officer appointed to prosecute the persons connected with the alleged abduction of Morgan. Judge Spencer was Secretary of State, 1839–41. He was first made Secretary of War and then Secretary of the Treasury in Tyler's Cabinet. Opposed to the annexation of Texas, he resigned in 1844 and resumed the practice of law. To Judge Spencer is due, to a great extent, the greater improvements in the common-school system of the State. He edited the first edition of De Tocqueville's *Democracy in America*.

* The apathy of the people concerning popular education in the State of New York at that time was most remarkable. It was stipulated that one copy of the *Common School Journal* should be sent regularly to the clerk of every school district in the State free of charge. "It is mortifying and painful to state," says Hammond, in his *Political History of New York*, vol. iii., p. 225, "what the truth of history requires us to record, that it is within our personal knowledge that the trustees of many school districts refused to take from the post-office this excellent journal, every number of which contained much important and useful information, the cost of which is paid from the State Treasury, because they were unwilling to pay from the common funds of their respective districts the sum of *one shilling a year for postage!*"—one cent a month.

The author of this volume was one of a few citizens of Duchess County who, at the beginning of 1837, formed a society for "The Improvement of Common Schools and the General Diffusion of Knowledge." Many of the best citizens of the county became members of the association, and meetings were held by the society at various places in the county with a hope of exciting public interest in the important subject. Yet such was the marvellous apathy of the trustees of the common schools and of parents in general, that after a trial of about fifteen months the effort was abandoned as useless.

antagonism of religious denominations, some of which had participated in the benefits of the public money placed under the control of the Public School Society (which was a close corporation and had supreme power in the distribution of the funds intrusted to it by the State), and others had been denied such participation. The subject was brought before the Legislature. That body by act transferred the whole matter of the distribution of the school fund in the city of New York to the Common Council, with full powers.

The trustees of the Roman Catholic Free Schools applied to the Common Council for a separate proportionate share in the distribution of the school fund. Their schools were numerous and were rapidly increasing. The Public School Society remonstrated, and the chamber of the Common Council became a notable arena for the display of argumentative oratory.

ARCHBISHOP HUGHES.

The Public School Society employed some of the best legal talent in the city to champion their cause. They were confronted by the astute Archbishop Hughes,* who appeared in behalf of the Roman Catholics.

The controversy became exceedingly hot, and great public excitement prevailed. The Common Council sustained the Public School Society. The Roman Catholics appealed to the Legislature. On the recommendation of Governor Seward that body extended to the wards of the city

---

* Archbishop John Hughes, an eminent Roman Catholic prelate, was born in county Tyrone, Ireland, in 1797; died in New York City in January, 1864. He emigrated to America with his father in 1817; received a good education at a Roman Catholic seminary in Maryland, and remained there as a teacher several years. In 1825 he was ordained a priest, and was settled in Philadelphia. In 1838 he became coadjutor to Bishop Dubois in New York, and on the death of the latter in 1842 he became bishop. He visited Europe in 1839, and in 1841 opened St. John's College at Fordham, which he had organized. He held the first diocesan synod in New York in 1842, where alterations were made in the methods of the administration of churches without trustees. In 1850 he was created archbishop. He held the first provincial council of his Church in New York in 1854. On the breaking out of the late Civil War Archbishop Hughes was sent to Europe with the late Thurlow Weed on an informal diplomatic mission in behalf of the United States Government. His health failed soon after his return. He was a powerful controversialist, and did much to advance the prosperity of his Church.

of New York the common-school system which had prevailed for many years throughout the State. The management of the schools (independent of those under the control of the Public School Society) was placed in the hands of inspectors, trustees, and commissioners elected by the people ; and so all schools were allowed to participate in the benefits of the public funds according to the number of their scholars ; but such participation was prohibited to any school in which any religious sectarian doctrine or tenet should be taught, inculcated, or practised.

Both contestants were dissatisfied. The friends of the Public School Society regarded the measure as a serious blow to popular education. The Roman Catholics considered the exclusion of all religious instruction from the schools as most fatal to the moral and religious principles of their children, and said : " Our only resource is to establish schools of our own." The Public School Society kept up its organization several years longer, but, convinced of the superiority of the State system, it was dissolved in 1853, and some of its members took seats in the Board of Education, which was organized in 1842. That board has ever since had the supreme control of public instruction in the city of New York.

Under the auspices of the Board of Education a normal school was established in the city of New York in 1869. An elegant, spacious, and well-equipped edifice for its use was completed in 1873, and the school was opened in September, that year, under the title of " The New York Normal College." * Already a State Normal School had been established at Albany (1844), as we have observed, under the control of an Executive Committee composed of the Superintendent of Common Schools and four other gentlemen.

In the fall of 1842 another political revolution in the State of New York occurred. The Whig Party was overthrown, and William C. Bouck, the Democratic candidate for governor, was elected by about twenty-two thousand majority.† The Democrats also elected a large majority of the members of both branches of the Legislature. The Abolitionists, who were chiefly Whigs, gave to their candidate for governor—Alvan Stuart—about seven thousand votes.

---

* The Normal College in New York is devoted to the training of female teachers. All its teachers, outside the faculty, are women. The building, fronting on Sixty-eighth Street, is an elegant one, four stories in height.

† William C. Bouck was born in Schoharie, N. Y., in 1786 ; died there in April, 1859. In 1812 he was appointed sheriff of Schoharie County. He was a member of the Assembly, 1813–15 ; State Senator in 1820, and canal commissioner, 1821–40. From 1843 to 1845 he was Governor of the State, and in 1846 was a member of the State Constitutional Convention. From 1846 to 1849 he was assistant treasurer in New York City, after which he devoted himself to agriculture.

Governor Bouck took his seat at the beginning of 1843. In February
Silas Wright, who now ranked among the ablest members of the Senate
of the United States, was re-elected to a seat in that body for six years.
The new State administration was moving on quietly and harmoniously,
when Colonel Samuel Young, the Secretary of State, created much
excitement in and out of the Legislature by declining to carry out one
of its important orders.

Several years before, the Legislature authorized a geological survey of
the State under the supervision of competent scientists. It was now
completed, and their elaborate report, in ten volumes, accompanied by
numerous illustrations, was submitted to the Legislature. That body
ordered three thousand copies to be printed and deposited with the
Secretary of State for distribution
among the State officers and members of the Legislature.

In a communication to the Legislature, in March, the Secretary of
State declined to carry out the provisions of the act. He declared it
to be unconstitutional, because it
had failed to receive the assent of
two thirds of all the members elected to each House, as directed by
the Constitution. He pointed out,
with stinging words of censure,
other violations of the Constitution
by the Legislature in the creation
of stocks and the grants of public
money. He said:

WILLIAM C. BOUCK.

"Millions of outstanding stocks are now impending over the State
which were created by laws in clear and direct hostility with the plain
provisions of the Constitution; null and void in their inception, and
imposing not even the shadow of a moral obligation for the fulfilment of
their ostensible demands."

These assertions created instant and warm debates in the Legislature
and alarm among the holders of these securities. That alarm was soon
quieted by resolutions adopted by the Legislature, declaring that the
State would sacredly fulfil all its obligations without regard to technical
informalities. The secretary, however, persisted in refusing to comply
with the law during his whole official term.

At this time the State was much agitated by the presentation of a social problem which had been pressing for a solution for some time. It was a question of land tenure.

We have noticed the acquirement of vast tracts of land in New Netherland, under the Dutch rule, by privileged persons called *patroons*. After the old war for independence, when the laws of primogeniture were abolished, a large proportion of the land of the settled part of the State of New York was held by these *patroons*, and the cultivators of the estates occupied farms on leases for one or more lives, or from year to year, stipulating for the payment of rents, dues, and services, somewhat after the manner of the old feudal tenures in Holland and England. These feudal tenures having also been abolished, the proprietors of manor grants contrived a form of deed by which the grantees agreed to pay rents and dues almost precisely as before. These tenures became burdensome and odious to the tillers; and in 1839 associations of farmers were formed for the purpose of devising a scheme of relief from the burdens. They were the tenants of *Patroon* Van Rensselaer, who had just died.

This movement soon became known as "anti-rentism." It speedily manifested itself in open resistance to the service of legal processes for the collecting of manorial rents. The first overt act of lawlessness that attracted public attention was in the town of Grafton, in Rensselaer County, where a band of anti-renters killed a man. Yet the criminal was never discovered.

In 1841 and 1842 Governor Seward in his messages recommended the reference of the alleged grievance and matters in dispute on both sides to arbitrators, and appointed three men to investigate and report to the Legislature. Nothing was accomplished, and the disaffection spread and was intensified. So rampant was the insubordination to law in Delaware County that the governor (Silas Wright) in 1845 recommended legislation for its suppression,* and declared the county in a state of insurrection. Finally the trial and conviction of a few persons for conspiracy

---

* The Legislature passed an "act to prevent persons appearing disguised and armed." It authorized the arrest of all persons who appeared having their faces concealed or discolored, who might be punished as vagrants. It authorized sheriffs to call a posse to his aid in making arrests.

At about the same time an Anti-Rent State Convention was held at Berne, in Albany County, at which great moderation was displayed by the chief actors in it. Eleven counties and a greater number of associations were represented. They disapproved the outrages that had been committed; appointed a State Central Committee and a committee to present petitions to the Legislature. A newspaper called *The Guardian of the Soil*, devoted to the anti-rent cause, was published at Albany, and was conducted with much ability and prudence.

and resistance to the laws, and their confinement in the State prison, caused a cessation of all operations by the masked bands.

There was so much popular sympathy manifested in behalf of the anti-renters that the association in 1839 organized a political party favorable to their cause. It succeeded in 1842, and for several years afterward, in electing one eighth of the Legislature, who favored anti-rentism; and in the revised Constitution of 1846 a clause was inserted abolishing all feudal tenures and incidents, and forbidding the leasing of agricultural lands for a longer term than twelve years.

The Democratic Party triumphed in the State and nation in 1844. James K. Polk was elected President of the United States, and Silas Wright was chosen Governor of New York by a majority of more than ten thousand votes over Millard Fillmore. His majority in New York city alone was three thousand three hundred and eighty-six.

The same year was made memorable by the successful establishment of instantaneous communication between distant places by means of the electro-magnetic telegraph, to which intelligence and a language had recently been given by a citizen of New York—Professor S. F. B. Morse. A line of telegraphic communication between Baltimore and Washington had just been completed, and the first public message sent over it was an announcement from Baltimore of the nomination of Mr. Polk for the presidency by the Democratic Convention then in session in that city. Other lines were speedily set up, largely through the wonderful executive ability of Henry O'Reilly, of New York, who was the editor of the first daily newspaper (at Rochester, N. Y.) established between the Hudson River and the Pacific Ocean.

Governor Wright's administration was a quiet one, disturbed only by the anti-rent excitements, which he did much to suppress. These excitements gradually subsided, and only in courts of law were the associations seen.*

Governor Wright, like Governors Marcy, Seward, and Bouck, made special efforts to increase the efficiency of the common-school system of the State. In his first message to the Legislature he said:

"Our school fund is not instituted to make our children and youth either partisans in politics or sectarians in religion, but to give them education, intelligence, sound principles, good moral habits, and a free and independent spirit; in short, to make them American freemen and

---

* Stephen van Rensselaer, the eldest son of the last patroon, and who inherited the estate, sold his interest in the lands of the great manor to a judicious kinsman by marriage, who made amicable arrangements with all the tenants for the rent, sale, and purchase of the farms.

American citizens, and to qualify them to judge and choose for themselves in matters of politics, religion, and government. . . . No public fund of the State is so unpretending, yet so all-pervading; so little seen, yet so universally felt; so mild in its exactions, yet so bountiful in its benefits; so little feared or courted, and yet so powerful as this fund for the support of common schools. The other funds act upon the secular interests of society; its business, its pleasures, its pride, its passions, its vices, its misfortunes. This acts upon its mind and its morals."

The common-school system of the State of New York is its chief glory. The annals of that system form the brightest and most important page in the history of the commonwealth. Whoever shall directly or indirectly conspire to use it for any other than its high and holy mission, to entangle it in the miserable meshes of political strife or the more unholy warfare of religious denominationalism, should be regarded by every true American citizen as a public enemy, and treated as such.

It was at about this time that the Democratic Party in the State presented two opposing factions, called respectively " Barn-burners" and " Hunkers." The former were progressive. They were for reform—radicals, anti-slavery men, and sympathizers with the anti-renters who had burned barns; hence the name given this faction in derision. The " Hunkers" were conservatives; non-progressive, " old fogies." The Native American Party, recently organized, was a disturbing element in both parties, and being largely composed of former members of the Whig Party, it somewhat diminished the political strength of that party.

The Democratic national administration took a bold step in 1845 in the interest of the slaveholders, who desired an expansion of the territory of the United States on its south-western borders in order to provide more ample breathing space for their peculiar institution, then threatened with suffocation by overcrowding. On that border lay the independent State of Texas, which had been wrested from Mexico by filibusters from the United States. Its annexation to our republic was determined upon. The South, as a unit, favored the measure; the North generally opposed it. President Tyler, who had deserted the party (the Whigs) which had elected him, favored the annexation. Texas consented. James K. Polk, of Tennessee, Tyler's successor in office, urged it; and on July 4th, 1845, the annexation of Texas was effected.

Mexico had never acknowledged the independence of Texas. It remonstrated in vain against the annexation. The United States sent an " Army of Observation" into Texas, on the border of Mexico; and in 1846 war between the two countries began. It ensued in the conquest by the United States troops of the Mexican territories of California and New Mexico.

Texas was so large that it was designed to divide it into five slave-labor States, and so increase the political power of the Southern oligarchy. Happily this scheme was never accomplished. In the whole iniquitous plan of annexation, and the more iniquitous war that ensued, citizens of New York—politicians and volunteer soldiers—bore a conspicuous part.

CHAPTER XXXVI.

The prescribed time for the consideration of amendments to the State Constitution was now at hand. There was a difference of opinion as to methods for the accomplishment of this object. Many preferred having amendments adopted by the Legislature and afterward submitted to the people for their ratification or rejection. Others preferred a convention of delegates chosen by the popular voice to discuss, form, and propose amendments to be submitted to the people.

Governor Wright, who was opposed to a convention, suggested to the Legislature of 1845 several amendments, which were submitted to the people and approved by them at the general election in the fall. To make them a part of the Constitution a vote of two thirds of the members of both houses of the Legislature was required. They failed to receive the requisite number of votes. Then a convention was authorized.

An election of delegates was held in April, 1846. In nearly all the counties it was made a partisan question, and a majority of the delegates chosen were Democrats. They assembled at Albany on June 1st, one hundred and twenty-eight in number. Only one of them—General James Tallmadge, of Duchess—was in the convention of 1821.

The convention was organized by the choice of ex-Lieutenant-Governor John Tracy for president. Thomas Stanbuck and Henry W. Strong were appointed secretaries. A committee of seventeen was appointed to formulate topics to be considered in the revision. They reported eighteen, and these were referred to as many standing committees. They embraced different and important subjects to be discussed.

The Executive, Legislative, and Judicial departments were first considered. No material alterations were made in the organization of the existing *Executive Department*. In the *Legislative Department* the only essential change was for the election of senators and assemblymen by single districts. The power of impeachment of public officers was vested in the Assembly. The Senate and the judges of the Court of Appeals, presided over by the lieutenant-governor, constituted the tribunal for the trial of such impeachments.

The *Judiciary Department* was reorganized. Its power was greatly increased, while the number of judicial officers was diminished. Centralization of judicial power was abolished, and the judges were made dependent upon the people directly by being chosen by the voters at general elections. A Court of Appeals was organized, to consist of eight judges, four to be elected by the people, the remainder to be selected from the class of justices of the Supreme Court having the shortest time to serve. The judges were made removable by a concurrent resolution of both houses of the Legislature. *Tribunals of Conciliation* were authorized for the voluntary settlements of litigated cases.

The prerogative of appointment to office was taken from the governor and Senate and given to the people. This change gave to the latter, acting in their sovereign capacity, the vast patronage which had been wielded by a central power. Some of the State officers composed the commissioners of the Land Office and of the Canal Fund, and, with the canal commissioners, constituted the *Canal Board*.

Provision was made for the certain payment and total extinction of the public debt (then about $17,000,000) within a comparatively short and defined period. The power of the Legislature in creating State indebtedness without the sanction of a majority of the people, declared at the polls at elections, was restricted, and certain means were provided for enlarging the grand canal and for the completion of canals already begun.

EXECUTIVE PRIVY SEAL

The banking monopoly was abolished by taking from the Legislature the power of granting special charters for banking purposes. Authority was given for the formation of banking and other corporations under general laws, but the Legislature was prohibited from sanctioning the suspension of specie payments. Bills or notes put into circulation by such corporations as money were required to be registered, and ample security given for their redemption in specie.

Provision was made for the preservation of the School, Literature, and State Deposit funds, and the legitimate expenditure of the revenues arising from them. The Legislature was also directed to provide for the organization of cities and villages, with authority to restrict their powers of taxation, assessment, borrowing money, contracting debts, and loaning their credit.

The tenure of all lands was declared to be allodial. All restrictions upon alienation were abolished, and the leasing of agricultural lands for a longer term than twelve years was prohibited.

It was during the sessions of this convention that the first movement was made for the establishment of absolutely free schools throughout the State. The subject was introduced by Robert Campbell, of Otsego, on June 15th, in the form of a resolution. With a memorial on the same subject from the State Convention of County Superintendents, it was referred to the Committee on Education. On July 22d that committee reported to the convention a series of resolutions, one of them providing for the establishment by the Legislature of a system of free schools, for the education of every child in the State between the ages of four and sixteen years, whose parents were residents of the State. This resolution was adopted on the day before the final adjournment of the convention, but, on being reconsidered, was rejected. This desirable measure was only postponed for a season.

The convention adjourned on October 9th, after a session of about four months. Although it was composed of warm partisans, there did not appear the shadow of partisanship in the debates. It exhibited to the world a spectacle never before seen.

The instrument then adopted became a mighty emancipator of the people—a marvellous and puissant supporter of popular liberty and the popular will. Before the convention of 1821 every officer, civil and military, with a few exceptions, was appointed by a board—the Council of Appointment—possessed of absolute power within its legitimate domain. It was composed of only five members, sitting at the State capital. At its own sovereign will it played at football with the offices of trust and emolument in the State, appointing and dismissing incumbents in obedience to the behests of partisan or personal favor or dislike, or the dictates of self-interest or mere caprice.

The convention of 1821 wrested some strength from this tyrannical oligarchy. The convention of 1846 wholly annihilated this terrible power, and placed the public interests under the direct control of the people, the true source of all political sovereignty.

In less than a month after the adjournment of the convention the people of the State, at a general election, adopted the revised Constitution by a majority of about one hundred and thirty thousand. At the same election John Young,* the Whig and anti-rent candidate for gov-

---

* John Young was born at Chelsea, Vt., in 1802; died in New York City in April, 1852. In his young childhood his father removed to Livingston County, N. Y., where John received a common-school education, and studied and practised law. He was a member of the State Legislature in 1831 and subsequently, and in 1841–43 he was a member of Congress. His political affinity was with the Democratic Party until he became an Anti-Mason in 1829, and was elected to Congress by the Whigs. He was

ernor, was elected over Governor Wright by eleven thousand majority, while Addison Gardiner, the Democratic candidate for lieutenant-governor, was elected over Hamilton Fish by about thirteen thousand majority. On the elevation of Gardiner to the bench of the Court of Appeals Mr. Fish was appointed to fill the chair of lieutenant-governor.

Governor Young gave special attention to the subject of common schools. The system of county superintendents had worked admirably, but a growing tendency of supervisors to make the appointments to that office on political grounds merely, caused widespread dissatisfaction. At the special session of the Legislature in the fall of 1847 the office was abolished and that of town superintendent was created. The best friends of popular education lamented the change. The schools steadily retrograded in efficiency. Finally, in 1856, the office of school commissioner was created, that of town superintendent was abolished, and that of county superintendent was practically reinstated.

JOHN YOUNG.

The free-school system was thoroughly discussed after the adjournment of the convention of 1846, and in the spring of 1849 an act was passed for the establishment of free schools throughout the State, and the abolition of the rate-bill system. The law was ratified by a majority of one hundred and fifty-eight thousand votes of the people, every county in the State but four giving majorities for it. The whole of the expense of the schools beyond the State appropriation was made a tax upon the property of each district. This act was sustained by a majority of three to one of the people. At the same session teachers' institutes, which had existed for some years as voluntary associations, were legally established.

The free-school system did not work satisfactorily, owing to inequality in the taxation imposed. The people murmured. They remonstrated, and clamored for a repeal of the law. The question was submitted to

---

elected Governor of the State by the Whigs and Anti-Renters in 1847, and in 1849–52 he was Assistant United States Treasurer in New York City.

them in 1850, and the law was sustained by a diminished majority.* It was repealed in the spring of 1851, and the rate-bill system was reinstated.

At the election in the fall of 1848 the Whigs were triumphant in the State and in the choice of President of the United States. Lieutenant-Governor Fish † was elected Governor of New York, and General Zachary Taylor, a brave, skilful, successful, and honest military leader in the war with Mexico, was chosen Chief Magistrate of the republic, with Millard Fillmore, of New York, as Vice-President. Mr. Van Buren accepted the nomination for President from the Free-Soil or anti-slavery Democrats, and thus diminished the strength of the regularly nominated candidate, General Lewis Cass. President Taylor died in the summer of 1850, and Vice-President Fillmore became his official successor.

HAMILTON FISH.

The administration of Governor Fish (1849–51) was a very quiet one, nothing of special importance in the history of the State occurring excepting the excitement concerning the repeal of the free-school law. There

---

* The vote in favor of the free-school law in 1849 was 249,872 against 91,951. In 1850 it was 209,347 against 184,208.

† Hamilton Fish, son of Colonel Nicholas Fish, a distinguished officer of the Revolution, was born in New York City in August, 1808. He was graduated at Columbia College in 1827, and was admitted to the bar in 1830. He took an active part in politics in early life as a member of the Whig Party, and in 1842 he was elected to a seat in Congress. He denounced the principles of the Anti-Renters, and in 1846 he was defeated by them as a candidate for the office of lieutenant-governor of the State. He was afterward chosen to fill that office, and in 1848 was elected Governor of the State by a large majority. In 1851 he was chosen United States Senator, and in 1854 he strenuously opposed the repeal of the Missouri Compromise. He was a most earnest supporter of the Government during the late Civil War. President Grant called him to his Cabinet as Secretary of State in 1869, and in that capacity he served eight years, retiring to private life on the accession of President Hayes. In 1854 he was chosen President-General of the Society of the Cincinnati, which office he yet (1887) holds. The next year he was chosen President of the New York State Society of the Cincinnati. He has been an active and influential member of the Union League Club from its organization, and has long been an efficient officer of the New York Historical Society. His hand and bounty are felt in many benevolent works.

was a very heated canvass of the matter, and at the fall election in 1850, as we have seen, there was a diminished majority against repeal. The rural counties were generally for repeal. Forty-two of the fifty-nine counties of the State gave an aggregate of forty-nine thousand votes for repeal, while the seventeen remaining counties, including the city of New York, gave an aggregate majority of seventy-two thousand against repeal. New York City and County alone gave thirty-seven thousand eight hundred and twenty-seven votes of that majority.

At the fall election of 1850 Washington Hunt,* Comptroller of the State, and a Whig, was elected Governor of New York by a small majority over Horatio Seymour. The Democratic candidate for lieutenant-governor, Sandford E. Church, was elected.

The administration of Governor Hunt was also a quiet one. The most exciting question was that of the repeal of the free-school law, in the winter and spring of 1851. The governor urged upon the Legislature the importance of making satisfactory amendments to the law, so as to secure its sustentation. The Legislature was beset with petitions for its repeal, from taxpayers of the rural districts especially. The pressure was so great that the law-makers yielded, and repealed the law in April. The governor, in a subsequent message, characterized the actions of the people of the State and of the Legislature as a "temporary compromise" between the advanced views of the advocates of free schools and the fears and prejudices of a majority of the taxpayers and

WASHINGTON HUNT.

---

* Washington Hunt was born in Windham, N. Y., in August, 1811; died in New York City in February, 1867. He was admitted to the bar at Lockport, N. Y., in 1834; was appointed first judge of Niagara County in 1836, and was elected to a seat in Congress in 1843, where he served until 1849 as chairman of the Committee on Commerce. In 1851 he was Governor of New York. He was a Whig, and in 1854 was one of the founders of the Republican Party. He became a leader of the conservative wing. He presided over the convention that nominated Mr. Lincoln for the presidency, but soon afterward joined the Democratic Party. In 1864 he was a delegate to the convention that nominated McClellan for President of the United States.

inhabitants of the rural districts long accustomed to the existing system. He said that the progress of public opinion might be relied upon to diffuse a more liberal view of the relations of the State to its future citizens. At that time the capital of the common-school fund was $6,500,000, of the revenue of which nearly $1,500,000 had been expended during the current year (1851-52) in the payment of teachers' wages and the purchase of school libraries. The number of pupils in attendance upon the several public schools was 726,000. The Legislature in 1852 authorized the governor to appoint a special commission for the revision and codification of the school laws of the State. For this task S. S. Randall, Deputy Superintendent of Common Schools, was appointed.

Again the Democratic Party in the State and nation acquired political ascendancy. In the fall of 1852 Horatio Seymour* was elected Governor of the State of New York, and General Franklin Pierce, of New Hampshire, was chosen President of the United States by a large majority over General Winfield Scott, the Whig candidate.

HORATIO SEYMOUR.

---

* Horatio Seymour was one of the most notable of the later governors of New York. He was born in Onondaga County, N. Y., in May, 1816, and went to Utica with his parents in early childhood. He was educated for a lawyer, but, inheriting a large estate from his father, he devoted his time to the care of it. Very studious, he acquired much and varied knowledge, which he used with skill. Becoming attached to the staff of Governor Marcy in young manhood, on which he served six years, he became enamored with public life. In 1841 he was elected a member of Assembly by the Democratic Party, and held the position four years. He was chosen Speaker in 1843. He had been elected Mayor of Utica in 1842. In 1852 he was elected Governor of the State. By vetoing a prohibitory liquor bill in 1854 he incurred the displeasure of the advocates of temperance, and he was defeated as a candidate for re-election. Mr. Seymour was again elected governor in 1862, in the midst of the Civil War, and he gave his support to the Government, though not very cordially. He was defeated in the fall of 1864. In 1868 he was nominated for the presidency, but failed to be elected. He then retired to private life, but keeping a lively interest in all passing events until his death at Utica in February, 1886.

The administration of Governor Seymour was also a quiet one, yet important measures were adopted. In his first message (1853) he urgently recommended provision to be made for the speedy completion of the canals, and the establishment of a State agricultural college and experimental farm. A charter for such an institution was granted that spring.

At a special session convened immediately after the adjournment of the regular session in 1853, an act was passed for the consolidation of the ward and Public School Society's schools in the city of New York, and placing them under the supreme control of a Board of Education, as we have already observed. At that time there were two hundred and twenty-four of these schools in the city, with about 1000 teachers and 123,530 pupils on register; also 25 evening schools, with 4000 pupils.

In the spring of 1854 the Legislature created the office of State superintendent of public instruction. The first incumbent of this office was Victor M. Rice. The superintendent is made, *ex-officio*, a regent of the University. At that session an amendment to the Constitution proposed the preceding year was ratified, requiring an annual appropriation of a sum not exceeding $2,250,000 for the completion of the canals. An act for that purpose was passed. The Whigs gained ascendancy in the State in the fall of 1854. Governor Seymour had lost the favor of the friends of temperance by vetoing an act passed by a large majority of the Legislature which aimed to prohibit the sale of intoxicating drinks. He pronounced it "unconstitutional, unjust, and oppressive," and declared his belief that intemperance could not be extirpated by prohibitory laws. The press and the pulpit denounced his action. He was a candidate for re-election in the fall. The Whigs were not represented in the canvass. A fusion convention, which met at Syracuse, nominated for governor Myron H. Clark,* of Ontario, a stanch advocate of prohibitory liquor

SEAL OF THE DEPARTMENT OF PUBLIC INSTRUCTION.

---

* Myron Halley Clark was born in Naples, Ontario County, N. Y., October 23d, 1806, and has been a resident of that county ever since. His father, Joseph Clark, was a native of Cunington, Berkshire County, Mass.; his grandfathers were natives of Connecticut. He attended the common schools of his native town three winter months each

laws, and he was elected over both Seymour and Daniel Ullman, the candidate of the Native American Party. There was a Whig majority in both branches of the Legislature.

During that year a new national party was formed, and grew vigorously. It was composed largely of progressive and independent Whigs and many Democrats. It is claimed that Jackson, Mich., was the place of its nativity, and July 6th, 1854, the time of its birth, when a political convention was held at that place pursuant to a call signed by more than ten thousand names. The chief planks in the platform constructed by the convention were opposition to the extension of slavery and its abolition in the District of Columbia. The name of "REPUBLICAN" was given to the new party.

Two years later the Republican Party was thoroughly organized and strong in numbers. They nominated Colonel J. C. Fremont for President of the United States in 1856. He was defeated by his Democratic competitor, James Buchanan. Fremont received one hundred and fourteen of the two hundred and eighty-eight electoral votes cast. At the next presidential election (1860) the Republican candidate, Abraham Lincoln, was elected by a majority of fifty-seven of the electoral votes over three other candidates—Breckinridge, Douglas, and Bell. It was the final political triumph of the anti-slavery men

MYRON H. CLARK.

---

year, and worked on his father's farm the remainder of the year until he was eighteen years of age, when he became a merchant's clerk in his town. At the age of twenty-one he became a clerk in Canandaigua. Two years later he returned to Naples and engaged in mercantile business on his own account with partners, and married in 1830. In 1837 he was elected sheriff of the county, and made Canandaigua his residence, where he still resides. At the close of his term of office he again engaged in trade. In 1851 Mr. Clark was elected State Senator, where he was distinguished for his advocacy of legislative enactments in favor of temperance. He was chairman of the committee that reported the "Bill for the Suppression of Intemperance," which, as we have observed, Governor Seymour vetoed. Senator Clark was the leader of the debates on the subject. He had served only one half of a second term in the Senate when he was elected Governor of the State, in 1854. He was appointed United States Collector of Internal Revenue in 1862.

and women of the Union, and led to the speedy emancipation of the slaves in every part of the Republic.

After Mr. Lincoln's inauguration, in the spring of 1861, the Republican Party retained its domination of the National Government for about a quarter of a century, and became a great historic party. Meanwhile, as usual, New York was an "uncertain" State in political calculations, for its political aspect frequently changed, the Republican and Democratic parties alternately holding the reins of power.

Governor Clark, in his first message to the Legislature (1855), called their attention to a pending controversy with the State authorities of Virginia concerning the force and operations of the infamous Fugitive Slave Law passed by Congress in 1850, which made every citizen a slave-catcher.[*] Its practical operations aroused the slumbering conscience of the people of the free-labor States and their intelligence to the danger foreshadowed by the increasing aggressiveness of the upholders of the slave system; and several of these States passed "Personal Liberty" bills in opposition to the obnoxious law.

The State of New York had statutory laws already which met the case, and when, late in 1852, Jonathan Lemon, of Norfolk, Va., brought eight slaves to New York City for reshipment to Texas, they were taken before Judge Paine, of the Superior Court, on a writ of *habeas corpus* to claim their right to freedom under the provisions of a law of the State which declared that every slave should be free on touching its soil when brought thither by his or her alleged owner. The judge set them free, and they fled to Canada. The case was brought before the Supreme Court of the United States, which sustained Judge Paine's decision.

This case produced very great excitement in the slave-labor States, and was the beginning of the preliminary skirmishes between the friends of freedom and of slavery which immediately preceded the civil war kindled in 1861 by the slaveocracy for the perpetuation and nationalizing of the system of hopeless bondage for the African race in the United States.[†] Some of the most violent of these skirmishes, resulting some-

---

[*] The law provided that the master of a fugitive slave or his agent might go into any State or Territory, and with or without legal warrant there obtained seize such fugitive and take him before any judge or commissioner, declare that the fugitive " owed labor" to the party who arrested him, when it was the duty of the judge to use the power of his office to take the alleged fugitive back to bondage. In *no case should the testimony of such alleged fugitive be admitted in evidence.* It further provided that no impediment should be put in the way of the slave-catcher by any process of law or otherwise, and any citizen might be *compelled to assist in the capture and rendition of the slave.*

[†] Threats of disunion freely uttered in 1850 to accelerate the passage of the Fugitive Slave Law were now heard echoing from State to State in the South. The Governor of

times in bloodshed, occurred in the then recently organized **Territory of Kansas.**

The decision of Judge Paine was followed by the flight of slaves from bondage, through New York and Ohio, to Canada. They were secretly aided in their exodus by the friends of freedom in New York City. The process was known as the " Underground Railroad," of which New York was the principal station. The consequence was Southern dealers became suspicious of New York merchants, and began to withdraw their trade. The effect was very demoralizing. Many merchants engaged in the Southern trade became obedient slaves of Mammon and the Southern oligarchy at the sacrifice of self-respect. " I am ashamed to own," said one of these merchants to me, " that when our Southern customers were in town, I felt compelled to order my clerks not to let the *Tribune* be seen in the store, for it would not do to let such customers know that I gave any countenance to that abolition sheet. From the bottom of my heart I despised myself."

JOHN A. KING.

Little of special importance in the history of New York occurred between the administration of Governor Clark and the kindling of the Civil War in 1861, when the State put forth its giant strength in defence of the life of the imperilled nation. Then the city of New York, so conservative before that crisis, became the foremost city in the republic in support of the National Government.

John A. King * succeeded Mr. Clark as governor in 1857. His

Virginia declared that if the decision of Judge Paine should be sustained all comity between the States would be destroyed, and the value of " slave property" be greatly diminished. Governor Howell Cobb, of Georgia, who, as Secretary of the United States Treasury in the Cabinet of President Buchanan, conspired to destroy the republic, declared that it was a sufficient cause for making war on the Union.

* John Alsop King, son of Hon. Rufus King, was born in the city of New York January 3d, 1788. He accompanied his father—who was Minister at the court of St. James—to England, and while there attended the famous school at Harrow. Among his fellow-pupils were his brother Charles, late President of Columbia College, Lord Byron, and Robert Peel. On his return home he studied law and was admitted to the bar. In

administration was quiet and uneventful. He recommended a judicious revision of the excise laws, and submitted to the Legislature a proposed constitutional amendment extending the right of suffrage to colored voters without a property qualification ; also a strenuous resistance on the part of the Legislature to the further extension of slavery in the Territories.

In the autumn of 1858 Edwin D. Morgan,* a distinguished merchant of New York City, was elected by the Republicans Governor of the State by a majority of about seventeen thousand. It was during his administration that the fierce Civil War in the nation was begun.

EDWIN D. MORGAN.

National affairs had now begun to attract unusual attention, and there was widespread uneasiness in the public mind. The slavery question had been brought conspicuously to the front in the arena of public discussion by the virtual repeal of the

---

the War of 1812-15 he served as lieutenant of a troop of horse, and continued in the service until the close of the contest, after which he took up his residence at Jamaica, Long Island, and there passed the remainder of his life in the business of agriculture. Six times Mr. King represented Queens County in the Assembly, and once in the Senate of his native State. In 1825 he was Secretary of Legation to Great Britain under his father. He represented his district in the Congress of the United States in 1849-51, and was very active in opposition to the compromise measures of the so-called " Omnibus Bill " of 1850, especially that of the Fugitive Slave Bill. He warmly advocated the admission of California as a free-labor State. Mr. King was an active member of the Whig Party, and in the organization of the Republican Party in 1854. In 1856 he was elected the first Republican Governor of New York, and was an earnest promoter of the canal system of the State. Governor Morgan appointed him a delegate to the notable Peace Congress at Washington early in 1861. He took his seat therein, and this was his last public act. On July 4th, 1867, he was addressing the young men of Jamaica, who had just raised a new flag, and as he uttered the words, " Life is all before *you*, but men like me are passing away," he was suddenly smitten with paralysis, and died three days afterward, in the eightieth year of his age.

* Edwin Dennison Morgan was born in Washington, Mass., in February, 1811. With a grocer in Hartford, Conn., he was first a clerk (1828), and in 1831 a partner in business. He removed to New York in 1836, where he pursued the same business successfully, and accumulated a large fortune. From 1849 to 1853 he was State Senator, and was made chairman of the State Republican Committee. In 1859 he took his seat as Governor of New York, and retained it until 1863, being one of the most active of the famous " war

Missouri Compromise, in 1854, and the violent struggle for the mastery in Kansas between the defenders and opposers of the slave system. Threats of disunion flew thick and fast from the lips of Southern political leaders, and the ominous mutterings of a gathering tempest were heard.

During the summer and early autumn of 1859 an unusual quiet seemed to pervade the political atmosphere. The violent agitation of the slavery question had almost ceased, and it was hoped by many that permanent public repose was nigh, when suddenly, in October, news flashed over the land that "an insurrection has broken out at Harper's Ferry, where an armed band of Abolitionists have full possession of the Government Arsenal." This was the famous "John Brown raid," which kindled a blaze of intense excitement in the slave-labor States, and which was fanned into the fearful conflagration of a four-years' civil war of unparalleled extent and destructiveness.

The events of the year 1860 rank among the most momentous in the history of our republic. In these events every State in the Union was a participant in feeling and interest. John Brown had been hanged for his foolish but philanthropic attempt to inaugurate a servile insurrection in favor of liberty in Virginia. The bitterness it engendered was nursed into the most intense implacability. The Republican Party was wrongfully charged with having originated and promoted John Brown's attempt to liberate the slaves; and in the canvass for the Presidency of the republic in 1860 the zeal displayed by the opposing parties was unexampled in warmth and persistence.

For many years a conspiracy for destroying the Union and establishing an empire, the corner-stone of which should be the system of human slavery, had been ripening in secret among leading politicians of the slave-labor States. They had clearly perceived that the "peculiar institution" and the domination of the National Government by the Southern oligarchy was foredoomed, by the power of public opinion, to a speedy close. They madly believed that in the crisis at hand was their golden opportunity to carry out their designs. They proceeded to "fire the Southern heart" by declaring that the success of the Republican Party in the pending presidential election would result in the ruin of the

---

governors" of that period. Stimulated by his zeal, his State Legislature voted men and money lavishly in support of the imperilled National Government. In 1861 he was created major-general of volunteers, but resigned in 1863. At about that time he was chosen to represent New York in the United States Senate. Governor Morgan was distinguished for his untiring zeal in philanthropic work and the promotion of Christian institutions. For these objects his gifts were munificent. He died on February 14th, 1883.

Southern States if acquiesced in, and that it would afford ample warrant for the secession of the slave-labor States from the Union, and the formation of an independent government.

To this end the few conspirators worked. They cast into the Democratic national nominating convention at Charleston in 1860 an apple of discord which caused a disruption of the party and gave strength to the Republicans, who nominated Abraham Lincoln, an avowed anti-slavery man, for the presidency of the republic. This the unwise conspirators, "deprived of reason," believed to be a sure prophecy of their triumph and a golden opportunity. They sent out their emissaries to "fire the Southern heart" by inflammatory harangues; and so well did they succeed that when it was known that Mr. Lincoln was elected, a larger proportion of the people in the slave-labor States, deceived by sophistry, misled by false statements, and benumbed by undefinable dread, were ready to submit passively to the will of these fiery politicians, who got up congenial conventions that passed ordinances of secession, which they never did (for they never dared), to ask the people to consider and act upon.

South Carolina, in which the serpent of secession was hatched from the egg of Nullification, was the first to "secede"—on paper—on December 20th, 1860, and having announced its "sovereignty," proceeded to make war upon the "foreign" Government of the United States. That Government, paralyzed by fear or something more serious, acted so feebly at first against rampant disloyalty in its very presence, and widespread treason, that conventions in State after State passed ordinances of secession, and made war upon the National Government in various forms, with impunity. The representatives of European monarchies at Washington sent home the tidings pleasing to the ears of the enemies of self-government, that the days of the great republic of the West were numbered. "The wish was father to the thought."

It is not the province of this work to give more than passing allusions to the history of the Civil War. Its chief task is to give a compendious narrative of the most important actions of the State of New York during that fearful struggle.

CHAPTER XXXVII.

At the beginning of the Civil War in 1861—the great crisis in our national history—the commonwealth of New York was, indeed, the "Empire State" of the republic. Its population then was 3,882,000. Its taxable property was assessed at $1,425,000,000. Its chief city, by the sea, contained a cosmopolitan population of more than 800,000. The foreign commerce within its revenue district, exports and imports, amounted in value to $375,000,000 in 1860. This population, wealth, and commerce fairly entitled New York to the honor of being the national metropolis.

New York City then (as now) was an eminently commercial mart. The influence of trade fashioned its general policy in a remarkable degree.

The best condition for commerce is peace. When the storm-clouds of civil war, though no "bigger than a man's hand," began to appear at the close of 1860, the business men of the city were ready to make enormous sacrifices of sentiment and pride for the preservation of peace. Hence, as we have observed, the citizens of New York were very conservative at the beginning of the trouble. They watched the approaching tempest as it gathered energy with mingled incredulity and uneasiness; and they anxiously observed the faint-heartedness or indifference of the National Government at that time of peril, with gloomy forebodings. Treason was then rampant and defiant at the national capital, and sappers and miners were working secretly and openly for the destruction of the great temple of liberty in the West. At that hour of greatest despondency, the trumpet voice of the newly-appointed Secretary of the Treasury (John A. Dix, of New York) rang throughout the nation, saying to an officer of the revenue service at New Orleans, "*If any one attempts to haul down the American flag, shoot him on the spot!*" That utterance was hailed by the loyal people of the land with hope and joy as a sure prophecy of salvation for the republic.

The Legislature of New York was then eminently loyal. There were thirty-eight Republicans and nine Democrats in the Senate, and ninety-eight Republicans and thirty-five Democrats in the Assembly. When that body assembled on January 2d, 1861, the whole country was in a fever of intense excitement. The message of Governor Morgan to the

518   THE EMPIRE STATE.

Legislature was calm, dignified, conservative, and even cold in comparison with the fervor of the public mind. In conciliatory tones he urged

> Treasury Department
> Jan. 29, 1861
>
> Tell Lieut. Caldwell to arrest Capt. Breshwood, assume command of the cutter and obey the order I gave through you. If Capt. Breshwood after arrest undertakes to interfere with the command of the cutter tell Lieut. Caldwell to consider him as a mutineer & treat him accordingly. If any one attempts to haul down the American flag shoot him on the spot. —
>
> John A. Dix,
> Secretary of the Treasury.

FAC-SIMILE OF DIX'S ORDER.

the duty of all legislators to act with moderation. Reflecting the sentiments of capitalists and business men specially, he said:

"Let New York set an example in this respect; let her oppose no barrier [to conciliation], but let her representatives in Congress give ready support to any just and honorable settlement; let her stand in hostility to none, but extend the hand of friendship to all. Live up to the strict letter of the Constitution, and cordially unite with other members of the Confederacy in proclaiming and enforcing a determination that the Constitution shall be honored and the Union of the States be preserved."

The governor even recommended the repeal of the statute which gave liberty to every slave whose feet should tread the soil of New York, and recommended other States to repeal their "Personal Liberty acts." There was naturally an earnest desire for peace, for war implied the cancelment of millions of dollars of debt due New York merchants by Southern customers.

The views of the Legislature were not in consonance with those of the governor. That body was more disposed to be defiant and uncompromising, especially when news arrived of the overt act of armed rebellion by South Carolinians in Charleston Harbor in firing upon the *Star of the West* when she entered those waters laden with supplies for the imperilled garrison in Fort Sumter. That act called out a patriotic message from President Buchanan, and the Legislature of New York spoke out in tones not to be misunderstood (January 11th, 1861), saying:

"*Resolved*, That the Legislature of New York is profoundly impressed with the value of the Union, and determined to preserve it unimpaired; that it greets with joy the recent firm, dignified, and patriotic special message of the President of the United States; and we tender him, through the chief magistrate of our State, whatever aid in men and money may be required to enable him to enforce the laws and uphold the authority of the Federal Government; and that, in defence of the Union, which has conferred prosperity and happiness upon the American people, renewing the pledge given and redeemed by our fathers, we are ready to devote our fortunes, our lives, and our sacred honor."

This patriotic proclamation by the representatives of the people of New York was in vivid contrast with the utterances of the disloyal Mayor of New York City (Fernando Wood) a few days before. He was in sympathy with the movements of the secessionists; and in a message to the Common Council (January 7th, 1861) he advocated the secession of the city from the State.

"Why should not New York City," he said, "instead of supporting by her contributions in revenue two thirds of the expenses of the United States, become, also, equally independent? As a free city, with a nominal duty on imports, her local government could be supported without taxation upon her people. Thus we could live free from taxes, and have cheap goods nearly duty free. . . . When disunion has become a fixed and certain fact, why may not New York disrupt the bands which bind her to a venal and corrupt master—to a people and a party that have plundered her revenues, attempted to ruin her commerce, taken away the power of self-government, and destroyed the confederacy of which she was the proud empire city."

The Common Council, in political accord with the mayor, ordered three thousand copies of this message to be printed in pamphlet form for free distribution among the people. The loyal citizens of New York condemned this revolutionary movement with great severity of utterance and patriotic deeds.

The message of Mayor Wood and the bold resolution of the Legislature alarmed a certain class of people, who were ready to make every concession to the insurgents consistent with honor and patriotism. A memorial in favor of compromise measures, largely signed by merchants, manufacturers, and capitalists, was sent to Congress on January 12th, 1861. It suggested the famous "Crittenden Compromise." * On the 18th a large meeting of merchants was held in the rooms of the Chamber of Commerce, when a memorial of similar import was adopted, and was taken to Washington early in February, with forty thousand names attached. On the 28th an immense gathering of citizens at the Cooper Union appointed three commissioners— James T. Brady, C. K. Garrison, and Appleton Oakes Smith—to confer with the "delegates" of six "seceded" States in conventions assembled, in regard to "the best measures calculated to restore the peace and integrity of the Union." At about the same time the Legislature, on the invitation of Virginia, appointed five representatives to a peace conference, to be held at Washington City, but with instructions not to take part in the proceedings unless a majority of the free-labor States were there represented.

Meanwhile the pro-slavery element in New York had been aroused to active sympathy with the insurgent slaveholders. An association was speedily formed which was styled "The American Society for the Promotion of National Union." They denounced the seminal doctrine of the Declaration of Independence, that "*all* men are created equal,"

---

* John J. Crittenden, of Kentucky, offered in the Senate of the United States, in December, a series of resolutions which was called a compromise between the people of the two sections of the country, but which virtually conceded to the slaveholders and their friends nearly everything for which they professed to be contending. It was before Congress during the whole session, and was finally rejected on the last day (March 3d, 1861) by a vote of twenty against nineteen.

and said: "Four millions of immortal beings, incapable of self-care, and indisposed to industry and foresight, are providentially committed to the hands of our Southern friends. This stupendous trust they cannot put from them if they would. Emancipation, were it possible, would be rebellion against Providence, and destruction of the colored race in our land."

How strangely mediæval appears such a sentence (written by one of the most distinguished scientists of the world) in the light of history to-day! This society, which sent its disloyal publications broadcast over the land, was the mother of the mischievous Peace Faction, which prolonged and increased the miseries of the Civil War. It was the parent of the brood of misguided men called "Copperheads" during that fearful struggle.

The exportation of fire-arms from the port of New York to the Southern insurgents was begun with the year 1861. Late in January the efficient chief of police (John A. Kennedy) caused to be seized a large quantity of arms consigned by an agent of the Governor of Georgia to insurgents in that State and in Alabama, which had been placed on a vessel bound for Savannah. This fact was telegraphed to the Georgia capital. Robert Toombs, a private citizen, took the matter in hand and peremptorily demanded of Mayor Wood whether or not the report was true. The mayor answered "Yes," and said he had no power over the police, or he would punish them for the act. The Governor of Georgia retaliated by ordering the seizure of some New York merchant vessels in the port of Savannah. The affair created intense excitement all over the Union. It was soon amicably adjusted.

Delegates appointed by secession conventions (not of the people) of six States assembled at Montgomery, Ala., on February 4th, 1861, and formed a league with the title, "CONFEDERATE STATES OF AMERICA"—a misnomer, for no States, as States, were there represented. A Provisional Constitution was adopted. Jefferson Davis, of Mississippi, was chosen "Provisional President," and Alexander H. Stephens, of Georgia, was made Vice-President.

Meanwhile the conspirators in Congress had been withdrawing from that body and organizing rebellion at home. President Buchanan remained a passive spectator of the rising rebellion. The general-in-chief of the national army (Scott) was feeble in mind and body; and when Mr. Lincoln was inaugurated (March 4th, 1861) the insurgents were organized and prepared for war. They had been materially assisted by treacherous members of the Cabinet of the retiring President, who became leaders of the insurgents.

South Carolinians had flocked to Charleston and piled fortifications around the harbor. On April 12th, 1861, the two hundred great guns of these forts opened fire upon Fort Sumter, which was occupied by a national garrison under the command of Major Anderson, a loyal Kentuckian. His provisions exhausted, he was compelled to evacuate (not surrender) the fort, carrying away with him the garrison flag. This event occurred on Sunday, the 14th. Just four years afterward Major Anderson again unfurled that flag over the ruins of the repossessed fort.

Twenty-four hours after the evacuation of Fort Sumter President Lincoln issued a call for seventy-five thousand militia from the several States, to serve for three months in suppressing this armed rebellion. The quota of New York was seventeen regiments, or thirteen thousand men. There was no longer hesitation in the Empire State. The governor sent the proclamation to the Legislature, then in session. In a few hours an act was passed conferring large powers on the chief magistrate, and authorizing the enrolment of thirty thousand men for two years, and an appropriation of $3,000,000.

The governor issued a proclamation ordering the troops to rendezvous at Elmira and New York City. An officer sent to Washington obtained the acceptance of the surplus regiments. The Secretary of War sent marching orders. Contracts for a large amount of supplies were immediately made. On April 24th an agent of the State sailed for Europe with a bill of credit for $500,000, with which to purchase arms; and very speedily nineteen thousand Enfield rifles, which cost $375,000, were landed at New York City.

The authorized thirty thousand men had been raised within thirty-six days after the President's call for troops; and early in July they were organized into thirty-eight regiments. An active committee in New York City added ten regiments; and on July 1st—seventy-seven days after the date of the President's proclamation—New York troops in the field numbered forty-six thousand seven hundred.

On April 20th an immense war meeting was held in Union Square, in the city of New York. So great was the multitude that it was divided into four sections, presided over respectively by John A. Dix, Hamilton Fish, ex-Mayor Havemeyer, and Moses H. Grinnell.*

---

* Moses H. Grinnell, an eminent merchant of New York City, was born at New Bedford, Mass., in March, 1803, and died in New York in November, 1877. He was educated at private schools and at an academy belonging to the Society of Friends, or Quakers. Bred a merchant, he frequently went abroad as supercargo. He removed to New York, and in 1829 he became one of the firm of Grinnell, Minturn & Company, a

Speeches fraught with intense fervor were made, and patriotic resolutions were adopted. That meeting effectually removed the false impression that the greed of commerce was stronger than patriotism in New York City. The insurgents, who evidently thought so, were disappointed. One of their organs, the *Richmond Despatch*, said : " New York will be remembered with special hatred by the South for all time."

At that meeting a Committee of Safety was appointed, composed of the most distinguished citizens of New York. They met on the same evening, and organized the famous Union Defence Committee.* Its room (30 Pine Street) was open every day, and at the Fifth Avenue Hotel every evening. The committee was charged with the duty of representing " the citizens in the collection of funds and the transaction of such other business, in aid of the movements of the Government, as the public interests may require." Its existence continued about a year, during which time

MOSES H. GRINNELL.

it disbursed about $1,000,000, which the corporation of New York appropriated for war purposes and placed at its disposal. It assisted in the equipment, etc., of forty-nine regiments, or about forty thousand men. It spent of the city funds for military purposes nearly $759,000, and for the relief of soldiers' families, $230,000. Within ten days after the

---

house founded many years before by Joseph Grinnell and Preserved Fish. Mr. Grinnell was one of the chief promoters of the expedition to the Arctic seas in search of Sir John Franklin, which was led by Dr. E. K. Kane, 1853-55. He was a member of Congress, 1839-41, and in 1869-71 he was Collector of the Port of New York.

* The members of the Union Defence Committee were : John A. Dix, *Chairman ;* Simeon Draper, *Vice-Chairman ;* William M. Evarts, *Secretary ;* Theodore Dehon, *Treasurer ;* Moses Taylor, Richard M. Blatchford, Edwards Pierrepont, Alexander T. Stewart, Samuel Sloan, John Jacob Astor, Jr., John J. Cisco, James S. Wadsworth, Isaac Bell, James Boorman, Charles H. Marshall, Robert H. McCurdy, Moses H. Grinnell, Royal Phelps, William E. Dodge, Green C. Bronson, Hamilton Fish, William F. Havemeyer, Charles H. Russell, James T. Brady, Rudolph A. Whitthaus, Abiel A. Low, Prosper M. Wetmore, A. C. Richards, and the mayor, comptroller, and the presidents of the two boards of the Common Council of the City of New York.

President's call for troops, that committee had sent to the field from the city of New York fully ten thousand men, well armed and equipped.

Among the regiments that went from the city of New York was the famous Seventh, National Guard, commanded by Colonel Marshall Lefferts. It was composed chiefly of young men of the best families in the city. Just as it was about to march news came of an attack upon Massachusetts troops in Baltimore by a mob. The regiment was furnished with ball cartridges. As it marched down Broadway it was greeted at every step by multitudes of the citizens on sidewalks and balconies, and from windows. At the ferry it was joined by a Massachusetts regiment accompanied by General B. F. Butler. Both regiments were speeding across New Jersey by railway at evening twilight.

Hundreds of families wooed sleep in vain that night. They knew that blood had been shed in Baltimore, and that their loved ones were in imminent peril. But patriotism triumphed over personal considerations. The enthusiasm of the people was marvellous. The women were as patriotic as the men. Five brothers of a New York family enlisted and marched away. Their mother was absent at the time. She wrote to her husband:

"Though I have loved my children with a love that only a mother knows, yet when I look upon the state of my country, I cannot withhold them. In the name of their God, and their mother's God, and their country's God, I bid them go. If I had ten sons instead of five I should give them all sooner than have our country rent in fragments."

This was the spirit of the loyal women all over the land during the fierce struggle that ensued.*

---

* The Society of Friends, or Quakers, were generally loyal. Their principles forbade them to bear arms, but they gave generous aid to the good cause by assiduous services in hospitals, etc. The society felt it a duty to publish a "Testimony" exhorting their brethren to resist "the temptations of the hour," and while anxious to uphold the Government, not to "transgress the principles and injunctions of the gospel." But many of the younger Friends especially gave little heed to the "Testimony," but bore arms and obeyed the injunctions of a patriotic Quaker mother in Philadelphia, who wrote to her son in camp: "Let not thy musket hold a silent meeting before the enemy."

In strong contrast with this was the letter of a Baltimore mother to her loyal son, a clergyman in Boston, who, on the Sunday after the attack on Fort Sumter, preached a patriotic sermon to his flock. She wrote:

"BALTIMORE, April 17, 1861.

"MY DEAR SON: Your remarks last Sabbath were telegraphed to Baltimore and published in an extra. Has God sent you to preach the sword or to preach Christ?

"YOUR MOTHER."

The son replied:

"BOSTON, April 22, 1861.

"DEAR MOTHER: 'God has sent' me not only to '*preach*' the sword, but to *use* it. When this Government tumbles, look among the ruins for

"YOUR STAR-SPANGLED BANNER SON."

After the President's proclamation, troops from the slave-labor States pressed eagerly toward the national capital, obedient to the shout of Alexander H. Stephens, as he moved northward from Montgomery to Richmond—"*On to Washington!*" Their object was the seizure of the Government, its archives and its treasury. At the same time thousands of men from the free-labor States were pressing as eagerly for the same goal, to save those precious possessions. News of a murderous attack upon a Massachusetts regiment in Baltimore by a mob flashed over the country accelerated the speed of preparation and march for the salvation of the Republic.

Major-General John E. Wool,* the second in command to the general-in-chief of the army (Scott), was at his home in Troy, N. Y. Though seventy-six years of age, he was then an active and vigorous soldier. He hastened to confer with Governor Morgan, at Albany. While they were in consultation the governor received a despatch from Washington urging him to send troops thither as quickly as possible. The general immediately issued orders to the quartermaster at New York to furnish transportation to Washington for all troops that might be sent; also to the commissary to furnish subsistence for them for thirty days.

JOHN ELLIS WOOL.

* John Ellis Wool was born in Newburgh, N. Y., in 1788, and died in Troy, N. Y., in November, 1869. He became in his youth a bookseller in Troy, studied law, and in the spring of 1812 entered the army as captain of a company raised in Troy. He served gallantly in the War of 1812-15. At the peace he was retained in the army. In 1832 he was sent to Europe to examine some of the military systems on the Continent. He became a brigadier-general in 1841, and performed excellent service in Mexico in 1846-48, especially in organizing and disciplining volunteers. For his bravery in the battle of Buena Vista, which he planned, he was brevetted major-general, and received the thanks of Congress and a sword. In 1856 he quelled Indian disturbances in Oregon. At the breaking out of the Civil War General Wool, in command of the Eastern Department, took measures which saved Washington City from capture by the Confederates. He was commissioned major-general in May, 1862, and he commanded the expedition that took possession of Norfolk that month.

The governor went to New York that night; the general followed two days afterward, and made his headquarters at the St. Nicholas Hotel. There he conferred with the Union Defence Committee and arranged plans for the salvation of the capital, which was then so isolated by a cordon of enemies that Scott could not communicate by telegraph to a regiment outside the District of Columbia; neither could any communication reach the President from beyond those limits. Under these circumstances General Wool assumed the gravest responsibilities, and with the assistance of the Union Defence Committee and the co-operation of Commodores Breeze and Stringham, succeeded in saving the capital.

The battle of Bull's Run, in July, gave a new impetus to the demand for troops, and Governor Morgan issued a proclamation for twenty-five thousand three years' men, the money to raise and equip them to be paid by the National Government. The quota of New York was increased from time to time, and on January 1st, 1862, it was one hundred and twenty thousand. Its troops had taken part in every engagement east of the Alleghany Mountains and south of Washington.

A called session of Congress opened on July 4th, for the purpose of providing means for carrying on the war then just begun. Authority was given for raising five hundred thousand soldiers, and appropriating $500,000,000 to pay the expenses. These acts implied a heavy loan from the people. Could it be obtained? The question was soon answered. At the close of the year the Secretary of the Treasury had borrowed $470,000,000 of the loyal people, of which sum New York alone had advanced $210,000,000. It was a wonderful exhibition of patriotism and of generous faith in the people. The risk was tremendous, but the jewel to be secured was beyond price. Without this advance arms could not have been bought, nor ships built, nor armies moved, and the Republic must have perished. Again New York saved it. Her sons appreciated the peril and the value of the endangered treasure, and flew to the rescue.

While thousands of loyal men were hastening to the field, loyal women were devising plans and taking measures for their aid and comfort. On the day when the President's call for troops appeared (April 15th), Miss Almena Bates, in Charlestown, Mass., took steps to found an association for the purpose. On the same day women of Bridgeport, Conn., organized a society to furnish nurses for the sick and wounded soldiers, and provisions and clothing for them. A few days later women of Lowell, Mass., did the same thing, and on the 19th women of Cleveland, O., formed an association for the more immediately practical purpose of giving assistance to the families of volunteers.

This spontaneous outcropping of the tenderest feelings of women suggested the formation, in the city of New York, of the powerful society known as the United States Sanitary Commission. Fifty or sixty benevolent women of New York met by appointment on April 26th, 1861, when a Central Relief Association was suggested. They formed a plan, and the women of the city were invited to assemble at the Cooper Union to consider it on the 29th. Many leading gentlemen of the city were invited to be present. The response to the call was ample in number, character, and financial resources. David Dudley Field presided. The Vice-President of the United States (Hannibal Hamlin) addressed the meeting. A benevolent organization known as the Women's Central Relief Association was effected, and the venerable Dr. Valentine Mott was chosen its president. The chief actor in this movement was the Rev. H. W. Bellows, D.D., pastor of All Souls (Unitarian) Church.*

HENRY W. BELLOWS.

The necessity for a much broader field of action was soon perceived, and early in June the Secretary of War authorized the formation of a "Commission of inquiry and advice in respect of the sanitary interests of the United States." Eminent civilians and soldiers formed the commission. Dr. Bellows, its real author, was chosen its president. He submitted a plan of operations which was adopted, and the association assumed the name of the UNITED STATES SANITARY COMMISSION.†

---

* Henry Whitney Bellows, D.D., an eloquent clergyman of the Unitarian Church, was born in Boston in June, 1814. He was graduated at Harvard College and at Harvard Divinity School at Cambridge, Mass. He was ordained pastor of the First Unitarian Church (All Souls) in New York in 1838, where he labored successfully forty-four years. He was the principal projector of the *Christian Inquirer*, a Unitarian newspaper, and its chief contributor. He was the real originator of the United States Sanitary Commission. Dr. Bellows died in January, 1882.

† The seal of the Sanitary Commission bore the device of an angel of mercy descending from the clouds upon a deserted battle-field, where a soldier is seen administering aid to a wounded comrade. The first officers of the commission were: Henry W. Bellows, D.D., *President;* Professor A. D. Bache, LL.D., *Vice-President;* Elisha Harris, M.D.,

Frederick Law Olmsted was appointed its resident secretary, and became its real manager.

The object of the commission was to supplement Government deficiencies. An appeal was made to the people for contributions. The response was most generous. Supplies and money flowed in from all quarters sufficient to meet every demand. All over the country men, women, and children were seen working singly or collectively for it. Fairs were held in cities and large towns which raised immense sums of money for the treasury of the commission. The city of Poughkeepsie, with sixteen thousand inhabitants, held a fair and contributed to the treasury of the commission *one dollar* for each man, woman, and child of its population—$16,000. The treasurer of the Soldiers' Sanitary Fair in the city of New York (John H. Gourlie) received from the treasurer of the commission a receipt for $1,000,000, the net proceeds of the fair. The commission established branches. Ambulances, army wagons, and steamboats were employed in transporting the sick and wounded soldiers under its charge. It followed the army closely in all campaigns. Before the smoke of conflict had been fairly lifted there was seen the commission with its tents, its vehicles, and its supplies.

SEAL OF THE UNITED STATES SANITARY COMMISSION.

The grand work of the United States Sanitary Commission was continually made plain during the war, and especially at its close, when the success of its labors was considered. The loyal people of the land, justly confiding in its wisdom, energy, and integrity, had given to it supplies valued at $15,000,000, and money to the amount of $5,000,000.

Later in the same year (1861) another and most efficient and important association was formed in the city of New York, the chief object of which was to promote the moral and spiritual welfare of the soldiers. It was suggested by Vincent Collyer, an artist, and a most earnest worker in the cause of Christian effort of every kind. It had its origin in the Young Men's Christian Association in New York. At a national convention of such associations held in their hall in November to consult

---

Corresponding Secretary; General George W. Cullum, Alexander E. Shiras, Robert C. Wood, M.D., Wolcott Gibbs, Cornelius R. Agnew, M.D., George T. Strong, Frederick Law Olmsted, Samuel G. Howe, M.D., and J. S. Newberry, M.D., *Commissioners.*

upon the best efforts to be made for the spiritual good of the soldiers, the UNITED STATES CHRISTIAN COMMISSION was organized, and George H. Stuart, of Philadelphia, was chosen its presiding officer.*

This commission worked upon the same general plan adopted by the Sanitary Commission. Its labors were by no means confined to spiritual and intellectual ministrations, but were extended to the distribution of a vast amount of food, hospital stores, delicacies, and clothing. It, too, followed the great national armies, and was like a twin angel of mercy with the Sanitary Commission. It co-operated efficiently with the chaplains of the army and navy, and cast about the soldiers and seamen a salutary hedge of Christian influence. The money collected for the use of the commission was mostly gathered by the women of various Christian denominations. It was a free-will offering, and amounted, in the aggregate, to about $1,000,000. The entire receipts of the commission in money and supplies were fully $6,000,000.

In this chapter we have an outline picture of the attitude of the people of the Commonwealth of

VINCENT COLLYER.

New York during that crucial period of its history—namely, the first few months of the kindling and progress of the great Civil War. We have seen how firmly they received the cruel and sudden shock ; how willingly they sacrificed their personal interests for the general good ; how generously they gave men and money for the salvation of the life of the Republic ; and what a wonderful system of philanthropic and patriotic effort they inaugurated and sustained in causing the loyal people of the land to lay at the feet of the defenders of our common country a free-will offering of $26,000,000 !

---

* The officers of the Christian Commission were : George H. Stuart, *Chairman ;* Rev. W. E. Boardman, *Secretary ;* Joseph Patterson, *Treasurer*, and George H. Stuart, Bishop E. S. Janes, D.D., Charles Demonds, John P. Croser, and Jay Cooke, *Executive Committee.*

CHAPTER XXXVIII.

There was a remarkable change in the political aspect of New York late in 1862. The Opposition charged the national administration with a design to destroy the institution of slavery. Countenance was given to this opinion because many of the Republican nominees for office at the fall election were known to be advocates of the anti-slavery cause. The Republican nominee for governor, James S. Wadsworth, held the most extreme radical views of his party on this subject.

The Democrats nominated Horatio Seymour for Governor. Both parties expressed, in the resolutions of their respective conventions, their firm determination to uphold the National Government in its struggle with its foes. The citizens of the State were then divided into two great parties, Republican and Democratic. There was a small party of adherents of the Bell organization of 1860, whose views were expressed in the phrase, "The Constitution, the Union, and the Enforcement of the Laws."

At the fall election ex-Governor Seymour and the Democratic candidates for State offices were elected by a majority of nearly eleven thousand votes. The Senate remained overwhelmingly Republican, while there was a tie in the Assembly at the beginning of 1863.

While the extraordinary expenses of the State on account of the war were increasing, and the commonwealth was pledged to pay its debts in coin, its revenues were diminished over $600,000 by the financial policy of the National Government at that time, in exempting its bonds from State taxation, etc. The banks of the State held $125,000,000 of these various untaxed bonds. The State debt (canal and funded) in the fall of 1862 was nearly $31,000,000.

Notwithstanding this diminution of its revenue, the State of New York continued its gigantic exertions in support of the National Government. It appropriated men and money with a lavish hand. During 1862 it sent one hundred and twenty regiments to the field in response to two calls of the President for troops for nine months and for the war —six hundred thousand in number. New York paid a bounty of fifty dollars each for volunteers, for which purpose $3,650,000 were required, making the war expenditure of the State $10,000,000. The subscriptions of towns and counties for the same purpose were equal in amount, making the contributions of the people of the State $20,000,000.

At the close of 1862 the number of soldiers furnished by the State of New York, including recruits for the regular army and for regiments in other States, was two hundred and nineteen thousand. Of the regiments raised seventy-one had their headquarters in New York City. At the close of the year the citizens of the State had contributed to the support of the Government in taxes, gifts, and loans to the nation $300,000,000 and eighty thousand volunteers.

The beginning of 1863 was the opening of a new era in the life of our Republic. On that day, by a proclamation of emancipation by the President of the United States, human slavery was abolished from every part of the Union, and our country became, for the first time, really

"The land of the free and the home of the brave."

Up to that period the fortunes of war had generally favored the enemies of the Republic. From that time until peace was secured by the wisdom, patience, and valor of the loyal people, almost continual triumphs rewarded the exertions of the national troops.

Horatio Seymour was again inaugurated Governor of New York on January 1st, 1863. His first message to the Legislature was a vigorous dissent from the entire policy of the national administration. He declared that Congress and the Government had violated the rights of the States. He traced the origin of the war to a disregard of the obligations of the Constitution, disrespect for constituted authority, and local and sectional prejudices. He believed the war might have been averted, but when its floodgates were opened the administration was inadequate to comprehend its dimensions or to control its sweep. He charged the Government with extravagance and corruption in every department, and violations of the Constitution and laws in making arbitrary arrests in disregard of the rights and authority of the States, suppressing journals, proclaiming martial law, and "attempting to emancipate the slaves." He declared that the administration had effected a complete revolution in the Government; that national bankruptcy and ruin were imminent; and that the Government, in its persistent attempts to subjugate the South, in violation of its solemn pledges at the beginning of the war, had failed in the attainment of its ends. At the same time he declared that the Union must be restored to its integrity as it existed before the war; that the situation as it stood must be accepted; that the armies in the field must be supported; that all the requirements of the Constitution must promptly be responded to, and that under no circumstances could a division of the Union be conceded.

This arraignment of the National Government at the bar of public opinion by the distinguished Governor of the great commonwealth of New York had a powerful influence in cooling the ardor of the loyal people, particularly in his own State. The patriotic tone of the message gave it greater puissance. The line of partisan demarcation between the two great political parties, which had been almost obliterated by the common effort to oppose the revolutionary movements of the secessionists, was now conspicuously restored. The Peace Faction made the message an instrument for the discouragement of volunteering, and demagogues at the North who sympathized with the insurgents made it a basis for inflammatory harangues intended to divide and distract the loyal people, and to excite a counter-demonstration in favor of the schemes of the conspirators.

Early in June a mass-meeting of members of the Peace Faction assembled in New York City and adopted a series of characteristic resolutions. They declared their fealty to the Constitution and to the " sovereignty of the States ;" denied that the National Government had rightful power to " coerce a State ;" asserted that the war was unconstitutional and ought to " be put an end to," and protested against the " cowardly, despotic, and inhuman act of banishing C. L. Vallandigham." * Administration and Democratic conventions were held in September, the former recommending a vigorous prosecution of the war, the latter pledging their support to the Government in subduing the rebellion and restoring the Union.

The obstructions which the Peace Faction continually cast in the way of enlistments compelled the President, under the authority of Congress, to order a general conscription or draft to fill up the rank of the armies. Organized resistance to this measure instantly appeared. The leaders of the Peace Faction denounced the law and all acts under it, with arbitrary

---

* In the spring of 1863 Clement L. Vallandigham, an ex-member of Congress from Ohio, was especially busy in sowing the seeds of disaffection to the Government among the people of Ohio. General Burnside, in command of the military department in which Vallandigham was operating, had issued a general order for the suppression of seditious speech and action, and threatened the punishment due to spies and traitors to such offenders. Vallandigham defied the military power and denounced the order. He was arrested at his own house at Dayton, was tried by a court-martial, convicted, and sentenced to close confinement in a fortress during the remainder of the war. This sentence was commuted to banishment within the Confederate lines. His Southern friends treated him so coldly that he left them in disgust, went to Canada, and tarried awhile with Confederate refugees there. Meanwhile the Democratic State Convention of Ohio nominated him for governor.

arrests for treasonable practices,* as despotic and unconstitutional. An obscure lawyer in New York named McCunn, who had been elected judge, so decided. He was sustained by three judges of the Supreme Court of Pennsylvania—Lowrie, Woodward, and Thompson. Supported by these decisions, opposition politicians opposed the draft with a high hand. Kindred newspapers and public speakers joined in the denunciations. The national anniversary (July 4th) was made the special occasion for their utterances.

Distinguished members of the Peace Faction exhorted the people to stand firmly in opposition to what they called the "usurpations of the Government." One of the most exalted among these opponents of the Government, in an address at Tammany Hall on July 4th, uttered sneers because Vicksburg had not been taken, and taunted the President with having uttered a "midnight cry for help" because of Lee's invasion of Maryland. At that moment Vicksburg and thirty-seven thousand prisoners of war were in the possession of General Grant, and Lee and his legions, discomfited at Gettysburg, were preparing to fly back to Virginia. These two decisive battles of the war had been fought and won by the National troops, and the safety of the Republic was assured in spite of the Peace Faction.

On the evening of July 3d an incendiary hand-bill, calculated to incite to insurrection, was scattered over the city, and a morning newspaper advised its readers to provide themselves with a "good rifled musket, a few pounds of powder, and a hundred or two of shot" to "defend their homes and personal liberties from invasion from *any* quarter." It is believed that an organized outbreak had been planned and would have been executed, but for the successes of the Nationals at Vicksburg and Gettysburg. The draft began in New York, on July 13th, 1863, in a building on the corner of Forty-sixth Street and Third Avenue. Suddenly a large crowd, who had cut the telegraph wires leading out of the city, appeared, attacked the building, drove out the men in charge of the

---

* Just after the proclamation for a conscription appeared, a public meeting was held in Albany to consider the arrest of Vallandigham. Governor Seymour was invited to attend. He declined, but sent a letter in which he expressed his views very freely. He denounced the act as a violation of the most sacred rights of every American citizen. He pronounced the order which, it was alleged, had been violated by the prisoner, invalid. He declared that the governments and the courts of some of the great Western States had sunk into insignificance before despotic military power. He said that, having given to the Government a generous support, the people would now "pause to see what kind of a government it is for which we are asked to pour out our blood and treasure;" to determine "whether this war is waged to put down rebellion at the South or to destroy free institutions at the North."

draft, poured kerosene oil over the floor of the room, and very soon that and the adjoining edifice were in flames. The firemen and the police were driven off. So began a violent tumult in which thousands of men and women, chiefly foreigners by birth and disloyal men from the Southern States, were engaged for three full days and nights. The draft was only a pretext. The cry against it soon ceased, and was supplemented by shouts of "Down with the Abolitionists! Down with the nigger! Hurrah for Jeff Davis!"

The mob compelled hundreds of citizens driven out of manufacturing establishments, which they had closed, to join them, and, under the influence of strong drink, arson and plunder became the business of the rioters. The special objects of their wrath were the innocent colored people. They laid in ashes the Colored Orphan Asylum. The terrified inmates, who fled in terror, were pursued and cruelly beaten. Men and women were pounded to death in the streets, and the colored people were hunted as if they were noxious wild beasts. Finally the police, aided by some troops, suppressed the insurrection in the city, but not until a thousand persons had been slain or wounded, fifty buildings had been destroyed by the mob, a large number of stores and dwellings not burned had been sacked or plundered, and property valued at $2,000,000 had been wasted. This riot was evidently an irregular outbreak of a vast conspiracy planned by disloyal men in both sections of the Union.

Governor Seymour, who was at the sea-shore a few miles from New York, interposed his personal influence to quell the disturbance on the second day of the riot. He came up to the scene of tumult, and after issuing a proclamation declaring the town to be in a state of insurrection, he repaired to the City Hall, and from its steps addressed the angry multitude in soothing words, telling them that he had sent his adjutant-general to the National Capital to demand a suspension of the draft until a judicial decision concerning it might be obtained. His mild exhortation was unheeded, of course. The mob while *waiting* went on plundering, burning, and murdering, until the strong arm of physical force —military and police—restrained them.

The governor's "demand" was not complied with. The exigency was too vitally important and the danger was too pressing to safely admit of delay. To save the Republic the army must be strengthened. The draft was resumed. General Dix asked Governor Seymour for military aid to enforce the measure. It was refused, when the Secretary of War ordered many regiments and batteries of artillery to the assistance of the commander of the Department of the East. An enrolment of the militia in New York, which was completed in September, showed that there were five hundred and thirty-nine thousand five hundred and thirty-nine men in the State subject to the draft.

Early in 1863 a powerful association was formed in the city of New York for the special purpose of giving support, moral and physical, to the National Government in its struggles with its foes, secret and open. It was organized on March 30th, 1863, with the title of the "Union League Club," and did noble service to the good cause during the remainder of the war. This club was essentially the child of the United States Sanitary Commission.

The Union League Club asked Governor Seymour to give them authority to recruit a regiment of colored troops. He refused, on the ground that he had not the power to do so. That authority was immediately given by the Secretary of War, and within a month a full regiment was recruited and placed in camp, for which duty the Club contributed $18,000. The regiment received their colors (presented by the loyal women of the city) in front of the club house. Six months after the riot, when no colored man dared to be seen in the streets of New York, this regiment marched down Broadway on its journey to the field, receiving tokens of respect and honor at every step.

In February, 1863, Congress passed an act for the establishment of a national paper currency that should circulate at par in all parts of the Union; also for the creation of national banking institutions. The author of this admirable scheme, which has worked so beneficently for the people and the nation, is the venerable John Thompson, then as now (1887) an eminent financier in the city of New York. He and Mr. Chase, the Secretary of the Treasury, were intimate personal friends. So early as June, 1861, Mr. Thompson, in a letter to the Secretary, proposed the plan, which Congress substantially adopted. When the law was passed Mr. Thompson showed his "faith by his works." He established in the city of New York the first bank under the law, and called it the "Chase National Bank."

As the war went on the State of New York continued to make striking displays of its vast military strength and other resources. The year 1864 was a memorable one in its history. General prosperity prevailed. The people bore the enormous burdens laid upon them with cheerfulness and alacrity. Careful of the credit and honor of the commonwealth, the Legislature early in the year adopted a joint resolution that no distinction should be made between the foreign and domestic creditors of the State in the payment of interest on the State debt. It was done, and the interest was paid to all alike in gold or its equivalent. At the same session provision was made to secure at the general election the votes of the soldiers and seamen who might be absent on actual duty at the time. At the Presidential election in the fall thousands of electors engaged in the naval and military service voted by proxy.

President Lincoln was renominated for the Chief Magistracy by the Republicans. General George B. McClellan, who had left the army, was the Democratic opponent, and received the solid vote of the Peace Faction. But Mr. Lincoln was elected by an overwhelming majority of the votes of the loyal people.

The National Government, having information that Confederates in Canada, acting as agents of the rebel government, had formed a conspiracy to interfere with the Presidential election and endeavor to inaugurate a counter-revolution in the Northern States, by sending refugees, deserters from the Union armies, aliens, and others to vote, precautionary measures were taken. General Dix, commander of the Department of the East, provided for the arrest and summary punishment of such offenders against the purity and freedom of the ballot and of social order. He was seconded by Governor Seymour. On November 2d the Mayor of New York City (Gunther) received a telegram from the Secretary of State (Seward) warning him that a conspiracy among the Confederate agents in Canada was on foot to burn the principal cities in the Northern States on the day of the Presidential election.

To protect the city of New York at that election about seven thousand troops were sent to the vicinity and placed on steamboats which were anchored in the surrounding waters, ready for prompt action at any moment. General B. F. Butler was sent from Fortress Monroe to take the chief command.

The Confederates and their Northern friends were foiled by this prompt and energetic action, and peace and good order were maintained at the elections throughout the State. Butler left the command of the troops with General Hawley on November 15th, when all danger seemed to be overpast. But ten days afterward the execution of a part of the conspiracy was attempted in the city of New York by setting on fire, at the same hour at night, of a large number of hotels and Barnum's Museum. One of the culprits, who was caught and hanged, confessed that he and several others had been sent by Confederates in Canada to lay the city of New York in ashes. They intended to start the conflagration on the night of the election, but some of their inflammable material was not then ready.

At the fall election in 1864 Reuben E. Fenton* was chosen Governor

---

* Reuben E. Fenton was born July 4th, 1819, in Chautauqua County, N. Y.; a descendant of one of the noted early settlers of Connecticut. He worked on his father's farm in the warm season and studied in a log school-house in winter until he was fifteen

of the State of New York by the Republicans, by a majority of over eight thousand votes. During that year the commonwealth had put forth its might in a surprising manner. It sent into the field from its farms and workshops and mercantile life 161,604 men. From April, 1861, to December, 1864, the State had given to the military service 437,701 men, of which number 409,426 had entered the army and 28,275 the navy. To preserve a record of every man sent from New York to the field, and for a depository of battle-flags and other trophies of the war, a Bureau of Military Statistics was established at the State capital, and for its use a fire-proof building was subsequently erected. Out of the enrolled militia of the State a National Guard was formed, consisting of about forty-six thousand men.

At the beginning of 1865 there was a glowing promise of a speedy termination of the war and the

REUBEN E. FENTON.

re-establishment of a Union strengthened and powerful. Brilliant victories had been won by the great armies led by Generals Grant and Sherman. The latter had marched triumphantly through Georgia—the "Empire State of the South"—from Atlanta to the sea, and discovered

---

years old, when he received a little academic education. In early life he became extensively engaged in the lumber business. At the age of twenty-three he was elected supervisor of his town, and held the office eight years. In 1840 he became a member of the Assembly, and in 1849 he was elected to Congress. He was a Democrat, but he firmly opposed the repeal of the Missouri Compromise, and fought against the Kansas-Nebraska bill, which effected it. With the passage of that act by the joint action of the Democrats and slaveholders, Mr. Fenton abandoned the Democratic Party, and became an active member of the Republican Party at its organization in 1854. He presided at the first Republican State Convention in New York. In 1856 the Republican Party elected him to Congress, wherein he served four terms successively. In 1864 he was elected Governor of his native State. Horatio Seymour was his opponent. An active war governor, he won the affection of all soldiers by the warm interest he always manifested in their welfare in or out of the army. His general policy during his administration was generally approved by the best men of both parties. He was engaged in the business of banking at the time of his death, which occurred very suddenly, from heart disease, in his private office at his banking-house at Jamestown, N. Y., on August 25th, 1885. In person Governor Fenton was tall and slender, and graceful in figure and movements.

the fatal weakness of the Confederacy ; the former, at Petersburg, was destroying the props of the Confederate capital, Richmond, which even then was tottering to its fall.

In his message to the Legislature (January, 1865) Governor Fenton congratulated the people of New York because of abounding prosperity in every part of the commonwealth, and the bright outlook of the future for the nation. He submitted to them the Thirteenth Amendment to the National Constitution proposed by Congress for the abolition of slavery, with an earnest recommendation for its prompt adoption. It was done.

The congratulations of the governor were justified by events. On April 9th the main Confederate Army under General Robert E. Lee was surrendered to General Grant at Appomattox Court-House, in Virginia ; and the next larger Confederate force, under General Joseph E. Johnston, surrendered to General Sherman near Raleigh, in North Carolina, on the 14th. These two events caused the speedy ending of the war.

The telegraph had thrilled the loyal people with the glad tidings of these auspicious events, when it checked the exuberance of that joy by imparting the sad news of the assassination of the President of the United States at a theatre in Washington, on the evening of the 14th of April. He expired the next morning. The Vice-President (Andrew Johnson) immediately assumed the functions of the exalted office, and the integrity and strength of the Government experienced no shock from the dreadful blow.

At the close of the war, in May, 1865, the State of New York had furnished for the conflict 473,443 men, including 16,000 militiamen mustered for a less term of service than three months. Of this number the city of New York gave 116,382 men for terms of one, two, three, and four years' service. The average cost for each man, including bounties, expenditures for the relief of their families, etc., was $150.47.

So rapidly did the great armies dissolve and become a part of the civil life of the nation,* that at the beginning of 1866 only seven regiments of infantry and two of cavalry of the New York troops remained in the service of the United States. In addition to other enormous expendi-

---

* The disbanding of the victorious armies of the republic began in June, 1865, and the soldiers returned to their homes. It was a most interesting and rare spectacle for the contemplation of the nations. In the space of one hundred and fifty days the vast multitude of defenders of the Union were transformed into peaceful citizens, and resumed the varied and blessed avocations of peace. There had been enrolled for duty 2,656,591 men, of whom 1,490,000 were in actual service. By mid-winter of 1866, 750,000 men had been mustered out of the service.

tures for the war, the State of New York disbursed over $35,000,000 to its soldiers in bounties alone from July 17th, 1861, to January 1st, 1866.

The population of the State diminished during the war. There were nearly forty-nine thousand less inhabitants in 1865 than in 1860. There were eighty thousand less in the city of New York than there were five years before. This diminution may be attributed to various causes directly or indirectly connected with the war. The total population of the State at the close of 1865 was about four millions.

Little of special historic importance occurred in the State after the close of the war until the meeting of the Constitutional Convention, in 1867. The Legislature, early in 1866, passed resolutions, by a large majority in both branches: (1) That no State in which rebellion had existed should be admitted to share in the national legislation until it should be presented in the attitude of loyalty and harmony in the person of representatives whose loyalty could not be questioned; (2) that the nation, by its professions and acts from the beginning of the war, and especially by accepting the President's proclamation of emancipation, and an amendment to the Constitution abolishing slavery, stands pledged to the world, to humanity, and, above all, to the freedmen, that in all lawful ways the liberty and civil rights of every human being subject to the Government of the United States shall be protected and enforced, regardless of race, color, or condition, against every wrongful opposing law, ordinance, custom, or prejudice; and "that the spirit which formed and organized and developed to the present strength that policy has not fulfilled its allotted work until every subject of that Government stands not only free, but equal before the law."

The Legislature of 1867 adopted the Fourteenth Amendment to the National Constitution proposed by Congress, which guaranteed equal rights to every citizen of whatever hue or social condition; defined the status in regard to public offices of men who had engaged in the rebellion; declared the validity of the national debt, and forbade the payment of any part of the Confederate debt by the nation or a State.

An act was passed for increasing the State tax for the support of common schools, declaring that all the schools of the State, including normal schools, should be "free," and providing for the establishment of additional normal schools in different parts of the State.

The Legislature also passed an act making eight hours' labor a legal day's work. This did not apply to farm laborers or men hired by the week, month, or year, nor did it prevent the making of contracts for any length of time.

In March (1867) a convention to consider a revision of the State Constitution was authorized. Delegates were chosen in April. The convention assembled in the State Capitol on June 4th. William A. Wheeler, of Franklin County (afterward Vice-President of the United States), was appointed President, and Luther Caldwell, of Chemung, Secretary. The number of delegates was one hundred and sixty, of whom ninety-seven were Republicans and sixty-three were Democrats. In September the Convention took a recess. It reassembled on November 12th, and continued its sessions into 1868, holding the meetings after January 1st in the City Hall, at Albany.

Various amendments were discussed. Some were adopted, by the provisions of which the right of suffrage was conferred on all male inhabitants of the age of twenty-one years and upward, without distinction of color; the payment of the canal and other State debts was secured; the time of office of Senators was extended to four years; the Assembly was increased to one hundred and thirty-nine members; the Court of Appeals was organized with a chief-justice and six associate justices; the existing Supreme Court organization was retained, with certain additional provisions for the despatch of business—the judges to be chosen by the people, and to hold their offices for fourteen years, or until they attain the age of seventy years. Provision was also made for submitting to the people in 1873 the question whether such judges should continue to be elected, or whether the position should be filled by appointment. The remaining provisions were substantially the same as the Constitution of 1846.

The amended Constitution was submitted to the people at the general election in the fall of 1869. The portions concerning the judiciary, taxation, and Negro suffrage were voted upon separately. The whole amended Constitution was rejected by the people by a negative majority of 66,521 votes, excepting the judiciary portion. That received an affirmative majority of 6798 votes. The amendment in favor of Negro suffrage was rejected by a negative majority of 32,601 votes.

During the autumn of 1867 Cornell University, one of the most useful of the literary and scientific institutions in the State of New York, was opened, under favorable auspices, at Ithaca. It was founded by Ezra Cornell, with the leading object in view of promoting instruction in agricultural science and the mechanic arts, and the literal and practical education of the industrial classes in the several pursuits and professions in life, without excluding other scientific and classical studies, including military tactics. The State endowed the institution with the proceeds of nine hundred and ninety thousand acres of public lands, its share of the domain given by Congress for such a purpose. The founder gave $500,000, and he and others afterward added $1,000,000 to the endowment funds. The institution is thoroughly equipped with buildings and apparatus, and a library of about forty-six thousand volumes.

At the November election, in 1868, the Democrats elected their candidate for Governor of New York, John T. Hoffman, by a majority of twenty-eight thousand votes, while the Republicans elected a majority of the members of the Legislature. At the same time General Ulysses S. Grant, the Republican candidate, was elected President of the United States by a large majority over Horatio Seymour, the Democratic candidate, with Schuyler Colfax, Vice-President. Mr. Seymour received a majority of ten thousand votes in his own State, while a majority of the Congressmen to represent New York were chosen by the Republicans.

CHAPTER XXXIX.

The first administration of Governor Hoffman* (1869-71) was distinguished by few important events in the history of New York. The Republican Legislature by concurrent resolution (1869) adopted the Fifteenth Amendment to the National Constitution proposed by Congress in the following words:

"Article XV. *Section* 1. The right of the citizens of the United States to vote shall not be denied or abridged by the United States or any State on account of race, color, or previous condition of servitude.

"*Section* 2. The Congress shall have power to enforce this article by appropriate legislation."

JOHN T. HOFFMAN.

This resolution was vehemently opposed by the Democratic members of the Legislature, and was carried by a strict party vote of 17 to 15 in the Senate and 72 to 47 in the Assembly. The governor did not com-

---

* John Thompson Hoffman descended from Martin Hoffman, who came to New York from Holland in 1671. His grandfather was Philip Livingston Hoffman, a grandson of Philip Livingston, of Livingston Manor. His father, Adrian Kissam Hoffman, after brief service in the navy, took up his residence at Sing Sing, N. Y., where his only son, John T., was born January 10th, 1828. At the age of eighteen he was graduated with honors at Union College, N. Y. He studied law with the late General Aaron Ward, and was admitted to the bar on his twenty-first birthday. A year before, he was a member of the State Central Committee of a wing of the Democratic Party. In 1849 he removed to the city of New York and formed a law partnership, soon rising to distinction in his profession. In 1854 he became a member of the Tammany Society, and was prominent in local politics. In 1860 he was elected Recorder of New York—the principal judge of criminal jurisdiction; and in 1865 he was elected mayor of the city over several opposing candidates. In 1868 he was elected Governor of the State of New York by the Democratic Party by a majority of over twenty-seven thousand votes, and was re-elected in 1870 by a majority of thirty-three thousand. In 1873 he retired from public life. Governor Hoffman's administration was conspicuous for the creation of the Constitutional Commission of 1872, which was his own device. The Legislature authorized it, and

municate this action to the proper authority at Washington until requested to do so by the Assistant-Secretary of State.

At the general election in November the political aspect of the State was entirely changed. At the opening of the sessions of the Legislature in 1870, the Democrats had the ascendancy in both Houses. There were eighteen Democrats and fourteen Republicans in the Senate, and seventy-two Democrats and fifty-six Republicans in the Assembly. On the first day of the session the notorious William M. Tweed, soon to be convicted as a plunderer of the public treasury in New York City and to be imprisoned for his crimes, offered in the Senate a series of resolutions withdrawing the assent of the State to the ratification of the Fifteenth Amendment. After reciting in the preamble the proposed Amendment, it was

"*Resolved*, That the Legislature of the State of New York refuses to ratify the above-recited proposed amendment to the Constitution of the United States, and withdraws absolutely any expression of consent heretofore given thereto, or ratification thereof.

"*Resolved*, That the governor be requested to transmit a copy of these resolutions and preamble to the Secretary of State of the United States at Washington, and to every member of the Senate and House of Representatives of the United States, and the governors of the several States."

The Legislature of 1872 rescinded these resolutions by an overwhelming majority.

During the session of 1870, the charters of the cities of Albany and New York were amended. That of the latter ostensibly restored self-government to the people of the city. Thenceforward the Mayor, Common Councilmen, Corporation Council, and the Comptroller were elected by the people. A Department of Public Works was created, which embraced the Street and Aqueduct Departments; also a Department of Docks. The heads of these departments, as well as of a Department of Public Parks, a Fire, Health, and Police Department, were appointed by the mayor under the new charter, an instrument obtained for a sinister purpose, as we shall perceive presently.

During this session an important change was made in the public-

---

Governor Hoffman appointed thirty-two citizens, composed of an equal number of Democrats and Republicans, to revise the State Constitution. The labors of that commission were of vital importance, rendering subsequent reforms in the administration of public affairs practicable. It was during his administration that the exposures of the "Tweed Ring" were made. For his veto of the City Charter presented by the Committee of Seventy the governor gave satisfactory constitutional reasons.

school system in the city of New York. The Board of twenty-one School Commissioners was dissolved and a new Board was created, consisting of twelve members appointed by the mayor, who were to hold office until 1871, after which their successors were to be elected by the people. As usual, the subject of common schools occupied a large space in the governor's annual message. He reported that the receipts of the Common School Fund in 1868 amounted to $10,500,000, of which amount $5,500,000 had been applied to the payment of teachers' wages during that year. There had been expended for the libraries, $26,726; for school apparatus, $234,432; for the support of schools for colored children, $64,765, and $2,000,000 for school-houses. In 11,731 school districts, 971,500 children had been taught by 27,000 teachers. The libraries contained an aggregate of 1,000,000 volumes. The National Census for 1870 gave to the State a population of 4,374,703, or an increase of nearly half a million in ten years.

The elections in the State of New York in the fall of 1870 resulted in the success of the Democratic ticket by a majority of about thirty thousand. Governor Hoffman was re-elected. The Democrats secured a little more than one half of the representatives of the State in Congress. The two branches of the Legislature were respectively almost equally divided politically, and a tie was produced in the Assembly by the compulsory resignation of a member from New York City because of his misconduct in the Legislative Chamber.

At midsummer (1871) a serious riot occurred in the city of New York between two Irish religious factions—namely, the "Orangemen" (Protestants) and the "Ribbon Men" (Roman Catholics). As the annual parade of the former was usually an incentive to personal collisions, the police authorities had forbidden it, but at the request of Governor Hoffman the order was revoked. The parade took place. A large body of both police and military turned out to protect the procession. At one point a mob attacked the marching line, and before order was restored several persons were killed.

Again the ever-oscillating political pendulum in the State of New York went to the Republican side in the fall, giving to the Senate twenty-four Republicans of the thirty-two members, and to the Assembly ninety-seven Republicans and thirty-one Democrats. This result was largely occasioned by the discovery during the summer of immense frauds perpetrated by municipal officers in the city of New York. The conspirators concerned in these frauds are known in local history as "The Tweed Ring," or the "Tammany Ring." For several years the metropolis was virtually ruled by William M. Tweed, a chair-maker by trade, and a politician of the baser sort by profession. Active, pushing, unscrupulous, he had worked his way up through petty municipal offices to the position of Supervisor of the County of New York, chairman of that Board, and Deputy Street Commissioner in 1863. The latter office placed him virtually at the head of the public works of the city, and gave him almost unlimited control of the public expenditures. At about the same time he was chosen Grand Sachem of the Tammany Society, which position endowed him with immense political power. This power, by means of his offices in the municipal government and the patronage at his command, he was able to wield with mighty force. He took advantage of this power to procure for himself election to the State Senate for three consecutive terms—1867 to 1871. Corrupt officials and hungry politicians swarmed around him. With three or four shrewd confidants—men who before had enjoyed a fair reputation for honor and honesty—he organized a system for plundering the public treasury unprecedented in boldness and extent. It comprehended the expenditure for streets, boulevards, parks, armories, public buildings, and improvements of every kind, in which the spoils were divided, *pro rata*, among the conspirators. These spoils consisted of sixty-five to eighty-five per cent of the public money paid to contractors and others, who were encouraged to add enormous amounts to their bills, often ten times the amount of an honest charge.*

To render plundering more secure, Tweed procured from the Legislature amendments to the charter just mentioned, by which the executive power of the city was vested in the mayor and the heads of departments, who were appointed by him. The mayor appears to have been one of the "ring" of conspirators, and appointed Tweed to the important office of Commissioner of Public Works. Tweed's confederates were placed at the head of other important departments connected with the city finances. The power of auditing accounts was taken from the supervisors and given to a Board of Audit, composed of the Mayor,

---

* For example: "On one occasion the sum of $1,500,000 was granted for pretended labor and expense of material, when a fair and liberal allowance would have been only $264,000. The sum authorized by the Legislature to be expended in the erection of a new county court-house in the city was $250,000; in 1871, when it was yet unfinished, $8,000,000 had ostensibly been spent upon it. Whenever any contractor or mechanic ventured to remonstrate, he was silenced by a threat of losing the city patronage or of non-payment for work already done; and so conscientious men were often forced to become the confederates of thieves. A secret record of these fraudulent transactions was kept in the auditor's office under the title of 'County Liabilities.' The incumbent of that office was a supple instrument of the plunderers, and did their bidding."—*Lossing's History of New York City*, vol. ii., p. 806.

Comptroller, Commissioner of Public Parks, and Commissioner of Public Works,* who were the chief conspirators.

The scheme for plundering the city treasury was now complete, and it was used with a free hand for the next fifteen months. In order to evade joint responsibility, the Board of Audit delegated their power to the city auditor, who was one of their willing tools. He signed all the fraudulent bills often without examining them, and paid over to the chief conspirators their commission of sixty-five or eighty-five per cent on the amount so audited. Within the space of less than four months the sum of $6,312,000 was paid from the city treasury, of which $5,710,000 was ostensibly on account of the new court-house. At least $5,000,000 of the $6,312,000 went into the pockets of the chief conspirators and their associates.

Their "sin found them out." The sheriff of New York happened to place an honest man in the auditor's office, named John Copeland. He stumbled upon the record of "County Liabilities." He made an exact copy of it, and showed it to the sheriff. The latter used it in endeavors to force the "ring" to pay a claim he held against the city. The conspirators refused compliance with his demand, and he threatened to publish the record in the *New York Daily Times.* Alarmed, they at once sent the auditor to negotiate with the sheriff, who, they supposed, was at a sporting tavern in a remote part of the city. Failing to find him, the auditor was returning, when he was thrown from his carriage and mortally hurt. He never regained consciousness.

For several months the sheriff unsuccessfully pressed his claim. At length he gave the damaging document to the proprietor of the *New York Times,* and in July, 1871, the tell-tale items were spread over its pages for the public eye. Amazement and hot indignation produced intense excitement in the city. Tweed, believing his fortress to be impregnable, sneeringly inquired :

"What are you going to do about it ?"

Day after day the *Times* dealt ponderous blows at the walls of the fortress of the conspirators, each day adding proofs of the black crimes of the plunderers. Week after week the inimitable cartoons of Nast in *Harper's Weekly* struck equally telling blows, for pictures are the literature of the unlearned ; and the most illiterate citizen could read and understand these cartoons. The conspirators were soon compelled to yield.

---

* A. Oakey Hall, Mayor ; Richard B. Connolly, Comptroller ; Peter B. Sweeney, Commissioner of Public Parks, and William M. Tweed, Commissioner of Public Works.

A meeting of citizens was held at the Cooper Union on September 4th, at which some of the principal men of New York City were active participants. An Executive Committee of Seventy, composed of leading citizens, was appointed, charged with the duty of making a thorough investigation, and to take action for relieving the city of the plunderers. The Committee sent forth an "Appeal to the people of the State of New York," and then entered upon their duties with vigor. Very soon the conspirators in office fled to Europe or were brought to the bar of justice. The Attorney-General of the State authorized the late Charles O'Conor to act for the commonwealth. He employed able assistants. The late Governor Samuel J. Tilden rendered conspicuous service in the matter. On the strength of an affidavit of the latter, Tweed was arrested and held to bail in the sum of $1,000,000. He was tried for and found guilty of forgery and grand larceny in 1873, and sentenced to a long imprisonment in the penitentiary on Blackwell's Island.* Very soon the city was purged of the plunderers. It was estimated that the "ring" had robbed the city of fully $20,000,000.†

The Committee of Seventy not only broke up the gang of official robbers, but procured an amendment to the city charter, by which the legislative power was vested in a board of twenty-two aldermen. The mayor retained the authority to appoint the heads of the several departments, but only with the advice and consent of the Board of Aldermen.

The State Legislature was called upon in 1872 to adjudicate the cases of five judges who had been impeached for corrupt official conduct. These were G. G. Barnard, A. Cardozo, J. A. McCunn, and George M. Curtis, of New York City, and H. G. Prindle, of Chenango County. Thirty-nine articles of impeachment were presented against Barnard, mostly accusing him of receiving bribes and corruptly using his judicial power. He was found guilty, was removed from the bench, and was

---

* In the summer of 1875 Tweed's friends procured his release on bail. He was immediately arrested on a civil suit to recover over $6,000,000 which he had stolen from the city treasury. Bail to the amount of $3,000,000 was required. He could not furnish it, and he was confined in the Ludlow Street Jail. One evening at twilight, being allowed to visit his wife in charge of the sheriff, he managed to escape. He fled to Europe, was arrested in a Spanish port, and brought back to New York in failing health, and lodged in jail. In March, 1876, in a civil suit for $6,537,000 the jury returned a verdict for that amount. He could not pay. He lingered in prison until January 12th, 1878, when he died at the age of fifty-five years.

† The Tweed Ring were not the only plunderers of the city at that period. Members of the dominant political party in the city Legislature (largely for political purposes) gave in lands and money, during three years previous to 1873, no less than $4,896,388 to one denomination of Christians in the city of New York for the support of its religious, benevolent, and educational organizations.

disqualified from ever afterward holding any office in the State of New York. Cardozo wisely resigned, and so avoided a trial. McCunn was found guilty, and was removed, and died soon afterward. Curtis and Prindle were acquitted.. The conduct of the four city judges was a part of the great official conspiracy to plunder the treasury of the metropolis.*

The colored population, availing themselves of their newly-acquired political rights, followed the example of the white people, and assembled in conventions in various parts of the Union to express their views. The first *State* convention of colored citizens ever assembled in the United States met at Troy, N. Y., on May 8th–9th, 1872. They expressed their gratitude to the Republican Party as their liberator; endorsed the administration of President Grant; pledged themselves to support the Republican nomination for President; asked the Republican State Convention, then about to assemble at Elmira, to send a colored delegate at large to the Republican National Convention, then soon to meet at Philadelphia, and demanded the recognition and the enforcement of the rights of the colored people.

The political aspect in the State of New York and of the whole country in 1872 was peculiar. A large faction of the Republican Party, who had become dissatisfied with the administration, had formed a separate organization under the title of Liberal Republicans, and arranged themselves in opposition to the great historic party as represented by that administration. At a National Convention held at Cincinnati on May 1st, they nominated Horace Greeley, the veteran editor of the *New York Tribune*, for President of the United States. The Democratic leaders, perceiving little hope of success for their party, sought and effected a fusion of the Democratic and Liberal Republican parties. Mr. Greeley accepted the nomination from both parties; but President Grant, who had been nominated for re-election, was chosen by a popular majority of over seven hundred and sixty-three thousand. Many

---

* When Tweed was at the height of his disreputable career a strange social phenomenon appeared. Dazzled by the magnitude of city " improvements" under his direction, and without inquiring whence he procured the means for dispensing his private charities on a munificent scale, some of the most reputable citizens of New York publicly proposed to erect a statue of him as a public benefactor ! And when his daughter was married sixty-two citizens, some of them of high social position, bestowed upon her wedding gifts to the aggregate value of $70,000. Only one present was as low as $100 in value. Twenty-one persons each gave presents valued at $1000. Ten persons gave $2000 presents, two, $2500, and five gave presents to the value of $5000 each. One of the donors of the latter amount was a woman. Some of the most munificent gifts were from persons connected with the " ring," but who were then accounted respectable members of society. See Lossing's *History of New York City*, p. 807. A list of the names of those donors may be found in Stone's *History of the City of New York*, Appendix.

straight-out Democrats, offended by the nomination of Mr. Greeley, their life-long political antagonist, nominated Charles O'Conor, of New York, and gave him over twenty-one thousand votes, though he declined to be a candidate. In the State of New York Grant's majority over Greeley was more than fifty-three thousand, and that of General John Adams Dix,* the Republican candidate for Governor of the State, was over fifty-five thousand. A large majority of the Republican Congressmen were elected, and the State Legislature, at the beginning of 1873, was overwhelmingly Republican. A greater portion of the Liberal Republican faction was afterward absorbed by their ally, the Democratic Party, in the State and nation, and disappeared as a distinct organization.

In the spring of 1873 a Civil Rights Bill was passed by the Legislature, forbidding the managers of theatres and other places of amusement denying equal enjoyment of the privileges of their exhibitions to any person on account of "race, color, or previous condition of servitude." During the same session a commission appointed to prepare and submit to the Legislature such amendments to the State Constitution as they might deem expedient completed their work and reported amendments of nine acts and two new acts. These amendments were referred to the people at the next fall election, when they were all ratified. They made some

JOHN A. DIX.

---

* John Adams Dix was born at Boscawen, N. H., on July 24th, 1798; died at New York on April 27th, 1879. He entered the army in 1812, a boy less than fifteen years of age; was promoted to captain in 1825, and soon afterward resigned and studied law. He made his residence at Cooperstown, N. Y., and was chosen Secretary of State in 1833 by the Democratic Party. In 1845 he was elected to the United States Senate to fill a vacancy. In 1848 he was the unsuccessful Free-Soil candidate for governor. While in the Senate he was chairman of the Committee on Commerce. He was succeeded in the Senate by Mr. Seward in 1849. In 1861 he was Secretary of the Treasury for about three months, in the Cabinet of President Buchanan, during which time he issued the famous order: "If any man attempts to haul down the American flag, shoot him on the spot!" He was made major-general of volunteers in May, 1861; commanded at Fortress Monroe in 1862, and performed eminent services of various kinds during the war. In 1867-68 he was United States Minister to France; also was made President of the Union Pacific Railroad. In 1872 he was chosen Governor of New York. In 1855 Governor Dix published *A Summer in Spain and Florence*, containing his reminiscences of travels in Europe.

notable alterations in the organic law of the State. Among other things, provision was made for securing equality in the exercise of the elective franchise ; for the punishment of givers and receivers of bribes at elections ; for the payment of a fixed salary of $1500 to the members of the Legislature ; for changing the official term of the governor and lieutenant-governor of the State from two to three years, making the salary of the former $10,000 a year, and of the latter $5000 a year ; for restricting the Legislature in the management of the finances of the State and the chartering of banks ; also for the prevention of official corruption.

For some years a topographical and trigonometrical survey of the Adirondack region of the State had been prosecuted. In 1873 a commission appointed to inquire into the expediency of setting apart a large portion of that mountain and lake district as a *State Park* reported in favor of doing so. It has been done. The domain surveyed embraces about five thousand square miles, and includes all the higher peaks of the group and many lakes. The principal object sought in the preservation of the forests which clothe the hills was their beneficial climatic effects and the furnishing and perpetuation of a healthful and delightful pleasure ground for the people—a vast and magnificent sanitarium.

At the State election in the fall of 1873, the following questions were submitted to the voters for their decision :

1. Shall the chief judge and the associate judges of the Court of Appeals and the justices of the Supreme Court be hereafter elected or appointed ?

2. Shall the judges of the Superior Courts of New York City and Brooklyn, of the Court of Common Pleas of Buffalo, and the several county judges throughout the State be hereafter elected or appointed ?

The majority for the election of the higher judges was 204,642 ; for the election of lower judges, 208,985.

Among the important events in the civil history of the State during the administration of Governor Dix was the passage of an act which became a law on May 11th, 1874, for the compulsory education of the children of the commonwealth. It met with much opposition. The law went into effect on January 1st, 1875. It requires all parents and those who have the care of children between the ages of eight and fourteen to see that they are instructed in spelling, reading, writing, English grammar, geography, and arithmetic at least fourteen weeks in each year, either at school or at home, unless the physical or mental condition of the child may render such instruction inexpedient or impracticable.[*]

---

[*] Eight of the fourteen weeks' attendance at school must be consecutive. Any person neglecting to comply with this requirement is liable to a fine of $1 for the first offence,

The political campaign in the State in 1874 was exceedingly interesting. A Prohibition Convention assembled at Auburn late in June, and nominated ex-Governor Myron H. Clark for governor. On the same day in the same city fifty temperance Republicans from various parts of the State met and passed resolutions condemnatory of Governor Dix, because he vetoed a so-called local-option bill for the repression of intemperance.* The Liberal Republicans met in convention at Albany in September, but did not make any nominations. The Democratic Convention held at Syracuse in the same month nominated Samuel J. Tilden for Governor.† The Republican Convention was also held at Syracuse in September, and renominated Governor Dix by acclamation. The result of the election in November was a Democratic

SAMUEL J. TILDEN.

---

and for each succeeding violation, after having been properly notified, the offender shall pay $5 for every week, not exceeding thirteen in a year, during which he shall fail to comply with the law. The fines thus collected are to be devoted to school purposes.

No person shall employ any child under the age of fourteen years to labor in any business during school hours, unless the child has been instructed, either at school or at home, for at least fourteen of the fifty-two weeks next preceding the year in which the child shall be employed. The child must also furnish a written certificate of having received such instruction. The penalty for violating this provision is $50 for every offence.

In every school district the trustees are required, in September and in February, to examine into the situation of children employed in all manufacturing establishments; and manufacturers must furnish a correct list of all children between the ages of eight and fourteen employed.

Trustees are required to furnish text-books where the parents or guardians are unable to do so. If the parent or guardian is unable to compel the child to attend school, and shall so state in writing, the child shall be dealt with as an habitual truant.

Boards of instruction and trustees in cities, school districts, etc., are authorized and directed to make all needful provisions and regulations concerning habitual truants, and children between the ages of eight and fourteen years found wandering about the streets during school hours, having no lawful occupation or business, and growing up in ignorance, and to provide for their instruction and confinement where necessary.

* Governor Dix expressed himself as favorable to the principles of the bill, but vetoed it because of its inconsistency and failure to meet the alleged exigency. It professed, he said, to leave to the people the largest liberty, while it in reality restricted them to the narrowest. This subject came up afterward, and a local-option bill finally became a law.

† Samuel Jones Tilden was an astute politician. He was born at New Lebanon,

victory. Mr. Tilden was chosen chief magistrate of the commonwealth by a plurality of 50,317 votes. Mr. Tilden took his seat as Governor of the State of New York on January 1st, 1875.

Columbia County, N. Y., in February, 1814. His physical constitution was weak from infancy. His father being a personal and political friend of Martin Van Buren and other politicians who composed the "Albany Regency," young Tilden was introduced into political circles at a very early age. He studied law with Benjamin F. Butler, and became a sound but not brilliant member of the profession. For a while he indulged in journalism, establishing the *Daily News* in New York City in 1844. He soon returned to the bar, was elected to the Assembly by the Democrats, and was a member of the convention that revised the State Constitution in 1846. Mr. Tilden was much sought after as counsel for corporations. He was a bitter opponent of the Republican Party, and blamed President Lincoln for not calling out 500,000 troops in 1861 instead of 75,000 to suppress the rebellion. He and Governor Seymour were in accord during the war. In 1874 Tilden was elected Governor of New York, and in 1876 he was an unsuccessful candidate for the Presidency of the United States. He died at his magnificent seat on the Hudson, near Yonkers, in August, 1886, leaving a fortune of fully $5,000,000. He was never married.

CHAPTER XL.

The year 1875 closed the first century of the life of the great republic of the West. The notes of preparation for a grand Centennial celebration and an exhibition of the industries of all nations were then heard throughout the land. The city of Philadelphia—the birthplace of the republic—was the chosen theatre of the wonderful display to which the State of New York made a notable contribution from its immense treasures of production of every sort.* At that centennial period—the end of 1875—I propose to close this compendious history of the Empire State of the Union. All events before that period have passed into the realm of completed and permanent history; all since then are components of current history with ever-changing phases, in which living men and women compose the persons of the drama.

The session of the Legislature began on January 6th, 1875, and adjourned on May 22d. Among the more important acts passed at that session were a general law for providing uniformity in the organization and administration of savings-banks,† empowering the Superintendent of the Banking Department to grant charters to such institutions, limiting the amount of deposits in the name of one person to $5000, and prohibiting their loaning money on personal securities and dealing in merchandise, or buying or selling exchange or gold and

---

* The exhibition was opened on May 10th, 1876, with imposing ceremonies. The most distinguished guests present were President Grant and the Emperor and Empress of Brazil. After prayers a thousand voices sang a beautiful Centennial Hymn written by John G. Whittier, the Quaker poet. The exhibition was kept open six months. The total number of admissions from the opening until the closing was 9,910,965, and the total cash receipts for admission was $3,813,725. The largest attendance for a full month was in October, when 2,663,911 persons were admitted. Twenty-six nations were represented among the products of industry.

† The first bank for savings in the State of New York was opened on Saturday evening, July 3d, 1819, in a basement room in Chambers Street, New York City. It was the fruit of the suggestion and efficient labors of John Pintard. An association was organized by the choice of twenty-six directors, with De Witt Clinton at their head. William Bayard was chosen president. The deposit office was open from six until nine o'clock that evening, when $2807 had been received from eighty-two depositors. The smallest amount deposited was $2; the largest amount was $300. That first savings-bank in New York is still a flourishing institution, located in an elegant banking-house of white marble on Bleecker Street. From 1819 until 1883 the aggregate sum of $162,032,515 had been deposited in that bank from 490,541 persons.

silver; also acts for the punishment for bribery at election; for general business incorporations; for the prevention of cruelty to children; for rapid transit in the city of New York; for creating a State Board of Audit, and for the suppression of intemperance.

During the recess of the Legislature several committees of investigation performed their tasks. One committee investigated the affairs of the quarantine, the Board of Health, and the management of emigrants and emigration at Castle Garden, New York; another sought to ascertain the causes of the rapid increase of crime in the city of New York, and another to investigate charges concerning the debtors' prison in the county of New York. Perhaps the most important committee of inquiry was appointed on the recommendation of Governor Tilden in a special message for an investigation concerning the management of the canals of the State. In that message he showed that for five years, ending September 30th, 1874, the total receipts for tolls had been $15,058,361, while the expenses for operating and for *ordinary* repairs had amounted to $9,202,434, leaving an apparent surplus of $5,855,927. During the same period the disbursements for *extraordinary* repairs had amounted to $10,960,644, causing a real deficiency of $5,104,697. Adding to this the payment on the canal debt and other outlays on account of the canals, an aggregate of over $11,000,000 was obtained as the amount expended by the State in five years for these works. The governor declared that the expenses for both ordinary and extraordinary repairs had been greatly in excess of what was required, and that there had been corrupt and fraudulent contracts for work and materials by which the State Treasury had been systematically plundered, something after the methods employed by the "Tweed Ring" in the city of New York.

The investigation showed among others as flagrant exhibitions of fraud, that the State had paid on ten contracts $1,560,769, while the amount to be paid upon the quality of materials exhibited in the proposals, at contract prices, would have been only $424,735. The governor recommended the adoption of measures at once for ascertaining the exact financial condition of the canals. It was done, and reforms in their management ensued.

There are thirteen canals in the State, two of them belonging to corporations.* Their total length, with navigable feeders and lakes and

---

* These are the Erie, Champlain, Oswego, Chenango, Chemung, Cayuga and Seneca, Genesee Valley, Oneida Lake, Chenango Extension, Crooked Lake Canal and Ithaca Inlet. The Delaware and Hudson and the Junction canals belong to corporations. The amount of work remaining to be done on the State canals, at the close of 1875, was contracted for at an aggregate of $892,397.

rivers artificially connected therewith, is 1393 miles. The length of the canals proper, with navigable feeders, is 907 miles. The number of tons of freight transported over these canals in 1874 was 5,804,588. The cost of this freight transportation was $4,335,536, and the receipts for tolls and freights were $6,882,921. The canals (excepting two) are the actual property of the people of the commonwealth, and had cost them up to 1875, for original construction and subsequent enlargements, fully $101,000,000. The aggregate cost of the canals and railroads of the State, with their equipments, at that time, was $735,862,282, which was equal to one third of the gross taxable property of the commonwealth, real and personal.

The railroads within the State are of far more value as vehicles of transportation for freight and passengers than the canals. The total length of steam railways in 1875 was 5210 miles, many of them with double tracks. There were seventy-six horse railroads, the aggregate length of which was 400 miles. The number of passengers carried on the steam railways within the State in 1874 was 34,719,018, and on horse railways, 228,372,112, making the total number of passengers 263,091,130. The receipts from freight carried on steam railroads within the State that year amounted to $65,085,604, and from passengers, $25,369,850. The receipts from passengers on horse railways were $12,003,654, making a total for passengers and freight of $109,342,029. The cost of transportation of freight and passengers on both steam and horse railroads in one year was $76,027,413.

These railways and their enormous business had been created in the space of forty-four years. The first railway put into operation in the State, as we have observed, was completed in 1831, and connected Albany and Schenectady by rail.*

The admirable common-school system of the State, so essential to the moral, intellectual, and social welfare of the people, has been frequently alluded to in preceding pages. It has been the object of the special care of the electors and the Legislature, and a topic for sugges-

---

* The first locomotive engine constructed in the United States was built by a native of New York, the late Peter Cooper, in 1830, at his Canton Iron Works, near Baltimore. It was made from his own designs, and was named "Tom Thumb." It was a very small tractor engine—too small for practical use. On a trial trip it drew a car with several Baltimorians in it from Baltimore to the Relay House, a distance of nine miles.

The first actual working locomotive built in America was made in New York City in 1830 from plans drawn by V. L. Miller, of Charleston, S. C., and used on a road between that city and Hamburg. It was named "Best Friend." The first projector of a land carriage, to be propelled by steam, was Oliver Evans, of Philadelphia.

tions and expressions of solicitude by the chief magistrates of the commonwealth, for almost half a century. Ample provision has always been made for the support and efficiency of the common schools, and for the wide distribution of their benefits. Every inhabited portion of the State has been divided into convenient districts, in each of which a school is taught some portions of the year, is open to all, and is within the reach of all. We have already observed (page 360) the origin of the common-school system in the State, and the methods used in providing funds for its support.*

In his synoptical report to the Legislature (January 5th, 1887), Hon. A. S. Draper, State Superintendent of Public Instruction, says: "The educational work in the State has been a wonderful growth and development. In 1850 we were spending $1,600,000 annually in the support of our public schools. During the past year we spent $14,000,000." He then propounded some pertinent questions suggestive of needed improvement in the methods of public instruction. He asked: "Is our education as practical as it might be? Do we reach all the children we ought? In our ardor over the high schools, which nine tenths of our children never reach, have we not neglected the low schools? Is there not too much French, and German, and Latin, and Greek, and too little spelling, and writing, and mental arithmetic, and English grammar being taught? Are not our courses of study too complex? Are we not undertaking to do more than we are doing well? Are we educating the *whole man?*" Some wise suggestions follow.

The State is divided into sixty counties. The first eight counties were established in 1683—Duchess, Kings, Queens, Orange, Richmond, Suffolk, Ulster, and Westchester. The last one organized was Wyoming, in 1841. For an account of the organization of each county, with a delineation of the seals and the population, etc., see pages 97 and 98, and Appendix.

The building of a new State House was authorized in 1868, and work

---

* There were in the State of New York at the close of 1875, 11,787 school-houses; 11,289 school districts, exclusive of cities; 19,157 teachers employed for the legal school term, and 29,977 during every portion of the year. There were 1,058,846 children attending public schools, and 185,098 of school age in private schools. There were 6207 persons attending normal schools. In the school district libraries there were 812,655 volumes. In the State were 1,579,504 persons between the ages of five and twenty-one years. The School Fund proper amounted on January 1st, 1875, to $3,054,772, and the revenue from it, $178,813. The total receipts on account of common schools that year were $12,516,362, and the total expenditures were $11,365,377. The amount paid for teachers' wages was $7,843,231. The estimated value of the school-houses and sites was $36,393,190.

upon it was begun soon afterward. The limestone and granite for the foundation were procured from the Lake Champlain, Adirondack, and Mohawk Valley regions of the State. The corner-stone was laid, with imposing ceremonies, on June 24th, 1871. Already $2,000,000 had been expended on the foundation (which rose seven feet above the ground), besides $650,000 paid for the land on which it was erected. It is built of drilled granite, four stories in height, two hundred and ninety feet wide, and three hundred and ninety feet long. When completed it will be one of the most costly buildings ever constructed in the United States —probably nearly $20,000,000.

The nominal funded debts of the State on September 30th, 1875, were $28,328,686, less the amount of sinking funds pledged for their redemption, which was $13,581,382, reducing the actual debt of the State to $14,747,304. The aggregate amount of the bonded debts of counties, cities, towns, and villages was very large, but was in rapid process of extinction. These debts were largely incurred by giving aid to railroads ; for public buildings ; for war and bounty expenses ; for roads and bridges, and for water-works and fire apparatus.

Let us here go forward five years from our intended resting-point, and take a general view of the Empire State in 1880, as revealed by the Tenth Census.

In size the State of New York is only nineteenth in rank. Its area is a thousand square miles less than that of North Carolina, and seven thousand less than Michigan. Although its territory includes less than one sixty-third of the whole country, its inhabitants then formed more than one tenth of the population. Its twenty-five cities contained between one fifth and one fourth of the entire urban population of the United States.*

One half of the inhabitants of the State lived in cities. The number engaged in agriculture was less than in Alabama, Georgia, Illinois, or in

---

* New York had drawn freely from and given liberally to the other States. In 1880 there were within its borders natives of Connecticut enough to make a city as large as Bridgeport ; of Maine, to repopulate Bath ; of Massachusetts, to repeople Lynn or Lawrence ; of Pennsylvania, nearly sufficient to twice repopulate its State capital ; of New Jersey, to fill Paterson, and more natives of Vermont than in Burlington, Rutland, and St. Albans together. New York had given to California people enough to populate two cities as large as Sacramento ; to Connecticut, almost enough to stock Hartford with men and women ; to Kansas, enough to make the three cities of Atchison, Topeka, and Leavenworth ; to Ohio, more than enough to make Columbus or Toledo ; to Wisconsin, in number equal to three fourths of the population of Milwaukee ; to Iowa, enough to fill her four largest cities ; to Pennsylvania, 100,000 ; to Illinois, 120,000, and to Michigan twice the population of Detroit. Nearly one fifth of the American-born population of Michigan were natives of New York.

Ohio. In acreage of improved land in farms, it was behind Iowa, Illinois, and Ohio; yet it is second only to Illinois as a farming State, taking as the basis of comparison the total value of all farm products during the year before the census. Illinois, with 26,000,000 acres and 436,000 farmers, produced value of $204,000,000. New York, with less than 18,000,000 acres and 377,000 farmers, produced $178,000,000. The average annual yield of the Illinois farmers was a little less than $8 an acre; of the New York farmers, a little more than $10 an acre.

New York raised more barley than any other State excepting California; more oats than any other State excepting Illinois and Iowa, and more rye than any other State excepting Illinois and Pennsylvania. Raising more buckwheat than any other State, it produced more than one third of the entire buckwheat crop of the country.

The hay crop of New York surpassed that of any other State. It was more than one seventh of the entire crop of the country. It also produced one fifth of all the so-called "Irish" potatoes grown in the United States, and more than twice as many bushels as Pennsylvania, the second potato-producing State in rank. It produced more than four fifths of the total hop crop of the country, and more than ten times that of the State next in rank.

New York is a great fruit-growing State. Its orchards yielded in the census year in value one sixth of the total fruit production of the United States, and almost twice that of its most successful rival, Pennsylvania. It is also pre-eminently a dairy State. In the year before the census it produced more than one seventh of all the butter of the United States, and nearly one third of all the cheese.

New York is the foremost manufacturing State in the Union. It is first in the number of establishments; second in the amount of capital invested; first in the number of hands employed; first in the amount of wages paid, and first in the value of manufactured products. It contained more than one sixth of all the mills, manufactories, and workshops of the United States that produced $500 in 1879. These establishments represented between one sixth and one fifth of all the capital invested in the mechanical and manufacturing establishments of the United States. Those industries gave employment to between one sixth and one fifth of all the hands at work in American mills and shops. The New York manufacturers paid more than one fifth of the total wages given to workingmen and women of this class. The total value of the manufactured products in the State was more than one fifth of the total for the Union.

Let us take a brief glance at the products of some of the vast and varied industries of the State in comparison with the same products in the whole Union, in 1879. New York produced nearly one sixth in value of all the agricultural implements made in the country; nearly one third of all the baking products; more than one half of the cheese, and nearly one half of the butter; between one third and one half of the men's clothing, and nearly two thirds of the women's clothing produced in manufactories; more than one fifth of the foundry and machine-shop products; between one fifth and one quarter of the furniture; more than one third of the hosiery and knit goods; nearly a quarter of the jewelry; more than one third of the beer and ale; more than one half of the millinery and lace goods; two thirds of the pianos; between one third and one half of the paints; more than half the perfumery and cosmetics; nearly one third of the books and periodicals; one quarter of the soap and candles; nearly one half of the refined sugar and molasses; more than one sixth of the smoking and chewing tobacco and snuff, and between one third and one half of the cigars and cigarettes.

New York then (1879) led the country in shipbuilding, both in the number of establishments devoted to the construction and repair of steam and sailing vessels and boats of all kinds, and in the annual value of all the products. While between one fifth and one fourth in value of all American vessels were built in the State, nearly one third of them were owned by New Yorkers.

Of all the steam craft owned in the United States, nearly one quarter belonged to New York, while the tonnage of these vessels was more than a quarter of the tonnage of the whole country, and their value nearly one third of the total value. New York had between one sixth and one fifth of the sailing-vessels of America; more than one fourth in tonnage and more than one fourth in value. Of the canal-boats of the country, New York owned about five eighths in value. In rank it is first in maritime commerce.*

Let us turn from a consideration of the pre-eminence of New York in agriculture, manufactures, and commerce, to that of its rank in intelligence and accumulated wealth.

While New York had one tenth of the population of the republic, its expenditures for popular education were more than one eighth of that of the whole Union. So general were the blessings of education diffused throughout the commonwealth, that only 4.2 per cent of the adult people were unable to read and 5.5 per cent unable to write. In 1875 the State spent nearly $290,000 in its nine normal schools for the edu-

---

* I am largely indebted to a writer in the *New York Sun*, in 1883, for the analysis and comparisons of the statistical facts here given.

cation of teachers for the public schools, and $18,000 for the aid of teachers' institutes. In the State were then nearly 250 academies or academic departments in Union schools, 27 colleges and universities, 7 scientific schools, 13 schools of theology, 4 law schools, and 14 medical schools.

A trustworthy measure of the intelligence of a large community is the activity of its printing-presses, especially those which distribute intelligence through newspapers and periodicals. New York produced nearly one third in value of the books published in the United States. It also issued one eighth of all the periodicals published in the country; also nearly one eighth of the newspapers issued. Of the aggregate circulation of the daily newspapers in the Union, New York furnished between one fourth and one third. Of the aggregate circulation of the weeklies and all other periodicals in the United States, it also furnished between one fourth and one third.

The assessed valuation of real estate and personal property in the State of New York in the census year was equal in amount to one seventh of the valuation of the entire real and personal property of the whole Republic. It was also almost exactly the same in amount as that of the six New England States—$2,651,940,006. One third of the registered bonds of the United States were held in New York—$210,264,250. But its enormous share of the wealth of the country cannot be computed from facts found in the census reports. Its financial interests are everywhere—in railways, in mines, in farms and factories in every State and Territory.

In nearly all the foregoing comparisons the figures of New York's part in the various forms of industry are merely the figures of its investments within its own borders. Great as is New York's ratio to the United States in population, it is greater still in almost every branch of human industry, and in the prosperity resulting therefrom.

New York is truly great in its magnificent and varied charities, public and private, and its provision for the promotion of morality and religion. Its institutions for special education—for the mute and the blind—its numerous reformatories, asylums, hospitals, and charitable foundations of every kind, as well as penal institutions, are of the highest order in equipment and management. The State abounds in literary and scientific societies; in large public and private libraries; in works and schools of art, and ample appliances for the intellectual and social advancement of every citizen of the commonwealth, of whatever race, color, or condition.

There were in the State, in 1875, 6320 church organizations, 6243 church edifices, 6115 clergymen, 1,177,537 church-members, with an adherent population of 3,934,690. The aggregate value of church property of every kind in the State was nearly $118,000,000.

The Hudson River, the grand and beautiful "River of the Mountains," as we have observed in the first chapter of this work, is clustered with the most interesting legendary and historic associations from the Wilderness to the Sea, a distance of three hundred miles or more. Its upper waters witnessed the fierce strifes for mastery between contending tribes of barbarians before the advent of Europeans, and the struggles

VAN RENSSELAER MANOR HOUSE.
(From a drawing made in 1866.)

for dominion of the French and English in later times. Then followed the victories of peace—the gradual blossoming of a large portion of that region into a paradise of beauty under the hand of skilled industry.

The tide-water region of the Hudson for fully sixty miles from the ocean has been for more than two centuries a theatre of most remarkable social and historic events. The principal of these have been briefly noted in preceding pages.

Among the social events on the borders of the great river, the creation of "patroons" and manorial estates and privileges at the earlier period of the history of the commonwealth appear the most conspicuous. Of these the manors of Rensselaerwyck, of Livingston, of Van Cortlandt, and of Philipse are most prominent.

The Van Rensselaer Manor and patroonship was, as we have observed, the first created, and survived all the others, its titles and privileges expiring with General Stephen van Rensselaer in 1839. The grant was made to Killian van Rensselaer, of Amsterdam, under a charter of privileges

JOHN AND MARY LIVINGSTON.

and exemptions passed in 1629. Van Rensselaer had co-partners at first. In 1685 the Van Rensselaer family became sole owners of the vast estate. The Manor House, modified several years ago, stands upon the site of the original Van Rensselaer dwelling, in the northern suburbs of the city of Albany.

The Livingston Manor was created by a preliminary act of Governor Dongan in 1685. Robert Livingston, the first of the name in America,*

---

* See page 108. The common ancestors of the Livingstons in America were John Livingston and his wife Mary. He was a great-great-grandson of Lord Livingstone, Earl of Linlithgow, Scotland. He was exiled, and went to Rotterdam, in Holland, where Robert learned the Dutch language, afterward emigrated to America, settled at Albany, as we have observed, and became the first Lord of the Manor of Livingston.

The above delineations of the heads of John and Mary Livingston I made many years ago from the original portraits then in the possession of Colonel Henry A. Livingston, of Poughkeepsie, N. Y.

married the wealthy widow of Rev. Nicholas van Rensselaer—Alida, daughter of Colonel Peter Schuyler, of Albany—in 1678. He bought of the Indians sixty thousand acres of land on the east side of the Hudson River, opposite the Kaatsbergs (Catskill Mountains). At the time of the creation of the manor, in 1715, it had increased by subsequent purchases to about one hundred and fifty thousand acres. The

LIVINGSTON LOWER MANOR HOUSE.

patent given by Dongan was confirmed by royal authority, with the title of "Manor of Livingston," and in 1716 the proprietor exercised manorial privileges.* He paid an annual tribute to the crown of three dollars and fifty cents. The manor was afterward divided into the Upper and Lower Manor. The latter was called Clermont. It was the home of Robert R. Livingston, the eminent chancellor. The manor house is not far from Tivoli, on the Hudson.†

---

* The privileges of the patroons have already been defined. Robert Livingston, by virtue of these privileges, took his seat in the Provincial Legislature in 1716. He had already built a substantial manor house of stone on a grassy point upon the bank of the Hudson, at the mouth of Roeleffe Jansen Kill, now Ancram Creek.

† The above picture is that of Clermont, or the Lower Manor House, built by Chancellor Livingston, a little below the old Manor House. After the British burnt Kingston in the fall of 1777, they proceeded to Livingston's manor and burnt both of the houses, the chancellor's mother then occupying the older one. They were both soon rebuilt. The chancellor erected a more spacious and elegant dwelling, and, as before, called the place

Stephen van Cortlandt,* one of the governor's council at New York, purchased large tracts of land in Westchester County, and in 1697 eighty-three thousand acres were by royal authority erected into "the lordship and manor of Courtlandt." The manor and its privileges were held by the tenure of paying an annual tribute to the crown of five

VAN CORTLANDT MANOR HOUSE.

dollars. The Van Cortlandt Manor House was erected at the beginning of the last century by John van Cortlandt, son of the first "lord of the manor." It stands on the right side of the Croton River, near where that stream enters the Hudson.

Late in the seventeenth century Frederick Philipse† bought of the

---

Clermont. The house is yet standing, and is preserved in its original style by its present owners, the Clarkson family, relatives of the Livingstons. It has a river front of one hundred and four feet, with very extensive and beautiful grounds around it.

* Stephen van Cortlandt was a son of Orloff Stevens van Cortlandt, who emigrated to New Amsterdam in Van Twiller's time. Orloff came from South Holland, and was soon engaged in public employment, holding alternately several civil offices. He was a burgomaster several years, and being "diligent in business," became wealthy. His wife was a sister of Govert Loockermans. His daughter Maria married Jeremiah van Rensselaer, the second Lord of the Manor of Rensselaerwyck. At the time of his death, about 1688, his son Stephen was a prosperous merchant. The family name was Stevens, van (from) Courtlandt, descendants of the Dukes of Courtlandt or Courland, in Russia. The first Lord of the Manor married Gertrude Schuyler, and died in the year 1700.

† The Philipse (Phillips) family descended from the Viscounts Felyps, of Bohemia. The first emigrant to New Netherland, Frederick Philipse, spelled his name **Vrederyck**

Indians large tracts of land on both sides of the *Po-can-te-co Creek*, in Westchester County, fronting on the Hudson River, and comprising about three hundred and ninety square miles of territory. In 1693 the domain was, by royal authority, erected into the "Lordship and Manor of Philipseburg," with all its privileges, subject to an annual tribute to the crown of a little less than five dollars. The manor house was

PHILIPSE LOWER MANOR HOUSE.

strongly built of stone in 1680, at the mouth of the *Po-can-te-co* at Tarrytown, with port-holes for cannons in the high cellar walls, and was called Philipse Castle. There the family lived until the lower manor house, yet standing, was built at Yonkers in 1745. Its interior exhibits some fine specimens of architecture executed nearly a century and a half ago.

Felypsen. The initials of his name—V. F.—may be seen on the wind-vane of the Sleepy Hollow Church, near Tarrytown. He arrived at New Amsterdam in 1658, purchased a large estate there and on the shores of the Hudson, and became one of the founders of the city of New York.

The last "Lord of the Manor" was Frederick Philipse, who was at one time a member of the Colonial Assembly and colonel of militia. At the breaking out of the old war for independence, he took the position of a firm supporter of the Crown. He finally felt compelled to abandon his home and take refuge with the British army in New York, whence he embarked for England. His estates were confiscated. The British Government gave him about $300,000 as a compensation for his losses. Colonel Phillips was an extremely large man. On account of his bulk, his wife seldom rode in the same carriage with him.

The city of New York, which had been scathed by flame and had lain prone under the heel of British military power for more than seven years, at once began its marvellous march toward greatness after peace was restored. It very soon became the chief commercial mart of the nation. It was the political capital of the State for several years,* and the first seat of the National Government. At the close of the war it was, in population, only an unusually large village; at the beginning of this century it embraced over sixty thousand inhabitants.

New York City has doubled its original territorial area within a few years, and has now (1887) fully a million and a half of inhabitants. It

GOVERNMENT HOUSE.

has become a mighty magnet, attracting everything, hence its marvellous growth by accretion. Possessors of wealth, of genius, and of enterprise have come to it from all parts of the republic to enjoy its manifold advantages of education for their children, the cultivation of æsthetic tastes, the blessings of scientific instruction, the facilities of commercial life, the chances of winning fortunes, and the pleasures of almost boundless social privileges and enjoyments.

Before and around New York City spreads out a magnificent harbor, spacious enough to float the navies of the world. One of the most

---

* On the south-east side of the Bowling Green a spacious and elegant mansion was built in 1790, for the purpose of a residence for the President of the United States. It was then supposed New York City would be the permanent seat of the National Government. When that Government was transferred to Philadelphia, this mansion was devoted to the use of the governors of the State of New York, while the city was the seat of the State Government. In it Governors George Clinton and John Jay resided, and it was known as the Government House. It was built of red brick, with Ionic columns forming a portico in front. The building stood on slightly elevated ground.

wonderful results of modern engineering skill—a suspension bridge—unites the city in loving embrace to Brooklyn, its superb offspring, of eight hundred thousand inhabitants. Near the portals of the city seaward stands the stupendous statue of LIBERTY ENLIGHTENING THE WORLD, wrought by Bartholdi, of Paris, and presented by the people of France. She bears aloft a mighty torch blazing with electric light,

LIBERTY ENLIGHTENING THE WORLD.

which spreads illumination over the broad bay, the great city, and its suburban municipalities.

"New York City is now the metropolis of the republic. By the close of this century it will probably be, in population, wealth, cultivation, and every element of a state of high civilization, the second city in the world. To the eye of the optimist the time appears not far distant when it will be the cosmetropolis."*

---

* Lossing's *History of New York City*, p. 866.

CHAPTER XLI.

LET us here take a brief retrospect of the life of the Empire State.

The Dutch, who first settled in the territory of New York and founded the city by the sea, gave special attention to the nurture of religion and learning. As we have observed on page 34, a clergyman and a school-teacher came from Holland to Manhattan together. It was ordered in the charter of the Dutch West India Company that the minister and schoolmaster should walk hand in hand in the high employment of educating the head and heart.

There were members of the Dutch Reformed Church among the early traders at Manhattan, and a congregation was formed by Rev. Jonas Michaelas in 1628. The functions of both minister and schoolmaster were performed by him until he was succeeded by Dominie Bogardus, in 1633, when Adam Roelandsen became the schoolmaster. The Dutch had been accustomed to the blessings of free schools in their fatherland, and they at once established one at Manhattan, which has survived until now, and is a very flourishing parochial school of the Collegiate (Dutch Reformed) Church of New York City.*

---

* This school is the oldest educational institution in the United States. It was founded in 1633, and has been in continual operation, excepting from 1776 to 1783 (when the British troops occupied New York), until now. It was supported by the Colonial Government for thirty years. The conquest of New Netherland by the English in 1664 did not materially affect the Dutch Church and its school. The latter then came under the exclusive control of the church. The petty tyrant Lord Cornbury gave them a little temporary trouble. Until 1748, when it was one hundred and fifteen years old, the school had no permanent habitation. In that year a small house was built for it in Garden Street, now Exchange Place. A new and more spacious house was erected on this site in 1773. Up to that time no one presumed to teach any but the Dutch language in this school. From the beginning until 1808 it was under the exclusive control of the ministers and deacons of the Church. The first feminine teacher was employed in 1792. It was not until 1804 that English grammar was taught in this school. Four years later the deacons gave up the control of the school to the rule of a board of trustees. For several years it was conducted on the Lancastrian plan.

This school has had, during its two hundred and fifty-six years of existence, only seventeen head teachers. James Forrester was the principal from 1810 until 1842, when Henry Webb Dunshee was appointed to take his place, and yet (1887) occupies that exalted station, having filled it for forty-three years consecutively. The present location of the school is in a building known as De Witt Chapel, at 160 West Twenty-ninth Street. That building was completed and the school first occupied it in 1861.

The doctrine and discipline of the Reformed Church was the "State religion" of New Netherland until the province was seized by the English in 1664, when the Church of England became dominant, through official influence, and so remained until the Revolution in 1775. Previous to the latter period the principal denominations in the colony, in numbers, as we have observed, were the Episcopalians (Church of England and Moravians), Dutch and English Presbyterians, Independents or Congregationalists, and Lutherans. The latter were among the earlier settlers at Manhattan, but had no minister; and when they were numerous enough to support a minister, Stuyvesant would not allow them to have one. They had full liberty under English rule, and built their first house for worship in New York in 1671. There were large accessions to their number from the emigration of the German Palatines, to the State in 1710.*

Although the Episcopalians in the province were as one to fifteen in numbers compared with other denominations, attempts were made from time to time to transplant into the province of New York the ecclesiastical establishment of the Anglican Church. To this end some of the colonial governors bent their energies, and often produced violent temporary excitements and permanent uneasiness. But the steady and determined opposition of the great body of the "dissenters," as the other sects were collectively but erroneously called, prevented such a calamity. As the quarrel before the breaking out of the old war for independence waxed hotter and hotter, the subject assumed a political aspect, and one of the most significant slogans of the patriots of the early period of the Revolution was:

> "A Church without a bishop,
> A State without a king."

The political condition of New York before the old war for independence was that of a dependent of the British crown, governed by the laws

---

* Early in the eighteenth century many of the inhabitants of the Lower Palatinate, lying on both sides of the Rhine, in Germany, were driven from their homes by the persecution of Louis XIV. of France. England received many of these Protestant fugitives. In the spring of 1708, on the petition of Joshua Kockerthal (evangelical minister of a body of Lutherans), for himself and thirty-nine others to be transported to America, an order was issued by Queen Anné in council for such transportation, and their naturalization before leaving England. The Queen provided for them at her own expense. This first company of Palatines landed on Governor's Island, in the harbor of New York, and afterward settled near the site of Newburgh, on the Hudson, in the spring of 1709. In 1710 a larger emigration of Palatines to America occurred, under the guidance of Robert Hunter, Governor of New York, as we have observed on page 137.

of Parliament, and compelled to suffer taxation and oppressive commercial regulations without the privilege of representation in the imperial legislature. The governor and his eleven councilmen were appointed by the monarch, but their salaries were paid by the colonists out of the revenue created by customs receipts. The freeholders elected a General Assembly of representatives, but the great mass of the " commonalty" had really no political privileges or powers. The relative position of the Council in legislation was that of the British House of Lords. They also had some judicial power, and were a sort of Privy Council, with the governor at their head during sessions. They assumed much dignity. Each was entitled " The Honorable," and the Council sent messages to the Assembly by one of their own members, when the " lower house" would rise to receive him.

The General Assembly consisted of twenty-seven members (in 1760), representing the several counties, two boroughs, and the three manors of Rensselaerwyck, Livingston, and Cortlandt. They met in the Assembly Chamber in the city of New York. Thirteen constituted a quorum for business. After they had taken the prescribed oath they were called before the governor, who recommended their choice of speaker, who was, of course, elected. They presented him to the governor in the Council Chamber, when the latter approved their choice. Then the speaker addressed the governor, and on behalf of the Assembly prayed " that their words and actions might have favorable construction ; that the members might have free access to him, and that they and their servants be privileged with freedom from arrests." After promising these things the governor read his speech to both Houses, and gave it to the speaker for the use of the Assembly. Then the latter proceeded to business.

The Assembly made the British House of Commons the model for their proceedings, and seldom varied from it. All bills were sent to the governor, who submitted them to his Council. When they were signed by him they were published by being read to the people in front of the City Hall, or State House, in the presence of the governor and both Houses. The continuance of the Assembly was unlimited until early in the administration of Governor Clinton, when it was restricted to seven years.*

---

* The pay of the members of the Assembly varied with the locality represented. It was as follows : City and county of New York, and the counties of Westchester, Kings, Queens, Richmond, Ulster, Duchess, and Orange, *six* shillings a day ; city and county of Albany, *ten* shillings ; Suffolk County, *nine* shillings ; the borough of Westchester, the town of Schenectady, and the Manors of Rensselaerwyck, Livingston, and Cortland, *ten* shillings a day.

The laws were administered by justices, Sessions and Common Pleas courts; a Supreme Court; a Court of Admiralty, which had jurisdiction in all maritime affairs; a Prerogative Court, the business of which related to wills, administrators, etc., the emoluments of which were perquisites of the governor, who acted ordinarily by a delegate; the Court of the Governor and Council, which was a sort of court of appeals, and the Court of Chancery, which was absolutely under the control of the governor. This court was an exceedingly obnoxious tribunal. All the courts were modelled after those of the same grade in England.

The trade and manufactures of New York before the Revolution suffered, in common with that of other colonies, from unwise navigation laws and oppressive restrictions inflicted by Great Britain; yet the very favorable geographical and topographical position of its fine seaport and commercial mart gave the province great advantages over other colonies for the prosecution of foreign trade. Its people grew rich and prosperous in spite of governmental obstructions.

The population of the province at near the close of the colonial period was not as large as many imagined it to be. Scarcely one third part of its tillable land was under cultivation. Its vast agricultural and mineral resources were almost entirely unsuspected. Connecticut, the area of which was one tenth that of New York, had forty thousand more inhabitants than its immediate neighbor on the west in 1760. There had been many discouragements to settlements in New York, the chief of which were the frequent and fearful incursions of the French and Indians, and the making of it a sort of penal colony by the British Government, which sent swarms of its criminals hither.*

All things were changed by the results of the war for independence. New York became a component part of a vigorous young nation. The fetters which had so long bound its industries and its commerce had been removed. It was an independent though not a sovereign state. It had a Constitution which guaranteed to its citizens political and religious freedom. Like a giant rising from refreshing slumbers, it went forth on its bounding career the very moment the clarion of peace was sounded. There was then assured safety for life and property within its border,

---

* "It is too well known," wrote William Livingston in 1752, "that, in pursuance of divers acts of Parliament, great numbers of felons, who have forfeited their lives to the public for the most atrocious crimes, are annually transported from home to these plantations. Very surprising, one would think, that these burglars, pickpockets, and cut-purses, and a herd of the most flagitious banditti upon earth, should be sent as agreeable companions to us!" Allusion has been made to the character of the people of the province at that time in Chapter XI.

and a tide of emigration flowed steadily in. The wilderness speedily began to "blossom as the rose."

Able statesmen and jurists have been abundant in New York from the time of its political organization. Among the most conspicuous names appear those of John Jay, Robert R. Livingston, Gouverneur Morris, Alexander Hamilton, De Witt Clinton, Chancellor Kent, Ambrose Spencer, Samuel Jones, Martin Van Buren, Silas Wright, William H. Seward, and Thomas J. Oakley.

Literature has had its representatives at every period in the history of the Empire State. John de Laet, one of the most active of the directors of the Dutch West India Company, and a resident of New Netherland for a while, gave to Europe a *History of the West Indies* (which included New Netherland) in 1640. In 1670 Daniel Denton wrote the first (it is supposed) *Description of New York, with the Country of the Indians*, in the English language; and in 1697 Daniel Leeds issued a pamphlet at New York against the Quakers of Philadelphia.

One of the most learned men of the province during the first half of the eighteenth century was Dr. Cadwallader Colden, author of a history of the Iroquois Confederacy and many scientific essays. William Smith wrote a history of the province down to his time, which was published in 1757. Mrs. Ann Eliza Bleecker, daughter of Brant Schuyler, wrote poetry and stories for the press, and Dr. Myles Cooper, President of King's College, and Dr. Auchmuty, on one side, and William Livingston on the other, were vigorous and prolific political and theological controversialists with the pen in the last colonial decade. There were also, during the stormy discussions before the kindling of the old war for independence, younger but equally able writers, such as Alexander Hamilton, John Jay, and Gouverneur Morris; while James Rivington was an able journalist.

The "Poet of the Revolution" was Philip Freneau, a native of New York City. Lindley Murray, a resident of New York since 1753, published his *English Grammar* and *English Reader* for the edification of millions, before the close of the century. At that period William Dunlap, painter, playwright, theatre manager, and historian, began his career. He wrote a *History of New York*, a *History of the American Theatre*, and a *History of the Arts of Design in America*.

Great intellectual activity was manifested in New York early in the present century. The most conspicuous of the many writers at that time were Washington Irving,[*] his brother, Peter, and James K. Paulding,

---

[*] Washington Irving was born in New York City, April 3d, 1783; died at Sunnyside, his seat on the Hudson, November 23d, 1859. His father was a Scotch **emigrant**,

their brother-in-law. They were joined by James Fenimore Cooper a little later. Irving began authorship in 1802 as a writer for his brother's journal, *The Morning Chronicle*. His work of rare humor, *Knickerbocker's History of New York*, appeared in 1808. Paulding had lately joined him and his brother in writing the *Salmagundi* papers. His *Sketch Book* charmed readers in both hemispheres. Later in life he became an eminent biographer and historian. Cooper began his literary career as a novelist about 1820, and produced over thirty volumes of fiction distinctly American in character.

Contemporary with Irving and Cooper* were De Witt Clinton, William L. Stone, Gulian C. Verplanck, Fitz-Greene Halleck, Joseph Rodman Drake, and Henry R. Schoolcraft, all (excepting Halleck) natives of New York. Stone, the

WASHINGTON IRVING.

---

and his mother an Englishwoman. At the age of nineteen he wrote a series of papers for *The Morning Chronicle*, over the signature of "Jonathan Oldstyle," which attracted much attention. His *Knickerbocker's History of New York*, a most humorous caricature of the Dutch dynasty on Manhattan Island, set everybody laughing, and much irritated some of the descendants of the first Dutch settlers at New Amsterdam. Irving was then only twenty-six years of age. He edited the *Analectic Magazine* during the War of 1812–15. Failing health induced him to go to Europe, where he resided seventeen years, and gained a great literary reputation. He was Secretary of the American Legation in London from 1829 to 1831, and received the fifty-guinea gold medal provided by George IV. for eminence in historical composition. In May, 1832, Mr. Irving returned to New York, and kept busy with his pen. He was appointed Minister to Spain in 1842, where he remained four years. On his return he revised all his works for publication. His last and greatest work was a *Life of Washington* in five octavo volumes. The honorary degree of LL.D. was conferred upon him by Harvard College, Oxford (Eng.) University, and Columbia College.

* James Fenimore Cooper was born at Burlington, N. J., September 15th, 1789; died at Cooperstown, N. Y., September 14th, 1851. He was a son of Judge William Cooper, one of the first settlers in Central New York. For six years he was in the United States Navy, and in 1811 he married a sister of the late Bishop De Lancey. His life was chiefly devoted to literature. His first novel was *Precaution*, published in 1821, which was rather coldly received. Then followed his *Spy*, *The Pioneers*, and the *Leatherstocking Tales* in quick succession, which gave him great fame as an American novelist.

eminent journalist, wrote lives of Brant, Red Jacket, and Sir William Johnson, the latter finished by his son. Verplanck was an accomplished essayist and one of the best-known men in the social circles of New York for fifty years. Drake was a gentle poet, of whom Halleck at his death wrote :

> " None knew thee but to love thee ;
> None named thee but to praise."

Schoolcraft became high authority concerning the Indians. The name of Samuel Woodworth, author of "The Old Oaken Bucket" and "The House I Live In," deserves special mention in this connection.

One of the most painstaking and trustworthy of the historians of New York was John R. Brodhead,* who died in 1873. By direction of the Legislature of New York, as its agent, he searched the historical archives of Holland, England, and France for documents relating to the colonial period of this State, and brought home copies of more than five thousand valuable papers, which the State published in eleven quarto volumes. He had published two volumes of an elaborate history of New York State, which he was preparing, when death ended his earthly career. Among the names of historians of portions of the State, those of W. W. Campbell, Jeptha R. Simms, Robert Bolton, Jr., Dr. Franklin B. Hough, Henry B. Dawson, and Martha J. Lamb appear

JAMES FENIMORE COOPER.

Mr. Cooper went to Europe in 1826, and remained there until 1833. He wrote a *History of the United States Navy, Lives of American Naval Officers,* in two volumes ; also wrote a comedy, which was performed in New York in 1850.

* John Romeyn Brodhead, son of Rev. Jacob Brodhead, was born in Philadelphia January 2d, 1814 ; died in New York City, May 6th, 1873. He was graduated at Rutgers College in 1831 ; admitted to the bar in 1835 ; was attached to the American Legation at the Hague in 1839, and procured for the State of New York copies of important documents, mentioned in the text. Mr. Brodhead was Secretary to the American Legation at London from 1846 till 1849. On his return he began the preparation of an exhaustive history of the State of New York, but did not live to complete it. The first volume was published in 1853 and the second in 1871, which brings the history down to the close of the seventeenth century.

most conspicuous. The latest and most trustworthy writer on the Iroquois Confederacy was Louis Morgan, who died in 1881.

In the realm of poetry New York is most prominently represented by William Cullen Bryant. Though a native of another State, he was a resident of this commonwealth from his young manhood. George P. Morris, also a resident from the period of his young manhood, ranks among its best song-writers.

Among scientific writers, Drs. Samuel L. Mitchell, David Hosack, John W. Francis, John Torrey, Professor James Renwick, and Dr. John W. Draper (all but the latter natives of New York) appear most conspicuous.

In no State in the Union are the fine arts more widely cultivated and fostered than in the commonwealth of New York. Besides the vast treasures of art found in New York City,* other cities and villages and private homes in various parts of the State exhibit rare and costly works of painters, sculptors, and engravers, while in every direction great taste in architecture is displayed.

Some of the more eminent resident artists of New York have not been natives of the State. Colonel J. Trumbull was born in Connecticut; John Wesley Jarvis and Thomas Cole came from England; Professor S. F. B. Morse (made more famous than any others by his scientific achievements in electro-magnetic telegraphy) was a native of Massachusetts, and A. B. Durand, the most eminent American engraver on steel,† was born in New Jersey. But Henry Inman and Charles L.

---

* The Metropolitan Museum of Art in the city of New York, under the direction of General L. P. di Cesnola, has already become the most attractive and important depository of rare works of art on this continent. Within the space of three months, in the spring of 1887, it was enriched by paintings from the studios of the most famous artists in the world, presented to the institution by generous citizens of the metropolis. The aggregate value of these gifts amounted to almost $1,000,000. Other valuable pictures have since been given.

† New York City was the birthplace of Alexander Anderson, the pioneer engraver on wood in America, who was born in April, 1775. His father was a Scotchman, and the publisher of a small Whig newspaper in New York entitled *The Constitutional Gazette*. He fled to Connecticut with his types and his family when the British took New York in 1776. Young Anderson graduated at the Medical School of Columbia College, and was a practising physician for a while; but, preferring art, he devoted himself to engraving first on type-metal and copper. His first knowledge of the use of wood for engraving pictures upon was derived from a copy of Bewick's *Birds*. He had then completed, on type-metal, about one half of the illustrations of the *Looking-glass for the Mind*, when he abandoned the metal and made the rest on wood. He practised that branch of art all the rest of his life. His last engraving was left half finished, when he was in the ninety-fifth year of his age. I have two of his first wood-engravings; also the half-finished one, his last. They were executed seventy-five years apart. He died in Jersey City, N. J., in January, 1870.

Elliott, the foremost portrait painters of their day, Robert W. Weir and Daniel Huntington, eminent portrait, historical, and *genre* painters, and Thomas Crawford, the sculptor, were all born in the State of New York. Professor Morse was the chief founder of the National Academy of the Arts of Design at New York, and Mr. Huntington is now (1887) its president. General Thomas S. Cummings, who for a generation or more was the leading painter of portraits in miniature in New York City, and was for forty years the treasurer of the Academy, is now, in the eighty-fourth year of his age, the sole survivor of the founders of that institution.

THE END.

CHAPTER XLII.

CONCLUSION.

To delineate with precision the kaleidoscopic features of contemporaneous history is a most difficult task, and the historian prefers to treat that period in the character of a mere annalist, for, as already observed, all events before that period have passed into the realm of completed and permanent history ; all since that period are components of current history, with ever-changing phases, in which living men and women are persons of the drama.

Yielding to the counsels of others, I depart from the original design of closing this history at an earlier period, and bring the narrative down to the time of this writing—the later days of the year 1887.

The energetic actions of Governor Tilden in his dealings with the "Canal Ring" (see p. 554) were generally commended, and he became very popular, for the people had become impatient for better work in the public service. Mr. Tilden was regarded as an aggressive champion of reform. The Democratic State Convention in 1876 commended him to the National Democratic Convention for nomination for the Presidency of the Republic, with assurances that he could command a majority of the votes of the great State of New York. His nomination was secured in the face of bitter opposition from a powerful faction in his own party.

Senator Roscoe Conkling, a leader of the Republican Party in New York, was a candidate before the National Republican Convention for nomination for the same high office, but failed to receive it. Rutherford B. Hayes, of Ohio, was nominated, with William A. Wheeler, of New York, for Vice-President. The canvass was close and hotly contested. Hayes and Wheeler won the prizes. Mr. Tilden's friends claimed the victory for him. Much excitement ensued, and at one time the public peace throughout the nation was menaced.

In 1876 Lucius Robinson was elected by the Democrats Governor of New York, by a majority of more than thirty thousand votes over ex-Governor E. D. Morgan, the Republican candidate. The policy of the national administration in 1877 concerning the Southern States and reform in the civil service caused a division in the Republican ranks in New York, and the Democrats elected the State officers that year. The next year the Greenback Party polled over seventy-five thousand votes, and the Republicans obtained a plurality of nearly thirty-five thousand votes for justice of the Court of Appeals, the only State office to be filled that year.

In 1878 the Court of Appeals declared the Civil Damage Act passed in 1873 to be constitutional. It holds the owner of a building wherein intoxicating liquors are sold liable for damages consequent upon such sale. The court declared that "all property is held subject to the power of the State to regulate or control its use to secure the general safety and the public welfare." Consonant with this opinion and applicable to every State in the Union was a decision of the Supreme Court of the United States, given early in December, 1887.

The new Capitol of the State was first occupied by the Legislature in 1879, though the edifice was then far from being completed. It is not yet (1887) finished, though nearly $20,000,000 have been expended on it.

True to their character as ever-changing in political complexion, a majority of the people of New York elected a Republican for governor of the commonwealth in 1879. They chose Alonzo B. Cornell, son of the founder of Cornell University. The Democratic Party had been severely rent by factions that year. A Tammany delegation to the State Convention protested against the renomination of Governor Robinson. Foiled, the delegation seceded, formed a new convention, and nominated John Kelly for governor. The vote for the three candidates in the field at the November election was as follows: Cornell, 418,567; Robinson, 375,790; Kelly, 77,566. Cornell's administration was a quiet one, marked by the general prosperity of the people.

Now appeared symptoms of the revolt in the Republican Party of New York, which became unparalleled in extent in the history of politics in that commonwealth. In 1880 the name of General Grant was presented to the National Republican Convention at Chicago as a candidate for the Presidency of the Republic for a third term. There was so much opposition everywhere to the idea of a third term, that the choice of delegates to the National Convention had been rendered a difficult task. Much controversy arose in New York concerning the independence of delegates in such a convention, some contending that each delegate should be free to vote as his judgment might dictate, while others insisted that delegates should be instructed as to who they should vote for, and obey such instructions.

The New York State Convention, by a considerable majority, instructed the delegates from the several districts to "use their most ear-

CONCLUSION. 576c

nest and united efforts to secure the nomination of U. S. Grant." The New York delegation in the convention at Chicago was divided in its choice of a Presidential candidate, for many refused to obey the instructions.

James A. Garfield, of Ohio, was nominated for President, and Chester A. Arthur, of New York, for Vice-President. They were elected, and entered upon their duties in the spring of 1881. At that time Roscoe Conkling and Thomas C. Platt represented the State of New York in the United States Senate. President Garfield sent to the Senate the name of State Senator W. H. Robertson as Collector of the Port of New York. The Vice-President and the Postmaster-General (Thomas L. James), both of New York, and the two Senators joined in a request for the withdrawal of the nomination of Senator Robertson. The President declined to do so, whereupon the two Senators transmitted (May 14th, 1881) to the Governor of New York their resignation, departed from Washington, and left the commonwealth unrepresented in the national Senate.

This movement created intense excitement throughout the State and beyond. The two Senators became candidates for re-election, but their seats were filled, after forty-eight ballots between May 31st and July 17th, by Elbridge G. Lapham and Warner Miller. The former was soon succeeded by William M. Evarts, and the latter, in 1887, by Frank Hiscock.

On July 2d, while this controversy was at its height, an incipient lunatic named Guiteau, crazed by the political excitement, shot President Garfield with a pistol at the railway station at Washington. The President died on September 19th, and was succeeded in office by Mr. Arthur.

Great bitterness of feeling continued to exist in the Republican Party, and when, in September, 1882, Judge C. J. Folger was nominated for Governor of New York by a State Convention to succeed Governor Cornell, the agitation and divisions in the convention and afterward among the people were most remarkable. In that convention a member of the State Republican Committee was represented by a substitute—a professed proxy—whose influence secured the nomination of Judge Folger. It was afterward proven that the proxy was a forgery. The nominee, innocent of all wrong, was denounced as a candidate of the national administration, opposed to the renomination of Cornell, and forced upon the convention by fraud. There was a general revolt at the polls in November, and Mr. Folger was defeated by a plurality of almost one hundred and ninety-three thousand votes. The Prohibition and Greenback parties also presented candidates. Grover Cleveland, the Democratic nominee for governor, received the unprecedented plurality of votes, and the Democrats secured a majority in both branches of the Legislature. The next year they elected their candidates for State officers.

The immense majority of votes given to Mr. Cleveland for Governor of New York made him a prominent candidate for nomination for the Presidency of the United States at the National Democratic Convention in 1884. He was nominated, but he was not the choice of all the New York delegates in that convention.

The Republicans nominated James G. Blaine, of Maine, for the Presidency. The canvass was a very active one, especially in the State of New York. Independent Republicans organized in favor of Cleveland, or omitted to vote. Upon the vote in the State of New York depended the fate of the candidates of the two great parties. The Greenback and Prohibition parties were also active in favor of their respective nominees.

On the eve of the election a remark made by a clergyman at a Republican banquet in New York City offended a large number of Roman Catholics who intended to vote for Mr. Blaine. It drove them to the other side in numbers, possibly, sufficient to defeat Mr. Blaine. Mr. Cleveland received about eleven hundred majority in the State of New York, and so won the great prize.

Lieutenant-Governor David B. Hill took the chair of State when Governor Cleveland left it, in the spring of 1885, and in the autumn he was elected governor of the commonwealth, which position he still (1887) holds. During his administration efforts were made to have a convention to revise the State Constitution, also to have the usual decennial census taken, the last having been accomplished in 1875. Neither of these measures has been effected.

Powerful and persistent efforts have been made in the State, in various ways, for the suppression of intemperance. Laws for the purpose have been made, but the fearful evil is yet strong. In 1886 a large number of Republicans formed a "Republican Anti-Saloon League," for the purpose of effecting the great reform by the action of that party. It was expanded to a national league. Meanwhile the Republicans had secured a working majority in both branches of the Legislature of the State, and efforts were made to obtain from the Legislature authority for submitting to the consideration of the people the propriety of holding a convention to amend the State Constitution in the interest of sobriety. These efforts failed. In the session of 1887 some temperance measures were adopted, but were annulled by executive interference.

EX-GOV. CLEVELAND.

GOV. DAVID B. HILL.

CONCLUSION.

The Republican State Convention, held early in the fall of 1887, adopted a resolution in favor of temperance measures. In the political canvass that ensued the liquor interest became very active ; so, also, did the Prohibitionists, who won a much larger vote in the State than ever before. There were five parties in the field, with their candidates. The Democratic Party elected the State officers, while the Republicans again secured a working majority in both branches of the Legislature.

During the last decade the Empire State has made immense progress in population, wealth, and influence. Its people have produced monuments which will forever commemorate their strength and enlightened civilization. In 1883 the two great commercial cities near the sea were united by an unrivalled work of human skill. They have established a vast park in the grand mountain region of the north. They have made the sublime cataract of Niagara and its surroundings a free pleasure resort ; and a corporation has bridged the beautiful Hudson River at the middle of its tide-water with a structure which overtops the highest masts of ocean ships, and connects, with railroads, populous and busy New England with the vast coal regions of Pennsylvania and the commerce of the West.

The population of the commonwealth of New York is probably not less than six millions at this time, while its industries, its charities, and its benevolent and religious work are commensurate.

APPENDIX.

I.

COUNTIES OF THE STATE OF NEW YORK.

On pages 97, 98 are given brief accounts of the organization of the ten counties in New York which were first established, with delineations of their respective seals.* Below may be found similar accounts of the remaining fifty counties with the population of each in 1875 and 1880.

Allegany County was formed from Genesee County, April 11th, 1806. A portion of Steuben County was annexed, March 11th, 1808. Portions of it were given to Genesee in 1811, to Wyoming and Livingston in 1846, and again to Livingston in 1856. Population in 1875 was 41,721; in 1880 it was 41,810.

Broome County was formed from Tioga, March 28th, 1806, and was so named in honor of Lieutenant-Governor John Broome, who gave it a silver seal. Oswego and Berkshire were annexed to Tioga County, March 21st, 1822. Population in 1875 was 47,913; in 1880 it was 49,483.

Cattaraugus County was formed from Genesee County, March 11th, 1808. Population in 1875 was 48,477; in 1880 it was 55,806.

Cayuga County was formed from Onondaga County, March 8th, 1799. It is a long, narrow county. Its name is derived from one of the Six Nations. Population in 1875 was 61,213; in 1880 it was 65,081.

Chautauqua County was formed from Genesee, March 8th, 1808. It lies upon the shore of Lake Erie in the southwest corner of the State. Population in 1875 was 64,869; in 1880 it was 65,342.

---

* In the accounts on pages 97, 98, the population of each of the ten counties is not given. The subjoined table will supply an omission:

COUNTIES.	POPULATION. 1875.	POPULATION. 1880.	COUNTIES.	POPULATION. 1875.	POPULATION. 1880.
Albany	147,530	154,890	Queens	84,131	90,574
Duchess	76,056	79,184	Richmond	35,241	38,991
Kings	509,216	599,495	Suffolk	52,088	53,888
New York	1,046,087	1,206,299	Ulster	88,271	85,888
Orange	85,252	88,220	Westchester	100,660	108,988

578　　　　　　　　　　APPENDIX.

COUNTY SEALS.

APPENDIX. 579

CHEMUNG COUNTY was formed from Tioga County, March 29th, 1836. The name is derived from the Indian title of the principal stream traversing it, and signifies, it is said, "Big horn in the water." Population in 1875 was 41,879 ; in 1880 it was 43,065.

CHENANGO COUNTY was formed from Herkimer and Tioga counties, March 15th, 1798. Sangerfield (Oneida County) was taken from it in 1804, and Madison County in 1806. It is an interior county. Population in 1875 was 39,937 ; in 1880 it was 39,891.

CLINTON COUNTY was formed from Washington, March 7th, 1788, and was so named in honor of Governor George Clinton. In 1799 Essex County was taken from it, St. Lawrence County was provisionally annexed to it in 1801, and taken off in 1802, and Franklin County was taken from it in 1808. It lies upon Lake Champlain, and is the northeast county of the State. Population in 1875 was 49,761 ; in 1880 it was 50,897.

COLUMBIA COUNTY was formed from Albany, April 4th, 1786. It lies on the east bank of the Hudson River, between Duchess and Rensselaer counties, and extends east to the Massachusetts line. Population in 1875 was 47,756 ; in 1880 it was 47,928.

CORTLAND COUNTY was formed from Onondaga, April 8th, 1808. It was named in honor of Pierre Van Cortlandt, the first Lieutenant-Governor of the State, who was an extensive owner of land in that region. It lies near the centre of the State. Population in 1875 was 24,500 ; in 1880 it was 25,825.

DELAWARE COUNTY was formed from Ulster and Otsego counties, March 10th, 1797. It lies upon the headwaters of the Delaware River. Population in 1875 was 42,149 ; in 1880 it was 42,721.

DUCHESS COUNTY. See page 98 and note, page 577.

ERIE COUNTY was formed from Niagara County, April 2d, 1821. It lies upon Lake Erie and Niagara River on the west line of the State. Population in 1875 was 199,570 ; in 1880 it was 219,884.

ESSEX COUNTY was formed from Clinton County, March 1st, 1799. In the erection of Franklin County in 1808 a corner was taken from Essex. It is upon Lake Champlain. Population in 1875 was 34,474 ; in 1880 it was 34,515.

FRANKLIN COUNTY was formed from Clinton County, March 11th, 1806. It was named in honor of Dr. Benjamin Franklin. On March 22d, 1822, a small portion of it was annexed to Essex County. Population in 1875 was 31,581 ; in 1880 it was 32,390.

FULTON COUNTY was formed from Montgomery County, April 18th, 1838, and was so named in honor of Robert Fulton. It lies north of the Mohawk River. Population in 1875 was 30,188 ; in 1880 it was 30,985.

APPENDIX. 581

GENESEE COUNTY was formed from Ontario, March 30th, 1802. It originally comprised all that part of the State lying west of the Genesee River, and a line extending due south from the junction of the Genesee and Canaseraga Creek to the southern line of the State. In 1806 Allegany was taken from it; Cattaraugus, Chautauqua and Niagara in 1808; parts of Livingston and Monroe in 1821; Orleans in 1824, and Wyoming in 1841. Population in 1875 was 32,551; in 1880 it was 32,806.

GREENE COUNTY was formed from Albany and Ulster counties, March 25th, 1800, and named in honor of General Nathaniel Greene, of the Revolution. It lies upon the west bank of the Hudson River. Population in 1875 was 32,554; in 1880 it was 32,695.

HAMILTON COUNTY was formed from Montgomery County, February 12th, 1816. It was named in honor of Alexander Hamilton. The territory was included in Herkimer County in 1791, but was reannexed to Montgomery in March, 1797. It occupies the central portion of the great northern wilderness. Its organization can only be complete when it has a population sufficient to entitle it to a Member of Assembly. Population in 1875 was 3,482; in 1880 it was 3,923.

HERKIMER COUNTY was formed from Montgomery, February 16th, 1791. "The name," says Dr. Hough, "was originally spelled Erghemar." It was named in honor of General Herkimer, fatally wounded at Oriskany, who signed his name Herkheimer. Onondaga County was taken from Herkimer in 1794; Oneida and part of Chenango in 1798; parts of Montgomery County were annexed to it, April 7th, 1817; and parts of Richfield and Plainfield, of Otsego County, were annexed in forming the town of Winfield in 1816. Population in 1875 was 41,692; in 1880 it was 42,669.

JEFFERSON COUNTY was formed from Oneida, March 28th, 1805, and named in honor of Thomas Jefferson, then President of the United States. Population in 1875 was 65,362; in 1880 it was 66,103.

KINGS COUNTY. See page 98 and note on page 577.

LEWIS COUNTY was formed from Oneida, March 28th, 1805, and named in honor of Morgan Lewis, the Governor of the State. Slight changes have been made in its boundary. It lies mostly within the Black River Valley. Population in 1875 was 29,236; in 1880 it was 31,416.

LIVINGSTON COUNTY was formed from Genesee and Ontario, February 23d, 1821. In 1846 a portion of Allegany was annexed, and in 1856 another portion. Population in 1875 was 38,564; in 1880 it was 39,562.

MADISON COUNTY was formed from Chenango, March 21st, 1806, and named in honor of James Madison, afterward President of the United States. Population in 1875 was 42,490; in 1880 it was 44,112.

COUNTY SEALS.

APPENDIX. 583

COUNTY SEALS.

MONROE COUNTY was formed from Ontario and Genesee counties, February 23d, 1821, and named in honor of James Monroe, then President of the United States. Population in 1875 was 134,534; in 1880 it was 144,903.

MONTGOMERY COUNTY was formed from Albany County, March 12th, 1772, under the name of Tryon County, so called in honor of the Royal Governor, William Tryon. Its name was changed on April 2d, 1784, in honor of General Richard Montgomery. Ontario was taken from it in 1789; Herkimer, Oswego, and Tioga in 1791; Hamilton in 1816, and Fulton in 1838. Population in 1875 was 35,200; in 1880 it was 38,315.

NEW YORK COUNTY. See page 97 and note on page 577.

NIAGARA COUNTY was formed from Genesee, March 11th, 1808. Erie was taken from it April 2d, 1821. It lies in the angle formed by the junction of the Niagara River and Lake Ontario. Population in 1875 was 51,904; in 1880 it was 54,173.

ONEIDA COUNTY was formed from Herkimer, March 15th, 1798. In 1805 Lewis and Jefferson counties were taken from it, also a part of Oswego County in 1816. In 1801 portions of it were annexed to Clinton County, and some to Madison County in 1836. In 1804 a part of Chenango County was annexed. Its name is derived from one of the Six Nations. Population in 1875 was 113,967; in 1880 it was 115,475.

ONONDAGA COUNTY was formed from Herkimer, March 5th, 1794, and included the "Military Tract." Cayuga was taken from it, March 8th, 1799, Cortland, April 8th, 1808, and a part of Oswego, March 1st, 1816. Its name was derived from one of the Six Nations. Population in 1875 was 113,223; in 1880 it was 117,893.

ONTARIO COUNTY was formed from Montgomery County, January 27th, 1789. Its name was derived from the great lake which originally formed its northern border. Steuben County was taken from it in 1796, Genesee in 1802; parts of Montgomery and Livingston in 1821, and Yates and a part of Wayne in 1823. A strip from Montgomery County, west of Seneca Lake, was annexed February 16th, 1791, and a small tract from Steuben, February 25th, 1814. Population in 1875 was 47,730; in 1880 it was 49,541.

ORANGE COUNTY. See page 98 and note on page 577.

ORLEANS COUNTY was formed from Genesee, November 11th, 1824. On April 5th, 1825, a portion of Genesee was annexed. Population in 1875 was 29,977; in 1880 it was 30,128.

OSWEGO COUNTY (an Indian name) was formed from Oneida and Onondaga, March 1st, 1816. It lies at the southeast extremity of Lake Ontario. Population in 1875 was 78,615; in 1880 it was 77,911.

APPENDIX. 585

OTSEGO COUNTY was formed from Montgomery, February 16th, 1791. It is also an Indian name. A part of Schoharie was taken from it in 1795, and a part of Delaware in 1797. Population in 1875 was 49,815; in 1880 it was 51,397.

PUTNAM COUNTY, so called in honor of General Israel Putnam, was formed from Duchess County, June 12th, 1812. It lies upon the Hudson River, between the counties of Duchess and Westchester, and extends to the State of Connecticut. Population in 1875 was 15,811; in 1880 it was 15,181.

QUEENS COUNTY. See page 98 and note on page 577.

RENSSELAER COUNTY was formed from Albany, February 7th, 1791, and named from the Van Rensselaer family. It included nearly all of the Van Rensselaer Manor east of the Hudson River. Population in 1875 was 105,053; in 1880 it was 115,328.

RICHMOND COUNTY. See page 98 and note on page 577.

ROCKLAND COUNTY was formed from Orange County, February 28th, 1798, and derives its name from its extensive mountain area. Population in 1875 was 26,951; in 1880 it was 27,690.

ST. LAWRENCE COUNTY was formed from Clinton County and parts of Montgomery and Herkimer counties, March 3d, 1802. Its northwestern boundary is the St. Lawrence River, from which it derives its name. It is the largest county in the State, its area being 2880 square miles. Population in 1875 was 84,124; in 1880 it was 85,997.

SARATOGA COUNTY was formed from Albany, February 7th, 1791. It lies in the angle formed by the junction of the Mohawk and Hudson rivers. It is an Indian name for a place. Population in 1875 was 55,233; in 1880 it was 55,156.

SCHENECTADY COUNTY was formed from Albany, March 7th, 1809. Population in 1875 was 22,892; in 1880 it was 23,538.

SCHOHARIE COUNTY was formed from Albany and Otsego, April 6th, 1795. The name is said to be the Indian term for "drift-wood." A small part of Greene County was annexed to it in 1836. Population in 1875 was 32,419; in 1880 it was 32,910.

SCHUYLER COUNTY was formed from Steuben, Chemung, and Tompkins counties, April 17th, 1854. It was named in honor of General Philip Schuyler. Population in 1875 was 18,928; in 1880 it was 18,842.

SENECA COUNTY was formed from Cayuga, March 29th, 1804. A part of Tompkins County was taken from it in 1817, and a part of Wayne in 1823. It derives its name from one of the Six Nations. Population in 1875 was 27,299; in 1880 it was 29,278.

STEUBEN COUNTY was formed from Ontario, March 18th, 1796, and named in honor of Baron Von Steuben. Parts were afterward annexed to Allegany County in 1808; to Livingston County in 1822, and to Schuyler County in 1854. Population in 1875 was 73,723; in 1880 it was 77,586.

SUFFOLK COUNTY. See page 98 and note on page 577.

SULLIVAN COUNTY was formed from Ulster, March 27th, 1809, and named in honor of General John Sullivan, of the Continental Army. Population in 1875 was 34,935; in 1880 it was 32,491.

TIOGA COUNTY was formed from Montgomery County, February 16th, 1791. In 1798 a part of Chenango was taken from it; Broome in 1806; a part of Tompkins in 1822, and Chemung in 1836. Population in 1875 was 31,744; in 1880 it was 32,673.

TOMPKINS COUNTY was formed from Cayuga and Seneca, April 17th, 1822. A part of Schuyler County was taken from it in 1854. It was named in honor of Governor Daniel D. Tompkins, then Vice-President of the United States. Population in 1875 was 32,915; in 1880 it was 34,445.

ULSTER COUNTY. See page 98 and note, page 577.

WARREN COUNTY was formed from Washington County, March 12th, 1813, and was named in honor of General Joseph Warren, of the Revolution. It lies on Lake George. Population in 1875 was 23,295; in 1880 it was 25,179.

WASHINGTON COUNTY was formed from Albany County, with the name of "Charlotte County" (in honor of Princess Charlotte, eldest daughter of George III.), March 12th, 1772. On April 2d, 1784, the name was changed to Washington. Clinton County was taken from it in 1788; the eastern portion was ceded to Vermont in 1790; a portion was annexed to Albany County in 1791, and Warren was taken from it in 1813. Population in 1875 was 48,167; in 1880 it was 47,871.

WAYNE COUNTY was formed from Ontario and Seneca counties, April 11th, 1823. It lies upon Lake Ontario, and was named in honor of General Anthony Wayne, of the Revolution. Population in 1875 was 49,882; in 1880 it was 54,700.

WESTCHESTER COUNTY. See page 98 and note on page 577.

WYOMING COUNTY was formed from Genesee County, May 14th, 1841. A portion of Allegany County was annexed in 1846. Population in 1875 was 30,595; in 1880 it was 30,907.

YATES COUNTY was formed from Ontario County, February 5th, 1823, and named in honor of Joseph C. Yates, then Governor of the State. A portion of Steuben County was annexed in 1824. Population in 1875 was 19,686; in 1880 it was 21,087.

II.

GOVERNORS OF NEW YORK.

COLONIAL.

Cornelius Jacobsen May..................................	1624
William Verhulst.......................................	1625
Peter Minuit..............................May 4.	1626
Walter (or Wouter) Van Twiller...............April.	1633
William Kieft.............................Mar. 28.	1638
Peter Stuyvesant..........................May 11.	1647
Richard Nicolls............................Sept. 8.	1664
Francis Lovelace...........................Aug. 17.	1668
Cornelis Evertse, Jr., and a Council of War....Aug. (n. s.) 12.	1673
Anthony Colve............................Sept. 19.	1673
Edmund Andros ....Nov. (n. s.) 10.	1674
Anthony Brockholls, Commander-in-Chief......Nov. 16.	1677
Sir Edmund Andros........................Aug. 7.	1678
Anthony Brockholls, Commander-in-Chief......Jan. (n. s.) 13.	1682
Thomas Dongan...........................Aug. 27.	1683
Sir Edmund Andros........................Aug. 11.	1688
Francis Nicholson, Lieutenant-Governor........Oct. 9.	1688
Jacob Leisler...............................June 3.	1689
Henry Sloughter...........................Mar. 19.	1691
Richard Ingoldsby, Commander-in-Chief........July 26.	1691
Benjamin Fletcher.........................Aug. 30.	1692
Earl of Bellomont..........................April 13.	1695
John Nanfan, Lieutenant-Governor............May 17.	1699
Earl of Bellomont..........................July 24.	1700
Eldest Councillor present, Pres. of the Council..Mar. 5.	1701
John Nanfan, Lieutenant-Governor............May 19.	1701
Lord Cornbury.............................May 3.	1702
Lord Lovelace..............................Dec. 18.	1708
Peter Schuyler, President ....May 6.	1709
Richard Ingoldsby, Lieutenant-Governor........May 9.	1709
Peter Schuyler, President ....May 25.	1709
Richard Ingoldsby, Lieutenant-Governor........June 1.	1709
Gerardus Beekman, President................April 10.	1710
Robert Hunter.............................June 14.	1710

APPENDIX.

Peter Schuyler, President	July 21.	1719
William Burnet	Sept. 17.	1720
John Montgomery	April 15.	1728
Rip Van Dam, President	July 1.	1731
William Cosby	Aug. 1.	1732
George Clarke, President	Mar. 10.	1736
George Clarke, Lieutenant-Governor	Oct. 30.	1736
George Clinton	Sept. 2.	1743
Sir Danvers Osborn	Oct. 10.	1753
James De Lancey, Lieutenant-Governor	Oct. 12.	1753
Sir Charles Hardy	Sept. 3.	1755
James De Lancey, Lieutenant-Governor	June 3.	1757
Cadwallader Colden, President	Aug. 4.	1760
Cadwallader Colden, Lieutenant-Governor	Aug. 8.	1761
Robert Monckton	Oct. 26.	1761
Cadwallader Colden, Lieutenant-Governor	Nov. 18.	1761
Robert Monckton	June 14.	1762
Cadwallader Colden, Lieutenant-Governor	June 28.	1763
Sir Henry Moore	Nov. 13.	1765
Cadwallader Colden, Lieutenant-Governor	Sept. 12.	1769
Earl of Dunmore	Oct. 19.	1770
William Tryon	July 9.	1771
Cadwallader Colden, Lieutenant-Governor	April 7.	1774
William Tryon	June 28.	1775
James Robertson, Military Governor	Mar. 23.	1780
Andrew Elliott, Lieutenant-Governor	April 17.	1783

The last two named are not recognized by the State of New York. They served during the occupation of New York City by the British from 1776 to 1783.

PRESIDENTS OF THE PROVINCIAL CONGRESS.

Peter Van Brugh Livingston	May 23.	1775
Nathaniel Woodhull, President *pro tempore*	Aug. 28.	1775
Abraham Yates, Jr., President *pro tempore*	Nov. 2.	1775
Nathaniel Woodhull	Dec. 6.	1775
John Haring, President *pro tempore*	Dec. 16.	1775
Abraham Yates, Jr., President *pro tempore*	Aug. 10.	1776
Abraham Yates, Jr.	Aug. 28.	1776
Peter R. Livingston	Sept. 26.	1776
Abraham Ten Broeck	Mar. 6.	1777

APPENDIX.

Leonard Gansevoort, President *pro tempore* .....April 18.   1777
Pierre Van Cortlandt, President of Council of Safety..................................May 14.   1777

GOVERNORS OF THE STATE.

George Clinton	July 30.	1777
John Jay	July 1.	1795
George Clinton		1801
Morgan Lewis		1804
Daniel D. Tompkins		1807
John Taylor, Lieutenant-Governor and Acting Governor	Mar.	1817
De Witt Clinton	July 1.	1817
Joseph C. Yates	Jan 1.	1823
De Witt Clinton		1825
Nathaniel Pitcher, Lieutenant-Governor and Acting Governor	Feb. 11.	1828
Martin Van Buren		1829
Enos T. Throop, Lieutenant-Governor and Acting Governor	Mar. 12.	1829
Enos T. Throop	Jan. 1.	1831
William L. Marcy	"	1833
William H. Seward	"	1839
William C. Bouck	"	1843
Silas Wright	"	1845
John Young	"	1847
Hamilton Fish	"	1849
Washington Hunt	"	1851
Horatio Seymour	"	1853
Myron H. Clark	"	1855
John A. King	"	1857
Edwin D. Morgan	"	1859
Horatio Seymour	"	1863
Reuben E. Fenton	"	1865
John T. Hoffman	"	1869
John Adams Dix	"	1873
Samuel J. Tilden	"	1875

MORE ELABORATE HISTORIES.

The reader of this compendious History of the State of New York who may desire more minute knowledge of the commonwealth may profitably consult the following works :

Documents Relating to the Colonial History of New York, obtained abroad by Brodhead.

Documentary History of New York, edited by E. B. O'Callaghan, M.D.

Brodhead's History of New York to 1691.
Macauley's History of New York.
Yates and Moulton's History of New York (colonial).
Smith's History of New York (colonial).
Dunlap's History of New York.
Roberts's History of New York.
Barbor's Historical Collection of New York.
O'Callaghan's History of New Netherland.
Jones's History of New York During the Revolutionary War.
Proceedings of the New York Historical Society.
Watson's Annals and Occurrences of New York City and State.
Colden's History of the Five Nations.
Schoolcraft's Notes on the Iroquois.
Morgan's History of the Iroquois Confederacy.
Ruttenber's Indian Tribes of the Hudson River.
The Jesuit Relations.
Stone's Biographies of Sir William Johnson, Brant, and Red Jacket.
Stone's History of Burgoyne's Campaign.
Lossing's Life and Times of Philip Schuyler.
Campbell's Border Wars of New York.
Simms's History of Schoharie County and Border Wars of New York.
Turner's History of Pioneer Settlements in New York.
O'Reilley's History of Rochester.
Munro's Description of the Genesee Country.
Watson's History of Essex County and of the Champlain Valley.
Palmer's History of Lake Champlain.
Onderdonk's Revolutionary Incidents on Long Island.
Thompson's History of Long Island.

MORE ELABORATE HISTORIES.

Prime's History of Long Island.
Stiles's History of the City of Brooklyn.
Histories of New York City by Miss M. L. Booth, D. T. Valentine, W. L. Stone, Mrs. M. J. Lamb, and B. J. Lossing.
Francis's Old New York.
Munsell's Annals of Albany.
Marshall's Niagara Frontier.
Public Documents Relating to the New York Canals.
Reports of the Regents of the University and of the State Superintendent of Public Instruction.
Hammond's Political History of New York.
Dunshee's History of the Collegiate (Dutch Reformed) Church School.
Ketchum's History of Buffalo.
Hunt's Letters About the Hudson.
Lossing's Hudson from the Wilderness to the Sea.
Bonney's Legacy of Historical Gleanings.
Numerous Town and County Histories.

INDEX.

A.

Abercrombie, James, Inefficiency of, 168; attacks Ticonderoga, 174.
Abraham, Heights of, scaled, 182.
Abraham, Plains of, 180; battle on the, 183.
Acadians or French Neutrals, 163.
Acland, Major, wounded, 278.
Acland, Lady Harriet (note), 278.
Adams, John, President of the United States, 363.
Aix-la-Chapelle, Treaty at, 157.
Albany City incorporated; municipal officers of, 102; name changed, 89; independent government at, 107; Colonial conventions at, 107, 162; Provincial Assembly at, 108; state of society at, 150, 151; canal celebration at, 464; charter of, amended, 543.
Albany County, Territory of, 98; extent of, 342.
Albany Regency, The, 452.
Alexander, James, counsel for Zenger, 144.
Alexandria Bay, Moonlight battle in, 416.
Algerine Corsairs, 458.
Algonquin Indians slain at Hoboken and Manhattan Island, 48.
Allen, Ethan, a bold popular leader, 190, 316; at Ticonderoga, 218; a prisoner, 229; and Beverly Robinson, 317.
Allen, Ichabod, killed at Cherry Valley, 291.
Allen, Ira, active in Vermont, 317; biography of (note), 318, 319.
Allen and Warner before the Provincial Congress of New York, 223.
Allerton, Isaac, at New Amsterdam, 49.
Allied armies besiege Yorktown, 322.
America, Position of affairs in, 172.
American Association, The, 211, 212.
American naval force in 1813, 419.
American Navy, Exploits of the, 397, 398.
American Society for the Promotion of National Union, 520, 521.
American System, The, 473.
Amherst, Jeffrey, at Louisburg, 173; biography of (note), 178; commander-in-chief on Lake Champlain, 179; receives the surrender of Montreal, 184.
Amphibious warfare, 418, 419.
Amsterdam Charter of the Dutch West India Co., Members of the (note), 23; action of the, 63.
Amsterdam merchants of trade at Manhattan (note), 14.
Anderson, Dr. Alexander, first engraver on wood in America; biography of (note), 575.
Anderson, Robert, Major, at Fort Sumter, 522.
Annapolis, Convention at, in 1786, 336.
André, Major John, complots with Arnold, 311; arrested as a spy, 312; executed; honored by his King, 315; captors of, 312; captors of, rewarded, 315.
Andros, Edmond, biography of (note), 91; Governor of New York; imprisons citizens, 92; at Albany; sends gunpowder to Rhode Island, 93; knighted, 94; long rule of, 96; Viceroy of English-American Colonies, 103; arrested in Boston and sent to England, 105.
Anne, Queen, crowned, 129.
Anthony, Allard, a *schepen*, 62.
Anti-Masonic movements, 471, 472; party dissolved, 476.
Anti-Masonry, Origin of, 471, 472.
Anti-Rentism, 499, 500.
Argus and *Pelican*, Battle between the, 418.
Armies, Disbandment of; the Union, 538.

INDEX.

Armstrong, John, Gates's aide-de-camp on Bemis's Heights, 276; author of the Newburgh Letters, 328; Secretary of War; biography of (note), 412; Hampton and Wilkinson and. 413, 414.

Arnold, Benedict, with Allen at Ticonderoga, 218; naval operations of; captures St. Johns, 222; joins Montgomery in an attack on Quebec; in command there, 230; naval career on Lake Champlain, 251; relieves Fort Schuyler, 273; in battle on Bemis's Heights, 275, 280; wounded, 280; military governor of Philadelphia; marriage of; convicted of crookedness; plots treason, 311, 312; flies to the *Vulture*, 314; receives his stipulated reward, 315; attempt to abduct, 315; a plunderer in Virginia; rewards offered for, 321.

Arnold and Morgan on Bemis's Heights, 281.

Arnold, Mrs., at her husband's headquarters, 313; distress of, 314.

Articles of Confederation, 319.

Asia, a British vessel, fires on New York City, 232.

Assembly, Popular, at New Amsterdam, Members of the, 74.

Assembly, The first General English, at New York, 96; laws passed by; Speaker of, 99.

Assembly, Anti-Leislerian, 123.

Assembly, Leislerian, 125; revokes fraudulent land-grants; victory over Absolutism, 150.

Assembly, The New York Provincial, prepares for war, 164.

Ato-tar-ho, first President of the Iroquois Confederacy, 8.

Attwood, William, Chief-Justice, 129.

Auchmuty, Rev. Dr., 572.

Autosee, Battle of, 406.

B.

Bainbridge, William, Commodore, 398.
Ballston destroyed, 308.
Baltimore, Attack on National troops in, 525.
Bank charter, A, in politics, 399, 400.
Barn-burners, a political faction, 501.
Barneveldt, John Van Olden, Death of (note), 16.

Barney, Joshua, Flotilla of, destroyed, 435.
Barré, Count de la, and Governor Dongan, 100.
Barré, Col. Isaac, Retort of, in Parliament (note), 185.
Bartholdi's Statue of Liberty Enlightening the World, 567.
Bauman, Lt.-Colonel, Death of, 269.
Baxter, George, commissioner at Hartford, 58; biography of (note); prepares an indictment against Governor Stuyvesant, 65.
Bayard, Nicholas, Secretary of the province of New York, 89; imprisoned, 92; opposes Leisler, 107; imprisoned, 109; receives grants of land, 125; a disturber of the public peace; convicted of high treason and reprieved, 130.
Beaver Dams, Affair at, 412.
Beeckman, Dr. Gerardus, Interview of, with Stuyvesant, 66; imprisoned, 92; convicted of treason and pardoned, 110, 111; biography of (note), 110.
Beeckman, William, a *schepen*, 62, 89; Vice-Director of New Amstel; biography of (note), 72.
Bellomont, Earl of, Governor of New York, 120, 121; administration of, 123, 124; favors the Leisler family, 124; death and character of, 125.
Bellomont and Livingston, 122.
Bellows, Rev. H. W., and the Sanitary Commission; biography of (note), 527.
Bemis's Heights, Battles on, 274-276.
Bennett, James Gordon, 483.
Bennington, Battle of, 269.
Benson, Egbert, first Attorney-General, 260; in New York Legislature; biography of (note), 337, 338.
Berkeley, John, Proprietor of New Jersey, 86.
Beverswyck, 45.
Biddle, Captain James, 439.
Billop House, Peace Conference at the, 244.
Binckes, Jacob, Proclamation of, 89.
Binnenhof, The, Hall of Representatives 16.
Bisshopp, Lt.-Colonel, Death of, 413.
Black Rock, Affair at, 413.
Bladensburg, Battle of, 436.

INDEX.

Blakely, Captain Johnson, Loss of, 438.
Bleecker, Ann Eliza, poet, 572.
Block, Adrien, Dutch navigator ; builds a ship at Manhattan ; discoveries of, 15.
Blommaert, Samuel, a patroon, 32.
Bloodshed, The last, in the Revolution, 326.
Bœrstler, Colonel, at the Beaver Dams, 412.
Bogardus, Rev. Everardus, first settled pastor in New Netherland, 34, 35, 568 ; rebukes the Governor, 52 ; death of, 53.
Bolingbroke, Lord, plans expedition against Quebec, 136 ; biography of (note), 136.
Bolton, Robert, historian, 574.
Boom at Ticonderoga and Mount Independence, 265 ; at West Point, 253.
Borgne, Lake, American flotilla on, 441.
Boscawen, Admiral, 173.
Boston massacre, The, 202.
Boston Port Bill, Effect of the, 206.
Boston, Siege and surrender of, 234.
Boston tea-party, The, 205 ; effects of the, 206.
Bostonians, Sympathy for the, 207.
Bouck, Wm. C., Governor ; biography of (note), 497.
Boundary line between New York and Connecticut ; The Oblong, 142.
Boyd, John Parker, at Chrysler's Field ; biography of (note), 416.
Braddock, Edward, meets Colonial governors ; death of, 163.
Bradford, William, and the *New York Gazette*, 143.
Bradley, Attorney-General of New York, 145, 152–154.
Bradstreet, John, provisions the garrison at Oswego, 168 ; biography of (note), 174 ; captures Fort Frontenac, 175 (note), 176.
Bradstreet, Simon, English commissioner at Hartford in 1650, 58.
Brandt (or Brant), Joseph, organizes scalping parties ; desolates Springfield and the Schoharie Valley, 290 ; Sir John Johnson and the Butlers, allies of, 291 ; (note) humanity of, 291, 292.
Brandywine Creek, Battle at, 286.
Brant, John, at Queenstown battle, 395 ; at the Beaver Dams, 412.

Brasher, Abraham, 110.
Breyman, Colonel, commands riflemen, 275 ; mortally wounded, 281.
Brewster, Elder Wm., leads the "Pilgrims," 24.
British expedition up the Hudson, 297.
British plan for dividing the Colonies, 238.
British posts in South Carolina captured, 324.
British troops, Depredations of, in South-East Virginia ; join Clinton at New York, 297 ; occupy only Charleston and Savannah in the South, 325 ; evacuate Savannah, 326 ; evacuate New York, 331.
Brock, General Sir Isaac, on Queenstown Heights, 394 ; death of, 395.
Brockholls, Anthony, Acting-Governor, 94.
Brodhead, John Romeyn, historian, 574 ; biography of (note), 574.
Brooklyn, Settlers at (note), 26.
Brown, Jacob, charged with the defence of the Northern portion of New York ; biography of (note), 390 ; invades Canada, 422.
Brown, Colonel John, in the rear of Burgoyne's army, 275 ; killed in battle at Stone Arabia ; biography of (note), 307.
Brown, John, Raid of, at Harper's Ferry, 515.
Brugh, Johannes Van, Alderman, 85 ; burgomaster, 89.
Brunel, Isambert, and the Champlain Canal, 349.
Bryant, Wm. C., Notice of, 482, 575.
Buchanan, James, President of the United States, 511.
"Bucktails" and "Clintonians," 453.
Buel, Jesse, Notice of ; biography of (note), 447.
Buffalo, Destruction of, 417 ; in 1813 ; growth of, 469.
Bull Run, Battle of ; effect of battle of, 526.
Bunker Hill, Battle of, 220.
Burgoyne, General Sir John, in Canada, 240 ; biography of (note), 263 ; embarks on Lake Champlain, 264 ; feasts the Indians ; arrives at Crown Point ; proclamation of, 265 and note, 266 ; takes Forts Ticonderoga and Independence, 266, 267 ; pushes on to the Hudson River, 268 ;

INDEX.

fights the Americans near the Hudson, 274–281; encamps on Saratoga Heights, 274; awaits tidings from Clinton; prepares for battle, 277; capitulation and surrender of, 281.

Burgoyne's invasion of New York, 263–284; troops of, sent to Virginia, 282.

Burnet, Governor William, Character of; biography of (note), 139; administration of, 139–141.

Burning vessels at Forts Clinton and Montgomery, 284.

Burns's Coffee-House (note), 198.

Burr, Aaron, Adroit management of, 364; biography of (note); Vice-President of the United States, 364; President of the State Constitutional Convention, 370; Democratic Candidate for Governor, 373; quarrel and duel with Hamilton, 373, 374; mysterious expedition of; tried for treason and acquitted; political death of, 375.

Burrites, The, 379.

Burton, Mary, and the Negro Plot, 153, 154.

Bute, Earl of, Prime Minister, 192; ruinous policy of, 193.

Butler, Colonel John, in the Wyoming Valley, 292–294.

Butler, Walter, at Cherry Valley, 291.

Butler, Colonel Zebulon, commands in the Wyoming Valley, 293.

C.

Campaign of 1755, 163; of 1756, 167; of 1758, 173; of 1759, 178, 179.

Campbell, Samuel, Family of, made captive at Cherry Valley, 292.

Campbell, Lt.-Colonel, attacks Fort Montgomery, 283.

Campbell, William W., historian, 574.

Canada, Invasion of, undertaken in 1690, 115; unsuccessful attempt to conquer, in 1711, 134, 135; surrendered to the English, 184; alliance with, or conquest of, 222; preparations to invade, in 1775, 227, 228; end of invasion in 1776, 240; Revolutionary movements in, 489.

Canajoharie settlement desolated, 306.

Canal companies organized, 348.

Canals in the State, 469, 554.

Cape Breton surrendered to the English, 156.

Carleton, Major, leads a marauding party to Lakes Champlain and George, 308.

Carleton, Sir Guy, succeeds Sir Henry Clinton in command, 323.

Caroline, Destruction of the, 490.

Carroll, Charles, commissioner in Canada, 239.

Carteret, George, Proprietor of New Jersey, 86.

Castine, Baron de (note), 100.

Centennial celebration and exhibition, 553.

Cesnola, L. P. di (note), 575.

Chamber of Commerce (note), 369.

Champlain, Samuel, in Northern New York; biography of (note), 9; in war with Northern Indians, 9, 10; in war with the Iroquois, 18.

Champlain Canal (note), 462.

Chancery, New Court of, established, 129.

Chandler, General, at Stony Creek, 410.

Charles II., Death of, 101.

Charter of Liberties and Privileges, 97.

Charter of Privileges and Exemptions, 81.

Charter of Special Privileges granted, 81.

Chase, Samuel, on a Committee in Canada, 239.

Chauncey, Isaac, Commander-in-chief on Lake Ontario, 392, 401; biography of (note), 401; blockades the British squadron at Kingston, 431.

Chauncey and Yeo on Lake Ontario, 415.

Cherry Valley, Massacre at, 291, 292.

Chesapeake and *Shannon*, Battle between the, 417, 418.

Chief-Justice of New York (Pratt) appointed by the crown, 189.

Children, cruelty to, Law for the prevention of, 554.

Chippewa, Battle of, 424.

Christian Commission, The, 528, 529.

Christianity of an Indian chief proven (note), 124.

Christiansen, Captain, 14; voyages of, to Manhattan Island and Albany, 15.

Christina, Fort, 41.

Christina, Queen, 41.

Chrysler's Field, Battle at, 416.

Churches in New York in 1750, 188.

Cincinnati, Society of the, 329, 330.

INDEX.   597

City Hall, First, in New Amsterdam (note), 63.
Civil Rights Bill, 549.
Clark, Myron H., Governor, 510; biography of (note), 510, 511; and Virginia authorities, 512.
Clarke, Sir George, Lieutenant-Governor; biography of (note), 152.
Clay, Henry, and the "American System," 473.
Clinton, De Witt, Appeal of, 234; first appearance of, in political life, 366; duel of, with Swartwout, 372; biography of (note), 385; and the Erie Canal, 386; candidate for the Presidency of the United States, 400; character of, 445; triumph of, 452; elected Governor, 453; removed from office of Canal Commissioner, 460; weds the Lakes to the Sea; death of, 473.
Clinton, George, first Governor of the State, 262; and the Highland Forts, 283; leads troops to Ticonderoga, 305; leads troops to the Mohawk Valley, 307; re-elected Governor, 353; Vice-President of the United States, 381; biography of (note), 398.
Clinton, James, and the Highland Forts, 283; biography of (note), 384.
Clinton, Sir George, Governor; biography of (note), 154; arrives at New York, 155; and the Assembly, 158, 159; administration of, 158.
Clinton, Sir Henry, at Sandy Hook, 234; march of, upon Forts Clinton and Montgomery; attacks them, 283; evacuates Philadelphia; in battle at Monmouth Court-House, 295; biography of (note), 297; sails for Charleston; captures that city, 308; deceived by misleading letters, 322.
Clinton's courier hung as a spy, 285.
Coalition, A political, 346.
Cochran, Admiral, 433.
Cockburn, Admiral, Marauding expeditions of, 418, 419.
Coerten, Myndert, arrested, 110.
Coffee, General John, in the Creek War, 406.
Colbert, French Minister, 91.
Colden, Cadwallader, remarks on the Five Nations (note), 8; a member of the Governor's Council, 139; and the Society Library, 187; Acting-Governor, 189; hung in effigy, and property destroyed by a mob, 196; notice of, 572.
Cole, Thomas, artist, 575.
College of Nineteen, The, 23, 31, 32, 52; changes the government of New Netherland, 53; gives a burgher government to New Amsterdam, 62.
Collegians in New York (note), 188.
Collegiate (Dutch Reformed) Church School, and two prominent principals of the (note), 568.
Colles, Christopher, on the canal system; biography of (note), 347.
Collier, Sir George, commands a flotilla in the Hudson River, 279.
Collyer, Vincent, and the Christian Commission, 529.
Colonial Congress at Albany, 107, 115.
Colonial Convention at Albany, 161.
Colonial Governors, Conference of, at Annapolis, 163.
Colored Orphan Asylum, New York, destroyed by a mob, 534.
Colve, Captain Anthony, Governor of New York; sketch of (note), 89; vigilance of, 90.
Commissioners of Congress sent to Canada, 239.
Commissioners of Indian Affairs (note), 140.
Committee of One Hundred (note), 217.
Committee of Safety, 523.
Committees of Correspondence, 210.
Committees of Fifty-one and Vigilance, Feud between the, 208, 209.
Common School Fund, Appropriations for a, 376; and the Roman Catholic Schools, 496, 497; condition of the, 360, 361, and note; notice of the, 555, 556.
Common Schools, Appropriations for, 376.
"Common Sense" and its effect, 236, 237.
Comptroller, Office of, created, 363.
Compulsory Education, 550; and note on, 551.
Confederate agents conspire to burn New York City, 536.
"Confederate States of America"—a league of politicians and a misnomer, 521.

Confederation, Articles of, Weakness of the, 327.
Confiscation and Attainder Acts, 261; persons affected by the (note), 262.
Congress, called, Session of, 526.
Congress, The First Continental; members of, from New York, 210.
Connecticut, Depredations on the coasts of; towns in, burned, 298.
Connecticut Valley, Contentions for occupation of the, 35.
Consolers of the sick, Duties of the, 32.
Constitution of the State of New York formed, 257; adopted, 258; published (note), 258; first revision of the, 370; government organized under the, 459, 460; third revision of the, 503, 504; amendments to, ratified, 549, 550.
Constitution and *Guerriere*, Battle between the, 397.
Continental Army, Disbandment of the, 328; last survivors of the, 329 and note; quotas for, furnished by States (note), 329.
Continental Congress, The first meeting of the, 210; resolutions of defiance; work of the, 211; effect of proceedings of the, 212; powers of the, 219; disarms Tories, 233; flight of the, to Lancaster, 287.
Continental paper money, Counterfeit, 319.
Convention of the State of New York; assembles at Kingston, 256; forms and adopts a constitution, 258; members of the new (note), 256.
Conway, General, Sketch of (note), 287.
"Conway's Cabal," 287.
Cook, Lemuel, Biography of (note), 329.
Cooper, James Fenimore, 573; biography of (note), 573.
Cooper, Myles, D.D., President of King's College, 213, 572.
Cooper, Peter, builder of the first American locomotive engine (note), 555.
Coote, Richard, Lord Bellomont, Governor; biography of (note), 120.
Cornbury, Lord, Governor, Character and career of, 129-132.
Cornell University, 540.
Cornwall County, Location of, 98.
Cornwallis, Earl, in battle of Long Island, 244; in command in South Carolina; invades North Carolina, 309; chases Greene; at Guilford Court-House; marches to the sea-coast, 324; in command in Virginia, 321, 324; at Yorktown, 321; surrender of, 322; effect of the surrender of, 323.
Corrupt judges, 547.
Cortlandt, Oloff Stevens Van, in the Council of Nine, 61; burgomaster, 85.
Cosby, Governor, Character of, 142; conflict of, with Van Dam and others, 143.
Council of Appointment, Composition of the, 259; actions of the, 459; powers of the, 505.
Council of Eight, 49, 50; send a memorial to the States-General concerning the conduct of Kieft, 50, 51.
Council of Nine, 61.
Council of Plymouth send a colony to Cape Cod Bay, 24.
Council of Revision, Composition of the, 259; (note), 454.
Council of Safety, Members of the, 260.
Cousseau, Jacques, Alderman, 85.
Covington, General, at Chrysler's Field, 416.
Cow Bay, Arms of Holland at, pulled down, 42.
Couwenhoven, Peter Wolfertsen Van, a *schepen*, 63.
Craney Island, Conflict at, 418.
Crawford, Thomas, sculptor, 576.
Credit system, Collapse of the, 481, 485; effects of the, 486.
Creek Indians, War against the, 406, 407.
Creek Nation, Ruin of the, 407.
Crittenden Compromise, The, 520.
Croghan, Major George, at Sandusky, 404.
Croton Aqueduct, The, 486.
Crown Point, Expedition against, 164; fort built at, 179; capture of, 219; possessed by the British, 252.
Cruger, John, Biography of (note), 369.
Cumberland County claimed by Vermont, 316.
Cummings, Thomas S., artist, 576.
Cunningham, William, British Provost Marshal (note), 250.
Curler or Corlear, Arendt Van, commissary at Rensselaerwyck, rescues Jesuit missionary, 46; biography of (note), 49.

INDEX.

Curler, Jacob Van, commands Fort Good Hope, 35.

D.

D'Anville, Duc, Expedition of, 156.
D'Aubrey, Colonel, commands French and Indians, 179.
Davis, Jefferson, President of the "Confederate States of America," 521
Dawson, Henry B., historian, 574.
Day, Benjamin H., publisher of the first "penny paper," 483.
Deane, James, Indian interpreter, 289.
Dearborn, Henry, commander of the Northern Department; biography of (note), 392; resolves to invade Canada, 408; resignation of, 412.
Debt, Imprisonment for, abolished, 478.
De Bougainville, Errand of, 182.
Decatur, Commodore Stephen, 398; commander of the *President*, 439; humbles the Barbary Powers; biography of (note), 458.
Declaration of Independence, 237; read to the army at New York; approved by the Provincial Congress, 238.
De Grist, Paul K. Van, a *schepen*, 62.
De Heister, leader of German troops, 244.
Delavall, Thomas, Councilman, 84.
De Laet, historian (note), 63, 592.
De Lancey, James, Chief-Justice, 143; presides at the trial of Zenger, 145; and Governor Clinton, 158; biography of (note), 158; Acting-Governor, 159; death of, 186; to Lords of Trade, 180; and Society Library, 187.
De Lancey, Oliver, in the Assembly; biography of (note), 213.
Delaware River, Settlers on the, 26; Washington crossing the, 254.
Dellius, Dominie, obtains land by fraud, 126.
De Milt, Anthony, *schout*, 89; imprisoned, 92.
Democratic Party overthrown, 49; schism in the, 373; disruption of the, 516.
Democratic Society song of "God Save the Guillotine," sung at meeting of (note), 357.
De Nonville, Dongan and, 102; invades the Iroquois country, 102, 103.
De Peyster, Abraham, Associate-Justice; biography of (note), 129; and the Society Library, 187.
De Peyster, Johannes, Alderman, 85; notice of (note), 85; burgomaster, 89, 92.
Dermer, Captain, at Manhattan, 23.
De Ruyven, Secretary, receiver of revenues, 90.
De Sille, Nicasius, Vice-Director-General, 67.
Detroit, Surrender of, 184, 185.
De Vries, David Pietersen, plants a colony on Delaware Bay, 32; leaves the colony, 50; prophetic words of, 51.
De Witt, a Dutch navigator, 14.
De Witt, Simeon, and the Erie Canal, 383, 384; surveyor-general, 460.
Dieskau, Baron de, defeated and wounded at Lake George, 166.
Dincklagen, Lubbertus Van, causes the recall of Van Twiller, 38; Provisional Governor, 51; joins in a memorial to the States-General, 62.
Dix, John Adams, and School District Libraries, 437; famous Order of, 517, 518; Governor; biography of (note), 549.
Donck, Adriaen Van der, one of the Council of Nine; imprisoned by Stuyvesant, 61; presents the memorial of the Council of Nine to the States-General, 62.
Dongan, Thomas, Governor, 96; biography of (note), 96; foreign relations of, 99, 100; refuses to obey the King, 101; is dismissed, 102.
Downie, Commodore, at Plattsburgh, 428.
Draft, The, 533.
Draft Riots in New York, 533, 534.
Drake, Joseph Rodman, 573.
Draper, A. S., Superintendent of Public Instruction, 556.
Draper, John W., 572.
Drummond, Lt.-General, with Wellington's veterans in Canada; commands the British forces in Canada, 424.
Duane, James, District Judge, 346; first Mayor of New York City after the Revolution, 350.
Duchess County, Territory of; name of (note), 89.
Dudley, Guilford D., 401.
Dudley, Joseph, Chief-Justice of New York (note), 116.

INDEX.

Duke of York, Character of, 92.
Duke's County, Location of, 98.
Duke's laws, The (note), 85.
Dunlap, Rev. Mr., at Cherry Valley, 291.
Dunlap, Wm., artist and historian, 572.
Dunmore, Lord, Governor, 203.
Duquesne, Fort, 162.
Durand, A. B., artist, 575.
Dutch, The, on Manhattan, surrounded by Indians, 18; liberality of the, 40; Christian charity of the, 46; embassy of the, to New Plymouth, and its results, 57; embassy of, to Maryland, 68, 69; retake New York, 88, 89.
Dutch West India Co., The, chartered; features of the charter; powers of the, 22; favored by the States-General, 22, 23; organization of the, 23; send colonists to New Netherland, 25, 27; success of the, 30; offer an asylum to the oppressed in New Netherland, 71.

E.

East and West Jersey, 94.
Eelkens defies Van Twiller, 34.
Election Riots in New York City, 483-485.
Elliott, Charles, artist, 575.
Elliott, Captain Jesse D., captures vessels near Buffalo, 402.
Embargoes and Orders in Council, 378-381.
Empire State, the, Retrospect of the life of, 568-576; religious denominations in 568, 569; political condition of, 569, 570; courts of; trade, manufactures and population of, 571; statesmen, jurists, literary men, and arts and artists in, 572-575.
Emuckfau, Battle of, 406.
England, Monarchy restored in; a royal state trick, 71; Revolution in, and its effect in America, 105.
English-American Colonists, Character and condition of, 185.
English, The, in America, 161.
English, The, in America, encroach on Dutch domain, 42.
Enterprise and *Boxer*, Battle between, 418.
Episcopacy in the Colonies, 185-189.
"Equal Rights" Party, Action of the; dissolution of the, 482.

Erie Canal, Genesis of the, 382, 384; beginning of the construction of the, 384, 385; preliminary measures adopted; meeting in favor of the (note), 450; ridiculed and opposed, 451; first boat on the, 453; influence of the; prophecy concerning the (note), 468; celebration of the opening of the, 463-468.
Erie, Fort, Capture of, by Americans, 422, 423; siege of, and sortie from, 426.
Esopus (Kingston), Settlement at, 26; trouble with the Indians at, 68.
Estaing, Count de, commands a French naval force on the American coasts, 295.
Europe, Condition of, in 1814, 420.
Eutaw Spring, Battle at, 325.
Evertsen, Admiral Cornelis, 88; proclamation of, 89.
Expedition against Canada, 115, 415-417.

F.

Falmouth (now Portland), burned, 252.
Fashions in New York changed, 476.
Faulkner, Major, at Craney Island, 418.
Federal Celebration at New York, 351; consequences of the, 352.
Federal Party, Chief leaders of the, in New York, 346; overthrow of the, 379; second overthrow of the, 386.
Federalist, The, 388.
Federalists and Anti-Federalists, 337.
Fenton, R. E., Governor; biography of (note), 536; and the Thirteenth Amendment of the National Constitution, 538.
Field, Cyrus W., erects a monument at Tappan, 315.
Field, David Dudley, and the Women's Relief Association, 527.
"Fields, The," Great meeting in, addressed by young Hamilton, 208.
Fillmore, Millard, Vice-President of the United States, 507.
Financial scheme, A, denounced (note), 201.
Fish, Hamilton, Governor, Biography of (note), 507.
Fitzroy, Lord, Reception of; marries Governor Cosby's daughter (note), 144.
Five Nations, Grant of land by the, to the English, 128.

INDEX. 601

Fletcher, Benjamin, Governor, 117; in conflict with the Assembly; at Hartford, 118.
Forbes, General Joseph, Tardy movements of, 176.
Forman, Joshua, and the Erie Canal, 383, 474.
Forsythe, Major Benjamin, at Ogdensburg, 401, 408.
Fort Amsterdam built, 29; treaty with Indians at, 52; taken by British troops and named Fort James, 78.
Fort Casimer built, 59; captured and named Fort Trinity, 66.
Fort Christina, 41.
Fort Clinton captured by the British, 283, 284.
Fort Duquesne, Capture of, 177.
Fort Edward, built by General Lyman, 165.
Fort Good Hope, 26.
Fort James, Name of, changed to William Henry, 89.
Fort Lee, 243; commanded by General Greene, 248; abandoned, 250.
Fort Montgomery captured by the British, 283, 284.
Fort Nassau on the Delaware, 26.
Fort Necessity, Surrender of, 162.
Fort Niagara captured by the English, 179, 180.
Fort Orange built, 26, 46; surrendered and named Albany, 78.
Fort Plain, 290; settlement desolated, 306.
Fort Schuyler besieged by St. Leger, 269; garrison of, 270; relieved (note), 273.
Fort Washington captured by the British, 249.
Fort William Henry, 166; winter expedition against (note), 171; massacre at, 171, 172.
Forts Mifflin and Mercer captured by the British, 289.
Forty Fort, Surrender of, 294.
France, Treaty of Alliance with, 294.
Francis, Dr. J. W., Notice of, 575.
Franklin, Dr. B., commissioner in Canada, 239.
Fraser, General, commands grenadiers; fatally wounded; death and burial of (note), 280.
Fraunce, Samuel (note), 331.

Free Colonists, Commercial privileges extended to, 44.
Free School District Libraries established, 487.
Free School Society, 376; members of the (note), 376.
Free Schools established by law, 505, 506; law for, repealed, 507, 508.
Free-will Offerings of the loyal people during the Civil War, 529.
Fremont, John Charles, candidate for the Presidency of the United States, 511.
French, Activity of the, in seeking power; settlements of the, 160; aggressive movements of the, 161.
French emigrants, Effect of, on New York society, 358.
French forces at Newport, 309.
French and Indian War, The, 162-184.
French Neutrals—Acadians, 163.
French Revolution, Influence of, in America, 353.
French vessel driven from Manhattan Harbor, 26.
Frenchtown, Massacre at, 404.
Freneau, Philip, "Poet of the Revolution," 592.
Friends or Quakers, Attitude of, during the Civil War (note), 524.
Frontenac, Count Louis, Governor of Canada; conduct toward the Five Nations; builds a fort, 91; invades New York, 114; performs an Indian wardance, 116; invades the Iroquois country, 118. 119; death of, 119.
Fry, Colonel Joshua, commands Virginia troops, 162.
Fulton, Robert, and navigation by steam; biography of (note), 377.

G.

Gabry, Timothy, Alderman, 85.
Gage, Thomas, fortifies Boston Neck, 215.
Gaines, General E. P., succeeds General Ripley, 425.
Galphin Fort, Capture of, 325.
Gardiner, Lyon, settles on Gardiner's Island, 42.
Gaspé, Burning of the (note), 204.
Gates, General Horatio, supersedes General

602 INDEX.

Schuyler; on Bemis's Heights, 274; conduct of, 276; jealousy of, displayed, 277; receives thanks and a gold medal from Congress, 282.

General Congress, A, recommended, 207; delegates to, from New York, appointed, 209.

Genet, Edmund C., Minister of the French Republic, 353; arrival of, 354; fits out privateers, 354, 355; reception of, at Philadelphia; banquet in honor of (note), 355; conduct of, 356; reception of, at New York; recalled; remains in America and marries, 357.

George III., First arbitrary act of, toward the Colonies, 189; ascends the throne, 192.

Germain, Lady Betty, Remark of, 373.

German mercenaries in Canada, 240.

Gerry, Elbridge, Vice-President of the United States, 398.

Gheel, Maximilian Van, a *schepen*, 62.

Glover, General, on Bemis's Heights, 280.

Godyn, Samuel, a patroon, 32.

Golden Hill, New York City, Skirmish on, 200.

Gorham and Phelps, purchase land in New York State, 335.

Gouverneur, Abraham, Leisler's secretary, imprisoned, 110; pardoned, 111.

Graham, James, first Recorder of New York (note), 100.

Granger, Francis, Anti-Masonic candidate for Governor, 476.

Grant, British General, in battle of Long Island, 244.

Grant, Mrs., of Laggan's description of social life at Albany (note), 151.

Grasse, Count de, in the West Indies, 321; before Yorktown with a French fleet, 322.

Great Britain and Holland, War between, 86; declares war against France in 1756, 167; causes of war between, and the United States, 387; United States declares war against, 387, 388; opposition to the war with, 388.

Greeley, Horace, candidate for the Presidency of the United States, 548.

Green Mountain Boys, 191; at Ticonderoga, 218; at Crown Point, 219; employment of, in the army, 223.

Greene, General Nathaniel, in command on Long Island; sick, 243; in South Carolina, 323; famous retreat of, 324; fights Cornwallis at Guilford Court-House; defeated near Camden; march of, toward Ninety-Six, 324; siege of Ninety-Six, by; on the High Hills of Santee; battle of, at Eutaw Springs; rewards given to, 325.

Grinnell, Moses H., at a war-meeting; biography of (note), 522.

Grotius condemned to imprisonment, 20.

Guilford Court-House, Battle at, 324.

Gustavus Adolphus of Sweden killed at Lutzen, 41.

H.

Hague, Residence of Counts of Holland at the, 16.

Hale, Nathan, Fate of (note), 246.

Halleck, Fitz-Greene, 573, 574.

Hamilton, Andrew, defends Zenger, 145; address of, to the jury, 146; triumph of, and honors to, 146, 147.

Hamilton, Alexander, speaks at "The Great Meeting" in The Fields, 208; at Arnold's headquarters, 313; in the National Convention, 336; biography of (note), 337; the chief writer of *The Federalist*, 338; in the State Convention at Poughkeepsie, in 1788, 341; Secretary of the United States Treasury, 346; helps in the establishment of the Board of Regents in New York, 362; death of, 375; allusion to, 572.

Hamilton and Burr, 373, 375; duel between, 374, 375.

Hampton, General Wade, in Northern New York; character of, 413, 415.

Hard-Cider Campaign, The, 494.

Hardy, Commodore Charles, Character of, 419.

Hardy, Sir Charles, Governor of New York, 160; leaves the province, 186.

Harlem, Village of, founded, 69.

Harlem Plains, Battle on, 247.

Harper, James, Mayor of New York, 485.

Harper's Ferry, John Brown's raid at, 515.

Harrison, Richard, United States Attorney for New York, 346.

Harrison, General Wm. Henry, marches for the recovery of Michigan, 403, 404;

INDEX.

builds Fort Meigs, 404 ; wins a battle at the Thames, and recovers Michigan, 406 ; becomes President of the United States, 494.

Hartford, Conference at, between the Dutch and English, in 1650 ; and the result, 58, 59.

Hartford Convention, The, in 1814, 443, 444.

Hathorn, Colonel, commands troops at Minisink, 301, 302.

Hattem, Arendt Van, burgomaster, 62.

Haviland, Colonel, at Montreal, 184.

Hawley, Jesse, and the Erie Canal, 383.

Hawley, Jesse, Superintendent of Public Instruction, 446 ; removal of, 454.

Heath, General William, in command in the Highlands, 248.

Heathcote, Caleb, Biography of (note), 132, 133.

Hell-Gate, 23.

Hendrick, King, at Lake George ; and William Johnson, 165 ; death of, 166.

Hendricksen, Captain, before the States-General, 16, 18 ; exploring voyage of, 18.

Herkimer, Nicholas, commands Tryon County militia, 270 ; defeated at Oriskany ; biography of, 271 ; death of, 272.

Heyn, Admiral, Exploit and death of, 30.

Hi-a-wat-ha, Death of daughter of, 4 ; services and departure of, 4, 5.

Hickey, one of Washington's Life Guard, Crime and execution of, 236.

Hobkirk's Hill, Battle of, 324.

Hoboken, Massacre of Indians at, 48.

Hoffman, John T., Governor, 541 ; biography of (note), 542.

"Holder of the Heavens," Legend of, 3, 4.

Holland, Prosperity of, anticipated ; social condition of, 19–21.

Hollandare, Peter, 52.

Holmes, Captain, puts a house on the site of Hartford, 38.

Holt's *Journal*, Devices on, 211, 212.

Hone, Philip, Mayor of New York ; biography of (note), 464.

Hongers, Hans, 14.

Hopkins, Commodore Esek, Exploits of, 252.

Hornet and *Peacock*, Battle between, 417.

Horseshoe Bend, Battle of, 407.

Hotham, Commodore, on the Hudson River, 283.

Hough, Franklin B., historian, 574.

Howe, Lord, on Lake George, 173, 174 ; death of, 174 ; biography of (note), 175.

Howe, Admiral Richard, before New York with a fleet ; a peace commissioner, 242.

Howe, General William, goes to Halifax from Boston, 235 ; before New York with troops ; joined by Sir Henry Clinton, 242 ; in battle on Long Island, 244 ; at White Plains, 248 ; captures Fort Washington, 249 ; in battle of Brandywine Creek, 286 ; takes Philadelphia, 287 ; succeeded by Sir Henry Clinton, 295.

Howe and Washington confront each other in New Jersey, 286.

Hubbardton, Battle of, 267.

Hudson, Henry, Biography of (note) ; seeks a northeast passage to India, 10, 11 ; discovers New York Bay, 11 ; voyages on the river that bears his name, 12 ; detained in England, 13 ; perishes in Polar waters, 14.

Hudson Highlands, Obstructions of the river in the, 253.

Hudson River, Names of the (note), 13 ; first trading vessels in the, 14 ; associations of the, 561 ; manors on the, 561–565.

Hughes, Archbishop, and the Common School Fund, 497 ; biography of (note), 496.

Hughson, John, a victim of the "Negro Plot" affair, 153.

Huguenots in New York, 148.

Hull, Captain Isaac, 397.

Hull, General William, in Michigan ; surrenders Detroit, 389.

Hunkers, a political faction, 501.

Hunt, Washington, Governor ; biography of (note) ; administration of, 508.

Hunter, Robert, Governor ; character of, 137, 138 ; brings Palatines to New York, 137 ; administration of, 137, 138.

"Hunters' Lodges" suppressed, 491.

Huntington, Daniel, President of the National Academy of the Arts of Design, 576.

Hutchings, William, one of the last two

604 INDEX.

survivors of the Continental Army (note), 329.
Hutchinson, Anne, Sketch of (note), 49.
Hyde, Sir Edward (Lord Cornbury), Governor of New York, 129.

I.

Independence, Yearnings of the people for; Paine's plea for, 236; resolutions for, adopted; Declaration of, adopted, 237, 238.
Indian Affairs, Board of Commissioners of, 93, 227.
Indian Fort (note), 17; Champlain's attack on the, 17, 18.
Indian tribes in New York, 3.
Indian war, A fierce, kindled by Kieft, 49.
Ingoldsby, Richard, demands possession of the fort at New York, 109, 110; notice of, 117; Acting-Governor of New York, 134; biography of (note), 186.
Inman, Henry, artist, 575.
Investigating Committee, concerning the Erie Canal, Work of the, 554.
Iroquois Confederacy, Origin of the, 3-5; Indian name of the, 6; polity of the, 6-9; totemic system of the, 7; customs of the, 8, 9; final disappearance of the, 334.
Irving, Peter, Reference to, 572.
Irving, Washington, Biography of (note), 572.
Izard, General George, on the Niagara frontier; biography of (note), 426.

J.

Jackson, Andrew, at war with the Creek Indians, 406; at Pensacola, Mobile, and New Orleans, 441; gains a victory at New Orleans; honors awarded to, 442; President of the United States, 474.
James II. King of England, and the New York "Charter of Liberties," 101; attempts of, to make the Roman Catholic the State religion; and French Jesuit missions in New York, 103, 104; flies to France, 104.
James, Major, Country residence of, desolated, 196.
Jarvis, J. Wesley, artist, 575.

Jay, John, and the State Constitution, 257, 258; biography of (note), 257; first Chief-Justice of the State, 260; one of the writers of *The Federalist*, 338; Chief-Justice of the United States Supreme Court, 346; Governor of New York, 363; a political writer, 572.
Jay, William, Notice of; biography of (note), 451.
Jay's treaty considered, 358, 359; burned by the populace; treatment of, at Charleston, 359.
Jefferson, Thomas, writes the Declaration of Independence, 227; his suspicions of the Federalists. 253, 254; his opinion of Hamilton; leader of the Republican Party, 354; Vice-President of the United States, 363; President of the United States, 366.
Jersey, The, a prison-ship (note), 149.
Jesuit missions in America, 90; active in New York, 140; influence of the, 160.
Jogues, Father, Notice of, 46.
Johnson, Guy, Indian agent, 224; holds Indian councils, 225, 226.
Johnson, Sir John, at Johnson Hall, 227; gives his parole; biography of (note), 231; breaks his parole, 240; flight of, to Canada; commissioned a brigadier-general, 241; leads Canadians and Indians, 264, 303; desolates his home neighborhood, 305; desolates Stone Arabia, 308.
Johnson, Lady, conveyed to Albany, 241.
Johnson, William, at a conference at Albany, 157; Indian commissioner in command of provincial troops, 164, 165; and King Hendrick (note), 165; in battle at Lake George; builds Fort William Henry, 166; knighted, 166, 167; captures Fort Niagara, 179; at Montreal, 184; biography of (note), 224.
Johnson, William, and the rebellion in Canada; biography of, 490.
Johnson, William Samuel, first President of King's College; biography of (note), 188.
Johnson and Lyman contrasted, 167.
Johnson's Royal Green, 270; defeated and dispersed, 271.
Johnston, Colonel, British commander at Stony Point, 300.

INDEX.

Jones, Captain Jacob, wins a naval victory, 397.
Jones, John Paul, wins a naval victory, 305.
Jones, Samuel, Chief-Justice; biography of (note), 474.
Joris, Captain Adriaens, commands the *New Netherland*, 25; constructs a fort on the site of Albany, 26.
Journalism, Revolution in, 482, 483.
Jumonville, French commander, slain, 162.

K.

Kalb, Baron de, in South Carolina, 309.
Keane, General, defeated below New Orleans, 441.
Kent, James, and Colonel Burr, 373; Chancellor, portrait of; biography of, 448.
Kentuckians, War-cry of the, 404.
Kidd, William, commands a privateer, 121; becomes a pirate and is hanged; treasure of, 122.
Kieft, Governor William, succeeds Van Twiller; De Vries's opinion of, 39; energetic rule of; builds a *harberg* and church, 40; snubbed by the people; calls heads of families to a consultation, 43–46; makes war on the Indians; sends soldiers against fugitive Indians at Hoboken, 48; asks the Commonalty to appoint a committee of conference, 49; recalled; threatened, 51; departure and death of, 53.
King George, Equestrian statue of, 199.
King George's War, 155.
King, John A., Governor, Biography of (note), 513; recommends the extension of the right of suffrage to colored men, 514.
King Philip's War, 93.
King William's War, 114.
King, Rufus, United States Senator; biography of (note), 341.
King's (now Columbia) College, founded and chartered, 187, 188.
Kings and Queens counties, Territory of, 98.
King's Mountain, Battle on, 309.
Kingston (note), 262; burned by the British, 286.
Kip, Jacob, Secretary of New Amsterdam, 63; alderman; imprisoned, 92.

Klock's Field, Battle at, 308.
Knowlton, Colonel, Death of, 247.
Knyphausen, General, leader of German troops, 244; in command of Germans at the capture of Fort Washington, 249.
Konick, Frederick de, commander of Stuyvesant's flag-ship in the Delaware, 67.
Kregier, Martin, burgomaster, 62.

L.

La Colle Mills, Battle at, 421.
Lafayette, Marquis de, joins the American army, 286; appointed to commission an expedition against Canada; loyalty to Washington; deceived by Gates, 288, 289; in Virginia, 321; in New York, the nation's guest, 461.
Lake Champlain, British force on, in 1776, 252; military affairs near, 414.
Lake Erie, Naval battle on, 405, 406.
Lamb, John, an active Son of Liberty, 205; addresses the people, 206; biography of (note), 206; removes cannons from the fort at New York, 232; home of, attacked by a mob, 352.
Lamb, Martha J., historian, 574.
Lancastrian and Pestalozzian systems of education, 488, 489.
Lansing, John, Chancellor, 371.
Lee, Charles, sent by Washington to New York, 234; disobedience and treason of, 253.
Lee, Gideon, Mayor of New York; wounded by rioters, 484.
Lee, Colonel Henry, in South Carolina, 324.
Lee, Richard Henry, offers resolutions for independence, 237.
Leggett, William, Notice of; biography of (note), 482.
Legislative reforms, 471.
L'Hommedieu, Ezra, and popular education; biography of, 362.
Leisler, Jacob, helps the Huguenots, 105; chosen chief ruler, temporarily, 106; organizes a provisional government, 107; tenders the fort and his power to the royal governor; arrested, 110; condemned to death, 111; executed, 112.
Leisler and Milborne, Property of, confis-

cated, and afterward restored, 112 ; remains of, lie in state at the City Hall, and buried in a cemetery, 124.
Leislerians or Democrats in political control, 129.
Lemon slaves' case, The, 512.
Levi, General de, attempts to recover Quebec, 183, 184.
Lewis, Morgan, Governor ; biography of (note), 374.
Liberty Pole erected, 199.
Liberal Republican Party, 548.
Life Guard of Washington tampered with ; origin of the (note), 235.
Lincoln, Abraham, President of the United States, 511 ; calls for troops, 522 ; re-elected President, 536 ; assassination of, 538.
Lincoln, General Benjamin, joins General Gates, 275 ; attack of, on Savannah, 305 ; surrenders Charleston, 308.
Liquor Bill, Prohibitory, vetoed, 510.
Literature Fund established, 361.
Livingston, Gilbert, in Constitutional Convention at Poughkeepsie, 341.
Livingston, John and Mary, 562.
Livingston, Philip, and the Society Library, 187 ; President of the Provincial Congress ; biography of (note), 221.
Livingston, Robert, Secretary of the Board of Commissioners of Indian Affairs, 93 ; controls the Provincial Convention ; accused of uttering treasonable words, and goes to New England, 108, 109 ; engages in a privateering scheme ; a friend of Kidd, 121, 122 ; changes his political position, 122.
Livingston, Robert R., first Chancellor of the State of New York, 264 ; administers the oath of office to Washington ; biography of (note), 345 ; Minister at the French Court, 371; becomes a Republican, 364 ; assists Fulton in his steam navigation scheme, 377 ; and the Manor House, 563.
Livingston, Walter, first Speaker of the New York Assembly, 262.
Livingston, William, a political and theological writer, 189, 213 ; prophetic appeal of, 201 : on immigrants into New York (note), 571, 572.

Livingstons in America, Ancestors of the, 562.
Livingston's Manor desolated, 286 ; account of the, 562.
Loco-foco Party, Origin of the name of the, 481.
Long Island, English settlements on, 42 ; revolt on, 73 ; preparations for battle on, 243 ; landing of British troops on ; battle on, 244 ; expedition against Tories on, 315.
Loudoun, Lord, succeeds Shirley in command of troops ; biography of (note) ; sends Abercrombie to America, 167 ; on expedition against Louisburg, 170 ; bad conduct of, 169, 170.
Louisburg, Expedition against, 155, 156 ; capture of, 173.
Lovelace, Francis, Governor ; biography of (note), 87 ; character of, 88.
Lovelace, Lord John, Governor, calls a new Assembly, 133.
Loyalists, Flight of, from New York ; confiscation of property of the; return of the, 330.
Lundy's Lane, Battle of, 425.
Luyck, Ægidius, burgomaster, 89 ; imprisoned, 92.
Lyman, General Phineas ; biography of (note), 164 ; lieutenant of General Wm. Johnson ; builds Fort Edward, 165 ; gains the victory at Lake George, 166.

M.

McArthur, Duncan, Raid of, 433.
McCrea, Jane, Tragedy of, 267.
McDonnell, Lieutenant-Colonel, attacks Ogdensburg, 408.
Macdonough, Thomas, on Lake Champlain, 414, 415 ; commands in a naval battle on Lake Champlain ; biography of (note), 429.
McDougall, Alexander, issues an offensive hand-bill ; imprisoned, and regarded as a martyr, 202.
McDougall, Sir Duncan, General Pakenham's aide, 442.
McEvers, James, stamp-distributor, resigns, 186.
McHenry, Fort, Bombardment of, 437.

INDEX.

Mackinaw, Attempt to take Fort, 432.
McKenzie, Wm. Lyon, and the insurrection in Canada, 489, 490.
McLeod, Trial and acquittal of, 491.
McLane, Secretary Louis, writes Jackson's nullification proclamation (note), 480.
Macomb, Alexander, an extensive landowner in Northern New York, 335.
Macomb, General, in command at Plattsburgh, 427–431; biography of (note), 430.
Macomb and Macdonough, recipients of honors, 431.
McNeil, Major, in battle of Chippewa, 424.
Madison, James, one of the writers of *The Federalist*, 338; elected president of the United States, 381; re-elected, 398.
Malden burned, 406.
Manning, Captain John, surrenders New York to the Dutch; punished (note), 89.
Manhattan Island, 1, 13; purchase of, from the Indians, 27.
Manhattan, Village of; an Indian murdered near, 29; flight of settlers to, 30.
Manhattan Water-works and Bank, 365.
Map of New Netherland, 36, 37.
Marauding expedition on the shores of Connecticut, 264.
Marcy, Wm. L., captures a British flag, 401; Comptroller of the State, 460; Governor; biography of (note), 479.
Marin, M., a French officer, 156, 170.
Marion, Francis, the "Swamp Fox," 309.
Mary, Queen, Death of, 129.
Maryland, Dutch Embassy sent to, 68; invasion of, 468.
Massachusetts, First emission of bills of credit of, 116; claims of, to New York territory adjusted; (note), 335.
Massasoit and his family (note), 93.
Matthews, Mayor, of New York, and a plot against Washington, 236.
May, Captain Jacobsen, and the Walloons, 25.
Mayflower, The, lands emigrants at Cape Cod, 24.
Medal, A descriptive French, 116.
Megopolensis, Dominie, with Stuyvesant, against the Swedes, 67.
Meigs, Colonel R. J., Exploit of, in Long Island, 316.

Meigs, Fort, relieved, 404.
Melyn, Cornelis, Notice of (note), 51, 62.
Mennonites settle near Swaanendael; plundered and ruined, 72.
Mercer, Colonel, in command at Oswego, 168; surrenders, 169.
Metropolitan Museum of Art (note), 575.
Michigan recovered, 403, 406.
Mifflin and Mercer, Forts, captured, 287.
Militia of New York, Arrangement of the, 389.
Milborne, Jacob, sent to Albany, 107, 108; addresses the people; leaves Albany, 108; condemned to death and executed, 111, 112.
Miller, Colonel James, Exploit of, at Lundy's Lane, 425.
Minisink, Raid upon the settlement of, 301.
Minuit, Peter, Director of New Netherland; purchases Manhattan Island, 27; Governor of New Sweden; defies Kieft, 41; death of, 52.
Minute Men, Organization of, 207.
Mitchell, Samuel L., Speech of, at the canal celebration; biography of (note), 466; notice of, 575.
Monckton, Robert, Governor, 192.
Monmouth, Battle of, 295.
Monongahela, Battle of, 163.
Montcalm, Marquis de, French commander, captures Oswego, 168; biography of (note); dances with the Indians. 170; captures Fort William Henry, 171; in command at Quebec, 181, 182; death of, 183.
Montgomery, John, Governor, Character of; administration of, 141; death of, 142.
Montgomery, Richard, at Albany, 227; biography of (note), 228; advances upon St. Johns, 228, 229; captures it and Montreal, 229; attacks Quebec; death of, 230.
Montmorenci, Falls of, Battle near, 181.
Montreal, Indians gathered at, 170; captured, 229.
Moody, Sir J. Henry, patentee of Gravesend (note), 49.
Moody, Lady Deborah, Sketch of (note), 49.
Mooers, General Benjamin, commands militia; biography of (note), 427; in battle of Plattsburgh, 430.

608 INDEX.

Moore, Sir Henry, Governor; administration of, 193; death of, 201.
Morgan, General Daniel, defeats Tarleton at the Cowpens; rewarded; joined by Greene, 323; in battle on Bemis's Heights, 275.
Morgan, Edwin D., Governor; biography of (note), 514; conservative position of, 518, 519; energetic action of, in upholding the National Government, 525, 526.
Morgan, Louis, historian, 575.
Morgan, William, and the Masonic fraternity, 471, 472.
Morris, George P., 575.
Morris, Gouverneur, Remarks of, concerning Zenger's trial (note), 147; biography of (note), 382; a political writer, 572.
Morris, Lewis, Chief-Justice, 143.
Moravian Towns, Battle near the, 406.
Morse, Samuel F. B., artist and scientist, 500, 575.
Mott, Samuel, to Governor Trumbull, 228.
Mott, Valentine, and Women's Relief Committee, 529.
Mount Defiance, taken possession of by the British, 266.
Mount Independence, Garrison of; surrender of, 265.
Munro, Colonel, surrenders Fort William Henry, 171.
Murray, General, 181; in possession of Quebec, 183, 184.
Murray, Lindley, author of English Grammar and Reader, 572.
Mutiny Act extended to New York; opposed by the Assembly, 200; and the people, 201.

N.

Nancy, a tea-ship, returns to England, 206.
Nanfan, John, Lieutenant-Governor; dissolves the Assembly, 128.
Nassau, Fort, below the site of Albany, built, 15; abandoned, 18.
National affairs, Critical state of, 514–516.
National Capital threatened, 525; isolated, 526.
National Convention at Philadelphia frames a new Constitution, 336, 337.
National Constitution framed, 336, 337; adopted by New York, 341; XVth Amendment of the, adopted, 542, and withdrawn, 543.
National currency, A, established, 535.
National Government, The, warned of danger, 436; weakly administered, 521.
Native American Party, The, 485.
Naval movements on Lake Champlain, 251.
Naval events on the ocean, 417, 418, and 438, 439.
Navigation, Steam, on the Hudson River, 377.
Navy, First Continental, 222, 252.
New Amstel founded and perished, 72.
New Amsterdam, 59; organized as a city; municipal officers of, 62; emigrants from New England at, 63, 64; popular assembly at, 64; city seal of, sent to, 66; menaced with destruction by Indians, 67, 68; social aspects of, 69, 70; described, 79; social condition of the people of, 80–82.
Neutrality, Proclamation of, 354.
New England coasts, Events on the, 433.
New Hampshire Committee of Safety, Action of the, 228.
New Hampshire Grants, The, 190, 191; events on the, 316.
New Haven Colony, The, 58.
Needham, Robert, councilman, 84.
Negro Plot in 1712, 138; in 1741, 152, 154.
Newburgh Letters or Addresses, The, 327; action of Washington on the, 328.
New Gottenburg, Fort, 52.
New Jersey, Latin name of, 78; given to Berkeley and Carteret, 86; Washington's flight across, 253.
New Netherland, Province of, created, 28; government of, under Dutch rule, 79.
New Plymouth, Relations between, and Manhattan, 56, 57; Dutch mission to, 57.
New Sweden, 41.
Newspapers in New York, 211.
New York City, Government of, 85; name of, changed to New Orange, 89; city and county of, 97; political divisions of (note), 99; state of society at, 151; important social events in, 186; British invasion of; great fire in 1776, 247;

INDEX. 609

evacuation of, by the British troops, 331; Washington with civil officers enters; civil government re-established in, 331; the foundations of its greatness laid, 332; residence of the National Government at; inauguration of President Washington at, 344; condition of, one hundred years ago, 350, 351; at the beginning of the nineteenth century, 367, 368; benevolent institutions in, 369; churches in, 370; patriotic popular movements at, 434; grand canal celebration at, 463-468; Mayor first elected by the people; conservatism of the merchants of the, 520; charter of, amended, 543; plundered by the "Tweed Ring," 545-547; other plunderers (note), 547; attractive features of, 566, 567; harbor of, 567.

New York Province; area, topography, and canals of, 1; farms, population, manufactories, birthplace of, 2; Indian tribes in, 3; first political organization of the; conduct of divine worship in the, 84; laws imposed upon the people of the, 85; divided into counties, 87, 88; consolidated with New England, 103; violence of party spirit in; social condition of, 148, 149; state of political society in, 204; delegate of, in the Continental Congress, 210, 215; Provincial Congress of, 215, 216; members of the Provincial Congress of (note), 216; patriotic efforts of the, 217, 218; condition of, 221; important events in, 256.

New York State, First Constitution of, adopted; features of the, 259, 260; choice of State officers of, 262; session of Legislature of; claims to the soil of, 333; seals of (note), 333, 334; reserves the right to collect import duties, 335; advocates more power for Congress in the matter of revenue, 336; Legislature of first, sanctions a movement toward the formation of a National Constitution (note), 336; Constitutional Convention of, 338, 339; members of the, 339; ratifies the National Constitution; first member of the National Congress from, 341; political divisions of, 342; early settlements in the interior of, 342, 343; emigrants from New England to, 342; political parties in, 343; power of the Governor of; number of voters in, 346; inland navigation of, 347; recuperation of, 349; ruling families in, 371; defences of, 380; measures for defence of, provided, 448; population, resources and influence of, 458; new era in history of, 462; condition of, 517; Legislative action of, 517-519; prompt response of, to the President's call for troops, 522; patriotism, generosity and faith of, 526; contributions of men and money for the Civil War, in 1864, by, 537, 538; decrease of, in population during the war; patriotic resolutions of the Legislature of; adopts the XIVth Amendment to the National Constitution; a free school system for, 539; revised Constitution of, rejected, 540; political divisions of, 556; new State House of; funded debts of; population of (note), 557; industrial products of, 558, 559; rank of, in intelligence and wealth, 559, 560; church organizations in, 560.

New York on the New Hampshire Grants, Relation of, 189-191.

Niagara, Fort, Artillery duel at, 402.

Niagara frontier in Canada seized by the Americans, 410; desolation of the Niagara frontier, 417.

Nicola, Colonel, proposes a kingship for Washington, 327.

Nicolls, Matthias, Secretary of the province of New York; provincial council of, 84 Speaker of the Provincial Assembly, 84.

Nicolls, Richard, commands an expedition against New Netherland; surrender of the province to, 75-78; Governor of biography of (note), 87.

Nicholson, Francis, Lieutenant-Governor, deserts his post, 107.

Nine, Council of, The, 56; papers of, seized by Stuyvesant; sends a memorial and remonstrance to the States-General; asks for a burgher government, 61, 62.

Ninety-Six, Fort, Siege of, 325.

Non-importation League, 197.

Normal College at New York (note), 497.

Normal School at Albany, 488.

North, Lord, Retirement of, 323.

North Point, Battle of; death of General Ross at, 437.

Northern New York, Events in, 420, 421.
Nullification movement suppressed, 480.
Nuptials of the lakes and the sea, 466.

O.

Oblong, The, 142.
O'Conor, Charles, and the "Tweed Ring," 547.
Ogden, Robert, 196.
Ogdensburg, Attacks upon, 401, 408.
Ohio country, Conflicting claims to the, 161.
Onondaga country protected, 128; expedition against the, 301.
Onrust (Restless), first ship built on Manhattan Island, 15.
Ontario, Lake, Vessels on, 390, 391.
Orangeburg, British forces at, and retreat from, 325.
Orange County, Territory of, 98.
Ordinance for special privileges, 15.
Osborne, Sir Danvers, Governor, 159.
Oswego, Capture of, by the British, 421.
Otis, James, opposes Writs of Assistance, 194.
Oxenstierna, Count of, sends a Swedish colony to the Delaware, 41.

P.

Paine, Thomas, writes "Common Sense," 236.
Paine, Judge, decision of, in the Lemon case, Effects of the, 512, 513.
Pakenham, General, commands the British at New Orleans, 441; death of, 442.
Palatines sent to New York, 137.
Paoli Tavern, Massacre near, 286.
Papineau, Joseph, and the insurrection in Canada, 489.
Paris, Treaty of, 185.
Parliament, Arbitrary acts of the, 201.
Partisan and personal warfare, 372.
Paterson, General, on Bemis's Heights, 280.
Patricians and Tribunes, 204.
Patroon estates, Features of the, 31.
Patroons, New charter for, granted, 44.
Paulding, James K., Notice of, 572.
Pauw, Michael, a patroon, 32.
Peace commissioners, Foolish acts of, 242, 246.

Peace commissioners appointed by Parliament, 295.
Peace faction, The, 420, 443; movements of the, and Vallandigham, 532, 533.
Peace with Great Britain, 442; rejoicing for the return of, 449; treaties of, signed, 323.
Pelgrave, Paul (note), 14.
Pemaquid, Indian runner from, to Frontenac, 116.
Penn, William, receives a grant of territory, 94, 95.
Pensacola, British driven from, 441.
People's Party, 460.
Pepperell, William, captures Louisburg; biography of (note), 156.
Perry, Oliver Hazard, on Lake Erie, 405, 406; biography of (note), 405; in an attack on Fort George, 410; wins a naval victory, 405, 406.
Petition to the King, 214.
Phelps and Gorham purchase lands, 335, 343.
Philadelphia menaced, 435; National Convention at, in 1787, 336, 337.
Philipse, Adolph, 143.
Philipse, Frederick, last "Lord of the Manor," 56; and Society Library, 187.
Philipse, Family and Manor of, 564, 565.
Phillips, General William, Burgoyne's lieutenant, 275; with Arnold in Virginia, 321.
Phipps, Sir William, naval commander, 115; before Quebec, 116; also note.
Pierce, Franklin, President of the United States, 509.
Pike, Zebulon M., attacks York; biography of (note), 409; death of, 410.
Pilgrims, The, found New Plymouth, 24.
Piquet, Father, 156.
Piracy during Fletcher's administration, 120.
Pitt, William, Prime Minister, 172; energetic and wise action of, 173; superseded by the Earl of Bute, 192; statue of, erected at New York, 199.
Plattsburgh, Naval battle near, 429; battle on land at; Americans victorious at; British retreat from, 430; "The siege of Plattsburgh," a song (note), 431.

INDEX.

Plockhoy, Peter, leader of the Mennonites, 72.

Plowden, Sir Edmund, Absurd claim of, 52.

Point Levi, English batteries at, 181.

Political division of the State, 556.

Political parties and schemes, 379.

Political and theological discussions, 213.

Pontiac's conspiracy, 185, 186 (note).

Poor, General Enoch, in battle on Bemis's Heights, 278.

Pope, The, and James II., 103, 106.

Popular education, Apathy of the people concerning (note), 495.

Porter, Captain David, Famous cruise of, 418.

Porter, General Peter B., at Black Rock, 413 ; at Chippewa, 422.

Poughkeepsie, Flight of Legislature to, from Kingston, 286.

Prence, Thomas, at Hartford, 1650, 58.

Press, Freedom of the, vindicated, 147.

Prevost, Sir George, in Canada, 408 ; at Sackett's Harbor, 411, 412 ; invades New York ; advances upon Plattsburgh ; biography of (note), 428 ; hasty retreat from Plattsburgh, 430, 431.

Prideaux, General, besieges Fort Niagara ; death of, 179.

Prince of Wales, Alleged birth of, 103.

Princess, The, wrecked, 53.

Princeton, Battle of, 255.

Printz, John, Governor of New Sweden instructions to, 52 ; friendly relations of, with Stuyvesant, 59 ; succeeded by John Risingh, 66.

Prisons and prison-ships, 249.

Privateers, American, 439, 440.

Privateering association, 120.

Privy Council, The British (note), 169.

Proctor and Tecumtha at Forts Meigs and Stephenson, 404.

Provincial Congress, Migration of the, 250.

Public Instruction, State Superintendent of, created, 510.

Public property, Seizure of, by patriots, 215.

Public School Society and ward schools in New York City consolidated, 510.

Public-school system in New York City, 544.

Putnam, Israel, Rescue of (note), 172 ; in command on Long Island, 244 ; commands the Highland forts, 283.

Q.

Quaker Hill, Battle of, 296.

Quakers at New Amsterdam, 71.

Queen Anne's War, 132.

Queen Esther, 294.

Queenstown, Battle of, 393-396.

Quebec, Surrender of, refused (note), 116 ; expedition against, 180 ; siege of, 181-183, 230.

R.

Railways in the State, and their work, 555.

Randall, S. S., and school district libraries, 487-495 ; Deputy Superintendent of Common Schools, 509.

Randolph, Peyton, President of the Continental Congress, 210.

Rangers of Putnam and Rogers (note), 172.

Raritan Indians attacked by the Dutch, 43.

Rawden, General, defeats Greene at Hobkirk's Hill ; abandons Camden, 324.

Rebellion, Beginning of the, 517.

Red Jacket, First public appearance of, 334 ; commands the Indians ; biography of (note), 422.

Regents, Board of, 362.

Reid, Captain S. C., and the *General Armstrong*, 440.

Rensselaer, Killian Van, a patroon, 32 ; power of, 45.

Rensselaerwyck, Colonie of, 33, 44, 46.

Renwick, James, Notice of, 575.

Representative Assembly at New Amsterdam ; defies Governor Stuyvesant ; names of members of the (note), 65.

Representative Council, A first, in New Netherland, 46, 47 : name of the, 47.

Republican Party, Formation of the, 511 ; character of the, 512.

Republicanism appears in New Netherland, 64.

Retreat of the American army from Long Island, 245 ; to Harlem Heights, 247.

Revolution in England, Effect of, in America, 105.

Rhode Island, D'Estaing at; military events on, 296; evacuated by the British, 305.

Riall, General, commands the British at Chippewa, 423, 424; retreats to Queenstown, 424.

Rice, Victor M., first Superintendent of Public Instruction, 510.

Richmond County, Territory of, 98.

Riedesel, General, commands German mercenaries, 240, 264; on Bemis's Heights, 276.

Riedesel, Baroness de, Sketch of (note), 264.

Riker, Richard, Duel of; biography of (note), 372.

Riot between religious factions, 544.

Ripley, General, on the Niagara frontier, 422–425; superseded by General Gaines, 425.

Risingh, John, Governor of New Sweden, 66.

River Indians imposed upon by Kieft and traders, 42.

Rivington, James, abuses the "Sons of Liberty;" printing-house of, destroyed; biography of (note), 233; notice of, 572.

Robinson, Beverly, Correspondence of, with Ethan Allen, 317, 318; biography of (note), 318.

Robinson, Rev. John, and emigration to America, 21.

Rochambeau, Count de, Arrival of, with French troops, 309; biography of (note), 320; leads French troops to the Hudson River, 321.

Rochester, Growth of, 469; Pagan rites at, in 1813 (note), 470.

Rodgers, Commodore John, at Sandy Hook; biography of (note), 397; long cruise of, 418.

Roelandsen, Adam, first schoolmaster at New Amsterdam, 34, 568.

Rogers, Major Robert, Biography of (note), 84.

Roman Catholic priests, Hanging of, authorized by law, 126.

Ross, General, commands British troops in Maryland, 435; death of, 437.

Royal commissioners with Colonel Nicolls at New Amsterdam, 75.

Ruggles, Timothy, in Stamp Act Congress, 196.

Ryswyk, Treaty at, 123.

S.

Sackett's Harbor, Hostilities at, 391, 411.

Safety Fund System, 474.

St. Clair, General, in command at Ticonderoga, 265; abandons Fort Ticonderoga and escapes, 266.

St. Johns, Capture of, 229.

St. Leger invades the Mohawk Valley; operations there, 264–270, 273; notice of (note), 273.

St. Regis, First trophy of the war (1812–1815), taken at, 401.

Sandford, Nathan, Chancellor, 459.

Sanitary fairs and the results, 528.

Saratoga, Destruction of, 156.

Savage, John, Chief-Justice, 459.

Savings-banks established, 553.

Schenectady, Destruction of, 114.

Schmidt, Claas, murdered, 43.

Schoharie Valley, Forts in the, 290; desolation of the, 306.

School System, the Common, Improvements in, suggested, 471.

Schoolcraft, Henry R., authority on Indian life, 573.

Schuyler, Captain John, menaces Montreal, 115.

Schuyler, Mayor Peter, opposes Milborne, 108; influence of, over the Indians, 134; goes to England with Indian sachems; biography of (note), 135; and the germ of the Society Library, 187.

Schuyler, Philip, Life and property of, destroyed at old Saratoga, 157.

Schuyler, Philip, at Oswego; leader of the Opposition in the Assembly, 213, 214; Commanding General of the Northern Department, 222; looks after the Tories in the Mohawk Valley; expedition of, to Johnstown; disarms the Tories, 231; authorized to invade Canada, 223; operations of, in the Mohawk Valley, 224; at Fort Edward; proclamation of, 267, 268; obstructs the march of Burgoyne, 267; indignant because of injustice at a council of war, 273; property of, de-

INDEX. 613

stroyed by the British army (note); entertains Burgoyne at Albany, 281; letter of, to Governor Clinton, 317; first New York member of the National Senate, 341; father of the canal system of New York, 347; journal of, in 1802, 349.

Scott, John, a disturber of the peace in Long Island, 73.

Scott, John Morin, member of a Council of Safety, 260; the first Secretary of State, 262.

Scott, Winfield, on Queenstown Heights, 395; at the capture of Fort George, 410; in command at the battle of Chippewa, 424; at battle of Lundy's Lane, 424, 425.

Seal, The Great, of the province of New York (note), 109; seals of the State (note), 141.

Sears, Isaac, a leading "Son of Liberty;" biography of, 208; arrest of, 216; destroys Rivington's printing-house, 233.

Seneca Nation, The, desolated by Sullivan, 304.

Seventh Regiment, National Guard, quells riots, 485; goes to the field, 528.

Seward, William H., in the State Senate, 476; Governor; biography of (note), 492; first encounter of, with the slave power, 493.

Seymour, Horatio, Governor; biography of (note), 509; vetoes a prohibitory liquor bill, 510; and the Draft Riots, 534.

Sharp, Jacob, gives books for a public library, 187.

Sharpe, Governor, of Maryland, commands Colonial forces, 163.

Sheaffe, General, succeeds Brock in command, 395.

Shirley, General William; biography of (note), 155; contemplates conquests, 157; meets Braddock in conference, 163; commands an expedition against Forts Niagara and Frontenac, which was abandoned; succeeds Braddock in command, 167.

Shute, Swen, commands Swedish soldiers at Fort Casimer, 66.

Simms, Jeptha R., historian, 574.

Six Nations, the, Conference of, with Shirley, 157; council with the (1778), 289; boundary of the territory of the, defined; cession and sales of the lands of, 334.

Skene, Philip, Biography of, 267.

Skenesborough, Flight of Americans to, from Ticonderoga, 266.

Slave trade, The, 138.

Slavery in New York, Abolition of, recommended, 363, 451; final abolition of, in the United States, 531.

Slechtenhorst, Brandt Van, commissary at Rensselaerwyck, defies the authority of Stuyvesant; sketch of (note), 60.

Sloughter, Governor Henry, 109; signs the death-warrant of Leisler and Milborne, 112.

Smith, William, on Lord Cornbury (note), 132; letter of, to Colonel Schuyler (note), 209; historian of New York, 572.

Smith, William, counsel for Zenger, 144.

Smith, William S., Marshal, 346.

Smythe, General, Absurd conduct of, 403.

Social phenomenon, A strange, 548.

Society Library, Founding of the; names of the founders of the, 187.

Sons of Liberty, The, work for Zenger, 145; members of the association of the (note), 195; activity of the, 217.

South Carolina, Partisan leaders in, 309; rebellious position of, 516.

Southwick, Solomon, 399; biography of (note), 447.

Spiegel, Laurens Van der, *schepen*, 89.

Spencer, Ambrose, Biography of (note), 452.

Spencer, John C., Superintendent of Common Schools; biography of, 494.

Stamp Act proposed and opposed, 194–198; effects of the, 197; repeal of the, 198.

Stamp Act Congress at New York, 196.

"Star Spangled Banner, The," Origin of the song of (note), 437.

Stark, John, reconnoitres Ticonderoga, 175.

State Constitutional Convention, Distinguished members of the, 455.

State Government put into operation, 260–262; plan of, arranged by a committee (note), 260.

State Constitution, Revision of the, 455–457.

State Lotteries, 459.

State Park, A, 550.
Staten Island, Colonies on, 42 ; claimed by Lady Carteret, 95.
States-General of Holland, 15.
Statesmen and jurists, 575.
Steamship, The first, that crossed the Atlantic Ocean ; of war, the first (note), 378.
Steenwyck, Cornelis, Mayor and wise councillor ; biography of (note), 88, 89 ; imprisoned, 92.
Stephens, Alexander H., and the Southern Confederacy, 521.
Stephenson, Fort, Defence of, 404.
Steuben, Baron von, in Virginia ; biography of (note), 320, 321.
Stewart, Captain Charles, and the *Constitution* frigate ; biography of (note), 438.
Stewart, Colonel, British commander, retreats from Orangeburg and fights at Eutaw Springs ; retreats to Charleston, 325.
Stirling, Lord, Charter given to, 42.
Stirling, General Lord, in battle on Long Island, 244; made prisoner ; biography of (note), 245.
Stone Arabia desolated, 308.
Stone, William L., reporter in the State Constitutional Convention in 1821, 455 ; historian of the canal celebration ; biography of (note), 463 ; historian and journalist, 574.
Stony Creek, Battle of, 410, 411.
Stony Point, Capture of, by Wayne, 299, 300.
Stony and Verplanck's Points captured by the British, 297, 298.
Stricker, General, in battle of North Point, 437.
Stuart Kings, The, chartered slave-trading companies (note), 138.
Stuyvesant, Peter, Biographical sketch of (note), 53 ; character of ; Director-General of New Netherland ; reception of, at Manhattan, 54 ; policy of, defined ; energetic administration of public affairs by, 55 ; calls a popular convention ; friendly relations with neighbors desired by, 56 ; attempts a settlement of disputes with New England, at Hartford, 58 ; demolishes Fort Nassau on the Delaware ; builds Fort Casimer; improves the capital of New Netherland ; names the capital New Amsterdam, 59 ; has trouble with Van Slechtenhorst and the Council of Nine, 60, 61 ; threatens to abolish The Council of Nine, 62 ; summoned before the States-General, 63 ; withstands the Representative Assembly, 65 ; interview of, with Beeckman ; ordered to retake Fort Casimer, 66 ; conquers New Sweden, 67 ; opposed to religious toleration ; persecutes Quakers, 71 ; alarmed by Captain Scott's statements ; orders an election of delegates to a Provincial Assembly, 74 ; stubborn resistance to the demands of English invaders, 75-78 ; receives a letter from the English commander ; urged to surrender ; tears up the letter in a passion ; the people demand it, 76 ; its fragments gathered up, 77 ; yields to the pressure of friends ; surrenders the city and province, 78 ; death and sepulture of, 83.
Stuyvesant and the Dutch West India Company, 82.
Suffolk County, Territory of, 98.
Sullivan, General John, succeeds General Thomas in Canada, 240 ; in battle on Long Island and made prisoner, 243 ; biography of (note), 302 ; expedition of, in Central New York, 303, 304.
Sumter, Fort, attacked and evacuated, 521.
Sumter, Thomas, the "South Carolina Game Cock," 309.
Sun, The, the first one-cent newspaper published, 483.
Surrender of Burgoyne, Effect of the, 282.
Sutherland, Jacob, Assistant Justice, 459.
Swaanendael, Colony of ; extinction of, 33.
Swartwout, General, in battle at Chrysler's Field, 416.
Swartwout, John, Duel of, with De Witt Clinton, 372.
Swift, Joseph G., at Chrysler's Field, 416.

T.

Talcott, S. A., first Attorney-General, 460.
Talladega, Battle of, 406.
Tallashatchee, Battle of, 406.
Tallmadge, Benjamin, on Long Island, 315.

INDEX.

Tallmadge, James, in State Constitutional Convention, 1846, 503.
Tallmadge, Nathaniel P., United States Senator, 479.
Tammany Society, Aims and character of the ; history of the (note), 360.
Ta-reng-a-wa-gon, Holder of the Heavens, 3.
Tariff System, 473.
Tawasentha Creek, Treaty at, with Indians, 19.
Taxation and Representation, 56, 193, 194.
Taylor, President Zachary, Death of, 507.
Tea Act introduced into Parliament, 202.
Tea, Importation of, opposed, 204-206 ; action concerning, at New York, 205, 206 ; destroyed at New York and Boston, 206.
Tecumtha, Death of, 406.
Tenbroeck, Abraham, in the Assembly, 214 ; in battle on Bemis's Heights, 278.
Ternay, Admiral, at Newport, 309.
Texas, Annexation of, 501 ; intention concerning, 502.
Thames, Battle at the, 406.
Thomas, General John, in command in Canada ; death of, 240.
Thompson, John, and the National currency, 535.
Throop, Enos T., Governor ; biography of (note), 478.
Ticonderoga, Attack upon, and repulse, 174 ; capture of, 218 ; evacuated, 266.
Tienhoven, Cornelis Van, *schout ;* biography of (note), 62.
Tiger, Block's ship, burned, 15.
Tilden, Samuel J., and the "Tweed Ring," 547 ; Governor, 551, 552 ; biography of, 551 ; institutes investigations concerning the canal, 554.
Tinicum Island, capital of New Sweden, 52.
Tompkins, Daniel D., Biography of (note), 280 ; character of, 445 ; declines the office of Secretary of War ; Vice-President of the United States, 449.
Tompkins, Governor, and Rufus King (note), 234.
Toombs, Robert, and Mayor Wood, 521.
Topping, Thomas, councilman, 84.
Torrey, John, 575.
Toryism, Prevalence of, in New York, 233.
Townshend, General, 181 ; assumes command of the army, 183.
Towson, N., at battle of Chippewa, 422, 424.
Transportation facilities of the State, 555.
Treaty of Alliance, Celebration of the anniversary of the, 364.
Treaty at Westminster, 1674, 90.
Trenton, Battle at, 254.
Trinity Church, Organization of ; vestrymen of (note), 119.
Troops, British, at New York, Conflicts with the, 200.
Trumbull, Governor Jonathan, sends troops to Lake Champlain, 223.
Trumbull, John, artist, 575.
Tryon, Governor William, attempts conciliation, 191 ; notice of, 203 ; reception of, at New York, 220 ; on board the *Asia ;* his council (note), 232 ; corresponds with leading Tories, 233 ; on board the *Duchess of Gordon,* 235 ; leads marauding expeditions, 264 ; allusion to, in "McFingal" (note), 298.
Tryon County, Extent of, 342.
Tuscaroras the sixth nation of the Iroquois League, 10 ; join the Iroquois, 137.
Tusten, Colonel, at Minisink, 301.
"Tweed Ring," The, attacked by the press its overthrow, 546, 547.
Tweenhuysen, L., 14.
Twelve, Committee of, 47, 48.
Twiller, Walter Van, Director of New Netherland ; description of, 33, 34 ; scolded from the pulpit, 34 ; absurd conduct of, 34 ; recalled, 38 ; no memorial of ; biography of (note), 39.

U.

Ulster County, Territory of, 98.
Underhill, John, assists the Dutch, 50.
Union, Conspiracy to destroy the, 515, 516.
Union Defence Committee formed ; members of the (note), 523 ; doings of the, 523, 524.
"Union Mechanics," Action of the, 260.
Union League Club ; raises a regiment, 535.
Union of the Colonies proposed, 161 ; result of (note), 162.

616 INDEX.

United Colonies of New England, 93.
United Provinces, The, 19.
United States Bank, Removal of Government deposits from the, 480, 481.
United States Sanitary Commission formed, 527, 528.
Ury, John, a victim of the Negro Plot delusion, 153, 154.
Usselincx suggests a Dutch West India Company, 22 ; proposes a Swedish settlement on the Delaware River, 40.

V.

Valley Forge, American army at, 287, 438.
Van Buren, Martin; biography of (note), 445 ; Governor of New York ; Secretary of the United States, 474; appointed Minister to England ; rejected by the Senate ; President of the United States, 480 ; the Free Soil Party and, 507.
Van Cortlandt, Mayor, Joy of, manifested, 103.
Van Cortlandt Manor, 564.
Cortlandt, Orloff Stevens van ; biography of (note), 564.
Van Cortlandt, Pierre, first Lieutenant-Governor of the State, 262 ; re-elected Lieutenant-Governor, 353.
Van Dam, Rip, Acting-Governor of the province, 142 ; conflict of, with Governor Cosby, 143 ; suspended from the Council Board, 151.
Van Dyck kills an Indian woman, and is slain, 67, 68.
Van Krieckenbeeck, Daniel, at Fort Orange, 29 ; makes war on the Mohawks and is killed, 30.
Van Ness, William P., Burr's second in his duel with Hamilton; attacks the Livingston family, 373.
Van Rensselaer Manor, 32, 33, 562.
Van Rensselaer, Robert, leads militia in the Mohawk Valley, 307, 308.
Van Rensselaer, Stephen, Lieutenant-Governor, 363 ; in command of the militia, 389 ; on the Niagara frontier, 393 ; biography of (note), 395 ; at the canal celebration, 463.
Van Rensselaer, Stephen, Jr., 500.

Van Ruyven, Stuyvesant's secretary (note), 78.
Van Schaick, Colonel, pursues Sir John Johnson, 305.
Varick, Richard, at a meeting of Federalists ; biography of (note), 358.
Vaudreuil, Governor of Canada, and the Indians, 170 ; at Montreal ; surrenders the city and the province, 184.
Vaughan, General, commands troops at the capture of the Highlands' forts, 283 ; at the burning of Kingston, 286.
Verazzano, John, Claim of, to the discovery of New York Bay (note), 11.
Vermilye, Johannes, arrested, 110.
Vermont, 191 ; leaders in, coquetting with the British authorities in Canada, 308, 317, 318 ; an independent State, 316 ; authorities of New York alarmed concerning, 317 ; becomes a State of the Union, 319.
Ver Planck, Gelyn, *schepen*, 89.
Verplanck, Gulian C., 513, 574.
Verplanck's Point, Headquarters at, 327.
Vestrymen of Trinity Church (note), 119.
Vigilance Committee of New York City, 203 ; of the State of New York, 260 ; operations of the, 261.
Vincent, General, commands British forces, 410.
" Virginia dynasty," The, 449.
Vulture, The, and André and Arnold, 311.

W.

Walker, Admiral Sir Hovenden, commands an expedition against Quebec and fails, 136.
Wallace, Hugh, receives Governor Tryon, 221.
Walloons, History of the (note) ; settle in New Netherland, 25.
Walters, Robert, Associate-Justice, 129.
Wampum, Uses of (note), 19.
War, Preparations for, by the Americans, 207.
War-meeting, A great, in New York City, 522.
Warner, Seth, before Congress, 222.
Warrington, Captain, Cruises of, 438, 439.
Washington, George, Mission of, 161, 162 ;

INDEX. 617

Major, builds Fort Necessity; fights French troops, and surrenders, 162, 163; Colonel, in command of Virginia forces, 169; General, reception of, at New York, 220; a plot to destroy, 235, 236; response to appeal of, 243; retreat of, across New Jersey, 250; crosses and recrosses the Delaware River; captures the British forces at Trenton, 254; gains a victory at Princeton; in winter quarters at Morristown, 255; Howe and, confront each other in New Jersey, 286; discovers Arnold's treason, 314; headquarters of, at Newburgh, 326, 327; final parting with his officers, 331; resigns his commission; retires to Mount Vernon, 332; presides over the Constitutional Convention, 336; letter of, to General Schuyler, 343; elected first President of the United States, 344; inaugurated, 345; interest of, in the canal system, 347; death of, 366.

Washington (the National Capital), menaced in 1814; attacked, and public and private property at, destroyed, 436.

Waterbury, General, captured on Lake Champlain, 252.

Watson, Elkanah, promotes canal projects, 347, 348; biography of (note); explorations and labors of, 348, 349.

Wayne, General Anthony, attacked near the Paoli Tavern, 286; takes Stony Point; biography of (note), 299.

Webb, General, Conduct of, at Fort Edward, 171.

Webb, James Watson, revolutionizes journalism; biography of (note), 482; defends his castle, 484.

Weed, Thurlow, journalist; biography of (note), 475.

Wellington's veterans sent to Canada, 420, 441.

Wells, William, councilman, 84.

Wells, Mr., killed at Cherry Valley, 291.

Wentworth, Benning, Governor, grants lands, 189, 190.

Westchester County, Territory of, 97; a British force invades, 248.

Weston, William, and the New York canals, 349.

West India Company, Prompt action of the, to save New Netherland, 51.

West Point Military Academy founded, 375.

Whig Party, history of its name, 477, 478.

Whiskey Insurrection, 358.

White, Hugh, in Central New York, 342.

White Plains, Battle at, 248.

Whitemarsh, American army at, 287.

Wilkinson, General James, in command of the Army of the North; biography of (note), 414; on the St. Lawrence, 415-417; leaves the army, 421.

Willett, Marinus, Sortie of, at Fort Schuyler, 271; mission of, to General Schuyler; biography of, 272; in expedition against the Indians, 301.

Willett, Thomas, commissioner at Hartford in 1650, 58; first Mayor of New York, 85.

William of Orange invades England; becomes joint monarch with his wife, Mary, 104; death of, 129.

William, the first English trading vessel on the Hudson River; driven off by the Dutch, 34, 35.

Williams, Colonel Ephraim, killed near Lake George, 166.

Williams, Major, a British officer made prisoner on Bemis's Heights, 278.

Williams, Thomas, arrested, 110.

Wiltwyck founded, 72; desolated by Indians, 73.

Winchester, General James, at Frenchtown, 403.

Winder, General W. H., at Stony Creek Battle, 410; commands troops in the District of Columbia; biography of (note), 458; commands at the Battle of Bladensburg, 436.

Winslow, General, leads provincial troops toward Canada, 115.

Wolfe, General James, Amherst's lieutenant, 173; commands expedition against Quebec, 180; on the St. Lawrence River (note); incidents of the death of, 183.

Women, Patriotism of the, 524.

Wood, Fernando, Mayor of New York, recommends the secession of New York City, 519, 520.

Woodhull, Colonel Nathaniel, in the Assembly, 214.

INDEX.

Woodworth, John, Associate-Justice, 459.

Woodworth, Samuel, Poem of, 434; notice of, 574.

Wool, General John E., Energetic action of, 525, 526.

Woolsey, Melancthon, on Lake Champlain, 390.

Wooster, General David, encamped at Harlem, 220; succeeds Arnold in command at Quebec; biography of (note), 230.

Wright, Silas, Comptroller of the State; biography of (note), 475; Governor, and the school fund, 500.

Writs of Assistance, Opposition to, 194.

Wyoming Valley, Invasion of, 293, 294.

Y.

Yates, J. Van Ness, Secretary of State, 459.

Yates, Joseph C., Governor of New York; biography of (note), 459.

Yates, Judge Robert, Patriotism of, 343.

Yellow fever in New York, 352.

Yeo, Sir James Lucas, on Lake Ontario; biography of (note), 411.

York, Duke of, receives a gift of all New Netherland from his brother, King Charles; Lord High Admiral; sends a force to seize the domain, 74.

York (Toronto), Expedition against, 409, 410.

Young, John, Governor of New York, 505; an advocate of popular education, 506.

Young, Samuel, Secretary of State; refuses to comply with an act of the Legislature, 498.

Z.

Zenger, John Peter, issues the *New York Weekly Journal*, a tribune of the people; attacks official authorities; trial of, for libel, 144, 147; acquitted, 147.